Thomas Jefferson

& The New Nation

Volume One
To the Vice Presidency

Thomas Jefferson

& The New Nation

Volume One
To the Vice Presidency

By

MERRILL D. PETERSON

Biography in two volumes:
To the Vice Presidency
Return to Monticello

Published by American Political Biography Press

Newtown, CT

All publications of
AMERICAN POLITICAL BIOGRAPHY PRESS
Are dedicated to my wife
Ellen and our two children
Katherine and William II

This particular book is
Dedicated to:

The Resilience of America
September 11, 2001

Professor Peterson dedicated his book to:

Jeffrey and Kent
"The Past is also stored in thee"

Contents

Three · Virginia Reformer

*

*

Four · War Governor

*

*

Five · Withdrawal and Return: Congressman

*

*

CONTENTS

Six · Minister to France

*

Seasoning in Paris 297

Hail and Farewell 385

*

Seven · Secretary of State

*

The Reluctant Nominee 390

Epilogue of Diplomacy 507

*

Eight · Withdrawal and Return: Vice President

*

Return to Felicity 518

Verdict in the House 642

*

CONTENTS

Nine · President: First Administration

*

Inauguration   652

Unquiet Empire   789

*

Ten · President: Second Administration

*

Inauguration   801

Failure and Triumph

*

Eleven · Sage of Monticello

*

In Retirement   922

Death in Jubilee   1005

*

Select Bibliography   1011

Index   1049

List of Illustrations

THOMAS JEFFERSON
AND THE
NEW NATION

Prologue to Fame

I confess, there are some men's constitutions of body and mind so vigorous, and well framed by nature, that they need not much assistance from others; but by the strength of their natural genius, they are, from their cradles, carried towards what is excellent; and, by the privilege of their happy constitution, are able to do wonders. But examples of this kind are few; and I think I may say, that, of all men we meet with, nine parts of them are what they are, good or evil, useful or not, by their education. It is that which makes the great difference in mankind. The little, or almost insensible, impressions on our tender infancies, have very important and lasting consequences: and there it is, as in the fountains of some rivers, where a gentle application of the hand turns the flexible waters into channels, that make them take quite contrary courses; and by this little direction, given them at first, in the source, they receive different tendencies, and arrive at last at very remote and distant places.

John Locke, Some Thoughts Concerning Education. *1693.*

To BECOME my own biographer is the last thing in the world I would undertake," Thomas Jefferson remarked in his seventy-second year. "No. If there has been anything in my course worth the public attention, they are better judges of it than I can be myself, and to them it is my duty to leave it." Few men ever left a richer or more abundant record of a life well spent. From the time he became conscious of his own fame and of posterity's immense stake in the events with which he was associated, Jefferson dutifully preserved the annals of his journey. Unfortunately, the road to fame is not so well documented. He did, it is true, five years after declining to become his own biographer, write for his family an unvarnished chronicle of his life to mid-passage, but this "autobiography," as valuable as it is, sheds little light on the child who became the man.

"The tradition of my father's family," Jefferson began his account, "was that their ancestors came to this country from Wales, and from near the mountain of Snowdon, the highest in Great Britain." This ancestor could not be definitely established. There had been Jeffersons in Virginia from the earliest times, but the great descendant traced the family line no farther back than his grandfather, Thomas Jefferson, Jr., who lived in Chesterfield County (then part of Henrico) some distance below the falls of the James River. Like a number of small planters, as well as large, Thomas turned his eyes to the virgin lands west of tidewater, and in 1718 patented several hundred acres at Fine Creek in what would become Goochland County. Upon his death thirteen years later, his youngest son Peter inherited these James River lands, which he promptly settled, if indeed he had not already done so.

Peter was then twenty-three or twenty-four years of age, a strongly built man with great force of mind and considerable ambition. His education, as his son would say, "had been quite neglected," and his circumstances were modest at best; but casting his lot with the new upcountry society, he quickly rose in the social scale, becoming a large landholder, a prominent member of the county squirearchy, and as a self-taught surveyor and mapmaker carved a niche for himself in the history of the province. Contributing to this rise was his marriage into one of the princely families, the Randolphs. "They trace their pedigree far back in England and Scotland, to which let every one ascribe the merit he chooses." Thomas Jefferson, the democrat, could thus lightly dismiss the aristocratic pedigree that helped to secure position and influence for himself and his children.

Jane Randolph was nineteen, the eldest daughter of Isham Randolph, of Dungeness, some miles farther up the James, when Peter Jefferson married her in 1739. "Captain" Randolph had been a seafaring man, sojourning a good deal in England, where Jane was born, before he settled down on a plantation seat in the Virginia piedmont. He thereafter played a prominent role in the military affairs of the colony. Botany was his amusement, as it was for so many planters, and he knew such eminent botanists as Peter Collinson in England and the Philadelphian John Bartram, who stopped at Dungeness on his southern excursion in 1738. Peter Jefferson's courtship there probably commenced about this time. He had become acquainted with the Dungeness branch of the family through his best friend, William Randolph, Isham's nephew, whose great estate Tuckahoe lay thirty miles or so to the east. The intimacy of these two men, William and Peter, would exert an influence on the latter's distinguished son beyond the incident of maternity.

The son, the first to Peter and Jane Jefferson, was born at Shadwell, in what soon became Albemarle County, on April 13, 1743. In this wilderness country, many miles up the Rivanna River from its confluence with the James, Peter Jefferson had patented a thousand acres in 1735, then cleared a tract for planting and built a modest frame dwelling, to which he brought his wife and two infant daughters not long before the birth of his son. The place, named for the London parish where his wife was born, lay in verdant rolling countryside between ramparts of the Southwest Mountains opening vistas of the Blue Ridge beyond the valley to the west. When the County of Albemarle was created in 1744 it embraced the entire Rivanna region. Indians called Saponi, of Sioux stock, once inhabited the region, but there were no Indians now except those who passed through, often stopping at Shadwell, on the road to the capital 120 miles or so to the east; and bear and buffalo had surrendered the forests to wolf and deer. The first settlers came in the 1730's; Jefferson thought his father the third or fourth in the region. They were nearly all, as he was, enterprising planters packing west from crowded or worn-out lands. His own landholdings, though they rapidly increased, were never as large as some of his neighbors'. As the region filled up, the gap widened between the magnates owning many thousands of acres, with the slaves to work them, and the mass of small farmers, many with fewer than a hundred acres. This was a frontier in the provincial Virginia fashion, free and open to middle-rank men of Peter Jefferson's means and enterprise but utterly recalcitrant to the leveling influence so often claimed for

5

the American frontier. If his son felt the force of the frontier, if the West constantly tugged at his mind, it was not from growing up in a democratic frontier society.

What counted in this respect was his emotional response to the natural landscape, his sense of the freedom and simplicity of up-country life, and, above all, his identification with Virginia pioneering and exploration. The last came chiefly through his father. Not only had he been in the vanguard of Virginia's westward settlement —always a source of pride to his son—but he had penetrated the Alleghenies, traversed the uncharted wilderness of southwest Virginia to extend the boundary with North Carolina begun by William Byrd many years before, and with his partner in this expedition, Joshua Fry, professor of mathematics in the College of William and Mary, drew the first correct map of the province. All of this happened when Jefferson was a child. His adventurous mind must have been touched by it. Something in Albemarle seemed to excite the westering imagination. Peter Jefferson's physician-friend and neighbor, Dr. Thomas Walker, also explored the mountain vastness, and later became the young Jefferson's preceptor on the West and the Indians. Walker was the leading spirit of the Loyal Company, a speculative enterprise in southwest Virginia in which Jefferson's father had a share. George Rogers Clark, conqueror of the Northwest during the American Revolution, and Meriwether Lewis, who later journeyed to the far Pacific, were natives of Albemarle, while William Clark, brother of the former and, in time, partner of the latter, only missed being born there. All would figure prominently in the life of Albemarle's most famous son. He was neither pioneer nor explorer, but the West was in his thoughts from an early age. The West was nature writ large, and though his own preference was for the humanized middle state between the wild and the civilized, such as he never ceased to celebrate in his native country, nature in the large had an enduring fascination for him. And his response to the softer and smaller, the tamed yet unspoiled and endlessly beautiful natural world of his childhood, enforced a sense of man's relationship to his environment that colored all his values. The openness, the freedom, the simplicity he found in this world set him on the road to the democratic ethic of his mature years.

Jefferson would never think of any place as home but the Albemarle of his birth. Actually, he spent six of the first nine years of his life at Tuckahoe. William Randolph died in 1745 leaving a will that requested his "dear and loving friend" Peter Jefferson to move down to Tuckahoe and look after his three motherless children until the son, four-year-old Thomas Mann Randolph, came of age. Peter honored the request, at least for a period of years, and packed off his entire family (there were now four children and a fifth on the way) to Tuckahoe. Thomas's earliest memories accordingly, were not of the simple farm house at Shadwell but of the airy and commodious frame and brick mansion on the James. "It is in the form of an H and has the appearance of two houses, joined by a large saloon; each wing has two stories, and four large rooms on a floor . . . the saloon that unites them is of considerable magnitude and on each side are doors. . . ." If it answered perfectly the purposes of Virginia hospitality, as the author of this description thought, Tuckahoe perfectly suited as well the needs of two families. Peter managed the large Randolph plantation, together with his own farms at Fine Creek and Shadwell, and was frequently away from home on surveying expeditions. His son's schooling commenced at the age of five. In a little one-room plantation schoolhouse Thomas and his sisters and cousins learned their reading, writing, and arithmetic from a private tutor.

About nine years old when the family returned to Shadwell, Thomas was promptly placed in a classical school conducted by the Reverend William Douglas, from Scotland, at his parsonage some distance to the east in Goochland County. In those days, of course, the classical languages were the indispensable foundations of education. His father had never acquired them, but he was sufficiently cultivated to know their value, for which his son was eternally grateful. "To read the Latin and Greek authors in their original is a sublime luxury . . . ," he said many years later. "I thank on my knees him who directed my early education for having put into my possession this rich source of delight; and I would not exchange it for anything which I could have then acquired, and have not since acquired." Perhaps he did not learn a great deal from the Reverend Mr. Douglas. Jefferson remembered him as "but a superficial Latinist, less instructed in Greek," though he got from him the rudiments of these languages as well as of French. In 1758, after several years

7

with the Reverend Mr. Douglas, he went to school with "a correct classical scholar," the Reverend James Maury. This delightful gentleman belonged to a prominent Virginia family of Huguenot descent and was among the better educated men of the province. He it was who, in 1763, brought to court the celebrated case of the Parson's Cause, which humbled the Anglican clergy and rocketed Patrick Henry to fame. Maury's Fredericksville parish, the first in the region, included part of Albemarle; in later years Jefferson, like his father before him, would serve on its vestry. The schoolhouse built of logs lay about a dozen miles from Shadwell, too far for commuting from home. For two years the young scholar soaked up Greek and Latin, got a mere smattering of English literature, perhaps a little geography and history and mathematics, and doubtless a heavy dose of the Bible. Partly because he boarded with the Maury family, riding home weekends, he was also introduced to the master's library of some four hundred volumes, by far the largest he had seen. Here at Maury's school he came to know the pleasures of study and caught his first glimpse of the world of learning.

He would remember these schooldays as among the happiest of his life. No friendships ever seemed sweeter than those he made then. Among his school chums were young James Maury, later American consul at Liverpool for many years; Dabney Carr, whom Jefferson loved as a brother and who would wed his sister Martha; John Walker, perhaps the only close friend Jefferson would ever lose; and James Madison—the *other* James Madison—afterwards president of the College of William and Mary. Their favorite pastime was hunting in mountains alive with deer, fox, turkey, partridge, and other game. Like most country boys, Thomas took to hunting at an early age, though loyalty to nature seemed to curb his ardor. It was later said that he would never shoot partridge or hare "settin'" but would "scare em up" first to give them a sporting chance. He was a good horseman in the Virginia fashion, but for exercise and diversion preferred walking in the woods and fields. Nature should be observed from the ground, not from five feet up in the air. Besides, a horse gave the body "but a kind of half exercise." From the little that can be known of his schooldays, Jefferson comes through not as the "All American Boy" but as the exceptionally diligent student. Even after classes were dismissed, "he used to be seen with his

Greek Grammar in hand while his comrades were enjoying relaxation." Not averse to games and fun, he studied first and played later. If a holiday was granted, the younger Maury recalled, "he would withdraw from the noisy crowd of his school fellows, learn the next day's lesson, and then, rejoining them, begin the day's pleasure."

He was only fourteen, and had not yet entered Maury's school, when he lost his father in 1757. Peter Jefferson had established himself as a first citizen of the county—local magistrate, county surveyor, county lieutenant (the chief military officer), even member of the House of Burgesses for a time. The pathway to power had been blazed for his son. He had also become wealthy, at least in land and slaves and the accoutrement of the tobacco planter. Had he lived longer he might have built the mansion that his estate plainly authorized; but this was left to his son. The "Colonel's" landholdings, mostly in Albemarle, amounted to about 7500 acres. Two-thirds of this, including the Monticello property, would eventually go to Thomas. The will made provision for the widow and all eight children, the youngest being two-year-old Randolph, but as was customary the distribution of the patrimony favored the first son. His mother lived many years yet. By his own reckoning she was a zero quantity in his life. He was especially fond of two of his sisters, Jane, the eldest, who shared his love of music, and Martha, who married Dabney Carr. With his only brother, Randolph, so much younger, he was never close. Indeed, except for the strong example and guidance provided by his father, his life course would not have been very different had all the members of his family been erased from the picture. He owed his father a great deal, not in companionship, for they were frequently apart, perhaps not even in affection, but in the tone and direction given to his life. Habits of industry, system, and responsibility are acquired early, and in Jefferson's case they were learned first from his father. He later expressed some astonishment that, when this force was removed at a tender age and there was no one to turn to, he did not lose his bearings, fall into bad company, and become quite worthless to society. Instead, the early thrust to maturity hardened the grain of habits already acquired.

Jefferson would have nothing to do with management of his inheritance until he came of age. Meanwhile it was in the hands of executors who also acted as guardians. In January 1760, when he was going on seventeen, he wrote a letter—the first from his pen that survives—to the principal executor, John Harvie. "I was at Col. Peter Randolph's [another executor] about a Fortnight ago," the letter began, "and my Schooling falling into Discourse, he said he thought it would be to my Advantage to go to College, and was desirous I should go, as indeed I am myself for several Reasons." He went on to explain that the move would put a stop to the distraction and the expense of company at Shadwell, widen his acquaintance with the world, and of course further his education. After two years at Maury's school he was ready for a richer and more varied fare. That he should go anywhere but the College of William and Mary seems not to have occurred to him or to his guardians. The College was in ill-repute in certain quarters; and some Virginia sons of well-to-do families still went to England for education, though the College of New Jersey, in Princeton, under Scottish Presbyterian auspices, was increasingly favored as an alternative. But the young gentleman of Albemarle set his sights on the provincial college. Here a new chapter opened.

A Williamsburg Education

This youth of seventeen who came down from the hills to Williamsburg in 1760 had taken on the physical characteristics so commonly ascribed to him in later years. He was tall and lanky, with large hands and feet, and seemed to be growing right out of his clothes. As straight and strong as a gun-barrel, he had the sinewy broad-shouldered vigor of his father. His tousled hair was of a reddish color, his eyes light and hazel, his face ruddy and freckled. His head, like his body, was spare of flesh. Lips thin and compressed suggested a mind in thought, while the angular nose and projecting chin added forcefulness to a countenance otherwise mild. He gave the appearance of the fresh country lad he was, rather more awkward than graceful, and by no stretch could he be considered handsome or polished at this stage. But he was bright, amiable, eager, and full of bounce, which more than compensated for any deficiency in looks.

Williamsburg was a new scene. To begin with it was a town, that rarity in Virginia young Jefferson had not known before. It was also the provincial capital, seat of empire in the New World, about as little felt in Albemarle as His Majesty's government across the ocean, but, nevertheless, the hub of Virginia politics, society, and culture. Close to 1500 people lived in the town. During "publick times" in the spring and fall, however, when the General Court and the House of Burgesses were in session, the population doubled. Between the College at one end and the Capitol at the other stretched a mile-long thoroughfare, Duke of Gloucester Street, through which coursed a colorful parade of humanity. In the years ahead Jefferson came to know every feature of this artery and its tributaries—the Bruton Church where he sometimes worshiped, the Raleigh Tavern where he danced and flirted and on occasion minded weighty affairs of state, the shops he patronized, the houses he visited. Williamsburg was not showy; but for the porticoed Capitol and the splendid Palace of the governor it might have been mistaken for a good English town. In the surrounding country were the princely estates of tidewater aristocrats who wielded power at Williamsburg. Sons of several of these patrician families—Harrisons, Burwells, Pages, and others—were among Jefferson's classmates at college, and he easily made his way into their society, so much grander than anything he had known in the upcountry.

Jefferson lived and studied for two years in the College. Chartered by the Crown in 1693, receiving its name from the reigning sovereigns, and floated on the profits of Virginia lands and tobacco, the College had a distinctive public character. It had a religious character too, being founded in part to provide ministers for the established Church of England and being under the control of the Church; but unlike the sister colleges to the north—more emphatically ecclesiastical in character—William and Mary failed miserably in this object. Few of the planters' sons who went there chose a ministerial career, with the result that the College was constantly at war with itself, torn between the brazen secularism of the community it served and its clerical mission. The College had grown into a miscellaneous assortment of schools: a preparatory or grammar school presided over by a master; an Indian school, the Brafferton, intended to Christianize the natives, also with a single master; the philosophy school, which was the equivalent of a liberal arts college, with two professors; and the divinity school, similarly staffed. Not more than a hundred students were enrolled in all the schools. Over the whole sat a president, who also usually occupied the position of commissary, as agent of the Bishop of London in the colony, and the pulpit of the Bruton Church, and who at the time of Jefferson's entrance into the College was a notorious drunkard. Jefferson, of course, enrolled in the philosophy school where "systems of logick, physicks, ethicks and mathematicks" were dispensed by the two professors.

"It was my great good fortune, and what probably fixed the destinies of my life," Jefferson wrote in his autobiography, "that Dr. William Small of Scotland, was then Professor of Mathematics, a man profound in most of the useful branches of science, with a happy talent of communication, correct and gentlemanly manners, and an enlarged and liberal mind. He, most happily for me, became soon attached to me, and made me his daily companion when not engaged in the school; and from his conversation I got my first views of the expansion of science, and of the system of things in which we are placed." This gentleman, the single non-clergyman on the faculty, had only recently come to the College, and he remained but six years. Judging by his later friendship, after his return to England, with James Watt, Erasmus Darwin, and others of the Birmingham scientific circle, Small was a man of talents not far below the mark assigned to him by his favorite student. He had been swept up in the enlightened thought of the age. His teaching was rational and scientific rather than religious and didactic; and he gave this cast to Jefferson's mind. He was, in fact, the first truly enlightened or scientific man the young student had encountered. Because of some rowdyism that led to the dismissal of his other teacher, the professor of moral philosophy, Jefferson was fortunate in having Small not only for mathematics, natural philosophy, and natural history but also for logic, ethics, rhetoric, and belles lettres. In fact, except for a few months, Small was his only regular teacher; and Jefferson continued in his company after leaving the College and commencing the study of law.

His choice of law as a profession was influenced more by chance and circumstance than by the conscious bent of his own mind. He never professed to love the law in the way he professed, repeatedly, to love science or the arts. A dark and gloomy study, the law was out of tune with his cheerful nature. The law was not his mistress but a profession of service and, incidentally, of livelihood. Now approaching twenty years of age, without the fortune to support a splendid retirement or any desire to spend his life planting tobacco, he sought a vocation that would challenge his mind, supplement his income, and render him useful to society. In Virginia the options were very few. The ministry held no charms for him, nor did any branch of the military service; like most Virginians he knew nothing of trade, which was a British monopoly; and there was no art or science or literature in which the colonial could make a career. Had he lived nearer the center of empire he might have found a calling that answered to his strongest impulses. And in retrospect it seems clear he might have excelled in almost any field of learning. (If the estimates of "historiometry," the technique of measuring the intelligence of historical figures, are to be credited, his IQ was about 150, in the same rank as Galileo, Handel, Michelangelo, and some other geniuses.) But in Virginia, on the fringes of empire, only law, and possibly medicine, though Jefferson always held a low opinion of the art, offered a calling at once learned and useful, if not especially profitable, and one which a gentleman could pursue while attending to his country estate. At Williamsburg the youth discovered models for emulation: Peyton Randolph, the king's attorney, who had been educated at the Inner Temple in London; Edmund Pendleton, the very popular home-grown product; and above all George Wythe, also native-born, bred, and educated, who became Jefferson's mentor. The magnates who sat on the Governor's Council and exercised great influence were, for the most part, planters, not lawyers; but as the contest with the mother country came on, and Virginians thought seriously about rights and government, a new generation of professional lawyers, their roots in the native land, rose to prominence. Themselves a part of the ruling class, they did not dethrone it but infused it with their own learning and ambitions. Jefferson and Patrick Henry were among the first of this Revolutionary generation of lawyers. Henry, who preceded him, came to the bar after six weeks of desultory reading while Jefferson spent five years in exhaustive preparation.

The presence of George Wythe in Williamsburg fixed Jefferson's determination and squelched any fugitive thoughts of going abroad for study. It was Small who brought master and pupil together. A man of the most exalted character and learning, entirely without the benefit of formal schooling, Wythe had become, as was said, "a scholar by the indispensable progress of his own industry in his closet." About thirty-five years of age when Jefferson came under his wing, he was already an ornament of the bar and on the point of learning the most eminent in the profession. To his knowledge of English and Roman law he brought a command of the whole field of humanistic learning and an irrepressible enthusiasm for classical languages and literature. "Mr. Wythe" it was said, "not only labored through an apprenticeship, but almost through life in the dead languages." Jefferson himself had spent several years in the same apprenticeship, and he did not in any formal sense continue it in Williamsburg. The burden of his education under Small was rational and scientific; but this new direction did not exclude the older one. His Attic and Roman tastes were further cultivated by Wythe, who pursued law and politics under the spell of the ancients. In a course of reading over five years, Jefferson learned law as a branch of the history of mankind. The relationship of master and pupil ripened into affectionate friendship through life. Wythe went on to become a signer of the Declaration of Independence, first professor of law at William and Mary, and finally chancellor of Virginia. Jefferson never tired of singing his virtues—integrity, generosity, patriotism, love of liberty—and thought he might be best remembered as "the Cato of his country without the avarice of the Roman."

The Williamsburg chain of influence from Small to Wythe terminated in the Royal Governor, Francis Fauquier, remembered by Jefferson as the ablest man ever to fill that chair. "They were"—Small, Wythe, and Fauquier—"inseparable friends, and at their frequent dinners with the governor (after his family had returned to England) he admitted me always to make it a *partie quarée*. At these dinners I . . . heard more good sense, more rational and philosophical conversations than in all my life besides. They were truly Attic societies." Coming to Virginia in 1758, the Governor had made himself popular with the leading gentry by exhibiting in his own character the fashionable culture to which they aspired. Elegant, urbane, learned, and witty, a man of almost Chesterfieldian manners, he brought the tastes and amusements of the metropolis to the province. He dabbled in science, patronized art and music, and introduced the taste for French literature and philosophy so much the vogue in England. The Governor, who was himself musical, recruited his young friend for the amateur ensemble that performed weekly at the Palace. Having taken up the fiddle on his own while still in school Jefferson found the first opportunity for instruction in Williamsburg. He must have attained at least a modest proficiency to play in Fauquier's concerts. The Governor's example of "taste, refinement and erudition," which he is said to have impressed on the colony, was not lost on Jefferson. However, he rejected the elegant vices that accompanied the Governor's virtues. Although he occasionally played at cards or backgammon or laid a bet on a horse race, he escaped the extravagant fashion of gambling, "the rage for playing deep, reckless of time, health, or money," that Fauquier was charged, not quite fairly, with spreading like wildfire among the great families.

Small, Wythe, and Fauquier: this Williamsburg circle was Jefferson's university. Small, the Scotsman, was his preceptor in mathematics, natural science, and modern philosophy; from him came the impulse toward scientific rationalism. Wythe extended his lines to the ancient world while at the same time opening before him a generous and humane path to the law. Fauquier, the man of the world, introduced him to the life of cultivated manners, taste, and sensibility, showing its pitfalls as well as its charms. All were, in their fashion, men of the Enlightenment. All were, if not heretics, suspiciously unorthodox in their religious opinions. All were models of conduct. Jefferson afterwards called Williamsburg "the finest school of manners and morals that ever existed in America." And the peak of felicity for him was undoubtedly the *partie quarée* around the Governor's table. Looking back on his youth for the instruction of his grandson, Jefferson said that when under temptations and difficulties he would ask himself, "What would Dr. Small, Mr. Wythe, Peyton Randolph, do in this situation? What course in it will insure me their approbation?" He never doubted that this way of deciding his conduct led him more truly than any mere process of reasoning through the "jaundiced eye of youth."

Student of Law

Once launched on his legal studies, Jefferson was more often at Shadwell than in Williamsburg. As he came of age his responsibilities to his family, his farms, and his country increased, but he was a "hard student" at all times, and in this period drove himself relentlessly. To get a good legal education in Virginia, or anywhere in North America, was more difficult, in some respects, than obtaining a good scientific education in the Congo today. There were no schools, no texts, no American law reports, and few books of any kind. The completion in 1769 of William Blackstone's grand outline, *Commentaries on the Laws of England*, marked a tremendous advance. Within a few years Blackstone was as popular in America as in England. But the work came too late for Jefferson, and in retrospect he was grateful for having missed the "honeyed" smoothness and treacherous systematizing of Blackstone's packaged course in four volumes at the commencement of his studies.

Jefferson started with Sir Edward Coke, that dreary and crabbed seventeenth-century legalist whose *Institutes of the Laws of England*—a "painful" work as he warned the reader in the preface—was unquestionably the fundamental treatise. Had he gone to the Inns of Court he would probably have started at the same place, but in England he would have found a highly organized legal profession that not only controlled entrance into this estate but sharply distinguished its various jurisdictions—common law, civil law, admiralty law, law of nations, and so on—and parceled out the business among tribes of specialists—barristers, solicitors, scriveners, and the like. In the simpler American world all of this was thrown together in disordered profusion. The practice was neither specialized nor even professionalized in the sense of conforming to rigid standards of its own. It developed helter-skelter in response to the needs and pressures of the community. Indeed, before it could develop very far at all, the law became so mixed up with the rising nation's political life that two generations passed before it began to acquire a life of its own. The process of training and admission to the bar was similarly free and loose. There were no patterned roads, as exemplified in the contrasting cases of Henry and Jefferson. The usual practice, however, was for the aspirant to read and work as an apprentice in a lawyer's office. Wythe started Jefferson along this route, but after a few months, whether because of the student's responsibilities in Albemarle or because of his manifest capacities of self-discipline, he turned him loose on an ambitious program of reading. Thereafter, only at brief intervals was Jefferson an apprentice. He disapproved of the system anyway, thinking it "rather a prejudice than a help" because it diverted the aspirant from books to business. "The only help a youth wants is to be directed what books to read, and in what order to read them," he said.

"Well, Page," Jefferson wrote from Shadwell to his college chum John Page, "I do wish the Devil had old Cooke [Coke], for I am sure I never was so tired of an old dull scoundrel in my life." It was enough to make one wonder if the quest for happiness through knowledge was not all humbug and delusion! But Jefferson struggled through the first part of the *Institutes*, *Coke upon Littleton*, an extended commentary on the classic treatise on tenures written in Law French during Edward III's time, then went on to other parts of the *Institutes*, treating statutory law since Magna Charta, criminal law, and jurisdiction; and he finally came to admire the "uncouth but cunning" legalist. Coke, of course, was best known to history as the common-law champion of English rights and liberties against the Stuarts, which was bound to ensure his reputation with the Americans as they took up what many believed to be the same cause nearly a century and a half later. In the aftermath of that struggle Jefferson would say of him, "a sounder Whig never wrote, nor of profounder learning in the orthodox doctrines of the British constitution, or in what were called British liberties." Blackstone, the champion of parliamentary supremacy become tyrannical, was a Tory by comparison, and in his later years Jefferson attributed the decline of Whig principles in the legal fraternity to the displacement of Coke's "black-letter text" by Blackstone. But in the 1760's, though his reading of Coke obviously faded into his developing political opinions, he was more immediately influenced by the jurist's precise ways of deciphering the mysteries of the common law, by his historical method, and his conception of legal science. Once alerted by Coke, Jefferson dug back to the roots of things before Magna Charta, before the Norman Conquest; unlike Coke, he came

17

to believe that these ancient Saxon foundations of English liberty had been corrupted in the succeeding centuries. His principal guides here were the work of Henry Bracton and the digest of Alfred's laws. Bracton, not Coke, he discovered, was the true foundation. Written a few years after Magna Charta, in technical Latin "abounding in terms antiquated, obsolete, and unintelligible but to the most learned," he later said, it gave the common law its ultimate form at exactly the point of division of the unwritten from the written, or statutory, law. Jefferson moved forward from Coke too, using Matthew Bacon's digest, various reports of cases, and treatises by Lord Kames and others.

But law was not to be studied in an intellectual vacuum. It was kindred of all the sciences and ought to be part of a large and varied diet of reading. Not long after Jefferson finished his own studies and began to practice, a young aspirant looked to him, as he had looked to Wythe, for direction. Although declining this responsibility, he supplied a complete course of reading all carefully scheduled for daily exercise. It was enough to rattle the brain of any man, so formidable a regimen, in fact, that Jefferson himself probably never followed it strictly; yet it conveys his own ardor for learning and the athletic rigor of the pursuit as well as the copious outlines, beyond mere technical competence, of his mentor's instruction. It was first necessary, Jefferson informed the aspirant, that a solid groundwork be laid: Latin and French, mathematics, natural philosophy, natural history—this was the minimum. Then the regular study of law might commence, mixed, however, with "its kindred sciences." From dawn until eight a.m. should be employed in the physical sciences, sparing some time for ethics and religion. Jefferson named the specific texts to be read under each of eight headings. From eight to noon, the best hours of the day, should be devoted to the black-letter of the law. From noon to one p.m., politics, beginning with Locke and Sidney. In the lazy hours in the afternoon, history, proceeding from ancient through modern to English and American. (At least the last appears in the 1814 revision of the letter, the only available text.) The evening hours until bedtime, usually about ten o'clock for Jefferson, should be given over to imaginative literature of all genres ("Shakespeare must be singled out by one who wishes to learn the full powers of the English language"), criticism, rhetoric, and oratory, on which Jefferson was very explicit. He also recommended the habit he had formed after getting through Coke of "commonplacing" pertinent cases and striking things encountered in his reading, sometimes adding his own reflections. These "commonplace books" reveal his careful way of working and provide a partial index to his reading from student days until the Revolution.

He was no recluse in these years. He could not escape company or the round of plantation visiting even had he wanted to—it was the custom of the country. If he was somewhat shy and reserved and inclined, as Page said, "to tear himself away from his dearest friends, and fly to his studies," he also had the normal youthful craving for companionship, male and female, and good times. Trudging the same round day after day at Shadwell he sometimes yearned for the gayer social life of Williamsburg.

This was especially true at the beginning of his legal study when he was caught up in a youthful romance. The lady, actually only sixteen years of age, was Rebecca Burwell, to whom he had been introduced by a college classmate, her brother, at the Burwell family seat, Fairfield, in York County. Back at Shadwell he was desperately afraid that this ripe young virgin would be plucked from the vine while he carried on his affair with old Coke. He did not wish to lose her, still less was he ready to take her. Not only was there Coke to think about, with all that involved, but he had vague ideas of a journey to England and other faraway places, perhaps Italy, where he could pick up a good violin. These ideas never matured. The farthest he traveled from home during the next twenty years was New York, which he visited on a northerly journey in 1766. At any rate, returning to Williamsburg in the fall of 1763, Jefferson saw Rebecca again. They danced at a ball in the Apollo Room of the Raleigh Tavern. Mustering all his courage, carefully rehearsing everything in advance, he determined to declare his affections. "But, good God!" the poor wretch wrote to Page the next morning, "When I had an opportunity of venting them, a few broken sentences, uttered in great disorder, and interrupted with pauses of uncommon length, were the too visible marks of my strange confusion!" Some days or weeks later he managed to make his little speech. It was not a proposal but the promise of a proposal to come, after he had arranged his own future. The damsel listened, returned no answer, and parted from this beau who could so coolly put romance on the shelf. Not long afterwards Jefferson learned of her engagement to Jacquelin Ambler. "Well the Lord bless her, I say! . . . Many and great are the comforts of a single state. . . ." He seems to have been none the worse for this amorous adventure. During the next several years, reconciled to the single state and the male companionship he usually preferred anyway, Jefferson took a harsh view of woman-kind in general. They would not cheat him of his freedom! "Marry!" he quoted a poet, "When I am old and weary of the world. . . ." He would rather be prudent than sorry; and it was not the last time he set duty, reason, and his emerging sense of destiny above the promptings of the heart. "Bold in the pursuit of knowl-edge," as he remembered himself in these young years, he would let nothing come in his way.

Lawyer, Builder, Husband

In 1767, three years after he came of age, Jefferson was admitted to the bar of the General Court. The highest court in the colony, it consisted of the Governor and Council and had appellate and origi-nal jurisdiction in both criminal and civil cases. Members of the Council, being appointed for life by royal grace and favor from among the leading families, having legislative and executive responsi-bilities as well, were not generally known for their legal or judicial attainments. It was a highly respectable court nonetheless, in part because of the advocates who appeared before it. Wythe and Pen-dleton were especially eminent at this time. Both men had risen from modest beginnings. One, Pendleton, was a striking figure, with a nimble mind and much popularity; the other, his rival, without surface brilliance of any kind, distinguished himself by plodding erudition. One was more learned, the other more successful in court. To an extent the contrast between them would be repeated in the two rising co-adjutors, Jefferson and Henry, though they seldom confronted each other at the bar. As Edmund Randolph observed, "Mr. Jefferson drew copiously from the depths of the law, Mr. Henry from the recesses of the human heart." Whatever advantage Jefferson derived from superiority of learning was canceled by

Henry's golden throat and folksy ways, which built for him a following Jefferson could never match. His deficiencies as a speaker were often noted in later years. As a lawyer, however, he seems to have acquitted himself respectably. Randolph, who knew him at the bar, said he was an impressive speaker who easily fixed the attention of his audience without the artifices of oratory.

At least half of the young lawyer's practice was in the county courts. These ruling bodies were even less judicial than the high court in Williamsburg; the litigation tended to be petty, the fees smaller; and the practice necessitated riding the circuit of the county seats. By law the two practices were to be kept separate, but the attorneys paid no attention to the law and pleaded indiscriminately in both jurisdictions. Like a plague of locusts, the pettifoggers of the counties descended on the General Court and, as Jefferson complained, "consumed the harvest." During the Revolution he tried to correct the evil by enforcing the separation of the two practices. Then men of legal science would not have to go marauding in the counties to make a living and the bar of the General Court would become the nursery of future judges. But the growing herd of lawyers had no interest in this system. Jefferson submitted to the drudgery of county practice and made the best of it. Mounted on horseback, his servant Jupiter in tow, he attended the courts of most of the counties of Virginia during seven years of practice. The circuit had its small rewards. It gave him firsthand knowledge of the society and politics of his native country and it established connections that would be useful to him later on. There was an *esprit*, an air of good humor and good fellowship, on the circuit that he enjoyed. And the court days were not without amusement. His account books, which he started with his law practice and in which he recorded every trifling expenditure to the end of his days, show that he attended the races, gambled occasionally at dice or cards, saw puppet shows, a "legerdemain man," an elk, a tiger, "a great hog," heard musical glasses, a woman sing, an organ grinder, and so on. Williamsburg offered plays and concerts and dances. Everywhere he searched out books for his growing library; once he bought a violin.

The account books with other records prove that he was a busy lawyer and, in the circumstances, a successful one. In Virginia, of course, litigation revolved around land and estate—there was little else. Not surprisingly, most of Jefferson's cases concerned tenures in one form or another, a subject grounded in *Coke upon Littleton.* His load of cases steadily increased, peaking in 1773, when he had more than 500 divided more or less evenly between the two jurisdictions, and dwindling the following year when the onrush of revolution closed the courts. Partly because the fees were fixed by law—a lingering trace of the old prejudice against lawyers—the financial return was rather paltry. The annual income on the average of seven years did not exceed $2000, and he was lucky if he collected three-quarters of this. Adding the tobacco income from his farms, he grossed in the neighborhood of $4000 a year, which was a substantial but far from princely income in pre-revolutionary Virginia. For him, as for Henry, as for John Adams in Massachusetts and so many others, the law laid the groundwork for a political career. His future was in the forum not at the bar. None of his cases produced public repercussions or became celebrated in the way the Parson's Cause brought instant fame to Henry. But his practice led to a widening circle of acquaintances and influence; even more important, it cultivated habits of mind that proved to be remarkably creative in the work of state-making. When he abandoned the practice in 1774 he did not abandon the law; rather he turned his legal skills to the greater cause of the Revolution.

The turn from law to politics had commenced five years earlier. In 1769 he took his seat in the House of Burgesses as a representative of Albemarle. This was almost sure to come in time: the service went with his position in the county. Still it was unusual for the freeholders to elect a young man of twenty-six who had not yet learned the ropes in the county magistracy. In the normal course one rose to the Burgesses on the ladder of local offices. Such had been his father's case. Jefferson reversed the procedure, starting at the top and taking in the local offices from that point. At least it does not appear that he was a justice of peace before he was a burgess; and he succeeded to the posts of county lieutenant and county surveyor, both formerly held by his father, in 1770 and 1773 respectively. Clearly the Albemarle gentry had taken the measure of young Jefferson and decided to promote him at once to the head of the class. Perhaps they were impressed by his legal attainments or his business-like approach to farming or, most of all, his enterprise in opening the Rivanna River to navigation. This was his first important public service and one that in later years he would count among the most useful. Until he came of age scarely a canoe navigated the Rivanna. Tobacco was transported overland to the stream's juncture with the James. Jefferson took a canoe, explored the river, and located the obstructions to navigation. He then started a subscription among his neighbors. Finally, with legislative authorization, the river was cleared as far as the falls at Milton just below Shadwell. Henceforth, the Rivanna floated most of the county's tobacco and produce to market.

As he was entering the public stage, Jefferson was also beginning to build at Monticello. The "little mountain" to which he gave the Italianate name was part of his father's original grant and had been a favorite haunt since he was a boy. It was now the chosen spot for his country seat. He began sawing lumber and planting fruit trees there in 1767; the next year he let a contract to level the summit; and in 1769 the foundations were dug, the brick kilns fired, and hardware ordered from England. He tried to get his English agent to send over an architect as well, but without success. He became his own architect. The versatility he demonstrated in this endeavor marked a permanent trait, exploding in all directions. The offspring of the meagerness of his cultural environment, it also expressed a powerful creative impulse in the man himself. Others might be content with what was; he could think only in terms of what should be. And he would not allow trifling obstacles, like those in the bed of the Rivanna, to bar his way.

To build a house with any pretensions to elegance in his remote country was difficult. But to rear it on a densely wooded summit seemed an act of folly. There was no precedent for it in America or in England; and though his reading of the Romans might have suggested the idea, it appears to have been entirely original with him. The simplest explanation is that he liked the view. From this eminence he surveyed a splendid panorama of nature, waves of forest, rolling hills and deep valleys, sharply etched, to the west, against the noble background of the Blue Ridge. The place appealed to his commingled sense of the beautiful and the sublime. He had probably read Edmund Burke's *Philosophical Inquiry into the Origin of*

Our Ideas of the Sublime and the Beautiful and noted his distinction between beauty in the classical sense of harmonious form and the sublime with its evocations of the boundless, the incomprehensible, the awesome in nature which, in Burke's view, communicated feelings of exaltation and power to the beholder. Whether or not he intended it, Jefferson achieved the latter in the setting and the former in his house. On the mountain nature was softened, proportioned, and improved by man; but all around wild nature inspired admiration and awe. The grandeur of the spectacle uplifted him. He felt bigger and nobler for having it at his command. "Where has nature spread so rich a mantle under the eye?" he exulted. "Mountains, forests, rocks, rivers. With what majesty do we ride above the storms! How sublime to look down into the workhouse of nature, to see her clouds, hail, snow, thunder, all fabricated at our feet! And the glorious sun when rising as if out of distant water, just gilding the tops of the mountains and giving life to all nature."

Learning to be his own architect, Jefferson first looked around his native country for models. The great plantation houses in the lowlands, Rosewell, Brandon, Westover, and others, some of which he knew well, were too elaborate, and the rough plans he obtained of newer and more modest dwellings did not suit him. So he turned to books. Later, when he felt he had earned the right, he was a harsh critic of Virginia building generally. Except for the Capitol in Williamsburg, no public building merited respect; and he cursed the prejudice against brick and stone and the sway of Georgian style in domestic architecture. "The genius of architecture seems to have shed its maledictions over this land." Searching for the first principles of the art, he acquainted himself with the books of certain English architects, Robert Morris and James Gibbs in particular, and they in turn led him to the master, the sixteenth-century Italian Andrea Palladio, whose *Four Books of Architecture*, virtually unknown in America, was the fountainhead of the art in Europe. Palladio had returned to Roman antiquity for his models—to surviving monuments where they existed, as in the case of theaters, temples, basilicas, and so on, and to the descriptions left by Vitruvius, Pliny, and others of Roman country villas. It was the last, of course, that now interested Jefferson. These villas, like his own, usually commanded an extensive landscape—Palladio recommended building on

24

an eminence—and as they were planned for productive estates employing slave labor, Jefferson discovered that their requirements, as in the relationship of the master's house to the service quarters, were remarkably similar to his own. But the greater and more enduring appeal of the Renaissance Italian to the Revolutionary Virginian lay in an aesthetic that not only confirmed but gave visible statement to his Newtonian faith in a rational and harmonious universe. In architecture the scientific modernist went back to the ancients because there, rather than in the vernacular of his own time and place, he found a definition of beauty that was as universal, chaste, and orderly as the laws of nature. The lesson of Palladio was that there were laws of architecture, equivalent to mathematical and physical laws, and that they were articulated in the buildings of ancient Rome. Escaping from mindless provincialism along this route, Jefferson ran the risk of falling into academic dogmatism. But he realized that in matters of taste, no less than in morals and politics, nature had constituted utility as the standard, thus the mind was free to adapt and transform the purest models in the light of environment and use. For himself, of course, and for the culture of his own country, he believed the classical ideal best expressed the dignity of free men in a free environment.

Palladio's influence made itself felt gradually, and never completely, in the design of Monticello. The early sketches show a one-story central block with pediment and flanking wings. Its principal source seems to have been a plate in Morris's *Select Architecture*. Later, after assimilating Palladio, he added a classical portico and other touches. The final plan combined features of both its predecessors. The elevation he drew exhibits a two-story central portico, Doric capitals below, Ionic above, with wings supporting a low attic story. Inside, a large entrance hall with staircase, a parlor or saloon, and a library on the second floor filled the central mass, while the wings housed the master's suite and the dining room and smaller bedrooms above. A Palladian villa in outline, the building was not a literal copy of anything. Many detail drawings, of orders, pediment, entablature, interior ornament, and so on, carefully calculated and scaled to correct classical proportions, show that Jefferson, who probably learned drafting skills from his father, had become a good craftsman. By 1772, when the house plan was settled, he had also worked out its relationship to the service buildings. Abandoning the first idea of a great terraced rectangle adjoining the house at one end, he decided instead on two L-shaped wings running out from the house. While this conformed to the idea of the Palladian court-yard, Jefferson imaginatively adapted it to his own taste and situa-tion by sinking these service wings into the slopes of the hillside at basement level, facing them outward rather than inward, and roof-ing them as terraces that flowed from the house to the lawns and gardens.

In planning his gardens Jefferson followed the new landscape style in vogue in England. He encountered it in the books of Wil-liam Shenstone and Thomas Whately and in the aesthetic theory of William Hogarth. The object of landscape, as distinguished from gardens in the formal French mode, was to reproduce artfully the beauties of nature in country estates. And since these beauties were irregular, waving, and rustic in outline—romantic rather than classi-cal—Jefferson's style in gardening contrasted sharply with his style in architecture. This was not a contradiction, since one comple-mented the other; the mingling revealed a man whose tastes, far from being narrow, were generous and eclectic. He made elaborate plans, including a park stocked with wild animals and embellished with cascading falls, temples (Chinese, Grecian, Gothic), and so on. But many years passed before these plans came to fruition, on a scale well below what he had envisioned.

The house itself was completed in about a dozen years, but the upper portico seems to have been omitted, and the service wings, or dependencies, existed only on paper until Jefferson rebuilt Monti-cello along its present lines in the 1790's. In a sense, he was always building Monticello. It was a lifelong passion, not simply as an ob-ject of taste and beauty but as an object of workmanship. He en-joyed building. A reflective or contemplative interest in the art did not satisfy him. He was excited more by the process itself than by the ultimate product. This went, too, for the other fine arts, such as music, that caught his fancy.

Jefferson took up residence on the mountain in November 1770. At the time only the little pavilion that in time would fix the termi-nus of the south service wing had been completed. "I have here but one room," he wrote, "which, like the cobbler's, serves me for parlor, for kitchen and hall . . . for bed chamber and study too." A devastating fire at Shadwell caused him to make the move somewhat earlier than he had anticipated. The fire consumed most of his papers together with a library estimated in monetary terms at £200 sterling, though it was the books, not the money, that he treasured. He set out at once to repair the loss, and within a few years boasted a library second to none in Virginia. His ambitions in this direction are suggested by the spacious quarters set aside in his house for the library. By the fall of 1770, too, Jefferson had commenced a courtship which, while its outcome remained uncertain, provided further incentive for him to hurry with the building of Monticello.

The lady was Martha Wayles Skelton, an attractive widow of twenty-three who resided at her father's place, The Forest, near Williamsburg. Jefferson had known Bathurst Skelton, the deceased husband, at college, and John Wayles, Martha's father, at the bar. By his own industry and cunning, both as a lawyer and trafficker in lands and slaves, Wayles had accumulated a large fortune. Martha, his eldest daughter, was the principal heir. Precious little is known of her. The fleeting glimpses that survive portray her as petite, pretty, vivacious, and unusually accomplished in the pleasing arts cultivated by Virginia belles. Indeed it is said that she favored Jefferson over several other suitors in part because he shared her love of music. He, at any rate, gave his sentineled heart to Martha and took her as his bride. They were married at The Forest on New Year's Day, 1772. After a round of festivities and a leisurely journey from the lowlands, they began housekeeping in Jefferson's bachelor quarters, transformed into "Honeymoon Lodge," at Monticello. The first child, Martha, was born in September. Of the six children born over ten years, only two survived infancy. The pain and the sorrow killed Martha. Jefferson, who regarded conjugal love, like religion, as an exclusively private matter, hid the emotional traces of his marriage from the world. Yet it was clearly a happy marriage even with its sorrows. He came to prize domestic felicity above any other. In his view the burden of attaining it rested mainly on the wife, whose whole life ought to revolve around husband, hearth, and children. Martha evidently measured up to the standard—and died under it.

John Wayles's death in 1773 led to a doubling of Jefferson's estate. He would never be so rich again. He came into possession, on behalf of Martha, of some 11,000 acres of land and 135 slaves. However, he promptly sold over half the land to cover his share, about £4300, of Wayles's debts to English creditors. Unfortunately, the bonds given him by purchasers of the lands, which were the security of his own bonds to the creditors, were finally paid off in depreciated Revolutionary currency as worthless as "oak leaves," as Jefferson said, and unacceptable in England. So he had to liquidate the debt all over again. In fact, it dogged him the rest of his life. The two valuable estates retained from the legacy, Elk Hill at the confluence of the Rivanna and the James, and Poplar Forest, to the west in Bedford County, were at first managed from Monticello, and there was a good deal of going and coming between these places. The management of so large an agricultural estate—over 10,000 acres with about 180 slaves, divided among three extensive plantations and several smaller ones—was not unlike the government of a miniature state. As the Revolution approached, Jefferson found less and less time for the affairs of this private domain, and two decades would pass before he could give it his earnest attention.

What manner of man was this thirty-year-old Virginian about to step to the center of the Revolutionary stage? Certain dominant traits of mind and character had formed a personal style destined to have profound public effects. While no complete accounting is possible at this point, before he was really known to history, some of the controlling features of his personality might be discerned.

One is struck, first of all, by the young Jefferson's intellectuality. He was pre-eminently a student, strenuous in the pursuit of knowledge. His mental discipline, his appetite for books, his omniverous curiosity, all marked the trait. He approached the world through his understanding rather than his feelings. It would be misleading to call him bookish, especially if that adjective is meant to suggest the pedant or the closeted philosopher, for he was neither of these; yet, far more than most men, he was dependent on books and inclined to take his knowledge from them rather than from direct acquaintance. As a result, his understanding spanned an immense field but spanned much of it at second- or third-hand, which gave a certain airiness to his traffic with reality. He gained a vantage point above or outside of things-as-they-are—the hard crust of history—from which to perceive, as through the eye of reason, things-as-they-might-be. The Baconian axiom, "knowledge is power," became the core of his faith; and he was never more typically a man of the Enlightenment than in his conviction that reason and inquiry would lead men away from whatever was false or capricious or twisted in human affairs toward the truth inherent in the natural order of things. With this went a tendency, already evident in law and architecture, to run everything back to its source, whence its inner nature could be defined, and to proceed from that point. A radical tendency, it would usually have radical effects. Because the quality of intellectuality was so marked in Jefferson, the principal wellsprings of his thought should be plainly defined. First in the course of education, though not in ultimate influence, was classical philosophy and literature. Second, modern scientific rationalism and natural religion, to which he was introduced by Dr. Small and the trio of tutors in Williamsburg. And third, English law and history, which became for him the main road to revolution.

A close companion of Jefferson's intellectuality was a characteristic forbearance and reserve in his intercourse with his fellow men. In part, this simply expressed his deference to the forms and proprieties of civilized society; but there was an added quality of austerity in Jefferson that, by Virginia standards, seemed more in keeping with the Puritan type. He was by all appearances an amiable and sociable person, never harsh or disagreeable, and he had a remarkable talent, seemingly effortless in its motions, for drawing men to him. But appearances could be deceiving. Most men caught him at the easy glasslike surface he exposed to the world. As Albert J. Nock has observed, "He was the most approachable and the most impenetrable of men, easy and delightful of acquaintance, impossible of knowledge." He kept a tight rein on his emotions. Only once in his youth, when he made "improper advances" to the wife of a friend, did the control slacken, and the narrowness of the escape may have caused him to strengthen his hold. He did not lack a sense of humor, yet it could not be considered a strong point of his personality. He was too fussy. What was ludicrous in life was more likely to be cause for regret than for amusement. Expecting so much of men, and of nations too, he could not laugh at their follies, least of all at his own. He discovered early, as early as his admission into the circle of mature scholars at Williamsburg, that high seriousness was the condition of any worthy endeavor, and he turned from this purchase of his youth, in the words of a favorite poet, "big with holy hope of nobler time to come." It remains to be seen what effects these traits would have in his public career. But one thing seems clear: he was not, in his nature, born for the public. The Pendletons and the Henrys and the Adamses—men who opened themselves freely to the currents of life and politics—were, but not Jefferson. None of the heroes of his early life was associated with political power. Intellectual and moral power yes, power of state no. Like Seneca he would "rather be quiet than in arms." And when arms swept him up, he could never resign himself to his fate. He held back, begrudging commitment to the public role, yet unable to make it in any other; and this pattern of forbearance, with its cycles of withdrawal and return, ran through his life.

No less characteristic was Jefferson's penchant for methodical industry, order, and system. In this he proved to be a rigorous man of business, like his father. He hated idleness. He was fond of detail. His personal records—Account Book, Garden Book, Farm Book, and so on—exhibit a profusion of minutiae. He recorded from year to year, for instance, the exact time and place of planting a given vegetable, when it sprouted, when it ripened and came to the table. His meteorological observations, regularly three times a day, extended over several decades. All was neatly ordered and arranged. He enjoyed poetry when young and heartstrong, even wrote a verse or two; but he was not a poet by nature and, as he matured, had little call for this muse. In nothing he ever undertook did he lack facts; and he felt more at home in the realm of empirical data than in the realm of abstractions. The logic of facts took nothing for granted. It dissolved phenomena into component elements, analyzed them, defined their natural relationship, then reconstructed the parts to express the newly discovered truth. Such at least was the intent. Clarity, precision, proportion—these qualities of his architecture expressed an essentially mathematical spirit—a Newtonian as well as a classical aesthetic—in the service of utilitarian objectives. Jefferson could not surrender gracefully to life. His whole tendency was to combat the chaos of experience and submit it to the dictates of reason which, of course, he identified with the laws of nature.

Related to this, though seemingly at odds with the traits of intellectuality and reserve, was the fundamentally activist temper of Jefferson's mind. With him, as with enlightened thinkers generally, ideas were meant to act on the world, not simply to reflect it. This functional interest in ideas exalted useful knowledge, practical workmanship, and mastery of nature. Even in the arts he was not primarily a passive observer or auditor; his greatest enjoyment came from participation. His temperament rejected the conventional dualism of mind and body, thought and work, theory and practice. He espoused bodily health and activity as the necessary condition of mental vigor; and partly for the same reason, he distrusted overly civilized environments cut off from physical nature. He loved to tinker, to work with his hands, as Monticello would demonstrate. The versatility that would become one of his claims to fame, the result of the workman-like temperament nurtured by his own environment, was already evident in the young Jefferson who, in James Parton's memorable description, "could calculate an eclipse, survey an estate, tie an artery, plan an edifice, try a cause, break a horse, dance a minuet, and play a violin."

An activist must, of necessity, be an optimist as well. The world of experience was malleable to the hammers of the mind. Only gloomy and hypochondriac souls thought differently. "My temperament is sanguine," Jefferson told John Adams in his seventy-third year, and he might have said the same in the thirtieth. "I steer my bark with Hope in the head, leaving Fear astern."

CHAPTER TWO

Philosopher
of Revolution

Charles Townshend: *Will these Americans, children planted by our care, nourished up by our indulgence until they are grown to a degree of strength and opulence, and protected by our arms, will they grudge to contribute their mite to relieve us from the heavy weight of that burden which we live under?*

Colonel Isaac Barré: *They planted by your care? No! Your oppressions planted 'em in America. They fled your tyranny to a then uncultivated and inhospitable country where they exposed themselves to almost all the hardships to which human nature is liable, and among others to the cruelties of a savage foe. . . .*

They nourished by your indulgence? They grew by your neglect of 'em. As soon as you began to care about 'em, that care was exercised in sending persons to rule over 'em. . . .

They protected by your arms? They have nobly taken up arms in your defence, have exerted a valour amidst their constant and laborious industry for the defence of a country, whose frontier while drenched in blood, its interior parts have yielded all its little savings to your emolument. And believe me, remember I this day told you so, that same spirit of freedom which activated that people at first, will accompany them still.

From the debate in the House of Commons on the Stamp Act, 1765.

THOMAS JEFFERSON entered the councils of the American Revolution in May 1769. Taking his seat in the House of Burgesses, he ceased to be an onlooker and became a mover and shaper of events. Pomp and circumstance befitting His Majesty's government in the Dominion of Virginia accompanied the initiation of the delegate from Albemarle. On the morning of May 8, standing with other newly elected burgesses in the Council chamber of the Capitol, he took the oath of office and, before returning to the House, watched the fanfare for the governor as he arrived in an elegantly liveried carriage drawn by six white horses. The Governor, Norborne Berkeley, Baron de Botetourt, had come to Virginia the previous year in succession to Francis Fauquier, dead and buried beneath the stone slab of the Bruton Church. He was a nobleman, of course, but significantly, unlike Fauquier and indeed all the royal governors since 1705, who had been lieutenants of titular heads in England, Lord Botetourt bore the commission of a full-masted viceroy, which the Virginians interpreted as a mark of respect from George III in troubled times. They looked upon this courtly but amiable man as a harbinger of peace and friendship.

Ceremony was the life of royalty. The burgesses—Jefferson one of the troop of perhaps 90 or 100 actually present—answer His Excellency's summons to attend him in the Council chamber. Gentlemen, he commands, return to the House and choose a speaker. They obey, and unanimously re-elect Peyton Randolph to that honorable post. The Governor, duly informed, again summons them and the burgesses again evacuate their benches and march to the other chamber, crowding around the room where the Council is seated at the great table. The Speaker is presented; the Governor reads his speech from the throne; the House retires. These formalities completed, it is now ready for business; not quite, however, for "a most humble and dutiful address" thanking His Excellency for his "very affectionate speech" must be drafted. The new member from Albemarle was given this task, and though his draft was virtually rewritten in committee, the address may be reckoned the first, and certainly the most innocuous, of Jefferson's state papers.

33

After all this parade, the assembly session lasted only ten days. The Speaker at once laid before the House an explosive piece of unfinished business from the previous meeting. In February 1768 the Massachusetts House of Representatives had adopted a vigorous protest against Parliament's Townshend Acts, and by a circular letter to the other colonial legislatures had appealed for united action. The Virginia House had answered with a circular letter of its own urging support of Massachusetts. It was the correspondence evoked by this action that was now laid before the house.

The several acts passed by Parliament in June and July 1767, and known collectively by the name of their principal sponsor, Charles Townshend, Chancellor of the Exchequer, revived the great controversy ignited by the Stamp Act of 1765. The repeal of that measure in the face of massive colonial resistance had given grounds for hope that the imperial government, though it persisted in claiming the right, would not again assert the power of taxing the colonists or otherwise interfere in their internal affairs. But Townshend shattered this illusion. Seizing on the distinction the Americans had supposedly made between *internal* taxes, which were prohibited, and *external* taxes, which were conceded, at least in so far as levied for the regulation of trade, Townshend proposed to collect £40,000 a year by duties in American ports on paper, glass, lead, paints, and tea. The act was a brazen reassertion of Parliament's sovereignty, a clear test of the power claimed by the Declaratory Act, which had passed on the repeal of the Stamp Act, to bind the colonists "in all cases whatsoever." The duties were *external*, but revenue, not trade, was their object; and the anticipated revenue was so paltry that the colonists could not fail to see the political motive and purpose of the act. This was further disclosed by the provision to pay the revenue into a special fund to support, in part, the salaries of royal governors, judges, and other colonial officials, thereby freeing them from dependence on the provincial legislatures. A companion of the revenue measure looked to the more vigorous enforcement of all trade laws by the establishment in Boston of an American board of customs commissioners directly responsible to the British treasury. Still another measure, the most audacious of all, suspended the New York Assembly for failure to furnish quarters and supplies for His Majesty's troops as required by the Quartering Act. New York's grudging eleventh-hour compliance lifted the suspension before it could take effect; but it was this act which submitted the very existence of a colonial government to the will of Parliament that particularly agitated the Virginians in 1768. Meanwhile, as Virginia and most other colonies endorsed the Massachusetts circular letter, the imperial government reacted angrily. All the governors were ordered to treat the letter as a subversive document and to dissolve, if necessary, any assembly that united in the protest against the Townshend Acts. Lord Botetourt carried the directive to Virginia. The Burgesses were under no misapprehension on this point and they had learned of new invasions of American rights brewing in Parliament, for instance, a proposition to transport American malcontents to England for trial.

Such was the challenge to the Burgesses in May 1769. Of course, it must be met. Jefferson may have been surprised that the Governor had chosen to risk a confrontation by convening the assembly. If he expected to pacify the Virginians, he was sadly mistaken. On May 16 the House unanimously adopted four resolutions: first, that the sole right of levying taxes on the inhabitants of Virginia rests with the local government; second, that the united action of the colonies to secure redress of grievances is lawful; third, that all trials for treason or other crimes committed in Virginia must be conducted locally with a jury from the vicinage; and fourth, that the King again be petitioned to intervene on behalf of the rights and liberties of his colonial subjects. A "humble address" to the King was adopted the next day. Immediately, the Governor summoned the House to attend him in the Council chamber. "Mr. Speaker and Gentlemen of the House of Burgesses," he announced, "I have heard of your resolves and augur ill of their effect. You have made it my duty to dissolve you; and you are dissolved accordingly."

Without further ado the burgesses, or rather ex-burgesses, reassembled in the Apollo Room of the Raleigh Tavern and there adopted a non-importation agreement, known as the Association, which bound the signers not to import or to buy any goods taxed by Parliament for the purpose of raising revenue in America. A long list of contraband articles was drawn up and measures taken to circulate the agreement. The Virginians were following the example of merchants and town meetings in the Northern ports; but for the first time a colonial legislature, stripped of its official status and re-constituted under its own authority, engaged in an act of rebellion. Several assemblies similarly situated now followed the Virginia ex-ample. The principal aim of the Association was to force repeal of the Townshend duties by unprecedented economic coercion of the mother country. In Virginia, where there were few cities or native merchants, the enforcement was poor; in the major seaports it was more effective. The merchants and treasury in Britain felt the ef-fects, and partly for this reason the new ministry under Lord Fred-erick North in 1770 brought about the repeal of all the duties, ex-cept the one on tea, and by other actions as well sought to conciliate the colonists. The experiment would have lasting consequences for Jefferson's career. He became a convert to the principle and the strategy of commercial coercion not only in the Revolutionary struggle against the mother country but in the larger campaign for national independence in the decades ahead.

In 1770 the American resistance promptly collapsed, despite North's vindication of the principle, in the continuing tax on tea, of the right and the power of Parliament to tax the colonists. Jefferson refused to accept the outcome. Nothing fundamental had been set-tled. Whatever the conciliatory gestures of the North ministry, the only security for America lay in a constitutional principle no closer to resolution than at the start of the controversy. In the spring, with some others of the same mind in Williamsburg, he signed additional articles of the Association demanding total repeal of the obnoxious duties and looking to the formation of county committees to en-force the agreement. But the movement had fallen beyond recovery at this stage. The Governor had charmed Virginians into a state of fawning admiration and treacherous insensibility to danger, Jeffer-son later said. Deftly playing the part of friend and reconciler, finess-ing every difficulty, Botetourt made himself so beloved by Virgini-ans in the few remaining months of his life that when he died the assembly voted to erect a statue of the noble lord in Williamsburg, where it remains to this day a monument of that "colonial subservi-ence" Jefferson deplored.

The second crisis in the contest with the mother country passed in 1770. Jefferson had witnessed the first, brought on by the Stamp Act, and played a modest role in the second, while in the third sure to come he had a still undisclosed appointment with destiny. As he went about the business of law and farming, building and marrying, politics began to have an important place in his life. Service in the assembly plunged him into the center of the colony's affairs. His reading shifted from law and literature, which had predominated, to the theory and practice of government, and with it went a change in the contours of his mind. Virginia was also changing. While it is difficult to say how conscious he was of these shifting contours of society and politics in his native country, it is equally difficult to explain his own career and convictions without taking some account of them.

Troubled Virginia

The remarkable unity of Virginia in support of the Revolution has tended to give a deceptively simple picture of the society and the impulses that moved it. In no colony was there greater solidarity in the ruling class or greater deference in the mass of people to the leadership. Nowhere did the Revolutionary movement produce so little internal discord or was the transition to independence accomplished with such ease. The smoothness of the entire operation has pointed up the importance of two causative factors. First, the structure of politics in Virginia consolidated power in a close-knit gentry class. Power was riveted solidly to wealth, breeding, and status. The House of Burgesses, which one historian has called "a tobacco planters' club" and others have seen as one huge cousinship, consisted of men who ordinarily had passed through the same experience, shared the same interests, and converged in the same outlook. Jefferson, however much he deviated from the type, was a member of the club and could always count half a dozen or more blood relations at the Capitol. Oligarchy was undergirded by democracy—the country democracy of all the landholders. But the electoral system favored the first gentlemen of the counties, and from ingrained habits of deference the freeholding yeomen looked to them for leadership.

The second factor, flowing from the first, was the extraordinary consensus among the leaders on the constitutional basis of Virginia's resistance to the mother country. Until the 1760's the colony had, in fact, enjoyed a high degree of self-government. When this period of "salutary neglect" ended after the Seven Years War, and the imperial government reasserted its claims, the Virginians described the movement as an assault on their ancient liberties and put forth their own claims, carefully buttressed with the defenses of the English constitution, to exclusive jurisdiction over the internal polity. From the Stamp Act forward, certainly, none of the leaders doubted the rightness of this position, though they might disagree on the means of holding it. The idea had been latent for some time. An astute observer in 1759 wrote of the gentry: "They are haughty and jealous of their liberties, impatient of restraints, and can scarcely bear the thought of being controlled by any superior power. Many of them consider the colonies as independent states, unconnected with Great Britain otherwise than by having the same common king." The House of Burgesses claimed for itself co-ordinate jurisdiction in Virginia with the House of Commons in England. Any interference from outside, any subordination of the representative body in Virginia, threatened gentry rule and could not be tolerated. The gentry, therefore, formed a united front against Britain. And precisely because they lacked other pressing grievances, they settled on the constitutional principle that, while it may also have been right and good in itself, secured their own power. When Jefferson finally worked the constitutional argument to a finish in 1774 he drew upon depths of thought and feeling in Virginia as well as upon his own capacious intellect.

Yet, admitting the importance of these forces of solidarity and consensus, revolutions are not made in the absence of social stress nor are the principles invoked an accurate reflection of the reality that moves them. If there were no sharp class or sectional or ideological or interest divisions in Virginia, such as could be found in other colonies, and if the gentry ruled without challenge except from abroad, it does not follow that the gentry had no serious problems of its own. It did; and the anxieties within the ruling class poisoned the imperial relationship. In their quarrel with the mother country Virginians objectified the tensions and strains of their own society. The process was largely unconscious. Jefferson himself was scarcely aware of it. But to a greater degree than anyone recognized, Virginia's antagonism to Britain arose from the ruling elite's troubles about itself.

Grave economic problems afflicted the colony in the 1760's. A debt of half a million pounds had been contracted in the imperial war against France; and lacking specie, the only way the colony would retire it was by the issuance of paper money. But the home government put a stop to this practice that threatened the sterling debts owed to British creditors. Currency remained a problem. Far more serious, however, was the sharp decline of tobacco prices. The planter's income dwindled while he continued to pay high prices to the British merchants who supplied him. The value of his lands and slaves depreciated. Some planters went under. The courts were crowded with suits for debts, and *capias* issued in great number, even against wealthy families. Several successive years of short crops added to the trouble. Planters observed a cooling trend in the climate and feared it would soon cease to support tobacco. Jefferson himself, guided by his thermometer at Monticello, came to this opinion sometime later. In the tidewater, planters worried over "our low land worn out soil." Everywhere the sordidness of slaves and the insolence of overseers stirred complaint. Worst of all, the shrinkage of income, rather than enforcing austerity, was accompanied by reckless extravagance. Chasing the fantastic image of themselves as transplanted English country gentlemen, the great planters lavishly indulged their taste for luxury, refinement, and idle pleasure. "Extravagance hath been our ruin," moaned one of the grandees in 1768. John Wayles, soon to become Jefferson's father-in-law, felt the same gloom. "In 1740," he observed, "I don't remember to have seen such a thing as a Turkey carpet in the Country except a small thing in a bedchamber. Now nothing are so common as Turkey or Wilton Carpets, the whole furniture, rooms, elegant, and every appearance of opulence." Had the Virginians risen to such heights to decline so soon? The history of some of the great families seemed to point the downward direction. William Byrd III had turned a great patrimony into a £100,000 debt. "Wild Bob" Carter, eldest son of Landon Carter of Sabine Hall, was a notorious rake. And ruin impended for the mighty Nelsons in the third generation. These squandering legatees of Virginia wealth and power, these ungrateful sons, figured in the general malaise which only a radical purgative could cure.

But if Virginians must castigate themselves for wanton extravagance, it was not as if they alone were to blame—the British merchants had lured them into the trap. On the whole, the planters were content to work within the mercantilist system, sending all their tobacco to the mother country, where 90 per cent of it was re-exported, after adding £200,000 a year to the British treasury and lining the merchants' pockets with the profits of the trade. The planters thus had no control over the market; yet such were the advantages of the system, especially the British mercantile expertise to which the Virginians laid no claim, that the trade laws were never a serious grievance against the mother country. The great irritant in this colonial subservience was credit, not trade. As Jefferson later explained it: "The advantages made by the British merchants, on the tobacco consigned to them, were so enormous, that they spared no means of increasing those consignments. A powerful engine for this purpose was the giving of good prices and credit to the planter, till they got him more immersed in debt than he could pay, without selling his lands and slaves. They then reduced the price given for the tobacco, so that let his shipments be ever so great, and his demand of necessaries ever so economical, they never permitted him to clear off his debt. These debts had become hereditary from father to son, for many generations, so that the planters were a species of property, annexed to certain mercantile houses in London." There is special pleading in this account, but what matters in the present context is the way Virginians viewed their plight; and, unquestionably, they attributed it in large part to this vassalage under British credit. Jefferson estimated the planter debts at two to three million pounds at the time of the Revolution. To unfriendly observers at the time, to historians since, the desire to throw off these debts was the hidden motive of the Virginia gentry's zeal for independence. The evidence fails to support this view, and as Jefferson's own experience would testify, the debts were not thrown off. Falling deeper and deeper into arrears, the planters directed their anger against Britain through her merchants, above all the Scottish resident factors who, coming to Virginia at mid-century, bought and sold to everyone and spread the web of debt and credit over the whole society.

Land rich, the planters too easily assumed that if forced to it they could sell parcels of their holdings to pay off their debts. But since nearly everyone was in the same boat, and specie or currency in any form exceedingly scarce, there were few buyers even at sacrifice prices. Indebtedness had become a chronic evil from which there seemed to be no escape.

The problem erupted in local politics in 1766. The death of John Robinson in May disclosed a major scandal in the ruling class. For nearly thirty years Robinson had held both the powerful offices of treasurer and speaker of the House of Burgesses. The clique that gathered around him, receiving his favors and doing his bidding in return, has been not inaccurately compared to a modern political machine. Now, after his death, it was discovered that Robinson had embezzled £100,000 from the Virginia treasury in order to help his friends in distress. (The paper money remitted during the war was to be retired when collected in the form of taxes, but instead of burning it as the law required, Robinson loaned it to hard-pressed planters, expecting that the transactions would be covered before they came to public notice.) Approximately 240 gentlemen were the beneficiaries of this largesse. They included Jefferson's father and his future father-in-law, who were indebted to the treasury for £52 and £445 respectively. The debts fell now to Robinson's estate, which in turn owed the money to the province. The administrator of the estate, Edmund Pendleton, patiently pressed the planters for payment. Many suits were instituted, and many of the debtors became bankrupts, if indeed they were not already. At the end of the Revolution the public account was finally closed in depreciated paper money, but before the Revolution the Robinson scandal shook the ruling class, wounded its morale, and damaged its prestige. Corruption and influence, it seemed, had spread from English shores and infected the virtuous heart of liberty in America. Virginians trembled for the future.

The Robinson affair did not split the ruling gentry since they had better reasons to stick together; but it joined with other influences to alter the complexion of Virginia politics. Men like Patrick Henry and Richard Henry Lee, "young hot-heads," Governor Fauquier called them, helped to expose the scandal and then used it to break the virtual monopoly of the Robinson coterie in the affairs of the assembly. Lee's ambitions were allied with the Potomac region, Henry's with the piedmont, both previously neglected in the distribution of power, and allied too, for both men, with more aggressive opposition to the mother country.

The "hot-heads" had won the first challenge a year before in the debate on the Stamp Act. In the waning hours of the assembly session, after most of the burgesses had gone home, Henry offered his resolutions against the Stamp Act and, in this connection, reputedly put down shouts of treason with the defiant line, "If this be treason, make the most of it." The resolutions, or most of them, were adopted over the strenuous opposition of Speaker Robinson, Peyton Randolph, and other members of the old guard. They did not disagree with the principle of these resolutions, which focused the constitutional claim of "no taxation without representation," one which they had, in fact, only a year before solemnly declared a "sacred birthright." But these gentlemen thought the resolutions too bold, perhaps treasonable now that the Stamp Act had become law, and quite aside from fiery implications for the contest with Britain, the resolutions and their upstart backers threatened the reign of the tidewater junto in Virginia. So the larger struggle for power enclosed a smaller one; and while the Virginia Stamp Act Resolves ignited a continent, they also shifted the balance of power in the Virginia gentry. The Robinson affair following in quick succession confirmed the change with added leverage. In general, power moved to the younger gentry, geographically to the upcountry and the Potomac; but these new forces did not so much take over as they were taken into the old leadership. It was a remarkable vindication of a law of conservative politics, phrased by a modern sociologist as "restriction by incorporation." Rather than lose the scepter altogether, the tidewater magnates consented, not without bitterness, to share it.

When Jefferson came into the House he naturally gravitated to the Lee-Henry pole, somewhat to the left of center—though it may be misleading to speak of poles when the political spectrum was so narrow. Lee and Henry remained suspect, but Jefferson was accepted by the old leaders as well as the new and thus helped to allay the little frictions between them. He had known Henry a long time, since a rollicking Christmastime in Hanover County before he entered college. As a law student he had stood in the door of the

House of Burgesses to hear Henry's great speech on the Stamp Act. "He appeared to me to speak as Homer wrote," Jefferson later recalled. From that moment, certainly, his own course in the imperial struggle was fixed. He always credited Henry, seven years his senior, with setting "the ball of revolution" in motion, and whatever he may have said about the Forest Demosthenes after their political estrangement, he insisted on the "exact conformity" of their opinions at this time. What he later said—that Henry was lazy, ignorant, coarse, ambitious, demagogic, and so on—was a fair summation of old guard opinion in the 1760's, though Jefferson had better ground for it. In the end Henry became the most conservative of provincials, while Jefferson, following the popular path he had blazed through densities of aristocratic conceit at the onset of the Revolution, became the hero of American democracy.

Certain areas of British policy in the 1760's not only aroused opposition in Virginia but slashed at the nerves of competing interests within the ruling class. This was notably the case with western lands. In the years between 1745 and 1754 the Governor and Council had granted over a million acres of Trans-Allegheny lands to several speculative companies. Different interests and coteries—a Robinson-Nelson group in the lower tidewater, a Lee-Washington-Mason group in the Potomac region, the Walker interest with which Jefferson's father was associated in Albemarle—jockeyed for favor and influence on Virginia's great frontier. So long as the French were in the Ohio Valley the home government encouraged this movement, believing that Virginia settlers would form a bulwark against the enemy. Various problems, including the war that followed, prevented the land companies from fulfilling the conditions of their grants, and the grants lapsed. After the fall of Fort Duquesne the Virginians attempted to revive the expansionist policy. The British ministry, on the other hand, more concerned now to keep peace with the Indians on the frontier, checked the Virginians at every turn. The Governor was enjoined from making grants on pain of removal from office, and the Royal Proclamation of 1763 prohibited settlement beyond the mountains. The policy broke down five years later. The companies, still without valid title to a single acre, faced a new obstacle in the form of the Grand Ohio, or Vandalia, Company, based in Philadelphia but with influential friends at court in

England, which capped four years of bargaining and intrigue by securing a huge proprietary grant lying south of the Ohio. Claiming
jurisdiction in this area, Virginia revived the old grants, issued new
patents, and pushed expansion westward, until new British restrictions in 1774 halted the march, so far as it could be halted by law.
In this enterprise the Virginians stood together on the issue of provincial versus Crown control but, otherwise, they were not always
united among themselves. There was rivalry between the companies;
the favors of Governor and Council were unevenly distributed; policies or tactics that benefited one speculative interest often injured
another; and the common people were left out of the reckoning altogether. Here again the smaller inner struggle generated some of
the heat for the larger one. Jefferson himself, a sworn non-specula-
tor, had only a remote personal interest—the inherited share of dubious value in Walker's Loyal Company—in this business, but western lands and expansion claimed his attention politically. And the
more he studied the matter the more convinced he became that no
satisfactory solution was possible within the imperial framework.

Looking back at this time in later years, Jefferson complained of
"the dull monotony of colonial subservience." What he meant, apparently, as he suggested in his autobiography, was that thought and
action were "circumscribed within narrow limits," not only by imperial rule but by colonial habits of mind. Insulated in his little
quarter of the globe, Jefferson's mind had nevertheless opened to
the enlightened spirit of his age, and he wished to give it effect in
the laws of Virginia. But what could be accomplished while the provincial mind was enthralled and an imperial authority 3000 miles
across the ocean fixed the country's destiny? During his first brief
session in the assembly he sought with one of the senior members to
secure legislation to ameliorate the condition, or possibly even permit the manumission, of slaves. The effort failed, and the senior
member, Richard Bland, who had taken the lead, was "denounced as
an enemy of his country." The Established Church, like slavery an
essentially colonial institution in Jefferson's eyes, enforced a "bigoted intolerance" at war with human rights, the peace of society,
and religion itself. Yet Virginians, who cared little for the Church,
could do nothing about it, except stave off such "pernicious projects" as the establishment of an American episcopate, which would

further undermine local autonomy. The obstacles to improvement, Jefferson later said, were more of habit and despair than of reflection and conviction. As he began to see government through the eye of first principles, he discovered many defects in both the Virginia and the English practice. The colonial judiciary, especially the mixing of legislative and executive powers in the General Court, assailed every sound principle. The case of John Wilkes, widely publicized in Virginia during Jefferson's first years on the political scene, vividly dramatized the corruption and deterioration of the home government. Wilkes's four successive elections to, and expulsions from, Parliament after his return from political exile seemed to prove that King and Parliament were tyrants at home as well as in America. The English constitution, although the whole world had been taught to admire it, appeared badly shattered. Jefferson increasingly despaired of its reform and feared the contagion of corrupt influence and arbitrary power in provincial affairs. Alienated from the source of authority, he in common with many other Americans set out to discover what the grounds of authority should be.

Enlightenment—Democracy—Nationality

The American Revolution was an intellectual as well as a political event. The political course to 1776 and beyond is well known in its outer manifestations. The inner movement of thought and sentiment —the history of the Revolutionary mind—remains obscure. Jefferson, who helped to make that mind and who epitomized the philosopher-statesman of the era, was remarkably inarticulate about the processes of thought that conducted him to the revolutionary event. Perhaps he did not understand them himself. Their channels were intricate, devious, and partly hidden from consciousness. Gradually, the heterogeneous elements, dissolved from their old associations, crystallized into a new body of thought. The future would disclose the full range of new associations, but the theoretical framework was set in 1776. It was articulated as a creed, notably in the Preamble of the Declaration of Independence, not as a philosophy, however. Jefferson, as has often been said, never reduced his thought to a system. He was distrustful of philosophical systems generally—

they were prisons of the mind. Thought with him was an instrument for reshaping life, not for reflecting it in some grand cosmic design. His philosophy was eclectic, dynamic, and pragmatic. Any attempt to give it the logical coherence of a finished system would be to rob it of the freedom and flexibility essential to its mission. So the philosophy was left in fragments, profuse but disordered, compatible but strangely dissimilar; and to reassemble them into something like the organic unity they must have had in his own mind is at once a difficult and treacherous undertaking. Even the fragments are distressingly scarce before 1776; but many things may be inferred from his reading, his writings, his education, and his experience.

Viewed as an intellectual movement, the Revolution drew on a cultural heritage as old as Western civilization itself. Picking and choosing from the vast concourse of traditions—Classical, Christian, English, Modern—the Americans, not omitting their own incipient tradition, framed a Revolutionary ideology that, while addressed to the unique task of national independence, exploited the sources and ideas and rhetoric of latent democratic revolution in the Western world. Certain dominant configurations emerged from this gathering of forces. For the purpose of analysis in Jefferson's thought, they may be broadly defined in terms of the critical spirit of the age in which he lived, the Age of Enlightenment, the central tradition of law and government on which he drew, the English, and the still shadowy but developing consciousness of the native environment. The terms are rough correlatives of the paramount themes of Jefferson's career in nation-building: Enlightenment, Democracy, Nationality.

Jefferson was the pre-eminent American exponent, along with Benjamin Franklin, of the eighteenth-century Enlightenment. Whether the Enlightenment is considered an intellectual movement, a temper of mind, or a climate of opinion, whether it is dismissed, denounced, or admired, Jefferson was one of its legitimate children, in the end one of its authentic geniuses. Its progenitors were English, Newton and Locke in particular, to whom Jefferson added Lord Bacon to form his trinity of heroes. His early exposure, beginning with the lesser trio in Williamsburg, was mainly to English and Scottish votaries of the Enlightenment. It had invaded the Conti-

46

nent, of course, and Jefferson was familiar with the writings of Montesquieu, Voltaire, Beccaria, Buffon, and several others before the Revolution; but it was not until he took up residence in Paris in the 1780's, then the capital of the Enlightenment, that he plugged the currents of his mind into the wider movement and became something of a *philosophe* himself.

The controlling assumptions of enlightened thought were so thoroughly assimilated in Jefferson's mind that he cannot possibly be understood apart from them. First, untrammeled free inquiry in the pursuit of knowledge. Nothing was to be taken for granted; everything was to be questioned, taken apart, traced back to its origins, and reconstructed in the light of intelligence. "Everything," Diderot enjoined in the great *Encyclopédie*, "must be examined, everything must be shaken up, without exception and without circumspection." Philosophy was a method of inquiry, not a static system of truths; and empirical science on the Newtonian model was good in all fields, the moral and social together with the physical. As Ernest Cassirer has said, the cosmos was no longer to be looked at but permeated. Second, the object of inquiry is the discovery of the natural order of things. Newton had demonstrated the order of the physical universe; Linnaeus had begun to put order into the chaos of life; and Locke, on the same empirical principles, had pointed the way to a science of mind. Were there not universal laws, roughly equivalent to the law of gravitation, in the moral and social realms? There were, the eighteenth-century philosophers insisted, but they lay buried under the rubble heaped up over the centuries by dogmatic authority and superstition. The political economists were gradually approaching the conception of an autonomous economic order governed by immutable laws of nature. The Newtonian model, which exalted a divine Creator, gave assurance that the laws of nature were universal, harmonious, and beneficent. Nothing in nature could be disharmonious, as Jefferson often said. Man, so long alienated from nature, could now begin to feel at home in it. Third, reason is the principal agent of criticism and inquiry—reason, that is, not as "eternal verities" but as a method of verification. Aggressively secular, enlightened thinkers exposed bigotry and superstition, denounced airy "metaphysical" speculation, and leveled the walls of mystery and authority separating man from nature. They did not claim om-

47

nipotence for reason, however. As the century advanced, more and more thinkers looked to the affections, or feelings, for a unifying principle in the moral world. And as Bacon taught, the mind should be freed from the burden or rationalizing grand mysteries beyond finite understanding in order to attack the concrete obstacles to human happiness in everyday life. The faith was utilitarian. "It is by witness to works rather than by logic or even observation that truth is revealed and established," said Bacon. "It follows from this that the improvement of man's lot and the improvement of man's mind are one and the same thing." Finally, the end of enlightened thought is happiness. "Man is unhappy only because he does not know nature," the *philosophe* Holbach declared. Knowing nature, man might come into harmony with the order of things and avail himself of its laws to secure happiness. Whether or not the "pursuit of happiness" was a right, as Jefferson would claim, it was certainly man's deepest desire. Individuals, like societies, differed in their definitions of happiness; hence an easy freedom, tolerance, and pluralism should reign in the determination of goals. Most, though not all, enlightened thinkers agreed that individual happiness, far from being a selfish propensity, was founded in social affections. Thus the pursuit involved an active and, on the whole, practical and humanitarian commitment to the well-being of others. Progress, one of the keynotes of the Enlightenment, was ensured by the conviction that man had all the necessary equipment to take possession of nature in the interest of the species. Illimitable progress, rather than the perfectibility of man, was the captivating vision. As Jefferson himself cautiously summed up this reasoned faith: "Although I do not, with some enthusiasts, believe that the human condition will ever advance to such a state of perfection as that there shall no longer be pain or vice in the world, yet I believe it susceptible to much improvement, and most of all, in matters of government and religion; and that the diffusion of knowledge among people is to be the instrument by which it is effected."

Jefferson's affinities to the ancient world were anchored in the world of thought of his own century. Perhaps in no way was he a more typical representative of the Enlightenment than in his deep feeling for antiquity. For the Enlightenment embraced, in Peter Gay's phrasing, both an "appeal to antiquity" and a "pursuit of modernity," the former being in the service of the latter. Hence it is quite misleading to polarize these two intellectual worlds and to say that Jefferson, for example, struck a balance between the "humanistic" interests of one and the "naturalistic" interests of the other. In fact, both were essentially humanistic by virtue of being essentially naturalistic, and one infused the other, just as Jefferson's appeal to classical forms infused a modern architecture. Men of the Enlightenment found in the pagan world of Greece and Rome a basis of perspective on their own age, one that liberated them from the claims of Christianity, and also furnished them with a whole armory of weapons for the assault on dogma, bigotry, and superstition. Except for the classical millennium, succeeded, it must be remembered, by the Christian "Dark Ages," there was scarcely an edifying page in the history of mankind. Darkness shadowed the ancient world too; nonetheless, the ancients exhibited ideals of learning, virtue, beauty, cultivation, the dignity of man, and the freedom of mind for the emulation of moderns. Their intelligence groped with fundamental problems of nature, religion, conduct, and governance. The questing mind of Socrates, the Horatian idyl to the art of living, Cicero on the duties of life, the competing moral schools of Cynics, Stoics, and Epicureans who yet united in the command "Follow Nature," Lucretius who conducted his own war of science against religion, the serenity of Seneca, the political wisdom of Tacitus, Tacitus who Jefferson thought "the first writer in the world without a single exception"—these and so many other classical authors threw shafts of light on the perplexities of modern men struggling for enlightenment.

Jefferson, like most of his contemporaries, was more attentive to Rome than to Greece. The Romans had absorbed what was best in Greek civilization and overcome its crucial weakness by the creation of a universal rule of law, the *jus gentium*, applicable to the farthest reaches of empire, to which, of course, the Western world fell heir. Politically, however, Rome too was a failure. Corruption, luxury, and ambition sank the republic in the second century of the Christian era. Not surprisingly, enlightened men, especially in America, focused their eyes on the republic and on Livy, Tacitus, and the others who sadly recorded its history and rebuked its sequel. Was the England of George III very different from Nero's Rome? The republic, indeed the entire course of ancient history, furnished a rich storehouse of analogies to eighteenth-century philosophers. The appeal to antiquity was not an antiquarian exercise; it had vitality, though with shallow men it could be a mere conceit, a badge of superficial learning. Some made a cult of antiquity and waxed nostalgic over "golden ages." Jefferson was not afflicted in this way. The darkness of the ancient world struck him fully as much as the light. He found virtually nothing to admire in ancient governments; and in time he would discover serious deficiencies in ancient morals. But none of this lessens his debt to the ancients.

In Jefferson's early thought on fundamental questions of religion and morals classical strains are subtly interwoven with the modern. In his youth, perhaps at college, perhaps soon after, he lost his inherited Anglican faith and became a convert to deistic natural religion. "I had never sense enough to comprehend the articles of faith of the Church," he later wrote in declining to be godfather to a child, "and it has always appeared to me that comprehension must precede assent." He did not sever all ties with the Church but was clearly alienated from it as early as 1770, by which time, too, the "episcopal palace" probably recognized him as an enemy, the dissenting sects as a friend, and the rising generation as a patron of the widest latitude in religious matters. He had no respect for the Established Church on any ground, and his reading of the modern rationalists, principally English and Scottish, conveyed him to that convenient via media of the Enlightenment, natural religion, between orthodoxy and atheism. The catalogue of his library in 1815 lists many of the English deistic tracts and treatises of the early eighteenth century, but with three or four exceptions one cannot be certain that Jefferson acquired and read these works when young. He probably did, for he would not have troubled himself at a later time. The works of these ponderous theologians—Matthew Tindal, Samuel Clarke, Thomas Chubb, Conyers Middleton, and others—together with those of more edifying philosophers like Lord Bolingbroke, belonged to a particular stage of religious controversy and staled rapidly. It was the stage that established two main propositions for enlightened men. First, that the Christianity of the churches was unreasonable, therefore unbelievable, but that stripped of priestly mystery, ritual, and dogma, reinterpreted in the light of historical evidence and human experience, and substituting the Newtonian cosmology for the discredited Biblical one, Christianity could be conformed to reason. Second, morality required no divine sanction or inspiration, no appeal beyond reason and nature, perhaps not even the hope of heaven or the fear of hell; and so the whole edifice of Christian revelation came tumbling to the ground.

Jefferson reached his own religious convictions along the lines of these propositions. He was a theist whose God was the Creator of the universe. Such a God exemplified workmanship and design; all the evidences of nature testified to His perfection; and man could rely on the harmony and beneficence of His work. Such a God could not be identified with the God of the Bible as commonly known. Tindal's *Christianity as Old as the Creation*, one of the classics of Deism, may have convinced Jefferson of the sufficiency of the laws of nature, the superfluousness of revelation, to explain the creation and the simple duties of man. He later attributed great influence to Middleton's writings. Middleton was both classical scholar and theologian. His *Life of Cicero* became a favorite with Jefferson. His *Letter from Rome*, a landmark in the pursuit of historical Christianity, explored its mythopeic origins in pagan idolatry and superstition, while the *Answer to Waterland* denied the literal inspiration of the Gospels and raised other doubts of Scriptural authority. From Middleton, rather than from Hume's scoffing *Essay on Miracles*, Jefferson probably learned to apply the test of historical evidence in religion and to withhold assent from the miracles and related supernatural phenomena. The same lesson was taught by Bolingbroke, that whirligig of eighteenth-century thought, whose writings Jefferson "commonplaced" at length. He copied Bolingbroke's Lockian injunction: "No hypothesis ought to be maintained if a single phenomenon stands in direct opposition to it." And also numerous passages that disparaged the Biblical God in comparison with the God of nature, rebuked Scriptural authority, and ridiculed sectarian pretensions to truth. He was inclined to agree with Bolingbroke's famous maxim on the tacit alliance between priests and atheists against true religion. In later years he traced the corruption of Christianity to the "whimsies" and "mysteries" excogitated by Plato's "foggy brain," inspiring "endless systems of mystical theology"; but at this stage, while never an admirer of Plato, he was not prepared to load the awful responsibility on him. Dismissing revelation, divine grace, and the future state of Christianity, dismissing, in short, the religion of the churches, Jefferson believed that natural reason and the evidence of the senses provided a sufficient basis of religion and ethics. Indeed, for the young Jefferson religion was absorbed in ethics; and he looked to the classical moralists, more than to the Christian, for his principles of conduct. He recognized, however, that this was only his private judgment. Others might disagree, and their truths, if reached after the same patient inquiry, were no better or no worse than his.

The conviction that religion is a private concern, that it merits honest inquiry, and that multiplicity of belief is the result, distinguishes Jefferson's thought on the subject. Unlike many Enlightenment thinkers, especially in the later and more radical stage, he did not form intellectual conceits about religion or scoff at faiths more pious than his or envision a grand unifying "religion of humanity." In a letter to a young nephew in 1787, he prescribed the method of inquiry he approved and had doubtless tried to follow himself. Fix reason firmly in her seat, he advised, shake off all bias in favor of novelty as well as all "servile prejudices" of orthodoxy, and boldly question everything, beginning with the existence of God. The religion of your own country merits respect—study it with care. "Read the Bible, then, as you would read Livy or Tacitus." Events that contradict the laws of nature must be weighed in the light of testimony, credibility, pretensions to inspiration, and so on. "The pretension is entitled to your inquiry, because millions believe it." Examine the character of Jesus. Was he the son of God? Read all the histories of Jesus, those of both the evangelists and the pseudo-evangelists. "Do not be frightened from this inquiry by any fear of its consequences," Jefferson said. "If it ends in a belief that there is no God, you will find incitements to virtue in the comfort and pleasantness you find in its exercise, and the love of others which it will procure you. If you find reason to believe there is a God, a consciousness that you are acting under his eye, and that he approves you, will be a vast additional incitement. . . . Your own reason is the only oracle given you by heaven, and you are answerable, not for the rightness, but [the] uprightness of the decision."

The uprightness of the decision: this conviction that true belief

is the result of an open mind and the courage of one's own understanding was the essence of Jefferson's doctrine. It was quite the opposite of both lazy conformity to prevailing canons of piety and
aggressive hostility to religion. It called for persevering search of
truth, not one and absolute, since the experiences of men and the
composition of their minds are much too varied to admit that, but
for the truth as one sees it. The doctrine would have profound public effects, for religion conceived in this way could have no public
authority. Moreover, the doctrine reveals Jefferson's concern for the
place of religion in his life; and although skeptical inquiry at the
threshold of maturity led him to assign it a rather small place within
the bland scheme of natural religion, there is no reason to question
the uprightness of his decision or his continuing responsibility to the
quest for religious truth.

Religion was valuable chiefly as an adjunct of morality. Partly
for this reason Jefferson never formulated a creed, and his library
catalogue assigned religion to a sub-division of a sub-division under
moral philosophy. Whether one acted on right principles considered
as the rule of God or considered as the rule of nature made little
difference. For himself, the latter was clearly indicated. In the ripeness of years he distilled a secular code from the teaching of Jesus,
the purest system of morals ever taught, he then thought; but when
young he could not separate the purities from the impurities of theology. He copied a passage from the contentious Bolingbroke denying that Christ revealed "an entire body of ethics." Instead of the
hodgepodge of inscrutable utterance, allusion, and parable contained
in the gospels, Bolingbroke recommended a code derived from the
ancient moralists. "A system thus collected from the writings of ancient heathen moralists, of Tully, of Seneca, of Epictetus, and others, would be more full, more entire, more coherent, and more
clearly deduced from unquestionable principles of knowledge."

Jefferson turned to these ancients less for a code than for a posture of conduct. Not committing himself to one school or another, he
took what he wanted from both Stoic and Epicurean. The former,
as exemplified in Epictetus, Seneca, and Marcus Aurelius, emphasized freedom from passion, aloofness from the swirling currents of
life, and resignation to fate, all to be achieved by stern self-discipline. The latter, the Epicurean, allowed more latitude to human pas-

53

sions and pleasures and was more cheerful generally. The Stoic creed, with its ideal of brotherhood, had been absorbed into Christianity, while the Epicurean had been smothered under the odium of libertinism. A seventeenth-century philosopher, Pierre Gassendi, much admired by men of the Enlightenment, had rescued Epicurus from this fate and, at the same time, established him as a classical precursor of the physics of Galileo and Newton. Jefferson read Epicurus through the eyes of Gassendi. Pleasure, rightly understood, conduces to virtue, for one cannot live a pleasurable or happy life without honor, goodness, and peace of mind. And since pleasure and pain, unlike virtue, which is an abstraction, are immediately experienced, the basis is laid in these sensations for an empirical science of ethics.

On the whole, Jefferson's posture was Epicurean. His desire to cultivate the senses, his concern for bodily comforts, his confidence in man's power to control events, his commitment to the pursuit of happiness—these directives were Epicurean. But the stiffer, the more ascetic, Stoic strain was always present and at times, when he sickened of the world, uppermost. His early commonplace book of the poets and philosophers, *The Literary Bible*, contains generous samples of melancholia, together with many fatalistic aphorisms and ordinances of self-denial. If much of this can be dismissed as youthful posturing, the fact remains that Jefferson's emotional reticence toward the world was characteristically Stoical. Like most men he found room in his life for both attitudes and shifted the accent according to his mood. In the final analysis, as Adrienne Koch has said, he employed rigorous Stoic self-discipline to the attainment of the Epicurean good life.

But what was the foundation of morality once the props of Christianity had been removed? Taking their cue from the ancients, who had found the moral in the natural, the enlightened thinkers developed a naturalistic ethics within the framework of empirical science. Human nature was the starting point for a moral Newtonianism. Early efforts to locate the source of moral judgement in reason failed. Reason was not an exciting force; it might be the stem but could not be the root of morality. The capacity to reason, in which men differed greatly, seemed to have no direct relation to moral capacity. So the inquiry turned to the sentiments or feelings.

One school, originated by Hobbes but popularized in the eighteenth century by Bernard de Mandeville, located the source of moral action in self-love. Jefferson was familiar with these teachings—several of Mandeville's books were in his library—and was repelled by them. The idea that selfishness led to virtue, that private vices produced public benefits—Mandeville's famous axiom—seemed to him a cynical assault on morality, in the same way that Machiavelli assailed the moral foundations of politics. He found his solution in the "moral sense" school of Lord Shaftesbury, Francis Hutcheson, and others. The ubiquitous Scot Henry Home, Lord Kames, whose writings on law, theology, natural history, and moral philosophy Jefferson mined when young, was the principal conveyer of this doctrine. He may have been introduced to Kames by Dr. Small. In any event, the moral philosophy taught by that good man was surely of this school.

Formulations differed, but in general the doctrine held that man is equipped with an inner sense of right and wrong, and that it approves conduct tending to the public good or, as Hutcheson put it, "the greatest happiness of the greatest numbers." Why is it, Jefferson asked, that benevolent actions give us pleasure? "Because nature hath implanted in our breasts a love of others, a sense of duty to them, a moral instinct, in short, which prompts us irresistibly to feel and to succor their distresses. . . ." (The fact that Jefferson used *instinct* interchangeably with *sense* suggests the deeper biological basis of the doctrine in his conception than in the formulations of leading proponents.) To act viciously is to be miserable; to act virtuously is to be happy—and to increase the happiness of mankind. The individual calculus of pleasure and pain, in the sensationalist psychology derived from Locke, thus had its social counterpart in a calculus of public happiness. "The Creator would indeed have been a bungling artist, had he intended man for a social animal, without planting in him social dispositions," Jefferson observed. Such a marvelous contrivance for harmonizing pleasure and virtue, self and society, implied a divine artificer, of course. Reason came into the system as a cultivator and regulator of the moral sense: the head informed and guided the natural dispositions of the heart. The moral sense was universal, as much a part of every man as the senses of sight and hearing; its exercise was defective from the want of educa-

55

tion or other circumstances. The fact that what was deemed virtue in one country was deemed vice in another did not disprove its existence. An internal directive toward the right and the good, it did not determine external standards. Utility, as Jefferson said, determined these. "Men living in different countries, under different circumstances, different habits and regimens, may have different utilities; the same act, therefore, may be useful, and consequently virtuous in one country which is injurious and vicious in another. . . ." He thus affirmed his belief in the fundamental uniformity and equality of mankind, while at the same time making allowance for the variations produced by history, culture, and environment. What was useful was good in Jefferson's philosophy; what was good was natural; and what was natural—an inherent human endowment—laid claim to the status of inalienable right.

The moral sense philosophy, with its facile logic and easy optimism, proved very useful to Jefferson, as to many of his contemporaries. In the breakdown of religious authority, it provided a secular analogue of Christian conscience. It helped to save him from nominalism and skepticism and, politically, from traffic with the Hobbesian Leviathan. The moral world had not been abandoned to chance. The same directing forces subsisted in the social as in the solar system. As the law of gravitation was the regulating power of one, the moral sense was the regulator of the other. Around the doctrine gathered Jefferson's faith in a divine Creator, in common humanity, and the natural sociability of mankind. It was the cohesive force in a philosophy pivoted on sense experience, wide open to the diversity of thought and the contentiousness of civil life, and running pell mell to individualism.

Jefferson's political thought, though it became the quintessence of Enlightenment liberalism, had its roots in English law and government. The American revolutionaries were fortunate in their heritage. The tradition of the English constitution gave a concreteness to their claims of personal and political liberty, even a color of legality to revolution itself, that no other modern revolutionaries possessed. Thus it has sometimes seemed that the Americans, far from finding a new political paradise, were simply regaining the one that had been lost somewhere in the tumultuous English past. The recovery strain is especially evident in the young Jefferson. He approached government from the law, and precedent was nine-tenths of the law. He approached law as a form of history. History, as the esteemed Bolingbroke had said, was philosophy teaching by example. Law was its most objective expression. Jefferson did not look to the past for political models. "History, in general, only informs us what bad government is." It was full of admonitions. More positively, however, historical investigation disclosed the sources of both truth and error in the modern constitution of society. By possessing this knowledge men might cultivate what was good, eradicate what was bad, and so, in a sense, escape altogether the tyranny of the past. Jefferson became an authentic spokesman of this hope of the Enlightenment, this vindication of human nature against the past, which seemed to be the peculiar mission of America. But he reached the position gradually. The progression of his political thought before the Revolution has been described as a movement from history to theory. It was that, and at the same time a movement from the particularism, the local patois, of English law and government to the rationalism and universalism of the natural rights philosophy. In the preliminary stage of the controversy with the mother country, he joined his fellow colonials in the appeal to the English constitution. And even after the ultimate appeal to nature in 1776, the shadow of the English heritage hovered over Jefferson's mind. His political imagination, partly clouded by old historical ideas, had not yet caught up with the principles of reason. The two main ideas that had great powers of prepossession in Jefferson's mind concerned the Saxon origins of English liberty and the "balanced" government of the English constitution.

Jefferson's study of law led him to the Anglo-Saxon conception of English liberty. The seeds were planted by the invading tribes from Germany in the fifth and sixth century, according to this theory. Tacitus, who had described these tribes in *Germania*, credited the Saxons with great virtue and political wisdom, and modern commentators embroidered his celebrated account. The Saxons, it was held, introduced into England an elective kingship, an annual assembly of tribal chiefs, the witenagemot—the true forerunner of Parliament—trial by jury, and the common law. The polity was pre-feudal. It presented an idyllic picture of simple independent farmers free of rents, entails, and other burdens. The Norman Conquest brought feudalism to England, and in the view of some commentators virtually destroyed the ancient Saxon laws. Against Norman tyranny the nation sought to reclaim the rights it had lost. The recurring struggle thenceforth characterized English history. Magna Charta opened a new epoch by restoring, substantially, the original constitution. Usurpation ever threatened, however, and under the Stuarts in the seventeenth century English liberty and self-government were again destroyed. The Long Parliament, the Commonwealth, the Restoration—these turbulent chapters were brought to a close by the Glorious Revolution of 1688. Alas, corruption and vice and new forms of oppression—standing armies, septennial parliaments, ministerial influence—soon spoiled the promising new epoch. In the eyes of belligerently libertarian Englishmen of the eighteenth century, at home and in the colonies, salvation lay in return to the track of the ancient constitution.

Such, in general, was the Saxon myth. Jefferson encountered it in whole or in part in the writings of legal commentators, historians, political theorists, and pamphleteers: in Tacitus, in "old Coke," in Lord Kames's *Historical Law Tracts*, Sir John Dalrymple's *Feudal Property*, Henry Care's *English Liberties*, Obadiah Hulme's *Historical Essay on the English Constitution*, Sir Robert Molesworth's *An Account of Denmark*, the "Cato Letters" of John Trenchard and Thomas Gordon, the martyred Algernon Sidney's *Discourse on Government*, which Jefferson thought "the best elementary textbook on the principles of government," the *History of England* by the Huguenot Paul de Rapin-Thoyras, which he always considered the most faithful ever written, and in numerous other works.

The Saxon myth in some form pervaded English historical thought. It entered into the prevailing Whig interpretation of the eighteenth century. Traces of it could be found even in David Hume's *History of England*, the great witness against the Whig theory. Hume was an ingratiating writer. Jefferson later recalled the enthusiasm with which he devoured the *History* when young—"and the length of time, the research and reflection which were necessary to eradicate the poison it had instilled into my mind." He must have eradicated the poison well before 1776, for beyond the admission of Saxon virtue there were few opinions in Hume's work he could approve, and he commenced a lifelong campaign against its insidious influence. Hume was a rank Tory apologist, he repeatedly insisted, who having begun with the vindication of the Stuarts wrote backwards, perverting all prior history, praising feudalism, deriving the constitution from the Norman Conquest, so as to sustain the enormities of the Stuarts. "It is this book which had undermined the free principles of the English government," he said. The Whig theory, identified with the ascendancy of Parliament after 1688, held to the idea of an immemorial constitution from ancient Saxon times. Thus the common law existed continuously, "time out of mind," undisturbed by conquest or usurpation, and Parliament, too, rested on the ancient foundation. Coke and the lawyer combatants of the Stuarts had invented this myth. In the eighteenth century it became the historical justification of the Whig ascendancy.

Jefferson absorbed the general theory, of course, but without at first realizing the implications, subscribed to a radical version. Unlike Coke and the Whig apologists, he believed that the Conquest had broken the line of continuity by introducing feudal tyranny, corrupting the common law, and so on; and that after all the struggles to root out these evils, they persisted, like some cancerous disease, in the English polity. So Jefferson celebrated the Saxon past as a kind of golden age, still to be recovered, rather than as a baptismal confirmation of the present regime. Many of the modern writers he read on English history and government—Trenchard and Gordon, Rapin, Hulme, James Burgh—held this view as part of a reform ideology. The heirs of a radical tradition born in the tumults of the seventeenth century, these "commonwealthmen," as they have been named, rejected the complacent Whig optimism of the age, decried luxury, vice, corruption, and arbitrary power, demanded the reform of Parliament, the purification of religion, the freedom of the press, the end of standing armies and other oppressions. Their voices were scarcely heard in Hanoverian England; but they struck a responsive chord in American breasts. The principles of the "commonwealthmen" fell in with emerging native ideals. If England had strayed so far from the paths of the ancient constitution, the Americans should look to its preservation on their own distant shore. Molesworth had shown how other northern nations, Sweden and Denmark in particular, sprung from the same Saxon origins as England, had lost their liberties during the past century. Heavy taxes, armies and navies, aristocratic influence at court, despotic kingship—these were parts of the story that Jefferson found sufficiently instructive to record in his commonplace book.

Early committed to the Saxon myth, Jefferson never abandoned it. His lifelong interest in the Anglo-Saxon language expressed a linguistic passion, involved as well, however, with the roots of law and government. Saxon laws of tenure and descent served him well in the reform of Virginia institutions commencing in 1776. And before that, in 1774, he invoked the Saxon myth to justify the colonists' claims against the mother country. This revealed a characteristic habit of mind: the appeal to ancient sources in behalf, not of conservatism, but of change and revolution. A good illustration is the little essay, "Whether Christianity is a Part of the Common Law," written in his commonplace book, perhaps about 1774. Interested at this time in the legal foundations of the Established Church, he questioned the doctrine first clearly enunciated by Sir Matthew Hale at the King's Bench in 1676, and solemnly repeated by Blackstone nearly a century later, that "Christianity is parcel of the laws of England." If true, Christianity must have been taken into the common law before Magna Charta, for it was never given the protection of statutory law. But the original Saxons were pagan; two centuries passed between the invasion and their conversion to Christianity, and the common law was in existence throughout. Jefferson searched the sources of the half-millennium before Magna Charta and found no evidence of Christianity's incorporation into the common law. The silence of Bracton, himself an ecclesiastic, offered cogent evidence of a negative kind. It was true that the codification of King Alfred in the ninth century incorporated the Ten Commandments and two or three chapters of Exodus. But the adoption of a part implied rejection of the rest; even more to the point, as Jefferson discovered in a French treatise on Anglo-Norman law, the interjection of ecclesiastical law into common law was an *"hor d'œuvre* of some pious copyist," "an awkward Monkish fabrication," proven a fraud by the whole nature of Alfred's laws. The ultimate fraud, however, originated in the seventeenth-century treatise of Sir Henry Finch. Finch mistranslated a phrase from an opinion in the Yearbook of 1458. The opinion held that the common law credited those laws of the Holy Church that were in ancient writing, *en an-*

cien scripture, that is, those precedents of the canon law shown to be part of the common law. But Finch rendered the Latin phrase as "holy scripture," thus installing bigotry and superstition in English law. "In truth," Jefferson concluded, "the alliance between church and state in England has ever made their judges accomplices in the frauds of the clergy; and even bolder than they are." His methodical inquiry, whether or not it led him to the right conclusion, proved his commitment to the rational laws of "our Saxon ancestors," which, far from existing in England's "immemorial constitution," had to be rediscovered under layers of fraud and usurpation.

The theory of "balanced government" had its origin with Aristotle, its revival with the late Renaissance political craftsman Machiavelli, and its modern exemplification in the English constitution. The celebrated freedom of the English government—the freest in the world—was a product of the balanced power of King, Lords, and Commons, each representing one of the great orders of society, royalty, nobility, and populace, and embodying in principle the three classical forms of government: monarchy, aristocracy, and democracy. These pure forms left to themselves ran to corruption: despotism, oligarchy, mobocracy. But properly mixed and balanced in association with the orders of hierarchical society, each checked the vices of the other without alienating or forfeiting the benefit of any one. This tripartite balance was the widely esteemed genius of the English constitution. The Americans not only looked to it for their freedom within the empire but conceived their provincial governments on the same model, at least in the royal colonies. The Royal Governor, the Council, and the Assembly became the rough colonial equivalents of King, Lords and Commons.

The theory was in the air, so to say, and Jefferson could not escape it. Its *locus classicus* in the eighteenth century was the eleventh book of the Baron de Montesquieu's *Esprit des lois.* Jefferson read this famous work around 1770. From it he made twenty-seven entries in his commonplace book—more than from any other book or author. He did not copy from Book XI, as it happens, probably because he took the exposition for granted, although Montesquieu introduced some new wrinkles. He admired this most astute of philosophers for the relativistic theory that associated laws and government with "climate" or, more generally, the entire cultural environ-

61

ment of a people; for the perception that the spirit of republican government was "virtue," a civic spirit subordinating selfish interests to the general welfare; for the generous humanitarianism of the work, as shown in the discussions of slavery and crime and punishment; for the advocacy of civil liberties and religious toleration; and for penetrating observations on federative republics, especially in ancient times. All of this was grist for Jefferson's mill. Yet he probably had reservations about Montesquieu even at this early stage, and two decades later he was an avowed antagonist. The theory of the English constitution was one thing, the perfection of its working quite another. He could not join wholeheartedly in the glorification of the English system in the years before the Revolution; and it would become an impertinence after the Americans evolved a system of their own. The aura of authority, the ensnaring charms of the *Spirit of the Laws*, easily led men into political heresies, Jefferson came to believe. The worst of these was the idea that a republic could exist only in a small territory, since the welfare of the whole could not make itself felt in a large state. Another reflected Montesquieu's class bias: his adherence to a hierarchical society and to aristocratic "honor" as the impulse of liberty.

In the reign of George III the Americans concluded, with the dissident Whigs in England, that this marvelous machine of reciprocating attractions and repulsions, this political counterpart of Newtonian law, the English constitution, had broken down. King and Parliament had combined to upset the balance. The Glorious Revolution established the supremacy of Parliament, more especially of the House of Commons. Locke, whose famous *Treatise on Civil Government* rationalized the event, clearly enunciated the principle: "the legislative must need be the supreme [power], and all other powers in any members or parts of society derived from and subordinate to it." Well and good; but it was not long before King and ministry, the latter becoming with the rise of the cabinet system a new fourth wheel of government, corrupted the new balance of the constitution by wickedly employing favors, bribery, and intrigue in the debasement of Parliament. George III, whose education was Tory, as Jefferson pointedly observed, pursued the scheme to alarming lengths. An invisible government, centered in the "King's Friends," manipulated Parliament for its own interest against the

public. If the King was the author of the system, Parliament had co-
alesced with him until the checks and balances of the constitution
were meaningless or, as Thomas Paine bluntly said, "farcical." The
old party distinctions, Whig and Tory, had also become meaningless. Politicians were locked into the system. "Influence," the favorite
word to describe its operation, bought elections with honors, titles,
pensions, money, and offices. The Commons was dominated by several self-perpetuating cliques who fought not over principles but
spoils. The "democratic" branch had never represented more than a
tiny fraction of the nation, and it was becoming steadily less representative all the time. Septennial election further weakened the
spring of the popular will. "As standing water stinks . . . ," wrote
James Burgh, "so a standing house of commons, will ever be a standing pool of corruption." The great check on the Crown, the power
of the purse, was no longer effective. According to the theory, the
King, receiving his authority from the people and responsible to
them for maintaining the constitution, should check any extravagance of Parliament, thus redressing the balance. Bolingbroke offered the old prescription in *The Idea of a Patriot King*. But George
III, unable to return to this discredited Tory model, perfected the
system of "influence," which instead of correcting the balance corrupted it.

The Americans observed the course of deterioration and feared
for their own governments. Taxes, armies, monopolies, venal offices
—all the arms of the octopus were reaching out to the colonies. The
dissident "old Whigs" and radical heretics in England warned the
colonials of their fate. The hope, of course, was that England would
reform. Americans closely followed the career of John Wilkes, not
only because the Crown's suppression of his voice and his rejection
by the Commons dramatized the tyranny of the government, but
also because they looked to Wilkes and his agitated following to
spur reform. At the peak of the agitation, between 1768 and 1771,
Wilkes was quoted in the gazettes published in Williamsburg more
often than any other man. Jefferson encountered him there, and he
obtained Wilkes's speeches for his library. In the end Wilkes proved
a disappointment, and there was no one to take his place. The obstinacy of Parliament to reform left the Americans no promising avenue of appeal except to the King, which was not very hopeful, ac-

tually, in view of his collusion with Parliament. Nevertheless, unrepresented in Parliament, increasingly scornful of its authority, the Americans were dependent on the King in theory and in fact. In 1774 Jefferson pointedly reminded His Majesty that he was "the chief officer of the people, appointed by the laws, and circumscribed with definite powers, to assist in the working the great machine of government, erected for their use, and consequently subject to their superintendence." This sounded a little like Bolingbroke: the "patriot king" as the great balance-wheel of the constitution. But Jefferson had shrugged off the Tory implications contained in the theory of balanced government. Only the awkward status of the colonies within the empire, all owing allegiance to a common sovereign, forced him to appeal to the Crown. He was a "True Whig" of 1688, a champion of legislative supremacy in the English constitution, in the American practice, and in political theory generally. It is notable that John Adams admired Bolingbroke's political theory but regretted his heretical religious opinions, while Jefferson accepted the latter but rejected the former. They were both Whigs in fact, yet their contrasting responses to Bolingbroke, the putative "father of modern toryism," would be reflected in the different emphases the two men gave to executive (monarchical) and legislative (democratic) power in the governments of the new nation. But these differences were unimportant before 1776 when American patriots agreed on the melancholy deterioration of balanced government in England and worried for the survival of this genie of freedom in America.

The ideas of Saxon origins and balanced government were so firmly implanted in Jefferson's mind that, while they could be transformed, they could never be uprooted. The Saxon myth persisted in curious ways. In the main, however, as a historical foundation of the rights of Englishmen, it was assimilated into a rational creed of liberty. Locke had pointed the way. When rights were subsumed under the law of nature, history was of no account. Rationalism conquered history. Jefferson did not go as far as Locke in this respect, for he appealed to ancient liberties to buttress the rational argument and to render concrete what otherwise was ethereal. The theory of balanced government was also historical, identified as it was with English constitutional development and premised on a historically given structure of power corresponding to the hierarchical orders of society. To erase from the political mind the vocabulary of orders, even in a society where there were none, and the forms of the classical trivium, and the categories of King, Lords, and Commons, was not easy. Jefferson encountered less difficulty than some of his notable contemporaries, John Adams for instance. Gradually, one form, one order, one category, democracy, effaced the others; and the old theory was transformed into a new theory of "separation of powers." Now the functional powers of government, legislative, executive, judicial, rather than the historically given orders, were to be checked and balanced, regarding nothing but natural rights and the sovereignty of the people. Driven by the force of the Revolution, Jefferson recast his essentially English political theory, retaining its strong constitutional and democratic elements, in the intellectual mould of the Enlightenment.

The American Revolution was a national as well as democratic movement—a colonial revolt that gave birth to a revolutionary ideology. It was accompanied by a growing consciousness of nationality, the sense of common experience and common culture, of unifying habits, beliefs, and aspirations, all parts of the process by which a people comes to identify itself as a nation. How far this had gone in the thirteen mainland British colonies by 1776 is problematical, and downright conjectural in Jefferson's case. The chicken-and-egg problem of whether revolution emerged from nationality or nationality from revolution is unsolvable. But more than most new nations the Americans achieved political independence before they had a conscious tradition and culture of their own; indeed the unique feature of the American fabric of nationality was its self-conscious creation in response to the achievement of nationhood. The frame came before the picture; in a sense, the Americans painted the picture themselves. Yet the process of transforming colonial Englishmen and assorted Europeans into Americans had been going on for a century and a half, and it was greatly accelerated by the alienation of affections after the Seven Years War. John Adams, more given to reflection on past times than his Virginia friend, observed in later years that "the Revolution was in the minds of the people, and this was effected from 1760 to 1775, in the course of fifteen years before a drop of blood was shed at Lexington." Jefferson, though he did not say, probably agreed in principle. His own emotional identifications were more Virginian than American or continental before 1775, and the transmutation of provincial loyalties into unifying national loyalties was another part of the process, as real in Massachusetts as in Virginia. But the inner revolution toward Americanism had already begun in him and would burst forth with tremendous energy once independence was declared.

Every philosophical American was aware of the debate among European savants on the prospects of the New World. The Abbé Raynal's *Histoire des deux Indes,* one of the most influential works of the age, brought the matter to a head in 1770. Whether America, North and South, should be considered a boon to civilization or a return to barbarism on a fantastic scale, whether America promised regeneration or degeneration for mankind, was the troubling question. Jefferson took it up when occasion offered in 1780, siding with the optimists against Raynal and others. To this school America, or at least the Northern British colonies, appeared as the land of Enlightenment dreams. Europeans caught between the impulses of primitivism and civilization, of retreat to nature and rush to progress, witnessed in America the emergence of civilization from nature. Here was a laboratory for the testing of eighteenth-century ideas. Beginning in the Lockian "state of nature," the Americans had an opportunity to create a new order of mankind. To many Europeans, Benjamin Franklin personified the ideal: provincial and cosmopolitan, rustic and philosopher, a man equally at home in the simple American world and the sophisticated salons of Europe. This hopeful New World image, as well as its dark opposite, crossed the Atlantic and forced its way into the consciousness of colonials. They began to think of themselves as Americans, to trace out the contours of the native environment, differentiating it from the European world they had fled, and to define its unique promise.

Montesquieu had taught that different physical and social environments give rise to different beliefs, manners, and laws. Human nature is everywhere the same but laws and government are moulded by circumstances of time and space, in a word by the culture of a people. What, then, was the American case? Or perhaps there were thirteen separate cases. Serious differences among the colonies became painfully evident in the First Continental Congress as delegates forged a common front against the mother country. Yet, sharing the same grievances, driven by the same fears, they perceived with increasing clarity that similar lines of development, under similar conditions, had produced a collective basis of national existence. "Love of freedom," in Edmund Burke's opinion the leading feature of American character, ran across the face of the country and up and down the social scale. It was not an abstract thing, as in most of Europe, but the sovereign force of law and opinion. The governments of the colonies were remarkably alike. Everywhere the public will centered in a representative assembly. Since a kind of revolutionary legitimacy was already contained in these bodies, it was unnecessary to go in search of it. English political institutions had been not merely adapted but transformed in the American environment. For example, the theory and practice of representation: as Bernard Bailyn has observed, the colonists developed the idea of "attorney-ship," wherein the representative literally re-presents the will of his constituents, while in England the prevailing theory ran to unitary or collective representation, Parliament being considered the assemblage of one nation with one overriding interest. Hence the idea that the Americans were *virtually* represented in Parliament made sense in England, where in fact not nine out of ten of the subjects of the realm were *actually* represented; but it made no sense at all in the colonies. In the light of peculiar American conditions, some imported institutions, such as the establishment of religion, began to seem incongruous with the society. Multiplicity, not uniformity, characterized religious life in America—the laws should be adapted to this condition. The wide diffusion of property meant that a more democratic frame of government was practical in America without incurring the risk, so much emphasized in conventional political wisdom, of splitting power from property. Characteristics of this kind, which philosophers abroad were already conceptualizing as "the American character," became more and more obvious to the colonists in the course of controversy with the mother country; and by 1776 some of them, like Jefferson, were ready to seize upon these *differentiae* for the reconstruction of civil life.

In his great Revolutionary pamphlet *Common Sense*, Thomas Paine dwelt on the absurdity of a continent's being governed by an island. "In no instance hath nature made the satellite larger than its primary planet; and as England and America, with respect to each other, reverse the common order of nature, it is evident that they belong in different systems. England to Europe: America to itself." This idea, too, had been breaking into American consciousness for some time. A quarter-century earlier Franklin, in his *Observations Concerning the Increase of Mankind,* noted that the population of the mainland colonies had doubled in twenty-five years, while the population of England had remained virtually stable. "What an accession of power to the British Empire by sea as well as land! What increase of trade and navigation. What numbers of ships and seamen," Franklin rejoiced. Clearly, he had a maritime conception of empire, an "empire of the deep," rated largely in trade, ships, and seamen. This was the prevailing conception. Under it the colonies were outposts of British dominion on the seas. They were not *in* and *of* the empire but existed *for* the empire. It was, Adam Smith wrote bitingly in 1776, an empire of "a nation of shopkeepers" run for "the sole purpose of raising up a people of customers." But Franklin, by locating the future grandeur of the empire in America, sounded a new note with startling implications. The perimeter was to become the center!

Before 1775, few if any Americans, whatever their hidden desires, admitted the intent of raising an independent empire. They advocated an empire of equal self-governing states owing allegiance to a common King. But this did not fit the British scheme. So gradually, almost imperceptibly, the earlier vision of America as the foundation of future British glory changed into a vision of America as potentially an empire within itself. This was a continental conception, though not excluding the maritime; and it looked to an empire of free and equal states, "an empire of liberty," as Jefferson would soon call the American experiment. It embraced the great West beyond the Appalachians, perhaps beyond the Mississippi, as well as the Atlantic seaboard. American nationality, inchoate and untried, was thus invested with high promise. Fulfillment was far off, but as independence dawned the promise grew in magnificence until it seemed, with Thomas Paine, that this new nation had it in its power "to begin the world over again."

Empire Theory and the American Cause

Many forces fed into the American Revolution, but the movement fed upon one great issue, the constitutional authority of Great Britain over the colonies. A struggle involving other and diverse interests and principles was conducted largely as a contest on the nature and limits of the English constitution. Jefferson addressed himself to this great question in *A Summary View of the Rights of British America* in 1774. Written as instructions for the Virginia delegates to the First Continental Congress, the tract was published on both sides of the Atlantic without his permission or ascription of authorship, though he quickly became known as the author and on that recognition moved to the front rank of America's patriot leadership.

Following the crisis of 1769, American resistance collapsed everywhere. The Virginians, Jefferson remarked, "seemed to fall into a state of insensibility to our situation." The new ministry in London headed by Lord North, a court favorite, showed strength at home and caution abroad. For three years North gave the American radicals no new fuel to stoke the furnace of agitation. Yet the Declaratory Act was still on the books and the Townshend duty on tea remained in force. In Virginia, returning prosperity and the popularity of the new Governor, Lord Dunmore, whose ardor for granting lands and pushing Western claims endeared him to many planters, contributed to the uneasy calm. Awaiting a new signal of alarm, Jefferson found it in 1773 in the British response to the burning of a revenue cutter, the *Gaspee*, off the coast of Rhode Island. A vice-admiralty court of inquiry was empowered to send the culprits to England for trial. The culprits were never identified, but this calculated usurpation could not be ignored, Jefferson thought. At the opening of the assembly in the spring of 1773 he met with several of the "hot-heads," Henry, Richard Henry Lee, Francis L. Lee, Dabney Carr, perhaps one or two others. They agreed to a series of resolutions calling for the institution of committees of correspondence in each colony to facilitate intercommunication and union in the common cause. Local committees had already been appointed in Massachusetts towns. But Jefferson always believed that the resolutions drawn up by his little group, introduced in the House, passed and circulated throughout the country were the first looking to colony-wide committees in a system of collective action. The Governor, sensing the threat of a revolutionary underground, promptly prorogued the House. Within a few months every colony but Pennsylvania had a committee of correspondence.

Before the legislature next met, in May 1774, the Tea Act had been passed, the Boston Tea Party had occurred, and British retaliation had commenced against Massachusetts. The Tea Act, which undercut colonial merchants by the special privileges it gave to the East India Company in the American market, little concerned Virginians. But they were aroused by the first of a series of measures, the Coercive Acts, against the sister colony to the north. News of the Boston Port Act reached Williamsburg while the assembly was in session. The trade and livelihood of a great city were to be sacrificed to revenge the action of a few militants who dumped several hundred chests of tea into Boston harbor. "This is administering justice with a heavy hand indeed!" Jefferson exclaimed. The little cadre of the previous year, minus Dabney Carr, now dead, again took the lead. They met, rummaged through John Rushworth's *Historical Collections* for precedents and forms drawn from the Puritan Revolution in England, and as Jefferson recalled, "cooked up a resolution . . . for appointing the 1st day of June, on which the port bill was to commence, for a day of fasting, humiliation, and prayer, to implore Heaven to avert from us the evils of civil war, to inspire us with firmness in support of our rights, and to turn the hearts of the King and Parliament to moderation and justice." They prevailed on Robert Carter Nicholas, "whose grave and religious character was more in unison with the tone of the resolution," to sponsor it in the House. It passed without opposition. The Governor, as on the push of a button, dissolved the assembly.

The burgesses reconvened, as it were, at the Raleigh Tavern and took the longest step yet recorded toward independence. The incipient revolutionary body declared that an attack on one colony should be considered an attack on all, instructed the Virginia committee of correspondence to propose the meeting of a continental congress, recommended to the counties the election of delegates to a convention to meet in Williamsburg on August 1, and adopted an

Association, more strongly armed than its predecessors, to interdict trade with Great Britain. The fast day, soon after the burgesses returned home, was a stunning propaganda success. "The people met generally, with anxiety and alarm in their countenance," Jefferson recalled, "and the effect of the day, through the whole colony, was like a shock of electricity, arousing every man, and placing him erect and solidly on his center." The counties chose delegates to the provincial convention, which in turn concluded its work in August by electing delegates to the First Continental Congress, convened in Philadelphia in September. A little "tea party" in Boston had mushroomed into a mighty storm uniting the continent.

Jefferson, from his part in this movement, might have been elected one of the seven delegates to the Congress had he taken his seat in the convention at Williamsburg. But falling sick on the road, he never reached the capital, and had to forward copies of his proposed instructions to Peyton Randolph and Patrick Henry. The paper was read by the members, admired by many, but thought too bold. Jefferson afterwards concurred in this judgment, saying that "the leap" he proposed was "too long as yet for the mass of our citizens." The difference between his paper and the humble instructions adopted by the convention showed, he added, "the inequality of the pace with which we moved, and the prudence required to keep front and rear together." The cooler heads of men like Randolph, Wythe, Pendleton, and Washington ensured a united, if slower, march toward the goal. The Virginia instructions of 1774 still turned on the constitutional distinction, worked out by John Dickinson several years earlier, between *external* and *internal* legislation, Parliament having rightful authority in one sphere but not in the other. Jefferson's paper, on the other hand, denied Parliament's authority altogether, or any connection with the mother country except through the King, and turned on natural as well as legal rights. "The young ascended with Mr. Jefferson to the source of those rights," Edmund Randolph recalled the division, "the old required time for consideration, before they could tread the lofty ground. . . ." Published by his friends as the *Summary View* in Williamsburg, at once reprinted in Philadelphia and in England, Jefferson's hastily penned instructions opened a new chapter in the polemics of the Revolution.

Yet, if the chapter was new, it was not without antecedents in Virginia. The *Summary View* carried to logical conclusion a line of argument broached by Richard Bland a decade earlier. In *The Colonel Dismounted* (1763) and, above all, his *Inquiry into the Rights of the British Colonies* (1766), Bland held that the colonies had never been part of the realm of England, hence could not of right be subject to the laws of Parliament, where they were not represented, but being dominions of the King, the colonies and the colonists owed him the same allegiance as his subjects in England or Scotland or Ireland. Bland seemed to lack the courage of his own premises, however. Jefferson, who admired this bookish elder statesman and upon his death at the beginning of the Revolution purchased his valuable library, later characterized Bland's rambling and indecisive argument: "He would set out with a set of sound principles, pursue them logically till he found them leading to the precipice which he had to leap, start back alarmed, then resume his ground, go over it in another direction, be led by the correctness of his reasoning to the same place and again back about and try other processes to reconcile right and wrong, but finally left his reader and himself bewildered between the steady index of the compass in their hand, and the phantasm to which it seemed to point." Jefferson took the compass and threw the phantasm of Parliament overboard.

From the beginning of the contest with the mother country the colonists had searched for some halfway house between total subjection to the authority of Parliament and its total rejection. Some, like James Otis of Massachusetts, had appealed to fundamental constitutional guarantees, such as the right to consent to taxes, which Parliament, supreme but under the law, could not transgress. Dickinson and many others had drawn the line between internal and external legislation. In imperial relationships any line was difficult, however; and just as it was anachronistic, with Otis, to regard Parliament as a high court that would void its own unconstitutional acts, it was equally so, and equally futile, with Dickinson to expect a body that since 1688 had made a fetish of its own "sovereign and uncontrollable authority" to yield limitations on its powers, regardless of hoary sanction or precedent. No modern Whig, not even the few, like Lord Chatham and Edmund Burke, friendly to the colonial cause, questioned the supremacy of Parliament. Burke's approach was to reconcile parliamentary supremacy and colonial rights on the level of expediency. "The question with me is," he said, "not whether you have a right to render your people miserable, but whether it is not your interest to make them happy." The Declaratory Act, "the system of 1766," set the proper course by claiming the right to legislate for the colonies while refraining from its exercise. But the colonists after 1774 demanded a solution founded in right and principle. Burke was no true friend of this cause; indeed he condemned "the dangerous spirit of disquisition," the fondness for "metaphysical questions," the speculation on rights and liberties, a foolish ministry had let loose in America. The myopia that persisted in treating issues of principle as issues of policy was a reproach to Whig politics. The Americans, seeking but not finding a halfway house, moved toward a theoretical position wholly incompatible with the Whig conception of the English constitution. What had been deemed liberty for Englishmen in 1688 was now deemed tyranny for the Americans. Returning to the ancient distinction between the realm and the dominions, Jefferson, together with the Adamses in Massachusetts and James Wilson in Pennsylvania, set forth the new theory of the imperial connection in which the colonies were equal self-governing states owing allegiance to the King.

The *Summary View* began with the proposition that the Americans were the sons of expatriated men who "possessed a right, which nature has given to all men, of departing from the country in which chance, not choice, has placed them, of going in quest of new habitations, and of there establishing new societies, under such laws and regulations as to them shall seem most likely to promote public happiness." This alleged natural right had no standing in English law, as Jefferson knew. Blackstone stated the rule: an English subject could not by any act of his own throw off his natural born allegiance. Jefferson could find the right of expatriation in Cicero, Grotius, Locke, and other eminent authorities, though he cited none of them. Instead he appealed to the example of the Saxon ancestors who had left the wilds of northern Europe and settled in England without their mother country ever making any claim of superiority over them. "And it is thought that no circumstance has occurred to distinguish materially the British from the Saxon emigration. America was conquered, and her settlements made and firmly established, at the expense of individuals, and not of the British public. . . . For themselves they fought, for themselves alone they have a right to hold." Much the same claim, it may be noted, had been made for the Americans in Parliament years before, during the debate on the Stamp Act, by Colonel Isaac Barré, whose speech on that occasion Jefferson considered one of the most eloquent ever uttered.

Exploiting the past for political ends, Jefferson was less interested in the historical truth than in the moral truth of the proposition. But he was not ready to dismiss history altogether, for to do so would be to dismiss the English constitution and imperial connection of any sort, and he was not ready for that. Proceeding with the argument, he conceded that when Britain discovered the commercial value of the wilderness colonies she extended protection to them. Receiving these aids, the colonists did not thereby submit themselves to British sovereignty. Certain errors crept into the relationship because the early settlers, being laborers not lawyers, failed to see the implications of practices that were, in fact, usurpations. Thus they were victimized by the "ficticious principle that all lands belong originally to the king . . . and accordingly took grants of their own lands from the crown." But this was the feudal principle introduced into Saxon England by William the Norman. The Americans, like their Saxon ancestors, claimed the wilderness lands in absolute dominion, disencumbered of any superior, whether feudal lord or king, and so escaped the terrible fate that overcame England. "America was not conquered by William the Norman, nor its lands surrendered to him or any of his successors." In principle, that is; in fact, feudalism sneaked in. So long as it worked easily the error went undetected. Only in recent decades had His Majesty's exactions on lands and control of grants caused severe hardship and the usurpation become evident. Confusion arose too, Jefferson said, from the early emigrants' adoption of the common law. They brought with them the rights of expatriated men, that is, natural rights, but they voluntarily chose to govern themselves by English law. Similarly, they chose to submit themselves to a common sovereign, the British monarch, "who was thereby made the central link connecting the several parts of the empire thus newly multiplied."

Jefferson dealt at length with the encroachments of Crown and Parliament on American rights. Freedom of trade, which he called a "natural right," fell before arbitrary power in the middle of the seventeenth century. Considering itself heir to the powers of the deposed king, Charles I, Parliament took the fatal step of legislating for the dominions. The trade and navigation acts from that point forward instanced a despotism without parallel in English annals. Yet Jefferson did not propose going back to the true principle. The commercial system, rightly conducted by the Crown, was one of the benefits of the empire. "The true ground on which we declare these acts void is that the British Parliament has no right to exercise authority over us." Until the reign of George III other violations of American rights had occurred at such distant intervals as to muffle alarm; since then they had followed in swift succession. "Single acts of tyranny may be ascribed to the accidental opinion of a day; but a series of oppressions, begun at a distinguished period, and pursued unalterably thro' every change of ministers, too plainly prove a deliberate, systematical plan of reducing us to slavery." Jefferson passed in review these oppressive measures beginning with the Revenue Act of 1764 and ending with the Boston Port Act. It was the responsibility of the King to check these encroachments; but not only had he failed in this duty, he had arbitrarily used his executive powers in the colonial governments, dissolving assemblies, refusing assent to some laws for trifling reasons, delaying consideration of others, interfering with the organization of legislative bodies, granting lands and advancing the terms of sale, standing an army among the people, and subordinating the civil to the military power. These charges against the King anticipated the long indictment in the Declaration of Independence. Jefferson's stated purpose in 1774, however, was not to convict the King but to reform him. "No longer persevere in sacrificing the rights of one part of the empire to the inordinate desires of another: but deal out to all equal and impartial right," he implored. "Let no act be passed by any one legislature which may infringe on the rights and liberties of another. This is the important post in which fortune has placed you, holding the balance of a great, if a well poised empire." The advice, unrelieved by humility or praise, was scarcely calculated to arouse the sympathies of George III. Nor was Jefferson's defiant conclusion: "The God who gave us life gave us liberty at the same time: the hand of force may destroy, but cannot disjoin them."

75

What was the purpose of the *Summary View?* Not conciliation, for Jefferson's language was anything but conciliatory. Did he and the other Americans who set forth this new theory of empire actually expect it to be adopted by the authorities in England? No, they were not naïve. There was, to be sure, historical basis for it in the tradition of the English constitution. In Jefferson's opinion the relationship of the colonies to England was exactly the same as that of Scotland after the accession of James I and before the Act of Union: equal states under a common king. And he was quite familiar with the case of Anglo-Irish, who claimed with some success at law the equality of their parliament with the English; yet their case was not as good as the American, for Ireland had been conquered by English arms. The idea of dominion status, not without precedent in history, also pointed to a creative solution to the problems of a multiplying empire; and Britain, after losing the American colonies, would slowly come to the conception of a "commonwealth of nations" anticipated by Jefferson and his American compatriates. But the conception was impractical given the structure of British politics in the reign of George III. That monarch gloried in the supremacy of Parliament and was intimately involved with it. The new theory of empire demanded the King's separation from Parliament— a monarch *above* many parliaments rather than *in* one Parliament. Besides, no English Whig could accept the idea that Parliament should be deposed and the Crown exalted in imperial affairs. Yet this seemed to be what the American militants advocated. Lord North sneered, "Their language therefore was that of toryism." The aberration was more glaring in Wilson's 1774 tract, *Considerations on the Nature and Extent of the Legislative Authority of the British Parliament*, than in the *Summary View*. Wilson made explicit what Jefferson left implicit: the King should be the colonies' protector, negative unjust acts of Parliament, and exercise his "prerogative" to regulate trade. The logic of the argument led embarrassingly to the aggrandizement of royal power, unless, of course, an imperial parliament miraculously came into being; but neither Jefferson nor Wilson advocated this, and when one was proposed in the First Continental Congress it was defeated. If Jefferson was not naïve, not a Tory, not a parliamentary unionist, what then, was he driving at?

He was advancing the contest to the next stage, not knowing where, once this act was played out, he would go next. The basic premise, that the Americans were expatriated men, a distinct people, endowed with natural rights and free to shape their institutions as they pleased, pointed directly to independence. But he still shrank from this last resort. Like Bland, whom he criticized for failure to leap the precipice of parliamentary authority, Jefferson, too, had a precipice, and he drew back, retreated along devious and at times treacherous trails of history and theory, rather than follow his premises to conclusion.

Events were rapidly driving him to that conclusion. The Congress at Philadelphia adjourned on October 26. "The colonists have taken such grounds that Great Britain must relax, or inevitably involve herself in civil war," John Dickinson, one of the delegates, wrote. "The first act of violence . . . will put the whole continent in arms from Nova Scotia to Georgia." He was right, in the main. Congress endorsed the Suffolk Resolves of Massachusetts, which declared the Coercive Acts unconstitutional and void, urged the formation of an independent government in that beleaguered colony, called the people to arm, and backed strong economic sanctions against Britain. Resolutions of the Congress repudiated the authority of Parliament, without specifically endorsing the new theory of empire. The system of non-intercourse copied with little change the Virginia Association. Local committees were to be elected throughout the country to enforce the economic coercion. In Virginia they were already in operation. Jefferson was a member of the Albemarle committee. With the suppression of commerce the county courts closed, and the local committees became the effective governing bodies. The Association brought the revolutionary movement to every man's door. The agreement served as a kind of loyalty oath; one either signed or faced suppression, boycott, or disrepute. In Virginia most merchants joined the planters in signing. Independent militia companies also sprang up in the fall of 1774. Jefferson found himself a private in the ranks—even his overseer was a sergeant—of the Albemarle company. The issue in the colonies was no longer between parties seeking different paths to conciliation, but between a radical party pushing toward independence and a moderate party holding back, still hopeful of conciliation. Jefferson kept in step with the radicals but patiently awaited the King's response to disillusion the moderates.

Nothing official had been heard from the King when the second provincial convention met at Richmond, out of the way of the Governor, in March 1775. Reports were discouraging, however. In his recent address to Parliament George III set a mad course of coercion and was applauded for it. Patrick Henry boldly announced in Richmond, "The war is actually begun," and vowed, "Give me liberty, or give me death." The old guard, still in control of the reconstituted Burgesses, wished to stand pat on the platform of Congress, pending the King's answer to the Virginia petition. But Henry moved a resolution to put the colony in a state of defense, not only at the local level, where volunteer companies were already forming, but colony-wide by raising an army. Jefferson spoke in favor of the motion. It passed, narrowly, though with little immediate effect. Jefferson also introduced a resolution denouncing the Governor for innovations in the established usage of granting lands. Poor Dunmore had just fought an Indian war, Dunmore's War, to defend the colony's claim to the Ohio Valley; but the Virginians, while grateful, would not brook royal interference with land policy. The Governor lost all standing in April, not long after the convention adjourned, when he succumbed to panic and removed the powder from the magazine at Williamsburg to a British vessel in the James, sent off his family, and barricaded himself in the Palace. Henry, in a grandstand play, put himself at the head of the Hanover militia and marched to the capital. The moderates spiked the burgeoning crisis, however. The militia turned back before reaching the capital.

The first shot had already been fired in Massachusetts. The encounter at Lexington and Concord, Jefferson wrote, "has cut off our last hopes of reconciliation, and a phrenzy of revenge seems to have seized all ranks of people." Incongruously, at this time, Dunmore called the assembly into session. The object was to deal with Lord North's "conciliatory proposition," under which Parliament would forbear to tax the colonies if they, individually, would make regular contributions to support the civil government and defense of the empire. Jefferson wrote Virginia's reply to the North proposal. In language firm but temperate he said that the plan "only changes the form of oppression, without lightening the burden." Parliament had no right to meddle in any way with the provincial government. "For us, not for them, has government been instituted here. . . ." A perpetual tax set by Parliament and subject to its disposal was totally unacceptable. "It is not merely the mode of raising but the freedom of granting our money for which we have contended." The plan made no provision for lifting other oppressions. It asked money of the colonies but continued the monopoly of their trade. And while this olive branch was held forth in one hand, the other unsheathed the sword—"a style of asking gifts not reconcilable to our freedom." Finally, now pledged to a common cause, the union of the colonies, Virginia could not accede to terms on its own authority. Jefferson praised Lord Chatham's more generous plan of reconciliation, brutally beaten down in Parliament, and invoked the God of Justice to point the way to peace.

On June 10 the House unanimously adopted Jefferson's resolutions, after passing over the moderate answer prepared by its own committee. By this time the Governor had taken refuge aboard a British man-of-war in York River, and Jefferson was on the road to Philadelphia. The convention had added him to the congressional delegation to serve in the place of Peyton Randolph, called from Philadelphia to preside over the House of Burgesses. That body would not convene again. The transition to revolutionary government was already far advanced in Virginia. Jefferson, having devoted his energies to this movement, now entered the continental theater in Philadelphia.

Congress and the Declaration of Independence

The Second Continental Congress had been in session several weeks when Jefferson took his seat in the downstairs chamber of the Pennsylvania State House (Independence Hall) on June 21, 1775. The assemblage was young, spirited, and distinguished. Benjamin Franklin, at sixty-nine, was the oldest member; Jefferson, at thirty-two, almost but not quite the youngest. Fifty to sixty members were usually in attendance. Omitting the Virginians, Jefferson recognized only one vaguely familiar face, Elbridge Gerry of Massachusetts, whom he had met in New York nine years before on his northern tour. His career in the future would cross Gerry's in unpredictable ways, as it would with many of these patriots: John Jay, an austere New Yorker, two years his junior; John Langdon, a Yankee commoner; the aristocratic Rutledge brothers, John and Edward, of South Carolina; John Dickinson, Pennsylvania's reluctant revolutionist; Charles Thomson, another Pennsylvanian and secretary of the Congress; and, of course, the leading zealots, John and Samuel Adams of Massachusetts. Next to Franklin, worshipped from the start, Jefferson was at once drawn to the bluff man from Quincy, John Adams, whose personality was of another genre but whose politics at this stage agreed with his own. The men who came to this Congress were accustomed to lead—all were generals bidding for new distinctions, commands, and followings—and while all were Americans, they were provincials still in their traits, attitudes, and interests. "Fifty gentlemen meeting together, all strangers, are not acquainted with each other's language, ideas, views, designs," Adams observed. "They are therefore jealous of each other—fearful, timid, skittish." If Jefferson found it difficult to keep front and rear ranks together in Virginia, it would be more difficult in Philadelphia, and infinitely more important because the cause of continental union depended upon it. Delicacy, tact, patience, a willingness to subordinate personal or parochial views to unity of action, were essential.

Jefferson's reputation had gone before him. As Adams recalled, he brought into Congress "a reputation for literature, science, and a happy talent of composition." His writings were known and admired for what Adams called their "peculiar felicity of expression." It was in this area, as a legislative draftsman, that he made his mark in Congress. On the floor of the House he never uttered a word, unless to untie some procedural knot. Yet his persuasive powers were not confined to a masterful pen. "Though a silent member of Congress," Adams said, "he was so prompt, frank, explicit, and decisive upon committees and in conversation, not even Samuel Adams was more so, that he soon seized upon my heart." Of course, he was an acquisition for the radicals. Lee and Henry, among the Virginia delegates, were on that side; but Henry's talents were exclusively oratorical and Lee's lay mainly in that line. The connection Lee established with the two Adamses aided the radical cause. Unfortunately, it also contributed to jealousy and division, especially in the Virginia delegation, where Lee was unpopular with moderate leaders like Harrison and Pendleton. Commanding the respect of all, Jefferson helped to hold the Virginia delegation together; and by virtue of his talents for legislative business and the drafting of papers, the radicals gained a valuable recruit from the most populous and most powerful of the thirteen colonies.

Just after he arrived in Philadelphia, news of the Battle of Bunker Hill reached the city. Amidst martial fanfare the next day, Congress sent off George Washington to take command of the Continental Army near Boston. Jefferson wrote home "that the war is now heartily entered into, without a prospect of accommodation but through the effectual interposition of arms." As civil war became the massive reality, he hesitated to embrace independence, which, as Adams said, was "a hobgoblin of . . . frightful mien." While not a "hobgoblin" for Jefferson, it clearly was for others, and he preferred to march in measured steps, in full force, to the Rubicon. Adams and several others wished to make the crossing at once, believing that only then would the country unite in the prosecution of the war. The Pennsylvania delegation under Dickinson, with strong support in the middle colonies, remained anxious for reconciliation. The prevailing sentiment seemed to be to fight and, for the present, keep the imperial quarrel open to negotiation. Jefferson could accept this, as could Adams and Dickinson, each with his own accent.

Jefferson's first important assignment came in connection with the Declaration of the Causes and Necessity for Taking Up Arms. A committee had reported, but the House, dissatisfied with the report, recommitted it and at the same time added Jefferson and Dickinson to the committee. The Virginian was asked to prepare a new draft. He did so with great care and deliberation, then presented the result. Dickinson objected to the paper as unnecessarily harsh and offensive. In this impasse the committee, as Jefferson put it, "indulged" Dickinson by asking him to try his hand. His draft, incorporating large parts of Jefferson's, was approved in committee and, subsequently, in the House. The Declaration was thus the product of collaboration at arm's length between Jefferson and Dickinson. Addressed not only to Great Britain but to the "Opinion of Mankind," the Declaration justified the appeal to arms as a cruel necessity forced by violent and tyrannical authority. "Our cause is just. Our union is perfect. Our internal Resources are great, and, if necessary, foreign Assistance is undoubtedly available." In strong but elevated language, the Declaration pledged unyielding resistance, "being with one Mind resolved to die Freemen rather than to live Slaves." With equal firmness it rejected independence, pleading instead for the restoration of union and concord. Jefferson's text had made the same appeal but less bluntly and without disclaiming independence. He had wished to express the true theory of imperial relations in the manifesto. Dickinson put a gloss on this question, alluding ambiguously to the theory without affirming it or explicitly repudiating the authority of Parliament. Dickinson's hand improved the style of the document if it somewhat weakened its theoretical basis. Yet both men aimed to produce the same effect: the justification of armed resistance not to divide but to reunite the empire on terms compatible with American liberty.

Having composed the Virginia reply to Lord North's "conciliatory proposition," Jefferson was asked to perform the same service for Congress. His argument was the same but the pitch was higher. He had not, in the Virginia answer, reflected on the motives of the British ministry in advancing this specious proposition; now he said it was "held up to the world, to deceive it into a belief that there was nothing in dispute between us but the *mode* of levying taxes" and to put the colonies in the wrong if they spurned the overture. In truth, this was far from the case, and the world when led to reflect on the bold succession of oppressions over the past eleven years would "believe with us, that nothing but our own exertions may defeat the ministerial sentence of death or abject submission." Congress adopted Jefferson's draft virtually unchanged. It also adopted a second humble petition to the King, again begging his intervention on the side of peace. Jefferson expected nothing from this appeal penned by Dickinson. Its cringing tone disgusted him and many of the delegates, yet it seemed necessary in order to mollify Pennsylvania.

Congress had other business than the drafting of manifestos, replies, and petitions. It was engaged in war. Officers had to be commissioned, a supply system organized, money raised, military regulations promulgated, strategy planned, Indian tribes won over or neutralized, new channels of trade opened, alliances broached, the union of the colonies consolidated. In the summer of 1775 the extent, the duration, and the course of the conflict were, as Jefferson said, "among the secrets of providence." Congress proceeded under a cloud of uncertainty, but it was best, he reflected, to be prepared for the worst.

When Congress adjourned briefly in August, Jefferson attended the Virginia convention at Richmond before going on to Monticello. The convention and its executive arm, the Committee of Public Safety, under Pendleton, ruled the province. Henry, panting for military glory, was put in command of Virginia's gathering forces, and operations were soon under way against Dunmore's paltry contingent of redcoats, loyalists, and blacks pillaging and plundering with the aid of several men-of-war in the vicinity of Norfolk. The convention elected a new set of delegates to Congress. Jefferson received the third highest vote, just behind Randolph and Lee, which was a fair indication of his standing in Virginia politics, though it must be remembered that several of his seniors—Henry, Pendleton, and Washington notably—were now unavailable for congressional service.

Detained at Monticello by the death of an infant daughter, Jefferson hurried back to Philadelphia early in the fall. The expedition against Quebec was in full tilt—Montreal fell to General Montgomery in November—and Jefferson confidently expected Canada's accession to the American union. He was busy with committees in the early morning hours, then in the House until late afternoon, and back to committee business late into the night. Congress set up a navy, appointed a secret committee of correspondence to arrange for foreign aid and support, and authorized several additional colonies, including Virginia, to establish their own governments, as Massachusetts was doing. The door was thus opened to internal revolution as Congress moved ever closer to independence. The radicals, generally, hailed this development, for they were eager to exploit the opportunity for democratic reform at home; the moderates, on the other hand, feared the specter of democracy that hovered ominously over the movement toward independence. In November, Congress learned of the King's refusal to receive the "Olive Branch Petition" —the second humble address—and his proclamation placing the colonies in a state of open rebellion. Congress answered by a disavowal of the authority of Parliament and a reaffirmation of allegiance to the King, though this was now a shabby fiction. Writing to a good friend, John Randolph, the attorney general, who had declared his loyalty to Britain and was about to leave Virginia, Jefferson made his last profession of affection for the empire and laid the blame for its impending dissolution squarely on the shoulders of George III. "In an earlier part of this contest out petitions told him that from our King there was but one appeal," he said. "The admonition was despised and that appeal forced on us. To undo his empire he has but one truth more to learn, that after colonies have drawn the sword there is but one step more they can take. . . . We want neither inducement nor power to declare and assert a separation. It is will alone which is wanting and that is gaining apace under the fostering hand of our King."

Near the end of the year Jefferson returned to Monticello. He was worried about his wife's health. Congress sat in continuous session, marking time on the great issue. The Virginia delegates, having only one vote together, agreed to spare him for awhile. He did not expect to be gone long, but his mother's death, followed by his own illness, kept him at home until early May. The personal malady was an "inveterate headache," which struck him periodically over the years, usually at times of emotional stress. (The first mention of the affliction is in a letter of March 1764 when he learned Rebecca Burwell would marry another.) At home he turned his thoughts to the reconstruction of Virginia's government and also, it seems, to the confederation of the colonies or states. He annotated a plan of union Franklin had prepared and extended his reading in the history of confederations both ancient and modern. But this problem, while much discussed, would not come on the carpet in Congress until after independence was declared, when Jefferson's mind reverted to Virginia. Reading in January the King's recent speech to Parliament, in which it was unctuously claimed that Britain had planted, nursed, and cared for the colonies, Jefferson indignantly rushed to his books to refute the pretension, filling in the details of the case outlined in the *Summary View*. "A King who can adopt falsehood, and solemnize it from the throne, justifies the revolution of fortunes which reduces him to a private station," he asserted after ransacking Hakluyt, Raleigh, Stith, and other authorities on the early English settlement of the New World. Presumably he intended this brief for publication, but it was technical and antiquarian, hardly calculated for the immediate crisis, so he filed it away.

A tract exactly calculated for the crisis was Thomas Paine's *Common Sense*. Published anonymously in Philadelphia in January, it spread the doctrine of independence across the land. Jefferson read the pamphlet at Monticello. Saying nothing about it at the time, he later praised its contribution, with all of Paine's services to the American cause, when most men preferred to forget him. A commoner by birth, a radical by temperament, a revolutionist by profession, Paine, though a newcomer to the American scene, perceived the absurdity of the imperial connection, the promise of continental union, and the greatness of the cause not only for Americans but for all mankind. "The sun never shone on a cause of greater worth. 'Tis not the affair of a city, a county, a province, or a kingdom; but of a continent—of at least one eighth part of the habitable globe. 'Tis not the concern of a day, a year, or an age; posterity are virtually involved in the contest, and will be more or less affected even to the end of time, by the proceedings now." Paine stripped the issues of their conventional legalistic dress and nakedly disclosed the "common sense" of independence. His political rhetoric was quite new. Earthy, naïve, direct, it addressed the people in their own language and evoked a qualitatively different response than the erudite polemics of constitutional warriors. He did not toy with error but strangled it; he did not toss truth into the philosophical air but grasped its stark simplicity. Appealing to the "simple voice of nature and reason," Paine pooh-poohed the elegant myth of balanced government, ridiculed monarchy and hereditary succession, and scoffed at the "papistical" idea of English parentage of America. Jefferson could agree with most of what Paine said, but he could not possibly have written *Common Sense*. The Virginian's language was elegant, not vulgar; his mind craved the historical and legal authority Paine contemptuously dismissed; his comparatively sedate politics reflected his membership in a governing class with which, of course, Paine had no associations and whose methods he eschewed. Yet the essentially naturalistic assumptions of Paine's pamphlet went right along with Jefferson's philosophy, and bringing these assumptions to bear on the question of national independence helped to free him from the inhibitions of law and history.

Independence had made great strides when Jefferson resumed his seat in Congress on May 14, 1776. Privateering had been authorized, American ports thrown open to all the world but Britain, and energetic steps taken toward securing foreign aid. The colonists had suffered a serious reversal in Canada, but the British had evacuated Boston. The military balance sheet, if not encouraging, was far from desperate. The middle colonies, in particular, still shied away from independence. "The novelty of the thing deters some," Franklin wrote from Congress in April, "the doubts of success, others, the vain hope of reconciliation, many." When Jefferson arrived Congress was just winding up debate on John Adams's motion calling on all the colonies to establish their own governments. The motion, "a machine to fabricate independence" in Adams's calculation, passed on May 15. On the same day the Virginia convention unanimously instructed its delegates to propose a declaration of independence, as well as to support foreign alliances and the confederation of the colonies. The convention proceeded at once to declare the independence of Virginia and to frame a government for the new state, adopted on June 28.

In Congress, meanwhile, compliant with the Virginia instructions, Lee introduced a resolution stating that the colonies "are, and of right ought to be, free and independent states." The laggards were coming up to the mark; even in the continent's mid-section, revolutionary patriot parties mobilized against the proprietary governments to force the issue of independence. "Every post and every day roles in upon us, Independence like a torrent," Adams rejoiced. The Lee resolution, incorporating as well the provisions for alliance and confederation, came up for consideration in committee of the whole on June 8. Jefferson recorded the arguments advanced pro and con in this debate. The spokesmen for the opposition—Jefferson mentioned Dickinson and Wilson, of Pennsylvania, and Robert R. Livingston and Edward Rutledge of New York and South Carolina respectively—narrowed the issue to one of timing. Congress should defer the final step until the united voice of the people drove them to it. The middle colonies, while ripening, were not yet ripe; and since their delegations were either expressly forbidden or unauthorized to vote for independence, premature forcing of the issue must produce secession from the union with all its perils. The more prudent course, the opponents said, was to await the outcome of the present summer's campaign, concentrating meanwhile on the formation of an alliance with France and consolidation of the union. To this the radicals, led by Adams and Lee, replied that a declaration of independence would simply recognize the *de facto* situation; that public opinion was ahead of Congress, even in the middle colonies, where the influence of proprietary power and immunity as yet from enemy attack, not the majority voice of the people, held them back; that the European nations would neither trade nor treat with rebel colonies until they established their independence *de jure;* that fears of secession were exaggerated, and military affairs might not for some time wear a brighter aspect than now. The debate continued on into the evening, was adjourned, and resumed the following Monday. A compromise was then adopted: the independence resolution would be postponed for three weeks, until July 1, and a committee appointed at once to prepare a declaration likely to be wanted at that time. The moderates won a brief reprieve; the radicals won the contest.

On the next day Congress appointed a committee of five, Jefferson, Adams, Franklin, Livingston, and Roger Sherman of Connecticut, to prepare the Declaration of Independence. (Two other committees were presently appointed to report a plan of treaties and a plan of confederation.) The naming of so young a man to head the committee caused some surprise. The resolution coming from Virginia, a Virginian was naturally named first; and Lee, standing as the sponsor, seemed the obvious choice. Adams later said Lee was passed over because of his unpopularity within the Virginia delegation. The probabilities are, however, that Lee did not want the job. He, too, had an ailing wife at home and wished for leave, not alone for that reason but also to share in the work of constitution-making at Williamsburg. Lee got his wish, while Jefferson remained, unhappily, in Philadelphia. The committee met, perhaps without Franklin, ridden by gout; and Jefferson agreed to prepare a draft of the Declaration. Adams remembered a conversation which began with Jefferson asking him to draw the paper:

"Oh! no.

"Why will you not? You ought to do it.

"I will not.

"Why.

"Reasons enough.

"What can be your reasons.

"Reason first—You are a Virginian, and a Virginian ought to appear at the head of this business. Reason second—I am obnoxious, suspected, and unpopular. You are very much otherwise. Reason third—You can write ten times better than I can.

"Well, if you are decided I will do as well as I can."

The recollection, if not correct in every detail, suggests how it happened that Jefferson became the author of the Declaration of Independence. Fortune of circumstance played a part; but his genius alone converted a merely political and diplomatic document into a monument of human liberty.

In his quarters on the second floor of a brick house at Seventh and Market Streets, during the third week of June, presumably before and after business hours in Congress, Jefferson composed the original draft of the Declaration of Independence. Only a fragment of the draft survives. What he called the rough draft, though it was almost certainly the second or perhaps even the third, was submitted to Franklin and to Adams for their corrections. "Their alterations were two or three only, merely verbal," he recalled. He then went through the work again, making many verbal changes and several additions. Satisfied now, he propped up the little portable writing table built to his own design by a previous landlord, and penned the fair copy of the Declaration. He reported this to the committee, and from there, unaltered, it went to Congress on June 28. This fair copy has been lost, but it can be reconstructed from duplicates Jefferson himself made apparently when the Declaration was before Congress.

In form the Declaration of Independence presents a syllogistic argument in three parts: a major premise stated in the introductory part, the Preamble; a minor premise, also stated there but demonstrated at length in what is sometimes misleadingly called the body of the work; and a conclusion following from the premises. The primary purpose, as stated in the opening paragraph, was to convince the world of the rightfulness of the colonies' separation from

Great Britain. Jefferson went beyond this, however, and seized the occasion to advance in axiomatic terms a political ideology for the new nation. This was compressed in the complex major premise of the second paragraph: just governments are founded on equal rights and the consent of the governed, and "whenever any form of government becomes destructive of these ends, it is the right of the people to alter or to abolish it, and to institute new government. . . ." Without attempting to define all the equal and "unalienable" rights, he epitomized them in the captivating phrase "life, liberty, and the pursuit of happiness." The strategy of the argument turned on the asserted "self-evidence" of the major premise. A moral truth beyond powers of demonstration, it carried immediate conviction to men of reason and good will. (If it did not, of course, the whole argument collapsed.) The minor premise was this: George III has repeatedly usurped the rights of the Americans with the design "to reduce them under absolute despotism." The demonstration took the form of a bill of indictment against the King—a list of eighteen incisively paragraphed charges, authenticated in historical events, and artfully exhibited as proof *prima facie* of guilt. The indictment issued against the King rather than Parliament because Congress had repudiated the latter authority, leaving allegiance to the King the only legal bond. Congress had not, it may be noted, formally adopted Jefferson's theory of empire as developed in the *Summary View*, and except for a passing allusion it refused to do so now when he attempted to smuggle it into the Declaration. The conclusion of the argument followed automatically. A corollary of the right to throw off a tyrannical government is the right to institute just government. So the Americans absolved themselves of allegiance to the British Crown and solemnly declared "that these United Colonies are and of right ought to be free and independent states."

Jefferson later said that in drafting the Declaration he turned to neither book nor pamphlet nor writing of any kind. This was not quite correct. He drew his charges against the King from the preamble of the constitution he had just drafted for Virginia and sent to Williamsburg. The Virginia Declaration of Rights, drawn by George Mason and available in Philadelphia before the middle of June, probably influenced the phrasing of the philosophical second paragraph. And Jefferson may have resorted to the *Summary View* for the passage on the imperial relationship struck by Congress. But ideas, as he once said, were of all things in nature the least capable of confinement or of exclusive appropriation. The ideas in the Declaration belonged to everyone and to no one. They were part of the climate of opinion, and they passed as coin of the realm among American patriots in 1776. Years afterwards, responding to criticism of the Declaration as a hackneyed performance, Jefferson lucidly stated his view of the task: "Not to find out new principles, or new arguments, never before thought of, not merely to say things which had never been said before; but to place before mankind the common sense of the subject, and to justify ourselves in the independent stand we are compelled to take. Neither aiming at originality of principle or sentiment, nor yet copied from any particular or previous writing, it was intended to be an expression of the American mind, and to give to that expression the proper tone and spirit called for by the occasion."

Yet the Declaration bore the unmistakable stamp of the author's genius. It possessed that "peculiar felicity of expression" for which he was already noted. It was simple, clear, and direct; crisp and angry when this was the tone required, as in the arraignment of the King; gracious and elevated in the soft passages enunciating the rights of man; solemn and stately in the concluding pledge of "our lives, our fortunes, and our sacred honor." Its rhetoric was faintly aristocratic, shrinking from the boldness, the enthusiasm, the popularity of Paine's writing, for example. But Jefferson was not penning a manifesto, and graciousness cannot be counted a fault in a production addressed to the opinion of mankind. Even so, he may have learned something from *Common Sense*, for the Declaration, far beyond any of Jefferson's earlier writings, suppressed recondite legalisms to fundamental human values and capsuled large ideas in electrifying phrases. In a document of less than 1500 words, most of it a bill of particulars against the reigning sovereign, ideas could not be developed, nor indeed even stated; they could only be conjured up by magical words and phrases in trim array. Jefferson managed to compress a cosmology, a political philosophy, a national creed in the second paragraph of the Declaration. This was a triumph. It raised the American cause above parochialism, above history, and united it with the cause of mankind. A philosophy of human rights attained timeless symbolization in words that inspired action; action became thought and thought became action. It was, as Hannah Arendt has said, "one of the rare moments in history when the power of action is great enough to erect its own monument."

Congress heard the Declaration on Friday, June 28, and promptly laid it on the table pending disposition of the Virginia resolution on independence. During the three-week interval just passed several of the delegations from the middle colonies received new instructions, representatives of the new revolutionary government in Pennsylvania came into Congress, and the Rutledge-dominated South Carolina delegation gradually gave ground. When the vote came on July 2 only New York, whose delegates approved the resolution but who were bound by previous instructions, was not recorded in favor. Congress then took up the Declaration, scrutinizing and debating it line by line for two and one-half days. The author squirmed under this ordeal. The introductory part was quickly approved, but Congress made many changes, mostly stylistic, some of substance, in the body of the work. It tempered overly vehement or extravagant expressions against the King, eliminated certain pejoratives, and here and there made a ceremonious bow to historical objectivity. For instance, "he has suffered the administration of justice totally to cease in some of these states" became "he has obstructed the administration of justice." The change was a gain for directness as well as balance. Most of the charges, it might be observed, concerned invasions of the representative assemblies, pointing up the crucial importance of this issue. Congress eliminated altogether the longest, angriest, and climactic count in Jefferson's indictment: the King's "cruel war against human nature itself" by the traffic in slaves. It was struck, Jefferson said, at the behest of South Carolina and Georgia, who wished to continue the African trade. But Congress had other reasons as well for removing this piece of bombast. True, as Jefferson knew from Virginia experience, the Crown had suppressed legislative attempts to stop the importation of slaves. But the Virginians had been motivated perhaps less by humanitarian than by selfish considerations, such as protecting the value of their property in slaves and securing their communities from the dangers of an ever-increasing slave population. It ill became the Americans, north and south, who had profited from this infernal traffic to lay the blame on George III. The charge simply did not ring true. And Jefferson's bloated rhetoric gave it away. Congress also cut deeply into the concluding portion of his composition, eliminating the capsuled restatement of the empire theory, which was water over the dam, and about two hundred additional words superfluous to the case. Jefferson seemed to feel that the Declaration, after passing through the gauntlet of Congress, emerged a weaker document. In fact, it gained in every respect. Congress corrected him precisely where he had allowed himself to go astray: in entering technical legal points, in making loose, circuitous, or wordy statements, and in using declamatory language. Cleared of these aberrations, the intrinsic merits of the work stood in bolder relief than when it passed from Jefferson's hands.

Adopted on the evening of July 4, the Declaration of Independence was promptly printed and put into circulation. Four days later, on a warm sunshiny Philadelphia morning, before a great concourse of people in the State House yard, it was publicly proclaimed for the first time. The people returned their huzzahs, then tore down the King's arms before the State House, and rang bells and lit bonfires on into the evening. It is pleasant to think that Jefferson shared in this celebration. He may not have, however. Congress worked without let-up. The Declaration of Independence, he realized, was no ordinary state paper, yet its immediate significance lay not in causing anything but in affirming an accomplished fact. It did not at once become popular. And several years passed before his authorship was generally known. It was some time, in fact, before he felt a marked pride in the authorship. In part, this was owing to the irritant of congressional tinkering; mainly, however, it was because neither he nor anyone else realized the far-reaching implications of the document. But the Declaration heralded the future, not alone in America but the world around; and in the longer run of time Jefferson's destiny rode with it.

Jefferson's progress from Virginia burgess to American revolutionist in seven years followed the main road of the patriot cause, beginning with the protective defense of traditional rights and liberties and ending with the radical ideology that became the birth-right and creed of a new nation. The line of advance intellectually ran, in general, from law to theory, from history to reason, from the prescriptive guarantees of the English constitution to the natural rights of man. In the course of asserting their claims within the empire, the colonists became increasingly disenchanted with the home government, distrustful of its designs, and anxious for the security of their own polities. They began to think for themselves and to search out their own identity; and swept along by the dialectics of the controversy, they assumed theoretical positions that placed them at odds not alone with the principles and practices of the imperial government but with the principles and practices of government everywhere. Discovering the bankruptcy of one system of politics, they invoked a new system. Viewed abstractly, it was founded on the ideas of the Enlightenment. But these ideas had a traditional base in English law and government, which facilitated the transition. Moreover, in America, the ideas were virtual mirror images of emerging social and political realities only dimly perceived before the birth of revolutionary consciousness. As liberal ideas called attention to these native realities, so did they enable Americans to release the substance of English liberty from its corrupted and constricted forms. The patriots did not invent these ideas, but they organized and condensed them into a revolutionary ideology, then proceeded to put it to work in the civil life of the new nation. Without quite realizing the implications for their own institutions, much less the world-wide import of what they had done, the patriots of 1776 had launched a radical new experiment in democracy.

In the philosophical second paragraph of the Declaration of Independence, Jefferson crystallized the ideas of that "transforming radicalism of the mind" that was, as Bernard Bailyn has said, the essence of the American Revolution.

First of all, *equality:* "all men are created equal." With Jefferson this was an article of science as well as of faith. All men were equal because all stemmed from a single divine creation. In an earlier draft he had written "that from that equal creation" they derive inalienable rights, but he dropped this infelicitous phrasing in favor of "they are endowed by their Creator." Believing in the unity of the human species—metaphorically, at least, in the Mosaic account of creation—and its indestructible place at the end of "the great chain of being,"

Jefferson considered all men equals in the order of nature, just as if the race had been carried forward by creation rather than generation. All men possessed an innate moral sense, the faculty of reason, and essentially the same biological needs. Hence the doctrine of equality was grounded in the facts of natural history.

Second, *natural rights:* "they are endowed by their Creator with certain unalienable rights; that among these are life, liberty, and the pursuit of happiness." The law of nature was furnished with the rights of man—a liberating, not a coercive law. Locke and other modern theorists had deduced the fundamental rights from an imaginary "state of nature." Jefferson neither liked nor used this fiction. The natural state of man was the social state; man realized his true nature as a civilized being. Moreover, the concept implied, as some said, that men gave up their natural rights when they entered under government. But these rights were not only antecedent to government, the whole object of government was to protect individuals in them. Even Locke, whose famous *Second Treatise* was the prototype of the theory, had been more concerned to establish the supremacy of Parliament than the supremacy of man. Jefferson's doctrine ran toward releasing the powers of free individuals. Government might help in this, especially by guarantees of liberty; but it must always be remembered that the moral right precedes the legal guarantee. The more striking departure from Locke was Jefferson's substitution of "the pursuit of happiness" for "property." In his *Essay on Human Understanding*, Locke had made the pursuit of happiness the mainspring of human action, yet he did not think it a natural right, as suggested by its omission from the *Second Treatise*. The idea of happiness, individual or social or both, as the supreme end was a commonplace of eighteenth-century thought. Jefferson declared it a right. Everyone had the right to pursue happiness in his own way, according to his own experience, his own talents, his own balance of pleasure and pain. There could be no objective definition of this good, therefore no way a government could obtain it for the multiplicity of citizens. Reason and the moral sense provided safeguards against the extravagances of individualism. Virtue being essential to happiness, and virtue consisting in the duty to others, it was negated by mere selfishness. Because the pursuit was a public activity, in part, dependent on public well-being, all men had a stake in the *res publica* and should have a voice in its affairs. Property, on the other hand, Jefferson apparently considered a civil rather than a natural right. Without the protection of the property that a man derived from his own labor, there could be no life, liberty, or happiness. So Jefferson did not intend to depreciate the right of property when he omitted it from the Declaration, but considering it an instrumental value, as a means to human happiness, and recognizing its civil character, he could not elevate property to the status of inalienable right.

Third, the *sovereignty of the people:* "that to secure these rights, governments are instituted among men, deriving their just powers from the consent of the governed." Sovereignty passed in 1776 from the Crown to the people of the newly free and independent states. There was no crisis of legitimacy: the people of each state possessed the ultimate authority, and they set about, through the device of civil contract, erecting legitimate governments on the old foundations. Always before sovereignty had been attached to the law-making power; the American theory placed it in the people, thus subordinating the rulers to the ruled. Always before sovereignty had been assumed to be one and indivisible—the British had conjured up the specter of an *imperium in imperio* to frighten the colonists. The American theory united sovereignty in one authority, the people, but delegated and divided the operative powers of government. Always before governments had swallowed up the rights of the people. The American theory made government responsible to the people, limited it to securing their rights, safety, and happiness, and bound it under a fundamental written law. Taking man as the starting point, the Declaration of Independence downgraded the role of government. At best government was, as *Common Sense* said, but "a necessary evil" in the work of securing the blessings of society. "Society is produced by our wants and government by our wickedness; the former promotes our happiness *positively* by uniting our affections, the latter *negatively* by restraining our vices." Jefferson agreed entirely, though he never said it so well. The conception of popular sovereignty, barely evoked in the Declaration, possessed many as yet unexplored or even undetected convolutions. Indeed the American democratic experiment would be largely an effort to come to grips with it.

Finally, the *right of revolution:* "that whenever any form of government becomes destructive of these ends, it is the right of the people to alter or to abolish it, and to institute new government." As the people made government so could they unmake it. The principle of revolution, which brought the American polity into being, was thus built into its foundations. The principle should be held under the dictates of prudence and forbearance, of course, in the manner of the patriots of 1776; and there could be no cause to exercise the right at all so long as government was free and popular. Nevertheless, the right of revolution was an inflammatory doctrine. It ignited combustible materials in other nations and conferred political legitimacy on radical democratic forces in the new nation.

The Declaration of Independence endowed the American Revolution with high moral purpose united to a theory of free government. Without this, the independence of thirteen colonies, three million people strung along the western Atlantic seaboard, would have been a significant but scarcely an epochal event in the history of mankind. As it was, it opened an age of revolution in old and new nations that is not yet spent. "We have it in our power to begin the world over again," *Common Sense* declared. This was inspired prophecy. Jefferson did not speak in these terms, and very few of the patriots of 1776 shared Paine's earth-shaking vision. The larger vision, this sense of destiny beyond national frontiers, came later, filtered through the French Revolution. Focusing on the task at hand—a war to wage, trade to secure, governments to erect, a federal union to form—the Americans had first to comprehend and work out the creed Jefferson had given them in the building of their own nation.

CHAPTER THREE

Virginia Reformer

You and I, my dear friend, have been sent into life at a time when the greatest lawgivers of antiquity would have wished to live. How few of the human race have ever enjoyed an opportunity of making an election of government—more than of air, soil, or climate—for themselves or their children! When, before the present epoch, had three millions of people full power and a fair opportunity to form and establish the wisest and happiest government that human wisdom can contrive?

John Adams, Thoughts on Government, in a Letter from
a Gentlemen to his Friend. *Philadelphia, 1776.*

THE REMAINDER of the story of Jefferson's service in Congress is little more than a footnote to the events that culminated in the Declaration of Independence. Throughout July and August, while his thoughts turned increasingly homeward, he worked in the day-to-day business of Congress. He took copious notes on the beginnings of the two-year-long debate on the Articles of Confederation, but made no significant contribution of his own. He served on numerous committees, among them the first of all congressional investigations, which looked into the failures of the Canadian campaign. Of the several reports he wrote, one at least had lasting importance: it first proposed the Spanish dollar as the standard money unit of the new nation. He communicated with his friends at home, exhorting them to rise above considerations of local defense and to throw the resources of the commonwealth behind the greater cause of the Union.

Virginia was secure. The pesky Dunmore, with his motley crew of Tories and blacks, dropped the royal standard and fled during the summer. The new government was in operation, lacking only the imprimatur of an official seal to dignify its acts. "We are very much at a loss here for an engraver to make our seal," John Page wrote to Jefferson. "Can you get the work done in Philadelphia?" Jefferson located an artist, but the seal was not actually cut until three years later in Paris. The United States waited even longer for its Great Seal. On July 4 Jefferson was appointed with Benjamin Franklin and John Adams to report an appropriate design. Adams proposed the figure of Hercules resting on his club, shunning sloth and pleasure, and beckoned by Virtue to ascend her rugged mountain. Franklin preferred a Biblical image: Moses in priestly robes causing the sea to overwhelm mighty Pharaoh, while a pillar of fire in the clouds evoked divine presence. Jefferson liked this, and proposed for the reverse side the figures of "Hengist and Horsa, the Saxon chiefs from whom we claim the honor of being descended, and whose political principles and form of government we have assumed." The confusing array of symbols, for all their incongruity, nevertheless fairly represented the different pasts Americans claimed heir to in 1776. Unable to agree among themselves, the distinguished committee recommended a thoroughly unhistorical plan submitted by the artist, Pierre Eugene Du Simitière. The Great Seal as finally approved by Congress in 1782 retained only its motto, *E Pluribus Unum*. A fitting emblem of the Union! But the spirit of the Revolution was better captured in the motto proposed by Franklin and Jefferson, one the Virginian later made his own: "Rebellion to Tyrants is Obedience to God."

Jefferson was more interested in revolution than in union. Without the latter the former must fail, of course, but the work of confederation was bound to lumber along for years, hobbled by the war's exigencies and the jangling interests in Congress. It was not yet a field for enduring accomplishment in the governing of men nor, as essentially the foreign department of the newly independent states, could it become the principal field until they were placed on proper foundations. The time was ripe for revolutionizing the colonial governments. It was, as Adams said, "a time when the greatest lawgivers of antiquity would have wished to live." Jefferson, with a sense of history and of his place in it no less acute than Adams's, wished to be a lawgiver to the new age. He was determined to seize the opportunity while the Revolutionary spirit flamed in every patriot breast. It would not last. "From the conclusion of the war we shall be going down hill," he later reflected. "It will not then be necessary to resort every moment to the people for support. They will be forgotten, therefore, and their rights disregarded. They will forget themselves, but in the sole faculty of making money, and will never think of uniting to effect a due respect for their rights."

So he must return to Virginia. There the work of reformation was under way, and Jefferson, three hundred miles from the scene, was deeply disturbed by the conservative course it was taking. In the opinion of many Virginians, the work was finished and done with upon the adoption of a constitution some days before Congress proclaimed independence. Such men were separationists—rebels against Britain but conservatives at home. Jefferson was a revolutionist. He had hoped that the Virginia delegates might have been recalled from Congress for a short time in order to have a voice in the making of the constitution. "In truth," he wrote to a friend in Williamsburg, "it is the whole object of the present controversy; for should a bad government be instituted for us in future it had been as well to have accepted the bad one offered to us from beyond the water without the risk and expense of contest." But in the momentous spring of 1776 Virginia could not be without a delegation in Congress. And had Jefferson got his wish he would not, in all probability, have become the author of the Declaration of Independence. He had to content himself with submitting a proposed constitution from afar, relying on his old teacher, George Wythe, to carry it to Williamsburg. It was late June when Wythe arrived at the convention. The weather was hot, the delegates were tired, and they had so far agreed on a plan of government widely at variance with this fresh proposal from Jefferson that they had not the patience to discuss it. They found it convenient, nevertheless, to tack on Jefferson's preamble, the parent of his arraignment of George III in the Declaration of Independence, and to incorporate two or three propositions of his in the finished document.

99

The constitution fell far below Jefferson's expectations, thus deepening his anxiety to return home. He was anxious in any event. Martha was not well; and the desire to be near his family was as strong as the spur of public responsibility. Against his declared will, the convention had re-elected him to another term in Congress. No sooner was he notified than he resigned, vaguely begging "the situation of my domestic affairs." But his correspondence with friends at home during the same months makes it abundantly clear that he was eager to take up the work of reformation where the convention had left off. He retired from Congress on September 2, and after a month at Monticello, took his seat in the House of Delegates, the old Burgesses, at Williamsburg.

The Virginia Constitution

The constitution Jefferson drafted and placed in Wythe's hands in Philadelphia was an epitome of his political science in 1776. Actually, this was the third draft. As one who believed the framing of new republican constitutions "the whole object of the present controversy," he probably gave to the task more time and thought than ever he did to the drafting of the immortal Declaration. There he boldly sketched the philosophy of the new nation; here, in planning a government for his countrymen, he endeavored to implement that philosophy and to secure the rights declared in the fundamental law of the new commonwealth. While some of his patriot friends looked upon the achievement of independence as the end toward which the Revolution aimed, it was for Jefferson only the beginning. The ultimate justification of American independence was moral: in the obligation to conform all conduct to the standard of right raised in the Declaration. Rhetoric was cheap, as Jefferson knew. Philosophers had talked of "natural rights" and "self-government" for centuries, but when had these theories been reduced to practice? Where had a government been instituted by "the consent of the governed"? Where had the rights of "life, liberty, and the pursuit of happiness" been held sacred? This was the harder part. And while it could not be finished in a day, a year, or a century, while it could never be accomplished with the nicety of abstract theory, the strongest possible beginning ought to be made lest the noble principles of 1776 be hooted down the corridors of time.

The constitution adopted at Williamsburg was undoubtedly more representative of Virginia political opinion than Jefferson's draft. Mainly the work of George Mason, a Fairfax planter close to the Lees, it steered a middle course between the conservatism of Edmund Pendleton, Carter Braxton, and the old guard generally, and the liberalism of Jefferson, Wythe, and many young Virginians. It did not in any way alter the distribution of power in Virginia society. It continued the freehold suffrage qualification under which one-third or more of the adult white males were disfranchised. It continued a system of representation in the legislature favorable to the smaller eastern counties. It actually increased the oligarchical power of the fountainheads of local justice and administration, the county courts. The most conspicuous change was in the executive office. Stripped of the vestments of monarchy, the Governor was annually elected by the General Assembly, and required to act with the consent of an eight-man Council of State, also elected by the assembly. Judges too, except for the self-perpetuating county courts, received their appointments from the assembly. All powers thus resided in the legislative body. In creating a bicameral legislature, Senate and House of Delegates, and in attacking such "monarchical" abuses as plural-officeholding, the convention went some farther way toward constituting an old and familiar Whig theory of government. The Virginia convention's originality lay not in the constitution but in Mason's Declaration of Rights appended to it. This was a magnificent achievement, even if its authority was uncertain. There were distressing disparities between the Declaration and the constitution, between the equalitarian phrases of the one and the aristocratic features of the other. The Virginia Declaration of Rights nevertheless set a model for governments of free men the world over.

Jefferson at once became the Virginia constitution's severest critic. His lifelong quarrel with it picked up more and more democratic accents in progress with his political opinions. He argued, first of all, that the constitution was illegitimate—a mere ordinance or statute with no permanent and binding power on the government. The convention that framed the constitution was, as he correctly observed, the Revolutionary successor of the House of Burgesses, its members elected in April 1776 to perform the *ordinary* business of government. "They could not, therefore, pass an act transcendent to the powers of other legislatures." The term "convention" as then employed in Virginia in no way conveyed the idea, still nebulous, of a constitutional convention: an especially elected body of delegates to draw the fundamental law of the state. This is what was necessary, Jefferson thought, for without it succeeding legislatures might freely alter the constitution to please themselves. Jefferson stated his objection through Edmund Randolph at the time of the convention's meeting. But Pendleton, Mason, and Patrick Henry, to whom Randolph talked, "saw no distinction between the conceded power to declare independence,"—a more than ordinary power the convention had exercised—"and its necessary consequence, the fencing of society by the institution of government." The fact that Jefferson went ahead and submitted his own proposal to the body whose rightful authority he denied suggested that his objection was captious and might not have occurred to him had he been in Williamsburg.

But Jefferson was not being frivolous. He was attempting to work out the practical means whereby a people, taking sovereignty to themselves, may create a government of their own choosing. There was, in his opinion, a vast difference between the revolutionary act of independence and the institution of government according to principles that alone jusified the act. "Necessities which dissolve a government, do not convey its authority to an oligarchy or to a monarchy. They throw the authority back, into the hands of the people . . . and leave them to shift for themselves." Thus figuratively thrown back into the Lockian "state of nature," how were the people to form a government over themselves? Neither Locke nor any theorist of the people's sovereignty had answered this question. It was to be answered in the actual process of state-making in the American Revolution.

As finally and fully developed, the process included three elements: a convention emanating from the people for the purpose of framing a constitution, popular ratification of the document, and provision for its periodic amendment and revision. None of the first constitutions, hastily framed in the face of the enemy, exhibited all these cardinal elements, nor did Jefferson or anyone grasp the finished theory in 1776. He had a good idea of it, however. It is interesting to notice in this connection the advanced position taken by numerous citizens of Albemarle County in the summer of 1776. In a document of unknown authorship, the citizens protested the undemocratic features of the new constitution and instructed their delegates, one of whom was Jefferson, to press for certain changes, to be followed, when made, by popular ratification of the entire plan of government. "It is our opinion," said Jefferson's constituents, "that among the rights, of which men cannot deprive, or divest their Posterity, the most important is that of approving, or disapproving, their own laws; which power ought forever to remain with the whole body of the people." The Albemarle instructions agreed on so many points with Jefferson's opinions as to warrant the inference that he had a hand in their preparation. Of the three draft constitutions he wrote, only the second demanded popular ratification. To the third, which Wythe took to Williamsburg, he appended a note proposing that the constitution, after approval by the convention, "shall be referred by them to the people to be assembled in their respective counties and that the suffrages of two thirds of the counties shall be required to establish it." But the convention, assuming the authority to establish as well as to frame the constitution, paid no attention to Jefferson's proposal; and in the long campaign he waged against the constitution of 1776, its failure to receive "the consent of the governed" was never the main ground of complaint. He made allowance for the hazard of popular ratification during the war. "True it is," he reflected, "this is no time for deliberating forms of government. While an enemy is within our bowels, the first object is to expel him." The same apology, if such it was, will not do for still another constitution he drafted, in 1783, for submission to a reform convention that never materialized. The war was over and despite the successful example of popular ratification of the Massachusetts constitution of 1780, he made no similar provision in his new proposal. In all but the very first of his draft constitutions, on the other hand, Jefferson supplied a method for regular amendment and revision by the consent of the people. He regarded this feature as indispensable if republican government was to advance "hand in hand with the progress of the human mind," and he made its omission from the Virginia constitution a leading count in his indictment.

The fact is that Jefferson, with many others, at first fumbled and groped in searching out a practical means of implementing the principles of the Revolution. "In truth," he reflected years later, "the abuses of monarchy had so much filled all the space of political contemplation, that we imagined everything republican which was not monarchy. We had not yet penetrated to the mother principle, that governments are republican only in proportion as they embody the will of the people, and execute it." If this can be said with respect to the foundations of authority, it can also be said with respect to the structure of government.

Here Jefferson was in substantial agreement with the moderate Whigs at Williamsburg. The question of the Senate was unusually perplexing. He had been disenchanted with the widely acclaimed "balance" of the English constitution, wherein the opposing forces of King, Lords, and Commons supposedly functioned with the perfection of the Newtonian laws of motion; still he was sufficiently influenced by the theory to conclude that the two houses of a consistently republican legislature ought to be bottomed on different principles and interests. How, then, should the upper house, the Senate, be differentiated from the popular branch of the legislature? In his first draft, Jefferson proposed life appointment of the senators, thus placing himself, on this issue, in the aristocratic camp of Pendleton and Braxton. He copied the same provision in the second draft, then pulled back, struck it, and called for election of senators to terms of nine years by the lower house. This was repeated in the final draft. The convention's solution was to have the Senate elected on a district basis, each district being composed of several counties, but by the same voters as elected representatives to the so-called popular branch. Jefferson disliked it. "I have ever observed that a choice by the people themselves is not generally distinguished for its wisdom," he avowed to Pendleton. The Senate should be entirely independent of the people and gifted with greater wisdom. Just how this would be achieved by making the senators elective of the lower house he did not explain. Perhaps he calculated on the maturer age, thirty-five years, he would require of senators and the combination of long terms with no re-eligibility. Confessing he would submit to almost "any thing rather than a mere creation by and dependence on the people," he nevertheless opposed return to the principle of life appointment and, as for the solution adopted in several states of basing the senate on property, he tartly remarked, "my observations do not enable me to say I think integrity the characteristic of wealth." He continued for some years to be troubled by the make-up of the Senate, perhaps less because it flouted conventional political theory than because it was, in fact, a lackey of the House of Delegates. In the final analysis he was unable to devise a basis of the Senate that satisfied both the demands of Whig political science and his republican convictions. When he again turned his hand to the reform of the Virginia constitution in 1783, he acquiesced in the system of election it provided.

Shedding aristocracy was a problem, but shedding monarchy was as easy as throwing off a badly frayed coat. The executive of Jefferson's plan was in some details even weaker than the one agreed upon at Williamsburg. His governor, whom he called Administrator, was elected annually by the House. He was ineligible for re-election until the expiration of three years after a term of service, whereas the convention allowed the Governor three consecutive annual terms. On balance, however, Jefferson's executive was definitely the stronger. He envisioned the Council as purely consultative, "to give advice to the Administrator when called on by him." Such an arrangement would have lightened Jefferson's later ordeal as Governor under the constitutional mandate to act with the "advice and consent" of the Council on all questions. Jefferson's plan also concentrated greater appointive powers in the Governor. The constitution continued the colonial practice of filling vacancies in the county courts on nomination of the respective court. Jefferson gave the appointments entirely to the executive. The provision, together with another making sheriffs and coroners elective, would have gone some way toward curbing the power of the courthouse cliques. Although Jefferson was to learn from hard experience the necessity of strengthening the executive, it would be many years before he would advocate the most obvious means of accomplishing the objective: election by the people.

Jefferson was farthest at odds with his compatriots in Virginia and elsewhere on the related issues of suffrage and representation.

His unhesitating advocacy of a broadly popular suffrage and of equal representation of the people in the legislature held the promise of making his constitution a vital instrument of democratic government. Although he did not entirely abandon the freehold suffrage qualification, he reduced it by more than one-half and, further, extended the suffrage to all taxpayers. Moreover, he ensured the enfranchisement of still other Virginians by a unique measure of both economic and political democracy: every person of full age who did not own fifty acres of land was entitled to a government appropriation of so many acres as necessary to make up that amount. Jefferson thus revived the old colonial importation or headright system, under which a fifty-acre grant was awarded to the person responsible for settling an immigrant in Virginia, and turned it toward democratic ends. But if he hoped to overcome the resistance of the planter class to universal white male suffrage by, in effect, making every man a freeholder, he was quickly disappointed. Young Randolph could not recall that any delegate in the convention uttered a word against the traditional freehold suffrage. It remained the rock of conservative influence for decades to come. Jefferson's reform would also eliminate special property qualifications for officeholders. Public office would be thrown open to a large electorate virtually identical with the community. Jefferson proposed to achieve fair and equal representation geographically by proportioning the legislature to the rule of numbers. Under the county-unit system of representation which the convention perpetuated, the tidewater counties controlled one-half the Senate and nearly one-half the House, though they possessed well under half the population and were steadily losing ground to the interior sections. The question was one of interest as well as of principle. The wealth and privilege of the state centered in the east. Jefferson identified himself with the aspirations of the west. But the point of equal representation struck him as "capital and fundamental" on whatever ground it was put, and he would not rest easy until it could be obtained.

Most of the remaining differences between Jefferson's plan and the one adopted at Williamsburg fall into the general category "rights and liberties." In view of his staunch advocacy of a federal Bill of Rights in 1788, it is surprising he did not add a similar document to the proposed Virginia constitution. He endeavored, he later said, "to reach all the great objects of public liberty" in the constitution itself. In fact, he reached only a few of them. The Virginia Declaration of Rights contained guarantees of the right against self-incrimination, the right of *habeas corpus*, and freedom from unwarranted searches and seizures, none of which were to be found in Jefferson's drafts. He upheld these rights, of course. They were in the common law. But in 1776 he evidently did not think it essential to give them constitutional protection. On the other hand, he incorporated in his constitution a number of liberal reforms—on religion, slavery, descent of lands, punishment of crimes—that were strangers to the Virginia constitution.

That frame of government proved utterly recalcitrant to change. Several times during the next fifty years Jefferson rode full tilt against it, each charge more democratic than the last, and each time he retired in defeat. But if he could not revamp the Constitution, he might, for the present, turn one of its vicious principles, the unfettered power of the assembly, to virtuous ends, and endeavor to achieve by ordinary legislation those fundamental reforms in Virginia law and institutions he had hoped to accomplish at one stroke by a liberal constitution.

In the House of Delegates

The House of Delegates Jefferson entered in October 1776 was, with the exception of several members like himself, the same body as formed the constitution. He took his seat, occupied by an alternate in his absence, by virtue of his election to the convention in April. Soon after he arrived in Williamsburg, a messenger from Congress notified him of his election as a joint commissioner, with Benjamin Franklin and Silas Deane, to negotiate a treaty of alliance at the Court of Louis XVI. Duty, the pleasures of France, the delightful company of Dr. Franklin—all inclined him to accept the charge. Although more sanguine than most men about the prospects of American arms, he knew the capital importance of the French mission, and he was honored by so distinguished an appointment. For three days he groped toward a decision; finally, on October 11, he dismissed the messenger with a letter politely declining the commission. The circumstances of his family, he explained, neither permitted him to leave them behind nor to expose them to the dangers of the crossing. "I saw, too," he later reflected, "that the laboring oar was really at home, where much was to be done, of the most permanent interest, in new modeling our governments. . . . " No task seemed more urgent to him, or more agreeable, since it permitted him to live as he was accustomed and be near his ailing wife. She joined him in Williamsburg. During Wythe's absence in Philadelphia, the Jeffersons occupied his modest house, which still stands facing the Palace green, a monument to an age of gentle simplicity.

A revolution had come, but the only noticeable change in the old capital was the new face in the Governor's Palace. Patrick Henry had been elected first Governor of the Commonwealth. The conservatives had put up an opposition in the person of Thomas Nelson, Sr., long-time secretary of the colony; but the popular orator drew support from both moderate and liberal men, and thus carried the election handily. It was a tribute owing to his unrivaled leadership in the Revolutionary movement. Despite his reputation as a "radical," Henry was satisfied with the new frame of government. The conservatives had nothing to fear from him. His powers were forensic; he was amiable and pliable; he was a Virginian to the core of his being, no less attached to the old ways than his arch-antagonist Edmund Pendleton. In 1776 Henry's great work was done; the work of his young friend and comrade Thomas Jefferson was just beginning. Henry led Virginia to the Revolution, but lacking either talent or zeal for constructive reform, he could not consolidate it. This was to be Jefferson's role. Elevated to the governorship, jealously guarded as it was, Henry lost much of the influence he formerly had. The vacuum he left in the legislative chamber, Jefferson hastened to fill. The delegate from Albemarle was one of the half-dozen most popular figures in the assembly. While this counted for much, the fact that he knew what he wanted, that he had a program for correcting abuses, righting wrongs, and expanding liberty, counted for more. Developing this line of politics, Jefferson did not displace Henry in the affections of the people—no one could do that —but made his brand of demagogical politics unnecessary to successful leadership in a republic of free men.

In the House of Delegates most of the faces were familiar. In

the Speaker's chair sat Edmund Pendleton, one of Jefferson's prized
friends among the elder statesmen of Virginia. The two men heartily liked and respected each other, though their political swords
were usually crossed. Genial, unaffected, and judicious, Pendleton
embodied the virtues of the ruling class without either its wealth or
its vices. Jefferson did not feel the same esteem for other leaders on
the conservative side, such as opulent Benjamin Harrison, of Berkeley,
with whom he had served in Congress, and Robert Carter Nicholas,
the former treasurer and guardian of the Church. He was perhaps
not yet well acquainted with George Mason, who best represented
the moderate element in the assembly and whose authorship of the
Declaration of Rights commended him to Jefferson. The master of
Potomac's Gunston Hall was a man of marvelous force and presence. A successful planter with a large family and a distinct preference for private life, he shied away from the leadership that might
have been his. During the next several years, when he served in the
assembly, Jefferson found him to be perhaps his "most steadfast, able
and zealous" colleague. Looking back on the time from the perspective of nearly half a century, Jefferson also remembered the assistance of two other men, more eager and more advanced in their
opinions than Mason but lacking his influence. One was George
Wythe, who returned from Congress in 1777, the other the new
delegate from Orange, James Madison. A delicate little man, reserved,
always garbed in black, and without surface brilliance of any kind,
Madison was wise and learned beyond his twenty-five years. He had
been educated at the College of New Jersey, in Princeton, where he
acquired clear ideas of civil and religious liberty from its Scottish
Presbyterian president, John Witherspoon. Several months earlier, in
the convention, he had posted his liberal colors by proposing a crucial amendment to the article on religion in the Declaration of
Rights. But Madison was not a man to invite instant attention or
friendship. Jefferson came to know and respect his abilities during
the first session of the assembly. Not until three years later, however, when he was Governor and Madison a member of the Council,
did they become intimate. In the years ahead Jefferson drew long
and well on "the rich resources of his luminous and discriminating
mind."

There were, of course, factions and followings in the government, and Henry was even accused of leading a party. Jefferson carefully skirted these political entanglements, with the personal animosities they often involved. The cordiality of his relations with men who were notorious enemies of each other—Henry and Pendleton, Lee and Harrison—bespeaks a mild temperament, a studied courtesy, and a revulsion from the dubious glories of political gladiators. This fact, combined with his forwardness in legislative business and the force of his ideas, ensured his ascendancy in the House of Delegates. Given the convenience of political labels, it is tempting to label Jefferson a "radical." A committed revolutionist, even if a gentle one, could hardly be anything else. And so he seemed to many Virginians of the old order. He was, certainly, more advanced in his thinking and objectives than the great host of his contemporaries in and out of Virginia. Yet he had none of the typical radical's rage against the past, intolerance of opposition, and perfectionist aspirations. With other philosophers of the time, he made a god of nature; yet, without idealizing the past, he embodied history in the cause of the future. He did not compromise his political convictions; but he recognized that they were *his* convictions, to be enjoyed with the same confidence he accorded to others, that perfect agreement was as unnecessary as it was unattainable, and that force could never substitute for reason and persuasion in republican government. He had no blueprint for a new society. He was, at bottom, attached to Virginia society, wishing only to reform its abuses—its feudal holdovers, unnatural privileges, its slavery, and massive ignorance. He would not go to radical lengths to achieve his objectives. And even his most progressive reforms were streaked with conservatism. If democracy was his destiny, he had yet to escape from the chrysalis of Whiggery in which he was born.

The initiative passed to Jefferson on October 12. On that day the House of Delegates gave him leave for the drafting of two bills: one for the abolition of the law of entail, the other for a general revision of the laws of the Commonwealth. He reported the former two days later. In retrospect, he bracketed it with three other measures, those calling for the abolition of primogeniture, for freedom of religion, and for general education, and viewed the whole "as forming a system by which every fiber would be eradicated of ancient or feudal aristocracy; and a foundation laid for government truly republican." Such measures were, as he said, "indicative of the strength and general pulse of reformation." But he also believed the entire code of law should be revised "with a single eye to reason, and the good of those for whose government it was framed."

The Revision of the Laws occupied Jefferson throughout his years in the assembly. The bill passed on October 26, and a few days later the two houses jointly elected a committee of five with instructions to repeal, amend, or revise the laws in force, to introduce others, and then to report the whole for the action of the legislature. Of the members nominated to undertake this work of "magnitude, labor, and difficulty," Jefferson received the most ballots, thus becoming chairman of the committee of revisers, whose other members were Pendleton, Mason, Wythe, and Thomas Ludwell Lee.

The committee met at Fredericksburg on January 3, 1777, to settle on a plan of operation. Disagreement arose on the first question: "whether we should propose to abolish the whole existing system of laws, and prepare a new and complete Institute, or preserve the general system, and only modify it to the present state of things." It was Pendleton, "contrary to his usual disposition in favor of ancient things," who advocated the former, and bolder, approach. As a philosopher of enlightenment, wishing to reform law "with a single eye to reason," Jefferson might have been expected to place himself unreservedly on the side of a new code. But law, for him, was a science of learning as well as of reason, and he shunned system-making heedless of the historic fabric of the law. He thought a completely new code or institute "would involve us in ages of litigation, and render property uncertain until, like the statutes of old, every word had been tried, and settled by numerous decisions, and by new volumes of reports and commentaries." Law should be reasonable, but stability and familiarity were essential elements of the law's reason. The question was settled in Jefferson's favor, though somewhat ambiguously, for what actually came to pass fell between two stools. For the most part the revisal simply recast the existing body of law, after discarding what was obsolete and useless; on the other hand, however, it introduced many new principles unknown to the law of Virginia in 1776. At Fredericksburg, the committee divided the work among themselves. But Lee died soon after and Mason resigned. Jefferson took over most of the portions assigned to them. The committee agreed on the style to be followed in drafting its bills. In general, it was thought better "not to vary the diction of the ancient statutes by modernizing it, nor to give rise to new questions by new expressions," but the style of the later statutes—involute, verbose, redundant—was to be reformed in favor of plain and direct diction.

The three remaining members of the committee finally submitted their report to the assembly in June 1779. "We had in this work," Jefferson wrote in his autobiography, "brought so much of the Common Law as it was thought necessary to alter, all the British statutes from *Magna Charta* to the present day, and all the laws of Virginia from the establishment of our legislature . . . which we thought should be retained, within a compass of one hundred and twenty-six bills, making a printed folio of ninety pages only." This was a triumph of brevity. Actually, though, the published *Report* omitted a good deal that was law in Virginia, and it exempted certain statutes from the final bill repealing all prior acts and ordinances. Before this time, too, a number of bills had been lifted out of the revisal, usually at Jefferson's instigation in order to quicken the pace of reform. Some of these were adopted in the ordinary course of legislation. But the major corpus was not taken up by the assembly until 1785, when to Jefferson's undying gratitude, "by the unwearied exertions of Mr. Madison, in opposition to endless quibbles, chicaneries, perversions, vexations and delays of lawyers and demi-lawyers, most of the bills were passed by the legislature, with little alteration." He was justifiably proud of the Revision of the Laws, even though the original aim of a revised code miscarried. The *Report* was never acted on as a unit; and the revisal became, to employ Madison's figure, "a mine of legislative wealth," rather than a single great monument of legislation. And a mine, it should be added, not only for Virginia but for many new American states over several decades.

The revisal, ample and compendious as it was, did not exhaust the labors of this republican Solon. In the day-to-day affairs of state Jefferson served on numberless committees and drafted reports and bills on every variety of subject. As Julian P. Boyd has observed, "He was in himself a veritable legislative drafting bureau." All this immense industry helps to reveal the mind of the Virginia revolutionist.

Lands

Jefferson's bill to abolish entail, enacted on November 1, 1776, pulled down the first of the pillars of landed aristocracy in Virginia. He subsequently proposed as part of the revisal the abolition of primogeniture, and the bill was adopted on Madison's motion in 1785. These measures, together with others abolishing quitrents and disposing of unappropriated lands, decisively settled the question of whether feudal or freehold tenure would prevail in the new state. Very likely the question would have been settled in the same way without Jefferson's assistance; in fact, social and economic forces having little to do with law had perhaps already settled it. Jefferson's bills capped the development and exalted the principle of freehold tenure.

From his earliest law reading Jefferson formed the opinion that entail and primogeniture—indeed all aspects of feudal tenure—were perversions of the common law. By the law of entail estates were perpetuated from generation to generation through a particular line of descent. By its twin, primogeniture, the lands and slaves of a person dying intestate passed exclusively to the eldest son. An estate held in fee tail might be alienated by a device known as "docking," which required a special act of the legislature. In 1774 Jefferson himself had applied to the Burgesses for permission to dock the entail on certain lands inherited by Martha. The procedure proved troublesome and doubtless contributed to his censure of it in the preamble to the abolition bill. Primogeniture could be avoided by the simple act of drawing a will. Wills were increasingly the practice among the great families. Land was plentiful in Virginia, thus the principal factor that sustained these feudal relics in England was absent. But the pride, opulence, and power of aristocratic families knew no country and continued to furnish motives for the perpetuation of great estates. The privilege of the laws had raised up a "patrician order," Jefferson said. "To annul this privilege, and instead of an aristocracy of wealth, of more harm and danger, than benefit, to society, to make an opening for the aristocracy of virtue and talent, which nature has wisely provided for the direction of the interests of society, and scattered with equal hand through all its conditions, was deemed essential to a well-ordered republic." Annuling the privilege, dissolving all property rights connected with it, the General Assembly at the same time fixed in the laws of Virginia the individualistic system of freehold tenure. Owners of land and slaves in *fee tail* were possessed of their estates in *fee simple*—that is, in absolute dominion, without limitation to a class of heirs or restriction on alienation—and intestate estates were henceforth to be divided equally among all the children. This was, in Jefferson's opinion, the system of reason and nature.

It was also "the happy system of our ancestors." In *A Summary View*, Jefferson had traced the introduction of feudal tenure in England to the alien Normans. The Saxons had held their lands in absolute dominion, but William the Conqueror granted the lands to the Norman barons in return for feudal dues and military services. There arose the fiction that all the lands originally belonged to the king, were received as gifts from him, and were forever beholden to him. This fiction founded on conquest was carried to America. But America had not been conquered by the Normans. The Saxon law of possession should have prevailed here. Instead, the Americans received their lands from the Crown, encumbered with quitrents acknowledging a superior, and were unable freely to hold or to alienate, as they did their personal property. In so far as this was so the Americans were servants of kings and lords rather than themselves free and independent lords of the soil.

Jefferson revived the argument in correspondence with Pendleton during the summer of 1776 when, as Pendleton dryly remarked, "it may be deciding by the sword in New York, whether we shall have any lands left to dispose of." The discussion in the letters centered on quitrents, only one element of the feudal tenure Jefferson wished to abolish. Pendleton favored continuing the system by transferring the right to these dues from the Crown to the Commonwealth. "To hold of the commonwealth by the payment of a certain sum, cannot interfere with the dignity of Freeman," Pendleton said. Jefferson objected, pointing to the danger of a perpetual and independent revenue, as well as to the rights of individuals. His reading of history told him that feudal tenure arose at a specific time for a specific purpose, Norman military discipline and defense, which had long since passed away. "Is it wanting with us for the purpose of military defense? . . . Are not we better off for what we have hitherto abolished of the feudal system? Has not every restitution of ancient Saxon laws had happy effects?" The conservative Pendleton could only smile at his young friend's enthusiasm to go forward by returning to the eighth century. "I highly esteem the old Saxon Laws in general," he remarked, "but cannot suppose them wholly unalterable for the better after an experience of so many centuries."

When the bill on entail came before the House in October, Pendleton opposed it and according to Jefferson offered an amendment that would merely give to the tenant in tail the discretion to convey his estate, both land and slaves, in fee simple. Jefferson dallied with the compromise, but seeing it would defeat his principle rejected it. The act as passed made mandatory the conversion to fee simple tenure, thus carrying out the proposal first advanced in his draft constitution. The Speaker continued his rear-guard action when the revisers met at Fredericksburg. The question of primogeniture was now on the carpet. He wished to preserve it, but finding no support proposed that the committee adopt the Hebrew principle of awarding the eldest son a double portion of the father's estate. "I observed," Jefferson recalled in his autobiography, "that if the eldest son could eat twice as much, or do double work, it might be a natural evidence of his right to a double portion; but being on a par in his powers and wants, with his brothers and sisters, he should be on a par also in the partition of the patrimony; and such was the decision of the members."

The committee went on to determine the precise course of descents, accounting for all possible circumstances, under the rule of co-parceny. The bill Jefferson drafted generally followed the committee's outline. The fundamental departure from the common law was, of course, in admitting all the children to the inheritance. The common law preference for "the worthiest of blood," beginning with the eldest son, had been carried all through the elaborate chain of descent, and had excluded kindred of certain degrees from representation. Thus bastards, aliens, and half-bloods could not inherit in

England. Jefferson manifested his humanity by admitting all three to representation. In the opinion of St. George Tucker, the distinguished Virginia jurist of Jefferson's time, the act of 1785 not only abolished primogeniture but introduced and established principles "in direct opposition to those of the common law, and scarcely agreeing with it in any one principle." It was "enlightened reason" replacing "feudal barbarism."

In later years it was not uncommon for the sons of the "old regime" to imagine that the overthrow of entail and primogeniture had accomplished at one stroke a virtual democratic revolution in Virginia society. Jefferson never made this mistake. He believed the laws "laid the axe to the foot of pseudo-aristocracy." But they did not destroy it. Only the "pseudo-aristocrats" themselves had a stake in that idea. The institution of fee simple tenure in the law of the commonwealth, while a radical act, was not socially revolutionary. A keen observer of the Virginia Tidewater early in the nineteenth century saw the same great inequalities of wealth and of social rank as in colonial times: "Here and there a stately aristocratic palace, with all its appurtenances, strikes the view; while all around, for many miles, no other buildings are to be seen but the little smoky huts and log cabins of poor, laborious, ignorant tenants. And, what is very ridiculous, these tenants, while they approach *the great house*, cap in hand, with all the fearful, trembling submission of the lowest feudal vassals, boast in their court-yards, with obstreperous exultation, that they live in a land of freemen, a land of equal liberty and equal rights." Jefferson had wished to change this picture, not by a leveling equalitarianism but by creating opportunities for "the aristocracy of virtue and talent" to rise. The eradication of entail and primogeniture—hopeless vestiges of feudalism—was only the first measure of his system. Unfortunately, he did not have the same success with the others.

The republican order Jefferson envisioned was bottomed on a mass of small, independent farmers. The husbandman was a poetic figure for him, associated with all the sturdy virtues a free government expected of its citizens; and agriculture was the most natural, as it was the most worthy, of all occupations. "Those who labor in the earth are the chosen people of God, if ever He had a chosen people, whose breasts He has made His peculiar deposit for substan-

tial and genuine virtue." This was not simply an ideal, such as philosophers and poets of other times and places had conjured with. It
was rooted in the American environment. It grew from Jefferson's
effort to define and interpret the values and the arts of a pioneering
society with an immensity of land at its disposal. In 1776 the Trans-
Allegheny West was in its infancy. Most of it, the vast expanses of
forest and prairie stretching westward to the Mississippi, was
claimed by Virginia. But the question of what should be done with
these lands, whether profiteering speculators or common farmers
should become the beneficiaries, was a question as yet vaguely defined and far from settled. Jefferson first seriously turned his
thoughts this way in 1774. Gradually he evolved a policy designed
to turn the western lands into a resource of freedom and democracy. The West, new Virginia, became in his eyes a ready-made
substitute for the revolution he was unable or unwilling to effect in
the landed order of old Virginia.

Before Virginia could make policy for the lands on the western
waters, she had first to re-establish her claim to them. While a colony her unappropriated lands belonged to the King to hold or to
grant at his pleasure. At least, the principle was universally assumed
until Jefferson denied it in the *Summary View*. "From the nature
and purpose of civil institutions," Jefferson there declared, "all the
lands within the limits, which any particular party has circumscribed
around itself, are assumed by that society, and subject to their allot-
ment; this may be done by themselves assembled collectively, or by
their legislature, to whom they have delegated sovereign authority;
and if they are allotted in neither of these ways, each individual of
the society, may appropriate to himself such lands as he finds vacant, and occupancy will give him title." An amazing statement!
Not only did Jefferson assert that the local government was right-
fully sovereign with respect to its land and boundaries—repudiated
by all colonial precedent—but also that individuals might themselves
take title to land after the manner of John Locke's theory of property. Jefferson too, like Locke, was dealing in theory, not in law;
but when Virginia became independent the theory could be put into
practice.

His draft constitution contained several provisions on the subject
of Virginia lands. One defined the boundaries of the new state in

conformity with the "sea to sea" charter of 1609. This first positive assertion of Virginia's jurisdiction beyond the mountains was copied into the constitution of 1776. The unappropriated lands within these boundaries were thus vested in the commonwealth to be disposed of on its authority, subject to the extinguishment of Indian titles. During the previous quarter-century, however, huge areas of the West had fallen into the hands of profiteering adventurers and land companies, who had obtained grants from the Crown, or negotiated purchases from the Indians, or both. Were these claims to be recognized? The question was complicated in the extreme, involving the interests of many Virginians and non-Virginians, and Jefferson did not propose to settle it by an outright constitutional bar to the claims. But he made his intention abundantly clear by providing that no purchases should be made of the Indians except by the authority of the General Assembly and "on behalf of the public." With one minor change, the convention adopted Jefferson's proposal. Some days earlier, probably under the influence of Jefferson's draft, for it was the only one to go into this question, the convention also adopted a resolution which condemned all private purchases from the Indians and ensured preemption rights to squatters on unappropriated lands. Still another proposal by the absentee delegate in Philadelphia contemplated the creation of new free and independent states in the West. But where Jefferson's draft made this mandatory, the constitution as adopted left it at discretion. Mason was against it entirely, and Article XIV of his Declaration of Rights explicitly barred the creation of new states within the limits of Virginia.

In sum, Jefferson's plan of government gave shape to a new policy for the West. Virginia asserted her political jurisdiction, which carried with it the heavy responsibility of defending this great domain. The lands would be alienated, after Indian titles were extinguished, to common farmers. And if Jefferson had his way, independent, self-governing states would be erected in the West. Significantly, he included these articles in the section of the draft constitution entitled "Rights Private and Public," under the subdivision "Lands," along with the provisions on entail and primogeniture and the fifty-acre grant. These were all spokes in the wheel of a freeholders' republic. The value of the lands as a source of public wealth and power did not seem to interest him at this juncture. The lands should not be sold but given away, he told Pendleton. "I am at the same time clear," he added, "that they should be appropriated in small quantities."

Once Virginia's western claim was officially declared, the land companies that sought to turn the West into a gigantic commercial adventure had no recourse but to Congress. Here they were not disappointed. The Articles of Confederation as first recommended to Congress placed the entire backcountry under its jurisdiction. The so-called landless states—those without western claims of any sort— took up the cause under the banner of union and common benefit from the western lands. This sounded good. But the intimate association between representatives of these states in Congress and powerful speculative interests centered in Philadelphia suggested that the land companies, and not the people, would benefit from congressional jurisdiction. The issue became the stumbling-block to the completion of the Confederation. Jefferson, in 1776, was aware of the stakes in the game, though it took him a little time to comprehend the rules and the characters of the players. Unlike so many of the prominent men of his day he never himself meddled in western lands and seemed to have no connections with speculative interests, though they were avid seekers of political influence. They lobbied at Williamsburg, for the assembly had yet to settle all the outstanding claims to ownership of Virginia soil.

Jefferson openly encountered the speculators in the first session of the assembly. The occasion was a conflict in the Kentucky lands. In March 1775 the Transylvania Company, headed by Judge Richard Henderson of North Carolina, acquired from the Cherokee some 20 million acres of land between the Cumberland and Kentucky rivers. Here Henderson planned to erect a new proprietary colony, Transylvania, which he hoped would be confirmed by charter from the King. In April, Daniel Boone led the first party of settlers into the region. Boonesborough was founded, a land office opened, and rudimentary government established. The coming of independence, followed by the unqualified assertion of Virginia's charter claims, upset Henderson's plan. He sought recognition from Congress but was unsuccessful. He turned to Williamsburg, now disclaiming any thought of "such an absurdity" as the erection of an independent government, but forcefully petitioning for title to the soil on the basis of Indian deed. Meanwhile, a group of settlers at Harrodsburg, in Kentucky, declared their opposition to Transylvania, acknowledged themselves citizens of Virginia, and begged to be represented in the government at Williamsburg. On October 8 the two "delegates" elected by the Harrodsburg meeting, Gabriel Jones and George Rogers Clark, presented the settlers' petition and asked to be recognized. They could not be seated in the House since the Kentucky region was then an appendage of the huge southwestern county of Fincastle; but a committee of three was appointed to bring in a bill which would convert this appendage, including most of Transylvania, into a distinct county. Jefferson was a member of this committee together with Nicholas and Braxton, both tidewater oligarchs with land company connections. Braxton, the chairman, reported a bill calling for the simple division of Fincastle. By some fast legislative footwork Jefferson blocked the bill's passage and got it recommitted to a new committee headed by himself. At the outset, at least, he seemed to have had no definite objective other than courting western favor. But as the struggle wore on during the next six weeks, he took the position that Fincastle should be divided into three counties, and incorporated this, with other liberal features, into the bill he drafted. He then secured its passage, thereby giving to the people on the southwestern frontier a net increase of four representatives. The position of leadership he assumed among the western delegates added greatly to his political capital. Either bill, Braxton's as well as Jefferson's, struck decisively at Henderson's ambitions by the extension of Virginia government to Kentucky. The question of ownership of the soil was left in suspension.

Land titles on the frontier were in a state of chaos. The pretensions of the land companies contributed to the situation. For several years, against discouragements first from the royal government and then from the revolutionary government, pioneers had traversed the mountains and settled on lands claimed by absentee proprietors. The settlers might be forced to make payment at any time on pain of eviction. But even if they had the means it was not always clear to whom they should pay. And after Dunmore's departure in 1775 no land office was open in Virginia. The government sold no lands; no lands could be patented. Pressure mounted on the frontier, especially in Kentucky lands. In 1776 the convention assured the squatters they might purchase the lands they occupied when a land office opened; and the next year the assembly taxed these people as if they had legal title to 400 acres. These were stopgaps. The liberals, led by Jefferson and Mason, favored a two-part program: first, the settlement of the multifarious and irregular claims outstanding; second, the establishment of a permanent policy for the disposal through a land office of the remainder of Virginia's domain, so far as cleared of Indian titles. Mason drafted the bill for the first object, Jefferson for the second. Introduced in January 1778, both bills met formidable eastern opposition. The tidewater, generally, showed little enthusiasm for Virginia's thrust westward. It drained off population, depreciated land values, offered a refuge for draft-dodgers and deserters, and incited costly Indian war. Conservative leaders like Harrison and Braxton had connections with northern land companies seeking to profit from Virginia lands. The liberals and western allies, anxious to secure these lands with settlers, nevertheless made progress in 1778. The House declared new claims prior to the opening of a land office invalid, and also permitted settlers to preempt 400 acres of land at whatever price the government might finally decide. At the fall session, after repeated delays, the land companies presented their claims. Henderson settled, rather handsomely, for "compensation" in the amount of 200,000 acres on the Green River in Kentucky, subject to Virginia law. The leading claimant from the North, the Indiana Company, received nothing, and such was the verdict on all the speculative combines except the old Loyal Company of Virginia, which was subsequently confirmed in its title to 200,000 acres in southwest Virginia.

The bills drafted by Mason and Jefferson, finally enacted by the assembly in the spring of 1779, were obvious twins. Mason's Bill for Settling Titles to Unpatented Land sought to clear away the existing chaos. It confirmed valid titles, granted 400 acres at a nominal price to all settlers prior to January 1778, and set up a commission empowered to render judgment on disputed claims. The bill passed with few changes.

Jefferson's Bill for Establishing a Land Office, on the other hand, was badly treated. It set up four classes of rights to Virginia's unappropriated lands: importation rights, native rights, military rights, and treasury rights. Any person qualifying under one or more of

these classes was entitled to so many acres of land. The first class revived the colonial practice of headrights. The second was unprecedented, though consistent with the 50-acre grant provision of the
draft constitution: every free-born native of the commonwealth
since its establishment was entitled to 75 acres of land upon his or
her marriage. Military rights referred to land bounties awarded in
varying amounts to officers and soldiers in the Revolutionary armies.
Treasury rights would arise from purchases through the Land Office
at a set price of £40 per 100 acres, the equivalent in the state's depreciated currency of the old colonial price of ten shillings the
hundred. But the House massacred Jefferson's plan for spreading
property among common farmers. It eliminated altogether the
grants to immigrants and natives. Of the many other changes made
in the bill, one was especially significant. In the case of purchases
not exceeding 400 acres, the bill authorized issuance of land warrants at any county court, while the act required purchasers, the
small with the large, to obtain warrants from the Register of the
Land Office at the capital. Virginia was a huge state. Jefferson's proposal to decentralize this business was clearly in the interest of the
small settler in the backcountry. The one crucial omission from the
bill, as from the act, was a limitation on the number of acres an individual might patent—a surprising omission in view of Jefferson's declared preference for small grants and his acquaintance with the insatiable appetites of speculators. Probably its cause lay in the desire
to turn the lands into a source of revenue for the state, which was
strongly felt as the costs of war mounted. Whatever the cause, the
omission contributed to the defeat of Jefferson's democratic aims
and to monopolization of a large part of the most valuable lands in
the West.

Jefferson took the lead in legislation on still another part of the
land problem in Virginia, the Tory estates. Most of the Loyalists,
never very numerous, had followed Dunmore's example and left the
state; the few who remained were effectively suppressed, though
they became a nuisance when British armies invaded Virginia. The
estates of these British subjects were both real and personal, involving not only valuable lands and improvements but planter debts
amounting to perhaps three million pounds. Jefferson's sensitive regard for the rights of personal liberty and property did not extend

to Tories. Their only standing at law was as enemy aliens; and his policy toward them, reflecting the feelings of most patriots, was tinged with malice. But he cast his eyes on the Tory estates from cold calculations of dollars and cents. He sought to bolster the state's credit and increase its revenue. In January 1778, simultaneous with the introduction of the Land Office bill, which had the same objects partially in view, the assembly passed Jefferson's Bill for Sequestering British Property. The act did not disturb titles or confiscate property; rather, it provided for the administration of Tory estates by government appointed commissioners and payment of the income into the treasury. In addition, it authorized the discharge of private debts owed to British subjects by legal tender payments into a state fund. The provision was confiscatory, in fact, since Virginia money had already depreciated four or five times over and would become, as Jefferson said, as worthless as oak leaves. But Virginians were required to accept it in payment of their debts, so it seemed fair enough to force it on enemy creditors. Surprisingly, comparatively few debtors took advantage of the law. Jefferson was one of them, motivated more by its public than its private benefits; for he subsequently repaid his British creditors in full value, and the Treaty of Paris in 1783 exacted no less.

From a financial standpoint, sequestration was a fiasco. The following year Jefferson drafted, and the assembly passed, a bill for the confiscation of Tory estates. The apologetical preamble suggests that he had little taste for this harsh measure. It marked, as he conceded, "a departure from that generosity which so honorably distinguishes the civilized nations of the present age." He resorted to the ancient common law of escheat and forfeiture for justification. The law of escheat derived from Jefferson's hated Normans. It was feudal, being founded, according to the eminent Blackstone, "upon this single principle, that the blood of the person last seized in fee-simple, is by some means or other, utterly extinct and gone; and since none can inherit his estate but such as are of his blood and consanguinity, it follows as a regular consequence, that when such blood is extinct, the inheritance itself must fail; the land . . . must result back again to the lord of the fee, by whom . . . it was given." Jefferson took this antiquated law, blended it with the English rule barring the transmission or inheritance of real property by aliens, and made the commonwealth, rather than feudal lord or king, beneficiary of the corrupted titles. The procedure called for the use of inquests to determine if the holders of real estate were, in fact, British subjects; if they were the property reverted by way of escheat to the commonwealth. The legality of the system was beyond question. It belonged to common law. It was specifically recognized by a provision of the constitution lifted from Jefferson's draft. It represented, nevertheless, an astounding revival of feudal practice. All the states confiscated British property, and some of them were far less generous than Virginia; but there alone, ironically by the most enlightened statesman of his time, was confiscation carried out in the shadow of feudalism.

Jefferson's attempt to prop up the state finances by the seizure and sale of Tory estates failed dismally. The return to the treasury in depreciated currency scarcely paid the state for its trouble. These measures, unlike his endeavors on behalf of the Virginia pioneers, had no place in his reform program. He did not conceive of the break-up and sale of Tory estates—far less extensive in Virginia than in several other states—as a means of distributing property among the common people. It did not have this effect, but neither did it have the effect Jefferson intended.

Crime and Punishment

The reform of criminal codes was a favorite pastime of the Enlightenment. All over Europe projects were afoot. Philosophers competed for prizes offered for humane solutions to problems of crime and punishment. Monarchs planned new and liberalized penal codes for their countries. Reformers gave a helping hand to criminals wasting away in jails and dungeons. Some of these stirrings reached Jefferson by way of books. He read the Marquis Beccaria's seminal work, *An Essay on Crimes and Punishments*, in the original Italian, copying long passages into his commonplace book. Similarly, *The Principles of Penal Law* by William Eden, a pioneer English reformer and collaborator with the great humanitarian John Howard. Montesquieu, Helvetius, Kames, even Blackstone put ideas of penal reform in Jefferson's head.

In this sphere there was no distinctly colonial body of law. Virginians were hanged, whipped, and pilloried; they were branded, dismembered, and cropped; but rarely were the crimes or the punishments set forth in any Virginia law. The English law, common and statute, was simply taken for granted. Only where local conditions required modifications, as in the case of slavery, did the provincial government concern itself. As an attorney practicing before the General Court, Jefferson had many opportunities to observe the vagaries and the brutalities of criminal justice in Virginia. Only in the privacy of his study, however, did he seem to entertain ideas of reform.

When the committee of revisers first met, the criminal law falling to Jefferson's portion, he got agreement on certain leading principles. The most important of these was that capital punishment should be abolished for all crimes except treason and willful murder. He had incorporated this principle in his proposed constitution. Proceeding from it now, he took up the several score of crimes which, as felonies, carried the death penalty, and to each of them assigned the punishment suited to reason. The lifting of the death penalty thus called forth a total reconstruction of criminal law. If Jefferson did not quite accomplish this, he made an important contribution of his own in one of the cornerstones of the revisal: A Bill for Proportioning Crimes and Punishments in Cases Heretofore Capital.

No other mere draft of legislation reveals so much of the mind and style of its author. It was definitely humanitarian in principle and design. Had it been enacted into law, Virginia would have taken the longest stride forward of any of the states and set an example to the whole of Christendom. Yet the bill contained shocking lapses from humane and liberal standards, which can only be attributed to the force of traditionalism in Jefferson's thinking. The subject was agreeable to his scholarly impulses. He avidly researched the books in his library, reviewed the passages earlier copied into his commonplace book, and wrote long notes as he went along. He lavished meticulous care on the drafting of the bill. "In style I have aimed at accuracy, brevity and simplicity . . . ," he explained to Wythe. "Indeed I wished to exhibit a sample of reformation in the barbarous style into which modern statutes have degenerated from their ancient simplicity." In the copious margins of the text, Jefferson bared

the massive erudition of the bill: extracts from ancient laws (in Anglo-Saxon, Latin, Old French, and English), citations of learned
sources, references to Beccaria and other philosophers, and little
notes and queries suggested by his own reflection. This was all very
artfully done, with more than a trace of pedantry, but glorious
withal. Here the philosopher declared his precedence to the statesman! An exquisitely penned copy of the bill for his own keeping
suggests his pride in it simply as a work of legislative draftsmanship.

The bill expressed Jefferson's passion for order and system in a
curiously perverse way. In the stately preamble, he said it was the
duty of lawmakers "to arrange in a proper scale the crimes which it
may be necessary to repress, and to adjust thereto a corresponding
gradation of punishments." This was the rational approach, but Jefferson did not follow it. Instead, he set up three basic classes, or
grades, of punishment—life, limb, and labor—and then fit the crimes
into this oversimplified system. One crime was related to another
not so much by its nature as by its penalty. From the standpoint of
legal science, Jefferson's classification was useless, perhaps even a re-
trograde step. More promising was his enunciation of three cardinal
principles derived from Beccaria and other votaries of reason. First,
since punishment is an evil in itself, it is justified only so far as it
produces greater happiness through the reformation of the criminal
and the future prevention of the crime. From this it followed,
among other things, that capital punishment should be "the last melancholy resource" of society. Second, punishments more severe than
necessary to prevent crimes defeat their object by, in Jefferson's
words, "engaging the benevolence of mankind to withhold prosecu-
tions, to smother testimony, or to listen to it with bias. . . ." Third,
crimes are more effectively prevented by the certainty than by the
severity of punishment; therefore, certain penalties should be clearly
associated with certain crimes and justice should be swift and sure,
protected from judicial caprice and special dispensation of any kind.
As Jefferson remarked to Pendleton, "Let mercy be the character of
the law-giver, but let the judge be a mere machine." The whole
tendency of the philosophy ran to the moderation of punishments.
And this was the dominant tendency of Jefferson's bill. However,
there were alarming chinks in its humanity.

In that category of "crimes whose punishment goes to *Limb*," Jefferson embraced rape, polygamy, sodomy, maiming, and disfiguring. All but polygamy were felonies (it was finally omitted) and there was local legislation covering two forms of mayhem endemic to Virginia: the gouging out of eyes and the biting off of ears. Travelers were shocked by these barbarous customs. "I have seen a fellow, reckoned a great adept in gouging," one outlander observed, "who constantly kept the nails of both his thumbs and second fingers very long and pointed; nay, to prevent their breaking or splitting . . . he hardened them every evening in a candle." These were hideous crimes. To them Jefferson applied the hideous punishment of the law of retaliation. No sooner had he done so than he was repelled by it. Presenting the bill for Wythe's inspection, he wrote, "The lex talionis, although a restitution of the Common law, to the simplicity of which we have generally found it so advantageous to return, will be revolting to the humanized feelings of modern times. An eye for an eye, and a hand for a hand will exhibit spectacles in execution whose moral effect would be questionable. . . . This needs reconsideration." It certainly did, and on the very principles declared in the preamble; but the *lex talionis* was allowed to stand in the bill as recommended by the revisers in 1779. Forty years later Jefferson was puzzled to account for the sanction given to this "revolting principle." The letter to Wythe indicates that he believed the principle had been adopted by the committee and that he "strictly observed" the decision "without being entirely satisfied with it." The committee did, in fact, give limited sanction to the principle, but Jefferson himself set up the category of "crimes whose punishment goes to *Limb*" and embraced mayhem, the most common of these crimes, within it. The old Saxon law, which exhibited the *lex talionis*, was a kind of political fetish with Jefferson. Always before it had been employed for liberal ends; here the effect was reactionary, as if he had been bewitched, though that was certainly not the case. He was fully convinced of the inhumanity and the inutility of maiming and stigmatizing offenders of certain crimes. Yet he proposed the very thing that revolted him and the sentiments of mankind. Other explanations failing, it seems probable that he was trapped by a misplaced desire for simplicity, such as he found in his threefold classification, and by the deceptive symmetry of "an eye for an eye and a tooth for a tooth."

Some other provisions of the bill embodied the same error. For example, "Whosoever committeth murder by poisoning shall suffer death by poison." But it was in this category of "crimes whose punishment extends to *Life*" that Jefferson made his principal contribution: the limitation of the death penalty to crimes of treason and murder. Manslaughter became a capital offense on the second conviction. Counterfeiting was punishable by labor and forfeiture of goods. But circumstances altered principles. Counterfeiting was a grave problem during the war, sapping the strength with the credit of the state, thus partaking, as it had of old, of the crime of treason; and in 1779 the assembly passed a bill drafted by Jefferson making it a capital offense. The bill on crimes and punishments lifted the penalty of forfeiture from the victims of suicide. Like Beccaria, Jefferson believed suicide not properly punishable. "As to the example, we need not fear its influence," he noted. "Men are too much attached to life to exhibit frequent instances of depriving themselves of it. At any rate, the quasi-punishment of confiscation will not prevent it." One of the fascinating curiosities of English law was the statute enacted in the reign of James I by which the mother's concealment of the death of a bastard child was made murder. In 1702 one Ann Tandy was convicted and executed in Virginia for the crime; and some years later the Burgesses took the unusual step of re-enacting the English statute, thus providing the only reference to the crime of murder in the colonial statutes. The law inferred guilt from the act of concealment, for the mother would choose to murder the child rather than to disgrace herself. Jefferson found the reasoning untenable. "If shame be a powerful affection of the mind, is not parental love also? Is it not the strongest affection known? Is it not greater than even that of self preservation?" Regardless of the moral arguments against the law, Jefferson thought there could never be justification for substituting presumption of guilt for the proof of it. In a note on breach of prison, a capital offense at common law, Jefferson gave full effect to the rule of the liberal penologists against laws at war with the sentiments of the heart. "It is not only vain, but wicked, in a legislator to frame laws in opposition to the laws of nature, and to arm men with the terrors of death. This is truly creating crimes in order to punish them," he declared. "The law of nature impels every one to escape from confinement; it should not therefore be subjected to punishment." Jefferson's bill released prison-breakers from penalty—a logical extension of the doctrine of natural rights. The bill abolished one of the least defensible features of English justice, the benefit of clergy. Under this privilege, which had originated as a protection of clerics in the civil-ecclesiastical conflicts of the Middle Ages, persons who could read Scripture were excused from punishment on first conviction of most felonies. Although criminal statutes steadily encroached on the privilege, it was recognized in Virginia until 1796.

Contracting the scope of capital punishment and such brute penalties as whipping, pillorying, and ducking, Jefferson had to devise some alternative method of punishment which, on the principles of the bill, ought to look to the reform of the criminal. Fines, forefeitures, and reparations might be relied upon to an extent, but they were insufficient. Imprisonment was not then a normal punishment for crimes. Prisons were rude jails, primarily places of custody for persons awaiting trial, execution, or discharge. The modern prison, or penitentiary, system developed logically from the philosophy of the eighteenth-century penal reformers. Already there were anticipations of the new system in Europe, but Jefferson learned nothing of these until later. He proposed instead a system of employing criminals at hard labor in the public works—mines, galleys, shipyards, foundries, roads, and so on. Thus the third and largest of his three categories: "crimes punishable by *Labor*."

Manslaughter, arson, burglary, horse stealing, larceny, and such crimes were to be punished by hard labor. Jefferson intended to carry the system into effect by a companion bill. The malefactors would "have their heads and beards constantly shaven, and be clothed in habits of coarse materials, uniform in color and make, and distinguished from all others used by the good citizens of this commonwealth . . . so they may be marked out to public note as well while at their ordinary occupations, as when attempting to escape from the public custody." Where he found the germ of this system is uncertain. It may have stemmed from his own reflections. He suggested one possible literary source, however, in Sir Thomas

More's *Utopia*. Of the punishment of thieves in the land of no-where, More wrote, "And they themselves be condemned to be common labourers: and, unless the theft be very henious, they be neither locked in prison, nor fettered in gyves, but be untied to go at large, labouring in the common work. . . . All and every one of them be apparelled in one colour. Their heads be not polled or shaven, but rounded a little above the ears." Closer at hand than this sixteenth-century work, the Pennsylvania constitution of 1776 authorized imprisonment at hard labor for punishment of crimes not capital; but this was not the same proposal as Jefferson's. In fact, there is more reason to believe that the direction of influence ran the other way: that his bill influenced Pennsylvania's adoption in 1786 of the system of "hard labor, publicly and disgracefully imposed." It failed after a brief trial, as Jefferson was to learn. "Exhibited as a public spectacle, with shaved heads and mean clothing, working on the high roads, produced in the criminals such a prostration of character, such an abandonment of self-respect, as, instead of reforming, plunged them into the most desperate and hardened depravity of morals and character." Regarding the experiment as conclusive, he turned, with the Pennsylvania reformers, to the penitentiary system on the principle of solitary confinement. While in Europe he learned of the success of this experiment in England and obtained from an architect in Lyons the plan of a prison adapted to solitary confinement. This plan, sent to Virginia, left its mark on the state penitentiary erected at Richmond a decade later. The peculiar horrors of the solitary system soon led to its replacement, but that is another story in no way involved in Jefferson's life.

When Madison, in 1785–86, systematically introduced each of the bills included in the *Report* of the revisers with a view to approximating the original aim of a revised code, the Bill on Crimes and Punishments proved a major stumbling-block. Twice introduced, debated at length, it was finally defeated in the House by a single vote in December 1786. Madison thought, so he reported to Jefferson, that most of the objections to the bill had been argued away. He did not explain these objections except to say, "The rage against horse stealers had a great influence on the fate of the Bill." Horse stealing had been a capital offense since the middle of the century; dozens of culprits had been hanged for it. Jefferson's bill would punish the crime with three years labor and reparations to the injured party. If a "rage against horse stealers" hurt the bill's chances, it is altogether probable that the mild punishments it proportioned to other crimes caused feelings of uneasiness among the legislators. There is no evidence that the *lex talionis* contributed to the bill's defeat. Virginians seemed to prefer "our old bloody code," as Madison put it. A decade later some of the good features of Jefferson's bill were finally enacted into law.

One provision of Jefferson's bill is significant because of its bearing on a notorious episode in the Revolutionary annals of Virginia. "No attainder shall work corruption of blood in any case," Jefferson wrote. While thus thinking to do away with one of the most revolting features of bills of attainder, Jefferson also assumed that such bills might be proper. Only a few months before, in May 1778, he had drafted the statute attainting Josiah Philips and his accomplices of high treason. Philips was a rank Tory who retired into the Dismal Swamp after Dunmore's exit and at the head of an insurgent band repeatedly sallied forth to pillage and terrorize the countryside. Captured once, he escaped and eluded all efforts of the government to take him dead or alive. The Governor, Patrick Henry, referred the problem to Jefferson. It was discussed in the House. A resolution to attaint Philips passed, and Jefferson drew the bill enacted on May 30, apparently without a whisper of dissent. The act accused Philips (and others unnamed) of levying war against the commonwealth and gave him one month to appear and submit himself to proper trial, at the expiration of which, if he remained at large, he would stand convicted of treason and become the lawful prey of any man. The attainder never actually took effect. Philips and three confederates were brought in within the month, tried on the charge of robbery, convicted, and hanged. They were quickly forgotten, but the act of attainder was not. It was later recalled to the republican mind of Virginia as a shocking example of legislative tyranny, violating the rights of individuals and usurping the powers of the judiciary. Jefferson, who felt the censure, defended the attainder of Philips. A special and limited act of attainder is always a legitimate instrument, he said in 1815, in the case of a person charged with heinous crime and who cannot by any other means be brought to justice. "No doubt that these acts of attainder have been abused in England as instruments of vengeance by a successful over a defeated party. But what institution is insusceptible to abuse in wicked hands?"

But this begged the question. His proposed revision of the Virginia constitution in 1783 prohibited bills of attainder; the United States Constitution barred them; and the execrable institution had few defenders anywhere. Did Jefferson really believe in 1815 that the question was one of its abuse? Probably not. Two considerations may help to make his role in the Philips case understandable. First, the original state constitutions, including Virginia's, imposed no bar to bills of attainder, and several of the Revolutionary governments used them. Pennsylvania attainted 490 persons of high treason in a single act; New York similarly attainted 59 persons. While such examples take none of the sting from Virginia's single act of attainder, they help to put it in perspective, and also to put Jefferson, who drew it, in the currents of passion and error with his Revolutionary comrades. Second, Jefferson always found the greatest difficulty in admitting a mistake either to himself or to others, even at the cost of deepening the guilt of the original error. After his renunciation in 1783, the defense of his actions in the Philips case offers the only evidence of continuing endorsement of the practice. Conscious of his own rectitude, he resented the imputation of trampling on the rights of liberty by the attainder of a traitorous scoundrel during the war. His pride was involved, and rather than admit the error as a Revolutionary aberration, he was led into a course of reasoning blatantly at odds with his own principles.

The Revolution was accomplished in Virginia without a single execution for treason, tending to bear out Jefferson's opinion that, despite occasional violence and unavoidable miscarriages, the record over-all was one of forbearance, moderation, and substantial justice. In the face of enemies within and without, the infant state had the problem of identifying those in allegiance. The test oath—a kind of naturalization oath—became the instrument of citizenship. Non-jurors (those who did not take the oath) were restrained, laws were enacted against Loyalists, and others to punish treason and lesser crimes stabbing at the state's existence. Jefferson subscribed to all these measures—the pains and penalties of revolution. With respect to treason, he may have influenced the statute enacted in 1776. The statute marked a great advance over the English law by narrowing the scope of the crime, defining the evidence required for conviction, and doing away with the hideous aftermath of hanging. In the Bill on Crimes and Punishments, he had only to embody the essential provisions of the treason statute of 1776.

Religion

The Church of England was established in the infancy of the Old Dominion and reigned virtually free of challenge for more than a century. Buttressed and safeguarded by many laws both local and English, aided by a long tradition, the Anglican Church functioned as an arm of the government. Its clergy, creed, and worship held a privileged status, while all others were subject to varying degrees of restraint, and it exacted support from believers and non-believers alike. The principles of the Revolution rendered this state of affairs intolerable. Jefferson at once set himself the task of tearing up the establishment by its roots. His draft constitution contained this sweeping clause: "All persons shall have full and free liberty of religious opinion, nor shall any be compelled to frequent or maintain any religious institution." This was too big a step for the Virginia convention. The constitution of 1776 pleaded mute. The Declaration of Rights, however, stated the true principle: "all men are equally entitled to the free exercise of religion according to the dictates of conscience." If the realization of this right became an object of legislation, the establishment was doomed.

The dissenting sects and others, secular liberals like Jefferson, who opposed the "spiritual tyranny" of the Anglican Church were alert to the opportunity. The first legislative assembly was crowded with petitions calling for disestablishment. "These brought on the severest contest in which I have ever been engaged," Jefferson reflected many years later. Soon after taking his seat, he was appointed to a nineteen-member committee on religion charged with the responsibility of reporting on these numerous petitions. The conflict must have been intense, resulting in stalemate, for after a month's deliberation the committee was discharged and the matter thrown into the House. On November 19 the House agreed to a set of six resolutions, all but one of which supported the liberal position as formulated in resolutions Jefferson had drafted. A new committee was now appointed, Jefferson again a member, to bring in a bill founded on the resolutions. Before this could be accomplished, the House drew back and instructed the committee to report a moderate bill. The upshot of these maneuvers was the act of December 1776 repealing oppressive acts of Parliament and exempting dissenters from taxes to support the Church. While this was an advance, it did not disestablish the Church or secure full freedom of religious conscience. Virginians might still be punished for heretical opinions, either under common law or Virginia statutes. Parish levies on members of the Church were suspended but not abolished. Finally, the act expressly reserved decision on the question, "Whether a general assessment should not be established by law, on every one, to the support of the pastor of his choice, or whether all should be left to voluntary contributions." This was a new issue going beyond the fate of the Established Church. It rapidly became the crucial issue in the long campaign for religious freedom. The climax came a decade later, when Jefferson was in France, with the enactment of his remarkable Bill for Establishing Religious Freedom.

When late in life Jefferson penned his epitaph, he named the Virginia Statute for Religious Freedom one of the three achievements for which he wished to be remembered. More than a statute, it was an eloquent manifesto of the sanctity of the human mind and spirit. It gave mature expression to convictions that, though they might have been reached wholly along the untroubled path of reason, were, in fact, tempered and formed in the crucible of religious controversy in Virginia. In denouncing the establishment and in advocating the fullest freedom in religious concerns, Jefferson drew on his experience as well as his philosophy.

Theological differences played a part in Jefferson's early alienation from the Virginia Church; but the Church was notably indifferent to theology in any case, so it could not have contributed materially to his growing disaffection. He came to oppose the union of Church and State in any form or dogma; and as the abuses of the Anglican connection more and more pressed upon him, he targeted it for dissolution in the holy cause of the Revolution. A pernicious colonial survival, the establishment in his eyes served neither religion

nor liberty. The clergy, weak, indolent, and ineffectual, shared the
worst vices of the community. "It is a melancholy fact," recalled a
leading churchman of the next generation, "that many of them had
been addicted to the race-field, the card-table, the ball room, the
theatre—nay, more, to the drunken revel." The Church had failed in
its moral and spiritual mission. Largely for that reason, and despite
its privileged status, as Jefferson observed, a majority of Virginians
were dissenters on the eve of the Revolution. The offices of some of
the parishes had actually been taken over by dissenters. Such anom-
alies made a mockery of the establishment. Possessing little intrinsic
strength, the Church depended all the more on the support of civil
authority, which was extrinsic in its nature. First, on the faintly aristocratic governing bodies of the parishes, the vestries, which levied
tithes, looked after church property, cared for the poor, and so on.
Second, on protective statutes such as required religious services
according to the articles of the Church of England, restricted marriage to its forms, and punished heresy. Finally, and ultimately, on
the ecclesiastical authority of the Crown. Independence abolished
the latter. Practically, it had never been important. The establishment had always been essentially colonial rather than imperial, and
not even Jefferson made it one of the grounds of revolt against
Britain. Yet political independence was a calamity for the Church.
At least one-third of the Anglican ministers affirmed their loyalty to
Britain, while still others silently opposed the patriots. In New
England, on the other hand, the Congregational clergy enlisted in
the cause of liberty. What subtracted from the Church's strength
added to the power and prestige of the strangely allied forces marshaled under the banner of religious freedom.

The Baptists, numbering in excess of five thousand, formed the
spearhead of sectarian opposition. Whether in spite of persecution
or because of it, they had grown remarkably during the previous
decade. Writing to a friend in Pennsylvania in 1774, the young
Madison bemoaned "the state and liberty of my country," citing the
imprisonment of five or six Baptist preachers in neighboring Culpe-
per. "That diabolical Hell conceived principle of persecution rages
among some and to their eternal infamy the Clergy can furnish their
quota of imps for such business." These preachers were of a particularly enthusiastic Baptist sect, the Separates. Their revivalistic style

of preaching, their coarse and provocative manners, their itinerant ministry, their appeal to the poor and ignorant combined to make them obnoxious not only to easygoing Virginians of the Anglican faith but to the less zealous, better-educated Presbyterians and old-style Baptists as well. "They cannot meet a man upon the road but they must ram a text of Scripture down his throat," said a prosecutor of these evangelists. The invariable charge against them was "disturbance of the peace." Under the English Act of Toleration, which legally extended to Virginia, dissenting Protestants were permitted to hold religious services provided their ministers and places of worship were registered. Most dissenters were content to work within the generous limits of the Act of Toleration. But the Separate Baptists, not finding them convenient, willfully violated the regulations society thought necessary for its peace and order, thereby furnishing the civil magistrates, prodded by the Anglican clergy, the handle of their persecution. In 1772 they began petitioning the House of Burgesses for religious freedom.

Jefferson became an outright champion of this cause in 1776. Prior to independence he had followed with concern the developments in the religious life of Virginia and unquestionably given a good deal of thought and study to the relationship between civil and ecclesiastical authority. His little essay on the fraudulent incorporation of Christianity into the common law has been noted. "We might as well say that the Newtonian system of philosophy is a part of the common law, as that the Christian religion is," he declared. As usual with him, history proved a convenient handmaid of his convictions. When he came to advocate the cause in the assembly he drew upon formidable legal and historical knowledge. Among his papers are several of the "scraps" he worked from: a list of the acts of Parliament and of the Virginia assembly concerning religion, a series of notes and observations on these acts, notes on episcopacy, on heresy, and so on. These notes, together with an abstract of Locke's views, formed the basis of a speech, probably delivered in November 1776, which compressed his whole philosophy of the subject.

Jefferson did not often rise to address the House, nor was he an eloquent speaker; but when the principle was as important as this one, he wished to expose it thoroughly to view, and the known strength of his ideas assured him a careful hearing. He first discussed the injuries of the establishment, with a detailed accounting of the statutory oppressions inseparable from it. Heresy might be punished by death; denial of the Trinity was punishable, on the third offense, by three years' imprisonment; Unitarians and freethinkers might be declared unfit parents and have their children taken from them; Roman Catholics were excluded from the mantle of toleration and burdened with legal disabilities; periodic church attendance was compulsory; profanity carried a fine of ten pounds for each offense; and so on. Yet, Jefferson observed, "most men imagine that persecution is unknown to our laws." He conceded that the statutes were dead letters for the most part. There were a few Virginians—Catholics, Unitarians, heretics—on whom the penalties might fall. "Happily, the spirit of the times is in favor of the rights of conscience." But when was this ever a sufficient reliance? "Everyone should know under what law he lives, and should not be obliged to recur to the spirit of the times for protection." Now, while the spirit was sound and union against the common enemy a necessity, now was the time to fix every right on firm foundations. Over one-half the inhabitants were dissenters from the Church they were nevertheless taxed to support, and despite the voluntary support many gave to the ministries of their choice. This, too, was a form of persecution. What kind of attachment might these people feel toward a government that so flagrantly, and in the face of declared principle, discriminated against them? Political realism as well as abstract right demanded that all religions be placed on a footing of freedom and equality.

Jefferson then posed this fundamental question: "Has the state a right to adopt an opinion in matters of religion?" His answer was an unequivocal no. The conclusion followed logically from the contract theory of government. Men unite in government to secure those rights they cannot secure themselves. The rights of conscience are not submitted to civil authority, first, because men are answerable for them solely to God, and second, because their exercise does no injury to others. Jefferson later gave memorable statement to the principle in the *Notes on Virginia:* "The legitimate powers of government extend to such acts only as are injurious to others. But it does me no injury for my neighbor to say there are twenty gods or no god. It neither picks my pocket, nor breaks my leg." In all this and more he simply followed Locke, particularly the first *Letter Concerning Toleration*. But as Jefferson observed in his "Notes on Locke," the great Whig failed to push his principles to conclusion, declining to extend freedom to Catholics, athiests, and some others. "It was a great thing to go so far . . . but where he stopped short, we may go on." Significantly, Jefferson, with Madison and others of the liberal persuasion, dropped the term *toleration*, which implied an official and preferred religion, in favor of the term *liberty*. The religious liberty advocated in 1776 involved both freedom *from* the privileges and oppressions of a state church and freedom *to* worship according to the dictates of conscience without legal hindrance or discrimination of any kind.

Irrespective of the question of right, as Jefferson went on to show, the intervention of government in the affairs of religion was neither necessary nor advantageous to either one. Some men feared the consequences of government showing religion to the door, turning it out like a pauper to struggle in the world of ideas, both sacred and profane, for a place in the minds of men. Such men hungered for Truth infallible and absolute. But it would forever elude them, Jefferson warned. "Millions of innocent men, women and children, since the introduction of Christianity, have been burnt, tortured, fined, and imprisoned; yet we have not advanced one inch towards uniformity. What has been the effect of coercion? To make one half the world fools, and the other half hypocrites." The history of progress in religion as in philosophy was the history of the march of free inquiry and private judgment against the coercion and error of public authority. "It is error alone which needs the support or government," Jefferson declared. "Truth can stand by itself." Religious differences were beneficial to the peace and order of society: "The several sects perform the office of a *censor morum* over each other." They were equally beneficial to religion, setting up a virtuous competition among the sects and forcing them to develop their own resources rather than to depend on external support.

As already recorded, the first contest in the assembly ended in a halfway measure. Dissenters of every description declined to stop there. During the next several years they kept the initiative and, propelled increasingly by the force of an idea, pressed the assembly to finish the work. The next victory came in 1779: repeal of the laws requiring members of the Anglican Church to contribute to its support. This pushed the establishment into irretrievable ruin, though vestiges of its exclusive status remained for a time. An act of the assembly in 1780 legalized marriages performed by non-Anglican clergy, and it was later liberalized in 1784 to overcome Baptist objections. The vestries continued for some years yet to discharge civil functions, such as the care of the poor. Not until 1802 were the parishes deprived of glebe lands for the support of the clergy.

These were details. Much more important was the new ground of contest: government support of Christianity as the established religion of the Commonwealth. Religious freedom being extended to all citizens, all sects and persuasions being put on an equal footing, churchmen and some other religionists, with strong political backing, called for a general assessment of all citizens for the support of all Christian ministers. The act of 1776 had specifically reserved this question for later decision. And in 1779, after the doom of the old establishment, its friends introduced the first general assessment bill. They sought thereby to prop up the decaying edifice of the Anglican Church, but the scheme committed them to a principle of far greater import. Historically, in America and throughout the Christian world, "the establishment of religion" meant official sanction and support of a single state church. In the course of religious controversy in Virginia, however, the concept acquired a new meaning: state encouragement and support of Christianity without preference as to sect.

The position staked out by liberals and dissenters in the early stages of the controversy was sufficient to meet the new challenge. Of course, their arguments had been directed against the existing establishment, and none of Jefferson's statements on record emphatically barred simple tax support of different faiths without discrimination. Yet this was the whole tone and tenor of his doctrine. If required to be more explicit about it, he certainly would be, and without revising anything. He believed with Locke that religion consists in "the *inward* persuasion of the mind," that a church is "a *voluntary* society of men," and that the jurisdiction of civil government cannot extend to either. He was far too sophisticated in his views of government, far too convinced of the tenderness of the private conscience, to believe that religious liberty, so conceived, could be se-

139

cured under the patronage of the state. He would have been equally opposed to the introduction of government support for all religions —the Jewish, the Mohammedan, the Hindu with the Christian— though such a program would have overcome powerful objections of another kind. "Hands off" was the only acceptable policy. Thus Jefferson's doctrine necessarily involved *the separation of church and state*, even if none of the reformers had yet uttered that doctrine.

Still, men who conceded the injustice of a state church might see nothing unjust or illogical in a general establishment of religion, all supporting the minister or church of their choice. It was partly to close off this fortuitous development that Jefferson drafted his Bill for Religious Freedom. Drawn in 1777 as part of the Revision of the Laws, it was not introduced in the House until two years later. The delay was probably a question of timing. The first protests against the "general assessment" plan reached the Assembly in the spring of 1777, and it was discussed in subsequent sessions, but the time grew ripe for it only after the old establishment was disposed of. Neither Jefferson's bill nor the first version of the plan to establish the Christian religion could command a majority in 1779 or for several years to come. The issue was well understood by the people. The contending principles and measures were identified with the two giants of Virginia politics, Jefferson and Henry. Starting as a champion against the Church, the famous orator came around to the cause of churchmen and conservatives like Pendleton and Nicholas without, in his opinion, the least change of principle. In 1784 the assembly entered upon the climactic stage of the long controversy. It called up a bill, principally sponsored by Henry, to levy "a moderate tax or contribution annually for the support of the Christian religion, or for some Christian church, denomination or communion of Churches, or for some form of Christian worship." The bill, somewhat more liberal than its predecessor, justified government support of religion not on any grounds of ecclesiastical authority but on the recognized power of the state to diffuse knowledge (Christian knowledge in this case), restrain vice, and preserve the peace of society. The idea that the state might thus, in the name of peace and morals, do what it could not do in the name of religion seemed to underscore the need to raise a wall of separation between church and state. The old dissenter coalition of rationalists and sectarians—the Presbyterians alone wavering for a time—blocked passage of the bill in 1784 and, under Madison's vigorous leadership, defeated it in 1785. Seeking to cap the climax, Madison then brought forward Jefferson's Bill for Religious Freedom.

As Jefferson reflected in his autobiography, he had drawn the bill "in all the latitude of reason and right" regardless of principles that might already have been established in law. Like the Declaration of Independence, to which it was a corollary, the great statute had more importance as an eloquent manifesto than as substantive legislation. But while the Declaration might be criticized for want of passion, the Statute for Religious Freedom burned with an ardor that belied mere rationality. Jefferson poured into the preamble—four times the length of the act itself—all his rage against the cant, the falsehood, the hypocrisy, the self-righteousness, the corruption, and the tyranny associated with the history of the alliance between Church and State. He did not stop with the assertion that it is "sinful and tyrannical" to compel a man to support opinions he disbelieves, but argued, no doubt with the assessment plan in mind, "that even the forcing him to support this or that teacher of his own religious persuasion" deprives him of liberty and the ministry of "incitement to earnest and unremitting labours for the instruction of mankind." He condemned religious tests and discriminations. He roundly declared "that the opinions of men are not the object of civil government, nor under its jurisdiction." The assembly struck this clause, but the statute in its entirety made evident how far the general cause of intellectual liberty—freedom of mind—was involved in Jefferson's argument for religious liberty. Of all men's convictions those of a religious nature were the most tender, most subjective, most private, and therefore, Jefferson believed, the least subject to authority or compulsion of any degree.

After several amendments which Madison termed "frivolous," the bill passed into law on January 16, 1786. Apparently no objection was raised to the enacting clause, only to the radical preamble. The legal effect of the statute was to make positive and unambiguous what had heretofore been the result of essentially negative actions, such as repeal laws and the defeat of the general assessment scheme. Never satisfied to leave fundamental rights to the hazard of statute, Jefferson had added an unusual final clause declaring that, though the act could not bind succeeding legislatures, nevertheless "if any act shall be hereafter passed to repeal the present or to narrow its operation, such act will be an infringement of natural right." Succeeding assemblies heeded the admonition. Reporting the conclusion of the campaign in which he shared equal honors with his friend in France, Madison grandly announced that the statute "extinguished forever the ambitious hope of making laws for the human mind."

The fame of the Virginia Statute for Religious Freedom rapidly spread beyond American shores. No other act of legislation so pointedly enforced the reality of the American Revolution on the enlightened heads of Europe. On the scene in Paris, proud of the honor the statute did to his country as well as to himself, Jefferson saw to its propagation. Before the year 1786 ran out, he reported to Madison on the wide acclaim. "I do not mean by the governments, but by the individuals which compose them. It has been translated into French and Italian, has been sent to most of the courts of Europe. . . . It is inserted in the new Encyclopédie, and is appearing in most of the publications respecting America. In fact it is comfortable," Jefferson continued, "to see the standard of reason at length erected, after so many ages during which the human mind has been held in vassalage by kings, priests and nobles; and it is honorable for us to have produced the first legislature who has had the courage to declare that the reason of man may be trusted with the formation of his own opinions."

The statute was the great testimony to Jefferson's conviction that "reason is the only oracle" of man. The question naturally arises of how far Jefferson's perfervid rationalism was hostile to the religion he professed to free. The statute repudiated the assumption common to most religions that there is an absolute standard of right and truth not to be known by reason alone. It denied to any religion the aid of civil authority to extend its sway. Was this position, expressing attitudes of skepticism, rationalism, and secularism, compatible with the ends of the statute: the full measure of religious profession and the strict neutrality of the state? Was Jefferson not arraying the state on the side of a new religion of enlightenment? These are questions for the logician, and he is not apt to be satisfied with Jefferson's logic. Theological presuppositions lurk in all great measures of legislation. Yet to find fault with the statute on this ground is but a sophistical way of quarreling with its principles and purposes.

Churchmen then and for generations after openly quarreled with them, charging that Jefferson was motivated by hostility to the Episcopal Church and, indeed, to all Christian profession or religious life of any kind. Nothing could be more mistaken. As a philosopher has said, "The power and eloquence of Jefferson's writings on religious freedom is due largely to his evident religious devotion." Unlike the anti-clericalism of the Old World, his hatred of establishments and priesthoods did not involve him in hatred of religion. He wished for himself, for all his countrymen, not freedom from religion but freedom to pursue religion wherever reason and conscience led, and the more sensitive and upright the pursuit the more respect it won from him. He attempted to say as much but, of course, the onus of his public work and utterance was on the side of tearing down, so he must appear to many as a mere destroyer of religion. His own deepest convictions he kept to himself, nor did the public know of the generous support he gave to various churches throughout his life. In 1777, for example, he subscribed six pounds to the annual support of the Reverend Charles Clay, St. Anne's Parish, Charlottesville. Jefferson may have had no personal call for the Reverend Mr. Clay's services but his neighbors did. His contribution—nearly twice the amount subscribed by any other parishioner—proved Jefferson's readiness to accept the consequences of his own principle: the voluntary support of churches and ministers.

In the liberality of his mind, as in his entire personality and background, Jefferson obviously had more in common with the mild and genial Episcopalians than with the evangelical Baptists and "New Light" Presbyterians who furnished the battalions for the campaign generaled by Madison and himself. It was a strange alliance: rationalists and enthusiasts, secularists and sectarians, skeptics and believers united by their common opposition to the established order. They were able to co-operate, in part, because they were so far apart, appeals to reason giving no practical trouble to sectaries who relied on the converting presence of the Holy Spirit. Thus by the unique logic of American history the seekers after God and the seekers after enlightenment were allies in liberty. Some of Jefferson's friends, like his boyhood chum John Page, were stunned by his stubborn support of the "bigoted and illiberal" folk after they had stolen the flocks and disrobed the shepherds of the "rational sect." "Nothing but a general assessment can prevent the State from being divided between immorality and enthusiastic bigotry," Page told Jefferson. The warning carried a partial truth, as Jefferson would discover in the course of time. Whatever the long-run effect of the newer sects on Virginia piety and morality, they were to do irreparable injury to the state's reputation for liberality and enlightenment. Yet even had Jefferson calculated this loss, it could have had no weight with him. "Reason and free inquiry are the only effectual agents against error." What he shared with Baptist ranters was more fundamental than his intellectual distaste for them. He looked to schools, not to churches, to improve the mass of people. Moreover, while Page with so many others thought the old church would go steadily downhill without public support, Jefferson's belief in the salubrity of freedom promised a better future for the Episcopalians. Viewing the progress several decades later, Bishop William Meade observed that "nothing could have been more injurious to the cause of true religion in the Episcopal Church, or to its growth in any way, than the continuance of either stipend or glebes." The revival of the Church commenced, Meade thought, when she was "thrown upon her own resources."

Jefferson's motives on the side of religion were entirely creditable, yet it would be quite erroneous to imply that he was motivated primarily by concern for religion. Religious freedom absorbed him most earnestly where it intersected intellectual freedom. The martyrs of science and philosophy, rather than the martyrs of religion, won his highest admiration. Both sectarian religionists and secular liberals sought separation of church and state; but the former feared most the power of the state to corrupt and tyrannize the church, while the latter feared, above all, the inquisitorial tendencies of the church. Religion and philosophy in all their amplitude do not comprehend the earnestness of Jefferson's purpose, however. A republican statesman who had made "the pursuit of happiness" his creed, he believed that the "voluntary system" would tend to produce loyalty in the state, moderation in the government, and peace and harmony

Monticello, the first version. Accepted elevation, 1771.

General plan of Monticello. Jefferson's drawing, 1772.

The Declaration of Independence July 4, 1776. Detail from the painting by John Trumbull.

Whosoever on purpose and of malice fore-thought shall maim another, or shall disfigure him by cutting out or disabling the tongue, slitting or cutting off a nose, lip or ear, branding, or otherwise, shall be maimed or disfigured in like sort: or if that cannot be for want of the same-part, then as nearly as may be in some other part of at least equal value and estimation in the opinion of a jury, and moreover shall forfeit one half of his lands and goods to the sufferer.

si soit le jugement tiel que il perde autiel membre come il avera tollé al pleintife. et si la pleynte soit faite de femme que avera tollé a home ses membres, en tiel cas perdra la femme la une meyn par jugement, come le membre dount ele avera trespassé.' Britton c. 25. Fleta. B. 1. c. 40. ll. Ælfr. 19. 40.

Whosoever shall counterfeit any coin current by law within this Commonwealth, or any paper bills issued in the nature of money, or of certificates of loan on the credit of this Commonwealth, or of all or any of the United States of America, or any Inspectors notes for tobacco, or shall pass any such counterfeited coin, paper, bills, or notes, knowing them to be counterfeit; or, for the sake of lucre, shall diminish case, or wash any such coin, shall be condemned to hard labor six years in the public works, & shall forfeit all his lands and goods to the Commonwealth.

[right column scholarly notes in Latin and Anglo-Saxon, largely illegible]

A page from Jefferson's draft of the Bill for Proportioning Crimes and Punishments, 1778.

in the society. The circumstances of war and revolution and nation-building gave an urgency to considerations of this kind. Writing to Jefferson in 1779 the Reverend John Todd, a leader of the famed Hanover Presbytery, stated the shared conviction "that people of different sentiments in religion will be all one in their love and fidelity to the State which secures to them everything dear and valuable: and the more catholic and friendly one to another, and free from *pride* and *envy* when the State rewards all men according to their merit." Two years later Jefferson thought the experiment had proved itself in New York and Pennsylvania, more varied religiously than Virginia. Unparalleled harmony prevailed amidst widest diversity. "They have made the happy discovery, that the way to silence religious disputes, is to take no notice of them." It would not prove quite so simple, but the history of American society justified his optimism.

Education

The backbone of Jefferson's republic was a system of public education. "If a nation expects to be ignorant and free in a state of civilization, it expects what never was and never will be," he once observed. The state of civilization being one of organization and power, of progress and improvement, it demanded commensurate means of enlightenment. Without the diffusion of knowledge through all the ranks of society, adapted to its different degrees and conditions, individuals could neither attend to their own happiness nor, as citizens, secure the freedom and the welfare of the state. It was axiomatic with Jefferson that the people were the only safe depository of their rights and liberties, always provided, however, that they were adequately informed and instructed. Education was too important a matter to be left to chance. It must be planned and carried out as a paramount responsibility of republican government.

Jefferson's "quixotism for the diffusion of knowledge," as he styled it, thus sprang from his political principles. The men of his class, favored by wealth and family, educated at private hands, had brought the country to freedom and self-government amidst colossal ignorance. There were no schools for children of the common people. Too many were raised up in the ignorance in which they were born. Much of Virginia was but a step or two removed from the reckless, brawling frontier, where education was a luxury and communal responsibility unformed, while the settled eastern portion was dominated by an haughty aristocracy notably more conscious of its rights than of its social obligations. Except for slavery, which added to the problem but raised peculiar dangers of its own, the ignorance and torpor of the people presented the main obstacle to the success of the republican experiment.

The Revision of the Laws gave Jefferson his first opportunity to attack the problem. Several acts of the old assembly relating to the College of William and Mary fell to Pendleton's portion, but the revisers agreed that a "systematical plan of general education" should be proposed and turned the entire subject over to Jefferson. He drafted three bills. The most important, A Bill for the More General Diffusion of Knowledge, in 1778, offered the blueprint of a system of education adapted to the condition and the capacity of everyone, as Jefferson thought, and reaching the objects of republican citizenship. The preamble defined two such objects. First, "to illuminate, as far as practicable, the minds of the people at large," which was called the most effectual means of preventing the degeneration of free government into tyranny. Second, to ensure "that those persons, whom nature hath endowed with genius and virtue, should be rendered by liberal education worthy to receive, and able to guard the sacred deposit of the rights and liberties of their fellow citizens, and that they should be called to that charge without regard to wealth, birth or other accidental condition or circumstance." There was nothing contradictory in these objects; but the first involved rudimentary instruction of the mass of citizens, while the second looked to the superior cultivation of the "natural aristocracy" from whom the state might draw its leaders. Citizenship and leadership: education for both ought to be supported at the public expense so far as practicable. To the question of which object was more important, Jefferson answered "that none is more important, none more legitimate, than that of rendering the people the safe, as they are the ultimate, guardians of their own liberty."

His method of reducing a problem to its components, analyzing them, then reassembling the parts into a new system was well displayed in the plan of general education. He projected three distinct grades of education—elementary, middle, and higher—the whole rising like a pyramid from the local communities. The latter, unfortunately, had almost no existence in Virginia. Jefferson proposed to create them. Counties would be laid off into *hundreds*, or *wards*, each of a size and population suitable for the maintenance of an elementary school. "At these schools all the free children, male and female, resident within the respective hundred, shall be entitled to receive tuition gratis, for a term of three years, and as much longer, at their private expense, as their parents, guardians or friends, shall think proper." Of course, the schools would teach reading, writing, and arithemtic. The aims of primary education included moral improvement, the acquisition of skills necessary for the common personal and business transactions of life, and instruction in the rights and duties of citizens. The last of these particularly absorbed his attention in 1778; and he specifically directed instruction in the history and experience of other ages and nations so that young citizens may come to recognize tyranny in embryo and exert themselves to crush it. Instead of drawing their moral lessons from the Bible, the children were to take the histories of Greece, Rome, Europe, and America as their texts. The Bible called for more mature judgment than children possessed, and was precluded in any event in a secular state. History furnished a secular guide to morality and promised to be even more useful as a monitor of the civil polity. "History, by apprizing them [the children] of the past, will enable them to judge of the future . . . it will qualify them as judges of the actions and designs of men; it will enable them to know ambition under every disguise it may assume; and knowing it, to defeat its views." This was expecting a good deal of the judgment of children! Jefferson was no Rousseau. His knowledge of the psychology and the learning processes of children was never very great. The design of an educational system deeply interested him; the theory of teaching it embodied clearly did not. He simply assumed with Locke that young minds were formed by the impressions passed before them, hence the right curriculum could make the right kind of citizens. Children were but incipient adults to him. Combined with the secularism and utilitarianism of his educational plan was a rationalism and a verbalism that were already being challenged by such European thinkers as Rousseau and Pestalozzi.

Above the hundred schools, freely educating all children, were the grammar schools, twenty in all, laid off in districts embracing several counties. These schools were also to be maintained by the state; however, most of the pupils coming from homes "in easy circumstances," they would be charged tuition and board. The exceptions were the "public foundationers," perhaps sixty or seventy of the most promising geniuses who, being also from poor families, would be annually chosen after rigorous examinations in the lower schools and awarded, in effect, state scholarships. One-third of these scholars would be eliminated after the first year's instruction, the remainder after two years, excepting the best scholar of each school, who would be at liberty to continue four more years. "By this means," Jefferson wrote of his ingenious selection system, "twenty of the best geniuses will be raked from the rubbish annually, and be instructed, at the public expense, so far as grammar schools go." And they would go to the teaching of the classical languages, English grammar, geography, and the higher branches of mathematics. At the top of the pyramid stood the College of William and Mary, which Jefferson sought by a companion bill to convert into a state university offering instruction in all the sciences. Every year ten seniors "of the best learning and most hopeful genius and disposition" would be chosen from the grammar schools of the state to be sent to the university, "there to be educated, boarded, and clothed, three years" on the public account.

William and Mary was to become not only a university but the supervisory head of the entire system of education. The College would determine the course of instruction in the lower schools, for example. Jefferson's plan for his alma mater, like the general education bill, was influenced in part by the desire to divorce education from religious guidance. Most of Virginia's private schoolmasters were Anglican clergymen. And, of course, the College was an Anglican institution. Publicly supported from its founding, the College was now of great interest to the commonwealth, for it was the only seminary "in which those who are to be the future guardians of the rights and liberties of their country may be endowed with science and virtue, to watch and preserve the sacred deposit." Jefferson proposed to amend the College's charter in three main respects. First, the self-perpetuating governing body of Anglicans would be replaced by a secular board receiving its appointment annually from the General Assembly. Second, the professorships would be raised from six to eight covering the principal fields of knowledge. Third, the public revenue of the College would be increased and placed on a secure footing.

Nothing came of this bill, but in 1779, when he became Governor, Jefferson was elected a visitor of the College, and he attempted in this capacity to make some limited progress toward his objectives. Restrained by the charter to six professorships, he succeeded in replacing three of them, in Divinity, Oriental Languages, and Greek and Latin, with professorships in Law and Government, Anatomy and Medicine, and Modern Languages. (Jefferson favored instruction in the ancient languages but felt it belonged to the academy or grammar school.) One of the professorships, called the Brafferton after the estate of its English donor, would be transformed from its stated mission, the conversion of the Indians to Christianity, into a kind of anthropological chair for the study of the American Indians. These changes struck very advanced secular and utilitarian notes in keeping with the idea of a university rather than a college. Their actual effect was small, however, and the assembly never got around to revising the charter or acting on other parts of Jefferson's bill. Nothing could erase the College's reputation as a Church institution. "The religious jealousies, therefore, of all the dissenters, took alarm lest this [the bill] might give an ascendancy to the Anglican sect . . . ," Jefferson accurately reported. "Its local eccentricity, too, and the unhealthy outward climate, lessened the general inclination toward it." Finally, the success of his own measure for removing the capital from Williamburg hurt the College by severing its connections with the seat of government. Decades later, when Jefferson revived his dream of a university, he brushed aside the claims of his alma mater and built from the ground up.

Still a third bill, for establishing a state-supported library, completed Jefferson's system. The function he had in mind for the library is obscure, but presumably it was to serve the needs of both public officials and scholars. He was zealous for the collection of historical records and artifacts, for the encouragement of learned inquiry in all areas, and, of course, he could not conceive of education without libraries. Years later, reflecting on the continuing education of adult citizens, he said "that nothing would do more extensive good at small expense than the establishment of a small circulating library in every county." But nothing ever came of this, or of the library bill proposed as part of the revisal in 1779.

The general education bill was nine-tenths of the system; the rest rose from it and could scarcely rise without it. "What a plan was here to give stability and solid glory to the republic!" The bill first went to the House in December 1778, then again a year and one-half later, and for a third time in 1785, when it passed in the House but died in the Senate. It was reconsidered and rejected for the last time the next year. "The necessity of a systematic provision on the subject was admitted on all hands," Madison informed Jefferson. The leading objections to the plan were "1. the expense, which was alleged to exceed the ability of the people. 2. the difficulty of executing it in the present sparse settlement of the Country." The objections mortgaged the future to exigencies of the present. Virginia *was* poor. But she would grow poorer still without the education of her people. The plan *was* impractical for large parts of the state. Each hundred was supposed to cover an area of five or six square miles at most—children could not be expected to traverse a greater distance daily—but many such areas had but a scattering of people. Yet the bill might have been revised to take account of this problem. There were still other objections, for the plan reached deep into the society and touched a number of sensitive interests. Religionists generally distrusted its secularism, while the Presbyterians in particular opposed the influence of William and Mary over the schools. The bill posed a threat to the county courts by the creation of potentially new units of local government, the hundreds or wards, with popularly elected officials called aldermen to administer the schools and perform other duties, such as poor relief and tax assessment, which were assigned to them by other bills of the revisal. Taxation to support the schools would fall most heavily on the propertied class, and from a purely selfish viewpoint the rich felt no interest in paying for the education of the poor. Whatever the reasons for the defeat of the plan, it was a terrible disappointment to Jefferson. "I think by far the most important bill in our whole code is that for the diffusion of knowledge among the people," he wrote to Wythe from France, which he thought the best school in the universe to cure Americans of the folly of seeking public happiness without public enlightenment. "Preach, my dear Sir, a crusade against ignorance; establish and improve the law for educating the common people," he implored. "Let our countrymen know . . . that the tax which will be paid for this purpose is not more than the thousandth part of what will be paid to kings, priests and nobles who will rise up among us if we leave the people in ignorance."

Regardless of defeat, Jefferson's Bill for the More General Diffusion of Knowledge was a landmark in the history of American education. The principle of public education was not new: common schools had existed in New England for generations. In fact, the principal difficulty of Jefferson's plan was the attempt to introduce a system borrowed from the close-knit town environment of New England into the spread-out rural environment of Virginia. But the plan broke sharply with the essentially religious ideal of New England education, substituting for it the citizen-republicanism of the new nation. Public responsibility for the enlightenment of the people was founded in the interest all men felt in freedom and self-government. Also significant was the conception of a complete and unified educational system, from the common schools at the bottom to the university at the top. There were no models for this, and whatever the possible literary sources of the idea—John Knox's sixteenth-century Scottish Presbyterian *Book of Discipline* has been suggested—it appears to have been an independent product of Jefferson's republican imagination. Three years of elementary education—all that Jefferson's plan guaranteed—seems very niggardly by modern standards, which must also condemn omission of the compulsory principle. But that principle was unheard of for many years yet, and a larger commitment to common schooling would have been hopelessly unrealistic. Jefferson perhaps would not have advocated it in any event. He did not believe the mass of citizens either required or were susceptible to education at advanced levels. But nature had sown talent and energy as liberally among the poor as the rich. As

Sir William Petty had observed a century earlier, "many are now holding the plough which might have been made fit to steer the state." The state had an obligation both to nature and to itself to prevent these abilities from running to waste. Jefferson's selection scheme aimed to scale education to merit; and he unreservedly placed the state on the side of talent by proposing to tax the entire community for the education of its most promising offspring of adversity. An audacious experiment indeed! It carried elitist overtones, though it was no part of Jefferson's purpose to establish an elite, even a natural one. Unforunately, the current neologism of the educators, "meritocracy," did not occur to him, for that is precisely what he had in mind when he spoke of "natural aristocracy." The ideal could find no place in the democratic ideology of public education in nineteenth-century America, and only recently have educators begun to catch up with it.

Other Reforms

Next to education as a means of improving the lot of his countrymen, Jefferson set his heart on the eradication of slavery. But he never underestimated the resistance he would meet on this question, and he would let it lie rather than risk the loss of all power of accomplishment by untimely advocacy of so arduous a cause. He had warmly denounced the African slave trade in his draft of the Declaration of Independence. His proposed constitution for Virginia prohibited holding in slavery any person henceforth coming into the country. In 1778 the assembly, while not going this far, slammed the door on the foreign slave trade. Although Jefferson's authorship of the statute cannot be definitely established, he claimed responsibility for it and there is no one else to whom it can be as fairly assigned. The original bill sought to encourage the private manumission of slaves, which existing law made virtually impossible, and firmly declared an anti-slavery position. As enacted the statute simply raised a bar to foreign importation.

The greater question of emancipation came before the revisers in connection with the codification of colonial slave laws. The bill they reported, and the assembly enacted after several amendments in

1785, contained no provision for emancipation and was for the most part "a mere digest" of the old laws. The principal difference lay in the limits set to the increase of slaves by confining this status henceforth to the descendants of female slaves currently in Virginia. The provision alone, by limiting the source of replenishment, would have gone some way toward eliminating slavery. As finally enacted, the bill did not have this effect. The revisers, according to Jefferson, prepared a plan of gradual emancipation under which all the slaves born after the passage of the act would become free at the age of adulthood and be colonized outside the limits of Virginia. "It was thought better that this should be kept back," Jefferson later wrote, "and attempted only by way of amendment, whenever the bill should be brought up." But, of course, he was abroad when the bill came up, and the amendment was never offered, perhaps because, as he observed, "the public mind would not yet bear the proposition." While he continued to favor the plan of gradual emancipation, first published in the *Notes on Virginia* in 1785, neither he nor any other prominent Virginian was ever willing to risk friends, position, and influence to fight for it.

Jefferson's work on the Revision of the Laws gave him a liberal education in most of the branches of political science. One of these, citizenship, was thrown into vast confusion by the American Revolution. Jefferson drew the principal bill intended to clarify the matter; detached from the *Report* of the revisers, it was enacted in 1779. The statute took over the basic English formula of *jus soli,* founding citizenship on native birth; however, both the conditions and the principles of the Revolution caused important departures from English law. (Jefferson drafted and introduced, also in 1779, the revisers' bill prescribing the oath of fidelity as the Revolutionary test of citizenship in Virginia.) The question of United States citizenship was covered in obscurity, but by extending to the citizens of the other twelve states all the rights, privileges, and immunities of the citizens of Virginia, Jefferson's bill placed his state in the path of the Confederation. The bill also offered liberal terms of naturalization. Jefferson had indicted George III for "obstructing the laws of naturalization of foreigners, and refusing to . . . encourage their migration hither." Indeed, English law did not recognize the validity of naturalization. The encouragement of immigration was, for Jefferson, the positive counterpart of his hostility to slavery, for as the number of slaves declined and Negroes were "colonized" their places would be "filled up by free white laborers." To accomplish this he was against any religious bar, such as the exclusion of Catholics, which Pendleton had proposed; he sought, unsuccessfully, to add the inducement of modest land and monetary grants to immigrants; and he placed naturalization on the simple basis of residence and oath of fidelity.

Of greater theoretical, if not practical, interest was still another feature of the citizenship statute. It declared that every citizen has a "natural right of expatriating himself" and laid down the method of exercising the right. The right arose logically from the principles of the Declaration of Independence. Free men could not be forced to remain members of that state "in which birth, or other accident may have thrown them." The right was unknown to English law, and Blackstone denied it any standing in the law of nations. The ancients had given precedence for it, however, and Jefferson, if he did not find it in Cicero, must certainly have discovered it in Locke. The Americans themselves had exercised the right, and they invited the citizens of other nations to do the same by coming hither. It became a fixed article of Jefferson's creed, and one might say of the American creed, though not in explicit legal terms. No sister state copied Jefferson's innovation. Virginia law ceased to recognize it in 1783, when the first citizenship statute was replaced by a less liberal one. And despite Jefferson's later efforts as Secretary of State, the right of expatriation—man's natural right to live on any portion of the earth that pleases him—went unrecognized in United States law.

Among the principal tasks Jefferson undertook during the first busy session of the General Assembly—any one of them enough to give him a name in history—was the organization of the Virginia judiciary. The constitution merely named the different courts of law to be established; their actual establishment, their powers, jurisdictions, procedures, and so on, was left to legislation. As chairman of the committee appointed to this work, Jefferson drew five bills, each covering a separate court. At the time only the inferior county courts were open for business. The old courts of more extensive jurisdiction remained closed to protect planters from suits for the recovery of debts. Wishing to set the entire judicial system in operation, Jefferson tried to allay the fears of debt-ridden planters by a measure to suspend executions for debts during the wartime interruption of Virginia's trade. But this compromise was unacceptable to the House. It promptly passed Jefferson's Bill for Establishing a Court of Admiralty, with jurisdiction over prizes, and deferred action on the others. The House never acted on the measure "for better regulating the proceedings in the County Courts"—all Jefferson's efforts to reform them failed. In 1778, when the planters were authorized to liquidate their debts in paper money, the House finally approved the bills for establishing a General Court and a High Court of Chancery, both to receive appeals from the county courts and to have original jurisdiction where they were incompetent, and also a Court of Appeals with ultimate jurisdiction in civil cases.

The judicial system thus established made no important departure from English practice. Jefferson liked to point to the innovation of jury trial in the Court of Chancery; but the reform did not last, and it is more significant that the Virginians chose to continue a separate court of chancery, or equity, rather than to mix this jurisdiction with the common law jurisdiction of the General Court. The latter course was advocated in England by the celebrated jurists Blackstone and Mansfield. Jefferson and the Virginians, on the other hand, thought it a matter of fundamental importance to keep the settled common law, which reached nine-tenths of the disputes before the courts, untroubled and uncorrupted by questions of equity. "This proportion then of our rights is placed on sure ground. Relieve the judges from the rigour of text law, and permit them, with pretorian discretion, to wander into its equity, and the whole legal system becomes uncertain. This has been its fate in every country where the fixed, and the discretionary law have been committed into the same hands." He recognized the dangers of the Court of Chancery, dispensing justice where the common law gave no relief, but thought they might be guarded against, as by the introduction of jury trial, and that they were less than the dangers to be apprehended from opening the common law courts to discretionary justice. The opinion was thoroughly characteristic of him. He wished always to bind judges, legislators, and executives to the fixed letter of the constitution and the laws, and where this was impossible always to keep the exceptions from spoiling the rules. The principal defect of the judicial system set in motion in 1778 arose from the inability of the General Court rapidly to dispose of all the business that crowded upon it. Even so the course of justice was several times speedier than in lazy colonial days. The bottleneck would have been avoided had the assembly not eliminated Jefferson's provision for assize courts as accessories to the General Court. The problem was overcome a decade later by the establishment of district courts.

Jefferson's name is omnipresent in the legislative history of Virginia during these formative years of statehood. He headed the committee of the House that brought in a fresh proposal for the settlement of the long disputed western boundary with Pennsylvania. For three successive sessions he was the protagonist of the House in a quarrel with the Senate over the asserted power of the latter to alter or amend money bills. Where there were bad feelings between rival factions Jefferson was the conciliator. In 1777, for example, he was appointed a committee of one to bring in a bill settling the terms of appointment of delegates to Congress, an issue that had embittered the Lee and Harrison factions. He remained on good terms with Governor Henry, who turned to him for counsel and assistance on matters too delicate to discuss openly, such as the attainder of Philips and George Rogers Clark's first expedition above the Ohio. He drafted and reported bills on every conceivable subject: the outfitting of soldiers and sailors, prices chargeable at grist mills, regulations for smallpox inoculation. He was responsible for the plan to move the capital from Williamsburg to Richmond, thus inaugurating the westward migration of the seats of government of many states. As he failed in several of his great enterprises, so he failed in a number of small ones; but these too reveal his mind and his hopes. He proposed to establish a state postal system, supplementing the national one, with a postmaster general, postriders and postroads running east and west across the north-south line of Congress, all with the view to promoting "the more general diffusion of public intelligence among the citizens of this commonwealth." He proposed a state system of vital statistics, a matter formerly in the hands of the parish clergy. But the assembly showed little interest in either of these measures.

Perhaps he attempted too much too soon. Disappointed by mindless and selfish opposition to reform, he had need of the philosophy commended to an impatient cohort a dozen years later: "the ground of liberty is to be gained by inches . . . we must be contented to secure what we can get from time to time, and eternally press forward for what is yet to get. It takes time to persuade men to do even what is for their own good." What he sought, most of all, was to create a more favorable public climate for the freedom and happiness of his countrymen. In order to create, it was first necessary to destroy—feudal holdovers, aristocratic privileges, the religious establishment. But Jefferson was not a happy destroyer and the balance of his effort was on the constructive side. Freedom was many things —suffrage and representation, land and mobility, education and learning—all interwoven in his republican design.

His creed, of course, was the simple philosophy of human rights of the Declaration of Independence. He had no Platonic conception of the perfect society. He had no thought of overthrowing the past and legislating for man as if he were just emerging from the state of nature. The Lockian idea of government originating in contract from that primitive state, while a useful fiction in the consummation of the Revolution, was rejected as a rule of action in the work of reconstruction. "For the nation was not dissolved, was not annihilated; its will, therefore, remained in full vigor: and on the establishing of the new organs, first of a convention, and afterwards a more complicated legislature, the old acts of national will continued in force, until the nation should, by its new organs, declare its will changed." The problem, then, was to save what was good and to reform what was bad in the received institutions. Jefferson worked for realizable goals, which is not to say that practicality was his standard but rather that he kept the needs and conditions of his own country in view and adjusted his principles and objectives to what, in his opinion, the society could sustain. His confidence in the reforming power of law was great, too great, in fact, for he expected much more from laws promoting the alienability and equalization of property, to cite one example, than they could accomplish apart from fundamental social change. He was a creature both of history and of reason. Either could lead him astray, and did; but as long as these two lights of truth converged steadily in his mind, bringing fact and logic, the actual and the ideal, the past and the future, into the alliance he found particularly congenial, the results were likely to be brilliant. It may be misleading to label him liberal or conservative, democratic or aristocratic, radical or moderate, for he was all these things in degrees and in different contexts. He called himself a Whig, which is the historical term, in America, that best describes his political outlook. He was a Whig, however, in a revolutionary situation, when there was both the opportunity and the determination to embody principles in the foundations of a new experiment. Embarked in this way, exalting reason, striking at privilege, opening rights, and releasing talents, Jefferson's direction was inescapably democratic in the line of American progress.

During Jefferson's three years in the Virginia assembly, the future of American independence was being decided in the camps and on the battlefields east of the Potomac and in the regal courts of Europe. General Washington led his tattered and beaten army from the heights above New York City across New Jersey to the rolling farmlands west of Philadelphia; then, after two desperate years when the question was not one of victory but of survival, Washington pursued the enemy back to New York and again camped his army on the bluffs above the Hudson. Nothing had been lost, only time had been gained. Jefferson kept himself posted on the ravages and fortunes of the war as best he could. During the bleak winter of Valley Forge, his friend John Harvie, who was with Congress some miles further west of Philadelphia, occupied by the British, told him of "the avarice and disaffection of the people here," "the shivering limbs of our poor naked soldiers," and "an almost universal discontent in the Army." "The waste of the enemy wherever they move is a scene of cruelty and distress," Harvie gloomily reported. If Jefferson was downcast by these things, he never admitted it. He was cheered by the surrender of Burgoyne's army at Saratoga, and when it was followed five months later, in February 1778, by the consummation of the French Alliance, he put aside any doubts he may have had for the outcome of the war.

Partly because of his optimism on this point, it never occurred to him that he served his country any less than the generals, the congressmen, or the ministers abroad by choosing a modest station suited to his public talents. He enjoyed a full life during these years, never long or far from his fireside, and free to indulge his intellectual curiosity. Twice annually, in the spring and in the fall, he journeyed to Williamsburg for the meetings of the assembly, which consumed perhaps four or five months of a year. His attendance was regular except when his wife was ill or expecting. She presented him with his first and only son in May 1777. He died, unchristened and unnamed, after three weeks of life. On August 1, 1778, "at 1 o'clock and 30 minutes A.M.," as he precisely noted in his prayer book, his third daughter, Mary, was born. Called Maria, or, affectionately, Polly, she grew to maturity with her sister Patsy, six years older. Jefferson's anxiety for his wife's recovery kept him away from the House of Delegates until the end of November, when he was brought in under the custody of the sergeant-at-arms. Of course, his public business was not confined to sessions of the assembly. Most of the work on the Revision of the Laws was done in his own library and could not have been done anywhere else. As county lieutenant of Albemarle he was responsible for the militia, for the recruitment and draft of regular soldiers, and, for a time, the supervision of prisoners-of-war lodged in the county. But these were minor duties. For the most part, while not in Williamsburg, he was the dutiful husband and father, the master of Monticello, and the student of everything that rubbed the surface of his mind.

Building, landscaping, and other improvements at Monticello continued to absorb him. He could not do as much as he would have liked because of wartime scarcities of labor and material. His attempts to recruit a house joiner, stonecutter, and other workmen in Pennsylvania failed. Despite these difficulties he was laying brick at Monticello almost from the moment he returned from Philadelphia. He began stocking his park with deer and drew the finished plan of his orchard, already well advanced. One of the local casualties of the Revolution was the experiment in Mediterranean fruits and viniculture started in 1774 by the middle-aged Italian immigrant, Philip Mazzei, whom Jefferson had enticed to settle on an adjoining property. Mazzei had planted his exotic vines and trees, imported Italian laborers, and planned an agricultural company, all with Jefferson's ardent patronage. In the fall of 1778 he brought from Colle, Mazzei's place, several shoots of a dying orange tree, one of a dead olive, and nursed them with the devotion of a true horticulturist. Not much else remained of the promising experiment. Now Mazzei was departing on a mission to his native Tuscany to raise money for the American cause he had made his own. This experiment, too, was doomed to failure.

"Tho' much of my time is employed in the councils of America I have yet a little leisure to indulge my fondness for philosophical studies," Jefferson wrote to an Italian correspondent and friend of Mazzei's, Giovanni Fabbroni. He wished to exchange information that would provide "a comparative view of the two climates," suggesting his method of taking daily high and low temperatures at Monticello. Mazzei and his friends had excited Jefferson's interest in things Mediterranean. He hoped the United States might cultivate trade and friendship with these sun-drenched countries, and receive from them workmen skilled in both agriculture and the fine arts. "I believe that had our country been peopled thence we should now have been farther advanced in rearing the several things which our country is capable of producing," he wrote to Lee in Congress. Other ventures were less speculative. Thus the critical shortage of salt in the early years of the war caused Jefferson to interest himself in a project to extract salt from sea water by means of large iron pans, which he had manufactured by his friend, the ironmaster Isaac Zane, in Frederick County.

On June 24, 1778, he made observations on the eclipse of the sun, a major astronomical event. At Williamsburg, as he learned from observers there, the eclipse was total. "Lightning bugs were seen as at night." It was not so dramatic at Monticello; the day was cloudy, and besides he had no timepiece he could depend on. All of which prompted him to write to David Rittenhouse, in Philadelphia, reminding him of his promise to make for Jefferson an accurate clock, "which being intended for astronomical purposes only, I would have divested of all apparatus for striking or for any other purpose, which by increasing its complication might disturb its accuracy." The belief that there was a correlation between the simplicity of a thing's construction and the accuracy of its purpose, it might be noted, was not limited to Jefferson's opinion of clocks. Rittenhouse was an ingenious mechanic, who had constructed a mechanical model of the solar system, commonly called the Orrery, which Jefferson greatly admired. (His bill to reform William and Mary in 1779 included provision for the Board of Visitors to engage Rittenhouse in the construction of "so great an ornament of astronomical science.") He thought Rittenhouse "the greatest of astronomers" and stood in awe of him. Imploring the astronomer, who was a good Whig, to shun affairs of state, he remarked, "No body can conceive that nature ever intended to throw away a Newton upon the occupations of a crown." It was a worshipful letter, conveying the sense of a man who felt himself in touch with greatness, the greatness of scientific inquiry, which Jefferson prized above any other.

Another letter, written in May 1777 to John Adams, marked the beginning of a brilliant epistolary dialogue. Again it is significant that Jefferson took the initiative, reaching out in this instance to a statesmen he admired and a man whose republican heart beat in unison with his own. Adams was then chairman of the Board of War in Congress, and Jefferson wrote to him matter-of-factly on subjects within his purview. He spoke of the needlessness and oppressiveness of a compulsory draft of soldiers; he repeated a suggestion earlier made to Adams in Philadelphia for closing the breach between the large and the small states on the delicate point of representation in the confederate government; and he urged "speedy and frequent communication of intelligence" from Congress. The primitive state of public intelligence troubled Jefferson throughout the war, and long after the war. Delays in printing the journal of Congress caused uneasiness, he told Adams. "In our assembly even the best affected think it an indignity to freemen to be voted away life and fortune in the dark." The postal system also required attention. "Our people merely for want of intelligence which they can rely on are become lethargic and insensible to the state they are in." Adams received Jefferson's letter ten days later in Philadelphia, as if to prove the point. Replying on the same day, he dealt with each of Jefferson's complaints in his characteristically open way, concurred in them, and closed with a warm appeal to "come and help us." "We want your industry and abilities here extremely. . . . Your Country is not yet, quite secure enough, to excuse your retreat to the delights of domestic life. Yet, for the soul of me," he added poignantly, "when I attend my own feelings, I cannot blame you."

No one blamed him then, but it is significant that Adams, and probably others, viewed Jefferson's station as more a private than a public one and was vaguely disturbed about it.

Early in 1779 Jefferson was diverted from his accustomed rounds by the arrival in the neighborhood of some 4000 English and German prisoners-of-war, the remains of the army Burgoyne had surrendered at Saratoga, commonly known as the Convention Army. Quartered for a year in the environs of Boston, the troops had been a heavy drain on the food and fuel supplies of the New England metropolis and a tempting prize to the British fleet cruising off shore. Congress ordered their removal to the area of Charlottesville. In the dead of winter, marching 700 miles over "break-neck roads," experiencing hardships of every description, the troops at last reached their destination, "the climax of all bad things," in the middle of January. Charlottesville, "this famous place we had heard so much of, consisted only of a Courthouse, one tavern, and about a dozen houses." The officers scurried about the countryside to find houses to rent. The soldiers were quartered on a wooded hill overlooking the town. "When they first reached here," wrote a German officer, "they found a few buildings, barracks *in name*, but *in fact*, nothing but some logs laid one upon another, without any covering, and the snow three feet deep on the ground." The barracks were to have been ready, but the unusual snows had scattered the workmen. No stores of bread had been laid in, much of the meat refrigerated in the ground had spoiled, and for days the troops made a diet of Indian corn. The populace round about gave a stony welcome to these Royalists and "dogs of Royalists," the Hessians, and feared that the want of provisions would create a dangerous situation.

The conditions and the spirits of the troops gradually improved, however. They finished the barracks, each consisting of a single room 24' x 14', built without windows and with precious few nails, adding chimneys and other improvements, caking the chinks between the logs with the orange-red mud of Albemarle—336 of these cabins, twelve in a row, four rows making a square, seven squares ranged across the top of the hill. Unfortunately, the weather was more freakish than usual during the early months of the year. After the heavy January snows, the weather turned mild, even warm, in February—peach trees and cherry trees put on their blooms—reverted to freezing cold in March, turned mild again, and wound up its crazy gyrations on April 17 with a blizzard that "totally blasted the forest and caused untold loss and hardship." Undaunted, the Germans sowed seed in the spring, and soon neatly trimmed and paled gardens, said to attract visitors from sixty miles around, adorned the tree-stumped hill. It was all very delightful, Jefferson thought. "There is little doubt that their own gardens will furnish them a great abundance of vegetables through the year. Their poultry, pigeons and other preparations of that kind present to the mind an idea of a company of farmers rather than of a camp of soldiers." The English, meanwhile, built a church and makeshift theater. "Having thus found the art of rendering captivity itself comfortable," as Jefferson observed, the troops seemed quite satisfied with their situation.

The officers made themselves as comfortable as possible in the places they had rented, often from Virginians who would sooner have the hard money rents than their own roofs over their heads. One of the articles of the Saratoga Convention provided that the officers were not to be separated from their men. This proved advantageous, for the officers not only cared for the needs of the troops but gave an honorable assist to the Virginia regiment of guards in the enforcement of discipline. Major General William Phillips, the British commanding officer, lived at Blenheim, Colonel Landon Carter's estate, while Major General Friederich von Riedesel, his German counterpart, with family in tow, rented Colle from Mazzei. Baroness Riedesel was a spirited trooper, affectionately known to the Brunswickers as "Madame General." She rode a horse astride, playfully sang Italian arias in exchange for farmers' butter, and fretted endlessly about Virginia rattlesnakes, wood ticks, and thunderstorms. Finding Mazzei's modest dwelling too small for his family— there were three young daughters—the Baron had a larger one built nearby. He kept the fields in production and set out his own gardens. "Very soon we wanted nothing," the Baroness noted in her charming memoirs. Jefferson later said that Riedesel's horses destroyed in one week what was left of Mazzei's vinicultural labors, "which from every appearance, would in a year or two have established the practicability of that branch of culture in America." Actually, most of the destruction seems to have been done by the horses of several British officers who briefly tenanted the place before the Riedesels' coming; and it is doubtful that Mazzei's experiment would ever have proven itself.

The hospitality enjoyed by the English and German officers at the seats of Virginia gentlemen suggests a kind of international community among men of rank and breeding that even the hatreds of war could not abate. Jefferson despised royalty and its trappings, but he was charmed by Phillips, Riedesel, and their like. He opened his doors to them, entertained them, loaned them books, tried to make them comfortable in the strange and primitive country they inhabited. There was a studied politeness in these relationships. Public questions were never discussed. Music was the happy *divertissement* when the Europeans were guests at Monticello. "As all Virginians are fond of Music," a German officer wrote home, "he is particularly so. You will find in his house an elegant harpsichord, pianoforte, and some violins. The latter he performs well upon himself, the former his lady touches very skillfully and who," he added, "is in all respects a very agreeable, sensible and accomplished lady." An English staff officer who played violin duets with Jefferson called him "one of the best amateur violinists" he ever knew. The opportunity to play with others, to make an ensemble, was rare at Monticello, and Jefferson must have made the most of it while it lasted. In writing to Fabronni, he wondered if it would not be possible to locate skilled tradesmen in Italy, where music was cultivated by every class, who would migrate to Virginia and who, in addition to serving as cabinet makers, stonemasons, and so on "could perform on the French horn, clarinet or hautboy and bassoon, so that we might have a band . . . without enlarging . . . domestic expenses." But the closest he ever came to realizing the dream of a "domestic band of musicians" was in 1779 with the captives he treated as guests.

The guests appreciated Jefferson's kindness and did what they could to repay him. One of the German officers, on departure, left to him all his music. Of course, the general officers entertained him in their temporary homes. On April 11 the following note was addressed to him from Blenheim: "Major General Phillips sends his Compliments to Mr. and Mrs. Jefferson, requests the favour of their company at dinner on Thursday next at Two o'clock to meet General and Madame de Riedesel. Major General Phillips hopes Miss

Jefferson will be permitted to be of the party to meet the young
Ladies from Colle." Sometime later, when Jefferson was Governor
of the sovereign state of Virginia and Phillips was commanding His
Majesty's forces there, he contemptuously addressed the Governor
as "Thomas Jefferson, Esquire." Jefferson was properly offended.
But nothing harsh or rude disturbed this beguiling interlude of
courtesy and civility in the midst of war. "The great cause which
divides our countries is not to be decided by individual animosities,"
Jefferson wrote to Phillips. "The harmony of private societies cannot weaken national efforts. To contribute by neighborly intercourse and attentions to make others happy is the surest way of
being happy ourselves."

Jefferson was not simply voicing an ideal of personal conduct; he
was also seeking to refute the proposition that between nations at
war "humanity was kicked out of doors." No sooner had the prisoners arrived than many Virginians called for their removal. They
were 4000 more mouths to feed out of the state's stock. They were
enemies in the bowels of the country. But Jefferson, when he
learned in March that the Governor was considering the removal of
all or part of the troops, indignantly opposed the measure in a
lengthy and carefully reasoned letter to Henry. Still another forced
removal of the Conventioners would be a breach of faith, he said.
He pointed to the financial rewards of the prisoners' presence in Albemarle, recommended a sensible plan of provisioning, expatiated on
their health and happiness, countered fears on the point of security,
and so on. Above all, he emphasized humanitarian considerations. "It
is for the benefit of mankind to mitigate the horrors of war as much
as possible." Applying the principle to the case at hand, his argument was unanswerable. The Convention Army was left undisturbed for the present. Over the next two years, however, he would
realize what a gossamer thing were the cosmopolitan sentiments of
humanity and philosophy in a country at war, and he would be
forced to approve what he had so vehemently disapproved in his address to Henry.

CHAPTER FOUR

War Governor

Certainly it must be a happy Climate, since it is very near the same Latitude with the Land of Promise. Besides, as Judea was full of Rivers, and Branches of Rivers; so is Virginia: As that was seated upon a great Bay and Sea, wherein were all the conveniences for Shipping and Trade; So is Virginia. Had that fertility of Soil? So has Virginia, equal to any Land in the known World. In fine, if any one impartially considers all the Advantages of this Country, as Nature made it; he must allow it to be as fine a Place, as any in the Universe; but I confess I am asham'd to say any thing of its Improvements, because I must at the same time reproach my Country-Men with a Laziness that is unpardonable. If there be any excuse for them in this Matter, 'tis the exceeding plenty of good things, with which Nature has blest them; for where God Almighty is so Merciful as to work for the People, they never work for themselves.

Robert Beverley, The History of the Present State of Virginia, *1705.*

THE GENERAL ASSEMBLY elected Jefferson Governor of Virginia on June 1, 1779. John Page, then at the head of the Council of State, was his principal rival for the office, though as Jefferson hastened to assure his old friend, "it was their competition, not ours," and the margin of victory was "too insignificant to give you a pain or me a pleasure had our dispositions toward each other been such as to have admitted those sensations." Nor were Page's feelings any different. His political strength lay in the tidewater, where he was a prince among planters; while Jefferson succeeded to Patrick Henry's following in the interior; but neither man was a creature of section or of party, and Jefferson's political course brought him into ever-increasing conflict with Henry. The "Forest Demosthenes," having completed the three consecutive terms allowed by the constitution to Virginia's governors, retired for a time to the seclusion of his modest estate Leatherwood. He remained a power to be reckoned with, however, as Jefferson was to discover before his governorship ended.

Honored by the office, Jefferson had no taste for it. He knew how far the duties of the chief magistracy of Virginia must break in upon his domestic happiness; yet he knew too that the public's claim on his services could not rightly be denied. "In a virtuous government, and more especially in times like these," he wrote to a friend, "public offices are, what they should be, burthens to those appointed to them which it would be wrong to decline, though foreseen to bring with them intense labor and great private loss." His election accurately measured his prominence in the state, and in view of his accomplishments both in Congress and in the assembly, his elevation to the state's highest office was as logical as it was merited. He was in Williamsburg at the time, having taken his seat in the House of Delegates early in May. He did not seek the governorship, but neither did he attempt to dissuade the friends who were active on his behalf. When formally notified of the assembly's decision, he responded with characteristic modesty. "My great pain is, lest my poor endeavours should fall short of the kind expectations of my country. . . ." This was one of the pleasantries the occasion demanded; it was not a confession of feebleness. And yet, if Jefferson paused at the threshold of the governorship, wracked by doubt, it can easily be forgiven him. Hitherto his abilities had been exhibited in the legislative chambers of the Revolution. Only now were they brought to the test of executive leadership in a crucible of foaming discord and disaster.

The Revolutionary War had entered a new and ominous phase. The British commander in chief, Sir Henry Clinton, unable to destroy General Washington's army in the North, determined to "unravel the thread of rebellion from the southward." Savannah fell to the British in December 1778, Augusta a month later, and in May the redcoats probed the defenses of Charleston. How far Clinton meant to pursue this strategy remained to be seen, but it broke upon the Virginians with lightning swiftness on May 10. A British fleet under Admiral Sir George Collier sailed into Hampton Roads, landed 1800 troops, which seized Portsmouth, raided the surrounding country, burned several towns, captured 130 vessels, destroyed 3000 pounds of tobacco and quantities of military and naval stores, and after sixteen days of plunder and ravage, returned to their ships and sailed back to New York without the loss of a man. Collier boasted, "the whole trade of the Chesapeake is at an end, and consequently the sinews of rebellion destroyed." Not since the departure of the Royal Governor's fleet in 1776 had Virginia been set upon. Surprisingly, in view of Collier's extraordinary success, nearly eighteen months were to pass before she was invaded again. Clinton was not yet ready for Virginia. The Carolinas must first be conquered. An early, hesitant probe of the strategy that would make the Chesapeake the principal theater of the war, first by disruption of supply lines, finally by conquest, the Collier expedition was a foretaste of things to come. The commonwealth, meanwhile, sped all possible assistance southward in the hope of defeating the enemy there.

"I see no better purpose to which they can apply their army in America," Washington sadly reflected on the enemy campaign in the South. The British had centered their operations in the North for three and one-half years, yet the southern states were more vulnerable on almost every count. And Virginia, the richest and largest of all the states, was the epitome of the whole. If instruction were needed on the defenselessness of her situation, it was furnished at Portsmouth. Chesapeake Bay and the several broad rivers emptying into it invited an enemy superior at sea. By blockading the bay at its mouth, the enemy could shut up the trade in tobacco which was the lifeblood of the state's economy. The rivers were navigable far into the interior, giving easy access to the principal towns and estates. Jefferson was convinced "that our only practicable defense was naval," but so ill-conceived and wasteful was the state's work in this sphere that he concluded six weeks after taking office, "we should be gainers were we to burn our whole navy" and start over. Virginia's naval investment exceeded that of any other state. Yet her total force consisted of three ships and a brig, mounting sixty-two guns altogether, four armed galleys, and a few boats, all badly cared for and chronically undermanned. Adequate naval defense was beyond the state's means in 1779, if indeed it was ever attainable, and Jefferson could only look, somewhat wistfully, to the aid of the French fleet.

The prospect on land was not much better. From the long, exposed coastline, the low country stretched upwards to 150 miles toward the Blue Ridge, with scarcely hill or vale to break its surface. Rivers and forests provided the only natural defenses against the marchings of armies. In the mountains and on the frontiers far beyond, there was the constant menace of hostile Indians aided and abetted by the British at Detroit and Pensacola. As Jefferson summed up the situation in 1780: "While we are threatened with a formidable attack from the northward on our Ohio settlements and from the Southern Indians on our frontiers convenient to them, our eastern country is exposed to invasion from the British army in Carolina." After subtracting the Ohio country, ceded to Congress in 1781, Virginia dwarfed the United Kingdom in size, and the more exposed portion east of the Alleghenies was as large as all New England. Thinly dispersed over this vast surface was an agricultural population estimated at something in excess of one-half million inhabitants, of whom approximately four in ten were slaves. The slaves were submissive, though a zero quantity at best in the reckoning of military strength. Among the whites were still a few Tories, pocketed in the Chesapeake region and in the mountains; but far more serious than Tory disaffection was the general languor of a rural populace, accustomed to peace, jealous of authority, and unmindful of danger. Habit alone would bring them to their senses, Jefferson later reflected, "a habit which must be purchased by calamity, but cannot be purchased too dear."

The defense of the country rested on the militia. Organized by county, the militia enrolled every able-bodied freeman between the ages of sixteen and fifty, with certain exceptions. While Jefferson was Governor it numbered fifty thousand. If the whole of the militia, including several thousand in the remote Trans-Allegheny counties, were distributed across the land east of the mountains it would have furnished but one makeshift soldier to the square mile. Supposedly like so many Cincinnati, militiamen rushed from the fields at the sound of alarm, then resumed their peaceful occupations after the suppression of danger. They were required by law to furnish themselves with arms, but most of the serviceable arms had been sent out of the state and, as a rule, only the mountain men—sharp-shooting riflemen—were well armed. "It is a melancholy fact," a Virginian wrote after the invasion of Portsmouth, "that there were not arms enough to put in the hands of the few militia who were called down . . . of which those which were to be had, a great number were not fit for use." Whether armed or not, untrained, un-disciplined militia, strangers to battle, ebbing and flowing like the tides, were no match for British regulars. Excessive reliance on militia was vociferously denounced in Congress and the camps of the Continental Army. Jefferson was quite aware of the militia's short-comings, but it was easier to denounce the system than to embody a sufficiency of regular troops for the state's defense. At the beginning of the contest, the state had done so. "Finding, however," as Jeffer-son explained, "that the dangers of our being invaded became less, our legislature made a tender of these battalions to the continental service." The ranks of the eleven Virginian battalions in the Conti-nental Army were but two-thirds full in June 1779, and recruits were desperately hard to find. Without a respectable force of regu-lars in the state, except for the regiment of guards at the Charlottes-ville barracks, the Governor was under constant pressure to fill up the Continental Line and succor the states to the southward. For the defense at home, there was only the shadow army of the militia.

The state's plight stemmed in part from acute financial disorders. Virginia had early embarked with Congress and the other states on the experiment of paying for the war with paper money. "I think nothing can bring the security of our continent and its cause into danger, if we can support the credit of our paper," Jefferson wrote in 1777. But depreciation had already set in, and by the time he be-came Governor the situation was desperate. The government's need for funds rose steadily. The presses printed more and more bills. As the volume swelled, their buying power diminished. The paper could not be maintained as legal tender, on a par with gold and sil-ver; so in May the assembly bowed to the inevitable and lifted all penalties for discounting the state's paper. Currency inflation under-mined the government's credit, soaked up its purchase funds, bred disaffection among soldiers and civilians alike, and let loose all the mean arts of pecuniary fraud and chicane. "The inundation of paper money appears to have overflowed virtue," one Virginian commiserated in June, "and I fear will bury the liberty of America in the same grave."

Virginia was not lacking in economic resources, but no application of them stemmed the torrent of depreciated paper. Her citizens were deeply averse to paying taxes to support a war originated in opposition to taxation. Light as the tax burden was, the habit of delinquency quickly took hold. Half the counties failed to meet their tax obligations in 1779. The amounts assessed steadily increased, but not as rapidly as the currency in which they were paid depreciated. Thus the government's revenue always lagged behind its needs. In May the legislature resorted to taxation in specifically enumerated commodities, but problems of collection and transportation were enormous. "Taxation is become of no account," Jefferson declared in June. At this time he hoped to realize substantial revenue from two statutes he had initiated in the assembly. The Land Office Act provided for the sale of western lands, partly with the aim to "increase the annual Revenue, and create a Fund for discharging the Public Debt." Five months later Congress bowed to the demand of the landless states and strongly protested this act. By holding out the prospect of "savage freedom" on the Ohio, it was wildly charged, the Virginia law "afforded both an asylum and a temptation for desertion." Some pointed to the increased burden of frontier defense exacted by the law. Untold thousands moved west and many who stayed home made fortunes in land warrants; still the finances of the state continued to deteriorate. Equally disappointing was the act of June 4 confiscating the property of British subjects. The statute remained on the books until 1784, but four months after its passage Jefferson advised the legislators to cast their eyes elsewhere for funds. The pleadings allowed by the courts were blocking the law's effects, "throwing the subject into a course of legal contestation which . . . may not be terminated in the present age."

Jefferson had once thought that public solvency could be secured by one of two steps: "Either to procure free trade by alliance with some naval power able to protect it: or, if we find there is no prospect of that, to shut our ports totally to all the world, and turn our laborers into manufacturers." Freed from British shackles, Virginia's tobacco entered the ports of France, Spain, Holland and their possessions in the West Indies. Tobacco brought hard money, and the sinews of war flowed from the trade. The French alliance of 1778 held the promise of naval protection. As already noted, however, the trade of the Chesapeake was easily bottled up by the British, and the risks of capture at sea were high. The tobacco trade was not enough. In June the new governor saw no escape from financial disaster except by "a plentiful loan of hard money." To secure loans, the government contracted with commercial agents abroad and sent special emissaries of its own, like Philip Mazzei, whose project to obtain assistance from Italian princes Jefferson had warmly supported. But nothing was accomplished. There was thus no alternative, as Jefferson saw it, even without a formal embargo, to the development of domestic manufacturers.

The weaving of cloth, the tanning of leather, the forging of iron, the making of gunpowder—simple manufactures of this kind made rapid strides in Virginia during the war. Jefferson took a keen interest in them. He embarked on a particularly ambitious enterprise at the outset of his governorship: the establishment of a large public arms factory on the James River. As he explained the plan to Benjamin Harrison, Speaker of the House of Delegates: "The depending on the transportation of arms across an element on which our enemies have reigned, for the defence of our Country, has been already found insecure and distressing. The endeavors of five years aided with some internal manufactures have not yet procured a tolerable supply of arms. To make them within ourselves, then, as well as the other implements of war, is as necessary as to make our bread within ourselves." The assembly authorized him to contract with the French firm of Penet, Windel & Company to build and operate the factory for the state and also to cut a canal around the Great Falls at Richmond in order to open navigation between the factory's site at Westham and the lower James. The project failed, mainly because the French government barred the emigration of munitions workers. The public foundry already at Westham turned out arms and munitions, though not at all on the scale envisioned by Jefferson's plan. Virginia remained dependent on outside sources of supply, not only for arms but many other articles of manufacture as well. Had transportation overland from the north been more convenient, or at sea less perilous, the situation would have been tolerable. Unfortunately, little reliance could be placed in either.

The system of government was badly designed for the exigencies of war that accompanied its revolutionary birth. Recoiling from the horrors of monarchy, the framers of the Virginia constitution had created a weak executive bridled by the legislature. Annually elected by the General Assembly, and rigidly separated from it, the chief magistrate was enjoined to "exercise the Executive powers of Government according to the laws of the Commonwealth; and . . . not, under any pretense, exercise any power or prerogative by virtue of any Law, statute, or Custom of England." The Governor could not very well rise above the level of the legislature; and nearly everyone agreed that the legislature of 1779 was not the equal of the body that brought on the Revolution and established the government. It was more democratic but less able, larger but less experienced, more complaining but less constructive. In addition, the constitution required the governor to work hand-in-glove with the Council of State. He could not make appointments, grant pardons, call out the militia except on advice of the eight-man Council. In a very real sense, the Council *was* the executive power, with the Governor merely its head. Almost invariably in executive matters, Jefferson spoke in the first person plural—the executive "we" not "I". Executive control over the cumbersome administrative apparatus was also limited. Military and commercial affairs were superintended by the Board of War and the Board of Trade respectively. Both were appointed by the assembly, an arrangement productive of confusion and delay since they must necessarily act under the executive. The Governor commanded the militia and relied on the local officers in the counties for its efficient functioning. In military as in civil administration, the government was decentralized, in conformity with the facts of geography, economics, and social organization.

Strength, energy, and dispatch, such as the times demanded, were simply not built into the Virginia government. The same could be said of the new governments in the sister states, for all were founded on Whig principles. The executive was usually the creature of popularly elected legislative bodies; and in this regard the Virginia executive was neither the weakest nor the strongest. But whether a wartime governor was weak or strong depended less on the constitutional powers of his office than on the political temperament he brought to it. George Clinton and William Livingston, governors of New York and New Jersey respectively during most of the war, gained reputations for vigor and resourcefulness. Their powers exceeded those of the Virginia governors, and allowance must be made for the greater compactness of the societies they represented, as well as for the almost constant presence of the contending armies; yet their personal inclinations toward forceful leadership probably counted for more. Jefferson's inclinations ran to the contrary. It would be exceedingly difficult for him to supply the kind of personal leadership that alone could overcome the deficiencies of executive power in the Virginia system. While no admirer of the frame of government, his objections at the time he became governor did not touch on the question of executive powers. A firm Whig, he believed in the strict separation of powers, the popular will embodied in the legislature, the supremacy of the constitution and the laws. Soon after he retired from office, he had reason to reflect on a proposition, first put forward in 1776 and later revived, to create a wartime dictator in Virginia. His impassioned denunciation of the scheme suggests his conception of the governor's office. "One who entered into this contest from a pure love of liberty, and a sense of injured rights," he wrote, "who determined to make every sacrifice, and to meet every danger, for the reestablishment of those rights on a firm basis, who did not mean to expend his blood and substance for the wretched purpose of changing this matter for that, but to place the powers of governing him in a plurality of hands of his own choice, so that the corrupt will of no one man might in future oppress him, must stand confounded and dismayed when he is told, that a considerable portion of that plurality had mediated the surrender of them into a single hand, and, in lieu of a limited monarchy, to deliver him over to a despotic one!" He thus took his bearings from the republican principles of the Revolution.

The Case of Governor Hamilton

Such was the state of affairs when Jefferson, sanguine and undismayed, took up residence in the Palace he had visited as a youth in

174

the days of the Royal Governors. His wife and daughters stayed at The Forest until in the August doldrums they all returned to Monticello. Family housekeeping commenced at the Palace in September. It was hardly on a palatial scale, and would be even less so when the government moved to Richmond the following April.

Jefferson had sponsored this move in the second year of the Revolution, chiefly on the grounds of the greater security and centrality of Richmond. The assembly finally and reluctantly consented just after his election. As grandly conceived by Jefferson, the new capital was to occupy six large public squares, each with a handsome edifice of brick brilliantly porticoed. But none of this work had even begun in 1780. Richmond, picturesquely set upon the hills above the murmuring cascades of the James, was a sleepy village of about 1800 inhabitants. "It is indeed a lovely situation," wrote a young lady unhappily transplanted from Williamsburg, "and may at some future period be a great city, but it will at present afford scarcely one comfort of life." Wishing to be as comfortable as possible, Jefferson rented perhaps the most elegant establishment in town—a brick house and garden on Shokoe Hill. There he brought his family, servants, and household goods—forty-nine boxes containing books, furniture, chandeliers, china, pictures, etc.—on a cold day in April, and there he remained with but one brief respite at Monticello until the government was forced to abandon Richmond a year later.

The work of the Governor involved the multitudinous details of countless transactions. The promulgation and execution of the laws, relations with Congress, Indian affairs, the care and exchange of prisoners-of-war, public works such as the gun factory and the lead mines, trade, taxes, purchasing and disbursement of funds, the raising of troops and the ordering of militia, naval affairs, fortifications, logistical support of the army—all these matters and others unmentioned occupied the Governor more or less constantly. As a rule, decisions were made "in Council." Jefferson met with the Council regularly at ten o'clock in the morning, laid the day's business before it, then proceeded to carry out the Council's actions. Clerks were employed to keep records and copy official letters, but the Governor, meticulous on all points of form and system, performed a large share of the drudgeries of the office.

The arrival in Virginia of a military escort bearing Sir Henry Hamilton and other British captives of Colonel George Rogers Clark's momentous conquest of Vincennes in the Illinois country at once confronted the new governor with a delicate problem. Hamilton's reputation for infamy had gone before him. As the Lieutenant Governor of Detroit in command of British operations in the Northwest, he had made formidable alliance with the Shawnee, Miami, and other tribes, and incited savage warfare on the distant Virginia frontier. "The Famous Hair Buyer General," Clark labeled him. He was a prize captive, and Clark, a state officer under state orders, sent Hamilton with part of the captured garrison to Virginia that they might receive the justice due them. At length, after a horrendous journey of three months through 1200 miles of wilderness, most of it on foot, the prisoners reached their destination, Chesterfield Court House. There Hamilton and his principal accomplice, Captain Guillaume La Mothe, were mounted, handcuffed, and marched to Williamsburg. Arriving on the evening of the next day, Hamilton later reported, "We were conducted to the Palace where we remained about half an hour in the Street at the Governor's door, in wet cloaths, weary, hungry, and thirsty, but had not even a cup of water offered to us." A jeering mob gathered, then followed them to the jail, where a tiny cell already inhabited by five common criminals and another of Hamilton's accomplices, Phillip Dejean, awaited them. "The next day," to continue Hamilton's account, "we three were taken out about 11 oClock, and before a number of people our handcuffs taken off and fetters put on in exchange—I was honored with the largest which weighed eighteen pounds eight ounces." Thus put in irons, they were further ordered by the Governor and Council "confined in the dungeon of the publick jail, debarred the use of pen, ink, and paper, and excluded all converse except with their keeper."

This cruel and unusual punishment embroiled Jefferson in a prolonged controversy. Despite the trouble it caused him, he seems never to have regretted the executive's action and always took full responsibility for it. The vengefulness of his feelings toward Hamilton may appear strangely out of character, particularly in view of the humanitarian plea he had recently made on behalf of the Convention prisoners; but those feelings were enmeshed in Jefferson's anxiety for the West, and when viewed in this context they are not so surprising.

In Jefferson's eyes British power in the Northwest presaged a dangerous extension of the Province of Canada and, more immediately, threatened the very survival of the new Virginia counties in Kentucky. The agent of this power was the Lieutenant Governor of Detroit. No doubt he took orders from the London government, but under his agency, the Indians, often with Tory troops, terrorized the Ohio frontier. Such was the destruction wrought by "the infernal rage and fury of those execrable Hellhounds" that in the summer of 1777 the Kentuckians withdrew into two garrisoned towns, and dared not venture forth to plow their fields or cut wood or herd cattle without arms. Dreadful atrocities were reported, and the Indians took scalps by the score to Detroit. "No people could be in a more alarming position," Clark said.

A native of Albemarle, Clark had settled in Kentucky in 1775. The following year the frontiersmen chose him to represent their claim to the protection of the government at Williamsburg. He was successful in this mission: the Kentucky settlements became an organized part of Virginia. But Clark realized the hopelessness of Kentucky's situation while the British held sway above the Ohio. The capture of Detroit was the obvious solution. As a first step in this ambitious enterprise, he formed the idea of conquering the towns in the Illinois country to which British power flowed from Detroit as along the fingers of a great outstretched hand. In the fall of 1777 he again journeyed over the mountains to lay his plan before the authorities in Williamsburg. Governor Henry favored the proposed expedition, declining, however, to hazard its chances by submission to the assembly or, on the other hand, to take full responsibility for it. He therefore called a council of three "select men," of whom Jefferson was one. How well Jefferson knew Clark is uncertain, but he instantly saw in this hardy and intrepid frontiersman a born leader of men—the hoped for savior of the West—and he gave himself wholly to Clark's bold enterprise. If successful, it would secure Kentucky, strengthen Virginia's disputed claim to the Northwest, open the Ohio River to trade with the Spanish at St. Louis and New Orleans, invite settlement beyond the mountains, and prepare the way for the decisive stroke on Detroit. What a leap forward of Jefferson's westering vision of an "empire of liberty"! In January 1778, Clark received his secret instructions. Money and supplies were placed at his disposal, and he was empowered to raise a troop of volunteers, allegedly for the defense of Kentucky. Jefferson and the others privy to Clark's true objectives gave assurance that the conquerors of Illinois would be rewarded with liberal grants of land.

Proceeding to Pittsburgh to assemble boats, ammunition, and supplies, Clark then descended the Ohio to the falls (the present-day site of Louisville), established a fortified base nearby, and from there embarked on the river with 170 men. At Fort Massac the troops landed and marched eighty miles to Kaskaskia. They took the town by surprise on July 4. Cahokia and the lesser villages in the vicinity soon fell; and in August the American flag flew over Vincennes on the Wabash nearly 200 miles to the east. None of these towns was defended. They were chiefly populated by Frenchmen, who generally welcomed the Americans and far outnumbered the few British officers and soldiers. The French used their influence to wean the Indians from their new allies, the British, telling them that their old father, the King of France, had come back to life and wished the tribes to make peace with the Big Knives. By bluff and cunning diplomacy at Kaskaskia, Clark won over several of the more powerful chiefs. "The British cause lost ground daily . . . ," he wrote, "and in a short time our influence over the Indians extended to the River St. Joseph and the lower end of Lake Michigan." Gloom descended with the winter snows, however. Supplies ran low. Hamilton's agents were once again among the Indians, and in December he retook Vincennes with a mixed force of regulars, redmen, and French volunteers. Clark's situation was desperate. "We saw but one alternative," he said, "which was to attack the enemy in his stronghold." Calculating the obvious madness of an attack "through a drowned country in the middle of winter" to catch the enemy off-guard, Clark resolved to try it after learning that Hamilton had sent his Indians to the Ohio preparatory to the spring campaign. He set out with his men on February 8. The unusual warmth of the season had turned the country into a veritable marshland. Alternately wading and marching for sixteen days "through difficulties far surpassing anything we had ever experienced," Clark came in sight of Vincennes on February 23. The town welcomed the Americans and joined in besieging the fort. It surrendered after a fight of eighteen hours, giving up seventy-nine prisoners and quantities of stores. Hamilton sought generous terms of capitulation from Clark, such as had been allowed to Burgoyne's army at Saratoga, but in vain. In effect, if not in law, he was forced to "surrender at discretion." His honor wounded, suffering Clark's contempt and the taunts of the victorious militia, Hamilton had yet to taste the dregs of the cup of humiliation at Williamsburg.

The Council of State publicly condemned the prisoner-of-war as a kind of war criminal. He was placed in irons because, in words that were doubtless Jefferson's, "They find that Governour Hamilton has executed the task of inciting the Indians to perpetuate their accustomed cruelties on the citizens of these states, without distinction of age, sex, or condition, with an eagerness and activity which evince that the general nature of his charge harmonized with his particular disposition." Proclamations and other papers implicating Hamilton seemed to place this point beyond reasonable doubt. But having established Hamilton's zeal in the incitement of Indian warfare, Jefferson and his colleagues went on to conjure up the demoniacal monster, The Hairbuyer, of the frontiersman's frightful imagination. The only witness actually to appear before the Council was one John Dodge, a native of Connecticut who had become an Indian trader in Detroit before the Revolution and, at its outset, been imprisoned by Governor Hamilton for disloyalty to Great Britain. Escaping two years later, he published at Philadelphia a sensational account of his captivity, and subsequently journeyed to Williamsburg to revenge himself on Hamilton, Dejean, and La Mothe. "They will be hanged without redemption," Dodge vowed. Despite the highly questionable character of Dodge's testimony, the Council accepted it and proclaimed its truth. Indeed, the Council's indictment of Hamilton was founded on little more than frontier opinion and rumor and the treacherous testimony of John Dodge.

Jefferson did not often allow his feelings to dictate to his judgment, but the celebrated case of Governor Hamilton exhibited the fault. He always justified the Council's action on "the general principle of National Retaliation." The original order, which was published in the *Virginia Gazette* and widely circulated, contrasted the British treatment of American prisoners-of-war, "savage and unprecedented among civilized nations," with the "moderation and humanity" practiced by the Americans. Since the British had apparently learned nothing from the American example, the time had come to try another method of persuasion. The Detroit butcherers were "fit subjects to begin on with the work of retaliation." Apparently the Governor was not aware of the improvement that had recently occurred in the lot of American prisoners. In any event, conscious of his own feelings of humanity and revolted by British "enormities," whether on the frontier, in Portsmouth, or in the pestilential holds of prison ships, Jefferson seemed convinced that an example of retaliation in the case of so distinguished an officer as Governor Hamilton would produce salutary effects. This was the official justification of his conduct, and Virginians applauded the courage of the example. Undergirding it, however, were considerations that could not be stated officially. Jefferson was closely identified with Clark's Illinois campaign. Its objectives were, in his view, of first importance both militarily and politically. They were realized beyond his fondest expectations: Virginia authority extended to the Wabash and beyond, greater security on the frontier, Kentucky's bond with the mother state strengthened. And the captive of Clark's conquest was the symbol not alone of the principal object yet to be attained but of the warfare that had brought untold suffering and sacrifice on western Americans. Was it not just as well as politic to celebrate his captivity? Had not Hamilton and his confederates forfeited honorable treatment by the betrayal of civilized warfare? Was it not imperative to take every precaution against Hamilton's escape or early parole? The new nation was playing for big stakes in the West. Jefferson would go to almost any lengths to see that they were won in the ultimate treaty of peace.

Three weeks after the spectacle at Williamsburg, General William Phillips, commander of the British prisoners in Albemarle, interceded on Hamilton's behalf. From the liberality Jefferson had shown toward him, Phillips was puzzled by the treatment of Hamilton. "I am led to imagine," he wrote, "it must have been very dissonant to the feelings of your mind to have inflicted so severe a weight of misery and stigma of dishonour upon the unfortunate gentleman in question." Unless there was mitigation of Hamilton's punishment, Phillips warned, the British would retaliate on Virginia prisoners. For the British general, the issue turned on the nice distinction between prisoners at *discretion* and prisoners on *capitulation*. Assuming for the sake of argument that Hamilton was the beast depicted by Jefferson, said Phillips, Clark might assuredly "have put the Lieut. Governor and every other person to the sword." But Clark granted a capitulation, "and it matters not how barbarous the disposition of the Lieutenant Governor might have been previous to the surrender, the capitulation was assuredly sacred, and should remain so. . . ." To this Jefferson answered that although Hamilton had capitulated, he had done so without any terms respecting the manner of confinement. Supposing that Phillips had not seen the straightforward surrender Hamilton had signed, Jefferson enclosed a copy for his perusal. In the usage of nations Hamilton might be a prisoner on capitulation, but he was liable to the treatment accorded prisoners at discretion, that is, said Jefferson, "gentle and humane, unless a contrary conduct in an enemy, or individual, renders a strict treatment necessary."

Jefferson at once forwarded Phillips's letter to General Washington and submitted the case to his decision. He had at first approved the Council's action, but now, on deeper reflection, thought that Hamilton's capitulation, regardless of its terms, "placed him upon a different footing from a mere prisoner at discretion." He allowed it might be expedient to continue Hamilton's confinement "from motives of policy and to satisfy our people." If so, he recommended the publication of a full and documented report of Hamilton's cruelties. No such report was ever made. Nor did Jefferson alter his opinion of the case. Washington's letter nevertheless had its effect. Hamilton's shackles were struck at once. In October the prisoners rejected paroles they thought too confining and offered, according to Hamilton, "from no other motive than to lay us open to the malice of the first informer," John Dodge. The paroles were, in fact, much more severe than those granted the Convention troops. Dejean and La Mothe soon changed their minds and accepted the paroles. Hamilton stood his ground. Meanwhile, having been taken to Chesterfield County, his health and circumstances improved. Finally, on October 10, 1780, he accepted a parole which, while still restricting his freedom of speech, permitted him to go to New York and await exchange.

By then Virginia's obstinacy in the Hamilton case seriously embarrassed the whole delicate business of prisoner exchange. Jefferson had refused to be bullied by British irons clamped on Virginia captives; he had rebuffed captive American officers paroled to Virginia in exchange for Hamilton; and only two weeks before issuing the final parole, he had informed Washington of the Council's grim determination to retain Hamilton. "You are not unapprised of the influence of this officer with the Indians, his activity and embittered zeal against us; you also perhaps know how precarious is our tenure of the Illinois country, and how critical is the situation of the new counties on the Ohio." Washington was not unaware of these things, nor was he inclined to interfere with the state's handling of Governor Hamilton. On the other hand, he was faced with the practical problem of prisoner exchange, and Hamilton had become a sticking point with the British. It was this consideration that finally forced Jefferson to retreat from "the hard necessity" he had so long felt.

All the while Jefferson kept an eye cocked on the frontier. Clark's victory at Vincennes upset Hamilton's plan for the summer of 1779 and brought a season of comparative calm to the Ohio. But Detroit, the key to peace, stood unmolested, and the Shawnee and other tribes breathed defiance of the Big Knives. Upwards to a thousand Virginia fighting men—men who became increasingly precious as the British advanced in the Carolinas—were employed in the West. The logistical difficulties were formidable. Hard money was non-existent, and the Illinois traders refused Virginia paper. Spanish New Orleans was a potential source of supplies. It could not be too much relied upon, however, because of the risks of the traffic and the tedious roundabout process of making payment on New Orleans bills with hard earned funds accumulated in France from the sale of Virginia tobacco. These troubles, combined with pressure from Congress, caused Jefferson in January 1780 to order Clark "to withdraw to the eastern [i.e. southern] side of the Ohio all the forces not absolutely necessary to sustain the spirits of the inhabitants of the Illinois, and for their real defence." Still determined to strengthen Virginia's position, Jefferson worked out with Clark a plan of operations for the succeeding summer. First, a fort was to be built near the mouth of the Ohio. The Mississippi trade would thus be secured, the neighboring Indian tribes subdued, and government firmly planted in the Illinois. Jefferson envisioned more than a military outpost. Land was promised to settlers around the fort, civil officers were to be appointed, and "a town of importance" was expected to rise. Second, Clark was to employ a force of regulars authorized by the assembly—only half the number Jefferson had wished—either in chastising the hostile tribes or in an expedition against Detroit, as circumstances might dictate. Jefferson prayed for the latter, and harder, of these alternate courses, but the Shawnee and their like, "troublesome thorns in our sides," could not be ignored. "The same world will scarcely do for them and for us," he reflected. Clark triumphed over the Shawnee during the summer. And a post, named Fort Jefferson, was established just below the mouth of the Ohio. Unfortunately, it was poorly situated for the purposes of trade and Jefferson's cautious recommendations for dealing with the neighboring tribes who claimed the land were neglected. Falling prey to hunger and attack, the fort was abandoned in June 1781.

Ardent, clearheaded, and persevering in his policy toward the West, Jefferson saw his ambitions exceed his grasp. Congress was either cool or downright hostile to Virginia's venture above the Ohio, and Virginia at this stage looked askance on congressional intervention. Faced with more pressing demands from other quarters, the state was unable to support Clark's command with the men and resources Jefferson knew to be necessary for complete success. In 1781, when the country lay stripped and naked before British arms in the East, the Governor was to make one last effort to drive the enemy from the Northwest. It was doomed to disappointment. He had finally to be satisfied with the gains already won. They proved sufficient in the final reckoning of 1783, and the entire Union became the beneficiary of Virginia arms and pioneering. The intensity of Jefferson's devotion to this enterprise antedated his governorship and had yet to show its fairest side in works of national statesmanship during three decades.

Against the Southern Thrust

One dominant force, the British thrust from the southward, controlled Jefferson's governorship. For the present Virginia was safe;

but invasion from the sea was a constant menace, and every triumph of British arms in the Carolinas brought the war closer to Virginia soil. Jefferson gauged the situation with increasing clarity. Hopes for a speedy conclusion of the war were set aside. The tempo of the executive, slow and cautious at first, quickened to the alarm, gathering energy with the acceleration of its movements. Spun upon the axis of military necessity, Jefferson struggled to perform duties for which he professed to have neither taste nor talent and, at the same time, to maintain the civilian deportment that alone suited his character and his principles.

One of his first objectives on taking office was to fill up the Virginia regiments in the Continental Army. Early in the war he had pleaded with friends at home to reconcile the defense of the state to the greater cause of the Union. Both military and political considerations recommended this course, and despite trials and difficulties, he never wavered from it. Neither was he able, however, to complete the Virginia Line according to the quota assigned by Congress. In the spring of 1779, Virginia was reported deficient one-third of its quota. The debt to the Continent was bound to increase, if for no other reason because of the expiration of short-term enlistments. Just before he entered office the General Assembly enacted legislation, which he had drafted, to meet the problem. The Governor was empowered to appoint an officer in every county to raise recruits for the duration of the war; the officers received premiums for the men they enlisted; bounties in land and money and other inducements were offered to the volunteers; and a draft was ordered in districts that failed to furnish them. Jefferson diligently implemented this measure. Every other month an officer rode "the circuit of the country" to gather the recruits. But few came forward, and the punitive draft was so feeble, distasteful, and unproductive that, Jefferson remarked, "we have not thought them worth the expense and trouble of gathering up." Supplementary acts of the assembly in the fall failed to improve Virginia's account with the Continent. It is difficult to say where the fault lay. The legislators might have offered stronger inducements: premiums and bounties figured in paper money were not as large as they seemed. The Governor could not, in the physical circumstances of Virginia, have ridden the circuit to rouse volunteers, even assuming his character admitted such activity.

Perhaps he might have made more effective use of influential men in the counties. But more than likely the blame, if such it was, lay in that nebulous thing, the public, whose ardor had cooled remarkably after four years of war. "But tell me," Henry queried his successor, "do you remember any instance, where Tyranny was destroyed and Freedom established on its ruins among a people possessing so small a share of virtue and public spirit?" But Jefferson's faith in the people and their attachment to the Revolution would not permit him even to entertain Henry's question, much less answer it.

Neglect of the Continental Army was not peculiar to Virginia. In fact, her record bettered that of most states. So depleted were the ranks in the fall, 1779, Washington resorted to the detestable expedient of calling 12,000 militia from nearby states. By this time, too, more urgent demands upon Virginia came from the South. "We have at present very pressing calls to send additional numbers of men to the southward," Jefferson informed Washington. "No inclination is wanting in either the legislative or executive powers to aid them, or to strengthen you: but we find it very difficult to procure men." Within two weeks, on December 9, Washington ordered the 2000 troops of the Virginia Line at Morristown, under Brigadier General William Woodford, to march to the aid of beleaguered Charleston. The Governor had legislative authority to send southward 1500 militia and as many of the state troops as could be marched under the terms of their enlistments. The latter, several small cavalry troops and a depleted regiment of infantry, were reserved for the defense of the commonwealth; but when other measures failed Jefferson used the power delgated by the assembly. He did not at this juncture order any militia to South Carolina, a last recourse in any event, and with nearly all the state's regulars marching south and west (the regiment raised for Clark's campaign) it was painfully obvious that the militia was the sole reliance for the state's defense.

Jefferson seemed less alarmed by this prospect than some others in his administration. In November the Board of War advised the Governor to expect a visit from the British in the winter months and recommended a series of defense measures. Governor and Council immediately approved most of these. The executive was cool to a plan for concentrating arms and militia in the exposed eastern counties, however, and flatly rejected the Board's call for the appointment of a general officer to direct the state's defense. "Civil bodies tho [they] may dictate to, are illy calculated to direct military ones," the Board declared. "The vigor and dispatch, necessary to military movements, can only be derived from full powers concentrated in one man. . . ." While Jefferson appreciated the merit of this position, it was one his political convictions would not permit him to endorse. Irrespective of its merits, the executive had no authority to appoint a general officer until an invasion or insurrection actually occurred and forces of resistance were organized.

An invasion seemed imminent on December 22, when Jefferson received a report, transmitted by the governor of Maryland, of a British naval expedition to the Chesapeake. Confirming intelligence reached Williamsburg some days later. Writing from Morristown on December 11, Washington advised that a powerful naval force carrying 8000 troops was about to sail from New York: "Their destination *reported* to be for Chesapeake Bay, on a combined operation in the 1st. place against the French Squadron there, and afterwards to attempt the rescue of the Convention troops." On the first report, Jefferson ordered precautionary measures, unhappily aware, with the Board of War, "that no place is defensible against a considerable force of the enemy." Defensive works were thrown up at York and Portsmouth, military stores removed from this sector, the few regulars concentrated there, recruits forming for South Carolina detained, and the Conventioners readied to march over the Blue Ridge. Jefferson deferred an immediate call for militia, pending opinion of the assembly. The procedure was unusual, suggesting some indecisiveness on the Governor's part. But for him to have called the militia in force on the mere suspicion of an invasion, founded on the first fragmentary report, would also have been unusual. Moreover, he was keenly aware of the economy wave that had swept over the assembly and seriously cut back both the land and the naval forces of the state. In addition to the expense of militia service, he was mindful of "the difficulties which attend a general call of the militia in the field, the disgust it gives them more especially when they find no enemy in place, and the extreme rigor of the season." The assembly's advice, if any, is unrecorded, and it promptly adjourned on December 24. Jefferson called a few militia

186

in the eastern counties in order, as he later said, "to convince the French of our disposition to protect their ships." For the rest, he quietly awaited the crisis. When it failed to materialize, his judgment was vindicated. Charleston, as he later learned and all along suspected, was the destination of Clinton's army. By the middle of January even "the most timid," he observed, had recovered from the panic, and the recruits marched southward.

Responsibility for the direction and disposition of Virginia's men and arms involved the Governor more or less constantly in decisions calling for the rapid assessment of numerous imponderables, for discerning judgment of military requirements and opportunities, and, above all, for an encompassing view of Virginia's commitments. These swept a wide arc from Charleston in the South, to the farthest reaches of the Ohio, and to the camps of the Continental Army in the East. Endeavoring always to employ Virginia's overtaxed resources in the best interest of the Continent, Jefferson was puzzled to determine where that interest lay from one crisis to the next. Nor could he forget his first obligation to defend the state's exposed frontiers. He had made the fateful decision, in which the legislature gave him little alternative, to risk the state's defense to the militia, whose "radical defects" he knew as well as anybody. But manpower was among the least of his problems. Men could not fight unless armed, equipped, clothed, and fed; and the pesky problems of supply were as stubborn as any he ever encountered.

The shortage of firearms caused genuine alarm in the summer of 1779. Returns from the state magazines showed at most 4000 stand of serviceable muskets. The invasion at Portsmouth had once again demonstrated that militiamen called from the field went home with their weapons. The stock was further depleted by arms furnished to the Virginia Line and to South Carolina. Rumors of invasion were afloat in the summer; and so when a vessel loaded with arms for delivery to Congress "seemed to be guided by the hand of providence into one of our harbors," the Council ordered the seizure of 5000 muskets for Virginia's use. Jefferson was absent at the time, but when Congress censured the action, he warmly defended it. Virginia could, he said, establish a right to 10,000 stand of arms freely furnished, with many other articles, to the Continent. In the distress then felt, the seizure was fully justified. "They were it's true the property of our friend, but of friends indebted to us for those very articles. They were for the common defence too, and we were a part of the body to be defended." The arrival from France of three vessels ladened with arms and military stores, the acquisitions of a resourceful commercial agent, replenished the state's stock in October. So rare was the safe conduct of any goods from Europe to the Chesapeake that Jefferson asked the assembly to award the agent, Jacques Le Maire, the brevet commission of lieutenant colonel. Meanwhile, his hopes for filling the arms gap by domestic manufacture were dashed by the failure of the contract with Penet, Windel & Company. Cannon, other ordnance, and military hardware were manufactured in modest quantities at Westham and Fredericksburg, and Jefferson gave these public works every assistance, including authorization for the purchase of Negro slaves to keep them in operation. But there were never enough arms.

Other shortages plagued the government in the autumn and winter. The late harvest was "the most unfavorable . . . ever known since the settlement of this Country," Jefferson said. The wheat crop gave little more than seed for the next planting, and Virginia went begging for flour to neighboring states she usually supplied. Maryland's executive approved the purchase of 2000 barrels of flour in that state, but before most of this could be forwarded, a new governor acting under a new statute seized the flour. Jefferson, considering the need desperate, protested the seizure. "Accustomed at all other times to furnish subsistence to others," he wrote, "it is the first instance where providence has exposed us to the necessity of asking leave to purchase it among our friends." But the seizure stood. A request to Congress for large quantities of flour to supply the Convention troops also failed. Still determined to alleviate the distressing shortage and the exorbitant prices of provisions, Jefferson proclaimed an embargo on export by land or water. He exercised judgment in its enforcement, however, approving trade in provisions that benefited the commonwealth. The British island of Bermuda, for example, depended on the United States for grain and gave precious salt in return. So precious, indeed, had salt become that it was rationed to families by county magistrates and could not be carried from one place to another except under bond. Without salt there could be no meat; and in order to obtain it Jefferson kept open the

Bermuda trade. Rum was an item almost as indispensable to armies as salt. The government endeavored to supply rum. Thinking it less than a prime necessity, Jefferson practiced restraint in this regard. The law required the Governor's approval of all purchase requisitions on the state's account; thus he was almost daily occupied in the tedious business of finding suppliers, comparing prices, estimating needs, making contracts, setting priorities, scrutinizing accounts, and —the worst of all his aggravations—paying the bills.

Financial deterioration, well under way when Jefferson became Governor, rapidly passed beyond recovery and left the state prostrate two years later. He at once saw the necessity of reducing the quantity of paper money in circulation. "Every other remedy is nonsensical quackery," he declared. He was a little inclined to look for fiscal scapegoats. "It is a cruel thought that when we feel ourselves standing on the firmest ground in every respect," he wrote to Richard Henry Lee, "the cursed arts of our secret enemies combining with other causes, should effect, by depreciating our money, what the open arms of a powerful enemy could not." No doubt there were such enemies—the avaricious and the speculators, the faint-hearted and the weak-headed—but Virginia's financial plight did not require their efforts. When the returns of the tobacco trade declined, when foreign loans failed to materialize, and revenue from the confiscation and land office acts fell so far below expectations, Jefferson was put at wits' end to devise other means of bolstering the state's finances. On no other subject did he defer so entirely to the assembly. The Revolution was partially staked on the principle of "fiscal liberty," and Jefferson had no desire to contradict it by entering the most jealously guarded of all the areas of legislative jurisdiction. Unfortunately, the assembly's only wisdom, aside from sudden bursts of frugality such as reduced the state's land and sea forces in the fall of 1779, was to increase taxes and speed up the printing presses. Fresh additions to the government's revenue were promptly wiped out by inflation. Public creditors declined to pay taxes because their bills had not been paid; the government could not pay its debts with the promptness the inflationary spiral required because citizens were delinquent in their taxes. And so the vicious circle went, gathering momentum from one session of the assembly to the next. The depleted treasury, as Jefferson observed during the December crisis, "presented an absolute obstacle to every military endeavor." It was his responsibility to enforce the revenue laws. For assistance where it counted, at the local level, he depended on the county governments, which were slow and stubborn. In this area, as in others, he governed with a gentle hand, believing that the good citizenry with burdens enough already would not endure a harsh one.

The deterioration of both state and Continental currencies led Congress to adopt drastic measures of reform early in 1780. The first of these, in February, assigned to each state a quota of supplies to be collected and delivered for the Continental Army. Thus Virginia was to supply so much corn, hay, flour, and rum. The state, in return, was forgiven two-thirds of the money she had previously been asked to raise monthly. The plan substituted supplies in kind for drafts of money to supply the army. The second resolution of March 18, projecting a "new plan of finance," was a companion of the first. The states were to retire the depreciated Continental currency by means of tax collections payable at the rate of 40 "continentals" to one dollar in coin. For each $20 of the old money thus collected the state could then issue one dollar of new, which Congress pledged to redeem in coin after five years. Meanwhile, Congress would print no money, relying on state supplies. Obviously, the plan required the full co-operation of the states. Since the two currencies circulated on an equal basis, state bills as well as Continental had to be retired. It was a hazardous experiment. James Madison, who had just taken a Virginia seat in Congress, summed up the situation: "An old system of finance discarded as incompetent to our necessities, an untried and precarious one substituted and a total stagnation in prospect between the end of the former and the operation of the latter." Madison favored the plan but was apprehensive for its success and deeply troubled by Congress' surrender of the one real power it had over its own affairs. So long as Congress exercised the power of issuing currency, the government had a margin of independence from the states. Now, as Madison explained to Jefferson, that was gone. "Since the resolution passed for shutting the press, this power has been entirely given up and they [Congress] are now as dependent on the States as the King of England is on the Parliament. They can neither enlist pay nor feed a single soldier, nor execute any other purpose but as the means are first put into their hands." Unless the states rose to the occasion, the tottering edifice of Union would fall in ruins.

Jefferson, too, was apprehensive. "The period . . . which will intervene between abolishing the old and establishing a new system of finance, will be distressing to the last degree," he observed. In the House of Delegates the plan met with strong opposition led by Patrick Henry, now back in harness. It was "repudiation," Henry charged. Under his influence the House defeated implementing legislation. But after he took leave of the assembly, the bill was revived and passed by a small margin, with the condition that its operation be suspended until a majority of the states enacted similar legislation. The condition was satisfied, as Jefferson had hoped, before the enemies of the plan could overturn it at the fall session. Unfortunately, it did not abate the twin evils of inflation and depreciation in Virginia. In order to see the government through the transition period, the assembly authorized another large issue of the old currency, thus at once cheapening the new. Balances still owed to Congress continued to drain the treasury. In May Congress urged payment in the amount of $1,900,000 so that the Army might be put on a footing to co-operate with the French forces soon to arrive. Jefferson made strenuous efforts to comply and by June 30 had scraped together nearly three-quarters of the total. As Madison had predicted, since the ability of the people to pay taxes derived from the sale of their commodities, the requisition of the latter made the former more difficult than before.

Virginia was already launched on the experiment of taxation in kind. The Provision Law enacted by the General Assembly in May 1779 assessed every white male of sixteen years of age or older and every female slave of like age the annual payment of one bushel of wheat, the equivalent in other grain, or twenty-eight pounds of tobacco. The repugnance of the tax, combined with problems of collection and storage and transfer, made the law, with its successors, an administrative nightmare. Jefferson probably did not welcome Congress' resort to the same expedient, though it sharply reduced Virginia's dollar payments. The state's compliance with the supply requisitions of Congress necessitated new executive powers. The assembly authorized the Governor to appoint commissioners in the counties to search out and purchase provisions at stipulated prices. The commissioners might break down doors, exact penalties for hoarding, and seize supplies. They were to hire, and if need be seize, wagons, boats, and men for transporting provisions. Congress left the states to struggle as best they could with the problem of moving the supplies to the armies. In Virginia it proved to be a task of Sisyphus. Jefferson assured Congress of "the strongest disposition" to contribute the quotas assigned but, though provisions were collected, he could not promise their delivery. "Transportation by land has been little practiced in this country. We have therefore few wagons, and a great part of these have been lately drawn to the southward. Transportation by water has been cut off for some time by the privateers which have been constantly cruising in our bay. . . . To them are added at present eight [enemy] frigates . . . In this situation nothing can venture out of our rivers." Some weeks later, on July 27, Jefferson was unable to say precisely what part of the quotas had been furnished, but he confessed disappointment at the state's performance.

Men, money, supplies: these were the items of account with the Continent. After summarizing the state of the account for the President of Congress in July 1780, Jefferson reflected on the circumstances that had prevented full and timely compliance. "It will doubtless occur," he wrote, "that some of these requisitions were difficult in their nature, that others were new in experiment, and all of them on as large a scale as the people think themselves equal to. In states more compact, experiments, tho' new, and difficult, are made with promptitude, their defects soon discovered and readily supplied. In those of greater extent they are carried into execution with less vigor and punctuality, and the time for complying with a requisition expires frequently before it is discovered that the means provided were defective. The time necessary for convening the legislature of such a state adds to the tardiness of the remedy, and the measure itself is so opppressive on the members as to discourage the attempting it, but on the last emergencies." Perhaps he was too much inclined to find fault with circumstances; but he spoke from hard experience and what he said was undeniably true.

While the Governor labored at these tasks in the early months of 1780, the British to the south grew stronger and still other enemies threatened in the southwestern part of the state. Indians of the Cherokee nation lived in settlements stretching for hundreds of miles along the Virginia and Carolina backcountry. Most of the Cherokees were "friendly," as a result of treaties forced upon them in 1777. Others withdrew to the Chickamauga River where, under the haughty chief Dragging Canoe, they started new towns, and assisted from the British posts in Florida, took to the warpath. They were badly punished by a joint expedition of North Carolina and Virginia in the spring of 1779, but violence flared again a year later. Jefferson ordered an expedition under the command of William Campbell to attack the hostile towns, and at the same time asked Clark's co-operation from Kentucky. Well aware of the frontiersmen's aversion to all Indians—"the only good Indian is a dead Indian"—Jefferson was anxious to protect the friendly Cherokees from harm. The state incurred much trouble and expense to supply them with clothing, liquor, and other scarce necessities. "Their present distresses are so great," Jefferson said, "that we have bought up every thing proper for them in our own country without regard to price." By purchasing their friendship, he hoped to defeat the machinations of British agents. He urged the same policy on the governors of the Carolinas. "The attachment which each settlement will by these means acquire to the particular state under whose patronage it is, perhaps will be a bond of peace, and will lead to a separation of that powerful people." Divide and rule, aid the friendly in peace, exterminate the incorrigibles—this was Jefferson's Indian policy. And in 1780 he wanted by every means possible to minimize the costly diversion of Virginia's manpower to Indian warfare. He was but partially successful. Before the attack on the Chickamaugas could be carried out, British agents prevailed on the chiefs of the old towns to resume their war-like ways. Retaliation was swift, as Virginia and Carolina backwoodsmen destroyed the towns in December 1780. Thereafter the danger lessened, but it was not extinguished.

More dangerous was the spirit of disaffection and insurgency that erupted in the southwest at this time. "Nothing can produce so dangerous a diversion of our force, as a circumstance of that kind if not crushed in its infancy," Jefferson wrote to Clark in the spring. Trouble had flared in the area before, but it now assumed a threatening aspect from the progress of British arms in the South, which rallied the disaffected and raised the prospect of Tory uprisings along a wide front. The disturbances centered in Montgomery County, whence came the lead for the bullets of American guns. William Preston, head of the Montgomery militia, alerted Jefferson to the conspiracy. As many as fifteen of the insurgents were operating under British commission, he said. Their principal object was the lead mines. Jefferson commended Preston for the measures he had already taken to capture the ringleaders, urged him to employ only legal means, and suggested he call new recruits from the vicinity to guard the mines. By July, however, the conspiracy had spread to several neighboring counties. Jefferson now ordered Campbell to forget the Chickamauga for the present and combine his force with the militia Preston had summoned to "take in hand these parricides." The border captains sent spies among the conspirators, discovered the plot before it could be sprung, and took captive about 60 men. Jefferson advised leniency toward the small offenders, if repentant, and prosecution of the ringleaders for high treason. He had nothing further to do with the proceedings in the case, which were sufficiently notorious to enrich the language with the euphemism "lynch law," derived from Charles Lynch, manager of the lead mines, who took a leading part, and also to cause the legislature later to pass an act of immunity for Lynch, Preston, and others who had suppressed the insurrection. An open insurrection, which must have been very damaging at that place at that time, was thus averted at a heavy price. The discontents that fed insurgency increased with the war's hardships until they became a factor in all of Jefferson's calculations.

Three days after he commenced his second term in office, Jefferson learned of the fall of Charleston to Clinton's army. The disaster, which actually occurred on May 12, was not unexpected, but coming on top of a mountain of troubles, and after he had strained every resource to help the city, he found it the least welcome event of the war. Public morale fell to a new low. The people grumbled at taxes and inflation, suspected everyone of growing rich but themselves, and in the spring elections exchanged many delegates of rank and experience for new men promising better things. The government was still recovering from the upset of its removal to Richmond. The boards of war and trade, handicapped by the move, ceased functioning in April. The General Assembly at its May session formally abolished these administrative monstrosities and, "for conducting the public business with the greatest expedition," authorized the Governor to appoint a commercial agent, a commissioner of the navy, and a comissioner of the war office. By other acts as well, the legislature seemed impressed with the need to strengthen and streamline the executive. It stiffend the Governor's powers to procure and transport provisions, authorized him to restore the navy it had dismantled six months before, and gave him a number of "extraordinary powers" in case of invasion or insurrection. While encouraged by these measures, Jefferson was disappointed by the failure of the legislature to meet the full request of Congress for militia and regulars to join the Southern Army.

The surrender of Charleston swallowed up nearly the whole of the Virginia Line. "There is really nothing to oppose the progress of the enemy northward but the cautious principles of the military art," Jefferson advised the commander in chief. Before the end of May, General Cornwallis crossed the Santee River with an army of 4000 men, steadily augmented as it advanced by recruits among the native inhabitants, who were the more susceptible to British intimidation as the hopes of American arms faded. North Carolina had neither the guns to arm nor the food to subsist its militia in the field. Jefferson concentrated his efforts, first, on forwarding the Continental troops of Maryland and Delaware detained on their march to Charleston, fortunately as it turned out, for want of wagons; and second, on assembling the force of 2500 militia that the legislature had now authorized for service in the Carolinas. On June 11 Jefferson informed Washington that the total force "in and about to be in motion" to oppose Cornwallis numbered 10,000 men; but the bulk of it was raw Virginia and North Carolina militia deplorably armed and accoutered. "Your Excellency will readily conceive that after the loss of one army our eyes are turned towards the other, and that we comfort ourselves that if any aids can be furnished by you without defeating operations more beneficial to the general union, they will be furnished." But this was poor comfort indeed. Congress could send no more than token assistance southward, and Washington dared not risk the further depletion of his army in the North. Later in the month, when Clinton returned to New York, Jefferson perceived Washington's embarrassment, "being situated between two fires," unable to attend to the new one in the South lest the old and still larger one in the North escape control. It became painfully evident that Virginia must shoulder the burden of southern defense.

The fact that Charleston was in enemy hands twenty-four days before news of the event reached Richmond pointed up the seriousness of the communications gap. Jefferson had already set up a team of express riders, stationed at intervals between the Virginia capes and Richmond, to speed intelligence of the long awaited arrival of the French fleet. (As it happened, on July 11, the fleet sailed into Rhode Island rather than Virginia.) The lamentable delay and unreliability of intelligence from the southward suggested the same remedy on a larger scale. To gather and transmit proper information from the vicinity of the enemy camps, Jefferson sought a sensible and judicious person with some knowledge of military affairs. He turned to a young acquaintance, James Monroe, who had served bravely and well in the Continental Army, left it for mysterious reasons, and then, after a period of deep perplexity and despair, commenced the study of law under Jefferson's tutelage. Believe me, Monroe wrote to him some months later, "I feel that whatever I am at present in the opinion of others or whatever I may be in future has greatly arose from your friendship." Jefferson's offer of a confidential mission precisely suited to his young protégé's talents and ambitions strengthened the bond between them, and thus had a significance far outrunning the mission itself. Jefferson directed Monroe to proceed southward from Richmond, stationing riders at forty-mile intervals to the vicinity of Cornwallis's army, from thence transmitting anything of military import, and opening channels of communication to commanders in the field and heads of government. At the same time, he arranged with Congress for the northern extension of the express line to Philadelphia. Monroe's first dispatch reached Richmond within forty-eight hours, which clipped five days off the time normally required by the post. Riders were sometimes negligent to the point of treachery, and commanders in the field unco-operative, but the express line largely fulfilled Jefferson's expectations. Congress was grateful for his innovation, and at the end of June undertook to maintain the full line at the expense of the Continent.

Unfortunately, no good tidings came from the South. Congress placed General Horatio Gates, the somewhat tarnished hero of Saratoga, in command of the Southern Army. Soon after arriving at headquarters the middle of July, he reported that the condition of the army was even more distressing than Jefferson had led him to expect. Only 1500 of the promised Virginia militia were on the scene; many were without arms, tents, and other necessities; all were obliged to forage for food. Jefferson attended to Gates's needs as best he could and congratulated him for advancing on the enemy. But the advance was more daring then wise. With a ragged and untried army numbering about 3000 men, Gates encountered Cornwallis at Camden on August 16, and was utterly crushed. One-third of the Americans were killed, another third captured, and the remainder, Gates at their head, fled in wild disorder. A more complete defeat could hardly be imagined. Jefferson was particularly disheartened by the behavior of the Virginia militia, as reported in vivid detail by its commanding officer, General Edward Stevens. On first fire the enemy charged with bayonets; the militia panicked and ran like a torrent, bearing all before them. "Their cowardly behavior has indeed given a mortal wound to my feelings," Stevens said. "I expect that near one half of the Militia will never halt till they get home." Stevens's mortification deepened when the stragglers, after being rounded up and ordered forward again, deserted in great number, as if to prove "they never had any intention of rendering their Country service." Jefferson refused to lose heart. "Instead of considering what is past . . . ," he philosophized to Stevens, "we are to look forward and prepare for the future."

In this spirit he returned to the arduous task of rebuilding the Southern Army. Fully realizing the difficulty of stopping the enemy in North Carolina, he knew it would be infinitely more difficult, and painful, to wage the combat on Virginia soil. Determined to act with all the vigor the laws permitted, he ordered the impressment of provisions, wagons, and other essentials; he pleaded with county lieutenants to arrest militia deserters, try them at court-martial, and exact the legal penalty of eight months' duty as regular soldiers; and he called for 2000 militia reinforcements to march south with new levies of Continental troops at the earliest opportunity. Jefferson told Washington nearly 7000 regulars and militia had been ordered from Virginia. But this was on paper. The number who actually marched fell well below the 5500 Jefferson, with his usual optimism, had counted on. Even so, many of the Virginians went south in an atrocious condition, and logistical support was as precarious as ever despite resourceful measures to overcome the bottleneck in transportation. "Sickness, Death, and Desertion," Gates repeatedly warned, "must certainly be the dire result of sending troops into the field" so badly equipped. "I must beg Sir this may be seriously consider'd by the Executive, whom I must request, will not send any men into the field, or even to this camp, that are not sufficiently clad, well furnished with shoes, blankets, and every necessary for immediate service, as I have not a single article here to supply them with." Jefferson patiently replied that adherence to this rule "would amount to a stoppage of every man." If the General wanted soldiers he would have to take them raw and ragged. Gates did not blame Jefferson for the situation; in fact, he thanked him for the "great care and assiduity" he showed. It was difficult to know who to blame. Jefferson refrained from blaming anyone. He sent the troops on, meanwhile trusting that Congress would eventually respond to his pleas for support.

For the rest, good news mixed with bad. At the beginning of October he cheered Clark's devastating blow to the Indians on the Ohio and, a few days later, the backwoodsmen's gallant victory over a joint force of British and Loyalists at King's Mountain, which aroused the flagging patriotism of North Carolina and sent Cornwallis hustling to safe quarters. Encouraged by Clark's success, Jefferson turned his thoughts once again to the long-deferred campaign against Detroit. To the south, time, at least, had been gained. But what of the eastern frontier? In September Gates had forwarded intelligence obtained from British deserters of a plan concerted between Cornwallis and Clinton to invade Portsmouth. Jefferson thought it most unlikely Clinton would provide the men for such an expedition, especially when the French could send a superior fleet to the Chesapeake; but he at once transmitted the report to Congress, observing that should the enemy "in this, as in so many other instances, go directly contrary to the principles of reason, they would find us in a condition incapable of resistance for want of small arms." Reason being a poor reliance in warfare, he would have felt more secure had the French fleet decided to pass the winter in the Chesapeake. But Washington, to whom he made this suggestion, assured him it was impossible: the enemy had blocked up the fleet at Newport since its arrival and, contrary to the Governor's opinion, continued its superior. Meanwhile, Washington informed him of an embarkation preparing in New York and bound, it was thought, either for Virginia or the Carolinas. Jefferson felt no more alarm at this report than at Gates's earlier one. He still thought an invasion improbable; if attempted, nothing could stop it, so he took no precautionary measures, except to employ an engineer attached to the Southern Army, Colonel John Christian Senf, in the long-term project of surveying the country of the lower James with a view to improving defensive capabilities there.

Senf was well along in this work when, on October 20, an enemy fleet stood in for Cape Henry, and during the next two or three days discharged its force of infantry and horse, commanded by Major General Alexander Leslie, on either side of the James River estuary. The army was first thought to number 5000 men, about twice its actual size. Jefferson learned of the invasion from General Thomas Nelson, who commanded a tiny corps of Virginia regulars on the lower James. "I hope you will lose no time in ordering a body of men down, that we may at least attempt an opposition," he pleaded. "I shall endeavour to collect a force from these counties, but the confusion is so great that much cannot be expected . . . . I never was in so bad a part of the Country for intelligence. The enemy might have secured every pass before I had any account of their landing." On receiving this report, which accurately conveyed the defenseless and bewildered state of the invaded country, Jefferson roughed out a breathless agenda of executive action: "Call on Lawson's troop of horse. . . . Call 10,000 troops. viz. . . . . Stop troops going on to Southward . . . Call vessels and stores from Ship yard . . . Provide batteaux at Foundry . . . Order away Conventioners . . . Beeves from Warm Springs come to Barracks . . . Officers . . . . Commrs. of provision law . . . Stores etc. at Wmsburg . . . Write to General Nelson Gates Congress. . . ." Obviously, Jefferson assumed the enemy would move up the James. Great numbers of militia were called, but his main reliance was on the militia and regulars already assembled and destined for the Southern Army. They were reluctantly, and temporarily, diverted to the task of driving the invaders back to their ships. "On this contemptible naval force," Jefferson wrote, "hangs the fate of an army; and yet contemptible as it is . . . it does not appear to be in danger."

While the enemy was thus unchallenged at sea, the want of arms, also of cavalry, checked effective opposition on land. Because the Convention troops furnished "perpetual fuel to that smothered fire," disaffection, and now a tempting object to the invasion army, Jefferson sought their removal to Maryland. (Only the more dangerous British troops were actually moved at this time.) As October gave way to November, no encounter, no action of any consequence occurred. The plains of Virginia spread like a brown carpet before the redcoats, but they showed no appetite for conquest and settled instead at Portsmouth. "Their movements have been truly incomprehensible," Jefferson noted with a trace of exasperation. "I rather believe that Lord Cornwallis had expected to have been in this state at this time, that they were intended to join him here; that his precipitate flight has left them without an object, and that they wait for further orders." Events soon verified Jefferson's hunch. Clinton had sent the expedition to the Chesapeake with the intention of establishing a permanent post, creating a diversion in favor of Cornwallis, disrupting the Virginia supply lines to the Southern Army, and rallying the disaffected on the lower James. But when Leslie learned of Cornwallis's retreat after the crippling blow at King's Mountain, he sent south for further orders. When they arrived about the middle of November, he embarked his whole force for Charleston. "But this is an end of all golden dreams in Chesapeake," Clinton sighed in New York.

Leslie's abortive expedition proved either the soundness of Jefferson's military sense or the weakness of the enemy's in the fall of 1780, but he took no comfort from this. It once again exhibited the defenseless state of the tidewater country, which the British could exploit at their convenience. With Leslie's departure the Governor returned to the principal business of reinforcing the Southern Army. As he did so, he gave the General Assembly a shrewd estimate of military prospects. "This event tho' relieving us in a certain degree by opening again the door to our commerce and also by putting it in our power to avail ourselves of the whole resources of our country, seems yet to call for an increase rather than abatement of military preparation," he said. "Should those now leaving us proceed to reinforce the hostile army already in the south: should the same be the object of a new embarcation said on good authority to be preparing in New York; we shall but too probably and speedily see our retreating enemy treading back their footsteps and menacing this country with a force to which the southern states have yet seen nothing equal. South Carolina and Georgia we are to consider as weighing nothing in our scale. North Carolina has been exhausted by the ravages of two armies. On this state therefore rests the weight of the opposition; and it is infinitely important that our efforts be such as to keep the war from our own country. Nor does it seem that we have a moment to lose, should the enemy be disposed to lose no time on their part." He concluded by asking the legislature for additional powers to procure supplies and transport, the money "to set every wheel in motion," and "men to form a permanent army."

The past several months had been wearisome to the last degree, and the months ahead promised to be worse. Since the Battle of Camden, Jefferson had been riveted to his desk, immersed in a thousand details that held no real interst for him, making plans and issuing orders that all too often crumbled at the touch of immitigable circumstance. He was uncomplaining. His sense of duty and devotion to the cause ensured that. But he felt keenly the impoverishment of his private life. He last visited Monticello in August. It was probably on that summer holiday, so harshly interrupted by the news of Camden, that he planned an ingenious contrivance for his house. "In his parlour," wrote one of the German officers, "he is creating on the ceiling a compass of his own invention by which he can know the strength as well as direction of the winds." But this was a rare pleasure. During the entire length of his governorship, Jefferson wrote scarcely a letter in which he permitted himself to indulge his curiosity on literary, scientific, and artistic subjects. He was all business. Anything in the course of executive business that awakened his slumbering intellectual interests—the running of a boundary line according to celestial observation, planning the government buildings at Richmond, securing Indian artifacts and records, purchasing for the state Diderot's *Encyclopédie*—gave him special delight. These were only crumbs from the executive table. In November a Virginia delegate to Congress placed in the Governor's hands an elaborate series of questions concerning the state of Virginia which François Marbois, secretary to the French minister, desired to have answered. "I am at present busily employed for Mons. Marbois without his knowing it," he was soon writing, "and have to acknowledge to him the mysterious obligation for making me much better acquainted with my own country than I ever was before." However, neither the leisure nor the requisite books were available to him in Richmond. He set the work aside until his retirement.

By September, not long after his last holiday at Monticello, he had decided to retire from office at the earliest opportunity. Confiding this decision to Lee, he wrote, "The application requisite to the duties of the office I hold is so excessive, and the execution of them after all so imperfect, that I have determined to retire from it at the close of the present campaign. I wish a successor to be thought of in time who to sound whiggism can join perserverence in business, and an extensive knowledge of the various subjects he must superintend. Such a one may keep us above water even in our present moneyless situation." What he meant by "the close of the present campaign" remains to conjecture. He presumably did not mean the expiration of his term of office, which ran to June, and of course he was eligible for a third term. At about the same time, he informed Page of his decision and suggested that he succeed him. Page flatly rejected the idea but could not persuade Jefferson to drop his plan. Hearing reports of it again in December, Page humored his old friend and beseeched him to stay on, not just for six months but for eighteen. "I know your love of study and retirement must strongly solicit you to leave the hurry, bustle, and nonsense your station daily exposes you to," Page wrote. "I know too the many mortifications you must meet with, but 18 months will soon pass away. Deny yourself your darling pleasures for that space of time, and despise not only now, but forever, the impertinence of the silly world." No one, unless possibly Lee, who was unpopular, was as eminently qualified for the office as he, nor was this merely a personal opinion, Page assured Jefferson. Whatever his reasons may have been, Jefferson dropped any thought of retiring in midstream and grimly resolved to stay on the job until June 1781.

Invasion

The new year began ominously. The traitor Benedict Arnold invaded the state from the coast, slashed through the low country, spreading panic as he went, and put the government itself to flight. It was a crippling blow to Virginia's morale. Some glittering military exploit was needed to revive it. Jefferson sorely taxed himself and the resources of the state in an effort to capture the perfidious author of Virginia's humiliation. All to no avail. He did not lose heart, but the fates seemed to have spiked all his guns. Even his little successes wore the face of disaster. As the energy of government increased, the more ineffectual it became, until it appeared to collapse altogether. In May, Cornwallis administered the last stroke in a long train of misfortune. The British army overran Virginia, and as if to add a crowning touch chased Jefferson within an inch of his life from Monticello, whither he had gone to escape "the impertinence of the silly world."

Leslie's expedition had in no way altered Jefferson's determination to combat the enemy outside of Virginia's borders. The state should be the arsenal, not the battleground, of the Southern Army. In this view he was encouraged by Congress, by Washington, and the commanders in the South. One of Washington's most trusted officers, General Nathaniel Greene, had been appointed to relieve Gates, who left the remnants of his military reputation at Camden. On November 16, Greene arrived in Richmond accompanied by "the Baron" Frederick William von Steuben, Inspector General of the Continental Army, assigned now to Greene's staff and ordered by him to command in Virginia "to put things in the most proper train for forwarding the reinforcements of men, and supplies of every kind to the Southern Army."

Greene and Steuben were two of the ablest officers on the Continent. Their assignment to the southern theater suggested that it was at last receiving the attention Jefferson had claimed for it. He welcomed them with the utmost cordiality and good will. Greene, a Yankee humbly born, corpulent, squint-eyed, lamed in one leg, and cocksure in his thirty-eighth year, had risen to great heights since that fateful day in 1775 when he marched the Rhode Island militia to Boston. Steuben, the Prussian drillmaster, was older than his friend, stocky in build, haughty in bearing, with soft lips, piercing dark eyes, and hair dressed in a slender queue after the manner of his former master and hero Frederick the Great. He had come to America in search of military glory, and after a period of three years spent in disciplining Washington's troops found himself, to his enormous satisfaction, one of the half-dozen top generals in rank. How little Jefferson understood either of these men, or they him, as they sat at the Council table in November! Remarkably different though they were, the two generals had much in common. In their inglorious staff positions under Washington, Greene as Quartermaster General, Steuben as Inspector General, both had aspired to line command. They prided themselves on being students of the military arts. In these matters they thought alike and had unshakable confidence in each other. Neither had any acquaintance with the southern country, so little suited to conventional rules and tactics, and they were quick to find fault with the government of Virginia. It is notable that Jefferson, despite much provocation, never found fault with either of them but, on the contrary, went out of his way to praise their talents and enterprise. He saw no more of Greene after he presented his requisition for the Southern Army and rode south to assume command. Steuben remained behind, dishing up to Virginians his "plate of *sauerkraut* dressed in the Prussian style" and hoping to prove to them, as he had earlier in the North, "by the force of 'God damns' that my cookery was the best."

Jefferson turned at once to the business of filling Greene's requisition. The assembly responded well to his appeal for an acceleration of military effort. That "last of all opppressions," in Jefferson's opinion, a draft, previously a punitive measure only, was authorized. Three thousand recruits enlisted for three years would hopefully complete the state's quota, however. Additional taxes were voted to pay the bounties; also, stiffer penalties for desertion and the harboring of deserters. Clothing, provisions, and wagons were to be obtained by a combination of purchase and levies on the citizenry. And the treasurer was empowered to emit an additional six million pounds in paper money. Jefferson seemed confident the executive could now meet Greene's requests on every article but that of guns. The state had attempted to arm its militia when necessary, he explained to Steuben, but Congress was responsible for arming Continental troops. If Jefferson wanted any instruction in the horrible poverty of the Southern Army, he received it in a typically lofty letter from Greene, expressing his shock at the wretched condition of the troops he had come to command. "Your troops may literally be said to be naked, and I shall be obliged to send a considerable number of them away into some secure place and warm quarters, until they can be furnished with clothing. . . . There must be either pride or principle to make a soldier. No man will think himself bound to fight the battles of a State that leaves him to perish for want of covering; nor can you inspire a soldier with the sentiment of pride whilst his situation renders him more object of pity than envy." A year earlier the Governor might have needed this sermon, but not now.

Steuben, meanwhile, hurried up reinforcements to Greene. There was no cause, he advised the Governor at the outset, to keep corps of regulars in the state, where no enemy was to be seen, nor bodies of militia that exhausted the state's magazines. All troops not destined for the Southern Army should be discharged, Steuben said; and this was promptly done. Complaining alternately of the insufficiency of the troops authorized and the poor provision of those actually raised, the Baron had great difficulty readying even a small detachment for the march. The executive must understand, he lectured, "the inhumanity of enlisting men and letting them die by inches." Too many of the recruits sent down from the counties were totally unfit, being decrepit old men or mere striplings. The recruiting system had operated on the principle of filling quotas rather than of furnishing fit soldiers. Some men made a profession of enlisting, pocketing the bounty, deserting, then enlisting again—an evil compounded by the assembly's fondness for short enlistments. Jefferson assisted the Baron in his attack on these abuses, but rot had sunk so deep into the system that measures to eradicate it produced costly delay and downright resistance. In other branches of military activity as well, Steuben took some of the burden off Jefferson's shoulders. With the help of his experience and forthright example, the executive set about to reform the war administration, eliminating waste and inefficiency, removing official deadwood, and appointing new and able officers to key posts. Unfortunately, no sooner had this work begun than Arnold's invasion threw everything into confusion.

Jefferson was forewarned of a possible invasion. On December 9,

Washington briefly mentioned at the end of a long letter, "I am at this moment informed from New York, another embarkation is taking place . . . supposed to be destined Southward." Steuben received the same intelligence, so similar to other reports in the previous weeks. Neither he nor Jefferson paid much attention to it. Preoccupied with the effort to support Greene, they resented any diversion to local defense. Had the Governor supposed Virginia threatened on every word of an enemy embarkation conjectured for the South, he would have had the militia constantly in the field, with disastrous results for the Southern Army.

In the present instance, the next news reached the Governor on a mild Sunday morning, the last day of the year. Twenty-seven sail of ships had been sighted entering the Virginia capes. Whether friend or foe, what force the ships carried, and what their destination might be—these things were as yet unknown. Jefferson ordered General Nelson to the lower country armed with full powers to act as exigencies should require. He informed Steuben and Benjamin Harrison, Speaker of the House, and, for the rest, awaited further information. None came until the following Tuesday morning: the fleet was British and it had advanced to near Jamestown. "From a fatal inattention to the giving us due notice of the arrival of a hostile force," he later reflected, "two days were completely lost in calling together the Militia." Always placing a high value on prompt intelligence, so singularly lacking in his crisis, he rightly emphasized the costliness of the delay; yet he might have posted the enemy's movements more carefully and made more efficient use of the intelligence he did receive.

In any event, he wasted no time on the 2nd of January. The Council met. Forty-six hundred militia were called into the field. Orders issued for removing official records and military stores to Westham, a few miles above the falls. And preparations were made for marching the remainder of the Convention troops across the Blue Ridge. The second and third of these measures were precautionary. Williamsburg was then believed to be the enemy's object. Taking full advantage of wind and tide, however, Arnold swiftly sailed up the river, destroyed the battery at Hood's intended to guard the upper James, and landed a force of 1500 at Westover, on the river's north shore where it bends toward Richmond. Jefferson was stunned. Even the elements had conspired with the enemy! "Winds favoring them in a remarkable degree," he remarked, "they almost brought the first news themselves of their movements." Richmond was the enemy's object. He ordered out the militia of the adjacent counties and asked Steuben to take command of the citizen army tumbling from the countryside to repel the invaders.

But not tumbling fast enough. On the 4th of January, two days after the first orders, only scattered militia were on the road to Richmond—more scattered at the redcoats' approach—and only 200 were in the town. The place was indefensible. Jefferson sent his wife and daughters to Tuckahoe, and at seven-thirty in the evening, as cannon announced the enemy, took his own solitary leave of the capital. He rode on horseback, was constantly active, yet managed to keep a record of his movements on scraps of paper taken out of his pocket at moments of rest. He went to Westham, stopping first at the foundry a mile below, to see that the records, arms, and stores earlier directed to these places were sent across the river. Mounting again about midnight, he rode another eight miles to Tuckahoe to look after his family. Early the next moring he returned to Westham, later crossed the river to Manchester, and there had a view of the enemy on the heights of Richmond. During the preceding eighteen hours, attending chiefly to the safety of records and stores, he had never been far in advance of the enemy. From Richmond, Arnold sent a detachment to Westham in search of stores; finding none, the troop succeeded in destroying the cannon foundry nearby. Jefferson, meanwhile, set out in futile search of Steuben. Riding up and down for two days—one horse had aready collapsed under him—he finally returned to Manchester through drenching rains and over heavy roads. Steuben was attempting to marshal the militia on the south side of the James, but the utmost confusion prevailed. He knew nothing of Nelson's movements on the opposite side, had the services neither of quartermaster nor of commissary, had exhausted his supply of arms on the militia coming in, and was frantic to discover the whereabouts of arms and stores sent off in several directions.

From the occupied capital Arnold sent a deputation to Jefferson proposing a ransom for its safety. He rejected it, of course. Arnold had neither the intention nor the capability of holding the town;

207

and after twenty-four hours, during which some houses and stores were burned, he retraced his steps to Westover. When Arnold reached there on the 7th he had completed a circuit of sixty-six miles in little more than two days and inflicted heavy damage at no expense to himself. At Westover he was reinforced by 400 troops whose transports had been separated from the main squadron off the capes. But by this time an equal force of Virginia militia was marshaled against him, and the fateful winds still blew from the east. Steuben's vigilance prevented the enemy from crossing the river. "Should they loiter a little longer and he be able to have a sufficient force," Jefferson informed Washington on the 10th, "I shall flatter myself they will not escape with total impunity." Almost at the moment of his writing, the enemy embarked on a fresh westerly wind, beating Steuben to Hood's where he had hoped to be ready for them. Informed of Steuben's approach, Arnold landed his army in the night and sent forward a detachment of 300 men. It encountered an advance party of 240 militia commanded by Colonel Clark, who had come to Richmond several weeks earlier to plan the next summer campaign in the West. Firing from ambush, Clark's men killed or wounded perhaps as many as thirty of the redcoats before fleeing from their bayonets. The next day Arnold made good his retreat down the river, landed on the 14th, and after collecting provisions around Pagan Creek marched to Portsmouth and rapidly covered himself behind barricades on the spot Leslie had abandoned.

Little ammunition had been spent or blood spilled on either side. Arnold's mission was the same as Leslie's earlier. And so far as it aimed at destroying stores and disrupting support of the Southern Army, his raid was a *tour de force*. After his return to Richmond, Jefferson gave Washington a full account of the physical damage: 300 muskets, some artillery pieces, and several tons of powder lost; quantities of clothing, artisans' tools, quartermaster's stores, including 120 sides of leather, destroyed; the boring mill and roof of the foundry consumed, but furnaces and chimneys secure; and the greater part of the papers of the Auditor and the Council of State gone. "Within less than 48 hours from the time of their landing and 19 from our knowing their destination they had penetrated 33 miles, done the whole injury and retired," he said. That the loss of records and stores was not greater was largely owing to Jefferson's diligence. But far greater were the damages that eluded his precise methods of accounting. Arnold succeeded in creating a diversion in favor of Cornwallis. Jefferson understood this, but unless he ignored the invasion, as he told Greene, he could not defeat the object. "When they came we were getting in a fair way of providing both subsistence and men. They have amazingly interrupted both operations." The militia ravenously consumed the provisions collected for Greene, tied up the meager facilities of the quartermaster, and so long as they were in the field, stopped the execution of the law for raising regular troops. Government was discredited by the invasion. Charges of supineness and neglect fell all around the Governor. Arnold's injury to the state's morale was quite incalculable. It was not so much the damage he did that hurt as it was the state's helplessness to return the blow. This slashed the tender nerve of Virginia pride, and the wound cut all the deeper because its author was the notorious traitor and parricide. Jefferson felt the humiliation, frankly conceded it, but unlike others who in losing honor lost all he did not exaggerate its importance or become demoralized in the face of it.

Against mounting difficulties, he set about repairing the losses and reopening the southern channel of men and materials. When the enemy barricaded itself at Portsmouth, the opposing force numbered 3700 men, nearly all militia, divided into three encampments: at Fredericksburg under General George Weedon for the protection of the iron works and other facilities there; near Williamsburg under the ailing Nelson; and on the opposite side of the river under Steuben until General J. P. G. Muhlenberg returned from furlough. Steuben advised Jefferson the enemy could not be dislodged, though it could be held in place. A small force would be sufficient; accordingly, the excess militia, who could not be armed anyway, should be discharged. By thus economizing on the state's defense, more men and supplies could be sent to Greene. Most stocks were desperately low in the weeks following Arnold's devastation. Of muskets, there were 3300 in service, two-thirds as many waiting repair, and only 68 in the magazines. Of shirts, shoes, and blankets, the situation was distressing to the last degree. The militia "are lousy dirty and ragged," a commander told the Governor. Ammunition stocks were all but gone. Lead, an article Virginia had furnished in great quantities to the Continent, was running dangerously low, partly from disaffection, partly from the ravages of the enemy, and a little later from the failure of the principal vein at the mines. No battle was lost for "the want of tacks," but this annoying deficiency held up the covering of wagons in February. Even money was exhausted for a time, not from any negligence of the legislature, which continued to authorize abundant issues, but from the enemy's destruction of the state's "money press." Only a single press was now available to the government, "and that has the newspapers, the Acts of Assembly, the advice and directions of the Executive, and many other things to print, so that money hardly gets its portion of time." These perplexing problems, while hardly novel, became terribly urgent toward the middle of February when Jefferson learned that Greene was retreating in all haste to Virginia.

The invasion offered instruction on a number of points concerning the state's defense. Steuben and several of the new staff officers spotted weaknesses and proposed reforms to the Governor, who was nearly always receptive, though less often able to effect changes. Colonel William Davies, a bluff, plain-speaking, and resourceful officer, in charge of assembling and equipping the state recruits at Chesterfield Court House, proved to be particularly useful. The troubles he had encountered during the invasion led him to conclude "that the former management of the military stores of this country was never adapted to the defense of it," and he soon proposed major reforms. The management of military stores was the responsibility of the Commissioner of the War Office, Colonel George Muter, a conscientious but weak administrator. Steuben, looking for the invasion's scapegoat, formally charged the Commissioner with neglect of duty, presented his case to the legislature, and forced Muter's resignation. Jefferson at once appointed Davies to the post. Given more latitude than Muter, showing more initiative and energy, Davies was to make himself indispensable in the trying months ahead.

Steuben took particular interest in a project to erect a small fort at Hood's, on a narrow, angular channel of the James, and when the work did not proceed as rapidly as expected he vented his rage on Jefferson. For sometime Jefferson had planned fortifications on each of the four principal rivers at the first points where the passage of vessels could be prevented. Priority was assigned to the James, at

Hood's. In November he informed the legislature that cannon had been removed there from the easterly posts, where they were quite useless, construction begun, and preliminary plans of the works sketched by Colonel Senf. These were submitted to the assembly, but it took no action on the proposal. After Arnold demolished the guns at Hood's and descended the river, Steuben directed Senf to finish his plans. They called for a battery of eight heavy cannon and several field pieces, blockhouse, redoubt, and barrack for a permanent garrison of sixty men, palisades, revetment, and impediments on an extensive scale. "This I insist on in the name of the United States," the Prussian thundered. "This shall be done," Jefferson promised. He must have been startled when he received Senf's request for men and materials two weeks later—10 artisans, 40 laborers, 560,000 bricks, wagons, and so on—but if he had misgivings on the state's ability to build the fortification, he kept them to himself. Labor, hard to obtain at any price, was the biggest obstacle. Steuben went to Jefferson and told him in blundering and blustering English that he meant to call a corps of militia from the surrounding counties to erect the fort or, that failing, to commandeer slave labor. Jefferson replied, "The Executive have not by the laws of this State any power to call a freeman to labor even for the public without his consent, nor a slave without that of his master." Steuben grudgingly bowed to the law upon being assured that voluntary laborers would be engaged and, he thought, made available at Hood's with the necessary materials on a specific day, February 7. The day passed and no workmen appeared. Steuben filed an indignant protest: "If Government think the work unnecessary [or if] they have it not in their [power] I have only to beg they would for my own justification give me their opinion in writing. I must beg your Excellency to consider that the shameful opposition made to the last incursion of the Enemy falls in some measure on me as the Commanding Officer in the state and I cannot but reckon it among my misfortunes to have been here at the time." Jefferson promptly gave him the explanation he demanded. The executive had not agreed to furnish the workmen at a specific time. Steps had been taken to hire both artisans and slaves, thus far with disappointing results. "Sensible that a necessary work is not to be abandoned because their means are not so energetic as they could wish them," he said, "and on the contrary that it is their duty to take those means as they find them and to make the most of them for the public good, they propose to pursue this work, and if they cannot accomplish it in a shorter, they will in a longer time."

And "a longer time" it would be. Jefferson tried first one means and then another to procure laborers. When the responsible officers failed, he turned to influential men in each of five counties surrounding Hood's, requesting them to hire the needed slaves. When this too failed ("Those who do not spare their labourers from principle will not for hire," one of the gentlemen sadly informed Jefferson), he proposed to the freemen of these counties a two months exemption from militia duty in exchange for eight days' labor. But the bargain, and a more liberal one later extended, had little appeal. Finally, Jefferson *ordered* every man of Prince George County to furnish a workman for a brief time in return for credited militia service. By then, however, the British were on the James again, and the few artisans and laborers at Hood's scampered. The fort was never finished. It might have been had Jefferson adopted Steuben's methods or come to his own final expedient at an earlier date. In this as in other matters, Steuben's arbitrary methods exacted a price he was reluctant to pay, and proceeding on characteristically sanguine expectations of public sacrifice, he had first to exhaust all voluntary remedies before resorting to the hated expedient of forced labor.

Virginia's shameful opposition to Arnold emphatically proved the error, if proof were wanting, of risking the state's defense to militia. Perhaps even the militiamen were convinced. "They have been so much harassed lately," General Nelson reported, "that they would give nearly half they possess to raise Regulars, rather than to be subject to the distresses they feel at leaving their plantations and families." Jefferson appreciated the defects of a citizen "army on paper". The disgraceful performance of the militia at Camden had instructed him further. And after Leslie's invasion he had suggested the formation of a "permanent army" to the legislature. The theory of militia—"the natural strength of a Nation, the cheapest and surest defence, on whose protection we are ultimately to depend"—appealed to Jefferson's republican feelings. He never raised his voice in the widespread and wholesale condemnation of militia. He took pride in their valorous achievements, at Saratoga, at King's Mountain and elsewhere; and where humiliation and defeat was their lot he made allowance for all the failings of leadership and arms and supply they were helpless to overcome. Nevertheless, the problems and difficulties he encountered in the wartime practice of the theory were enough to make the British yoke seem almost inviting.

Militia duty, being rather like the payment of taxes, should fall with equality and justice, which required exact returns from the officers, regular rotation, and careful bookkeeping by the Governor. Jefferson was scrupulously fair, though he could not overcome all the delinquencies of county lieutenants and field commanders. In theory, militiamen were to respond at the call of alarm and accept the lot of soldiers until relieved or discharged. But they were, for the most part, farmers with families dependent on their labors. Where did the obligation to their families end and the obligation to the state begin? Drawn into the service, they remained more citizens than soldiers and easily found excuses for returning to their firesides, which while desertion in the eyes of the law appeared in a different aspect to them. Their misfortunes were often heart-rending. A county lieutenant thus explained to the Governor why 240 of his men left the field and came home in the spring of 1781: "As meany of them who will Now have goe [back] has Not a Creature to act for them but a wife and Small Children, unavoidable they will lose their Crops and of Corse thear famaly starve." He assured the Governor that they "always Discovered the Greatest Alacrity and Zeal in our Cause," and observed "that if their Conduct is not altogether Defensible, it is not so bad but might be plead in their Excuse."

Jefferson was moved by such pleas in the name of humanity. He realized, moreover, that in the face of "murmerings almost amounting to mutinies," or of widespread desertion, it was sometimes foolish to stand on impeccable rules of military discipline. But the pitfalls of too freely temporizing with discontented militia were equally obvious. He checked his feelings and, with few exceptions, adhered to a stern and impartial course. "We are sensible that the circumstances of hardship . . . are just and have to lament that the public situation should have called such hardships into existence," he wrote typically to one petitioner, "but they must perceive that it will be vain for them to sow or plant and leave the enemy to reap." Losses of food for the camps and the sinews of war were, nevertheless, among the hidden costs of the militia system. How its costs compared with those of a regular army could not be determined, but experience exploded the idea that it was cheap. No possible mode of carrying on the war, Jefferson told the legislature, "can be so expensive to the public and so distressing and disgusting to individuals as by militia." Militiamen served for such short terms—Jefferson attempted to standardize the term at two months—that dividends of training and experience were unappreciable. They were "here today and gone tomorrow." They had to be freshly supplied each time they came into the field. And nothing was more annoying than their habit of carrying guns from the field. Jefferson repeatedly pressed officers to recover the arms, and before his term was over actually committed the anomaly of *disarming* the militia not on active duty.

Just as the theory, and the law, of the system assumed that every man furnished his own weapon, it also assumed that men were called to service in the defense of their own homes and firesides. In fact, of course, they were called to distant parts, out of the state, where they were subjected to the rigors of the continental Articles of War. Incongruously, as James Innes, a top-flight militia commander, philosophized to Jefferson, the militia belonging to the country most in danger were the least effectual in combating the enemy. "The feelings of the man, may in a fatal moment, swallow up the sentiments of the patriot," Innes said. "During my little experience in the Northern Army, I learned by observation one truth—which I ever found invariable—which was that no militia could ever be drawn from the part of the Country immediately invaded. The strong impulses on the heart . . . forever produced inactivity, but transfer the scene of war from their own doors, and the very men who before had been so tame and inactive, flew to arms with fierceness and unanimity, and were of very important service." Governor Clinton of New York, among others, also noted this paradox, and Jefferson seems to have been convinced of its truth. Within the state, at any rate, he preferred to rely on militia called from a distance. But he placed little trust in militia called to service beyond the state's borders. So he exerted every effort to send Greene regulars. Unfortunately, no sooner was the recruiting system set in motion after one invasion than it was immobilized by the next, for it could not function in any county whose militia was in the field. His hopes for escaping this vicious circle were not very high in 1781. For all its faults the country was stuck with the system, and must either cherish the militia or give up the contest.

Dissatisfaction with the militia as the state's sole means of defense was one of the reasons Jefferson convened the assembly in special session on March 1. (The call went out on January 23.) "Whether it be practicable to raise and maintain a sufficient number of regulars to carry on the war is a question," he impassively announced to the assembly. He did not seek to answer it; that was the assembly's job, but he transmitted a plan developed by Steuben for the establishment of a regular army. The assembly demurred. The treasury was empty. Legislation authorized the issuance of £10,000,000, half again as much if exigencies required, and pledged the public faith to redeem the bills in specie at the old ratio of forty to one. The act further provided that Virginia paper should be legal tender in the discharge of all debts, thus restoring the principle abandoned nearly two years before. The principle, maintaining a parity of specie and paper on a fixed ratio, had been impracticable then; it was now hopelessly so, and a fraud on creditors besides. The paper actually had less than half the legally stipulated value and was falling rapidly. Some of the consequences were described by the officer commanding the regiment of guards for the Convention troops in Winchester: "The Regiment have just received their pay at 40 to one, but it is of little value to them. Every merchant here refused to receive it for goods, and those persons who will take it demand three hundred or more for one." The problems encountered by procurement officers—commissaries, quartermasters, purchasing agents—may well be imagined. Jefferson could only listen to their troubles, throw them more and more paper that bought less and less, expand the despised alternative of impressment, and trust their ingenuity. Finally, in March, he requested the legislature to extend the time allowed for the execution of the acts of the previous session for recruiting the quota of Continental troops and for supplying the army with provisions, clothes, and wagons. The invasion had interrupted the former and so far delayed the printing and promulgation of the latter that the time set for execution had passed before it could be received in the counties. Jefferson was criticized for these delays, which were perhaps longer than necessary. He did not scruple to enforce the stiff supply act, however, having directed the county magistrates to assess the levies of wagons, provisions, and clothing at once. "While we have so many foes in our bowels and environing us on every side, he is but a bad citizen who can entertain a doubt whether the law will justify him in saving his country, or who will scruple to risk himself in support of the spirit of a law where unavoidable accidents have prevented a literal compliance with it." The assembly approved Jefferson's extra-legal actions in this instance.

Arnold had delayed everything. In December the assembly had resolved to send a special emissary to Congress beseeching immediate assistance in the form of men, arms, ammunition, clothing, and other necessities. But it was February before Benjamin Harrison, the appointed emissary, journeyed northward. "Have you cried aloud to Congress, and to *The Commander in Chief of The Army*, for succor; have they listen'd to your cry?" Gates implored the Governor. He assured the rusticated General, "I have been knocking at the door of Congress for aids of all kinds, but especially of arms ever since the middle of summer." Repeatedly called on the carpet by Greene for failure to fill his November requisition, Jefferson politely suggested that he too should take his complaints to Congress. "Every moment . . . brings us new proofs that we must be aided by our Northern brethren," he went on. "Perhaps they are aiding us, and we may be uninformed of it. I think near half the enemy's force are now in Virginia and the states south of that. Is half the burthern of opposition to rest on Virginia and N. Carolina?" His hopes now rode on Harrison's mission, not alone for military assistance in the South but also for the settlement of other serious matters: the continuation of the illicit Bermuda trade "without umbrage to Congress or the French minister," removal from the state of the 1400 German Conventioners and release from the task of provisioning the English prisoners transferred to Maryland, assistance in the transportation of a valuable cargo belonging to the state but held in Rhode Island, and the immediate shipment of four tons of powder to Pittsburgh for Clark's campaign.

Harrison skillfully attended to all this business and reported encouraging progress to Jefferson on February 19. The next day Congress voted to add the Pennsylvania Line to the Southern Army, to furnish 10,000 suits of clothes, 400 wagons, and sufficient arms and military stores. As Harrison foresaw, Congress would discover "very great difficulty in their carrying their resolution into effect, they being extremely poor and their credit but low." The problem of moving any supplies from the North, or from Europe, was illustrated by the balky cargo at Newport. It had been dispatched from Nantes on the ship *La Comité* in May 1780. The ship was taken as a British prize, then recaptured by American privateers and brought to Rhode Island, where one-half of its cargo of arms, clothing, and other military supplies was awarded to its former owner, the Commonwealth of Virginia. Informed of this odyssey in September, Jefferson directed the Virginia delegates in Congress to arrange for the conveyance of the precious cargo to Virginia. With the assistance of the French minister, it was finally loaded on a French frigate, where it still reposed in February. Jefferson expected to receive it when several French warships came to Virginia about this time but was disappointed. On April 3 Madison informed him the cargo was in harbor at Philadelphia. Realizing its "infinite importance" to the state, the delegates decided to forward it immediately by land. There arose, however, "insurmountable difficulties." The shipment got into transit near the end of April and reached the state magazines one week before Jefferson's retirement from the governorship. Such were the exasperations of "circumstances beyond his control."

On the issues of the Bermuda trade and the Convention prisoners, Harrison had little success, though the latter was finally settled to Virginia's satisfaction; but he accomplished the remaining, and in Jefferson's eyes more important, task assigned to him: the purchase and shipment of powder to Clark at Fort Pitt. As long ago as September, after hearing of Clark's devastation of the Indian towns above the Ohio, he had begun planning the next campaign in the West, with Detroit the object. "Could that post be reduced and retained it would cover all the States to the south-east of it," he wrote to Washington. Virginia could not carry out so large an enterprise unassisted. He therefore reversed standing policy and asked that it be pursued jointly with the Continent.

Various factors entered into this decision, among them the hard realities already stated. Of fundamental importance, as he suggested to Washington, was the fact that Congress was about to resolve the divisive issue of western lands on terms acceptable to Virginia. Those lands would be ceded to Congress by Virginia and the other claimant states, then disposed of for the benefit of all the people, rather than of a few speculators, and formed into new self-governing states. The cession would remove the only obstacle to the completion of the Confederation. When finally effected, as Jefferson had every confidence it would be, Virginia's lands north of the Ohio River would become the property of the Union. And the expedition against Detroit in the coming spring, as it would be for the "general good," ought to be at the "general expense." Washington at first responded coldly to Jefferson's overture but subsequently promised to furnish Clark all possible assistance at Fort Pitt, perhaps even a detachment of Continental troops. Jefferson, meanwhile, moved ahead with his plans. Recent intelligence warned of a powerful confederacy of British and Indians forming to terrorize the frontier in the spring. "Should this take place we certainly lose in the south all aids of militia from beyond the Blue Ridge besides the inhabitants who must fall a sacrifice in the course of the savage irruptions. There seems to be but one method of preventing this," he said, "which is to give the Western enemy employment in their own country." Clark came to Richmond in December, and Jefferson spent Christmas Day 1780 penning his orders, which ran to approximately 2800 words. Everything was covered in detail: the force numbering 2000, mostly crack militia from nine western counties; arms, munitions, supplies of all kinds, their anticipated quantities and locations; the times and places of rendezvous, calculated on Clark's leaving Fort Pitt no later than March 15 so as to drop down the Ohio and move up the Wabash soon after the ice broke.

But the plans, so carefully laid, went all awry. Not long after Clark left Richmond in January with a brigadier general's commission, the militia officers of three of the counties informed the Governor their men would not march. Jefferson cast about for replacements, but Clark's anticipated force steadily dwindled. The commandant at Pittsburgh, Colonel William Brodhead, a Continental officer, was jealous of Clark and threw obstacles in his path. Aside from authorizing the powder, Congress showed little interest in Clark's project. The expedition was doomed long before the sorely frustrated General set forth on the Ohio in August. Jefferson was disappointed, of course. He was right in the importance he attached to the project, not in the short-range, but in the longer course of history. The Treaty of Peace would confirm American sovereignty in the Northwest, but British power and Indian alliances were left undisturbed. Had Clark's campaign succeeded, the United States would have been spared much trouble and grief in the years ahead. Yet in 1781 that issue had almost no bearing on the question of victory or defeat in the war against Britain.

"History," General Greene wrote to a Virginia officer, "affords no instance of a nation being so engaged in conquest abroad as Virginia is at a time when all her powers were necessary to secure herself from ruin at home." Jefferson might have answered this, and other charges of "going on some wild goose Chase," by another vindication of the military as well as political soundness of aggressive policy in the West. But the argument was circuitous, and Greene could not wait for the roundabout relief it promised to the Southern Army. He crossed the Dan River into Virginia, on February 14, with Cornwallis in hot pursuit. "Unless our Army is greatly reinforced I see nothing to prevent their future progress," he warned Jefferson. The militia rallied in the southern counties. Greene gathered new strength. While Cornwallis lingered in North Carolina, he seized the initiative, recrossing the Dan on the 21st. It was a tense moment. Jefferson felt he could have been of more service to Greene at the Dan, and also better prepared to meet the enemy in Virginia, had the General kept him posted on the movements of the two armies. Not until he was in Virginia did Greene apprise the Governor of his retreat. To improve communication Jefferson sent his own confidential representative, Major Charles Magill, to Greene's headquarters. Gates had welcomed Monroe in a similar capacity; but Greene, underscoring "the necessity for secrecy," gently rebuffed the Governor and kept Magill at arm's length. Although he bore Jefferson no personal ill-will, Greene, with typical military conceit, believed the prosecution of war to be the business of generals, and he deeply distrusted the Virginia government. "I have long endeavored to impress upon the different Legislatures the impossibility of accommodating the operations of the Army to civil convenience . . . ," he lectured Jefferson on another occasion. "Indeed civil polity must accommodate itself to the emergencies of war, or the people submit to the power of the enemy." No sensible man, certainly not Jefferson, disputed the need for such "accommodation," but he insisted on the authority of civil government to determine its conditions, bounded by what a free people could accept; and this required the confidence of military commanders, as well as ultimate superiority over them. Carefully avoiding fruitless argument on so basic a disagreement, Jefferson must, nevertheless, have been affronted by the preaching tone of Greene's letters and his use of Steuben, a man of monumental ineptitude off the drillgrounds, as the main pipe of comunication with the Virginia government.

While Greene artfully parried Cornwallis in North Carolina, Jefferson entered eagerly into a plan to capture Arnold and rout the invaders from Portsmouth. A virtual stalemate prevailed there: except to forage, the British never ventured from behind the barricades, and the Virginians lacked the strength to expel them. But the longer the enemy remained, the greater the dangers of timidity and disaffection in the surrounding counties. Jefferson frustrated this in part by a timely proclamation aimed at the British practice of taking unarmed citizens and, on the pretext they were prisoners-of-war, extorting pardons with the condition they would not in any way assist the enemies of Britain on pain of life and fortune. The practice was, as Jefferson declared, unauthorized by the law of nations, though perfectly consistent with the British view of the war as a rebellion. Regardless of the principle, the policy jeopardized the patriot cause wherever the British were in a position to exchange the safety of the citizen for his loyalty. "They have conquered South Carolina by paroles alone," Jefferson said. "They will conquer us also if we admit their validity." By his January proclamation such paroles were null and void, and citizens who did not avail themselves of release were ordered behind the enemy lines. Subsequently, when British umbrage threatened death to civilians who violated their paroles, Jefferson promised retaliation in kind on enemy prisoners-of-war.

Having brought this danger under control, he was still anxious to revive Virginia's flagging morale by some exploit at Portsmouth. A spectacular scheme to send a "fire ship" into the enemy fleet, its sole means of escape, aborted; and nothing came of a cloak and dagger plan to capture Arnold. Then a stroke of fortune put it in the power of the French fleet to answer his persistent pleas for assistance. Late in January, a fierce gale crippled the British squadron off Gardiner's Bay, Long Island, at last securing the ascendancy of the French navy. "Heavenly Storm!" A detachment under Commodore Tilly soon sailed from Newport, arriving in the Chesapeake on February 15. But unable to take his strongest ship of 64 guns into the shallow waters of Elizabeth River, where the enemy vessels lay at anchor, the Commodore returned as abruptly as he had come.

The disappointment was momentary. On February 28 Jefferson heard from Washington of a joint sea and land operation planned at the highest level against Arnold at Portsmouth. Washington had ordered a detachment of 1200 troops commanded by General Marquis de Lafayette to march from the Hudson to Head of Elk, at the upper reaches of the Chesapeake, fall down the bay on transports, and in concert with the militia around Portsmouth and the French squadron lead the expedition against Arnold's forces. (Washington was as yet uninformed of Tilly's departure from Virginia waters.) Jefferson, with Steuben and others, worked feverishly to mobilize men, provisions, ordnance, and articles of all kinds. With unabashed eagerness, dreams of glory dancing before him, young Lafayette drove his troops hard, arriving at Head of Elk on March 3, three days ahead of schedule. There he waited until boats could be gathered and a French squadron could command the bay. In a long letter to Jefferson, he sketched in bold words the preparations wanted of Virginia, emphasizing men, boats, and horses. Jefferson had already called for militia reinforcements of 1100 men, which he estimated would place a total of 4000 Virginia militia, plus another 1000 from North Carolina, at Lafayette's command.

A week passed, and Jefferson was dismayed to learn from Steuben "of the refusal of considerable numbers of militia within certain counties to come into the field, and the departure of some others in defiance with their arms." Excessive duty, desertion with impunity, and downright fear contributed to this disobedience. The fear arose, Jefferson thought, from a widespread rumor "that the militia now called on are intended to storm the enemy's works at Portsmouth." In fact Lafayette did intend to storm Arnold's fortifications, though Jefferson continued to entertain the idea of a siege. "Were it possible to block up the river," he told Washington, "a little time would suffice to reduce them by want and desertion and would be more sure in its event than an attempt by storm." At any rate, the crisis would not admit of disobedience by militia. He referred Steuben's complaint to the assembly with recommendation for amendment of the Invasion Law. Stiffening amendments were introduced and debated but finally defeated. Meanwhile, he ordered additional militia into the field to make up for deficiencies that baffled all his calculations.

Impressment offered the only means of obtaining boats and horses. The deserted and plundered Virginia navy was useless in this crisis, as in every other. Fearing inadequate naval protection at Portsmouth, Jefferson took the extraordinary measure of directing the impressment of private vessels and crews on the James and Appomattox rivers. He asked the assembly for authority but did not wait to receive it. One ship and three brigs mounting a total of 36 guns, exceeding the combined power of the state vessels in readiness, were thus drawn into service. The greater need was for small craft to carry men and cannon across the James. Jefferson had first issued orders to obtain boats of this description, under armed guard apparently, when Tilly was at the mouth of the James. The orders were renewed in March. Nevertheless, he had to report to Lafayette a shortage of boats.

The impressment of horses was an even more arduous, and indeed inflammatory, business. If Virginians were not necessarily averse to parting with their horses, they expected outlandish prices for them. "The Thirteen United States are not rich enough to remount the two regiments of this state," Steuben declared. Horses taken under impress warrants were appraised by two citizens, who knew their own property was as likely to be taken as another's and, therefore, had a personal interest in inflated prices. "To retain the horses at such enormous prices threatens ruin on one hand," Jefferson said, "on the other, to discharge them endangers an enterprise which if successful would relieve us from an enemy whose presence is attended with continued expense, fatigue and danger." He referred the problem to the assembly, which promptly authorized the executive to appoint appraisers charged with the responsibility of affixing just prices. But, once again, he had waited until the crisis was upon him. The problem was not wholly one of valuation and price. The much harassed Continental Quartermaster in Virginia, Richard

Claiborne, insisted the needed horses could be obtained only with an armed force. With Steuben's support, he repeatedly asked Jefferson's authority to employ a troop of militia in this work. The executive repeatedly denied the application. An impress force was "as unnecessary as it was new," Jefferson said. The fact was that citizens had parted with their horses "too easily by delivering them to every man who said he was riding on public business and assumed a right of impressing." The militia had troubles enough already, and while the executive could not prevent commanding officers from ordering militia to assist the Quartermaster, it could not itself countenance their employment in this capacity. "We did not think proper to resign ourselves and our Country implicitly to the demands of a Quarter-master," Jefferson indignantly wrote, "but thought we had some right of judgment left to us."

He was perhaps peculiarly sensitive to the issue because a little earlier, without a stitch of legislative authority, he had told Greene to taken horses for his cavalry, and the abuses committed by Greene's officers in this nasty business caused an uproar in the assembly at the very time hundreds of the beasts were demanded for Lafayette's expedition. It was alleged that valuable stud horses and brood mares were taken, that fine covering horses were castrated, that others unfit for service were impressed at exorbitant prices. Jefferson felt some responsibility for these abuses, which of course stung the Virginians' pride in good horseflesh and made them all the less willing to part with their mounts. He sent vigorous protests to Greene, appealing for corrective action; but he was not prepared to support the angry resolution of the assembly calling for the return of all horses valued in excess of £5000 Virginia money. Few could be had at that price, and their return would accomplish nothing. So while urging Greene to rectify abuses, Jefferson told him to ignore the resolution as "inconsistent with the public good." This bold exercise of executive discretion showed that Jefferson would not allow trifles of economy and punctilio to override military requirements. In the circumstances of Caliborne's appeal, however, when passions ran high against impresses generally and especially of horses, he did not think it either desirable or necessary to substitute force for reason and persuasion.

The pressures and frustrations became too much for Steuben. On

March 9 he exploded to the Governor: he would "not be answer-able for the consequences" of a slack militia, he would give "no future orders for impressing horses or any thing else," he would, unless he received immediate satisfaction from the government, bare its failings to the Marquis and the commander of the French fleet "that they may not engage too far in an enterprise which there is no prospect of carrying through." Steuben had had mixed feelings about the Portsmouth expedition from the start. He was jealous of the dashing Marquis, many years his junior but his senior in rank, and was singularly devoted to Greene. "The Baron wishes to be with you," his aide-de-camp wrote Greene near the end of February. "He would rather Obey in an Army, than Command in Virginia." Steuben was rapidly losing what popularity he had in Virginia, partly from clumsy handling of staff and line officers, partly from constant badgering of the government. On the other hand, the Portsmouth expedition held out the prospect, however dimly, of fame and glory. This overruled contrary feelings, and the apprehension of losing that stake, or of another failure at the expense of honor, prompted Steuben's angry outburst under the strain of preparing for the expedition. Jefferson did not make light of it. He at once conveyed Steuben's letter to the House of Delegates and also to Lafayette. If the state's support of his command fell short of expectations, he assured the Marquis, the fault did not arise from any want of zeal in the executive. "Mild laws, a people not used to war and prompt obedience, a want of the provisions of war and means of procuring them render our orders ineffectual, oblige us to temporize and if we cannot accomplish an object in one way to attempt it in another." Lafayette's answer was like a cheerful breath of spring to the Governor. He thanked Jefferson for the exertions already made, confident that new ones would ensure the success of the operation, and understood that, of course, every measure must be accommodated to the temper of the people. "Long since have I been used to those inconveniences that are so far compensated by the numberless blessings of a popular government."

Lafayette wrote from Williamsburg, having arrived there with an advance party on March 14. It is not likely he journeyed to Richmond, though Jefferson assuredly met him there, for the first time, at a critical hour in April. But Jefferson was prepared to love this celebated young Frenchman whom Mazzei described to him as "sensible and clever, lively, smart and modest, and all together one of the most amiable characters I ever saw." He might have wished that other commanders showed the same plucky, uncomplaining spirit of Lafayette: "When we are not able to do what we wish, we must do what we can." Steuben, fortunately, soon recovered his composure and apologised for his conduct. He did not so much blame Jefferson for his difficulties as he did the lethargy of the people, the laxity of the laws, and the bureaucracy that botched the best efforts of the executive. Yet the responsibility, if it was to be meaningful, had to be placed somewhere in particular. The appeal to "circumstances" was self-defeating. As one whose entire training inculcated responsibility under military chain of command, Steuben could not comprehend, much less accept, the justification Jefferson offered—and underscored for effect—in his letter to him: *We can only be answerable for the orders we give, and not for their execution.* An executive disclaiming responsibility for the execution of its orders must have struck Steuben as strange. On the usual administrative canons it was untenable. Yet in the actual context of "obstinacy of spirit or want of coercion in the laws" Jefferson's assertion was perfectly reasonable.

In the end, the expedition against Portsmouth went astray not from any backwardness on the part of Virginia but from the tardiness of the French fleet. Its commander, the Chevalier Destouches, was under orders to sail from Newport for the Chesapeake on March 7; unaccountably, he was delayed more than twenty-four hours, long enough to permit a British squadron reinforcing Arnold to overtake him outside the Virginia capes. He fought a brief, indecisive action on March 16, laid off during the night, and discovered the next morning that the British ships had quietly sneaked into the James. Risking nothing further, he returned to Newport. Thus ended one of the intriguing "might have beens" of the war. For it is not unrealistic to suppose that the design on Portsmouth would have succeeded with the necessary naval support. "With a naval superiority our success would have been certain," Lafayette insisted. And success at Portsmouth would have altered British strategy. Had Cornwallis then rushed to Arnold's rescue, the climactic battle of the Revolution might have been fought in Virginia while Jefferson was Governor, thus redounding to his fame, rather than at York-town months later, when the victory could not erase the defeats and disappointments of his leadership.

As it was, the enemy at Portsmouth doubled its strength and now threatened to break out at any time. Jefferson stoically turned to the task of dismantling the project that had cost so much trouble and expense. At the same time he made a crucial decision on the strategy now to be be pursued. On March 27 Steuben presented his plan to a military board convened at Williamsburg. He would draw together the 4000 Virginia militia before Portsmouth and by forced marches lead them to Greene's camp. The Baron, of course, discovered sound military reasons to support the plan that agreed so precisely with his feelings and desires. "After four weeks' suspense," he un-burdened himself to Greene, "our hopes of doing anything are de-stroyed and the Marquis returns to the Northward, leaving me ex-posed to nothing but affront, whilst every prospect of glory was re-served for others." The military board, consisting of Lafayette, Weedon, and a French colonel, endorsed Steuben's plan, and he set out for Richmond at once. Two days later he met with Jefferson and the Council. After discussing the plan at length, they rejected it as unjustifiable in the present circumstances, the enemy having been greatly reinforced in Virginia. Steuben was crushed. Weedon, who owed his command to Steuben, sourly commented, "I was fear-ful our scheme would be rejected by the Executive who have not an idea beyond local security." The impudence of the man challenges belief! Greene was more restrained, though he complained of the presumptuousness of the executive in vetoing a plan of operations recommended by the Continental officers commanding in the state.

But events rapidly proved the folly of Steuben's strategy and the wisdom of the executive's decision. The plan assumed, first of all, that Arnold, or rather General William Phillips, who now com-manded at Portsmouth, would not break out and overrun the state. There was an element of sophistry in this reasoning, for Steuben ad-mitted to Greene that the enemy troops would in all probability advance through the country when they pleased. No reliable intelli-gence came from the enemy's camp, but within three weeks Phillips started his advance. Secondly, Steuben calculated that Greene, greatly strengthened from Virginia, would overwhelm Cornwallis before he could repair his damanged army or receive assistance from Phillips. But both Greene and Cornwallis, to say nothing further of Phillips, upset the calculation. Greene had already elected a totally different strategy. "I think it will be our true plan of policy to move into South Carolina. . . . This will oblige the enemy to follow us or give up their posts there." Thus Greene abandoned the center in order to recover the rear. Cornwallis decided to leave Greene alone and march his army from Wilmington to Virginia, the real seat of rebellion in the South.

Jefferson did not foresee this course of events as the spring bloom returned to Virginia. He still viewed the southern theater as "the interesting scene of action to us." In its critical decision of March 29, the executive had voted to reinforce Greene with a minimum of 1500 militia; and on through April and part of May, despite Phillip's ravages along the James, the state continued to succor Greene's army. Jefferson wrote to Lafayette near the end of April: "The British force may harass and distress us greatly but the Carolinas alone can subdue us. . . . We therefore think it our first interest to keep them under in that quarter, considering the war in our own Country but as a secondary object." Knowing better than ever that Virginia could not alone withstand the enemy armies in the South, he took a bolder tone toward "our Northern Brethren." On this ticklish subject, he bared his feelings to the French minister, the Chevalier de la Luzerne. "The Northern States are safe: their independence has been established by the joint efforts of the whole," he said. "It is proved as far as testimony can prove any thing that our enemies have transferred every expectation from that quarter and mean nothing further there than a diversion in favor of their Southern arms. It would be unfortunate indeed should it be again proposed to lose a campaign in New York and to exhaust on that the efforts of the Confederacy as those of Spain on Gibraltar,* to give up Provinces in the South for towns in the North." Though he did not exactly say so, Jefferson clearly felt that Washington, fearing to lower his guard at New York, fearing his army would evaporate if divided or marched south, played into the British hands. Washington supposed that he thereby created a useful diversion in favor of southern arms

* A reference to the Spanish ally's almost exclusive interest in acquiring Gibraltar from Great Britain.

when, in fact, it was really Clinton who was diverting him. In Jefferson's opinion, as he told Luzerne, the solution lay in large part with French sea power. "Should a superiority on the Continental Seas be obtained by our fleet, it will save everything from North to South. If the detachments of the British Army can once be insulated, they will be whittled down by the militia, by famine, by sickness and desertion to nothing." He was right on both counts. Washington's army and the French navy did, in due time, come to Virginia, but too late for him to share the glory of their victory.

The problems of the Governor were essentially no different from before, but they threatened to pass out of his hands entirely. "The affliction of the people for want of arms is great," he wrote tiresomely to Congress, "that of ammunition is not yet known to them." And to the Virginia delegates: "It is impossible to give you an idea of the distress we are in for want of lead." Fortunately, he had anticipated this deficiency, rummaged the state for quantities to meet immediate needs, and pushed, successfully, to get the mines back in operation. The state's credit was all but gone. The British conquest of the Dutch free port of St. Eustatius in the Caribbean deprived Virginia of a principal outlet for tobacco. At the end of March the state's Commercial Agent, David Ross, informed Jefferson that tobacco could not be sold in Philadelphia and merchants flew from Virginia money. "Sweet Virginia goes on as usual," a fellow countryman remarked of Ross's efforts in Philadelphia. "The agent is sent up to purchase an immense quantity of articles without a farthing of cash in his pocket: As to the credit of the state, I don't believe anybody would trust her for half a crown." But Ross was not easily defeated. If tobacco would not do, he would try hemp; and he managed, with hemp, to pay for repairs of 2000 stand of arms in May. Promising reforms had been made in the quartermaster department, but it was hopelessly bogged down in the state's financial and moral troubles. More than once Claiborne told Jefferson his department must shortly collapse altogether for want of money. He depended for wagons, teams, and forage on the county commissioners of the Provision Law; if they failed him, or if the supply thus obtained was used up, he must either purchase or impress, and he might succeed in neither. When Jefferson directed him to furnish wagons for the transportation of ammunition from the northward,

Claiborne threw up his hands: "However easy it was for your Excellency to issue such an order, the business is attended with so many difficulties that I am very fearful it will not be in my power to comply with it." *He* would not be answerable for orders he had not the means to execute!

The Governor could scrape through problems such as these. How he was to cope with the breakdown of authority in the militia system and the recruiting system was more difficult to discern. The calls on the militia were exceedingly heavy in April, when upwards to one-half of the men in the camps around Portsmouth and 1500 with Greene were due for replacement. Jefferson carefully chose the counties now to be called with a view to minimizing interference with recruitment. Most recruits were, in fact, drafted. The draft was restored in counties whose militia were recalled, suspended in counties with militia in the field or freshly called. But results were poor all around. In May, Steuben had 954 men in the Virginia Line, about one-sixth of the quota. Seven of the eleven counties ordered to send militia reinforcements to Greene applied for excuse—the Council indulged only one. Specific examples illustrate the range and the seriousness of the problem: *Charlotte:* Of its rank and file numbering 565, some 142 were on duty at Portsmouth, 170 marched with Greene from the Dan, 30 volunteered on the same occasion, and 70 were with General Lawson's corps—412 in service, leaving but 153 men to answer the executive's call for 156. *King George:* The militia of this Potomac county was occupied with the protection of life and property close at hand from enemy vessels raiding and plundering along the river as far north as Alexandria; furthermore, not one-third of the militia had servicable arms, and there were no gunsmiths to repair the others. *Fayette:* This Kentucky county had furnished men to Clark and had scarcely enough bodies at home to hold its forts against the Shawnee; it therefore begged to be excused from the draft of eighteen men for the Continental Army. *Montgomery:* Disaffection had spread to half the militia, who would withdraw to the mountains or start another insurrection rather than obey the laws; many of the others were exposed to the savages and could not leave their families at this dangerous season. *Hampshire:* Open insurrection had broken out in this county at the northern tip of the state. The trouble began with defiance of a collector. "A certain John Claypole Said if all the men were of his mind they would not make up any Cloathes, Beef or men and all that would Join him Should turn out. Upon which he Got all the men present to five or Six and Got Liquor and Drank king George the thirds health, and Damnation to Congress." Claypole, thereafter, rallied a great number. Jefferson instructed the county lieutenant to mount loyal militia, sweep down in the night, "and take them out of their beds." Not for two months were the insurgents rounded up and order restored in Hampshire. As discontents deepened and multiplied, government drifted in an expanding vacuum of power. Jefferson can only be accused of understatement in what he wrote to the Virginia delegates in Congress: "Should this Army at Portsmouth come forth and become active (and as we have no reason to believe they came here to sleep) our affairs will assume a very disagreeable aspect."

Phillips came forth on April 18. At six-thirty the next morning, Jefferson received a dispatch from Colonel Innes commanding the troops at Williamsburg: fourteen sail of enemy vessels dragging numerous flat-bottomed boats at their sterns were standing up the James. Still suffering the grief of his infant daughter's death but three days earlier, the Governor called the Council into session, and within an hour issued orders to the militia of nine counties to rendezvous in all haste at Richmond, Petersburg, and Manchester. Soon, more militia and also volunteer cavalry were called. Richmond was feared to be the enemy's object; accordingly, Jefferson prepared for its abandonment. Records and stores were promptly removed. "We can never proceed with any degree of certainty in any of our public works while the enemy command the rivers," Davies observed. On his advice the government moved works and magazines to Point of Fork, far up the James at its juncture with the Rivanna. As events unfolded, Richmond did not appear to be Phillips's destination. He aimed at disruption and depredation in advance of Cornwallis. On the 20th, a sizable detachment of infantry and cavalry landed near Jamestown and marched on Williamsburg. Innes quickly withdrew his inferior force, and the enemy retraced their steps to the James. Another detachment on the Chickahominy took possession of the shipyard, burned its buildings and some vessels and stores, then chased after Innes. His alertness and agility, while it occupied his pursuers, kept them at a distance, until by a circuitous route he approached Richmond from the east. Meanwhile, the fleet carried the main body of troops farther up the James. It lay opposite Westover on the 23rd, when Phillips feinted toward Richmond. The capital was indefensible as before. Of the militia called there but 500 had reported, only 200 of them armed. Jefferson prepared to leave the city. Neither he nor Steuben, who was on the south side of the James, had yet unraveled the enemy's plan or organized an effective resistance.

The Prussian was disconsolate as ever. Militia came in slowly, arms were wanting, cavalry was wanting, the fort at Hood's was not half finished: "Every thing is in the same confusion as when Arnold came up the River." On the 24th, while reconnoitering the fleet, Steuben watched it ascend the river toward City Point on the southern side of the confluence of the Appomattox and James. There Phillips landed his force of approximately 2300 men, declaring his object to be Petersburg, a few miles to the west. At Petersburg, Steuben marshaled about 1200 militia of Muhlenberg's command, and in the heat of the following day, April 25, battled the enemy for two hours, at first disputing the ground "inch by inch," then, ammunition exhausted, making an orderly retreat across the Appomattox. Steuben congratulated the militia on its performance. After burning tobacco and warehouses in Petersburg, Phillips marched to the place called Osborne's, or Coxe's Dale, on the south bank of the James. Here Captain James Maxwell, Commissioner of the Navy, had ranged his pitiful fleet, adding several impressed vessels, for a last stand. A curious engagement between land and sea forces followed. The British set up a deadly fire of musket and cannon from shore positions. Some of the ships surrendered, others were destroyed by enemy fire, still others were burned or scuttled by their officers. None escaped. As one participant recalled, "we saved nothing but the clothes we had on." Two days later, the 29th, Phillips marched to Manchester.

If Phillips had any intention of attacking Richmond on the opposite bank, he was dissuaded by the view it suddenly presented: 900 Continental troops with Lafayette at their head. The Marquis, on hearing at Baltimore of Virginia's plight, left baggage, artillery, and stores behind, and by forced marches under the most trying condi-

231

tions reached Richmond in ten days. It was a timely arrival. The British retired to their waiting fleet in the James, burning as they went. "Six or eight hundred of their picked men of light infantry with General Arnold at their head . . . ," Jefferson gloated, "fled from a patrol of 16 horse every man into his boat as he could, some pushing north and some south as their fears drove them." Before reaching the camps at Portsmouth, the fleet abruptly turned about, ascended the river, and came to anchor at Brandon, just below Hood's, where the troops landed. "We have not yet heard which way they went or whether they are gone," Jefferson informed Washington on May 10, "but having about the same time received authentic information that Lord Cornwallis had on the 1st instant advanced from Wilmington half way to Halifax we have no doubt putting all circumstances together but that these two bodies are forming a junction."

Jefferson braced himself for this gloomy event. It was essential, he told the county lieutenants, "to turn out . . . as many men as there are arms to be found in the County." One-tenth should be mounted and equipped as cavalry. Other troops of cavalry, earlier authorized by the assembly at his request, were also in formation. In a country as wide and open as Virginia, especially when the enemy commanded the rivers, a formidable cavalry was indispensable. On the surface, nothing should have been easier. But the people had been so revolted by the commandeering of horse as to put the objective out of reach. And instead of Virginia gaining the benefit of its cavalry potential, it fell to the enemy by plunder. Determined to reverse this disastrous course, Jefferson formed the policy of requiring the removal, and military impress as necessary, of all servicable horses from within twenty miles of the enemy. A first step toward the proclamation of martial law in the areas of the contending armies, Jefferson's action was subsequently sanctioned by the legislature. He kept his wits about him, however, and urged "a high tone of conduct" upon the responsible officers, lest the people take umbrage as before and defeat the measure.

Evidences of panic and collapse were all around him. Claiborne declared "all faith in the public agents is lost and the citizen will do nothing without being compelled by military force." Jefferson stayed at his post and almost alone gave some semblance of direction to the government. During Phillips's invasion, as in Arnold's before, the members of the Council scattered. The Council did not again meet, for want of a quorum, until May 7, and from May 15 through the remainder of his term in office Jefferson was without its services. The assembly was to convene on May 7, but neither house could muster a quorum. The members present issued a call to meet in Charlottesville on May 24. Jefferson now put everything in motion to transfer the seat of government to Charlottesville. Davies had already centered the operations of the War Office at Point of Fork some miles below. Steuben made this inland location his training grounds for recruits intended for the Southern Army. The dispersal of the government from Richmond added to the sum of confusion. But it was unavoidable. Richmond was surely in Cornwallis's line of March. Jefferson kept in constant touch with the different commands and departments as the government endeavored to draw its energies together again at the base of the Blue Ridge.

More support was coming from the North. By May, after agonizing delay, no one could doubt that Washington, Congress, and the nothern public were at last awake to the needs and opportunities of the southern states. The Virginia congressmen maneuvered and scraped to obtain 2000 rampart muskets which, after being sawed to proper size and repaired, were shipped to Virginia. The Board of War promised more arms. Ross's agent in Philadelphia, on the credit of private citizens, purchased and dispatched hundreds of guns and tons of powder. To these shipments was added the cargo of *La Comité*. By the end of May, for the first time in Jefferson's governorship, the state had a sufficiency of arms. Soldiers too were coming. Troops of the Pennsylvania Line under General Anthony Wayne, after weeks of exasperating delay, finally marched to join Lafayette. "No means in the power of Congress will be left unessayed to give you all necessary aids," the President assured Jefferson. What a welcome change! For months Jefferson had pleaded and plotted for this commitment. On May 16 Washington wrote that he would soon meet with General Rochambeau to plan a summer campaign looking to the relief of the southern states. When the two commanders met at Wethersfield, Connecticut, they decided to move their combined armies against New York, and thereby force Clinton either to risk its loss or recall troops from the South. The decision was disappointing. It favored Virginia only with a questionable diversion at New York. But the French fleet was as yet incapable of wresting the Chesapeake from the British, and Washington declined to risk his army in an overland march of 450 miles in the heat of the summer. The commanders agreed, however, to resort to the alternate plan, a campaign in Virginia, should circumstances dictate. They did, after Jefferson went into retirement.

Unopposed in his march, Cornwallis joined forces with the British army in Virginia, at Petersburg, on May 20. Five days later he crossed the James, and with the reinforcements he then received led an army of 7000 men. His first objective was to destroy Lafayette's army, vastly inferior, yet the principal force in the state. "The boy cannot escape me!" Cornwallis gloated. Lafayette retreated above Richmond in a northerly direction, holding to the upper part of the country and hoping to effect a juncture with Wayne. "We are in the outmost want of Cavalry," he informed Jefferson. General Banastre Tarleton's intrepid dragoons moved with lightning speed, plundering the stables of fine mounts all along the line of march, until it became impossible, Lafayette said, "either to stop or reconnoiter their movements, and much more so to send impressing parties around their camp." Despite the handicap, Lafayette made good his escape. Cornwallis gave up the chase halfway to Fredericksburg, turned about, and ravaged the defenseless country to the south. Before leaving his camp, he sent Tarleton's dragoons and Colonel Simcoe's rangers on separate missions to the west: the former to rout the government at Charlottesville and capture the Governor, the latter to destroy the arms and stores under Steuben's protection at Point of Fork.

Steuben was eagerly preparing to march southward at the head of 500 recruits equipped and outfitted at Point of Fork. Believing his usefulness to the state was at an end, he had written to Greene on May 14, "I will with pleasure fly to put myself under your orders and I beseech you . . . to call me as soon as possible, for be assured I am heartily disgusted at the conduct and proceedings in this quarter." Greene also wanted Steuben, "an officer educated in the Prussian school," and orders calling him south were already on the way. Cornwallis's presence, Lafayette's retreat—all the needs of the state that so far exceeded Greene's—did not deter Steuben. He was blocked, however, first by the pressure of events, second by a resolution of the assembly holding the recruits in the state, and finally by Lafayette's order. The responsibility of protecting the magazines at Point of Fork fell to him. As Lafayette retreated northward, the security of that place came into jeopardy. Steuben directed the removal of the stores to the south bank of the James, whence they were to be transported beyond the mountains. In the midst of this work, on June 4, he was surprised by Simcoe's rangers. By the ruse of kindling superfluous campfires over a long stretch of the river's north bank, Simcoe led Steuben to believe the entire British army lay opposite. Beating a hasty retreat in the night, he abandoned most of the stores to the enemy's torch the next morning. The loss was of minor importance. But Steuben's conduct was such that, as Lafayette reported to Washington, "every man, woman and child in Virginia is roused against him." Jefferson, certainly, never "roused against him." Despite serious differences between them, he had trusted the Baron, humored his faults, and quieted his enemies. But nothing now could prevent the legislature, enraged by Steuben's flight, from voting an inquiry into his conduct; and while he remained in Virginia he lay under its shadow.

Tarleton was foiled in his objectives by an alert militiaman, Jack Jouett, who spotted the white-coated dragoons on the main road at Louisa, mounted his steed, and sped along a back trail to Charlottesville heralding their approach. On his way, at sunrise June 4, he stopped at Monticello to warn the Governor and several members of the assembly who were his guests. They breakfasted, then descended the mountain to the town. The assembly convened hurriedly, and just as hurriedly adjourned to meet again at Staunton, across the Blue Ridge, on June 7. As Tarleton swooped down on the fleeing delegates, capturing some of them, a detachment under Captain McCleod took the road to Monticello. Jefferson, meanwhile, ordered his favorite horse freshly shod at Shadwell, looked after his papers, and sent his family to a neighboring plantation. What passed through his mind as he occupied himself in this deliberate manner for nearly two hours, it is impossible to say; but in view of the infamous reputation of Tarleton's legion, he must have contemplated Monticello with mournful affection. Alerted to McCleod's approach, he walked to the road between Monticello and adjacent

Carter's Mountain, where his horse awaited him. Riding up the mountain, he stopped and trained his telescope on Charlottesville. The scene dispelled any lingering hope that he might reverse his steps. He went on and took refuge with his family. Not for many years did anyone suggest that the "flight" to Carter's Mountain was an act of pusillanimity.

McCleod, arriving a few minutes after the prey departed, proved to be as considerate of Monticello as Jefferson could have wished. Martin, one of the house servants, met the Captain at the door and escorted him through the house. "On reaching the study, the depository of the Governor's papers," according to a family tradition, "McCleod gazed about him a few moments, and then locking the door gave Martin the key, and bade him refer any of his soldiers inquiring for it to himself." Nothing was disturbed. After eighteen hours, McCleod rejoined Tarleton. The dragoons followed the Rivanna down to the main army on the James. Here Cornwallis set up headquarters at Jefferson's Elk Hill plantation. In later years he bitterly recalled the "spirit of total extermination" the British commander loosed on this property: the barns and fences burned, the crops in the field and the quantities of corn, wheat and tobacco destroyed, the number of horses, cows, sheep, hogs eaten or carried away, and the number of slaves, 27, captured. "Had this been to give them freedom he [Cornwallis] would have done right," Jefferson reflected, "but it was to consign them to inevitable death from the small pox and putrid fever then raging in his camp." This, indeed, was the fate of most of the slaves, and Jefferson recovered only five of them.

Before these events took place, actually before his narrow escape at Carter's Mountain, the curtain fell on the agonizing drama of Jefferson's governorship. His term of office expired on June 2. This was the day fixed for his retirement, though he in effect occupied the office until Tarleton chased the government from Charlottesville. Not until June 12, after the assembly convened at Staunton, was General Nelson chosen as his successor. It was the least propitious time imaginable—at the piercing crescendo of all the havoc and defeat Virginia had endured—for Jefferson calmly to withdraw from the scene. "You will then judge the situation of this country," Richard Henry Lee solemnly wrote to the Virginia congressmen, "without either executive or legislative authority, everything in the greatest possible confusion, the enemy far superior in force to that with the Marquis, and practicing everything that force and fraud can contrive."

Infected by the panic that struck the state, Lee took a chapter from the book of the ancient republics and proposed that Congress dispatch Washington to Virginia vested with dictatorial powers. A faction of the assembly also looked for salvation from a dictator, though their candidate, so Jefferson believed, was Patrick Henry. The subject was delicate, the proceedings of the House of Delegates veiled in obscurity; but the motion to appoint a dictator was apparently introduced by George Nicholas, seconded by Henry, and after some debate defeated. Jefferson afterwards learned as much from an eyewitness. He was writing the *Notes on Virginia* at the time, and entered a passionate denunciation of the scheme in that work. The experience of the past two years, while it had lowered still further his opinion of the Virginia constitution, had in no way diminished his attachment to republican government. He did not disguise to himself or to others the perilous situation of the state. In one of his last acts as Governor, he had pleaded with Washington to return to his countrymen, assured "that your appearance among them, would restore full confidence of salvation, and would render them equal to whatever is not impossible." But he looked to Washington for generalship, not dictatorship. "The very thought alone was treason against the people . . . a people mild in their dispositions, patient under their trial, united for the public liberty, and affectionate to their leaders." Writing in retrospect, Edmund Randolph stated Jefferson's opinion more pointedly than he ever did himself: "The power which may have saved Rome, would have made Virginia revolt."

Rage succeeded to panic. On June 12 the House of Delegates resolved on an inquiry into the conduct of the executive. This motion, too, was made by young Nicholas, though Jefferson believed, as with the former one, "his natural ill-temper was the tool worked with by another hand"—the hand of Patrick Henry. By the terms of resolution, the executive, not simply the Governor, was called on the carpet. And, of course, the Council being an integral part of the executive authority, no inquiry of the sort proposed could be fairly pressed on the Governor alone. Yet this was the upshot of the resolution. Several members of the Council threatened to resign if the sword of censure hung over them. Faced with the dilemma of either depriving the state of a lawful executive or of simply by-passing the record of the Council, the assembly chose the latter. Jefferson viewed the resolution as an implied censure of him; accordingly, with his friends in the assembly, he invited the inquiry as a means of vindication.

In July he addressed Nicholas for information on the charges against him. Nicholas replied, "I shall exhibit no charges but only join in an enquiry," and then proceeded to list five, which were later revised and enlarged to the number of eleven. All referred to Arnold's invasion: Why had the executive not acted on the receipt of Washington's notice of an embarkation? Why had not lookouts been stationed at the capes? Why had there not been carriages for heavy artillery? Why had the fortifications at York and Portsmouth been abandoned? And so on. Jefferson sought affidavits where pertinent and penned his own impatient answers. In December he attended the House of Delegates as a member solely on this business. A committee was appointed to conduct the inquiry, but neither Nicholas nor anyone else offered information. There was no inquiry. The committee simply reported to the House that the original resolution had stemmed from rumors which, in its opinion, were groundless. After the delegates heard the report, Jefferson rose and read the paper he had prepared during the summer. The House then, without further ado, voted Jefferson a resolution of thanks in which, after amendment, the Senate concurred: "The Assembly wish in the strongest manner to declare the high opinion which they entertain of Mr. Jefferson's Ability, Rectitude, and Integrity as chief Magistrate of this Commonwealth, and mean by thus publicly avowing their Opinion, to obviate and to remove all unmerited Censure."

But the assembly, while it might obviate, could not prevent censure, and it pursued Jefferson through life and beyond the grave. He was stung by the original resolution, far beyond anything that had befallen him in public life. As usual, he checked his feelings and avoided personal recrimination. "If pride of character be of worth at any time," he had observed, "it is when it disarms the efforts of malice." For whatever reason, his critics were disarmed in 1781, the assembly relieved of embarrassment, and Jefferson accorded the expression of public gratitude he deserved, though not without the tormenting suggestion that some censure might be merited.

His governorship could not be reckoned brilliant or even successful. Yet if faithfulness to duty, courage in distress, calmness and forecast of mind, devotion to republican principles, flexibility in the face of danger, and an enlarged view of Virginia's place in the grand strategy of the Union—if these things were important, then Jefferson was more deserving of praise than of blame. He certainly never claimed more for himself. He knew, and frankly conceded, how far character and training unsuited him to the role of a wartime governor, and he endorsed the assembly's choice of a military commander, General Nelson, to succeed him. But he knew that some circumstances are unyielding, that some evils are mild when compared with the evils likely to result from their suppression, and, as he stated to Lafayette, "that public misfortunes may be produced as well by public poverty and private disobedience to the laws as by the misconduct of public servants."

The panic that accompanied his retirement was unjustified. The government had not collapsed. The assembly was in being, the War Office and other administrative departments continued to function, and the executive was fully restored by the middle of June. The state maintained its independence and the loyalty of its people. Its military strength constantly increased while Cornwallis exhausted himself in useless marches. "Overrunning a Country is not to conquer it," Lafayette wisely observed of the lord commander's movements, adding by way of illustration, "and if it was construed into a right of possession, the French could claim the whole German Empire." Virginia's situation would have been much worse had the executive, bowing to the wishes of Steuben and Greene, stripped the state of all defensive capabilities in the spring. The nucleus of defense remained. Lafayette's force engaged Cornwallis until fresh militia could be mobilized, until Steuben's recruits were diverted from a fruitless march southward and drawn into the field, and until Wayne's army arrived from Pennsylvania. All of this occurred at the time of Jefferson's retirement. By the middle of June, Lafayette's army, now numbering perhaps 8000 men, was superior to the enemy's. The second division of the French fleet, with 24 warships and 3000 troops, lay poised in Caribbean waters. Congress was making every endeavor to aid Virginia. And Washington closely watched the developments there. When Cornwallis, in short order, withdrew his fever-ridden army into Yorktown, the outcome was a military certainty. Going into retirement, Jefferson could not foresee in detail the culmination of this chain of events; but he had never once doubted the ultimate triumph of American arms, and he turned to the long deferred pleasures of private life confident of an early victory and an early peace.

CHAPTER FIVE

Withdrawal and Return:

Congressman

Our style and manner of thinking have undergone a revolution more extraordinary than the political revolution of the country. We see with other eyes; we hear with other ears; and think with other thoughts, than those we formerly used. We can look back on our own prejudices, as if they had been the prejudices of other people. . . .

The people of England not having experienced this change, had likewise no ideas of it. They were hugging to their bosoms the same prejudices we were trampling beneath our feet; and they expected to keep a hold upon America, by that narrowness of thinking which America disdained. What they were proud of, we despised; and this is a principal cause why all their negotiations, constructed on this ground, have failed. We are now really another people, and cannot again go back to ignorance and prejudice. The mind once enlightened cannot again become dark.

Thomas Paine, Letter to the Abbé Raynal. Philadelphia, 1782.

DAYS AND MONTHS of anguish, eighteen dreary months, descended on Jefferson after his retirement. The Nicholas resolution wounded him more than he was at first willing to admit. The charges themselves were a mere impertinence; but to be exposed to the public on the suspicion of delinquency, to be made a mark for

the slings of malice and the sport of rumor and gossip, to be forced
to defend a record that needed no defense—all this was painful and
more than a little disillusioning. The adulation of the public he
could do without, but he did require its respect. Duty as high-
minded as he believed his to be was insupportable in the face of censure. It poisoned his affections, and he determined to quit the public stage forever. The December resolution of the assembly cleared
him of ill-founded suspicion or blame, but the wound, being to the
spirit, could "only be cured by the all healing grave."

Sickened to his heart's core, Jefferson nursed the injury and embraced suffering as the only solace in a cruelly misshapen world.
The response, so out of proportion to the offence, revealed sensitiv-
ities of no ordinary degree. Perhaps there lurked in Jefferson's consciousness some unavowed sense of failure or inadequacy such as
men accused him of. He had learned that governing was a perilous
thing, perhaps unworthy of further venture in his case. Several
years later he confessed to a friend how ill-suited he was to a scene
of troubles. "I do not love difficulties. I am fond of quiet, willing to
do my duty, but irritable by slander and apt to be forced by it to
abandon my post." Writing thus, the memory of his retirement
from the governorship may not have entered his head, but the
words suggested that ordeal. It was followed by a succession of personal misfortunes and one final, almost mortal, blow. Worn down
by the grueling pace of the last five months in office he was chased
from Monticello before he could catch his breath. At Poplar Forest,
where he took refuge with his family, he fell from a horse and was
immobilized for several weeks. His James River plantation was ravaged, the slaves carried away and consumed by pestilence, the tobacco crop destroyed. As a result, he found it hard to pay his taxes
the following year. Apprehensions for his wife's health rose steadily
while she was carrying their sixth child. A daughter was born in
May 1782. Martha sank beyond recovery and died in September.
Jefferson seemed to pass the threshold of misery.

All through these months his friends in Congress and the General
Assembly tried to soothe his feelings and draw him back to the public stage. But without success. In July 1781 he was notified of his
appointment as a commissioner to negotiate peace with Great Britain. He promptly drafted his refusal, then held the letter for four

weeks. Again, as five years before, he was tempted by a European mission. But he must yield the opportunity, he said, in order to confront his accusers in the fall session of the legislature. Writing from Congress, Edmund Randolph hastened to assure him that he might discharge this obligation and still reach France before the negotiations commenced. He replied that there were still other obstacles, unspecified, to his acceptance of any public post. "I have taken my final leave of everything of that nature, have retired to my farm, my family and books from which I think nothing will ever more separate me." Randolph shot back: "If you can justify this resolution to yourself, I am confident, that you cannot to the world." Madison agreed. Jefferson's conduct in the fact of adversity, while it manifested "a keen sensibility and strong consciousness of rectitude," could not be justified by philosophy or patriotism. Even before the adoption of the December resolution, the assembly showed its confidence in the former governor by electing him to Congress. He declined to serve; and after leaving Richmond the day before Christmas wrapped himself in a mantle of oblivion uninterrupted by word or letter for a period of three months. The silence was broken, though not the oblivion, by another "act of renunciation": the repudiation of his Albemarle constituents who again elected him to the House of Delegates. His protégé James Monroe, just now embarked in politics as a member of the House, took alarm at Jefferson's absence. The talk of the streets and the corridors was full if it. "It is publicly said here," Monroe reported, "that the people of your county informed you that they had frequently elected you in times of less difficulty and danger than the present to please you, but that now they called you forth into public office to serve themselves." He implored Jefferson to overcome his morbid resolution and shoulder the burden of republican service. To this appeal, the Speaker of the House, rejecting Jefferson's resignation, added the threat of arrest and attendance in custody of the sergeant of arms should he persist in his disobedience.

Jefferson deigned no reply to the Speaker, but to Monroe he wrote a long and pathetic letter which revealed the tortures of his soul and set forth, with what reason he could muster, the grounds of his defense. His beloved Martha had given birth to her last child twelve days before. She was slipping from him. He did not, however, offer her illness as his excuse. He returned instead to the feelings that had motivated his retirement: the exhaustion of political ambition, the preference for private life, the care of his disordered estate, the obligation to his family, and, above all, the distressing evidence "that by a constant sacrifice of time, labour, loss, parental and friendly duties, I had been so far from gaining the affections of my countrymen which was the only reward I ever asked or could have felt, that I had even lost the small estimation I before possessed: that however I might have comforted myself under the disapprobation of well-meaning but uninformed people yet that of their representatives was a shock on which I had not calculated. . . ." He then undertook to refute the proposition that "the state may command the political services of all its members to an indefinite extent." Reason and law were against it. "This would be slavery and not that liberty which the bill of rights has made inviolable. . . . This to men of certain ways of thinking would be to annihilate the blessings of existence; to contradict the giver of life who gave it for happiness and not for wretchedness, and certainly to such it were better that they had never been born. However with these I may think public service and private misery inseparably linked together, I have not the vanity to count myself among those whom the state would think worth oppressing with perpetual service. I have received a sufficient memento to the contrary," he bitterly concluded. More because of his wife's condition than his own apology, the House left Jefferson to his misery. At the fall session, however, after her death, he was ordered into custody, appeared in the House, and obtained release for good cause.

During the first few months of retirement, Jefferson picked up the threads of an idealized private life that, like a phantom, seemed always to escape his grasp. He took an increasing interest in the education of his eldest daughter, Patsy. His sister Martha Carr and her six children, a "sacred charge" since the death of their father, came to live at Monticello; and to Peter Carr, in particular, Jefferson was a devoted guardian and tutor. There was little he could do in the distressed situation of Virginia to improve his estate. The practice of law offered an obvious recourse, and Jefferson took it, though not very seriously. Early in 1782 he undertook at Madison's urging to prepare a defense of Virginia's title to the western territory; but it was interrupted by his wife's illness and never completed. Unquestionably the most important product of these months was the *Notes on the State of Virginia*. Whatever his countrymen might think of his withdrawal from public life, they, and indeed all Americans, had reason to be grateful to him for this work. Commenced in the fall of 1780, set aside after Arnold's invasion, Jefferson brought it near completion during the weeks of enforced idleness at Poplar Forest, leaving only a few gaps to be filled up after his return to Monticello later in the summer.

There, in the first blush of spring the following year, Jefferson received a memorable visitor, the Chevalier de Chastellux, a member of the French Academy and a major general in Rochambeau's army encamped at Williamsburg. When he returned to France, Chastellux published his *Travels in North America*, subsequently translated into English. His felicitous portrait of Monticello and its master was the first to present Jefferson to the world in philosophical colors. The amiable Frenchman at first found Jefferson "serious, nay even cold," but within two hours they were as intimate as if they had spent their lives together. They walked up and down Jefferson's little mountain, conversed on all variety of subjects—politics, natural philosophy, fine arts—and passed an entire evening around a bowl of punch, spouting the bardic verses of Ossian, in whom they discovered a mutual enthusiasm. "Let me describe to you a man, not yet forty, tall, and with a mild and pleasing countenance, but whose mind and understanding are ample substitutes for every exterior grace. An American, who without ever having quitted his own country, is at once a musician, skilled in drawing, a geometrician, an astronomer, a natural philosopher, legislator, and statesman . . . a philosopher, in voluntary retirement from the world, and public business, because he loves the world, inasmuch only as he can flatter himself with being useful to mankind. . . . A mild and amiable wife, charming children, of whose education he himself takes charge, a house to embellish, great provisions to improve, and the arts and sciences to cultivate; these are what remain to Mr. Jefferson, after having played a principal character on the theater of the new world, and which he preferred to the honorable commission of Minister Plenipotentiary in Europe." Chastellux described Monticello in some detail, for it had a charm, an elegance, a character not to be found in other Virginia mansions. "Mr. Jefferson," he observed, "is the first American who has consulted the fine arts to know how he should shelter himself from the weather." The visit of four days passed like so many minutes, Chastellux recalled, and he set out to view the spectacle of the Natural Bridge convinced that his host was a supremely enlightened man. "It seemed as if from his youth he had placed his mind, as he had done his house, on an elevated situation, from which he might contemplate the universe."

Chastellux saw little of Mrs. Jefferson, which is a pity, for it would be pleasing to know something more of her than that she was "mild and amiable." Of course, she was also charming and accomplished in the manner of Virginia ladies of that day. But what else she was, what set her apart, what she contributed to the life of her husband other than six children in ten years (three of them living) and an abiding love—on the person of Martha Jefferson history is silent. Death lingered at her bedside for four months. Jefferson was never out of calling and daily attended her as a nurse. When she died on September 6, according to his eldest daughter's recollection, he fell into a state of insensibility from which it was feared he would not revive. When he did, his torment was indescribable. "He kept [to] his room three weeks, and I was never a moment from his side. He walked almost incessantly night and day, only lying down occasionally, when nature was completely exhausted, on a pallet that had been brought in during his long fainting fits. . . . When at last he left his room, he rode out, and from that time he was incessantly on horseback, rambling about the mountain, in the least frequented roads, and just as often through the woods. In those melancholy rambles, I was his constant companion," Patsy said, "a solitary witness to many a violent burst of grief. . . ."

From this stupor Jefferson gradually emerged in October. Monticello was now full of anguished memories. He found himself "absolutely unable to attend to any thing like business," and saw in prospect "a gloom unbrightened with one cheerful expectation." Then, in November, Congress threw him a lifeline: renewal of the commission as Minister Plenipotentiary to negotiate peace. Congress acted on the well-founded assumption that the loss of his wife had caused a change in Jefferson's sentiments toward the public service. He lost no time accepting the appointment. In little more than three weeks he was on the road to Philadelphia to embark for France. Jefferson had lost a wife; the country regained a statesman.

With overtones of heroic mythos, the passing of Jefferson's beloved freed him from the prison he was making for himself and returned him to the path of destiny. "Before that event my scheme of life had been determined," he wrote to Chastellux on the very day he announced his return to duty. "I had folded myself in the arms of retirement, and rested all prospects of future happiness on domestic and literary objects. A single event wiped away all my plans and left me a blank which I had not the spirit to fill up." His withdrawal served him well. Not only did he have the *Notes on Virginia* to show for it, but it also taught him to take adversity in stride, stoically shore up his feelings, and view his favored life of retirement with more becoming modesty. These lessons did not change his character, or overcome its pivotal ambivalence, but they improved its balance and resiliency. After passing through the great private ordeal of his life, he returned to the public a stronger and wiser man.

The Notes on Virginia

"The subjects are all treated imperfectly, some scarcely touched on," Jefferson wrote of the *Notes on Virginia* in 1787. "To apologize for this by developing the circumstances of the time and place of their composition, would be to open wounds which have already bled enough." Of all Jefferson's compositions this one alone assumed the character of a book; yet it did not begin as one or with intentions of publication. It began in response to the request of the secretary of the French legation, François de Marbois, for information on the state of Virginia. The information might have been furnished in perfunctory fashion, as indeed it was, so far as furnished at all, by the secretary's informants in other states. But Jefferson converted the occasion into an opportunity for the intellectual discovery of his own country. In the philosophic view Americans were yet strangers to the land. Its rivers and mountains, its flora and fauna, its laws and institutions and productions—"What a field have we at our door to signalize ourselves in!" Jefferson exclaimed. The information sought by an enlightened foreigner for his government was information of infinitely greater value to the enlightened patriot. And thus, as Jefferson answered Marbois's queries, the manuscript became a vehicle for the interpretation of his country to himself.

While he had no desire to appear before the public as an author, and was actually averse to it, Jefferson sensed that the work so modestly begun had taken a character to interest other Americans of a philosophical turn of mind. He returned the answers to Marbois in December 1781, but this was not the end of it. His friend Charles Thomson, Secretary of Congress and a fellow counsellor of the American Philosophical Society, encouraged him to present it to that body. Jefferson held off. Some parts required more complete and reliable data. He continued his investigations, communicated with well-informed friends, and as leisure permitted, revised and enlarged the manuscript until, in 1784, it had "swelled to nearly treble bulk." By then many persons in Virginia, Philadelphia, and other places had seen or heard something of Jefferson's "Notes." They wished to possess it. Being now too much for manuscript copies, such as he had endeavored to provide, Jefferson decided "to print a dozen or 20 copies to be given to my friends, not suffering another to go out." He opposed outright publication from the fear that his severe strictures on slavery and the Virginia constitution would expose him to renewed censure in his native state and prove more a hindrance than a help to the reform of these institutions. The plan for a limited edition was deferred until Jefferson, at last, reached Paris. An edition of 200 copies was ready for private distribution in the spring of 1785.

The book was born. It contained no avowal of authorship, however, and he still hoped to confine his opinions to a small circle, whose co-operation he asked to prevent the book from falling into untrustworthy hands. But a corps of secret agents on two continents could not have prevented this. On the decease of a friend who had received a copy, the book came into the possession of a French bookseller. Jefferson had no choice but to make the best arrangement he could for French translation and publication. Even worse was the prospect of a botched English edition, retranslated from the already botched French. So in 1787 he arranged for the publication of the *Notes* in England, submitting also to the acknowledgment of authorship. Meanwhile, Madison overcame his opposition to the circulation of the book in Virginia. He sent numerous copies home, a total of thirty-seven to George Wythe alone for distribution to favored students in the College. His political feelings, still tender after six years, could not be protected in any event. The book had escaped his control. Months before the English edition crossed the Atlantic, American newspapers were publishing the work piecemeal. The first, and unauthorized, American edition appeared at Philadelphia in 1788. Four editions in four years, with many more to come: such is the record of a book Jefferson never meant to write and, having written it, seemed determined to keep from the general public.

Viewed in one aspect the *Notes on Virginia* was simply a glorified guidebook, descriptive, crammed with facts, informative on a broad range of subjects from cascades and caverns to weights and measures, all treated in clear, effortless prose touched with philosophy. Viewed in the light of eighteenth-century knowledge, it was a work of natural and civil history, uniquely interesting as a guide to Jefferson's mind as well as to his native country. Taking his cue from the Baconian faculties of the time—memory, reason, and imagination—Jefferson divided all knowledge into three great branches: history, philosophy, and fine arts. Each in turn was subdivided until every species of knowledge found its logical place. When he first made a catalogue of his library in 1783, he classified the books according to this system. History, the principal realm occupied by the *Notes on Virginia*, was divided between natural and civil. Much of Jefferson's discussion of Virginia society and government belonged to the field of civil history; other parts of it, such as the strictures on slavery and the constitution, belonged in his system to the realm of philosophy, including among its lesser branches ethics, law, and politics.

Natural history was one of the two vast fields of scientific inquiry in the eighteenth century. For Jefferson, as for most Americans, it was a more spacious, a more agreeable, and a more practical field of investigation than natural philosophy, which embraced astronomy, physics, and chemistry. Natural history comprehended the entire earth as a scene of life: land, water, and climate, the kingdoms of plants and animals, the races and the descent of man. Some of the particular sciences were peculiarly attractive to Americans. Botany, for example, was not only useful, it might be pursued as a charming pastime. "No country gentleman," Jefferson observed, "should be without what amuses every step he takes into his fields." Both botany and zoology had been reduced to orderly system by the Swedish naturalist Linnaeus. Even the untutored investigator could discover, describe, and classify according to the Linnaen system. A triumph of rationality, it appealed to Jefferson's mind; and the infinitely subtle gradations of plant and animal life confirmed his faith in the perfection of the divine Creator. The study of American nature was, moreover, a patriotic as well as a scientific obligation. Astronomy and physics—all the sciences Jefferson called "mathematical" and considered of greater import in the long run—were the same the world around. But America had its own natural history, and from this standpoint was still a *terra incognita*. The unique task of American science lay along the paths of self-discovery. This conviction animated Jefferson's scientific work, set the tone of the *Notes on Virginia*, and, with that book, secured him a reputation among the savants of two continents. It was, according to Charles Thomson, "a most excellent Natural History not merely of Virginia but of North America and possibly equal if not superior to that of any country yet published."

Marbois's twenty-two queries came to Jefferson's hand in a jumble. Questions on colonial laws and charters and the constitution preceded questions of a geographical nature, for instance, and some questions combined incongruous subjects. Jefferson sorted and arranged the whole under twenty-three heads, the order proceeding from the natural through the civil to the generally social and moral. Viewing Virginia as an environment of life, he thought it important to begin with nature, which so profoundly conditioned every human part. The greater Virginia he described, broken in the middle by the Allegheny Mountains, had no geographical unity. But the coastal and the western rivers might be joined together, or nearly so, making strong bonds between the two regions. Questions of western navigation and commerce occupied him when he revised the original manuscript. He described all the principal rivers from the James to the Missouri in remarkable detail, traced their courses, measured their length and breadth and depth, noted their rapids and other obstructions to navigation, and so on. His interest was factual and utilitarian; still he could not refrain from observing that the Ohio was "the most beautiful river in the world," and that the passage of the Potomac through the Blue Ridge, at Harper's Ferry, was "one of the most stupendous scenes of nature . . . . worth a voyage across the Atlantic." A lover's pride in the bigness and grandeur of his country shone through Jefferson's prose, without any traces of the braggadocio that was later to characterize native depictions of American nature. He was capable of wildly subjective emotion, as in his response to the Natural Bridge, which was located on his own property in Rockbridge County. "It is impossible for the emotions arising from the sublime to be felt beyond what they are here; so beautiful an arch, so elevated, so light, and springing as it were up to heaven! The rapture of the spectator is really indescribable." Even here, however, the paroxysm was momentary, the sublimity faded, as he became the geometrician again and exactly measured every element of the "semi-elliptical" arch through the mountains. The Potomac passage was similarly affecting. Regarding it as a stupendous monument of "a war between rivers and mountains, which must have shaken the earth itself to its very center," he supposed that an ocean had once filled the valley behind the Blue Ridge until the waters rose to a great height, broke over, tore the mountain down from its summit to its base, and cut the channel of the Potomac.

The notion of an inland sea suggested explanation for the phenomenon of shells discovered in Virginia, as in other countries, thousands of feet above sea level. The curiosity was of unusual interest because of its implications for the emerging science of historical geology. Two schools of thought, Neptunists and Vulcanists, were at loggerheads on the theory of the formation of the earth's crust. The Neptunists held that it emerged gradually from a universal ocean. The theory easily disposed of the mystery of shells atop mountains, and it appealed to learned and unlearned alike because of its compatibility with the Biblical deluge. The Vulcanists held that the earth's chaotic surface was formed by volcanic explosion from intense heat within its bowels. On this theory the shells were supposed to have been thrown from the earth's bed onto the mountains by a gigantic convulsion. Jefferson, neither Vulcanist nor Neptunist, rejected both explanations. Nothing in the history of nature pointed to a force sufficient to warrant the Vulcanists' conclusion. Equally "out of the laws of nature" was the hypothesis of a universal deluge —an opinion that contributed to Jefferson's reputation as an infidel. Still a third solution to the riddle of the shells had been advanced by Voltaire: they were not shells at all but calcareous earth and stone formed by some process of nature into the image of shells. Jefferson took this position in the first edition of the *Notes on Virginia*. When David Rittenhouse, among others, disagreed, he reconsidered, altered the text, and stamped Voltaire's hypothesis unproven with the others. "Ignorance is preferable to error; and he is less remote from the truth who believes nothing, than he who believes what is wrong." Yet the theory of "mineral simulacra" of shells was the only one that did not run in the face of the laws of nature. It had the singular merit, moreover, of being subject to Jefferson's personal investigation. It was founded on observation of a spot of earth near Tours, in France. In 1787 Jefferson visited Tours to satisfy his curiosity in this matter. "What are we to conclude? That we have not materials enough yet to form any conclusion." He began to think the entire question "beyond the investigation of human sagacity." And soon historical geology, as differentiated from the useful applied science of mineralogy, appeared a senseless muddle: "the dreams about the modes of creations, inquiries whether our globe has been formed by the agency of fire or water, how many millions of years it has cost Vulcan or Neptune to produce what the fiat of the Creator would effect by a single act of will, is too idle to be worth a single hour of any man's life." His own idle hours with the mystery of the shells revealed both the strength and the weakness of Jefferson's scientific attitude. A hard-headed skepticism toward all explanations not grounded in observed facts of nature and a dominant utilitarian purpose. But impatience with imaginative generalizations which, while neither verifiable nor useful, held the promise of entire new orders of truth. The early geologists were wrong, yet they were on the right track, the track of evolution, while Jefferson slumbered in the pious faith of divine creation "by a single act of will."

In treating the animals of Virginia, Jefferson entered the first important rebuttal of European theories of degeneracy in the New

World. Georges Louis Leclerc, Comte de Buffon, the greatest naturalist in the world—"the pope of eighteenth century zoologists"—had said the New World exhibited fewer species than the Old and, of the animals common to both, those of the former were smaller, meanly formed, "very few ferocious, and none formidable." The niggardliness of American nature was owing to three facts: the coldness of the climate in comparison with other lands in similar latitudes, the excessive moisture that overlaid the ground and filled the atmosphere, and the very newness of America from the standpoint both of geologic time and human habitation. Buffon was a Neptunist. The American continent had emerged more recently from the deluge; it was, accordingly, more primitive. "In these melancholy regions," Buffon wrote depressingly, "nature remains concealed under her old garments, and never exhibits herself in fresh attire; being neither cherished nor cultivated by man, she never opens her fruitful and beneficient womb. . . . In this abandoned condition, every thing languishes, corrupts, and proves abortive. The air and the earth, overloaded with humid and noxious vapours, are unable either to purify themselves, or to profit by the influence of the sun, who darts in vain his most enlivening rays upon this frigid mass, which is not in a condition to make suitable return to his ardour. Its powers are limited to the production of moist plants, reptiles and insects, and can afford nourishment only for cold men and feeble animals." The savages of America formed no exception to the rule of degeneracy, according to Buffon. But it was left to others to take the next step, condemning the transplanted European to waste and decay in the wretched New World. The Abbé Raynal, the Swedish naturalist Kalm, the Dutchman De Pauw, the Scotsman William Robertson, whose *History of America*, published in 1777, won a large audience—these freely elaborated the theory until Buffon himself was moved to refute their extravagances.

Jefferson's vindication of American nature attacked the Buffon theory in its conclusions rather than in its premises. That the natural environment basically determined institutional life was the assumption of the age. But whether America was, in fact, comparatively more humid, whether moisture was unfriendly to animal growth, whether there had been a deluge or America had emerged late from it, were questions scientists could not answer. Prompted by Franklin, Jefferson later pursued evidence to prove that Europe was actually more humid than America; but knowledge of these matters was still very primitive, as he said in the *Notes*, giving neither proof nor disproof of degeneracy theories. He proceeded instead on the assumption that America was equally adapted with Europe to animal life. "Let us then take a comparative view of the quadrupeds of Europe and America, presenting them to the eye in three different tables, in one of which shall be enumerated those found in both countries; in a second, those found in one only; in a third, those which have been domesticated in both." The truth would then emerge from comparisons of number and size. He put his friends to work weighing and measuring animals "from the mouse to the mammoth." "I Killed a bear, not fat which waighed 410 lb after he was Quartered," Archibald Cary reported, "and have seen much larger but had no oppartunaty of Trying their Weight." Weasel and woodchuck were never more meticulously gauged and scaled than by James Madison! As the data came in, Jefferson filled up his tables. They remained very imperfect, as he conceded, not only because comparable weights were unavailable for comparable animals, but also because the state of the science and the differences in nomenclature between the two continents often made it impossible to identify the comparable animals. Nevertheless, so far as the evidence went, Jefferson was justified in his conclusions: that of the quadrupeds common to both continents, those of America were generally as large; that the types peculiar to America were much more numerous than those peculiar to Europe and built on as generous a scale; that while the domestic animals were perhaps smaller in America, the cause was to be found in the miserable animal husbandry of the country rather than in its climate; and finally, taking all the tables together, that America produced more than her share of the world's quadrupeds. As great a zoologist as Buffon was, in Jefferson's opinion, he showed "more eloquence than sound reason" in support of his theory.

One animal particularly, the mammoth, fascinated Jefferson, and it furnished the *coup de grâce* in his encounter with Buffon. Tusks, grinders, and bones of this huge creature of Indian legend had been found on the Ohio. While Governor of Virginia, inspired perhaps by Marbois's queries, Jefferson had asked George Rogers Clark to procure the necessary bones to reconstruct a skeleton of this most desirable of all objects of natural history. Not for many years was the mission accomplished, by Colonel William Clark (of Lewis and Clark fame) under Jefferson's auspices; but thus began Jefferson's long interest in paleontology, his one great passion in pure science. Certain European naturalists, including Buffon, had said that the relics of the so-called mammoth belonged to the family of elephant. But the elephant, Jefferson pointed out, was a native only of the torrid zone and its skeleton was probably but one-fifth that of the mammoth. He thought the mammoth a distinct species, "the largest of all terrestial beings," and believed it still roamed the frozen northland. The Old World elephant was but a mouse to the New World mammoth! "It should have sufficed to have rescued the earth it inhabited, and the atmosphere it breathed, from the imputation of impotence in the conception and nourishment of animal life on a large scale; to have stifled, in its birth, the opinion of a writer, the most learned, too, of all others in the science of animal history . . . that nature is less active, less energetic on one side of the globe than she is on the other."

There was a touch of the fabulous in Jefferson's account of the mammoth, as if to answer European pessimism with a tale of American giants; but he checked himself and kept the discussion on a high plane. Although his comparative data supported a claim for American superiority, he asked only for equality, consistent with the enlightened principle of uniformity in the operations of nature. He had no desire, not yet anyway, to encourage a delusion the opposite of Buffon's: America the land of noble savagery or Arcadian simplicity in contrast to the civilized decadence of Europe. It was against this romantic conception, nourished by the primitivism of Jean Jacques Rousseau, that Voltaire, Buffon, and the partisans of civilization had risen in protest. Jefferson did not take sides in this contest. But in the *Notes on Virginia*, as it happened, the criticism was all on one side, and several of the book's most eloquent passages contributed mightily to the idealization of American nature. Revolutionary nationalism accented nature. Philosophical Europeans, responding to the achievement of the American Revolution, established correlations between the natural environment of the Americans and the principles of liberty. The New World image projected by Raynal, Buffon, and the other degenerationists was fading fast, at least as to the United States, when Jefferson undertook to refute it. The *Notes on Virginia* blended in with the ascendant revolutionary cult of America, though idealization was far from Jefferson's intention.

For the Abbé Raynal the great crime of the New World was the ruthless slaughter, plunder, and enslavement both of the Indian aborigines and the imported Africans. Jefferson treated at considerable length each of these races, the conquered and the enslaved, as well as his own race of conquerors.

For all his enlightenment, Jefferson suffered the color prejudice of Western man. He believed the race of "whites" of superior beauty, possibly of superior intellect, though morally no better or worse than others. Civilization in the United States was the white man's enterprise and responsibility. Any other hypothesis was inconceivable to him. But he did not idealize the prospect. From the end of the Revolution the country would probably be "going down hill." In Virginia the people had yet to secure a constitution of their own or the education of their posterity; they would, he feared, become caught up in the race for riches, forget about their rights, and lose their chance of happiness. The natural history of government, as he always said, was for liberty to lose and tyranny to gain ground. Such had been the fate of Rome, and Britain's sun had already set. What saved him from pessimism was the dominant fact of the American environment: "an immensity of land courting the industry of the husbandman." The economic values of agriculture concerned him, of course, but the moral values were of first importance. Agricultural industry put man into relationship with the natural world, and through that to the divine Creator; it nourished a virtuous way of life; it secured dignity, competency, and independence, so essential to the support of free government. "It is the manner and spirit of a people which preserve a republic in vigor," he wrote. Jefferson's hymn to the husbandman became famous:

> Those who labor in the earth are the chosen people of God, if ever He had a chosen people, whose breasts He has made His peculiar deposit for substantial and genuine virtue. It is the focus in which He keeps alive that sacred fire, which otherwise might escape from the face of the earth. Corruption of morals

in the mass of cultivators is a phenomenon of which no age nor nation has furnished an example. It is the mark set on those, who, not looking up to heaven, to their own soil and industry, as does the husbandman, for their subsistence, depend for it on casualties and caprice of customers. Dependence begets subservience and venality, suffocates the germ of virtue, and prepares fit tools for the designs of ambition. This, the natural progress and consequence of the arts, has sometimes perhaps been retarded by accidental circumstances; but, generally speaking, the proportion which the aggregate of the other classes of citizens bears in any State to that of its husbandmen, is the proportion of its unsound to its healthy parts, and is a good enough barometer whereby to measure its degree of corruption. While we have land to labor then, let us never wish to see our citizens occupied at a work-bench, or twirling a distaff.

This was an ideal, drawn from poetry more than from observation, and not meant to describe any American reality; but it was meant as a moral directive consonant with the American environment. In 1782 Hector St. Jean Crèvecœur struck the same bucolic note in his *Letters from an American Farmer*, which became the bible of a European cult of republican simplicity. It was not so much the farmer or farming that Jefferson, or Crèvecœur, idealized, but a state of life midway between the primitive and the civilized, possessing the virtues of both and the vices of neither. This dreamy state captured his feelings and his hopes for the culture of man in America.

For Jefferson, clearly, the American land was a regenerative force. Taking up the application of the degeneracy theory to "the race of whites," Jefferson focused on Raynal's statement of amazement that America had not yet produced a good poet, an able mathematician, or a man of genius in any science. In war Washington, in physics Franklin, in astronomy Rittenhouse: these names, Jefferson declared in answer, would be remembered long after the philosophy defrauding the Western day was forgotten. America, "though but a child of yesterday," with a population not one-third that of Great Britain or one-sixth that of France, had contributed her full share to the world's genius. He claimed nothing in poetry but, with ill-disguised indignation, asked for time. "When we shall have existed as a people as long as the Greeks did before they produced a Homer, the Romans a Virgil, the French a Racine and Voltaire, the English a Shakespeare and Milton, shall this reproach be still true, we will inquire from what unfriendly causes it has proceeded, that the other countries of Europe and quarters of the earth shall not have inscribed any name in the roll of poets." The European reproach to American culture rang down the years. Jefferson's response, while more realistic and restrained than many to come, unmasked the patriotic ardor that animated his entire vindication of American nature.

The Virginia philosopher keenly perceived the dilemma of the American Indian and, in a sense, entered into it himself. As children of nature, the aborigines were admirable. They recalled man to his original freedom. He sometimes wondered if their condition, without organized government, was not the best; it was certainly preferable to the government of "wolves over sheep" as in Europe. But civilization was the natural state of the white man. As he pushed back the wilderness, the Indian way of life was doomed. Fortunately, these people possessed equal powers of body and mind with the whites; hence they could be civilized, fully incorporated into the white man's society, indeed racially amalgamated as well. Ultimately, the Indians could be saved from extinction only by losing their racial identity—by becoming Americanized.

Buffon had condemned this race to stupidity and impotence. Mere automatons of nature, feeble in body and mind, without manly ardor or parental affection, their fundamental defect, according to Buffon, was one of sexual incapacity. The picture was false, Jefferson said. In a superficial view certain characteristics of the race (the beardlessness of the males, the fewer childbirths of the females) supported the theory; but these were cultural rather than physical characteristics. "With them it is disgraceful to be hairy on the body," for example. "They say it likens them to hogs. They therefore pluck the hair as fast as it appears." Making allowance for the "circumstances of their situation which call for a display of particular talents only"—talents of war and chase—"we shall probably find that they are formed in mind as well as in body on the same module with the *Homo sapiens Europaeus*." Even in their savage state the Indians showed the germ of higher talents. "They astonish you with

258

strokes of the most sublime oratory; such as to prove their reason and sentiment strong, their imagination glowing and elevated." Jefferson introduced into the *Notes* the affecting speech of the Mingo Chief Logan, related to him at Williamsburg in 1774. The speech had been published before, in the United States, England, and France, but the *Notes* gave it immortality. Schoolboys across the land later declaimed this grave lament on the white man's murderous destruction of the chief's family and his proud revenge, closing with the familiar line, "Who is there to mourn for Logan? Not one."

Jefferson's interest in the redmen was essentially anthropological. The *Notes* provided an informed summary of the numbers and locations of the tribes of North America. He described his own careful excavation of a large barrow in Albemarle and speculated on the origin of the aborigines. Whether they were the product of a "special creation," as Buffon and Lord Kames thought, or descended from an ancient people—Hebrew, Tartar, Carthaginian—was a much debated question. In Jefferson's opinion they were of the same race as the people of Northern Asia, Tartar, having probably crossed from one continent to the other by way of the Bering Strait. The conjecture was not original; but he went on to argue against the principal authorities that the migration had been from North America to Asia rather than the other way around. He inferred the greater antiquity of the Americans from the greater profusion of tongues and dialects among them. At any rate, the comparative study of languages held the key to the puzzle of origins. He lamented that many tribes had passed away without leaving any record of the languages they spoke. At the time of writing the *Notes*, he commenced a remarkable collection of Indian vocabularies, eventually numbering some forty tribes. He thus employed the tools of ethnology, archaeology, and linguistics in his study of the Indians.

Jefferson's vindication of the American Indian was at the same time a vindication of the American environment; the children of Africa, on the other hand, had no natural place in that environment, and his solution for them was not amalgamation but expulsion. The double standard toward Indians and Africans was at least two centuries old. The great Hispanic priest Las Casas, while he had envisioned a Christianized utopia for the Indians of the New World, had condemned the Negroes of the dark continent of the Old World to perpetual slavery. The Indians of the Northern latitudes had not, with few exceptions, been enslaved, which seemed to Jefferson all the more reason to bring them under a different rule than the unfortunate blacks, redeemed by neither nature nor civilization. But this rule did not justify their enslavement.

Jefferson's impassioned denunciation of slavery occurred in answer to the query on "the particular customs and manners" of Virginians. Basically, his position was a moral one, founded in the immutable principles of human liberty. No abolitionist of later time ever cried out more prophetically against slavery. "And can the liberties of a nation be thought secure when we have removed their only firm basis, a conviction in the minds of the people that these liberties are the gift of God?" he demanded. "That they are not to be violated but with his wrath? Indeed I tremble for my country when I reflect that God is just. . . ." He even threatened "supernatural interference"—an event unheard of in his philosophy—should civil emancipation fail to take place. But Jefferson was moved as much by the debasement of the master as by the misery and oppression of the slave. Like Montesquieu, he believed that slavery created an evil social environment, retarded public improvement, and corrupted the master class. "The whole commerce between master and slave is a perpetual exercise of the most boisterous passions, the most unremitting despotism on the one part, and degrading submission on the other. . . . The man must be a prodigy who can retain his manners and morals undepraved by such circumstances." And he added, "With the morals of the people, their industry also is destroyed." Jefferson sketched the plan of gradual emancipation earlier withheld by the revisers, and looked hopefully to young men growing up, who had "sucked in the principles of liberty as it were with their mothers' milk," to turn the fate of this question. Young men still in college: this was the audience Jefferson wished to reach. Outside a small circle of friends, they were the first Americans to receive his book.

The colonization feature of the plan of emancipation led Jefferson into a discussion of the racial attributes of the Negro; and here he broached opinions that seriously embarrassed his philosophy. It was unthinkable, he said, to incorporate the mass of freed blacks into the commonwealth. "Deep-rooted prejudices entertained by the whites; ten thousand recollections, by the blacks, of the injuries they have sustained; new provocations; the real distinctions which nature has made; and many other circumstances, will divide us into parties, and produce convulsions, which will probably never end but in the extermination of one or the other race. To these objections, which are political," Jefferson continued, "may be added others, which are physical and moral." The color of the Negroes, "that immovable veil of black," which in its "eternal monotony" was aesthetically inferior to "the fine mixtures of red and white" of the Caucasians, posed a powerful objection to the racial blending that must ensue from a simple act of emancipation. There were differences of figure, of hair, of glandular function, all unfavorable to the Negroes. "Many of their advocates," among whom Jefferson counted himself, "while they wish to vindicate the liberty of human nature, are anxious also to preserve its dignity and beauty." In a moral view the Negroes had several engaging, if somewhat child-like qualities. But they had little capacity for reflection or forethought; in reason they were much inferior to the whites, in imagination "dull, tasteless, and anomalous"; and, while sexually ardent, their affections were neither tender nor lasting. Many Negroes, unlike the Indians, had associated with the whites, some were liberally educated; yet never had Jefferson known a black to utter an eloquent thought, compose a piece of music, paint a simple picture, discover a single truth. The criticism came with ill grace from the man who demolished Raynal for employing the same line of argument against the American whites!

Great allowance ought to be made for "the difference of condition," Jefferson conceded, but too many proofs offered that the inferiority of the Negroes was not the effect merely of their servile status. The slavery of ancient Rome was infinitely more wretched than the American; nevertheless, the Roman slaves excelled in the arts and sciences. "But they were of the race of white," Jefferson reasoned from the analogy. "It is not their condition then, but nature, which has produced this distinction." The very thought was treason to his heart and head. Still he advanced the opinion, though "a suspicion only" and "hazarded with great diffidence," "that the blacks, whether originally a distinct race, or made distinct by time and circumstances, are inferior to the whites in the endowments both of body and mind."

261

Honest, disinterested, and no doubt true to his personal observation and knowledge, Jefferson's opinion was also a product of frivolous and tortuous reasoning, of preconception, prejudice, ignorance, contradiction, and bewildering confusion of principles. Was he not simply voicing the master's conceit in observing that, while the Negroes "seem to require less sleep," they are disposed to sleep more than the whites? Their disposition to theft he readily ascribed to condition, but the transiency of their griefs he supposed a defect of nature, never stopping to consider the slaves' inordinate need for a psychological mechansim to check grief. The analogy to Roman slavery was badly misplaced. The discussion of the comparative beauty of the two races betrayed an insensibility to standards other than his own. Many of his observations, paraded as scientific, were but thinly disguised statements of folk belief about Negroes. This was blatantly true of his causual reference to the uniform preference shown by the orangutan for the black woman over the female of his own species. Yet even Buffon, "the greatest scientist in the world," had credited this notion. Deplorably, Jefferson was not out of tune with the scientific teaching of his day. Edward Tyson's monumental treatise on the orangutan, with which Jefferson was probably familiar, had established the close proximity of ape to man, and from this some scientific and pseudo-scientific observers—it is not always easy to distinguish them—went on to infer the Negro's intermediate place in the chain of being. Whether the Negro was equal or inferior to European man, if the latter whether his inferiority stemmed from genetic or environmental causes, and whether he was to be considered a different species or an inferior variety of the same species, the offspring of a unitary or a separate creation of God—these questions scratched the minds of the Enlightenment. The tendency was toward a humane, generous, and hopeful view of the Negro, as in *Esprit des lois* or, even better, the later work of Jefferson's philosophical friend in Paris, the Marquis de Condorcet, which he began to translate into English and never finished. But there were heretics, like the great Hume, who argued the natural inferiority of the Negro.

Jefferson's basic assumptions touching race were liberal and enlightened, but they were upset by his observation from the post of a Virginia planter. He could account for the observed inferiority of the Negro in one of two ways: either the Negro was a distinct species with an ancestry other than the white man's or an environmentally produced variety of the same species. But neither explanation was satisfactory. The first degraded a whole race of men in the order of Creation, exploding the equality doctrine founded in the unity of the species. The second was inconsistent with the conception of a fixed chain of being wrought by the Creator in the beginning. If the Negro was created equal, he could not lapse in the scale of being; if created unequal, time and improvement could not raise him on the scale. Jefferson evaded the problem, declining to accept either the explanation that assailed his faith in human equality or the explanation that played havoc with the system of nature. Nevertheless, overwhelmed by the physical distinctions between the races and the limited testimony of his senses, he raised the awful doubt of Negro inferiority.

Why? A quarter-century later, still not allowed to forget what he had written, Jefferson said, "It is impossible for doubt to have been more tenderly and hesitatingly expressed than it was in the *Notes on Virginia,* and nothing was farther from my intention than to enlist myself as the champion of a fixed opinion, where I have only expressed a doubt." Fair enough, in view of the abuse he had taken. Yet his "doubt" had been the conclusion of a long argument that carried the tone of conviction, and the opinion he chose to "hazard" was inferiority rather than equality. He might have been expected to place the emphasis on the inhibiting effects of slavery. In defense of the noble redmen he repeatedly appealed to "the circumstances of their situation." He argued that the conquest of the wilderness would ameliorate the American climate. Even the size of the asses of America was the effect of circumstances, not of nature. Yet he was unable to see the Negro in the same light. He reproached his countrymen for their failure to view either of the minority peoples living among them as subjects of natural history, which was to say, in effect, that these races were still unknown to scientific intelligence. Perhaps he wished, by broaching the subject, to open the way to investigation. But he broached it, it will be recalled, in order to demonstrate the practical impossibility of incorporating the emancipated blacks into the free American society. The twin imperatives were emancipation and colonization. To support, in his own mind to justify, the latter, he offered his damning appraisal of Negro capacities. Perhaps in this way he hoped to hasten a solution—the only workable one in his opinion—to the most menacing problem of the new nation.

Still, in the final analysis, what is astounding is that he chose to advance any conclusion at all, albeit a guarded one. He always commended the skeptical attitude: believe nothing rather than what is unproven. "To justify a general conclusion, requires many observations, even where the subject may be submitted to the anatomical knife, to optical glasses, to analysis by fire or by solvents. How much more then where it is a faculty, not a substance, we are examining; where it eludes the research of all the senses . . . ," as in the case of a race of men little known to natural history. Instead of adhering to this rule, he reached a tentative conclusion on the Negro that he knew to be indefensible morally and unproven scientifically. He soon retreated under fire from assorted Christians, speculators, abolitionists, and political enemies, though the latter usually seized upon his condemnation of slavery. Unable to affirm the natural equality of the Negro, unwilling to deny it, he suspended judgment and closed his mouth, meanwhile keeping his mind open and, as a practical matter, adhering to the liberal principle. "Whatever be their degree of talent," he declared, "it is no measure of their rights."

The *Notes on Virginia* ensured Jefferson a scientific and literary reputation to accompany his reputation as a political philosopher and statesman. Its information on all sorts of phenomena natural and civil, its sometimes dazzling erudition, its flights of speculation—these made it a book fit for the appetites of learned men. The circle of its readers steadily increased as the restraints on its circulation were lifted and as its author became better known to the American people. While never a popular book, it was constantly involved in public discussion. In Virginia, particularly, its politcal parts became virtually a handbook of liberal opinion. The *Notes on Virginia* acted as a catalyst in several fields of intellectual activity. It set an enviable standard for the writing of state histories and, of course, spurred this enterprise. It stimulated the investigation and inventory of the natural resources of the new nation. When Jedediah Morse, "the father of American geography," published his pioneer work in

1785, all he had to do with respect to Virginia and the vast western domain was to reprint the account from the *Notes on Virginia*. (Some travelers offered Jefferson's depiction as their own!) It set the stage for the literary battles of the next half-century between the Old World and the New. Much of the book, having served its purpose, soon became outmoded, and Jefferson never found the leisure to revise it as he wished to do. It would be longest and best remembered for the triumphant vindication of American nature. "Mr. Jefferson," an American scientist later declared, "in stepping forward as he did in favour of American power, may be almost said to have proclaimed emancipation a second time."

The Vagabond Congress

Jefferson was at Ampthill, Archibald Cary's place down the James, having his children inoculated against smallpox, when he was notified of his reappointment as Minister Plenipotentiary to negotiate peace. There was no time for delay. He placed little Polly and the infant Lucy in the care of their Aunt Eppes, arranged the management of his affairs, and left Monticello accompanied by ten-year-old Patsy, whom he was determined to keep at his side, on December 19. They were in Philadelphia a week later. Jefferson armed himself for the negotiations, poring over papers in the office of the Secretary of Foreign Affairs, and wondering if he would have anything to do upon his arrival in Paris but to toast the victory. Dispatches from the commissioners on the scene had already announced a preliminary accord. Then the brief stopover he had planned lengthened to a month, as the French warship in which he was to sail lay locked in ice below Baltimore.

The month passed pleasantly enough. Jefferson attended the meetings of the American Philosophical Society, then struggling to recover from the war's paralysis. He dipped into his pocketbook to help the cause of "useful knowledge," and at one of the meetings proposed that the Society present the King of France with an orrery to be made by the great Rittenhouse. (The Society agreed to the resolution, but the orrery was never completed.) He drew up at this time the first "catalogue" of his library, listing as well the books he wished to procure in France. From it Madison compiled a desideratum of some 300 titles to be embodied in a report to Congress recommending, unsuccessfully, the establishment of a congressional library. With Madison he concerted the first of many ciphers to be employed in political correspondence in order to evade snoopers and tattlers on both sides of the Atlantic.

The resumption of his friendship with Madison proved of lasting consequence. They lived under the same roof in Philadelphia, ate at the same table, and spent long hours in conversation. After the passage of a month, the friendship became something more, a partnership of two philosophic statesmen, enduring with scarcely a ripple between them as long as they lived. They had unlimited confidence in each other. Each in his own station was the eyes and the ears and the helping hand of the other. Madison, younger by several years, readily acted the part of the faithful lieutenant, undertaking assignments from Jefferson such as he would never ask him to perform. Yet Madison was a general in his own right, "the greatest man in the world," Jefferson called him in 1790; and in the constant exchange of ideas and services between them the account balanced. Men who were enough alike to work together, yet sufficiently different to complement each other, their alliance was remarkably beneficial. Madison had the more penetrating mind, sharp, probing, and persistent. Jefferson was the bolder thinker, more inventive, more talented in generalization and synthesis, and easily caught up in any idea that promised improvement to mankind. Madison had the keener sense of realities: he helped to keep Jefferson's political feet on the ground. In the new nation's search for an equilibrium between liberty and power, Jefferson's stress typically fell on the first term of the equation, Madison's on the second. Jefferson possessed the gift of brilliant rhetoric, Madison of skillful analysis. Jefferson had political magnetism, Madison none. About Jefferson there was an aura of greatness from the moment he stepped into fame: he stood, like his house, on a mountain, and celebrated himself in splendid achievements. Madison radiated neither mastery nor charm, but he had infinitely more patience with the drudgeries of politics and shone in caucuses and committees. Men respected Madison, even in opposition. They worshiped, or hated, Jefferson.

Toward the end of January 1783, Jefferson and his daughter

rode to Baltimore to board the French frigate *Romulus* for passage to France. Again he was delayed, by winter ice and a British fleet blocking Chesapeake Bay. No flag of safe conduct having been asked or received for Jefferson's passage, his capture was a calculable certainty were he to venture forth. "I am exceedingly fatigued with this place," he wrote to Madison after a fortnight, "as indeed I should be with any other when I had neither occupation nor amusement." He was soon rescued. Reports that a provisional treaty had been signed reached Congress the middle of February, and Jefferson's orders were suspended. Returning to Philadelphia, he waited another month to learn what final disposition would be made of him. When the earlier reports were verified, Congress gave him his discharge. The disappointment he felt at the defeat of his plans was submerged in the glad tidings of peace. On April 11 he sent a letter of congratulations to the commission in Paris, and the next day departed for Virginia.

He did not intend to fall back into the retirement he had so recently left. Stopping at Richmond, he discussed public affairs with members of the assembly. Under Madison's prodding at Philadelphia, he had enlisted in the campaign to strengthen the Confederacy. The first point to be gained from the states was the power of Congress to raise its own revenue by means of an impost. No doubt Jefferson lobbied for this measure at Richmond. With the end of the war, the question of a convention to "new model" the Virginia constitution was seriously agitated. Nothing was closer to Jefferson's heart. The chances of a convention seemed to him good. When he collected his family and returned to Monticello in May, he prepared a new draft constitution which, as noted earlier, made some advances over his previous thinking. He sent it to Madison and later incorporated it in the *Notes on Virginia*. But the convention never materialized. In June the assembly placed Jefferson at the head of the newly elected delegation to Congress. The news probably came as no surprise. He had discussed congressional duty with Madison in Philadelphia, and he could not have avoided the subject in Richmond. If he would accept employment in Congress, the assembly was eager to put him there. And so, after a lazy summer at Monticello, Jefferson again parted with his two younger daughters, arranged his affairs, and set out for Philadelphia, Patsy in tow, the middle of October. He traveled a westerly route, through the Shenandoah Valley bedecked in fall colors, leisurely viewing caves and caverns and the spectacle at Harper's Ferry—scenes new to his eye and depicted in the *Notes on Virginia*—thence to Philadelphia.

Unfortunately, a soldiers' mutiny had driven Congress from Philadelphia. It was temporarily quartered in the insignificant village of Princeton, New Jersey, "utterly undecided," as Madison informed his friend, "both as to their ultimate seat and their intermediate residence." Jefferson hurried off to Princeton, and took his seat on November 4, the same day Congress adjourned to reconvene at Annapolis, Maryland, three weeks later. Wherever Congress might set, he meant to settle Patsy in Philadelphia, the metropolis of America, for her education. He now arranged for her to live with the widowed mother of his friend, the genial poetaster, composer, and gadgeteer Francis Hopkinson, and canvassed the city for the best tutors in French, music, dancing, and drawing.

His familiar letters to Patsy, which commenced on his arrival at Annapolis, portray a keenly solicitous and demanding father. His wife gone, he clutched his daughters to his heart, the eldest especially, and transferred to them his hopes of personal happiness. "I have placed my happiness on seeing you good and accomplished," he told Patsy, "and no distress which this world can now bring on me could equal that of your disappointing my hopes." It was a dreadful onus to place on a child. Patsy carried it better than her younger sister. The daily regimen Jefferson prescribed was rather forbidding: "From 8 to 10 o'clock practice music. From 10 to 1 dance one day and draw another. From 1 to 2 draw on the day you dance, and write a letter the next day. From 3 to 4 read French. From 4 to 5 exercise yourself in music. From 5 till bedtime read English, write etc." Patsy was to write by every post. "Inform me what books you read, what tunes you learn, and inclose me your best copy of every lesson in drawing." Father was crushed when weekly epistles, and the drawings, failed to arrive. Mixing endearments with admonitions, his letters usually taught some little lesson in deportment. "Take care that you never spell a word wrong. . . . It produces great praise in a lady to spell well." "I do not wish you to be gayly clothed at this time of life, but that what you wear should be fine of its kind; but above all things, and at all times let your clothes be clean, whole, and properly put on. . . . Nothing is so disgusting to our sex as a want of cleanliness and delicacy in yours." "Determine never to be idle. No person will have occasion to complain of the want of time who never loses any." The man who found himself equal to whatever he undertook expected the same ability and application in his children. Deeply devoted to her father, Patsy did her best, which was really very good, and continually promised to do better; but sometimes she was at her wits' end to please him.

After the peregrinations of the past year, Jefferson was glad to come to rest at last in Annapolis. James Monroe, newly elected to Congress, had arranged temporary quarters for them in the home of a widow lady. Then in February the two men rented a house, hired a French major-domo, and lived quietly as two bachelors until Jefferson's departure in May. Annapolis was a charming, pleasure-loving town. It boasted a theater but no church, and "plays, balls, concerts, routs, hops, fandangoes and fox hunting." Jefferson did not partake of these amusements. He hated the cold, and the winter in Annapolis was "severe beyond all memory." Through most of it he was ill: a prolonged infection, with intermittent high fever, later complicated by his old headache affliction. Not until spring was he on the mend. The public business was demanding; but since Congress was slow to organize, and then frequently stalled for want of a quorum, he read a good deal and worked sporadically on the *Notes on Virginia*.

A young Dutch nobleman, Gijsbert Karel van Hogendorp, whom Jefferson befriended at Annapolis, portrayed him in words that have the ring of authenticity. "Retired from fashionable society," Hogendorp said, "he concerned himself only with affairs of public interest, his sole diversion being that offered by belles lettres. The poor state of his health, he told me occasionally, was the cause of this retirement; but it seemed rather that his mind, accustomed to the unalloyed pleasure of the society of a lovable wife, was impervious since her loss to the feeble attractions of common society, and that his soul, fed on noble thoughts, was revolted by idle chatter. . . . He has the shyness that accompanies true worth, which is at first disturbing and which puts off those who seek to know him. Those who persist in knowing him soon discern the man of letters, the lover of natural history, Law, Statecraft, Philosophy, and the friend of mankind." Hogendorp persisted. Jefferson liked him, thought him brilliant, took him into his household, fed his curiosity about things American, and seemed to open his heart to this presumptuous young man.

Congress was in deep trouble as the nation emerged from the war. The Confederation had slowly gathered strength in the presence of the common enemy; now, the enemy gone, the incentive to tighten the continental belt seemed gone too. When Congress failed to obtain additional powers from the states, the promising nationalist movement of the later war years subsided, and several of its young leaders, like Madison and Alexander Hamilton, of New York, retired in disgust. New faces predominated in the Congress Jefferson entered at Annapolis, itself a symbol of congressional impotency. The problem began with obtaining a quorum. The presence of a majority of the states was required to transact any business at all. Seven states must concur in the adoption of ordinary legislation, nine in decisions of greater import. These numbers proved formidable in themselves; but when it is considered that most of the states in attendance were represented by only two delegates, who must therefore concur if the vote of that state was to affect the decision on any question, the predicament of Congress becomes truly staggering. "There are 8 states in town, 6 of which are represented by two members only," Jefferson wrote to Madison in February. "Of these two members of different states are confined by the gout so that we cannot make a house. We have not sit above 3 days I believe in as many weeks. Admonition after admonition has been sent to the states, to no effect." The numbers changed from time to time, but the problem was constant. What could it signify but indifference to the government of the Union or inability of the states to support it? Jefferson preferred the latter, the more charitable, explanation. While he advocated the accession of new powers and the more vigorous employment of existing ones, he made every allowance for the havoc wreaked by the war in most of the states. "The greatest difficulty we find is to get money from them. The reason is not found in their unwillingness, but in their real inability." The Confederacy had labored under this difficulty for years; now, however, it reflected itself in the niggardly policy of the states toward their delegations, if any, in that "vagabond, strolling, contemptible crew," the Congress of the United States. Jefferson felt it in his own purse. He was on public duty for four months before he received one cent of pay. Other congressmen were in tighter straits. "There is really no standing this." And, of course, good men would not stand it for long. Everyone's energies were quickly exhausted in vain efforts to do business, and the interminable sessions, which necessarily followed from the lack of an executive head, were beyond endurance. After all was said of the feebleness of Congress on the point of constitutional powers, the fact remained, in Jefferson's opinion, that it lacked the political backing of the states, the internal organization, the caliber of leadership required for the effective exercise of the powers it had.

Jefferson at once encountered the problem in the ratification of the treaty of peace. When Congress finally reconvened on December 13, he was appointed to a committee to report on the definitive treaty. The report recommending its approval was submitted in his hand three days later. Seven states only being present, when the Articles of Confederation required the assent of nine to a treaty, the question of how Congress should proceed caused heated debate. Nor was it merely an abstract question. The treaty, having been signed on September 3, allowed six months, until March 3, 1784, for the exchange of ratifications to take place in Paris. Congress was reaching the ultimate point of time for ratification, after which the British government could regard the treaty as void. A number of congressmen ingeniously argued that seven states were competent to sanction the treaty. Jefferson called this course "a dishonorable prostitution of our seal," and led the opposition, less on grounds of law than of policy. The treaty was a solemn engagement. In the nature of the Confederation, its enforcement would rest with the states. Although nine states had approved the treaty in its provisional form, several of its articles—on the return of Tories and the restitution of confiscated estates, for instance—were already resisted. What excuses and evasions might not be found if the treaty was riveted on the states by a body representing less than one-third of the whole citizenry! The only statesman-like course was to remove every possible source of cavil. If this was true with regard to the United States, it was equally true with regard to Britain. Jefferson did not minimize the

271

risks of delay. War was kindling in Europe, and if France were to be involved Britain might jump at the opportunity to scrap or amend the treaty. But the risks of fraud and deception were far greater, he thought. It would be easy enough to explain a delay; it would be impossible to explain or to justify an improper ratification, should Whitehall choose to make a point of it. Jefferson had the votes to defeat the move for immediate ratification. Having done so, he yielded to the opposition, "very restless on the loss of their motion," and proposed to meet them on "middle ground." He prepared a resolution declaring ratification by seven states so far as they were competent and requesting the commissioners in Paris to obtain an extension of three months for the exchange of the treaty. In this way the integrity both of the Confederation and of the treaty would be protected. The resolution appeased the opposition. Fortunately, events made it unnecessary. On January 13 the delegations from Connecticut and New Jersey took their seats. Nine states formally endorsed the treaty on the next day. The instrument of ratification was Jefferson's report of December 16. He also wrote the public proclamation. So the author of the document declaring American independence became, seven and one-half years later, the author of the state papers announcing its consummation.

The celebration of the peace was anti-climactic in Annapolis. Just before Christmas, Congress witnessed the imposing spectacle of George Washington's resignation as Commander in Chief. Since taking leave of his officers in New York on December 4, the General had been on a homeward journey that was one long triumphal procession. He arrived in Annapolis on December 19, and only on the next day announced his intention of surrendering his sword to Congress. Jefferson was named chairman of a committee hurriedly appointed to make the arrangements for Washington's "public audience," set for the noon hour, December 23. People crowded the Maryland State House, the meeting place of Congress, to witness the ceremony. "The spectators all wept, and there was hardly a member of Congress who did not drop tears." The General's hand shook, his voice faltered, it was said, as he read his solemn address. "Having now finished the work assigned to me," he concluded, "I retire from the great theatre of Action; and bidding an Affectionate farewell to this August body under whose orders I have so long acted, I here offer my Commission, and take my leave of all the employments of public life." So saying, he drew his commission from his chest and presented it to the President of Congress, who replied in an address that showed "the shining traces of Jefferson's pen." The ceremony concluded, Washington "bid every member farewell and rode off from the door, intent upon eating his Christmas dinner at home." Jefferson had little liking for ceremony of any kind, but the voluntary retirement of the victorious general who might have become a Caesar was an event so honorable to the young republic that it left an indelible impression on his mind.

National Cornerstones

Jefferson must have wished that Congress had the "august" character Washington generously attributed to it. "Our body was little numerous, but very contentious," he recalled in his autobiography. "Day after day was wasted on the most unimportant questions." On one occasion of "trifling but wordy debate," a member asked him how he could sit impassively while men spouted nonsense. "I observed to him, that to refute indeed was easy, but to silence was impossible; that in measures brought forward by myself, I took the laboring oar, as was incumbent on me; but that in general, I was willing to listen; that if every sound argument or objection was used by some one or other of the numerous debaters, it was enough; if not, I thought it sufficient to suggest the omission, without going into a repetition of what had been already said by others: that this was a watse and abuse of the time and patience of the House, which could not be justified." He observed that Washington and Franklin, with whom he had served in the old Burgesses and in Congress respectively, had never spoken more than ten minutes on any question. "They laid their shoulders to the great points, knowing that the little ones would follow of themselves." It was a good example, and he followed it. In Congress he showed the same talent for legislative business, for modest leadership, and for bold political design he had earlier demonstrated in Virginia affairs. Immediately, without a trace of effort, he became the dominant figure. Indeed, whatever merit Congress had during his five months of service was mainly owing to his presence.

When the treaty of peace was out of the way and Congress had the majority, at least for a time, to tackle its new problems, Jefferson reported the formidable agenda to the Governor of Virginia: "1. Authorizing our foreign ministers to enter into treaties of alliance and commerce with the several nations who have desired it. 2. Arranging the domestic administration. 3. Establishing arsenals within the states, and posts on our frontiers. 4. Disposing of the Western territory. 5. Treaties of peace and purchase with the Indians. 6. Money." His hand was present in all but the third item of the agenda. He chaired the principal committees and wrote the principal reports. In connection with the fourth and sixth items, his contributions were of the highest importance. But the list does not begin to encompass Jefferson's work in Congress. As the head of the Virginia delegation, no doubt remembering his own experience as governor, he inaugurated a regular system of communication with the state government. Only in this way could the Confederation gain the support it required. Questions stemming from the treaty, questions of commerce and navigation, questions of congressional power— none could be settled satisfactorily, even with the best will in the world, unless there was co-operation between the governments. "We seem to blunder here more for want of information than design," Benjamin Harrison, the Governor, told Jefferson. Harrison was grateful for the new plan of correspondence. Each member reserved the right to dissent from the reported views of the delegation as a whole, a right often exercised by two of the five Virginians in particular. With Monroe and young Samuel Hardy, whose one foible was excessive good humor, Jefferson was on the best of terms. With Arthur Lee and John F. Mercer, men of distinguished northern Virginia families, his relations were less fortunate. Both were vain and quarrelsome, both fed on faction and intrigue, both lusted for the same office, the Secretary of Foreign Affairs, which Robert R. Livingston had vacated and because Jefferson stood in the way of their ambitions, they often opposed him.

Judged by the space he gave to the subject in his autobiography, Jefferson thought his attempt to establish "a visible head of the government," though unsuccessful, worthy of historical notice. In 1776 he had advanced the idea of a "committee of the states" to exercise executive powers during the recess of Congress. The Articles of Confederation made provision for this incipient executive, but Congress had never put it to work. Jefferson hoped to remedy the deficiency. The idea that the business of the Confederation must grind to a halt in the recess of Congress was, of course, preposterous. In the eyes of foreign nations, the adjournment of Congress virtually effaced the government of the United States. Keeping Congress in more or less permanent session was equally preposterous, and Jefferson associated this idea with the notorious ills of that body. Three months a year ought to be a sufficient term, he thought. "Then," as he explained to Hogendorp, "intelligent men from each state will be pleased to enter Congress for a short period, whereas now it is a sacrifice. . . . We will never again have in such a Congress obscure men who do its business badly." In January he moved the appointment of a committee of the states, to consist of a member from each state, empowered during the recess of Congress to exercise executive responsibilities. The resolution was sent to a committee he headed. The report as finally submitted, then amended, did not go the lengths Jefferson wished. He conceived of the interim executive as a device to strengthen the Confederation; Congress agreed only to a committee of caretakers. Such a committee was appointed prior to adjournment in June. Soon after it went into operation, as Jefferson recalled, the members quarreled, "split into two parties, abandoned their post, and left the government without any visible head, until the next meeting in Congress." The plan was not revived. In addition to all the congressional bickerings and fears of executive authority, the Articles of Confederation offered a very poor framework in which to rig an independent executive. The lesson was not lost on Jefferson, nor on the framers of the Constitution three years hence.

Money was the ubiquitous problem of Congress. Jefferson, first as a member, then as chairman of the Grand Committee, struggled to make economies in the domestic administration, procure funds from the states, and meet pressing obligations at home and abroad. In these difficult matters he often found himself at odds with the Philadelphia banker Robert Morris, the former Superintendent of

Finance, whose wizardry, practiced with so much success at the close of the war, no longer cast a spell over Congress. But this was all patchwork. Jefferson's plan for a national system of coinage, on the other hand, was a landmark in monetary history. Here, too, he clashed with the financier.

Jefferson's connection with the subject went back to 1776 when he first recommended the dollar as the standard money unit of the new nation. Nothing was done until Morris revived the subject six years later. Coinage and monetary reckoning were in a state of chaos. Congress minted no money, and while the states were free to do so, the supply of domestic coins fell far short of the demand. As a result, English and French guineas, Spanish pistoles, Portuguese "joes," and many other coins circulated side by side, their values varying from one part of the Union to another. As Morris observed, "The ideas annexed to a pound, a shilling, and a penny are almost as various as the States themselves. . . . A farmer in New Hampshire for instance can readily form an idea of a bushel of wheat in South Carolina weighing sixty pounds and placed at one hundred miles from Charleston, but if he were told that in such situation it is worth twenty-one shillings and eight pence, he would be obliged to make enquiries and form some calculations before he could know that this sum meant in general what he would call four shillings." The situation was productive of fraud and, of course, it obstructed trade among the states. Morris asked for a standard money unit based on silver. By intricate calculations he fixed the unit at the 1440th part of a dollar, this being the one by which the currencies of all the states save one were divisible without a fraction. The new money would thus be intelligible in terms of the old. The mint, which he also urged Congress to establish, would turn out coins in several denominations: two copper coins of five and eight units, and silver coins rising in decimal proportions of 100, 500, and 1000 units. While his report languished in Congress, he proceeded independently with his plan for a mint and actually had specimen coins struck before Congress killed the project in 1783. By then Morris had resigned.

Jefferson revived the subject. He avoided the controversial, and subsidiary, question of a mint and returned the discussion to the primary point of the money unit. The paper he then prepared, Notes on Coinage, while not actually a legislative report, assumed that character in history. A remarkably lucid analysis of a complex problem, it was intended to overcome congressional reluctance to tackle an issue covered with confusion and difficulty. It also set forth a clear alternative to the financier's system of coinage. Jefferson adopted the dollar as the unit of coinage, and attached it to gold as well as silver; but what distinguished his plan was the use of the decimal ratio to proportion the values among the different coins. "Every one knows the facility of decimal arithmetic. . . . The bulk of mankind are school boys thro' life. . . . Certainly in all cases where we are free to choose between easy and difficult modes of operation, it is most rational to choose the easy." And what could be easier than a system of coins in multiples and divisions of ten: the dollar, ten dollars, one-tenth and one-hundredth of a dollar. Morris's unit, on the other hand, preserved the monstrous strength of calculation required of monetary systems the world around. A loaf of bread, one-twentieth of a dollar, or five cents, would be 72 units; a pound of butter, 20 cents, 288 units; a horse, perhaps $80, 115,200 units; and so on. Morris conceded the desirability of the decimal ratio, but he thought it necessary to devise a unit consonant with the existing currencies. His merchant's head told him that no merchant kept his books in dollars, and that however convenient a scheme such as Jefferson's might appear in the abstract, it was not in keeping with the life of trade. To this objection Jefferson replied: "The conversion of the merchant's accounts is but a single operation. Once done it is done forever. He is skillful and equal to the task. Tho' the adoption of the Financier's Unit may relieve this one operation of the merchant yet it would throw the difficulty on the farmer who knows what a dollar is but not what the Financier's Unit is. The farmer is ignorant." The planning of a system of coinage was "a work proper . . . to mathematicians as well as merchants," Jefferson said. Seldom would he have the opportunity to demonstrate so pointedly and so conclusively the superiority of a statesmanship founded on rational principles to one founded on narrowly practical considerations.

The theory, in this instance, would prove sound in practice. Jefferson left Congress before he could offer his plan in the form of a resolution. He had communicated it to several of his colleagues, however, among them David Howell, of Rhode Island. Howell had an odious reputation as an obstructionist and a demagogue, in keeping with the reputation of his state; but Jefferson was friendly with this professor turned politician and found him a staunch ally in several contests. Pleased with the Notes on Coinage, Howell sent a copy to the Governor of Rhode Island, who saw to its publication in *The Providence Gazette*. When the subject was again brought forward in 1785, mainly on Howell's initiative, Congress reprinted the newspaper version of Jefferson's plan and proceeded to adopt its basic principles. In Paris, meanwhile, Jefferson was preparing the Notes on Coinage for what he supposed to be its first publication. The dollar thus became the money unit of the United States, and history was made by the adoption of the decimal system in the coinage of a nation. Several years passed before the system was implemented by the first secretary of the treasury, Alexander Hamilton.

The fortuities that guided Jefferson's plan of coinage to a happy conclusion were somewhat less evident in the case of his plans for the West. Two ordinances, one a plan of government for the western territory, the other a system of land survey and sale, were cornerstones of national policy, meriting rank with Jefferson's most important legislative accomplishments. The first, however, while enacted into law in 1784, remained a dead letter and was practically erased from the page of history by the famous Northwest Ordinance of 1787; the second ordinance was not enacted, though major parts of it survived in the first federal land law of 1785. The way was prepared for these plans by Congress's acceptance, after prolonged and angry controversy, of Virginia's cession of lands northwest of the Ohio. From the time Jefferson transmitted Virginia's original act of cession in January 1781, the creation of a national domain scarcely admitted of doubt; but whether it would be premised on Virginia's declared title to these lands, and therefore formed on the conditions she laid down, was a question to exhaust the talents of legal casuists and land speculators. Virginia stood firm, reserving tracts of land to satisfy bounty claims on the state, combating the pretensions of land companies, and calling for the formation of new republican states to be admitted to the Union on an equal footing with the original thirteen. Congress received Virginia's final act of cession in February 1784. A committee recommended its acceptance in the form of a deed executed by the Virginia delegation. At first only five states approved. New Jersey, the main opponent, offered an amendment declaring that acceptance should not amount to an acknowledgment of Virginia's title. "We told them we were not authorized to admit any conditions or provisoes," Jefferson reported the debate, "that this acceptance must be simple, absolute and unqualified or we could not execute." The amendment was lost, the subject dropped. Then the dissenting member of the Pennsylvania pair asked leave to change his vote, and this, with the vote of the New Hampshire delegation just arrived, furnished the majority. Never did a state have so much difficulty disposing of an empire! Jefferson, with Madison, Joseph Jones, and several others, had played a leading part in the entire transaction, as honorable to Virginia as it was beneficial to the nation.

Jefferson's thoughts were never far from the West, and now, in 1784, he sought to fix its future. Time was running out. The debt-ridden and land-hungry poured across the mountains, pushed down the Ohio, the Kanawha, the Kentucky, and the Cumberland. Treaties must be made with the Indians. An orderly system of land survey and sale must be instituted. Provision must be made for the temporary government of these lands, extending westward to the French towns of the Illinois and southward, pending cessions from North Carolina and Georgia, to the Spanish border. The British in their posts on the Great Lakes, the Spanish in command of the great river that drained the entire country, had it in their power to do untold mischief. The Kentuckians, looking down the Mississippi, grew restive under Virginia's sovereignty. There was no holding them, Jefferson thought, and he advocated their independence from the mother state and admission to the Union.

As Jefferson studied these problems, he realized that political ties alone would not secure the West. Economic ties were also necessary. The waters flowing to the Mississippi furnished the natural arteries of western commerce; but the hazards of this traffic, the difficulty of upstream navigation, along with Spanish control at New Orleans, seemed likely to check the Mississippi trade for some time to come. The bulk of western commerce might, therefore, be drawn to the Atlantic, helping to bind the Union together even as it expanded. Navigation being essential to an extensive inland commerce,

Jefferson believed the principal competition would be between the Hudson River and the Potomac. Geography had declared in favor of the Potomac, provided its upper waters, with those of the Ohio, were joined and cleared for navigation. Virginia ought to undertake this great work, Jefferson argued. "This is the moment in which the trade of the West will begin to get into motion and to take its direction. It behooves us then to open our doors to it." And not only through the Potomac system. The James and its headwaters reached toward the Kanawha, thence to the Ohio. The development of both the James and the Potomac systems would complete a vast network of navigation such as promised "to pour into our lap the whole commerce of the Western world." In March Jefferson outlined his plan in a long letter to Washington and begged him to put himself at the head of the Potomac project. "What a monument of your retirement would it be!" Washington was no stranger to the subject, having dreamed of a Potomac route to the West before the Revolution. In the summer he toured some of the western country, where he had speculative holdings, and on his return persuaded the legislature to adopt elaborate plans to extend the navigation of the Potomac and the James. Hopes rode high for a few years. But the design of a Virginia commercial empire in the West was doomed to failure. Jefferson followed its course, meanwhile offering his solution to the manifold problems of allocating and governing this new and unpredictable domain.

He reported his plan of government when Congress accepted the Virginia cession on March 1, 1784. The national domain was a reality. Whether the title deed to the land itself, as distinguished from the right of political jurisdiction, still belonged to the Indian tribes or had fallen to the Americans by right of conquest was another issue awaiting settlement. Jefferson worked at this problem too; and it would finally be resolved, technically in favor of the Indians, practically of the Americans. Whatever the solution, he simply assumed the advance of civilization over the whole domain. Obviously, a plan of government was needed. The fact that Congress had no delegated authority to govern territory was irrelevant, for the constitutional limits were breached, irrevocably, when Congress acquired the lands it had no authority to acquire. "The public interest, the necessity of the case," as Madison later said, "imposed upon them the task of overleaping their constitutional limits." But how should the country be laid off into political jurisdictions? Should Congress deal with the problem piecemeal, making political arrangements as exigencies of settlement beyond the mountains required, or should it draw a blueprint of government for the entire West? And what should be the character of this government? A centralized colonial administration like the old imperial government, with Congress taking the place of King and Parliament? Or a government consonant with the principles of the Revolution? Far-reaching questions of this kind had been bandied about Congress for months. Nothing had been decided when Jefferson was appointed chairman of a committee to "prepare a plan for temporary government of western territory." He interpreted this vague commission in all possible latitude. The committee deliberated several weeks, then reported the plan of Jefferson's authorship. Congress adopted it, after amendment, as the Ordinance of 1784.

The first feature of Jefferson's plan was its application to all the territory ceded *or to be ceded* to the United States. It thus encompassed the entire western country between the Mississippi and the British and Spanish borders, though approximately one-half of this area was not yet under congressional jurisdiction. Jefferson divided the whole into fourteen states, arranging them longitudinally in two tiers, one bounded by the Mississippi on the west and the meridianal line drawn from the falls of the Ohio to the tip of Lake Michigan on the east, the other from this line to the meridian of the mouth of the Kanawha, with one state to be formed between this line and the Pennsylvania border. These lines were crossed by parallels allowing each state two degrees of latitude. The approach was severely geometrical, taking almost no account of physiographical features. At an early stage of his plan Jefferson had attempted to do so, but cartographical knowledge of the West, which he possessed thoroughly, was as yet too imperfect. Moreover, he was working under a mandate contained in the Virginia cession to organize states not less than 100 nor more than 150 miles square. If the political geography was arbitrary, it was not entirely through fault of his own. It was abritrary, too, where it touched the old states. The Kanawha meridian fixed the western boundary of several states some degress east of existing claims, cutting off a large chunk of Virginia, for example.

Congress approved Jefferson's geographical divisions with but one or two modifications. But it eliminated the names he had thought to give ten of the proposed states. These curious polysyllables—Cherronesus, Assenenisipia, Metropotamia, Polypotamia, Pelisipia, and so on —provoked an unending stream of hilarity and ridicule. Congress mercifully dropped them, less because it objected to the names themselves than because the subject was premature. The names, most of them Indian derivatives with classical endings, were not as eccentric in Jefferson's generation as they would seem later, and they testified to his mingling of Roman civility with American wildness.

The great idea of the Ordinance of 1784 was the creation out of the wilderness of new republican states eventually to be taken into the Union on perfect equality with the original states. Many had advocated the basic principle, Jefferson for the first time in 1776 in connection with the Virginia Constitution. While generally accepted in 1784, the opposition was sufficient three years later to prevent a guarantee of the equality of new states from being written into the federal Constitution. The progression to statehood, on Jefferson's plan, would be in three easy stages. In the earliest stage all the free adult males would meet together to form a temporary government modeled on the constitution and the laws of one of the states. When the free inhabitants numbered 20,000 they would be authorized to call a constitutional convention for the purpose of establishing permanent self-government. The final stage, statehood, would be attained when the population of a territory equaled the population of the least numerous state, approximately 160,000 in 1784. The plan allowed wide freedom to the territories and their inhabitants. Manhood suffrage was guaranteed at the outset. Not a single state had as yet taken this step toward democracy! Control by the central government was severely limited, thereby encouraging the freedom and initiative of a pioneering people. They were to elect their rulers, make their own laws, lay off counties and townships to suit themselves. Congressmen who imagined a frontier populated by marauding banditti incapable of self-government—and many respectable men held this opinion—sought to increase the measure of congressional control. An amendment to this end failed, though at the last minute Jefferson acquiesced in an amendment empowering Congress to take measures necessary for the preservation of peace and order in any of the new lands prior to the organization of temporary self-government.

In so far as Jefferson's plan placed restrictions on the territories, they were in the form of five so-called "compact" articles. The new governments must be republican in form, subject to the jurisdiction of Congress, liable for the payment of the federal debt, and forever remain a part of the United States: thus far the "charter of compact" merely embodied conditions implicit or explicit in Virginia's deed of cession. The fifth and final article was totally unprecedented: "That after the year 1800 of the Christian era, there shall be neither slavery nor involuntary servitude. . . ." Jefferson thus proposed that Congress, without a shadow of authority, pre-empt the decision on the question of slavery in the territories. He had deep convictions on many important questions of public policy, such as religious freedom and common schools. He did not attempt to decide these questions for the westerners. Slavery had become in his mind a matter of fundamental national importance overriding considerations of local autonomy. The majority of congressmen agreed with him, yet the anti-slavery clause was lost. Jefferson's own delegation abandoned him. Of the southern delegates only his good friend Hugh Williamson, of North Carolina, voted with him. But for the absence of a New Jersey delegate, ill in his lodging, the clause would have been retained. "Thus we see the fate of millions unborn hanging on the tongue of one man," Jefferson later reflected, "and heaven was silent in that awful moment."

Factors intrinsic and extrinsic rendered the Ordinance of 1784 ineffectual. Delays in the extinguishment of Indian titles and the failure of Congress to enact Jefferson's land law presented the first obstacles, for these were prerequisites of any political organization in the West. Then it was discovered that the plan's political divisions were impractical. Many congressmen came to this conclusion, among them James Monroe, who traveled in the West after leaving Annapolis in 1784 and again the following summer. "A great part of the territory is miserably poor," he reported to Jefferson, "especially that near Lakes Michigan and Erie, and that upon the Mississippi and the Illinois consists of extensive plains which have not had from appearances and will not have a single bush on them, for ages."

283

So, Monroe said, with reasoning history would make laughable, the territories as bounded by Jefferson "will perhaps never contain sufficient numbers of inhabitants to entitle them to membership in the confederacy." He and other critics were right, however, in seeing that the low ratio of land to people in Jefferson's plan would delay the progress to statehood; indeed confusion and delay might occur at the start from the provision making the settlers rather than Congress responsible for organization of the territories. The defects of Jefferson's rigid grid also became evident: some of the proposed states were inconveniently divided by mountains and rivers or deprived of effective navigation.

In 1786 Monroe was named chairman of a committee to devise a modified plan of government, and this became the entering wedge to upset Jefferson's plan entirely. Fear that the virgin lands would drain off the population of the East to its economic harm, distrust of the frontier as a scene of lawlessness, apprehension of western power in the Union—these sentiments were not new, but now they produced a reaction led by Rufus King and Nathan Dane, of Massachusetts, against Jefferson's plan of government. The result was the Northwest Ordinance of 1787. As the title indicates, it was framed solely for the area above the Ohio River, from which three to five states were to be carved. Like Jefferson's plan, the new one provided for territorial government through stages culminating in statehood. It also restored Jefferson's anti-slavery clause in a modified form. But it tore from his plan the provisions for democratic self-government. The Ordinance of 1787 legislated a freehold suffrage, combined with residence qualifications, and high property qualifications for officeholders. It imposed a centralized colonial government, "similar to that which prevailed in these States previous to the Revolution," in Monroe's opinion, with Congress-appointed governor, secretary, and judges. Its "compact" articles, so very different from Jefferson's, also breathed hostility to the West, for they purported to fix the fundamental laws and institutions of the new lands forever, even after statehood was attained. Still, with all its defects, the Northwest Ordinance was a more workable offspring of his original conception of an expanding continental empire of free and independent states. Monroe's fears were not unjustified, but the American "empire of liberty" followed a different course from European colonial empires.

Jefferson's land ordinance of 1784 projected the rectilinear land survey system of the American West. Anyone who has flown across the prairies of the Old Northwest or the Great Plains beyond, and viewed the seemingly endless rectangular patchwork of the fields below, is familiar with the effects of the system. It is not quite the one Jefferson planned with Hugh Williamson and the other members of his committee, however. That plan called for dividing the land into "hundreds"—Jefferson's favorite Anglo-Saxon unit—of ten miles square, lines running due north and south at right angles, which would then be subdivided into lots one-mile square. This was a unique conception: the use of parallels and meridians to bound lands uniformly over a vast area regardless of topography. It could only have originated in a country planning to take possession of an immense unexplored terrain, and at a time when rational philosophers were at the helm of state. Addicted to decimal measurement, Jefferson proposed to use the geographical (or nautical) mile surveyed by a chain of 100 links, 100 chains to the mile, 10 square chains to the acre, 1000 acres to the square mile, 100,000 acres to the hundred. The large lots of this grid were on a scale more suggestive of southern than of northern practice. The plan also incorporated the southern system of indiscriminate settlement, even prior to survey, provided, however, that the final grants conform to the grid. Jefferson reported the plan just before he left Congress in May. When finally brought to a vote, it was defeated, only twenty-three delegates being present. Revived and revised at the next session, it eventuated in the Land Ordinance of 1785. This plan, the basis of the federal survey system, retained the rectilinear grid on the smaller scale of six-mile square townships, rather than hundreds. It abandoned altogether decimal measurement and indiscriminate settlement, substituting for the latter the New England practice of discriminate settlement after survey.

One of the innocent restrictions Jefferson had thought to place on the republican governments of the territories was that they "shall admit no person to be a citizen who holds any hereditary title." Congress kept the requirement of republican government but dropped this clause, no doubt because it would be interpreted as a direct slap at the controversial Society of the Cincinnati. The Society had been organized the previous year by a group of army officers, General Steuben at their head. The elitist character of a society of military officers was objectionable; and the provision for hereditary membership through the eldest son sent shivers through the country. A fiery pamphlet accused the Society of aiming at hereditary aristocracy. Several state legislatures passed resolutions against it. As the alarm spread, Washington, who had been named temporary president of the Society, was puzzled what stand he should take and asked Jefferson's opinion. "The subject has been at the point of my pen in every letter I have written to you," Jefferson replied in the middle of April. While acquitting the Society of devious intent, military or monarchical, he nevertheless felt that it ran contrary to the spirit of American institutions, that the dangers men feared from it were, even if remote, founded in all human experience, and that Washington's association with the Cincinnati sullied his character and renown. Passing through Annapolis a week or so later on his way to the first national meeting of the order in Philadelphia, the General stopped at Jefferson's house, dined in style, and talked of the Cincinnati. "It was a little after candlelight, and he sat with me till after midnight, conversing almost exclusively on that subject." He left, Jefferson later recalled, "with a determination to use all his influence for its entire suppression." In this he was not successful, though his impassioned appeal to the officers resulted in the elimination of the hereditary principle. The victory belonged in some part to Jefferson.

When spring came to the village at the mouth of the Severn, and Congress seemed, week after week, on the point of winding up its affairs, Jefferson pondered a summer trip across the mountains as a commissioner of his state in fixing the ultimate boundary with Pennsylvania. Congress had other plans for him. On May 7 he was appointed Minister Plenipotentiary to join Benjamin Franklin and John Adams in the negotiation of treaties of amity and commerce with European nations. The American ministers abroad had for some time been engaged in commercial negotiations of the highest interest. Jefferson had been one of a committee charged with the reformulation of policy on this subject. The committee's report lay untouched for several months. Then, on May 7, being officially informed that John Jay, one of the ministers, was sailing for home, Congress appointed him to the vacant post of Secretary of Foreign Affairs, named Jefferson as his replacement in Europe, and adopted the new instructions he had helped draft and would now receive.

His career as a legislator thus came to an abrupt and final close. Now the long-deferred career in diplomacy on the European stage opened before him. While he professed to be indifferent to the appointment, the haste with which he penned "valedictory" letters to friends and loved ones in Virginia, settled his affairs, and abandoned Annapolis suggests feelings of another kind. He had come out of retirement with the expectation of going to Europe. Instead, he had landed in Congress, and his experience with the "justlings of states" in that vagabond and lackluster body, while remarkably creative on his part, had not been pleasant. So with no apparent regrets he set out for Philadelphia four days after his appointment.

He lingered there two weeks, packing Patsy's trunk as well as his own, fetching a favorite servant, Jame, from Monticello, and awaiting the papers he was to take to Paris. His plans for a prolonged absence had been laid eighteen months before; he had only to reactivate them. To his entourage he added a secretary, William Short, a young friend and protégé unhappy with his prospects as a member of the Governor's Council and anxious to serve Jefferson in Europe. Balloon ascensions were all the rage in Philadelphia. Jefferson witnessed three of them. (He had read one of the first books devoted to the wonderful discovery of the French Montgolfier brothers a year before.) A serious breach in the Franco-American alliance also drew his attention. A disgruntled Frenchman named Longchamps brutally attacked the secretary of the French legation, Marbois, in the streets of Philadelphia. The affair dragged on. Jefferson, meanwhile, co-operated with Marbois in taking the exact measurements of a four-year-old bull: more ammunition against Buffon. Discovering that the cost of printing his manuscript in Philadelphia was prohibitive, he packed it up, and all in readiness near the end of May, departed for Boston to catch a ship bound for France.

A Strategy of Trade

"I mean to go thro' the Eastern states in hopes of deriving some knowledge of them from actual inspection and enquiry which may enable me to discharge my duty to them somewhat the better," Jefferson explained his overland journey to Edmund Pendleton. Much of the United States he had not seen—most of it he would never see. Only twice had he crossed the Delaware. Now duty happily comported with desire, and he sought first-hand knowledge of the country to the east. With the commerce of the Chesapeake he was familiar, of course, and all the staple producing states had much in common. He had been an easy choice to replace Jay, a New Yorker, on the European commission, for in addition to his other merits he was a Virginian. The interests of the South deserved an advocate in a body whose other members were Franklin and Adams. But Jefferson did not regard himself as the representative of a section. In foreign commerce the United States was "one nation," he insisted. The diversified productions and extensive carrying trade of the eastern states thus claimed his attention. With his usual penchant for order and system, he devised a questionnaire covering all aspects of trade for the purpose of eliciting information from merchants and officials as he passed through the principal cities.

The future of American commerce, perforce of American wealth and power, was very uncertain in 1784. The return of peace had brought prosperity more delusive than real. Americans found ready markets and good prices for their productions, but they let their starved appetites for European finery run away with them, buying far more than they could afford, depleting the country's money stock, and saddling it with a huge debt. The signs of economic depression—money scarcity, falling prices, stagnation of trade—had begun to appear when Jefferson traveled to Boston. In Connecticut, he learned, European imports exceeded exports in more than a tenfold proportion. The carrying trade of the eastern ports languished. Key industries, like shipbuilding and whaling, failed to revive after the war. With respect to the mainstay of Virginia's economy, tobacco, production was well below prewar levels, and the planters were still in the grip of the Scottish merchants. These were some of the alarming weaknesses. While their causes were various, Jefferson agreed with most Americans in tracing the manifold problem to a common root: Great Britain.

From the first, the economic hopes of the new nation had been tied to the kite of commercial freedom. The United States stood ready to trade freely with all comers who would recognize its independence and enter into liberal commercial arrangements. "Our plan is commerce," *Common Sense* had declared, "and that, well attended to, will secure us the peace and friendship of all Europe; because it is the interest of all Europe to have America as a free port. Her trade will always be a protection. . . ." Acting on this calculation, Congress, in 1776, adopted the "plan of treaties." It failed of conspicuous success except in the case of France, where, however, the treaty of commerce was coupled with a treaty of alliance involving political commitments inconsistent with the "commerce only" principle of the original plan. That plan, for all the troubles it encountered, was the natural offspring of the union between revolutionary necessity and revolutionary aspiration. Seen in the light of the policies of nations, rather than of their forms of government, the American Revolution looked to the dissolution of mercantilism and the liberation of trade, together with a new openness, trust, and pacific temper in the international community. It was this emphasis on commercial freedom that made the Revolutionary event and the simultaneous publication of Adam Smith's *The Wealth of Nations* something more than a coincidence; that gave substance to the Earl of Shelburne's abortive project for a commercial union between Britain and the United States at the conclusion of the war; and that conveyed the message of the American Revolution to many enlightened Europeans who, while they exalted commercial freedom, either feared or had little hope for republican government.

Jefferson had no direct responsibility for the "plan of treaties" and probably had not thought much on commercial questions before he returned to Congress. But he was in complete accord with the spirit of the standing policy. "Our interest," he wrote in the *Notes on Virginia*, "will be to throw open the doors of commerce, and to knock off all its shackles, giving perfect freedom to all persons for the vent of whatever they may chuse to bring into our ports, and asking the same in theirs." With the conclusion of the war, it was thought that nations reluctant to treat with a rebel government would be eager to treat with a legitimate one whose only interest was mutual trade and profit. To take advantage of these friendly dispositions, Congress had appointed the three-man European commission. The undertaking had assumed a new importance. Lacking the old privileges of trade within the empire, the Americans had secured few privileges of trade outside of it, and so they suffered the same colonial dependence as before the Revolution. It became increasingly evident that Britain, though she had lost the thirteen colonies, was determined to hold the Americans in commercial vassalage. The Earl of Sheffield, in his influential *Observations on the Commerce of the United States*, in 1783, had demonstrated how easily it could be done. Exploit the feebleness of the Confederacy. Exploit the British merchants' mastery of the American market. Above all, destroy the American carrying trade by imposing the navigation law that had secured its growth within the imperial system. A new ministry, with other dispositions than the discredited Shelburne ministry had shown toward the United States, adopted this line of policy. The crippling blow fell in July 1783. An order in council excluded American ships from the British West Indies; and this, together with the restoration of old restrictions in the French and Spanish colonies, closed off the most profitable branch of American trade.

There were several possible lines of attack on the problem, and in different contexts Jefferson advocated all of them. When moral and political considerations were uppermost, he held up the ideal of a hermit nation. "Were I to indulge my own theory," he wrote characteristically, "I should wish them [the Americans] to practice neither commerce nor navigation, but to stand with respect to Europe precisely on the footing of China. We should thus avoid wars, and all our citizens would be husbandmen." He thus expressed his sense of the unique opportunities of American society, which modified the orthodox canons of European political economy. "But this is theory only," he hastened to add, "and a theory which the servants of America are not at liberty to follow." The people were accustomed to foreign commerce; great interests depended upon it; it was essential for the disposal of agricultural surpluses. Jefferson never let the dreamy ideal control his search for a viable system of political economy. A variation of the insular approach looked to the development of internal commerce. The Americans are peculiarly blessed and have no need of foreign trade, no cause to incur its vices, enmities, and debaucheries, Richard Price counseled in 1784. "They are spread over a great continent, and they make a world within themselves." The English radical was gifted with prophesy. In time the Americans would realize his conception of a great home market—"a world within itself"—but few had as much as a glimpse of it in 1784. Even with regard to western navigation, Jefferson, and nearly everyone else, viewed inland commerce as an accessory to foreign commerce. Still another strategy called for the creation of a countervailing system of mercantilist restrictions by the United States. Jefferson was not averse to retaliatory measures of this kind. In the condition of American affairs he did not believe trade should be left to regulate itself, though that was his theoretical preference, of course. He helped to draft the congressional address of April 30, 1784, recommending that the states "vest Congress with so much power over their commerce as will enable them to retaliate on any nation who may wish to grasp it on unequal terms; and to enable them . . . to pass something like the British navigation act." The Confederacy must be strengthened primarily, in his opinion, for the purpose of regulating foreign trade. But the states held back, defeating a truly national system, and regulation by the states severally raised more problems than it solved. Madison and some other nationalists inclined to believe that so long as the vacuum of commercial power existed in the Confederacy there was really nothing to do but to fill it. Jefferson, always sanguine, did not take this desperate view. The front door to commercial regulation was closed but the back door was already open. In its power to make treaties the United States could act as "one nation," and so acting not only develop its commercial system but strengthen the bonds of Union as well.

The new instructions Jefferson helped to draft for the European commission carried forward the liberal policy with some practical modifications. Each party to a commercial treaty should be free to carry exports and imports to or from the other in its own bottoms. Duties should be based on the principle of the "most favored nation," which simply offered a guarantee against treatment less favorable than accorded another nation. The principle was European, far short of the American objective of free trade. Although the commission was authorized to go as far toward the ultimate goal as conditions might permit, it was recognized that the "most favored nation" formula offered the only realistic starting point. Mercantilist prejudice and practice, deeply embedded in the European states, had to be reckoned with. Jefferson willingly accepted this concession to expediency, yet was steady in his pursuit of the goal. With respect to the American colonies of European powers, trade was to be put on a reciprocal footing if at all possible; at the very least, United States ships and productions must be admitted into direct trade with these possessions. This was asking a good deal when scarcely a foreign port in the Western Hemisphere was open to American vessels. Other provisions covered the rights of enemy aliens and neutral carriers in time of war—matters of pacific and humanitarian import under the law of nations, in which Jefferson built on the work already begun by Franklin.

Congress authorized commercial treaties with sixteen European states, as well as the Barbary powers. The decision to pursue this general European plan was of considerable importance. Freedom from British domination was to be found in the widening of markets. A strong minority in Congress, primarily New England men, advocated a different approach, one which would give precedence to a commercial treaty with Britain. The restoration of the British trade to something like its old footing was so vital, in their opinion, that it should not be complicated by trifles; and no doubt some objected to the European plan because it would tend to pivot on France, thereby increasing that nation's influence in American affairs. Jefferson opposed the re-establishment of a partial connection with Britain. And he envisioned the French treaty not as a new axis of American commerce replacing the discredited British one, but rather as the point of departure for the creation of a far-flung system.

It was an incredibly ambitious undertaking: nothing less than a diplomatic mission to convert all Europe to the commercial principles of the American Revolution. The end in view was a system of purely commercial relations with foreign states, which, being based on the exchange of mutual surpluses for mutual wants, need not plunge the new nation into the blood-drenched rivalries of the Old

World or, alternately, force the country into isolation and penury. Clearly, however, the end could not be reached along purely commercial lines. In order to overcome mercantilism it was first necessary to play the mercantilist game and exploit trade as a political weapon. Although no threats were issued, it was well understood—Congress had so declared—that nations declining to enter into treaty relations with the United States would be liable to discriminatory regulations in the American market and would, of course, be denied other valuable privileges in peace and in war. How much these considerations could be made to count in the European balance of power depended on the progress of reform at home. But in the end every nation, on a rational view of its own interest, must see the advantages of entering the American consortium.

Instructions in hand, gathering what information he could as he traveled northward, Jefferson first stopped in New York. He lodged on Maiden Lane, next door to Crèvecœur, the French consul, known to Jefferson not only as the author of the *Letters of an American Farmer* but also as an ardent horticulturist who had earlier written to him about the reported talent of Virginians in distilling potatoes. From Virginia, Jefferson had sent him seeds of cypress, cedar, magnolia, and myrtle, a bushel or two of each. In his letters at this time, Crèvecœur was despondent over the prospects of French commercial success in the United States. The French merchants in New York were a bad lot, and the goods shipped not much better. Perhaps he did not speak so candidly to Jefferson, but he would soon hear a good deal of this problem. In New Haven, Jefferson took a holiday, touring Yale College in the congenial company of Ezra Stiles, the president. The Puritan educator thought the Virginian "a most ingenious naturalist and philosopher, a truly scientific and learned man, and every way excellent." They exchanged information on their respective colleges, talked of electrical apparatus, and speculated on the bones of the mammoth. As Jefferson passed through New England he made mental notes on the character of the people, checking these impressions with his knowledge of the Virginians. Writing to Chastellux months later, he thought the different characters, North and South, might be depicted schematically:

In the North they are	In the South they are
cool	fiery
sober	voluptuary
laborious	indolent
persevering	unsteady
independent	independent
jealous of their own liberties, and just to those of others	zealous for their own liberties, but trampling on those of others
interested	generous
chicaning	candid
superstitious and hypocritical in their religion	without attachment to pretentions to any religion but that of the heart

"These characteristics," Jefferson said, "grow weaker and weaker by gradation from North to South and South to North, insomuch that an observing traveller, without the aid of the quadrant may always know his latitude by the character of the people among whom he finds himself." Cued by Montesquieu, he ascribed these differences to a cause, the comparative warmth or coldness of the climate; and, of course, in Pennsylvania, with its moderate climate, the two characters blended "to form a people free from the extremes both of vice and virtue."

Jefferson had hoped to reach Boston in time to accompany John Adams's wife and daughter across the Atlantic, but he was too late, and while still uncertain of his passage, journeyed into New Hampshire as far as Portsmouth. When he returned to Boston, the General Court appointed a committee to confer with him on the commerce of the state. "No small part of my time too," he wrote Elbridge Gerry, his Massachusetts ally in Congress, "has been occupied by the hospitality and civilities of this place which I have experienced in the highest degree." Jefferson's reputation had preceded him. A Boston newspaper thus announced his presence: "Governor Jefferson, who has so eminently distinguished himself in the late glorious revolution is a gentleman of a very amiable character, to which he has joined the most extensive knowledge. He is mathematician and philosopher, as well as a civilian and politician, and the memorable declaration of American independence is said to have been penned by him." The tribute suggests Jefferson's rising fame as the author of the Declaration of Independence as well as his reputation, even before the publication of the *Notes on Virginia*, for philosophy.

He finally booked passage on the *Ceres*, a merchant ship owned by Nathaniel Tracy, of Newburyport, himself one of the passengers. The ship weighed anchor for England on the morning of July 5, 1784. "We had a lovely passage in a beautiful new ship that had made one voyage before," Patsy later reported. "There were only six passengers, all of whom papa knew, and a fine sun shine all the way, the sea as calm as a river." Jefferson amused himself learning Spanish with the aid of *Don Quixote* and a dictionary he had purchased in New York. Tracy was an amiable companion, possessing a great fund of commercial knowledge, and Jefferson recorded his answers to the questionnaire prepared in New York. After a fast crossing of twenty days, father, daughter and servant landed at Cowes. Detained for a time by Patsy's illness, they embarked for Le Havre on June 30, suffered the agonies of the Channel crossing, and, arriving on French soil, encountered the everlasting hardships of the foreign traveler. The nuisances of baggage and customs! Jefferson read French like a native but could speak the language scarcely at all. "It is annoying to see how they cheat strangers," Patsy noted. Journeying overland along the Seine to Paris, she thought it "the most beautiful country" she had ever seen, though the siege of beggars at every stop was disagreeable. "One day I counted no less than nine while we stopped to change horses." Thus the Virginians had their first encounter with the paradox of the beauty and the misery of France.

They first lived as transients in Paris, then in the middle of October settled in a handsome house, the hôtel Landron, as it was called, in a fashionable quarter of the city. With the aid of Chastellux, Patsy was entered in the stylish convent-school, the Abbaye Royale de Pentemont. "It is a house of education altogether the best in France, and at which the best masters attend," Jefferson wrote. "There are as many Protestants as Catholics, and not a word is ever spoken to them on the subject of religion." (He later had occasion to question this assurance.) Short, who soon arrived from Virginia, and David Humphreys, secretary of the commission, joined Jefferson's household. Humphreys had been one of Washington's trusted aides during the war. Jefferson was charmed by this elegant gentleman who, with Joel Barlow, John Trumbull and several other Yale men, belonged to a patriotic literary circle known to history as the Hartford Wits. The mission on which they were engaged was limited to two years. But it would be half-a-decade and another revolution later before Jefferson returned to his native land.

CHAPTER SIX

Minister to France

North America is become a new primary planet in the system of the world, which while it takes its own course, in its own orbit, must have effect on the orbit of every other planet, and shift the common center of gravity of the whole system of the European world. . . . It is earth-born, and like a giant ready to run its course."

> *Thomas Pownall,* A Memorial . . . to the Sovereigns of Europe.
> *London, 1780.*

It is not enough that the rights of man be written in the books of philosophers and inscribed in the habits of virtuous men; the weak and ignorant must be able to read them in the example of a great nation. America has given us this example.

> *Condorcet,* The Influence of the American Revolution on Europe.
> *Paris, 1786.*

I N THE VILLAGE of Passy outside Paris the venerable Dr. Franklin still presided, as he had for eight years, over the fortunes of the American Revolution in Europe. The friends of liberty and enlightenment had beaten a path to his door, and Jefferson made haste to follow it in August. Franklin, seventy-eight years old now, surfeited with honors, worn down by the cares of his office, punished by gout and a bladder stone so painful he could not bear the joltings of a carriage or even write without discomfort, was impatient to return home, and he could muster little enthusiasm for the ambitious project his young friend brought from Congress. Later in the month John Adams, with his wife and two children, came on from his post at The Hague and rented an elegant mansion in Anteuil, just beyond Passy. Adams doubted the success of the commission, but he took heart from Jefferson's appointment. "He is an old friend with whom I have often had occasion to labor on many a knotty problem, and in whose abilities and steadiness I always found great cause to confide."

These three giants of the Revolution, who had last labored together on the "knotty problem" of the Declaration of Independence, met officially at Passy on August 30 and more or less daily thereafter until their commissions to the various countries were put in a train of execution. "We proceed with wonderful harmony, good humor, and unanimity," Adams reported after six weeks. Even Franklin, with whom he had quarreled and whose popularity he resented, seemed amicable. With Franklin, Jefferson had anticipated no difficulty. Their tempers were as congenial as their politics, and Jefferson rejoiced in the old man's fame. With the astringent New Englander, he had been put on guard by Madison and Randolph, who had observed Adams critically from their former posts in Congress. Since he had gone abroad, they warned, Adams had become vain, cantankerous, morbidly suspicious of Congress, of the French, and of course of Franklin. Only after many months of scrutiny did Jefferson lower, though not by much, his high opinion of Adams. "He is vain, irritable and a bad calculator of the force and probable effect of the motives which govern men," he wrote to Madison. "This is all the ill which can possibly be said of him." He was honest, utterly disinterested, and often wise. Both Adams and Franklin were happy with Jefferson. Through him the official circle, not forgetting Humphreys, became agreeable all around.

Jefferson's relationship with Franklin, now almost a recluse at Passy, was for the most part confined to official business; but his relationship with Adams, the captivating Abigail, and their children, quickly ripened into a family friendship that brightened Jefferson's dreary initiation into Paris and glowed for many years. He dined often at Anteuil, which was a domestic idyll straight from America. He enjoyed the company of John Quincy, 17, and his older sister "Nabby." The whole family was charmed by the Virginian's sparkling conversation and gracious manners. Adams had earlier made some choice friends in the French capital, to whom he introduced the newcomer from Virginia. Americans kept turning up. The phenomenon of "the American in Paris" was born about 1784: merchants, adventurers, artists, scientists, fashionable sycophants—strangers all, as Abigail said—visited the American ministers and usually expected invitations to dinner. In January the Marquis de Lafayette returned from a triumphant tour of the United States. Jefferson had already been introduced to Lafayette's family. Their magnificent new home on the rue de Bourbon became the center of the American colony. No mere native of the land could equal the gallant Frenchman's enthusiasm for the United States. Lafayette's desire to serve, combined with his fame and position, smoothed many a path for Jefferson both in official and social circles.

If the universe were a gaily colored ball surrounded by a gaseous intellectual nebula, then Paris was the center of the universe. The city was not easily discovered, however. Jefferson lived on its lonely fringes for several months. Sights, diversions, people: he seldom babbled about these commonplace things in his letters, and those he wrote home during the first season offer surprisingly few glimpses of the kaleidoscopic scene. Man's conquest of the air was still the craze of Paris. Each flight of the gaudy silk bubbles was more daring than the last, until one exploded at a height of 1600 feet, making martyrs of its pilots, in an attempt at aerial navigation of the English Channel. The craze, too, burst. Jefferson regretted it, for he envisioned great things from "the aeronautical art." It was only a temporary setback. "As the birds and fish prove that the means exist, we may count on human ingenuity for its discovery." He looked askance upon another pioneering venture, Friedrich Anton Mesmer's fantastic probings across the boundaries of the conscious mind. Mesmerism was the sensation of Paris. The doctor's flamboyant style, the mumbo-jumbo of "animal magnetism," and the bewitching sorcery of the séance won a fashionable following for this alleged new science of healing. The Queen was a patron. Lafayette was an ardent disciple and actually lectured on Mesmerism before the American Philosophical Society in 1784. Jefferson, with most learned men, regarded Mesmerism as quackery. This was the verdict, in essence, of a royal commission on which Franklin served in 1785. Another bubble burst; and if the discovery of hypnosis dangled from the occult trappings, Jefferson and his peers can scarcely be blamed for failing to recognize it.

He kept his American friends informed of these rages and of all useful discoveries. Phosphorous matches: "They are a beautiful discovery. . . . The convenience of lighting a candle without getting out of bed, of sealing letters without calling a servant, of kindling a fire without flint, steel, punk etc. are of value." The Argand cylinder lamp: "It gives a light equal as is thought to six or eight candles." The screw propeller: "It is in fact a screw which takes hold of the air and draws itself along by it: losing indeed much of its effort by the yielding nature of the body it lays hold of to pull itself on by." Jefferson thought the invention could be applied to water with much greater effect.

The newcomer was alarmed by the low opinion of the United States prevalent in Europe, at court, in public print, among merchants, everywhere outside the small circles of ardent admirers of the American Revolution. Opinion and fact were wide apart. He blamed the disparity on English newspapers which blanketed Europe with lying stories of riot and anarchy in the United States. While with one hand he combated these false reports, with the other he urged the invigoration of the American government, citing the reports as evidence of the need. "All respect for our government is annihilated on this side of the water, from an idea of its want of tone and energy," he wrote Elbridge Gerry. "It is a dangerous opinion to us, and possibly will bring on insults which will force us into war." For months after his arrival he expected war between Austria and Holland and their respective allies over the navigation of the Scheldt. It would not likely involve the United States, but Britain, he warned, would surely exploit the opportunity to embarrass American peace and trade. Jealousy of the new nation's commercial rivalry, even more fear of its doctrine, Jefferson thought, was largely responsible for the British propaganda barrage.

His European initiation was edged with sadness, loneliness, and miseries of the body as well as of spirit. No sooner had he got settled than the illness that had plagued him in Annapolis returned. He continued his work and correspondence, but kept to his house most of the winter, during one stretch for six weeks without stirring. "A seasoning as they call it is the lot of most strangers: and none I believe have experienced a more severe one than myself," he wrote in March. By then the sun, "my almighty physician," had returned; he was walking four or five miles a day, and hoping to complete his recovery in the south of France. During this dreary siege Lafayette returned from America with a letter telling him of the death of little Lucy, "a Martyr to the Complicated evils of teething, Worms and Hooping Cough," the physician reported. Nothing could return this sun of his happiness.

Long accustomed to drawing information of home and friends from a thousand channels, Jefferson felt isolated and forgotten at so great a distance, dependent on the dreadfully slow transatlantic pipeline. Some letters, he remarked, "like the histories of ancient times . . . detail to us events after their influence is spent." And the letters seldom told him what he wanted to hear. "Political events are scarcely interesting to a man who looks on them from high ground. There is always war in one place, revolution in another, pestilence in a third interspersed with spots of quiet. These chequers shift places, but they do not vanish; so that to an eye which extends itself over the whole earth there is always a uniformity of prospect." Of political correspondents he could find enough, Jefferson wrote an old friend in Richmond, and there were always the newspapers forwarded from the United States. "But I can persuade nobody to believe that the small facts which they see daily passing under their eyes are precious to me at this distance: much more interesting to the heart than events of higher rank." Home was much in his thoughts. He had not been in Paris four months before he revived a favorite plan to seat his most congenial friends, Madison, Monroe, and Short—one or two others were sometimes mentioned—in the neighborhood of Monticello. "Looking back with fondness to the moment when I am again to be fixed in my own country, I view the prospect of this society as inestimable."

There were also distresses of an official nature. The question of salaries and allowances of the ministers abroad had for years been a bone of contention with Congress. At home accused of living like kings, the ministers, comparing their establishments with those of other nations, claimed they could not even keep up appearances. When Jefferson was appointed, Congress struck $2000 from the ministers' salaries and discontinued the allowance of an outfit—furniture, clothing, carriage, and so on. Congress seemed determined the ministers should not "eat the bread of idleness" and, Franklin added dryly, "that we may not eat too much, our masters have diminished our allowances." Jefferson immediately went into debt $4000, and though he lived modestly, about as they had in Annapolis, he told Monroe, he could not possibly repay it out of his annual salary. There was no end of expenses—of court, of fashion, of household— to be avoided only at the sacrifice of national dignity. The Americans were, unquestionably, "the lowest and most obscure of the whole diplomatic tribe," and Jefferson, of course, was the most obscure of the Americans. As yet he was virtually unknown in Europe, in diplomacy untried, and his position, while of ministerial rank, hung on a two-year commercial project most of the embassies little understood or cared about.

Life assumed a sunnier aspect in the spring. Not only was his health restored, but he was appointed to succeed Franklin as Minister to France. Franklin was returning home at last, and Congress had decided to keep but two ministers abroad, one in England, where Adams was appointed, and one at Versailles. Jefferson celebrated with a festive dinner. The Adamses were there, also the Lafayettes, Luzerne (the former Minister to the United States), John Paul Jones, and several others, American and French. On May 17 he presented his credentials to Louis XVI and went through the usual ceremonies. What they were, he did not care to remember and could not be troubled to describe. He was utterly indifferent to the pomp and pageantry of the Court. His curt dismissal of the subject contrasted with the lofty and effusive account Adams gave of his reception at the Court of St. James's. It had not been pleasant for the Adamses, against the soft spring beauty of Anteuil, to contemplate London. Most of all they regretted the loss of Jefferson's companionship. "He is one of the choice ones of the earth," Abigail said. Jefferson presented them with a copy of the *Notes on Virginia*, just off the press, and bade them adieu. "The departure of your family has left me in the dumps," he wrote Adams several days later. The afternoons, when he had often been at Anteuil, now hung heavily and he imagined himself a fit candidate for "the dark and narrow house of Ossian." He and Adams still had business to transact—the unfinished work of the commission—so they would not be out of touch. Franklin retired with his laurels in July. Jefferson afterwards said it was "an excellent school of humility" to step into the position of so great a man. When being presented to strangers in Paris as Minister of the United States, they were apt to say, "So you are Dr. Franklin's replacement?" And Jefferson would answer, "No one can replace him, sir; I am only his successor."

The succession raised Jefferson's diplomatic stature, put him more at ease with Europe, clarified his objectives, and enhanced the prospects of accomplishment. Although his responsibilities touched other countries, they centered increasingly on France, the surest friend of the United States in an alien world. He succeeded to Franklin's policy as well as his office, for Jefferson was equally convinced with him that France alone gave the infant nation weight in Europe and that rupture of the alliance would lead the country back into colonial subserviency. Requiring more becoming quarters now, he at length rented the elegant Paris hôtel of the Comte de Langeac, located at the end of the Champs Elysées near the city wall passed on going to Versailles. "It suits me in every circumstance but the price—being dearer than the one I am now in—it has a clever garden to it." His desire for gracious living, which Paris might gratify above any other place in the world, upset all resolutions of mean economy. He added a *maître d'hôtel* to his staff of servants, acquired a carriage, powdered his hair in concession to fashion, frequented splendid salons, and by all the outer insignia of life appeared perfectly at home in Paris. The one thing still necessary was the presence of his younger daughter. "I must have Polly," he wrote to her uncle Eppes on learning he would be away from America for at least three more years. Although this emptiness remained for some time, the cup of his happiness gradually filled, not with work only, but with the infinitely varied pleasures of mind and spirit.

Commercial Diplomacy

Considered from the standpoint of political economy, the American Revolution aimed to emancipate commerce from the myriad restrictions with which the jealous nations of Europe beggared their neighbors and exalted themselves in the benighted age of mercantilism. How far Jefferson had absorbed the new doctrine of "perfect liberty" of trade may be gleaned from one of many summary statements: "Instead of embarrassing commerce under piles of regulating laws, duties and prohibitions, could it be relieved from all its shackles in all parts of the world, could every country be employed in producing that which nature had best fitted it to produce, and each be free to exchange with others mutual surpluses for mutual wants, the greatest mass possible would then be produced of those things which contribute to human life and human happiness; the numbers of mankind would be increased, and their conditions bettered." With this idea Jefferson went to Europe and, despite frustrations and disappointments, with it he would return to America. The aspiration was not unrealistic. It had a dynamism of its own, but more substantial was the inducement of American trade: necessities of life and materials for manufacture which the United States stood ready to exchange with any nation on a footing of freedom and equality. Of course, mercantilist prejudice and practice had to be reckoned with. Jefferson willingly adapted principles to specific situations without yielding the one or suffering total defeat from the other. America's trade, he believed, was a potent political weapon. By granting or withholding commercial favors, the United States might weigh in the European balance of power to the advantage of its own strength and well-being. No trading nation could be indifferent to America's effort to achieve economic independence by opening new channels to the commerce that had built Britain's supremacy. American idealism, as embodied in Jefferson, thus plucked the strings of Old World diplomacy.

Political calculations of another kind influenced Jefferson's commercial diplomacy. The escape from British bondage was, as previously noted, the main objective; but Jefferson also said, repeatedly, "that my primary object in the formation of treaties is to take the commerce of the states out of the hands of the states, and to place it under the superintendence of Congress, so far as the imperfect provisions of our constitution will admit, and until the states shall by new compact make them more perfect." The treaty-making in Europe was an elaborate shadow-play, Jefferson seemed to say, for securing the consolidation of the American Union. "The moment these treaties are concluded the jurisdiction of Congress over the commerce of the states springs into existence." The argument that Congress might do by treaty what it could not do by legislation had dangerous implications; and, indeed, when fears of congressional usurpation in this way had been voiced in the Virginia assembly on the question of approving the Articles of Confederation in 1777, Jefferson emphatically declared that Article IX, the treaty clause, "no more gave such power over our commerce than over every thing else." By 1784, however, he was beginning to construe every power to the advantage of the Union. He had written into the commission's instructions the article declaring the United States to be "one nation" toward others: an implicit denial of state authority so far as commerce was covered by treaties. It was a very delicate point, he later informed the ministers, and swallowed with difficulty by Congress. "The majority however is for strengthening the bond of Union," he added, "they are the growing party, and if we can do any thing to help them, it will be well."

Such were the general considerations in Jefferson's mind when the commissioners went to work at Passy near the end of August. While they awaited replies to letters addressed to the envoys of the different governments at the French court, informing them of their power to treat, Jefferson drafted a model treaty. With his invariable bent toward "style and structure," he reduced the jumbled articles of existing treaties to orderly system and introduced clear and simple grammatical usage. As long as the commissioners were reforming the principles of treaties, he observed, they ought to reform their manner as well. Jefferson's model treaty expressed the "New Diplomacy" of the Age of Enlightenment. For example, Article XXIII exempted peaceful shipping from capture in time of war and gave protection to the civilians of either party then residing in the other. Franklin had unsuccessfully proposed this piece of "platonic philosophy," as Adams dubbed it, to the British commissioners during the peace negotiations. Jefferson introduced an article of his own devising for the abolition of contraband of war. This, along with the principle of "free ships make free goods," was intended to protect America's neutral commerce in case of war involving the European party to the treaty.

A treaty was concluded with Prussia on the model in 1785. Prus-

sian commerce was of small account, but prestige attached to anything old Frederick the Great did. "Of all the powers not holding
American territory, a connection with him will give us the most
credit," Jefferson said. Some difficulties arose over Article IV's
granting to each party the right to carry for the other and freely to
buy and sell on the terms accorded the most favored nation. The
commissioners showed their accommodating spirit by admitting one
specific exception to these principles and further reserving the right
to prohibit trade "when reasons of state require it." The benevolent
Article XXIII was at once agreed to, though the recognition lost
some of its force from the remote chance of belligerency between
Prussia and the United States. Much more valuable to the United
States, if not to the hopes of mankind, was a provision opening
Prussia's neutral ports to the vessels and prizes of the United States
during war with another European power. The privilege would
prove of great consequence, Jefferson thought, in the event of war
with Britain. Given access to Prussian ports, American vessels, both
public and private, might prey on British shipping in the Baltic and
cut off the supply of naval stores from Russia.

Negotiations went on with several other nations, Denmark, Portugal, and Tuscany chiefly, but no treaties were concluded. There
were particular obstacles in every case. Larger difficulties of an in-
tangible nature proved harder to overcome, however. The commissioners had counted on a growing European interest in the United
States. Instead, most of the powers met their overtures with colossal
indifference. "They seemed, in fact, to know little about us," Jefferson later recalled, "but as rebels, who had been successful in throwing off the yoke of the mother country. They were ignorant of our
commerce, which had always been monopolized by England, and of
the exchange of articles it might offer advantageously to both parties." Not understanding this, the rulers felt no disposition to offer
the transatlantic stripling privileges no European country had ever
before granted. The good will that had existed toward the United
States in the triumph of the peace had been suffocated by the English newspapers, Jefferson added. Believing the country was falling
apart, nations were wary of treaty-making. Perhaps the ministers
erred in confining their negotiations to Paris, asking other countries
to come to them, as it were, yet, given the magnitude of the task,

the immovability of one of the commissioners and the periodic illness of the other, the alternative seemed out of the question. Had
the commissioners been warmly supported at home, they might have
fared better. Little more than a year after the adoption of the instructions of May 1784, John Jay, the new Secretary of Foreign Affairs, reported to Congress that, in his opinion, a purely national system for the regulation of trade should be established before more
encumbering treaties were negotiated. This was certainly putting
the horse before the cart, whereas the treaty policy, as Jefferson
conceived it, was intended to back into a national system of political
economy. Jay expressed a common nationalist view. Simultaneously,
another party attacked the plan of treaties on constitutional
grounds, recommending, in effect, that the entire operation be
scrapped. Hearing of this from Monroe, one of the leaders of the
party, Jefferson defended the right and the wisdom of the treaty
policy.

By this time, however, July 1785, even Jefferson felt discour-
aged. From the outset he had considered the negotiation of treaties
with nations holding possessions in the West Indies "the important
part of our business." Trade with other European countries, such as
it was, would go on covered by treaty or not. But Britain, France,
Spain, Portugal, the Netherlands: not only was their commerce with
the United States substantial, but entrance into their dominions took
priority over everything else. In order to gain it the United States
must have something to give in return. The privilege of free trade in
American ports would be attractive, Jefferson thought, but it would
be no privilege at all, he came to realize, if every piddling kingdom
of Europe could claim it on the ordinary ground of the "most favored nation." Therefore, wishing not to embarrass negotiations
with the colonial powers, the ministers "protracted designedly" with
all others and anxiously awaited the expiration of their commissions.

But the new tactics met with no better success. Britain stalled,
pointedly questioned the commission's authority to make a treaty
binding on the states, then pretended the Americans were averse to
negotiating, though Adams didn't see what more they could have
done "unless we had all three flown over in an air balloon." When
Adams became Minister to Britain, the task of negotiation with that
court fell to him. Since the restoration of the Navigation Act in

June 1783, Britain's policy of monopolizing the trade of her American colonies had been placed upon virtually impregnable foundations by the exhaustive report of a special investigating committee appointed by William Pitt, the Prime Minister. The committee had enthusiastically endorsed the restrictive system, and government was stuck with it. The sugar islands and the Canadian maritimes could be subsisted and supplied without the commerce of the United States, it was optimistically argued. British naval supremacy rested on the monopoly of the colonial carrying trade, that "nursery for seamen," as the shipbuilders and shipowners trumpeted. "The words 'ship and sailor' still turn the head of this people," Adams remarked. "They grudge to every other people, a single ship and a single seaman." And what cause had Britain to make concessions to the United States when she already possessed 75 per cent of the Anglo-American trade? Retaliatory legislation by the state legislatures, which Jefferson applauded when it appeared in 1785, held no fears for the British, who believed their command of the American market was unbreakable. "The infatuation of that nation seems really preternatural," Jefferson remarked with more than a trace of bitterness. "Nothing will bring them to reason but physical obstruction, applied to their bodily senses. We must show that we are capable of forgoing commerce with them, before they will be capable of consenting to an equal commerce." An interdict of all commerce with Britain, he wrote to Madison, would bring that nation to its senses and purge the United States of debilitating luxuries at the same time. This was idle speculation, of course. Retaliation in the hands of miscellaneous state governments was useless, in fact positively harmful to the conception of "one nation," and the country could not do without British commerce until there was something to replace it.

The negotiations at St. James's hinged on the negotiations at Versailles and vice versa. Success at either court would provide diplomatic leverage in the other. The French government was not indifferent to the opportunity of diverting American trade from the British. Indeed, this had been the anticipated gain from French support for American independence. But circumstances demanded caution. The French economy was depressed. Merchants raised a furor when, in August 1784, American vessels were given limited entrance to the colonial ports. "As yet nothing has been opened here," Jefferson wrote soon after he became Minister, "the times did not admit it." In the regular course of diplomacy over the next four years, he would achieve modest success. But that is another story. With Spain and the Netherlands, very protective of their colonies, the commission accomplished nothing. With Portugal, a treaty was negotiated at the eleventh hour of the commission's life, only to be rejected by the government in Lisbon.

Months before their commissions expired, Adams and Jefferson were trying hard not to negotiate. Repelling Austria's advances, earlier invited, Jefferson expressed his dilemma to Jay. "Our instructions are clearly to treat. But these made part of a system, wise and advantageous if executed in all its parts, but which has hitherto failed in its most material branch, that of connection with the powers having American territory." Under the circumstances it might become necessary for Congress to adopt a defensive commercial policy, which would be hampered by commitments of small value to the United States. Earlier he had seen the plan of treaties as a means, however imperfect, of arming the Union. Now he stressed the limitations of this plan and wondered if it should not be abandoned for the frontal attack of nationalists like Madison and Jay. "My letters from members of Congress render it doubtful," he wrote Adams in September, "whether they would not rather that full time should be given for the present disposition of America to mature itself and to produce a permanent improvement in the federal constitution, rather than, by removing the incentive, to prevent that improvement." Jefferson was soon advocating coercion of the states, if need be, to strengthen the Confederacy. He continued to support the movement to vest Congress with power over commerce, the movement that eventuated in the Constitutional Convention in 1787. "*Nil desperandum*" was truly the motto of Americans: if Europe repelled their pacific overtures, they would arm "the hand of the Union" to achieve security and well-being.

This realistic awareness in no way dimmed Jefferson's vision of friendly intercourse among nations. That vision actually grew in boldness. In July 1785 he communicated to Adams a proposition to place the rights of citizenship between contracting nations on a thoroughly reciprocal basis. A citizen of the United States in England, for example, would thus have all the rights, privileges, and immunities of Englishmen. As the circle of friendship widened, men would truly become citizens of the world. The proposal is as revolutionary today as when Jefferson made it, specifically, for inclusion in the project Adams would submit to the British government. It was beyond the commissioners' authority, as Jefferson conceded, and wildly impractical. Adams shelved it. Jefferson, after mentioning it at Versailles, did the same. But the ideal of a family of mankind tugged at his mind, even as he struggled for practical solutions within the limits of circumstance.

American amity and commerce with the piratical Barbary states was a case by itself. The commission was authorized to conclude treaties with Morocco, Algiers, Tunis, and Tripoli. For two centuries the Muslim states of North Africa had preyed on the commerce of the Mediterranean, the more daring sending their fleet corsairs past Gibraltar and into the Atlantic every spring, plundering ships and cargoes, enslaving their captives in hideous workhouses, where torture, pestilence, and starvation were the lot of untold numbers. Exemption from this fate was given in exchange for lavish tribute, and the major European powers, with a heavy stake in the commerce of the Mediterranean, paid it year after year. It was an important stake for the Americans too. Jefferson estimated that before the war the countries washed by the Mediterranean annually took about one-sixth of the wheat and flour exported by the thirteen colonies, one-fourth of their dried and pickled fish, along with rice and other articles, and gave employment to 80 or 100 ships and 1200 seamen. The trade was then under the protection of the British flag. When the flag came down, the trade fell, the spoil of marauders. Moroccan capture of the American brig *Betsy* in October 1784 pointed up the urgency of the problem.

Uncertain how to proceed with the Barbary states, the commissioners sent to Congress for further instructions. Meanwhile, they sought to enlist assistance at Versailles and to obtain reliable information on the price of peace with the pirates. The King had earlier pledged to intercede for the United States in the Mediterranean, but now his ministers begged off. Diplomacy with the Barbary powers was unusually delicate and secretive. The French treaty of a century's standing with Algiers, the mightiest of these states, was about to expire; and it was not in France's interest, nor indeed in the interest of any European nation at peace in the Mediterranean, to remove obstacles to American trade east of Gibraltar. Were it not for little fish like the United States the marauders would prey on the big ones. Above all, the British, whose trade easily supported tributes, fattened themselves on Algerine piracies at the Americans' expense, Jefferson thought. Lloyds was charging 25 per cent for insurance on American vessels bound for Cadiz or Lisbon, whereas the usual rate for English vessels to these Atlantic ports was 1.5 per cent. Britain might thus virtually eliminate American freights to Spain and Portugal. Sometime later, in April 1785, Jefferson learned from the American chargé d'affaires in Madrid, William Carmichael, that the British agent in Algiers was probably exciting piratical warfare on American traders. Spain was then at war with Algiers, and Carmichael was able to throw some light on the costs of peace. Lafayette, utilizing his connections, furnished detailed accounts of the presents given by different governments on various occasions: gold, cloth, jewelry, carriages, food, and the arms, lumber, and naval stores with which Christian slaves built and outfitted the pirate vessels. From this information it appeared that the commissioners' original estimate of $300,000 as the cost of peace with the Barbary chiefs would have to be multiplied many times.

Acting without this knowledge, Congress authorized $80,000 and pressed the ministers to negotiate peace "immediately, earnestly, and vigorously," sending whatever agents they pleased to the Moorish courts. "The interests of humanity as well as commerce," Jay wrote, "urge Congress and the public to provide and to desire that no time or pains may be spared to bring this matter to an advantageous and happy conclusion." While doubting the wisdom and the policy, and smiling at the paltry means, Jefferson accepted it and awaited the arrival of the confidential agent Jay had dispatched with the official papers. The agent, John Lamb of Connecticut, required six months to reach Paris. Impatient at the delay, anxious to take advantage of the friendly disposition of the Emperor of Morocco, who had released the captives of the *Betsy* on the intercession of the Spanish minister, Jefferson arranged to send Thomas Barclay, the Consul General, to purchase peace with Morocco. (His bag of "trinkets" included a pair of gold inlaid pistols, a blue enameled gold snuff box, a crimson silk umbrella, perfume, a sword, phosphorous matches, and "a clock in the bottom of a cage, with an artificial bird, that sings every hour or when the string is pulled, and sings six times.") When Lamb finally arrived in September, he was sent to Algiers. Perhaps Jefferson and Adams together would have made no impression on the imperious Dey; but Lamb, so warmly recommended by Jay, lacked even a trace of diplomatic skill. The Algerines had recently captured two American ships off the coast of Portugal, their captive crews totaling twenty-one men. The mission to Algiers became, therefore, one of ransom and redemption as well as peace. Neither was accomplished. The price on the head of each captive was $1200; as for peace, Lamb said, "it will cost a Tower of Constantinople." At Morocco, on the other hand, Barclay negotiated in 1786 the most advanced treaty of any Christian nation with a Barbary power. No annual tribute was required, and American ships and citizens received the protection accorded the most favored nation. The treaty cost only $30,000.

From the beginning, Jefferson considered the path of diplomacy with the Barbary states not only futile and humiliating but in the long run disastrous for the United States; and despite the Moroccan peace, experience served to strengthen this conviction. No peace founded on ransom and tribute could endure. A naval war would be less expensive, more effective, and highly honorable in the United States. "Nor does it respect us as to these pirates only, but as to the nations of Europe," he told Monroe. "If we wish our commerce to be free and uninsulted, we must let these nations see that we have the energy which at present they disbelieve." He conceded that the question of war or tribute was no longer debatable; Congress had made the decision and he must obey. All the while, however, he adroitly planned for war. From information supplied by Carmichael, by the American emissaries, and friends and ministers in Paris, he formed an opinion of the contemptible weakness of the Barbary powers, of the jealousies among them, and of the interest of the Italian states, in particular, in coercive measures. No lightning blow from a great armada was contemplated; rather, a small naval force of perhaps half a dozen frigates and as many tenders to blockade the Barbary ports into submission. He learned from Lafayette that such an operation had once been employed successfully by France against

Algiers. As the scheme matured in Jefferson's mind it took the form of a confederacy among the nations at war with the pirate states to force a perpetual peace without price. In the spring of 1786, wholly without the knowledge of Congress, he communicated the proposed articles of this confederacy to the ministers of several European governments at the French court.

John Adams was acquainted with his colleague's thinking. For several years they kept up an epistolary dialogue on the question of war or tribute. The crusty New Englander, strangely enough, took the part of the dove to the gentle Virginian's hawk. Adams thought peace ought to be purchased as rapidly as possible. "At present we are sacrificing a million annually to save one gift [to the Algerines] of two hundred thousand pounds. This is not good economy. We might at this hour have two hundred ships in the Mediterranean, whose freights alone would be worth two hundred thousand pounds, besides the influence upon the price of our produce." And where, Adams asked, would the United States find a navy to pursue an offensive war? "The same facts impress us differently," Jefferson replied. Justice, honor, economy, and enduring peace called for war. Naples and Portugal would join the United States, he confidently predicted. "And many, if not most of the powers of Europe (except France, England, Holland, and Spain . . .) would sooner or later enter into the confederacy, for the sake of having their peace with the piratical states guaranteed by the whole." The anti-piratical confederacy would produce indirect benefits of the highest import. It would win European respect for the Americans, and respect, he added, is the safeguard of national interest. While Adams underscored the feebleness of the United States as an argument for peace, Jefferson thought that very feebleness one of the best arguments for war. What better occasion could the nation have for beginning a navy? "It will arm the federal head with the safest of all instruments of coercion over their delinquent members." Here, as elsewhere, he calculated the effect of diplomatic projects on the power of the American Union. He expressed his opinion even more forcefully in a letter to Monroe at this time: "Were the honor and advantage of establishing such a confederacy out of the question, yet the necessity that the United States should have some marine force, and the happiness of this as the ostensible cause for beginning it, would decide on its propriety. It will be said there is no money in the treasury. There never will be money in the treasury till the confederacy shows its teeth. The states must see the rod; perhaps it must be felt by some of them. . . . Every national citizen must wish to see an effective instrument of coercion, and should fear to see it on any other element but the water. A naval force can never endanger our liberties, nor occasion bloodshed; a land force would do both." Europe, it is sometimes said, made Jefferson a democrat; far more it made him a nationalist.

The last word, after all, belonged to Adams, the pessimist. "I perceive that neither force nor money will be applied. . . . Your plan of fighting will be no more adopted than mine of negotiating." Jefferson never sent his plan to Congress, though Congress got wind of it, no doubt as he intended, through Lafayette. In 1787 Congress resolved that the United States should enter an anti-piratical confederacy such as Lafayette had outlined, and it asked Jay to submit a report on the motion. The report was negative, essentially on the ground of Congress's inability to support the proposed confederacy. Neither was there the ability to buy peace. Not until Jefferson succeeded Adams as President would the problem be solved—by war, as Jefferson had advocated from the start.

Negotiating with France

While bringing the Prussian treaty to conclusion, preparing the Barbary negotiations, and accustoming himself to the varied rounds, official and unofficial, of the American Minister in Paris, Jefferson gradually took up the principal work of the embassy, the promotion of commercial intercourse between France and the United States. With the failure of the general European plan, he became convinced that France held the key to America's commercial problem. The British monopoly could be broken, the main avenues of American trade shifted to France and her colonies, if Versailles would abolish antiquated restrictions, open the ports to American productions, and pay for them in manufactures, oils, wines, tropical produce, and other articles. France had everything to gain. Her hopes of permanently displacing Britain in the American market as a result of the war had been cruelly disappointed; but the commercial war was still on, in Jefferson's opinion, and France might yet succeed. He did not have to look far in the French capital—to Americanists like Lafayette, to physiocrats like Dupont de Nemours, to philosophes like Morellet and Condorcet, even to the Comte de Vergennes himself—for men of influence who sympathized with the commercial goals of the American Revolution. As for the United States, the infant prodigy needed France's friendship. Britain was hostile. War was an ever-present danger. Aside from the economic benefits of a strong commercial union, it would undergird the treaty of alliance. All considered, the course of prudence for the United States, Jefferson reasoned, was to develop a Franco-American commercial axis as the first step in a free-trading system.

The ministry at Versailles seemed cordially disposed. Vergennes, Louis XVI's foreign minister, architect of the war alliance, had already initiated a plan of trade concessions calculated to maintain French ascendancy in American affairs after the war's inducements to co-operation were withdrawn. Vergennes was the acknowledged master of European diplomacy, with a sly and crafty reputation. But Jefferson, shunning diplomatic subtlety and deceit, found Vergennes, in turn, frank, honorable, reasonable, altogether an agreeable person in business, and inclined toward economic, if not political, liberalism. "His devotion to the principles of pure despotism render him unaffectionate to our governments but his fear of England makes him value us as a make weight," Jefferson thought. Fear and hatred of Britain were Vergennes's ruling passions. The United States was only a pawn on his European chessboard, yet an exceedingly useful one, and Jefferson hoped to duplicate Franklin's feat of winning for it the favors usually accorded a queen.

The first cautious ministerial attack on the old restrictive system produced the August 1784 *arrêt* opening the West Indies to trade in certain articles. Lafayette had played a leading role in this development. Popular, zealous for the American cause, craving the spotlight, the youthful Marquis was a perfect front for Vergennes's scheme, and he used him to ward off official and mercantile opposition. Unlike Vergennes, Lafayette was an ardent devotee of the United States, eager to promote its interests in any way compatible with his French nationality. Visitors to his Paris home experienced the strange sensation of being suddenly transplanted to America. One was sure to meet Americans there and to converse on things American. The Marquis spoke English as readily as French; his children, Virginia and George Washington Lafayette, spoke English and sang American songs; two American Indian boys were part of his household; an engraved copy of the Declaration of Independence hung on the wall of his study in one side of a double frame, the other side empty, "waiting for the declaration of the rights of France." Washington was his god, the Declaration of Independence his Bible. It was a sacrilege, he said, "to mention any day as the beginning of the year but the blessed 4th of July." Lafayette began his year 1785, the tenth of American independence, magnetized at Jefferson's table. Franklin's departure threw them closer together for business reasons. But their relationship was more than a business one. An intimacy sprang up between the two families; and the headstrong aristocrat, whose education was exclusively military, found in Jefferson a friendly counselor and political mentor to lead him, and France, into the promised land of republican liberty. Words could scarcely express Lafayette's admiration for Jefferson. "No better minister could be sent to France," he wrote to a friend in America. "He is everything that is good, upright, enlightened and clever, and is respected and beloved by every one that knows him." Lafayette was pleased to serve as the American Minister's aide-de-camp. He was Jefferson's liaison in nearly all matters touching the relations between the two countries. "In truth," as Jefferson years later recalled their campaign for Franco-American commerce, "I only held the nail, he drove it."

The first attack had failed, and Jefferson reviewed the entire subject in a series of conversations with Vergennes from August to December 1785. He wisely refrained from asking further concessions in the West Indies, since the government was hard pressed to hold the position taken the year before and, in fact, commenced a tactical retreat in September. He centered his efforts on opening direct trade between the two countries in the productions each could furnish the other. But here, too, he met the spirit of monopoly and a vertible wilderness of fees, duties, and commercial regulations whose roots ran deep into the economic and political order. Especially formidable was the Farmers-General. To this company of wealthy and influential men the government "farmed out" the collection of several indirect taxes and customs' duties, including the tobacco duty. The latter filled the coffers of the King and proved very lucrative to the farmers, who were granted a monopoly in the importation of tobacco. Tobacco was America's leading export. Any attempt to free the French market for American commerce must begin with an attack on the tobacco monopoly. Yet the Farmers-General was so interwoven with the French system of finance, there seemed little chance of success. In 1783 Vergennes had collaborated with the Comptroller, Ormesson, in a move to abolish the Farmers-General. The result was Ormesson's dismissal and his replacement by Charles-Alexandre de Calonne under conditions that made him a captive of the system.

The French, of course, were still strangers to the American market. English merchants had generations of experience in managing the trade, catering to American tastes, finding vent for American productions. So it was, with the peace, that the trade flowed back into the old channels. Angry and resentful at this commercial bondage, the Americans nevertheless indulged their prejudices in favor of English wares and, falling into debt, found no way to escape the liberal credits allowed by English merchants on consignment. These credits, Jefferson said, "are the actual links which hold us whether we will or no to Great Britain." The French merchants, on the other hand, were not accustomed to advancing credit and trading on consignment; they had no established commercial connections in American ports. Their first big venture in the market, in 1783–84, had been a disaster on both sides. The French felt cheated, many abandoned the field in disgust, while the Americans looked upon their agents as "a set of needy adventurers, without fortune or character, who by importing the refuse of the French manufactures, have effectually strengthened our prejudices in favor of the British." When several of the American states embarked on commercial retaliation, they made no exception in favor of French imports. Vergennes lodged a strong protest with Jefferson. He defended the laws at court, though he privately believed they should be repealed except against Britain and other countries not in treaty relation with the United States. "The selfishness of England alone will not justify our hazarding a contest of this kind against all Europe," he told

Adams. In every conversation with Vergennes, Jefferson combated ideas of the Americans' irrevocable attachment to English manufactures, of infidelity in their commercial engagements, and so on. "Were national prejudice alone listened to," he said, "our trade would quit England and come to France." The real obstacle was the Americans' inability to make exchanges in the French market. American commerce might be coaxed from Britain if France would abolish antiquated regulations and enter into a free exchange of productions. "It will be a strong link of connection," Jefferson said, "the more with the only nation on earth on whom we can solidly rely for assistance till we stand on our own legs."

Tobacco was substance and essence of the entire proceeding. "The monopoly of the purchase of tobacco in France discourages both the French and the American merchant from bringing it here, and from taking in exchange the manufactures and productions of France." The Americans, Jefferson continued, are reluctant to enter a market where there is but one buyer, who sets the price, and that buyer one that does not engage in mercantile exchange but pays in coin. As a result, France purchased large quantities of tobacco from Britain, and of that purchased directly from Americans the coin was remitted to Britain, thus supporting the industry of the common enemy. No one in the United States or in France, except the monopolists, benefited from the enormous trade in tobacco. Jefferson proposed the abolition of the monopoly, leaving the trade freely to French and American merchants. The latter would, by their competition, ensure France's receiving the best tobaccos at the lowest prices, take their returns on the spot in merchandise, not money, and accustom the American consumer to French wares. The trade in tobacco would pave the way for other articles. To Vergennes's objection that such a change of system would imperil the King's revenue, Jefferson replied that a modest customs duty, like Britain's, would actually bring more money into the treasury. "Ma foi," said the old Count, "c'est une bonne idée." Encouraged, Jefferson pressed the matter. The time was propitious, for the Farmers-General five-year contract was up for renewal. Vergennes wished to withdraw tobacco from the contract and so advised Calonne, in whose department the business belonged. Calonne objected on fiscal grounds, adding that the negotiation of a new contract was so far advanced it was impossible to suppress the tobacco monopoly without "unravelling the whole transaction." But the true obstacle had gradually penetrated the covering veil, Jefferson observed. Calonne dared not buck the Farmers-General without risking loss of office. Jefferson kept the issue alive but no longer hoped for an early abolition of the monopoly. "I have struck at its roots here, and spared no pains to have the farm itself demolished," he wrote Patrick Henry, again Governor of Virginia, in January. "But it has been in vain. The persons interested in it are too powerful to be opposed, even by the interest of the whole country."

Two developments, meanwhile, altered the complexion of affairs. Jefferson learned near the end of the year that the monster he was combating had not one but two heads. The Farmers-General had awarded Robert Morris, of Philadelphia, an exclusive three-year contract for the supply of American tobacco. To the long-established monopoly in the purchase of tobacco was added a new monopoly in its sale. It seemed sure to depress prices in the Chesapeake, working solely to Morris's benefit, since the farm's price to him was fixed. He had struggled to slay monopoly in Europe only to find that the monster had straddled the Atlantic! At this point Lafayette, just returned from Prussia, came to Jefferson's aid. The Marquis and several men engaged with him urged Jefferson to press Vergennes for the appointment of a special committee to study means of promoting Franco-American commerce. Jefferson demurred, thinking it an improper proposal from a foreign envoy, but agreed to back it if it came from the Marquis. The proposal was made, Vergennes adopted it, Calonne acquiesced, and the so-called American Committee was appointed in January. Lafayette was a member, leading the assault on the double monopoly, ably assisted by the physiocrat Dupont de Nemours and Simon Bérard, a prominent L'Orient merchant enlisted on the side of free trade. Calonne and representatives of other government departments and the Farmers-General completed the committee of twelve. Jefferson and Vergennes remained very much in the picture as the protracted negotiations between them were replaced by the deliberations of the American Committee.

Soon after the committee commenced its work, Jefferson was called to London to join Adams in commercial negotiations with the envoys of Portugal and Tripoli. During his absence the farm's contract was renewed with provision for alteration or discontinuance at the King's pleasure. Accepting this as a foregone conclusion in any event, Jefferson pinned his hopes on a strong report from the committee, which would strengthen the King's hand, perhaps break the Morris contract, and smooth the way to freer commerce in the future. On his return at the end of April, he conferred with Lafayette and his allies, also with Vergennes. As before, the Count agreed with Jefferson's principles and objectives, but he felt the delicate financial condition of the country barred tampering with the annual revenue of 29 million livres from the tobacco monopoly. The American Committee had studied six different memoirs on the tobacco trade and considered at least as many propositions. The showdown meeting, Vergennes attending, was held at Calonne's estate in Berni on May 24. While acquiescing to the domestic monopoly, the committee resolved to break Morris's by obliging the farm to purchase annually 12,000 to 15,000 hogsheads of American tobacco over and above the 20,000 Morris had contracted to supply. The tobacco was to be carried in French and American vessels only, and purchased at prices consistent with the Morris contract. When that contract expired, no similar one was to be made.

Whether considered as a partial victory or a partial defeat, Jefferson thought the committee's decision, which the King endorsed, "the least bad of all the palliatives." He foresaw, accurately, that the farm would make all kinds of difficulty with the Berni agreement. He questioned its value, even as an expedient to keep the American trade open until the monopoly could be demolished. Nothing less would satisfy him. The committee was forced to be practical. Jefferson could afford the luxury of radicalism. "The committee's views have been somewhat different from mine," he wrote to Monroe, his confidential correspondent in Congress. "They despair of a suppression of the farm, and therefore wish to obtain palliatives which would coincide with the particular good of this country. I think that so long as the monopoly in the sale is kept up, it is of no consequence to us how they modify the pill for their own internal relief; but on the contrary the worse it remains, the more necessary it will render a reformation. Any palliative would take from us all those arguments and friends who would be satisfied with accommodation." He demanded the whole loaf on the familiar principle that half-a-loaf merely dulls the appetite for real reform.

The committee now turned its attention to other aspects of American commerce. Jefferson's views reached the group through Lafayette's unfailing agency. The final report took the form of a letter that Calonne addressed to Jefferson on October 22, 1786. It confirmed the concessions previously granted American trade, as in the instance of tobacco and free ports. It announced the suppression of duties on a large number of American imports from furs to ships, the reduction of export duties on French wines, and promised concessions on still other items. Jefferson was delighted. Viewing Calonne's letter as "an ultimate settlement of the conditions of our commerce with this country," he hastened its dispatch to Congress and the seaport towns.

But, alas, when shipmasters arrived claiming the benefit of these regulations for their cargoes, they found nothing changed. Calonne, whether because of real hostility to the concessions or because of the mounting fiscal crisis that would tumble him from office the succeeding April, could never bring himself to register the letter in the King's council; and thus it remained, literally, a dead letter. Not until December 1787 did it obtain the force of law. At that time Jefferson received assurances from Lambert, the third Comptroller General since Calonne's downfall, on the strict enforcement of the agreement of Berni. The chicaneries, vexations, and evasions practiced by the Farmers-General had substantially annulled even the modest gains expected for American tobacco. Jefferson scrambled for these gains while continuing to advocate his more radical solution. "By prohibiting all his Majesty's subjects from dealing in tobacco except with a single company, one-third of the exports of the United States are rendered uncommerciable here . . . ," he preached to Vergennes's successor. "A relief from these shackles will form a memorable epoch in the commerce of the two nations. It will establish at once a great basis of exchange, serving like a point of union to draw to it other members of our commerce. . . . Each nation has exactly to spare the articles which the other wants. . . . The governments have nothing to do but *not to hinder* their merchants from making the exchange." But the power of the Farmers-General defied government itself. A mighty revolution would be needed to destroy it.

In reporting the December *arrêt* to Jay, Jefferson said the principal difficulty arose on the article of whale oil, for which he had demanded free entry but finally acquiesced in the continuance of a modest duty in order to keep the sympathetic Lambert in office. "It hung on this article alone for two months, during which we risked the total loss of the *arrêt* on the stability of M. Lambert." Next to tobacco, the precious oils of the mammoth of the deep enlisted Jefferson's diplomacy from beginning to end. He had learned of the desperate plight of the Yankee whalemen during his journey through New England. The whale fishery had flourished before the war. From barren Nantucket Island and several mainland ports, 300 ships employing 5000 hardy seamen had sailed the distant seas in search of whales, returning with cargoes that lighted millions of lamps and furnished an important item in the colonies' balance of payments with the mother country. After the Revolution, Britain levied prohibitive duties on American whale oil and rapidly built up her own fishery. The American industry was badly crippled. Nantucket whalemen, for whom the trade was a way of life, were encouraged to abandon their island and migrate to Nova Scotia or across the Atlantic, thus throwing both industry and seamen into the scale of British power. The migration began in 1784. It was checked briefly by a Massachusetts law laying a bounty on whale oil and by timely French maneuvers to defeat the British plan. Setting out to revive the French fishery, Calonne competed with the British for the Nantucketers; and a number of the clan, after striking the best bargain between the rivals, settled at Dunkirk in 1786. But Calonne's scheme was doomed to failure. Taking a different tack, Lafayette sought to open the French market to American whale oil, thereby permitting the Nantucketers to remain on their island, depriving Britain of an enormous asset, and furthering Franco-American trade. Just at the time Jefferson became Minister, a contract for the supply of American oil, free of duties, to a company franchised to light the streets of Paris and several other cities was completed under Lafayette's auspices. It helped to check the flight of the Nantucketers, who showed their gratitude by presenting the Marquis with a 500-pound cheese.

Jefferson, of course, endorsed Lafayette's objectives, though he disapproved of the exclusive privilege in the contract with the French company. Some months later a prominent Massachusetts merchant arrived in Paris asking privileges of the same kind. Jefferson took him to the Marquis's house, and the question of a contract was discussed. "I proposed, however, to the Marquis, when we were alone," as Jefferson reported the meeting to Adams, "that instead of wasting our efforts on individual applications, we had better take it up on general ground, and, whatever could be obtained, let it be common to all." When the right political path was pointed out, Lafayette took it. He pressed the matter on Calonne, with the result that the American oil was put on an equal footing with the Hanseatic towns, the most favored European nation in this article, which amounted to about a two-thirds reduction of duties. The oil must be brought in American or French ships, and the indulgence was limited to one year. Jefferson was not at all satisfied with this arrangement. By right, it represented no concession whatever, since the United States was entitled by treaty to the privileges accorded the most favored nation. Moreover, in his opinion, the duties on whale oil ought to be suppressed entirely. The indulgence, so-called, proved even less beneficial than Jefferson had expected. After a trial of two years, whale oil remained an insignificant article of commerce between the two countries, the American fishery continued to languish, while the French drained the royal treasury without supplying the nation's needs. Britain alone profited from this disastrous policy. Yet it was continued by the regulations of December 1787 for the encouragement of American commerce.

Pursuing the whale through treacherous political waters required, as Jefferson discovered, all the cunning and tenacity of the mariners' hunt. The December *arrêt* provoked "violent opposition." With an eye to appeasement, the ministry seized on the modest privileges granted the American fisheries. The first to go, in February, was the provision for an entrepôt, whereby the produce of the fisheries, including whale oil, might be re-exported from French ports without payment of duties. (Merchant ships often went from port to port in search of the best market.) Jefferson was fully informed of this change, actually participated in ministerial conferences where it was agreed upon; yet he afterwards said that the withdrawal of the privilege was meant to apply only to codfish, a minor article cheerfully sacrificed, and that its extension to whale oil arose from bureaucratic error or fraud. In truth, this was an excuse to cover his embarrassment. He had been taken off guard, and he did not realize it until he returned to Paris from a tour of the Rhineland near the end of April. Another month passed before he could bring himself to communicate the new *arrêt* to Congress. Coming so closely on the heels of a much acclaimed diplomatic victory, it was bound to be interpreted as a setback. Rather than risk a blow to American confidence in French commercial regulations, Jefferson emphasized the ministry's stubborn adherence, in the face of opposition, to other more valuable concessions it had granted. With respect to revocation of the entrepôt for whale oil, he continued to employ the fiction of trickery or error, which left him an opening to get it restored, as he promised to do at the first opportunity.

But the pressures that produced the February directive were even more formidable when Jefferson tried to overcome them in May. These pressures came from both inside and outside the government. The objective of a great national fishery, in which the ministry of marine was particularly interested, ran counter to the foreign ministry's policy of fostering American commerce. The Nantucketers at Dunkirk, to whom the success of the whale fishery was confided, artfully kept the government's hopes alive and used their influence to check American competition. The British, however, offered the more serious threat. Aided by elaborate subsidies and the Anglo-French commercial treaty of 1786, the British fishery glutted the market, underselling all rivals, and caused the Nantucketers to press for higher premiums and protection just as Jefferson again took up the American case. Britain's success was truly astounding, he said. "Before the war she had not 100 vessels in the whale trade, while America employed 309. In . . . 1788, 314, nearly the ancient American number; while the latter is fallen to about 80. They have just changed places then, England having gained exactly what America has lost. France by her ports and markets holds the balance between the two contending parties, and gives the victory, by opening and shutting them, to which she pleases." Not for many years, and after heavy financial sacrifice, could France harpoon her own needs. "Is it not better then, by keeping her ports open to the U.S. to enable them to aid in maintaining the field against the common adversary . . . ? Otherwise her supplies must aliment that very force which is keeping her under." Whether the whale fishery was viewed as a political or a commercial institution, the logic of Jefferson's position was unassailable. It concluded, of course, in the proposal to exclude European oil from France. This would not conflict with the new Anglo-French treaty, that ambiguous triumph of French physiocracy, since it granted Britain only the privileges accorded the most favored European nation. Jefferson was dumbfounded in September when an *arrêt* prohibited the importation of all foreign whale oils.

For the next two months, while also bringing to conclusion the long-delayed consular convention between the two countries, Jefferson labored to repel this new blow to Franco-American commerce. Again, in representing the matter to the Comte de Montmorin, successor to Vergennes in the foreign ministry on the latter's death the previous year, he took the tack that it was all a mistake, that the *arrêt*, despite its wording, was not meant to reverse the "uniform disposition . . . which his Majesty and his ministers have shown to promote the commerce between France and the United States," and that the exclusion really had in contemplation the nations of Europe only. He asked the issuance of an explanatory *arrêt*, lest more Nantucket whalemen flee to Britain and American merchants recoil from the uncertainties of French commerce.

Finding in his conferences with Montmorin and other ministers considerable ignorance of the whaling industry, Jefferson took the data he had studiously gathered over the years and wrote a small treatise, *Observations on the Whale-Fishery*. It exhibited his mastery of this intricate subject: the properties of different illuminating oils; the fisheries of Britain, France, and the United States; whaling as a source of naval power; whaling in all its commercial and political aspects. No more interesting or authoritative guide had been written. But its historical importance lay with a specific purpose: the reopening of French ports to American whale oil. Jefferson had a number of copies printed and sent the pamphlet to the ministers concerned. Some days later he and Lafayette conferred with Montmorin, who now agreed to exempt the United States from the prohibition. The *arrêt* was finally issued on December 7, 1788. Thus, as Jefferson wrote triumphantly to Jay, "this branch of commerce, after so threatening an appearance, will be on a better footing than ever, as enjoying jointly with the French oil, a monopoly of their markets." It was the paramount concession France made to American commerce. The government threw itself into the scale of American power, and against strong political and mercantile opposition left its own industry to the hazard of American competition.

Jefferson saw still another raw product, the rice of the steamy Carolina tidelands, as a promising article of exchange with France. Rice was the second major export of the southern states, as important to South Carolina and Georgia as tobacco was to the Chesapeake country; and, like tobacco, it suffered severely from the war. Rice exports were less than one-half of pre-war averages. Britain continued to dominate the trade—a highly profitable re-export trade on her part—through the controls of debt and credit and the excellent facilities of the entrepôt at Cowes. Of the next most important pre-war markets, the British West Indies were closed, unless carried in British bottoms, and Portugal, now supplied by Brazil, excluded American rice. The economy of South Carolina was further depressed by the need to replace 20,000 slaves lost to the ravages of war and by the virtual disappearance of the foreign market for indigo, the state's second major staple.

Taking up this problem, Jefferson endeavored to channel part of the rice trade directly to France. French consumption of rice, already large, increased yearly; yet very little was bought from the Americans. Monopoly and restriction, such as burdened the tobacco trade, had no bearing on the problem. Rice entered virtually free of duties. Versailles could do nothing. Where, then, did the trouble lie, and what could the American Minister do about it? On the basis of preliminary inquiries, he informed the Carolinians that their rice, either because of the seed or the preparation, was not adapted to the French taste, thus explaining the ascendancy of Piedmont and Levantine rice in the market. To David Ramsay, the South Carolina legislator and historian, whose *History of the American Revolution*

Jefferson was trying to peddle in France, he sent samples of the Mediterranean rice sold in Paris. "Our house of assembly was then sitting," Ramsay replied. "I produced the samples of rice on the table of the house for the inspection of the members who were planters." Ramsay also published Jefferson's letter, which made a hit with the planters. Jefferson continued in every way possible to educate the Carolinians in the culture and preparation of Mediterranean rice. When he toured the south of France in the spring of 1787, he extended his itinerary to the fields of Piedmont and Lombardy in hopes of discovering the clue to the supposed superiority of their rice. Perhaps a different machine was used to clean it, thereby lessening the number of broken grains—a culinary complaint he had often heard against the American grain. But no, the machine was the same as the one Edward Rutledge had described to him when they sat together in Congress in 1775. (As a precaution against faulty memory, however, he sent an iron tooth from a Piedmont machine to Charleston.) "It is a difference in the species of grain," he concluded, "of which the government of Turin is so sensible, that . . . they prohibit the exportation of rough rice on pain of death." Undaunted, Jefferson filled his pockets with enough grain to put the Carolinians in seed, and with greedy determination, hired a muleteer to smuggle a couple of sacks across the Appenines. What fate may have overtaken the poor muleteer, Jefferson never learned; and the Carolinians, though they dutifully planted the Piedmont seed, thought it inferior to their own and soon gave it up. Nor did they share Jefferson's enthusiasm for the upland, or dry, rice he procured from China and Africa. Some of this seed spread wild in the Georgia uplands, he afterwards learned, and the people relished it.

Despite the exacting requirements of the French cuisine, American rice found increasing favor. Jefferson came to believe it might capture the market if it could be brought directly to France. "But it is first carried and deposited in England, and it is the merchant of that country who sends it here, [drawing] a great profit himself, while the commodity is moreover subjected to the expenses of a double voyage." No respectable French mercantile house had ventured in this business, and the debtor position of the planters, combined with the liberal advances on consignment given by the merchants and the facilities at Cowes, ensured British control of the trade. Moving against these difficulties, Jefferson tried to induce solid French houses to offer attractive terms to the Carolinians. In the summer of 1787, after returning from his southern tour, Jefferson approached Simon Bérard, one of the liberals on the American Committee, and the Bérard Company of L'Orient made proposals that Jefferson sent to Charleston. They were warmly received. Jefferson had "opened the door" to release from British bondage! Several large shipments were made. Unfortunately, though they gave umbrage to the British, they lost money for the planters, who persevered nonetheless. In 1789 more shipments cleared the Charleston customs house for France than ever before. Jefferson was honored by the South Carolina Agriculture Society and lavishly praised for his efforts on the state's behalf.

On the whole, Jefferson's labors to build a Franco-American commercial system were out of proportion to the results obtained. After five years the French Revolution intervened, disrupting further progress along the lines he had laid out. Britain maintained her commercial supremacy, yet American ships and cargoes moved into new avenues of trade, above all French, partly because of his efforts. The available statistics on the trade of the two nations during this period point to several conclusions. First, the total volume, though there were ups and downs in key articles, fluctuated very little and was not significantly greater at the end of the period than it was at the beginning. Second, the trade with the French colonies far exceeded the direct trade with the mother country. And third, in both branches, the Americans had much the better of it. The balance of trade in the island commerce favored the United States on a ratio of nearly two to one, the direct trade on a ratio of perhaps five or six to one. A bonanza for the Americans, the trade was a small disaster for the French.

What, then, becomes of Jefferson's constant plea for markets? Obviously, it did not go the heart of the problem. He naturally fixed his attention on obstacles to American imports (and navigation) to the neglect of France's difficulties in making exchanges for them. He knew very well that an enduring commerce between the two countries must be more or less equal in its benefits; and near the end of his ministry especially, he was urging the French to look beyond the luxury trade in wines, oils, dyes, silks, and linens, and to adapt their industry more deliberately to the American market. But French manufacturing industry was sluggish and inefficient; the Anglo-French commercial accord of 1786 flooded the market with English goods, in the process drowning many merchants and manufacturers; and in the deepening depression of the following years capital was simply not available for the improvements Jefferson had in mind. At any rate, though he did not fully appreciate it, the difficulty of his system was less one of French markets than of French supplies. By 1789 the markets were open to an astonishing degree, largely due to his efforts and the influence of liberal commercial ideology at Versailles. The Americans exploited these markets, then transferred most of the money balance in their favor to the support of British industry. This was the very problem that Jefferson and his French allies had endeavored to overcome. As liberal commercial policy gained in official favor, the country's merchants, manufacturers, *fabricants*, and shopkeepers, who were losing by it, drifted toward revolution. The American Minister had little contact with this bourgeoisie. He moved in a narrow circle, the enlightened nobility for the most part—friends of agriculture and free trade, of America and republicanism—and so it is not surprising that some of the most disturbing realities of the French economy eluded him. Some years later, when these realities were painfully obvious, Gouverneur Morris, who succeeded him at Versailles, fastened the skeptic's slur, *visionary*, on the Jeffersonian plan of direct commerce between France and the United States.

The plan was an important phase of Jefferson's, and America's, search for a viable commercial system. It was oriented to France primarily by virtue of its being against Britain. Britain was still the enemy in his eyes, and so long as she dominated the American economy, national dignity and independence were more illusory than real. The advantages of direct trade with France were self-evident from an economic standpoint. On moral and political grounds they appeared to be overwhelming, as a means of curbing British power and of multiplying ties of interest and affection with the only nation that had earned American friendship. The true policy toward foreign nations was one of perfect freedom and equality in trade and of strict political neutrality. Unfortunately, the world was not yet ready for this policy. Denied the "natural right" of free trade, requiring foreign outlets for growing agricultural surpluses, dependent on their exchange for necessary manufactures, encircled by the colonial outposts of European powers—the United States could not escape foreign involvements or withhold itself from the balance of power in the Atlantic world or ignore the ever present danger of war, particularly with Britain. The young republic must make the best commercial arrangements it could, and everything pointed to France as the surest partner. Jefferson was thoroughly cognizant of the political risk this policy entailed—the danger that in throwing off British chains the country would put on French ones. But this risk was manageable; the risk on the other side, with the former mother country jealous of her supremacy, was not. For the new nation, France offered imposing political support in Europe and an opportunity, an entering wedge, for the free commercial system on which American wealth and welfare depended.

The Vaunted Scene

"Behold me at length on the vaunted scene of Europe!" Thus saluting a friend at home, Jefferson went on to express the ambivalent feelings—attraction and repulsion—that generations of Americans after him would experience in their encounters with the Old World. "But you are perhaps curious to know how this new scene has struck a savage from the mountains of America" he wrote with self-conscious parody. "Not advantageously I assure you. I find the general fate of humanity here most deplorable. The truth of Voltaire's observation offers itself perpetually, that every man here must be either the hammer or the anvil." And he went on to compare the misery of the European masses crushed under the weight of panoplied kings, priests and nobles with the uniform happiness of the American people. Government was a tyrant; society was a whore. "Conjugal love having no existence among them, domestic happiness, of which that is the basis, is utterly unknown." The Americans could congratulate themselves on the easy domestic felicity that kept the wine of passion unclouded and sweet. "In science, the mass of people is two centuries behind ours, their literati half a dozen years before us." On the other hand, in polite manners and breeding the Europeans were far ahead of the still unpolished Americans. "Here it seems that a man might pass a life without encountering a single rudeness." And for the lover of the fine arts Europe was a glittering paradise. "Were I to proceed to tell you how much I enjoy their architecture, sculpture, painting, music, I should want words." Yet their splendor only magnified the awful shadow cast by the hosts of the damned. "My God!" Jefferson exclaimed to another friend. "How little do my countrymen know what precious blessings they are in possession of, and which no other people on earth enjoy. I confess I had no idea of it myself. . . ."

I had no idea of it myself. In the act of discovering Europe, Jefferson discovered America as well. Not the land or people or institutions, for he came into intellectual possession of these things before he set foot in Europe; but America as a spiritual ideal, harbinger of a new era, vision of an earthly paradise, bearer of the hopes of mankind—the American dream—this seized Jefferson's heart and mind only after he was enabled to view his native land from the perspective of Europe. The Americans, having the reality, had no need to invent the dream. The Europeans, above all the French, required the dream to sustain their hopes. It was the French philosophes who made of Franklin a living exemplification of their Heavenly City. It was Lafayette, at the head of the returning soldiers, who planted the tree of liberty at Versailles. It was the Americanized Crèvecœur who conducted earthbound Europeans on a spiritual pilgrimage to the land where homely virtue and enlightenment, liberty and prosperity, dwelled together. It was the Marquis de Condorcet, philosopher of human progress, who saw in the United States a model for revolution and living proof of progress in affairs of state. This idealized image rapidly eclipsed the older theory of New World degeneracy. Jefferson reflected it back to his homeland. The more he saw of Europe, the dearer his own country became, taking a luster to all its parts that no one bound to the farther shore could know it merited.

In his growing awareness of the peculiar blessings of the United States, Jefferson was uncertain whether "Americanism" ought to be a bridge to Europe, as its devotees intended, or a protective wall against European vices. If these blessings were, in fact, peculiar, his reform-minded friends in France, Holland, England, and elsewhere were chasing after false dawns. And the blessings Europe could not attain were America's to cherish in a world happily set apart. Jefferson seemed often to hold this opinion. An almost puritanical feeling about American manners and morals led him to preach hellfire sermons against the corruptions of European education. "Of all the errors which can possibly be committed in the education of youth, that of sending them to Europe is the most fatal." Young Americans, some of whom he observed in Paris, were likely to acquire a "fondness for European luxury and dissipation . . . a partiality for aristocracy or monarchy . . . a spirit of female intrigue," all certain to make them miserable aliens to their own country. Yet, in day-to-day diplomacy, Jefferson worked to strengthen the bonds between the United States and France and to free that most efficient of all contagions, commerce. His numerous unofficial labors facilitated intercourse in the arts and sciences. He was of too liberal a mind to entertain parochial views, too admiring of Europe's civilizing arts to renounce them for America, too cosmopolitan in his principles to suppose his people held a perpetual monopoly of them. With the rumblings of the French Revolution, he seemed convinced that the European lump could be broken and he entered wholeheartedly into the movement impelled by the American example. Jefferson's stance toward Europe was, therefore, shifting and complex. He shared Franklin's catholicity of outlook, though not his easy acceptance of French society. He shared Adams's puritanical indignation toward European vice and luxury, though none of his stony austerity. Because Europe stirred very contrary feelings in Jefferson's heart it was impossible for him to formulate a simple and unambiguous conception of America's role in the Atlantic world.

Jefferson denounced Europe, yet under the cover of his rhetoric made a marriage of convenience with the wicked temptress. Except for occasional "squalls of work," the duties of the embassy left him ample time for his own pursuits. Always an early riser, he generally worked at his desk until noon. Several hours, more or less daily, were given over to correspondence, both official and unofficial. No American minister reported with such regularity to the government at home or with a keener eye to European affairs. There was always some "tedious business" to deal with: the settlement of Commodore Jones's prize account with the French government, the recovery of arms intended for the United States but seized by French creditors during the war, the release of an American crew imprisoned for smuggling tobacco, and so on. In the absence of a consular convention governing the rights of American citizens, they often sought Jefferson's intervention with French authorities. The greatest discretion was necessary to keep these claims within proper bounds lest by constantly troubling the ministry for small favors he wear out his welcome for large ones. "Worn down every morning with writing on business, I sally at 12 o'clock into the bois de Boulogne, and unbend my labours. . . ." Sometimes the sallies were on horseback, more often on foot, for walking was the "sovereign invigorator" of the body. For a summer or two he devoted every free afternoon to the bookstores, "turning over every book with my own hands, and putting by everything which related to America, and indeed whatever was rare and valuable in every science." He would return home with books to occupy 250 feet of shelves. Dinner was at the peak of a leisurely afternoon, and whether host or guest Jefferson savored the pleasures—the wines, the cuisine, the conversation—of the French table. Perhaps the theater, the opera, or a concert, capped by the entertainment of some glittering salon, climaxed the day. Paris shone in all the arts. Jefferson fixed upon music in particular. "I am almost ready to say it is the only thing which from my heart I envy them, and which in spite of all the authority of the decalogue I do covet."

He went often to Versailles to transact business, attend the court, or take a pleasurable excursion through the spacious avenues, bright gardens, and classic glories of Louis XIV's monument to his grandeur. Versailles was amusing but scarcely deserving of superlatives, and he wasted none on it. Nor was he enamored of the court. A young American, Thomas Lee Shippen, whom Jefferson presented at Versailles, described the "obsequious adulation," "empty ornament," and "unmeaning grandeur" of these regal ceremonies, adding "that although Mr. Jefferson was the plainest man in the room, and the most destitute of ribbands, crosses and other insignia of rank . . . he was most courted and most attended to (even by the Courtiers themselves) of the whole Diplomatic corps." The corps was the most distinguished in Europe. Jefferson took a dim view of these titled ambassadors and ministers, however. They were not worth knowing, he said, and, in fact, he had only a trifling acquaintance with any of them. The Baron de Grimm, man of letters and critic of the arts, struck Jefferson as the best of the tribe: "No heart, not much of any science, yet enough of every one to speak its language." The entire court followed the King to the pleasure grounds of Fontainbleau in the fall of each year. Jefferson went along, though only for several days, in October 1785. Neither his finances nor his dispositions would support an annual residence there. A more satisfying retreat was afforded by the hermits of Mont Calvaire, beyond the bois de Boulogne. He sometimes occupied an apartment there, where he could work in perfect silence and stroll in the brothers' gardens.

The American Minister moved quietly in a select social circle. He was not seeking amorous adventure. The incessant whirl from one drawing room or boudoir to another held no charms for him. He was not a celebrity, as his predecessor had been, shunned popularity, and remained as inconspicuous as his office permitted. The reading public seldom came upon his name. Chastellux, of course, portrayed him in flattering colors in his *Travels;* but this was an exception, and it embarrassed the self-effacing American. Neither through the anonymously published *Notes on Virginia*, nor through American state papers circulated in France, like the Virginia Statute for Religious Freedom, nor in other productions of his pen did he show the slightest desire to attract notice to himself.

He was known best to the initiated of the American sect. Franklin had introduced him to the Comtesse de Houdetot, a woman reputedly ugly but radiating charm, wit, and goodness, the beloved of the poet-philosopher St. Lambert, and at the time Jefferson met her the priestess of the Crèvecœur cult of Arcadian America. Jefferson was often at her salon, where the literati congregated, and they shared a mutual interest in the education of Crèvecœur's sons. When Phillip Mazzei turned up in the summer of 1785, he at once took Jefferson on an afternoon round of his friends, starting with the poet-dramatist Marmontel, Secretary of the Académie Française, then to the great chemist Lavoisier, then to Condorcet, finally to the Duc de La Rochefoucauld, an aristocrat renowned for his liberalism. With Condorcet and La Rochefoucauld, Jefferson was probably already acquainted, as he certainly was with the Abbé Morellet, translator of the *Notes on Virginia*, who belonged to the same liberal circle. Perhaps he did not yet know the two men he later described as the most powerful in France at the approach of the Revolution, Jacques Necker and the Comte de Mirabeau. The latter, "this glittering monster," he thought an unscrupulous adventurer, while Necker, the Genevese banker, showed a limited capacity for statesmanship in his desperate efforts to save the *ancien régime* from itself. Jefferson sometimes attended the fashionable salon of Madame Necker, a woman who suffered from what Virginians called "the Budge," that is, she bounced and fidgeted; and he admired the brilliant daughter and young priestess of the salon, Madame de Staël. The salons of Madame Helvetius, Franklin's great friend, and of Madame d'Holbach, whose Encyclopédist husband had written the *Système de la nature*, which Jefferson had read years before—each presented a distinctive segment of the enlightened society of Paris.

But no salon appealed to him more than that of Comtesse de Tessé, at her country place Chaville, near Paris. An abiding affection grew up between the Virginian and this captivating little lady of the *ancien régime*, Lafayette's aunt and confidante, partroness of the arts and letters, friend of liberty and humanity. The Comtesse was an enthusiastic horticulturist, Chaville a botanical paradise. Jefferson went to great pains to obtain for her whole catalogues of seeds and plants from America. At the conclusion of his ministry, she presented him a marble pedestal inscribed, in Latin, "To the Supreme Ruler of the Universe, under whose watchful care the liberties of North America were finally achieved, and under whose tutelage the name of Thomas Jefferson will descend forever blessed to posterity." The American long remembered the Comtesse as his "particular botanical friend."

The botanical exchanges Jefferson conducted between the two worlds, exchanges that found him planting Indian corn in his garden at the Grille de Chaillot, for instance, while American collaborators experimented with European varieties of grass, rice, melons, and so on, were part of a larger enterprise in the transmission of useful knowledge. "Science is more important in a republican than in any other government," he wrote many years later. "And in an infant country like ours, we must depend for improvement on the science of other countries, longer established, possessing better means, and more advanced than we are." The *Encyclopédie méthodique*, successor to Diderot's work, was in preparation when he arrived in Paris. He patronized, and silently contributed to, this project, purchased it for the College of William and Mary, and entered subscriptions for his American friends. He sent trunks full of books to Madison, who balanced the account by payments made for the education of Jefferson's nephews, the Carrs. To the Reverend James Madison, of the College, among others, he periodically passed on "the crumbs of science" from the European table. A single letter reported Jan Ingenhousz's experiments on the effects of electricity on vegetation, an impressive new theory, upsetting Newton, on the phenomenon of the rainbow, LaPlace's latest astronomical work, the alleged discovery of the lost books of Livy which, as suspected, turned out to be a hoax, and encouraging developments in the as yet infant science of chemistry, "among the most useful of sciences," he remarked, "and big with future discoveries for the utility and safety of the human race."

This Virginia Yankee's curiosity about gadgets and machines of all kinds was insatiable. From England he imported a copying press —a simple instrument for making a duplicate of a letter. He was much taken with it, got French workmen to make presses on the same principle, presented them to a number of friends, and carried a portable version on his travels. He said he would gladly have given ten times the cost of his copying press to have had it from the date of the Stamp Act. He was similarly fascinated with a new process, called polytype, for the multiplication of facsimiles of original documents, drawings, or other images. Witnessing the process at the Paris shop of the inventor, he had 100 copies of a handwritten dinner invitation struck off in 45 minutes. Remarkable! He was never content to hear or read about a new invention: he must see it. Learning of an improvement in the production of muskets by standardized interchangeable parts, he went to the inventor and with his own hand put together several musket locks, "taking pieces at hazard as they came to hand, and they fitted in the most perfect manner." The significance of this technical advance did not escape Jefferson. He reported it to Congress. Sixteen years later Eli Whitney would perform an almost identical demonstration before astonished eyes in Washington. A Swiss established in Paris, Jean Pierre Droz, had made virtually "a new art" of coinage by the invention of a machine for stamping the two faces and the edge of a coin at one stroke. Jefferson investigated and informed Congress that Droz's services could be obtained for the United States. "It would be very desirable that in the institution of a new coinage, we could set out on so perfect a plan as this, and the more so, while the work is so exquisitely done, it is done cheaper." But Congress was still far from the establishment of a mint. No new contrivance was too trifling for Jefferson's attention. For instance, the pedometer: an ingenious device strapped between waist and knee to calculate strides in walking. He conducted a little experiment, ticking off his steps from place to place in winter and summer, proving that he did indeed go at a brisker pace and with longer strides in winter—a difference of exactly 331 steps to the mile. Jefferson saw that Madison got a pedometer.

The commerce in ideas and inventions, like the commerce in goods, ought to be reciprocal, so Jefferson worked hard to overcome the debit side of the account. Fortunately, two of his countrymen, Thomas Paine, of *Common Sense* fame, and James Rumsey, "the greatest mechanical genius" he knew, came to Europe to promote two very promising inventions. Paine brought the model of his revolutionary iron bridge to Paris in 1787. Jefferson's efforts to win French acceptance of the bridge led to a lasting friendship, though, ironically, Paine got the patents and support necessary for his work in England rather than in France. Rumsey sought exclusive patents and rights for steam navigation in France. The American Minister did everything possible to help him, seeking the patronage of nobility, the imprimatur of the French Academy, and approval of Rumsey's application at Versailles. "I have been frequently at Mr. Jefferson's . . . ," Rumsey wrote admiringly. "He has got all that ease, affability, and goodness about him, that distinguishes him as a good as well as a great man." But the time was not propitious. The efforts of "the most popular ambassador at the French Court" were in vain, and Rumsey died before his dreams could be realized.

Jefferson's patience in these matters was not easily exhausted. The trials of the long ocean voyage set back his plans to introduce American plants to Europe; yet he kept defying the odds so that the Old World might enjoy the superior productions of the New. "They have no apple here to compare with our Newtown pippin. They have nothing which deserves the name of a peach. . . . Their

337

cherries and strawberries are fair, but I think less flavored." Worst of all was the corn which, he said, "cannot be eaten, either in the form of corn or of bread, by any person who has eaten that of America." A patriot's pride shown in this work. It was a task of first importance "to do justice to our country, its productions, and its genius," he declared in a letter acknowledging an honorary doctor of law degree from Harvard University, the third institution so to honor him. "It is the work to which the young men, whom you are forming, should lay their hands. We have spent the prime of our lives in procuring them the precious blessings of liberty. Let them spend theirs in showing that it is the great parent of science and virtue; and that a nation will be great in both always in proportion as it is free."

In this same letter, Jefferson noted that the natural history of America was "totally mistaken and mis-represented" in Europe. He had been in Paris little over a year when Chastellux took him to the country residence of the great Buffon. "I was introduced to him as Mr. Jefferson, who, in some notes on Virginia, had combated some of his opinions. Instead of entering into an argument," so Jefferson recalled the meeting, "he took down his last work, presented it to me, and said, 'When Mr. Jefferson shall have read this, he will be perfectly satisfied that I am right.'" Undaunted by this grand gesture, Jefferson said Buffon had confounded the American deer, or elk, with the red deer of Europe and the moose with the reindeer. "I told him that our deer had horns two feet long; he replied with warmth, that if I could produce a single specimen, with horns one foot long, he would give up the question. . . . I told him also that the reindeer could walk under the belly of our moose; but he entirely scouted the idea." Whereupon Jefferson sent to America for the specimens. John Sullivan, of New Hampshire, to whom he had applied earlier, was pressed for the horns, skin, and skeleton of a moose. The former Revolutionary general, as Jefferson subsequently learned to his dismay, conducted a regular campaign. "The troops he employed sallied forth . . . in the month of March—much snow —a herd attacked—one killed—in the wilderness—a road cut 20 miles —to be drawn by hands from the frontier to his house—bones to be cleaned etc, etc, etc. . . ." Jefferson's tilt with Buffon cost him dearly. Sullivan submitted a bill for 45 pounds! By the time it arrived, before the consignment, Jefferson had forgotten about his request. He paid, of course, and thought the moose a valuable acquisition, despite the disappointing smallness of its horns, for which he apologized to Buffon. He hoped it might be reconstructed and mounted in the King's Cabinet of Natural History under Buffon's supervision. But the great scientist was soon dead. Jefferson never learned if he had repented the error of his ways.

Science and diplomacy combined to interest the Minister in geographical explorations, for knowledge and power were uncomfortably blended in these quests of discovery. One particularly engaged Jefferson. It revolved around an eccentric Connecticut genius, John Ledyard. This self-styled "slave of accident and son of care" had sailed with Captain Cook on his third Pacific voyage. He had come to Paris with the plan of a company to trade in furs between the northwest coast of America and China. The plan had not prospered when Jefferson met Ledyard early in 1786. He urged upon him the exploration of the American Northwest by journey eastward, through Siberia to Kamchatka, thence to the North American continent, and on to the Atlantic coast. The wild scheme excited Ledyard. He became obsessed with the idea of becoming "the first circumambulator of the globe." Through Baron de Grimm, the Empress Catherine's correspondent at Versailles, Jefferson and Lafayette undertook to obtain Ledyard's freedom of passage across Russia. She refused, thinking the enterprise chimerical. Ledyard would not relinquish it, however, and after the abortion of an alternate plan to sail from England to the Pacific, he returned to the original scheme, confident Catherine would acquiesce or even approve. He actually got within several hundred miles of Kamchatka before Catherine's couriers caught up with him and turned him back. Ledyard thought he had at least solved the ethnological riddle, the relationship between the Tartars and the American Indians, that had chiefly interested Jefferson in the venture. "They are the same people—" Ledyard wrote from Siberia, "the most ancient, the most numerous of any other, and had not a small sea divided them, they would all have still been known by the same name." Jefferson saw Ledyard again a year later, in 1788, when he passed through Paris on an expedition to Africa. He promised on his return to go to America and make the continental crossing westward from Kentucky. But Ledyard never returned from Africa. The path of destiny he had charted would be traveled by Lewis and Clark years later, under Jefferson's auspices of course.

In the fine arts Jefferson believed the Old World should furnish models for the New. The subject engaged him seriously chiefly in its public, or monumental, aspect. None of the commissions he performed in Paris gave him greater pleasure than two of this kind on behalf of his native state. No sooner had he arrived than he received the resolution of the Virginia assembly authorizing a statue of George Washington, with instructions to him and Franklin to select the artist and otherwise look after the execution of the work. The responsibility fell largely to Jefferson. After satisfying himself that the greatest living sculptor was the Parisian Houdon, he sent for him. Houdon leaped at the opportunity. He would gladly "leave the statues of kings unfinished," even go to America, which had not been contemplated, in order to copy Washington's features. Jefferson fell in with Houdon's thinking. Nothing should be spared in so noble a work; the statue should be life-size, and the bust, at least, taken from life. Houdon voyaged to America, "panting after glory," in company with Franklin. He returned six months later with plaster bust and measurements. The inscription for the statue provoked fanciful suggestions in Paris, including one from Jefferson, though the straightforward inscription earlier written by Madison was finally adhered to. Equally interesting was the question of dress. Benjamin West, in England, had successfully introduced modern garb into heroic portraiture. Despite his taste, and the taste of Paris, for things Roman, Jefferson thought "a modern in an antique dress as just an object of ridicule as a Hercules or Marius with a periwig and chapeaux bras." He was relieved when Washington himself deferred to the judgment in favor of modern dress. While the work went forward, Jefferson occasionally visited Houdon's studio, a cluttered museum of sculptured monuments of the great. The artist executed busts of several Revolutionary heroes—Franklin, Jones, Lafayette, Jefferson himself—and the American Minister would return home with plasters of these and others. The great noble pedestrian statue of Washington, "une Epoque dans les Arts," as Crèvecœur called it, was still unfinished when Jefferson left Paris in 1789.

Not long after, however, it would adorn the Virginia Capitol, at

Richmond, which Jefferson designed. His original plan for the new government buildings proved too ambitious for the state's resources. Rather than the complex of structures Jefferson had envisioned, the Directors of the Public Buildings decided to consolidate the whole under one roof. This single building, the Capitol, must have appropriate magnificence. The directors entreated Jefferson to consult on a plan in Paris, adding a request for drawings of a prison as well. He entered upon the assignment with the utmost deliberation. First the style was decided: Roman classical, as befitted the aspirations of the new republic. Then the model: one Palladio had made familiar to him, the Maison Carrée at Nîmes, thought by Jefferson "the best morsel of ancient architecture now remaining." Then the consulting architect: Jefferson finally chose Charles Clérisseau, who had published drawings of the antiquities of Nîmes. Finally, the adaptation of the model, a Roman temple, to the purpose at hand. Changes were made in the dimensions, the ordonance, and many details; windows were substituted for the pilasters of the outer walls; one of the three rows of columns was dropped from the portico. This last was at Clérisseau's suggestion in order to admit more light. Jefferson consented reluctantly, for he was anxious to preserve the purity of the ancient form. "What is good is often spoiled by trying to make it better," he observed. He sketched plans for the interior rooms and chambers, while Clérisseau drew the elevation and prepared a plaster model to guide workmen inexperienced in the fine art of building.

With what mortification did he then learn, in September 1785, that work was proceeding at Richmond on another, a less elegant and less costly, plan! He wrote the directors, Madison, and others imploring delay. "But how is a taste in this beautiful art to be formed in our countrymen," he demanded, "unless we avail ourselves of every occasion when public buildings are to be erected, of presenting to them models for their study and imitation?" No miserable expediency ought to decide the question between the copy of a sublime structure approved by the centuries and "the brat of a whimsical conception never before brought to light." "You see I am an enthusiast on the subject of the arts," he told Madison. "But it is an enthusiasm of which I am not ashamed, as its object is to improve the taste of my countrymen, to increase their reputation, and to reconcile to them the respect of the world and procure them its praise." His pleas were heeded. Foundations and bricks were already laid when Jefferson's plan reached Richmond many months later, but the directors endeavored to conform everything to his model. When finally completed a decade later, the Capitol gave visible form, if imperfectly, to Jefferson's grand conception. A touring Frenchman, La Rochefoucauld-Liancourt, then pronounced this building "beyond compare, the finest, the most noble, and the greatest in America." As the first monument of the classic revival, the Virginia Capitol exerted enormous influence on the public architecture of the United States.

Life for Jefferson was a perpetual study, and while on "the vaunted scene" he naturally sought to further his education by travel. Except for the brief sojourn at Fontainbleau, he had scarcely set foot outside Paris since his arrival when, in March 1786, Adams called him to London on the business of commercial treaties. Jefferson was prepared to dislike England. In friendly banter with Abigail Adams he had declared he would not give "the polite, self-denying, feeling, hospitable, goodhumored people of this country [France] and their amiability in every point of view . . . for ten such races of rich, proud, hectoring, swearing, squibbing, carnivorous animals as those among whom you are." The prejudice behind the banter was political—the freed colonial's prejudice against the mother country—and the visit to England only deepened it. Adams proudly carried his Virginia friend to court for presentation to the King. George III, who had been civil to Adams, pointedly snubbed the author of the Declaration of Independence. The Americans' overtures to the Foreign Secretary on the subject of a commercial treaty fell flat. The United States had friends in England—Richard Price, Thomas Brand-Hollis, Benjamin Vaughan, the Marquis of Lansdowne (Shelburne)—and Jefferson enjoyed their company; but they were few and without influence. Even the studied politeness of the dinner table offered no bar to English rudeness and insolence. "That nation hates us," Jefferson concluded after his visit, "their ministers hate us, and their king more than all other men."

The Adamses welcomed Jefferson as one of their own to the house on Grosvenor Square. They showed him London, from Drury Lane to the British Museum. He conceded the city was hand-

somer, cleaner, and roomier than Paris, though its architecture was
the most wretched imaginable. In the mechanical arts, London stood
at the head of the world. "I could write volumes on the improvements which I find made and making here in the arts," he wrote
Charles Thomson. With the Adamses he saw the great steam mill at
Blackfriars Bridge on the Thames. Powered by huge Boulton and
Watt engines, it was one of the wonders of the industrial revolution.
Unfortunately, he could not inspect the machinery itself. The English took extraordinary precautions against foreign larceny of industrial secrets. But not all useful inventions came from England or
all thievery from foreigners. While in London he visited a shop
where patented wagon wheels were made from a single piece of
wood. The New Jersey farmers first perfected the process, Jefferson
insisted, and Franklin had carried it to London, where it was patented, wheels produced in quantity, and exported around the world,
which thought it an English discovery. Jefferson's patriotic ardor
would not permit him to claim the discovery exclusively for the
Americans, however. The idea was in the *Iliad*, whence the Jersey
farmers, "the only farmers who can read Homer," got it! Visiting
the shop of London's leading maker of harpsichords, he attempted,
unsuccessfully, to promote a technical improvement introduced by
his Philadelphia friend Francis Hopkinson. Patsy continued to study
the harpsichord, and her father wanted her to have a fine instrument
made to order in London. It was to be one of the bulkier items later
carried home from Paris.

During a lull in negotiations with the Portuguese ambassador,
and after talks with the Tripolitan ambassador reached an impasse,
the two Americans made a leisurely tour of celebrated English
country estates and gardens. Armed with Thomas Whately's *Observations on Modern Gardening*, an infallible guide as he discovered, Jefferson viewed every park, walk, riding, hedge, garden, and
ornament of the spring infested English verdure with the practiced
eye of a landscapist. He jotted down useful observations, supplementing Whately, on the slope of a lawn, the cost of a grotto, size
of a lake or pond, style of an arch, effect of a temple or other ornament, number of deer inhabiting a park, and so on. While his taste
in architecture ran to classicism, his taste in landscape ran to the baroque. Here, at least, he agreed with William Hogarth, whose pro-

343

vocative essay on beauty he knew, in preferring the curved and waving lines of nature to the precise formality and regularity of the classical. And because the style of English pleasure-gardening, unlike the French, generally imitated nature in rococo profusion, Jefferson was charmed by it. He liked surprises to the eye, varying levels, asymmetrical balances. "Art appears too much," he wrote of Blenheim; and he repeatedly noted disapproval of straight lines, while particularly praising a "most lovely mixture of concave and convex" in one of the gardens he toured. For him, as for Hogarth, the serpentine was the line of nature.

The New Englander did not share his companion's enthusiasm. The gardens were lovely, of course, but scarcely deserving of a chaste republican's study. "It will be long, I hope, before ridings, parks, pleasure grounds, gardens, and ornamental farms grow so much in fashion in America," Adams jotted in his diary. The historic sites they visited aroused Adams's pride in his English heritage. On the battlefield at Worcester, where Cromwell defeated Charles II, Adams was amazed to discover the farmers at the local tavern ignorant of the encounter, and he gave them a little lecture. "Tell your neighbors and your children that this is holy ground; much holier than that on which your churches stand." Jefferson undoubtedly agreed, but, except for his infernal accounting of shillings and pence, he was as silent as the grave about this and every other historic scene. At Stratford-upon-Avon they followed the tourists' custom and cut a chip from the chair in the chimney corner where Shakespeare supposedly sat. Adams entered a tribute to the poet's genius in his diary. Jefferson's dry record of the excursion runs as follows: "paid postillion 3s; for seeing house where Shakespeare was born, 1s; seeing his tomb-stone, 1s; entertainment, 4s.2d; servants, 2s; horses to Hockley, 12s." It would be wrong to conclude that because he did not record his feelings he therefore had none; but his mind was on the future, on useful knowledge rather than historical sentiments.

The Portuguese treaty continued to drag after Jefferson returned to London the middle of April. While awaiting its completion, the two ministers endeavored to reach an agreement with the chairman of a committee of British merchants on the settlement of American debts. The treaty of peace provided for the recovery of these debts, and Jefferson never questioned the justice of the measure. But the violations of the treaty on the British side, as in the refusal to withdraw from the Northwest posts and to make restitution for captured slaves, furnished the excuse to demagogues, like Patrick Henry, to keep up the spirit of opposition at home. The stalemate might be broken, Jefferson thought, if reasonable terms of repayment could be agreed upon. He recommended a term of five years, which was acceptable, but his demand for the renunciation of interest during the war was too bitter a pill for the merchants to swallow. The negotiations broke down. Jefferson, meanwhile, tried to make private arrangements with his own creditors. Spurning the protection of Virginia laws, he put a heavy burden on his estate—selling land and slaves, renting out plantations—in order to pay his just debts. "I am miserable till I shall owe not a shilling," he later wrote; "the moment that shall be the case I shall feel at liberty to do something for the comfort of my slaves." Unfortunately, that moment would never come. At length, near the end of April, the ill-fated Portuguese treaty was signed, and Jefferson hurried back to Paris.

On leaving London he paid a young American artist, Mather Brown, ten pounds for an oil portrait, so far as is known the first ever made of him. The portrait was Abigail's idea. She wished it for John and herself; and Jefferson agreed to sit for Brown if Adams would reciprocate. The Adamses actually got the replica, which they hung in their residence on Grosvenor Square, while the original went to Jefferson two years later with Brown's portrait of Adams. Brown painted a dandified Jefferson: hair powdered and rolled and tied in a queue, fancy lace, soft face, exquisitely feminine hands. It was not thought a good likeness. "It has no feature like him," Short said, adding that everyone in Paris considered it an *étude*. The opinion was shared by John Trumbull, another young American artist Jefferson met in London. He was at once taken with Trumbull. His was one of several new friendships Jefferson took back to Paris. Another was with William S. Smith, secretary of the legation and the betrothed of young Abigail Adams. Smith, Trumbull, and the Adams family were always performing little commissions for him in London, while he and Short did the same for them in Paris. He preferred to dress in English cloth, for which

345

he apologized to the French ministry. Abigail looked after his orders for shirts, and he supplied her with silk stockings woven by the hermits of Mont Calvaire. Nothing abashed in these matters, the new Mrs. Smith asked the American Minister to obtain two corsets for her from a Parisian mademoiselle she had patronized three years before. Forwarding the corsets, Jefferson noted her failure to provide current measurements. "Should they be too small however," he added with an amusement Mrs. Smith seemed not to appreciate, "she will be so good as to lay them by a while. There are ebbs as well as flows in this world. When the mountain refused to come to Mahomet, he went up to the mountain."

The tobacco trade was on the carpet when Jefferson returned to Paris, and he was much occupied with the affairs of the American Committee, as well as the Barbary negotiations, for the next several months. Eager for every opporunity to create a favorable image of the United States in Europe, he had, in January, entered into a silent collaboration with Jean Nicholas Démeunier, who was responsible for the article on the United States in the authoritative *Encyclopédie méthodique.* Rochefoucauld had brought the two men together. Before going to London Jefferson had written out detailed answers to two sets of queries presented by Dameunier. The manuscript article of nearly 300 pages was then given to Jefferson for his observations, which he finished and returned in June. Aside from correcting Démeunier's mistakes, most of them derived, Jefferson thought, from the Abbé Raynal's *Histoire,* he supplied information on current American affairs interpreted in the most advantageous light. His true opinion of the Cincinnati, for example, left no ground for apology or equivocation; yet he urged upon Démeunier a face-saving explanation of that institution, not only in charity to the United States but to the numerous French officers who proudly wore the badge. Démeunier's article, first published in book form, disappointed him. "He has still left in a great deal of the Abbé Raynal, that is to say a great deal of falsehood, and he has stated other things on bad information." Nevertheless, it was a useful work, clearly the better for Jefferson's trouble, which Démeunier paid for "in the true coin of his country, most unmerciful compliment."

The charms of winsome romance touched the 43-year-old widower's heartstrings in August. The lady was Maria Cosway. An artist in her own right, she had come to Paris with her husband Richard Cosway, a fashionable London painter and renowned miniaturist. There Trumbull met them. He had accepted Jefferson's invitation to see and study the art treasures of Paris while making the hôtel de Langeac his home. Trumbull had brought along for engraving the first fruits of his epic enterprise in patriotic portraiture, *The Death of Montgomery* and *The Battle of Bunker's Hill;* and with Jefferson's assistance he began the composition of the still more famous painting, *The Declaration of Independence.* On an August afternoon Trumbull introduced Jefferson to the English couple at the Halle aux Bleds, the great domed grain market of Paris. A market was to be built in Richmond: how wonderful if it could be as beautiful and commodious as the Halle aux Bleds! But this utilitarian object was quickly forgotten as Jefferson fell under Maria's charms. A camaraderie seized the company, everyone of whom had dinner engagements. "Lying messengers were . . . dispatched into every quarter of the city with apologies for . . . breach of engagement." The American Minister sent his excuses to the Duchesse d'Anville; and they all drove off to St. Cloud, four miles distant, dined and toured the gallery there, returned to Paris under a glow of fireworks to match their spirits, and before separating made a late evening call on a celebrated harpist Maria admired.

Until October 5, when the Cosways returned to London, Jefferson and Maria were almost constant companions, usually with Trumbull and the Comte d'Angeville, director of the King's gallery. (Cosway was occupied with painting the portraits of the Duchesse d'Orléans and her children.) They toured the galleries, attended concerts at the Tuileries, sported at the Palais Royal, walked in the bois de Boulogne, and journeyed into the countryside. When the interlude passed, Jefferson let his memory wonder over these ecstatic days. St. Germain! "How beautiful was every object! The Port de Neuilly, the hills along the Seine, the rainbows of the machine of Marly, the terras of St. Germain, the chateaux, the gardens, the statues of Marly, the pavilion of Lucienne. . . . The wheels of time moved on with a rapidity of which those of our carriage gave but a faint idea, and yet in the evening, when one took a retrospect of the day, what a mass of happiness had we travelled over!"

The enchantress was Maria, not St. Germain. A little wisp of a woman, soft and delicate, deep blue eyes set in an oval face, with a head of frothy golden curls, she seemed to step out of one of her husband's cameos. But she possessed other charms as well. Although English, she had grown up in Florence, and the lightness of the Italian air was in her disposition, the music of the Italian tongue in her voice, the artistry of Florence in her fingertips. Introduced into London art circles when she was but twenty years of age, she soon married Richard Cosway, like Jefferson many years her senior. The marriage was not a happy one. Cosway was a vain and pompous dandy, caricatured by his enemies as "the macaroni miniature painter," jealous, or at least unappreciative, of Maria's talents, and holding her like a bird in his slightly tarnished cage of gilt. London was oppressive, but she turned their home on Stratford Place into a brilliant salon. Her musical evenings—"great concerts" they were called—became the height of fashion. It was a highly sophisticated world. Gossip connected Cosway with other women, and men buzzed around Maria like bees around a flower. "You make every body love you," Jefferson once said to her. "You are sought and surrounded therefore by all."

Jefferson's feelings toward Maria, while no doubt sexual in origin, had an airy quality that leaves no suggestion of ardent desire. They were gay and lighthearted with each other, affectionate in a pleasant way, flirting at love with neither choosing to embrace it. It was as if they were playing a game, delightfully free and even reckless, but which he at least knew all along would end in a perfectly conventional fashion. He was never happier in Paris than during this late summer of 1786, when the days, were they as long as Lapland's, would have been filled to overflowing. An evening or so after Maria's departure, Jefferson sat at his fireside, "solitary and sad," and composed a long letter to her in the form of a dialogue between his head and heart. The head upbraids the heart for its follies; the heart, unable to deny them but unrepentant, claims its rights from the prudent tyrant. "Let the gloomy Monk, sequestered from the world, seek unsocial pleasures in the bottom of his cell! Let the sublimated philosopher grasp visionary happiness while pursuing phantoms dressed in the garb of truth! Their supreme wisdom is supreme folly. . . . Had they ever felt the solid pleasure of one generous spasm of the heart, they would exchange for it all the frigid speculations of their lives, which you [the head] have been vaunting in such elevated terms. . . . Fill paper as you please with triangles and squares: try how many ways you can hang and combine them together. I shall never envy nor control your supreme delights. But leave me to decide when and where friendships are to be contracted." It wasn't that simple, however; in the end, the head (Jefferson) coolly put the heart (Maria) in its place. Reason and sentiment might divide life between them, yet, for him, one was the master, the other the servant. With the seraphic Maria he slackened the reins on his emotions but did not drop them. The following summer she was again in Paris, this time without her husband, but Jefferson saw less of her than before. "Your mere domestic cortege was so numerous, *et si imposante*, that one could not approach you quite at their ease," he apologized afterwards. Their affection endured for many years, long after he became President of the United States and she, widowed and returned to Italy, the beloved Baroness of Lodi.

During one of his perambulations with Maria, feeling friskier than usual, Jefferson attempted to jump a fence, fell hard, and dislocated his wrist. This was one of those follies the head upbraided him for. He suffered pain and sleepless nights for several days. For much longer he was unable to write except with his left hand, which required the superhuman effort reserved for such letters as the *adieu* to Maria. Short, meanwhile, was his amanuensis. The best surgeon in Paris had been called in to set the wrist, but obviously he bungled it. "The fingers remain swelled and crooked, the hand withered, and the joint having a very confined motion," Jefferson wrote nearly a year later. He had to lay aside his violin and never recovered full use of his right hand. The injury caused him to postpone a journey he had planned to the south of France in the fall of 1786. But as the months passed and the wrist failed to mend, his doctors prescribed the mineral waters of Aix-en-Provence. Government was at a standstill in February. Financial crisis had led to the extraordinary measure of convening an Assembly of Notables. This passage of affairs was likely to prove interesting—but not interesting enough to hold the American Minister in Paris. He attended the opening session of the Assembly, mapped out the tour, and took to the road the last day of February.

He traveled incognito with only a trunk and a servant. To complete his circuit would require more than ten weeks, but he was in no hurry. "I am constantly roving about, to see what I have never seen before and shall never see again," he wrote to Lafayette. "In the great cities, I go to see what travellers think alone worthy of being seen; but I make a job of it, and generally gulp it down in a day. On the other hand, I am never satiated with rambling through the fields and farms, examining the culture of the cultivators, with a degree of curiosity which makes them take me to be a fool, and others to be much wiser than I am." In place of ministers, dukes, and duchesses, he courted the society of gardeners, vignerons, coopers, and farmers, and at night took refuge in some simple *auberge* where, "unknown to all, unheeded, undisturbed," he dined, read, reflected, recorded the day's observations, and slept. He encountered difficulties, of course, and saw many things disagreeable to him; but, as he philosophized to a Parisian friend, "The plan of my journey, as well as of my life, being to take things by the smooth handle, few occur which have not something tolerable to offer me." His tour was a continuous inquiry, and as his notes make clear, mainly an agricultural inquiry. He traveled "to see the country and not its towns." Agriculture was the most useful field for the studious American with an eye cocked to his own country; and the mass of Frenchmen being farmers of one description or another, the countryside furnished the clues to the comparative misery or felicity of the nation. Jefferson commended his procedure to Lafayette: "You must ferret the people out of their hovels . . . look into their kettles, eat their bread, loll on their beds under the pretense of resting yourself, but in fact to find if they are soft. You will feel a sublime pleasure in the course of this investigation, and a sublimer one hereafter when you shall be able to apply your knowledge to the softening of their beds, or the throwing a morsel of meat into the kettle of vegetables." The peripatetic inquirer might thus become the wiser statesman.

Striking out through the Champagne—corn country which reminded him of the neighborhood of Elk Hill—he thought the cultivation and the cultivators poor. There were no farm houses, the people being gathered in villages, as around feudal manors, where he was sure they were "less happy and less virtuous . . . than they would be insulated with their families on the grounds they culti-

350

vate." The women too worked in the fields, "an unequivocal indication of extreme poverty," for the position of women in any society
was an infallible index to its well-being. The conditions of French
agriculture varied enormously from one region to another. As he
moved through Burgundy and into the Beaujolais, Jefferson thought
the country the richest he had ever seen. The people lived on their
farms, but unfortunately, because of the system of tenancy on short
leases, the husbandry was not equal to the land. He agreed with Arthur Young, the English agriculturist who toured France at about
the same time: "Give a man the secure possession of a bleak rock,
and he will turn it into a garden; give him a nine year lease of a garden, and he will convert it into a desert." Of French agriculture
generally, Jefferson had a higher opinion than Young. The latter, of
course, wrote as a professional observer and for an English audience
just after the French Revolution, while Jefferson's observations on
the wing were intended for no one but himself and his friends. In
any event, taking things by "the smooth handle," he expressed none
of the Englishman's outrage at the sight of bad husbandry and a miserable peasantry.

He came upon vineyards in Burgundy. "I mounted a *bidet*, put a
peasant on another and rambled thro' their most celebrated vineyards," he reported to Short. Throughout the tour he paid the closest attention to viniculture, wines, and vintages, not with a view to
American agriculture, for he discovered that the vine was "the parent of misery," but rather as a connoisseur for whom good wines
had become a necessary part of the art of living. Before reaching
Lyons, after two weeks of travel pelted with rain, hail, and snow, he
briefly departed from his usual plan of avoiding "good dinners and
good company" and stopped at a great chateau whose seigneur was
known to his friends the Abbés Arnoux and Chalut. There he fell in
love with a sculptured Diana, the most precious work of the chisel
he had ever seen.

Bent as he was on utilitarian objects, Jefferson did not entirely
ignore the fine arts in his travels. In painting and sculpture his taste
was quite uncultivated. Yet he could be transfixed by a statue or a
painting. He seemed indifferent to the canvases of the great masters,
"the old faded red things of Rubens," for example, and saved his
praise for contemporary works portraying Biblical or classical scenes

351

in a baroque manner: Marius pleading with his assassin, by Drouais; Van der Werf's picture of Sarah delivering Agar up to Abraham; and "republican" paintings in the same vein by Jacques Louis David, leader of the neo-classical school in Paris. "I am but a son of nature," he once said to Maria Cosway, "loving what I see and feel, without being able to give a reason, nor caring much whether there be one." When his ramblings were over, in 1788, he set down some observations for the guidance of two young Americans in their European travels. Here he listed the "objects of attention for an American." Agriculture came first, then mechanical arts (forges, quarries, boats, canals, bridges), then manufactures, though it would be a waste of time to examine them minutely, since the United States would not soon become a manufacturing country. Gardens ought to be studied, for the Americans might make the noblest gardens with the least expense. "Architecture worth great attention. As we double our numbers every 20 years we must double our houses . . . and it is desirable to introduce taste into an art which shows so much." As for painting and sculpture: "Too expensive for the state of wealth among us. It would be useless therefore and preposterous for us to endeavor to make ourselves connoisseurs in those arts. They are worth seeing, but not studying." Politics were worth while so far as they influenced the happiness of a people, but one might as well see the menagerie at Versailles, with its lions, tigers and other beasts of prey, as to seek out the courts of nobility. The advice was all very American—damning in the eyes of cultivated Europeans. Utility was Jefferson's standard; but if he thereby downgraded aesthetic enjoyments, it was because he knew the American tourist would find them easily enough, whereas the discovery of the more prosaic and practical arts with which to build a civilization called for disciplined effort.

Proceeding down the Rhone Valley, Jefferson's eyes feasted on "the remains of Roman grandeur"—palaces, arches, aqueducts, amphitheaters. Nîmes abounded in antiquities, and Jefferson loved it. "Here I am, Madame," he addressed Mme de Tessé in Paris, "gazing whole hours at the Maison Quarrée like a lover at his mistress." The chaste beauty of the building riveted his attention, fully justifying his expectations for the temple chosen as the model of the Virginia

Capitol. Arriving at Aix near the end of March, he spent several days bathing his wrist, without any sensible benefit, and soaking up the sun. "I am now in the land of corn, wine, oil, and sunshine. What more can man ask of heaven? If I should happen to die in Paris," he instructed Short, "I will beg you to send me here, and have me exposed to the sun. I am sure it will bring me to life again." In the country around Aix, he studied the culture of the olive and the making of oil. Of the several useful plants of the Mediterranean —fig, caper, mulberry, apricot, and others—the olive was the least known and the most worthy of being known in the United States. The plant lived forever and grew in any soil. It might be cultivated by slaves in South Carolina and Georgia. "Having been myself an eyewitness to the blessings which this tree sheds on the poor," he wrote to one of his Charleston correspondents, "I never had my wishes so kindled for the introduction of any article of new culture into our own country." At Aix he was amused to discover that he understood the Provençal dialect more because of his command of Italian than of French. Speculating on the reason for this in a letter to Short, he also expressed his disappointment that Provençal, a language next to Italian and Spanish in point of beauty, had lost out to the French and seemed certain to disappear.

From Aix, Jefferson went to Marseilles, chiefly to gather information on the port. There he decided to venture across the Alps in order to unravel the mystery of Piedmont rice. Leaving his carriage at Nice, he mounted a mule that faithfully brought him through the mountains to Turin in four days. The road he traveled struck him as one of the greatest works of man. "It did not cost as much as one year's war." He carried with him some writings purporting to explain Hannibal's passage across the Alps, and concluded they were all guesswork. Passing through the rice country, Jefferson also saw how Parmesan cheese was made, discovered a new method of storing rice, and acquired a taste for macaroni. (Later, when Short toured Italy, he obtained for Jefferson a machine to make macaroni, seldom if ever put to use.) He went as far as Milan. The famous cathedral was "a worthy object of philosophical speculation" because of its gaudy extravagance. "On viewing the churches of Italy it is evident without calculation that the same expense would have sufficed to throw the Apennines into the Adriatic and thereby render it terra firma from Leghorn to Constantinople." And he did not believe the soul of man would be any the worse for it.

Jefferson would always regret that he did not go to Rome. "I calculated the hours . . . . . But they were exactly more than I had to spare. Was not this provoking?" he asked Maria. Nor did he see Palladio's country, which lay too far to the east. Instead, he returned to Nice by way of Genoa—a sickening sea voyage followed by a fatiguing climb on muleback. Resting briefly, he then proceeded on the westward leg of his journey. At Avignon he admired the tomb of Laura, the lovely lady of Petrarch's passion, and made an excursion to the celebrated fountain of Vaucluse. "It gushes, of the size of a river, from a secluded valley of the mountain, the ruin of Petrarch's chateau being perched on a rock 200 feet perpendicular above. To add to the enchantment of the scene, every tree and bush was filled with nightingales in full song." The nightingales along the Seine had not been the same; he had judged them inferior to the Virginia mockingbirds. The warblers of the Mediterranean had a more varied song and a fuller tone. "It explains to me . . . ," he wrote in a typical flight of fancy, "why there never was a poet north of the Alps, and why there never will be one. A poet is as much the creature of climate as an orange or palm tree. What a bird the nightingale would be in the climates of America! We must colonize him thither."

The Mediterranean spring in all its glory found the questing American on the Canal of Languedoc, "cloudless skies above, limpid waters below, and on each hand a row of nightingales in full chorus." His carriage, *sans* wheels, was mounted on a light bark and towed on the canal. "I walk the greater part of the way along the banks of the canal, level, and lined with a double row of trees which furnish shade. When fatigued I take seat in my carriage where, as much at ease as if in my study, I read, write, or observe." All in all, it was the pleasantest mode of travel he had ever come upon. The waterway linking the Mediterranean with Bordeaux via the Garonne River was a grand work of engineering, deeply interesting to the Virginian who had ideas of connecting the James and the Potomac with the waters of the Ohio. He measured its every dimension and distance, studied its locks, and investigated its sources of water.

After nine lyrical days and 200 miles on the canal, he mounted the wheels to his carriage and drove to Bordeaux. This gleaming white city, hailed by Young as the most beautiful in France, made no particular impression on Jefferson, though the celebrated vineyards of the surrounding countryside claimed his ardent attention. Six dozen bottles of "the very best Bordeaux wine" were packed up and sent to Francis Eppes in Virginia. A few months later he ordered 250 bottles of vintage sauterne for his table in Paris. With the knowledge of the vineyards gleaned on his tour, Jefferson stocked his celler in handsome style for years to come.

From Bordeaux to Nantes and by way of Tours and Orleans to Paris, Jefferson returned to his starting point on June 10. "I . . . never passed three months and a half more delightfully," he said. He might have tarried longer, perhaps taken Rome or Palladio's Vicenza into his tour, but for the anxiously expected arrival of nine-year-old Polly. Jefferson had asked the Eppeses to send her to him the previous spring. His letter arrived too late, much to the relief of the Eppeses, for the little girl put her foot down. "I am very sorry you have sent for me. I don't want to go to France, I had rather stay with Aunt Eppes." The succeeding spring found her more stubborn than ever, but she was inveigled aboard ship, attended by a servant, Sally Hemings, less than twice her age. The voyage was uneventful; the captain doted on the child, and after landing in England carried her to Abigail Adams. Polly was wretched to leave him. "I tell her that I did not see her sister cry once," Abigail reported to Jefferson. "She replies that her sister was older and ought to do better, besides she had Pappa with her. I show her your picture. She says she cannot know it, how should she when she should not know you." Abigail promised to take her to Sadlers Wells. "I had rather . . . see Captain Ramsey [sic] one moment, than all the fun in the world," Polly sulked. But soon she became as attached to Abigail as she had been to the Captain. Abigail, and John too, fell in love with her. They were dismayed when Jefferson, offering the excuse of a backlog of work, sent a servant, the faithful Petit, to fetch her. Polly refused to see him, burst into tears, and clung to Abigail as her only refuge in a deceiving world. After several days she went with Petit, arriving in Paris the middle of July.

Reunited at last with a father and sister she scarcely knew, Polly soon became everyone's favorite. Jefferson was delighted with her. "Her reading, her writing, her manner in general show what everlasting obligation we are all under to you," he wrote to Mrs. Eppes. Polly was placed in the convent school, which Abigail Adams heartily disapproved of, and under Patsy's charge rapidly adjusted. The sisters were strikingly different: Patsy, like her father, tall and angular, reddish hair, and "the sunshine of heaven" in her temperament; Polly slight-of-build, high-strung, the prettier and more bewitching of the two, and the less studious. The crimson-frocked girls visited their father weekly, often with Kitty Church, whose mother Angelica Schuyler Church, American-born but married into fashionable London society, Jefferson admired. For him no pleasures equaled those of the family circle, whether passing a leisurely hour at tea, coaxing Polly to write letters, helping with a cursed Latin text, or seated at the fire and listening to Patsy play the harpsichord.

History had marched with quickening strides during Jefferson's absence, and he hastened to catch up. The Assembly of Notables had met, listened incredulously to Calonne's report, and rather than endorse his bold program of reform had driven him from office. Even so, there was room for encouragement in the Assembly's work, and Jefferson, with Lafayette and most liberal men, was disposed to find it. He praised, for instance, the provision for provincial assemblies as an important first step toward bringing the people into the affairs of government. Calonne's retirement offered the opportunity, at last, to get the government to honor the Berni agreement. Jefferson pressed the matter as much as he dared in view of the troubles besetting the ministry. As already noted, the decree—"the sheet-anchor of our connection with France"—finally issued in December. Meanwhile, the nation's disorders mounted. Mobs raged in Paris; every scribbler denounced the government, which seemed helpless to arrest this "revolution of public opinion." "The king, long in the habit of drowning his cares in wine, plunges deeper and deeper; the queen cries but sins on," Jefferson reported. He believed reform would work its way to a peaceful conclusion, but the high confidence he felt in June subsided by September.

At the same time, affairs in Holland threatened to erupt in a European war. Foreign powers had become entangled in the long and bitter contest between the Patriot, or democratic, party, which dominated the States General of the United Netherlands, and the mingled array of royalists, aristocrats, and local burghers who supported the Stadtholder, the Prince of Orange. France was pledged to the former, Britain and Prussia to the latter. When the civil conflict produced an insult to the Princess of Orange, her brother, the King of Prussia, sent 20,000 troops into the Netherlands, and Britain prepared to enter the fray if France intervened. Jefferson pondered the effect of such a war on his own country. It promised great commercial benefits, of course, since the United States would become the neutral carrier for the belligerents. "But," he wrote to Washington, "in the first place no war can be safe for us which threatens France with an unfavourable issue. And in the next, it will probably embark us again into the ocean of speculation, engage us to overtrade ourselves, convert us into sea-ravens under French and Dutch colors, divert us from agriculture which is our wisest pursuit, because it will in the end contribute most to real wealth, good morals and happiness." The British ambassador at Versailles asked Jefferson what the policy of the United States might be in the event of war. He replied without hesitation that the country would be neutral, unless Britain should be so foolish as to attack French possessions in the West Indies, which the United States was bound by treaty to defend. "Then it will be war," the ambassador said. War was averted, and the Dutch Patriots were crushed, principally because Louis XVI, his treasury empty, his hands full at home, dishonored his commitments. The United States could take no satisfaction from France's perfidy. Britain, seeing with what case France abandoned her friends, might think the moment propitious for regaining the lost colonies. "It conveys to us the important lesson," Jefferson wrote to Jay, "that no circumstances of morality, honor, interest or engagement are sufficient to authorize a secure reliance on any nation, at all times, and in all positions." He hoped Congress would fill the magazines and prepare for any eventuality.

Europe was turbulent from the Black Sea to the English Channel in the summer and fall of 1787. In the United States, meanwhile, a new federal constitution was framed by an assembly of notables at Philadelphia. Jefferson had applauded every effort to strengthen the bonds of union. A year before he was disturbed by alarming reports of dissension between the eastern and southern states on the question of the navigation of the Mississippi River. Congress had instructed Jay, in his negotiations with the Spanish Minister Diego de Gardoqui, to insist on the American right to navigate the river; but Gardoqui's instructions were just as emphatic on the opposite side, and after a year of fruitless talk Jay got authority from Congress, on a sharply sectional vote, to suspend the Mississippi claim for a period of twenty-five years in return for a treaty of commerce with Spain. Jefferson's Virginia friends accused Jay of selling out the West for eastern gain. In the face of angry opposition, Jay dropped the plan; but it produced a revulsion against federal measures in Virginia, west of the Alleghenies, and, indeed, in all the non-carrying states. Madison feared dire consequences. Jefferson shared his fears, and fully realized now, what he had only half believed before, that western commerce must flow to the Mississippi. "And I venture to say," he wrote Madison, "that the act which abandons the Mississippi is an act of separation between the Eastern and Western country." He did not expect Spain to relinquish the river, but he did expect it to be opened, either by the westerners themselves, perhaps in alliance with another nation, or by the agency of the United States, which was the only course consistent with the interests of the Union. The time would be ripe to pursue it when European nations jealous of American power were at war with each other.

While disturbed by the Jay-Gardoqui affair, Jefferson received the news of Shays' Rebellion with amazing aplomb. The uprising of Massachusetts' debt-ridden farmers was a frightening spectacle to Americans, but viewed from Jefferson's European perch it offered a not unpleasing picture of republican liberty flexing its muscles. The first report, from Jay, bristled with repressive outrage against the insurgents. Liberty was losing its charms, the Foreign Secretary suggested. But could it be that this immoderate reaction, rather than the insurgency, posed the real danger? Republican governors must not lose faith in the people in moments of waywardness, Jefferson lectured. "They may be led astray for a moment, but will soon correct themselves. The people are the only censors of their governors: and even their errors will tend to keep them to the true principles of their institution." Jefferson did not condone the insurgency, nor did he doubt the grievances of the insurgents, who were, in fact, very unjustly taxed; but he asked that it be weighed in the scale of European tyranny. Then a little insurgency would be found but a small price for the blessings of liberty. Abigail Adams, to whom Jefferson avowed this opinion, was indignant. "Instead of the laudable spirit which you approve, which makes a people watchful over their liberties and alert in the defense of them, the mobish insurgents are sapping the foundation, and destroying the whole fabric at once." Jefferson stood his ground. The spirit of resistance to government was so valuable on some occasions, it ought to be tolerated even when wrong. "I like a little rebellion now and then. It is like a storm in the atmosphere." He changed the metaphor, but nothing else, when he learned that Shays' Rebellion had taken a toll in lives. "The tree of liberty must be refreshed from time to time with the blood of patriots and tyrants," Jefferson flourished his pen. "It is its natural manure." The simple arithmetic of the matter was that the thirteen states had had but one rebellion in eleven years, which figured out to one rebellion per state in approximately 150 years. "What country before ever existed a century and half without a rebellion? . . . What signify a few lives lost in a century or two?" Better this insurgency and tumult, better this blood, than a European government of wolves over sheep.

This attitude conditioned Jefferson's first reaction to the Constitution framed in the shadow of Shays' Rebellion. In Philadelphia, men feared the breakdown of republican government from rampant democracy in the states; in Paris, Jefferson feared overzealous reaction to this democracy. "How do you like our new constitution?" he addressed Adams as soon as he saw it. "I confess there are things in it which stagger all my dispositions. . . ." The good it contained, he thought, "might have been couched in three or four new articles to be added to the good, old, and venerable fabric," the Articles of Confederation. He would have been satisfied with the addition of a federal commerce power, probably the tax power as well, and a separate executive and judiciary. But the convention at Philadelphia created a radically new frame of government. While the existing government was too weak, the new one promised to be too strong. "Our Convention has been too much impressed by the insurrection of Massachusetts: and in the spur of the moment they are setting up a kite to keep the hen yard in order." Unlike the adversaries of the Constitution at home, Anti-Federalists, as they were called, Jefferson was not apprehensive for the survival of the states in the invigorated system. As he assured Madison, he liked whatever strengthened the Union.

His first and principal objection was founded on European rather than American fears. The perpetual re-eligibility of the President raised dreaded monarchical alarms in Jefferson's mind. There was scarcely an evil in European countries not traceable to their kings, he said, and an American President re-eligible every fourth year would soon become a king, albeit an elective one, like the king of Poland, and like him too in that he would become the focus of foreign bribery, force, and intrigue. The recent chapter in the history of Holland also colored Jefferson's thinking on this subject. His second major objection to the Constitution, its omission of a bill of rights, seems not to have occurred to him at first. But the point was much agitated by the Anti-Federalists in the controversy over ratification, and when these reports came to hand Jefferson urged on Madison and others the addition of articles securing fundamental personal liberties. The friends of the Constitution, the Federalists, denied the need for a bill of rights, since the new government was granted no power in the sphere of personal liberties. But these rights were too important to be left to inference, Jefferson replied; and whatever the inconvenience or inefficacy of a parchment guarantee, it was far better than no guarantee at all.

As the weeks and months passed, and one state after another ratified the Constitution, Jefferson became more and more friendly toward it. "At first," he said, "though I saw that the great mass and groundwork was good, I disliked many appendages. Reflection and discussion have cleared up most of these." Some of the discussion was carried on with Lafayette and Paine. According to the Marquis, the three men debated the Constitution in a convention of their own as earnestly as if they were to decide its fate. Jefferson continued to protest the re-eligibility of the President; but finding that it excited no fears in America, chiefly because of the universal confidence in General Washington, whose election to the office was a foregone conclusion, he gave up the hope of correcting the provision. Increasingly, he concentrated on the attainable object, a bill of rights. But how could this demand be met without endangering the ratification of the Constitution? The document had been sent to the states for simple acceptance or rejection, without complicating reservations or amendments. Thus, in the mouths of Anti-Federalists like Henry in Virginia, the clamor for a bill of rights was a stratagem to defeat the Constitution. Jefferson unwittingly played into their hands. Writing to a friend in Virginia, he suggested the last four states should refuse to come under the new roof until a bill of rights was laid over it. Henry learned of the letter and used it with telling effect in the Virginia ratifying convention. "This illustrious citizen advises you to reject this government till it be amended," he declared. Henry barely failed to block ratification in Virginia, and Jefferson's letter, introduced in the North Carolina convention, contributed to the initial defeat in that state. Actually, Jefferson's plan called for the adoption, not the defeat, of the Constitution by nine states, which would put it into operation, trusting that the demand of the last four would produce the concession of a bill of rights. Virginia appeared to be the ninth state (in fact, New Hampshire ratified four days earlier) and so ought not to be a hold-out under the 9-4 plan. Moreover, unknown to Jefferson's friends at this time, June 1788, he had given up this idea in favor of the Massachusetts plan of unconditional ratification by all with recommended amendments. "It appears to me . . . from all information that its [the Constitution's] rejection would drive the states to despair, and bring an event which cannot be foreseen: and that its adoption is become absolutely necessary," he said. "It will be easier to get the assent of 9 states to correct what is wrong in the way pointed out by the Constitution itself, than to get 13 to concur in a new convention and another plan of confederation." A sense of despair over anything that would upset or impede the course of ratification had been communicated to him by Madison. In this crisis, as in others, the two Virginians compensated for each other's deficiencies. While Madison, with keen political realism, overcame Jefferson's hesitancy toward unconditional ratification, Jefferson, with superb political vision, overcame Madison's aversion to a federal bill of rights. The two men corresponded at length on this subject. Later Madison, almost singlehandedly, carried through the First Congress the first ten amendments—the Bill of Rights—to the Constitution.

While the new Constitution was winning a sure place in his political affections, Jefferson faced a crisis in the European finances of the United States. No sooner had he returned to Paris in June than he was informed by Ferdinand Grand, the Paris banker of the United States, that American funds were exhausted with no early prospect of replenishment. "We are thus left to shift for ourselves . . . ," Jefferson told poor Carmichael in Madrid. The poverty of the Confederacy was an old story, which it was hoped the Constitution would end. For years the United States had lived on borrowed money. Dutch banking houses, in particular, had raised the funds to make American remittances in Europe and to succor the credit of the infant republic. Florins borrowed in Holland kept American dollars at home where, however, there were never enough to meet domestic needs. New loans were floated in Holland in order to pay principal and interest on old loans, as well as to maintain the embassies and pay the other costs of European diplomacy. Jefferson had hoped that western land sales would replenish the Treasury and permit the government to extinguish its foreign debts. But this was a delusion. He was especially anxious to get rid of the French debt, both the part owed to the Crown and the part owed to French officers. On the former, not a franc's interest had been paid or demanded. Still it was a potential source of friction with France, and in view of the government's fiscal distress, payment of the debt amounting to 24 million livres was bound to produce a capital effect in favor of the United States. The debt to the Revolutionary officers for salaries and arrears of interest since 1785, though a trifling sum, sapped the good will of this very influential group at the French court. In 1786, and repeatedly, Jefferson pressed the home government to pay the debt with additional money borrowed from Dutch bankers, in effect transferring the French debt to private hands in Holland. The plan was politically astute, yet it risked American credit in Holland on the chance of cementing American friendship with France. Congress, thinking the risk too great, rejected the plan.

The risk was not wholly imaginary, as Jefferson learned near the end of 1787. No money came, or was in prospect, from Congress; and the Amsterdam bankers serving the United States, the brothers Willink and the brothers Van Staphorst, informed Jefferson that the loan floated a year before was but one-third filled. It would be impossible, therefore, to make remittances in Europe the ensuing year, or discharge the principal due on a small loan, or perhaps to pay the June interest amounting to 270,000 florins on outstanding loans. American credit faced collapse just when the new Constitution promised to secure it. Jefferson was at a loss what to do. Adams, who had conducted affairs with the Dutch bankers, was about to take leave of his post in London. There was no time to await instructions from Congress, more helpless than usual because of the interregnum. The bankers, meanwhile, pressed upon Jefferson their solution to the problem: the payment of a year's interest, amounting to 180,000 florins, on certain certificates of the American *domestic* debt held by Dutch speculators, as the pre-condition for filling up the current loan. It was wholly outside his or Adams's province to decide anything touching the domestic debt. Congress had made no arrangements for it. Jefferson abhorred speculation in general, scrupulously avoided it; and this particular piece of jobbery by the Amsterdam bankers struck him as a brazen attempt to exploit the foreign debt in order to reap handsome profits on the domestic. Squeezed between the jaws of an impossible proposition, on the one hand, and American default on its European obligations, on the other, Jefferson begged Adams for his advice. Adams returned a fiery blast against "the immeasurable avarice of Amsterdam." Willink and Van Staphorst were themselves speculators in American domestic securities, and by their plan would force payment at full value in Europe. Yet they were too deeply involved in American finance to do it injury. "Depend upon it," Adams wrote reassuringly, "the Amsterdamers love money too well to execute their threats." Lacking his experience in these matters, Jefferson still felt anxious. "Our affairs at Amsterdam press on my mind like a mountain." When he learned in March that Adams was going to The Hague to take formal leave as the American Commissioner there, Jefferson hurried to meet him.

Holland presented a melancholy scene. The Patriots—those who had not fled to France—were cruelly suppressed. The Orange cockade was everywhere. Jefferson passed through Rotterdam on the evening of the Prince's birthday. "The illuminations were the most splendid I had ever seen and the roar of joy the most universal I had ever heard." Catching Adams at The Hague in the nick of time, the two men went to Amsterdam, the banking capital of the world.

Their first object was to get the bankers to abandon the plan involving the domestic debt. This was accomplished, though with difficulty, Jefferson reported. The bankers agreed to push the loan on other grounds. But the million florins from this loan, if successful, would meet the country's European demands only during the current year. It would be at least another year, probably two, before the new government could make remittances to Europe. So Jefferson and Adams arranged, provisionally, for another loan of a million florins "to place the government at its ease and our credit in security during the trying interval." The estimated European account, balancing receipts and expenditures, was then drawn up for a period of three years.

Adams returned to London and soon sailed for home. Jefferson stayed on in Amsterdam for two weeks, familiarizing himself with unpleasant "money business" and anxiously watching the progress of the current loan. The condition of American credit was less desperate than he had dared hope in Paris. The Amsterdamers considered the United States "the surest nation on earth for the repayment of capital," he told Washington; the difficulty arose on the punctual payment of interest. American credit in Europe was a matter of first importance for the new government under the Constitution, which already brightened the dour countenances of bankers and brokers. A nation without foreign credit was handicapped in waging war and easily made the prey of great powers. "My wish would be to possess it in the highest degree, but to use it little," he said. In the present circumstances the principal danger lay in European speculation in the fallen domestic debt, potentially so much more profitable than the foreign. Before leaving Amsterdam, Jefferson implored the authorities at home to throw every obstacle in the way of the transfer of the domestic debt to Europe.

Jefferson saw much of interest in Amsterdam—elegant homes, wind-driven sawmills, canals and bridges, porcelain and ironwear, which he purchased—and he decided to seize the opportunity for a tour through Holland and the valley of the Rhine. He set forth at the end of March, traveling alternately by canal and road, to the Rhine at Nijmegen. "The transition from ease and opulence to extreme poverty is remarkable on crossing the line between Dutch and Prussian territory," he noted. "The soil and climate are the same.

The governments alone differ." (Six months before he had condemned misery and misrule in Holland.) Skirting the plains along
treacherous roads over barren, broom-covered hills, observing the
haggard populace and the run-down lands, Jefferson felt he had
come face to face with unmitigated European despotism for the first
time. "There are no chateaux, nor houses that bespeak the existence
even of a middle class. Universal and equal poverty overspread the
whole." He viewed a "sublime" gallery of paintings in Dusseldorf,
observed the hog of Westphalia whence came the celebrated ham, at
Cologne made inquiries about the city's world-famed millstones and
commenced notes on the Rhine wines. Only when he entered
Frankfort, a bustling commercial town and a republic, did he note
the reappearance of wealth. Here on the fringes of the Palatinate,
whence swarms of Germans had immigrated to America, he felt he
was in "a second mother country." "I have been continually amused
by seeing here the origin of whatever is not English among us," he
wrote to Short. "I fancied myself often in the upper parts of Maryland and Pennsylvania." In Frankfort he enjoyed a reunion with a
friend of Revolutionary days, the Baron de Geismar. At his garrison
in nearby Hanau were several of the officers who had lived in captivity in Albemarle.

Jefferson traveled southward through Hesse and Baden as far as
Strasbourg. Spring came on, the wines improved, and so, gradually,
did the country. He visited the famous *Schloss* at Heidelberg,
thinking it the noblest ruin he had ever seen and even more romanti-
cally situated than Petrarch's chateau at Vaucluse. He toured the
great estate of the Margrave of Baden in Karlsruhe. In Strasbourg
he browsed and made purchases in "the best shop of classical books"
he had ever encountered, and climbed to the top of the steeple of
the magnificent cathedral. Hurrying through the Marne toward
Paris, he stopped briefly only in the neighborhood of Epernay to
study the making of champagne.

While on the road Jefferson's observing eye fell on men and
oxen straining at plows in freshly turned fields. Noting the awkward
figure of the plows' moldboard, he was led to consider what its
form should be. From the function of the moldboard, "to receive
the sod after the share has cut under it, to raise it gradually and reverse it," he deduced that it ought to be so constructed as to oppose

the least resistance to the sod. He then made rough mathematical calculations, sketched the principle of the thing, and determined exactly how it should be built. Years later, in America, Jefferson returned to the idea and perfected "the moldboard of least resistance," acclaimed on two continents as an important technological improvement. That is another story; but Jefferson's encounter with the plow on the road to Nancy in April 1788 epitomizes the *modus operandi* of this attentive traveler: eyes turned to the land and the way men live on it; the mind excited by things seen and felt in the flow of experience, reducing them to mathematical form; the man endeavoring always to add to his store of useful knowledge for the good of humanity.

Back in Paris near the end of April, Jefferson was up to his ears in whale oil for the next several months, tracking that slippery subject through another round of diplomacy. Nor had he finished with the Dutch bankers, speculators in American funds, and the vexing problem of the national credit. Encouraging reports came from Amsterdam in the spring. The current loan filled up, Congress soon approved the new loan he and Adams had negotiated. But Versailles now called for the payment of interest, and he was troubled, too, by the renewed activity of a group of speculators in American securities. They sought, among other things, to purchase the debt to the French government at a substantial discount. Spurred by the prospects of the reformed government in the United States, Dutch bankers, French intellectuals, and American adventurers, some in high places at home, others operating in Europe, speculated extensively in the foreign and domestic debt. Their profiteering schemes were obscure. Jefferson did not comprehend them in detail but perceived their injurious tendency. He again appealed to the authorities at home to stop the speculative transfer of American debt to Europe. "This is a momentous object," he told Jay, "and in my opinion should receive instantaneous attention." The rise of speculation made him more eager to shift the French debt to Holland. He proposed the consolidation of the entire foreign debt in Holland, and worked out a careful plan for funding and extinguishing it over a dozen years. Nothing came of this proposal channeled through Madison, probably because William Duer, secretary of the Treasury Board in Philadelphia, was himself at the head of a ring of Americans promoting the European speculations. Afterwards, when Alexander Hamilton put the national credit on its feet, no one remembered Jefferson's earlier efforts to prop up this prodigy. Instead, Hamilton himself, doubtless prompted by Duer, accused his cabinet colleague of culpable irresponsibility in proposing to transfer the French debt to Holland.

The ensuing winter Jefferson had an unpleasant quarrel with the Dutch bankers. Several important diplomatic objects had been postponed pending the success of the loans in Holland. One involved the payment of interest to the French officers, now threatening open agitation of their cause. Before going to Holland he had prevailed on their spokesmen to wait until July; July passed and he begged their patience until February. Even more distressing was the deferment of plans Jefferson had made to redeem Amercian captives in Algiers. In January 1787 he had enlisted the aid of an order of priests, the Mathurins, whose mission of mercy embraced the victims of Barbary piracy. Procedures and modest ransom money were agreed upon for fifteen American survivors. The plan required the greatest secrecy, indeed a feigned indifference in official quarters to the fate of the captives, lest Algiers persist in demanding a princely sum. This humane endeavor, like the obligation to the French officers, hung fire because the bankers refused to advance the money. An amount had been allocated for the secret project when Jefferson was in Amsterdam, but the bankers now contended they had been instructed by Congress to place the payment of interest ahead of any other claims whatsoever on American funds. Under this mandate, they argued in February 1789, current income from the sale of bonds must be held against the June interest. While not denying the instructions, Jefferson sharply disputed the inference that income could not be applied to other objects until the next installment of semi-annual interest was provided for. Congress must have intended that salaries and other commitments were to be paid as they arose and interest paid as it arose. Otherwise, American diplomacy in Europe was at an end, except as the bankers chose to permit it. "I have observed," Jefferson wrote to Jay, "that as soon as a sum of interest is becoming due they are able to borrow just that, and no more or at least only so much more as may pay our salaries and keep us quiet . . . . I think it possible they may choose to support our credit to a certain point and let it go no further but at their will; to keep it so poised as that it may be at their mercy. By this they will be sure to keep us in their own hands." The stalemate continued for several months. Finally, in July, after the new loan was completed and the interest paid, Jefferson received funds to discharge the arrears due foreign officers and for his "particular purpose" in Algiers. He thought Willink and Van Staphorst had exerted themselves to fill the loan because of the threat of competition from another banking house and the prompt passage of a revenue bill by the First Congress. Before leaving for home he had the satisfaction of honoring the debt to the officers, but the devious plan to redeem the captives came to nothing, as the Mathurins, like so many orders ecclesiastical as well as civil, were caught up in the whirlwind of the French Revolution.

Just before the Revolution unhinged diplomacy at Versailles, the American Minister concluded the negotiation of the consular convention that had been promised by the treaty of 1778. Congress had refused to ratify the convention signed by Franklin in 1784. Contradictory attitudes toward the consular institution, inflammatory incidents touching the consuls or envoys of both countries, obstructionism growing out of American fears of French influence—these factors contributed to the delicacy of the task that fell to Jefferson on new instructions from Congress in 1786. The business was quite deliberately pigeonholed for two years while he worked to improve Franco-American commerce and to create a conciliatory atmosphere for the settlement of the consular question. He brought it forward on his return from the Rhine, pursuing it to conclusion in November. His opinion of consular establishments in general did not differ materially from Jay's, the man chiefly responsible for defeating Franklin's project. The institution was a relic of barbarism, neither necessary nor desirable to nations that had emerged into the light of peace, liberty, and justice. Unlike Jay, however, whose aggressive feelings toward France had been a persistent obstacle to his diplomacy, Jefferson thought amicable relations between the two countries more important than theoretical and technical differences on the issue of consuls. "That this government thinks them useful," he told Montmorin, "is sufficient reason for us to give them all the functions and facilities which our circumstances will admit." Negotiating in this spirit, Jefferson achieved an accord satisfactory to

The Maison Carrée at Nîmes.

The Virginia Capitol. Plaster model.

Minister to France. Replica of the portrait by Mather Brown, 1786.

Jefferson in 1789. Marble bust by Houdon.

Secretary of State. Portrait by Charles Willson Peale, 1791.

both nations. Even Jay commended him. It was promptly ratified by the United States, the last act of the old Congress, the first of the new.

The pleasure which the Versailles court took in the American Minister was generally reciprocated at home, as earlier shown by his appointment to a second three-year term, not unanimously, but without a negative vote in Congress. Unfortunately, his French counterpart in the United States, the Comte de Moustier, was unpopular from the moment he stepped off the boat in December 1787. "He is unsocial, proud and niggardly and betrays a sort of fastidiousness toward this country," Madison summarized the general opinion of Moustier after a year's trial. Jefferson was surprised. He had warmly recommended Moustier as a generous and amiable person who would easily adapt to the American scene. Usually a good judge of character, he erred badly in this instance. Moustier suffered too, Madison said, "from his illicit connection with Madame de Brehan which is universally known and offensive to American manners." The Marquise de Brehan, the Minister's sister-in-law, had accompanied him supposedly for her health, her son's education, and love of America, or rather, Crèvecœur's image of it. Reality failed to answer her expectations, of course, and when this bucolic cultist "appeared, in a considerable company, with a three-cornered muslin handkerchief tied round her head . . . in the fashion of the Negro women in the West Indies," the native ladies thought they were being snubbed. Her disenchantment with America soured Moustier's feelings as well. A subtle treachery lurked in the Arcadian dream of America, so fashionable in French republican circles. Jefferson did not wish to kill the dream—it had become too much a part of himself—but he sought to contain it. (He reprinted Franklin's down-to-earth pamphlet, *Information to Those Who Would Remove to America*, both as a time-saver in answering inquiries and as a cheerful but honest view of the United States.) Moustier, at any rate, rapidly lost his usefulness in the United States. Jefferson presented the problem to Montmorin, who at once arranged for the Comte's return and the appointment of a successor chosen with Jefferson's blessing in 1789.

To the Bastille

The times were grave and eventful, Jefferson reported after his return to the capital in the spring of 1788. "The gay and thoughtless Paris is now become a furnace of politics. All the world is run politically mad. Men, women, children talk nothing else. . . . Society is spoilt by it, at least for those who, like myself, are but lookers on." The insouciance of Parisian society was one of its charms, and for all the gravity of his political convictions Jefferson could not suppress a sigh over the loss. He pictured himself as a mere spectator of the events propelling France toward a revolution that would make the American seem innocuous by comparison. Yet he could not entirely escape the role of a participant in the drama unfolding before him. In his circle of friends and admirers he stood as the oracle of the revolutionary nation that inspired France. Naturally, they sought his advice. How could he be indifferent? Sincerely attached to the French people, he wished they might throw off the mass of misrule and oppression. His devotion to the cause of human rights transcended narrow calculations of national interest. But cause and interest united in making him a partisan to the reformation of the Bourbon monarchy. Whatever the outcome might be, it seemed certain to introduce potent elements of republicanism into the French constitution, break the shackles on trade and industry, push back the boundaries of freedom on every side, and in this way create a stronger basis of Franco-American friendship. As France went, so would go Europe, Jefferson thought, and the destiny of the United States must be linked for a future too long to measure with the destiny of freedom in Europe.

From the convening of the Notables a reformation was assured, though no one could predict its course or extent. By the time Jefferson left Paris in September 1789, it would have gone much farther than he had any idea of in the preliminary stages. For two and a half years he had repeatedly to adjust his thinking to a course of events always leaping ahead of him. He kept expecting the movement to come to rest, the revolution to stabilize itself, at some reasonable point along the line of advance. When it did not, but rolled dizzily onward with a logic all its own, Jefferson hurried to catch up and offer counsels of conciliation at the next favorable turn. Like his liberal friends, Lafayette chief among them, with whom he was in communication at all times and whose opinions usually swayed his own, Jefferson hoped for a final settlement more on the terms of the English constitution than the American. A nation could not go from absolutism to democracy all at once. France had not yet had her revolution of 1688. And Jefferson doubted she was ready for more. Since this is what he looked for, he did not really see the revolution of 1789 until it was fast upon him. Even so his perception of the movement was better than most men's, and he realigned his thinking at each critical juncture with a swiftness that would put a closet philosopher to shame. Because he responded to the French Revolution in this *ad hoc* fashion, he thought differently about it at different times. But the Revolution grew more and more radical, and so did Jefferson.

In the first preliminary stage, opened by the Assembly of Notables, Jefferson supported the aristocratic resurgence against royal absolutism in the belief it would produce a constitutional monarchy with guarantees of individual liberty, fiscal reform, and the beginnings of popular representation, all together "a vast mass of improvement in the condition of the nation." Lafayette and most of Jefferson's friends shared this belief. As the *noblesse*, the *parlements*, the provincial estates, and other aristocratic bodies combated the King, they appeared as the champions of liberty, and virtually the entire nation cheered them on. They wrung important concessions from the King, agreed to bear a fairer share of taxes, and gradually evolved a program of moderate reform. Yet the nobility had no intention of surrendering its privileged status. It aimed to rule the nation, not to be absorbed into it. In any aristocratic reformation, ancient orders and distinctions would remain, and the mass of the nation, the Third Estate, counting 96 of every 100 Frenchmen, would be subordinate to the privileged orders of Nobles and Clergy. The fate of the experiment with provincial assemblies in 1787 offered useful instruction in the motives and aims of the aristocratic revolt. As proposed by Calonne the assemblies were to be popularly elected without distinction of rank. Jefferson thought the innovation the most fundamental of all promised reforms. The provincial assemblies would be perfect representatives of the people, counteracting the evils of centralized monarchical power, and slowly setting the populace in the ways of self-government. But the nobles brought about Calonne's downfall, and the new ministry headed by the Comte de Brienne, yielding to aristocratic pressures, made the assemblies appointive bodies (one-half the members named by Brienne, the other half by co-optation), had them meet in three separate orders, and gave the presidency of each to the privileged ranks. The experiment thus lost its democratic character. The facts were clear; yet Jefferson seemed unable to recognize them, and continued for at least a year to view the provincial assemblies as incipient republican legislatures according to the mental image he had first formed of them. In this, as in the general support he gave to the aristocratic revolt of 1787–88, he allowed his fears of royal absolutism and his hopes of constitutional liberty to obscure the conservative animus and direction of the entire movement.

His perception improved markedly at the peak of the aristocratic resurgence in the spring and summer of 1788. He became as apprehensive of the nobility as he had previously been of the court, and gave up any idea that either, or both, could achieve a reformation for the good of the people. The struggle was between the centuries' old contenders, king and nobles, for "a monopoly of despotism over the people." "The nation is no otherwise concerned but as both parties may be induced to let go some of its abuses to court the public favor." A reformed constitution which curtailed the monarchy but excluded the people must still be a despotism. The question naturally arose, Jefferson reflected in a letter to Madison, "whether a pure despotism, in a single head or one which is divided among a king, nobles, priesthood, and numerous magistracy is the least bad. I should be puzzled to decide: but I hope they [the French] will have neither, and that they are advancing to a limited, moderate government, in which the people will have a good share."

But here, too, was a rub. Unfortunately, the people were not yet ready for the blessings of liberty and self-government. Jefferson doubted they would accept even a habeas corpus law if one were given to them. "The danger is that the people," he observed, "deceived by a false cry of liberty may be led to take side with one party, and thus give the other a pretext for crushing them still more." Something like this had happened in Holland, and the fiasco of the democratic revolution there colored Jefferson's counsels of moderation to the French. He was convinced the Dutch Patriots had aimed at too much democracy, thus frightening the moderate aristocrats into the arms of the Stadtholder. Events in France should take a happier turn, he thought. The "real patriots," as he called them, were united with the liberal nobility; the King, though weak and incompetent, was well-disposed toward the people; all parties showed commendable restraint; neither violence nor popular commotion threatened the advance toward a balanced constitution on the English model.

Such was Jefferson's appraisal of the situation in the fall of 1788. The King and the *parlement* of Paris had composed their differences. The momentous call had gone forth convening the Estates General in May. The popular financier Jacques Necker had been named to head the ministry. It was the quiet before the storm. In retrospect, Jefferson could be accused of bland insensitivity to the psychology of revolutionary movements. Had his temperament been different, his mind less rational, his knowledge of France better, he might have sensed, with Alexis de Tocqueville several decades later, that "the most perilous moment for a bad government is when it seeks to mend its ways."

The calling of the Estates General was an appeal to the nation, the first since 1614. The Third Estate was invited into the revolution, but whether it would have a major or a minor role depended on the forms and procedures to be followed in the convocation of the Estates General. The Patriot party, including many of Jefferson's friends—Rochefoucauld, Dupont, Condorcet, and, of course, Lafayette—demanded that the bourgeoisie have as many deputies as the nobility and clergy combined, and then pushed for constituting the assembly without distinction or vote by order, thus absorbing the old elements of estate and privilege into a single uniform nation. The first demand prevailed over angry aristocratic opposition that cost the *parlement* of Paris the popularity it had enjoyed while fencing the King. Whether voting would be by head or by order, the next crucial question, was left to the decision of the Estates General itself. But the Third Estate, being assured of a majority with the addition of liberal nobles and clerics, claimed a signal victory. The King was now virtually out of the dispute. Influenced by ministers sympathetic to the revolution, feeling the pressure of the court for money, which could be squeezed from an obstinate aristocracy by the only agency powerful enough, the people, Louis XVI must make valuable concessions. So, Jefferson said, "the dispute is between the privileged and unprivileged orders [over] how they shall divide these concessions between them." The outcome was sure, provided the Patriots did not seek too much at the threshold of power. On the whole, Jefferson thought they should ask no more than the King showed a readiness to grant and the aristocracy to tolerate, "lest they should shock the dispositions of the court, and even alarm the public mind, which must be left to open itself to successive improvements." The right of the Estates General to convene periodically, their exclusive right to raise and appropriate money, their participation in legislation, and, in time, the right to originate laws, probably a declaration of rights, possibly a habeas corpus law —this was the conciliatory agenda Jefferson set forth in January 1789.

It would soon seem hopelessly inadequate. The rise of public expectations and the surprising intransigence of the aristocracy, according to his calculations, caused Jefferson to grow bolder without, however, shifting his position as a prudent counselor of moderation. In the engine of revolution he acted as a balance wheel against dangers of extremism. He feared that in attempting too much the Patriots, like their Dutch friends, would lose everything. He feared an appeal to arms at court. He feared aristocratic reaction. He feared social chaos. He feared foreign intervention—at a time when France had lost most of her European friends. The course of the Revolution justified his fears. In this sense, then, his judgment was realistic. It was the judgment not of a radical or a visionary but of a practical statesman who refused to mix the American case with the French, who was more impressed by political than by social injustice, who wished to preserve the bonds of continuity and consensus in the society and to maintain the stability of government even in the throes of revolution. In a deeper sense, however, he was neither right nor realistic. For the Revolution proved to be a good deal more than Jefferson's idea of it. Not merely a constitutional reformation but a vast social upheaval, it could not be accomplished in the amiable spirit Jefferson advocated.

The winter of 1788–89 was the worst in memory. The Virginian

374

had never been so cold. The mercury plummeted to 20 degrees below zero in Paris. (He had to order a new thermometer from London to take the temperatures.) Loaded carriages passed on the Seine, and thousands skated from morning to night. The laboring poor were without work. Crowds of people huddled around great fires built in the streets. To the pangs of cold were added the pangs of hunger. The summer's wheat harvest had been disastrous. At every baker's shop, long queues waited scanty allowances of bread. Soup kitchens, furnished by the well-to-do, Jefferson among them, fed the hungry; and dinner invitations to the richest houses notified the guests to bring their own bread. At Necker's request near the end of November, Jefferson sent word to America of the bread shortage and the bounty offered for cargoes of grain and flour. American shipments helped to relieve the distress, which continued for many months, though neither Jefferson nor Necker deserved the credit. Both men acted more slowly than the crisis demanded—mercantile intelligence preceded Jefferson's by several weeks. Subsequently, in July, the stormy petrel of the National Assembly, Mirabeau, recklessly accused Necker of declining an *offer* from the American Minister of great quantities of flour. Being caught in a political quarrel between Necker and Mirabeau on this seething issue was scarcely a laughing matter. With Lafayette's aid, Jefferson managed to extricate himself, and Necker, without offense.

Sensible as he was to the hardships of the prolonged freeze and the bread shortage, Jefferson seems not to have connected them with the rise of revolutionary violence in the cities and the countryside. A riot among Paris workmen in April 1789, taking a hundred lives, struck him as the "unprovoked" mischief of "abandoned banditti," therefore justly "unpitied." He did not see that the distresses of workers and peasants incited smoldering hatred of aristocratic privilege and injustice, or that mobs and riots were more than coincidental to the mounting crisis, because he viewed the Revolution as an almost self-contained political affair to be negotiated by responsible persons from above. A social revolution from below was no part of his experience or his theoretical equipment. The main effect of the bread shortage on the political rejuvenation, he thought, was the additional burden its relief placed on a treasury already drained to the bottom.

Jefferson weathered the season as best he could. One, or both, of the girls was sometimes ill, Polly seriously for a period of two or three months; and there were weeks when he seldom stirred out-of-doors. In February a distinguished compatriot, Gouverneur Morris, arrived in Paris bearing letters of introduction from Washington and others. The Pennsylvanian with a wooden leg, who had won laurels as the stylist of the Constitution, came to unravel the tangled financial affairs of Robert Morris. While attending to this business, he found time for new speculations (one of them in the French debt), for becoming a Parisian *bon vivant*, and falling in love with the enchanting Madame de Flahut. Jefferson enjoyed this amiable, if somewhat garrulous, American. He was often at the hôtel de Langeac, warming himself at Jefferson's fire, taking "a dish of tea," dining *en famille*, talking of his own affairs and of the busy scene, of which he left fascinating glimpses in his diary. The two men did not agree in their politics. Morris felt that Jefferson was too advanced, too American, too democratic, in his ideas. They were not suited to the circumstances or the dispositions of the French people. Jefferson, he said, "with all the leaders of liberty here, are desirous of annihilating distinctions of order. How far such views may be right respecting mankind in general is I think extremely problematical, but with respect to this nation I am sure it is wrong and cannot eventuate well." Morris was impressed with royalty. The sight of Louis XVI brought tears to his eyes. Mobs and murders reinforced his skepticism of the populace. By comparison with Condorcet or Mirabeau or the Abbé Sièyes, Jefferson's views were moderate; by comparison with the Pennsylvania Federalist, the only other American on the scene who recorded his opinions, they were liberal and, indeed, becoming radical.

The Estates General convened at Versailles on May 5. "Viewing it as an opera it was imposing," Jefferson remarked. The King mounted on the throne, Queen two steps down, panoplied Princes of the Blood seated below, courtly retinue, officers of the household, and guards in ancient costume all ranged about; in front of the stage, ministers of state; on the benches to one side, marshals and other great officers, on the opposite side 300 clergy in robes of all colors and the same number of nobility garbed in black and gold; finally, the bourgeoisie in somber black. It was a striking tableau of the Old Regime. The King spoke, impressively, Jefferson thought.

The Keeper of the Seals, inaudible to the crowded spectators, was followed by Necker, whose long address disappointed nearly everyone. Louis XVI left the hall to the shouts of *vive le Roi* and his imperious queen heard the sweet music of *vive la Reine* for the first time in months. The next day the three orders commenced their meetings in separate chambers of the "hall of states." For several weeks Jefferson was a daily observer, most often of the debates of the Third, which he remembered as temperate and rational despite the size of the body—600 Frenchmen "among whom there are always more speakers than listeners"—and the crowds that hissed, clapped, shouted, flowed onto the floor, and mixed with the delegates.

"It is now for the first time," he reported to Jay, "that their revolution is likely to receive a serious check, and begins to wear a fearful appearance." The Third refused to organize itself as a separate order but invited the others to join in a single national assembly. The clergy, to Jefferson's surprise, showed a willingness to coalesce. The nobles, whom he had expected to divide, stood virtually united in defense of the ancient principle of representation and vote by order. Jefferson supposed the King would end the stalemate happily for the nation by intervening on the side of the Third. But the King was mute. As the crisis entered the fifth week, Jefferson suggested a decisive course of action to the Patriots. During an evening's conversation with Short, Lafayette, and Rabaut de St. Etienne, the Protestant leader, he threw out the idea of the King coming forward in a *séance royale* with a "charter of rights" signed by himself and every member of the three orders. The dramatic idea, with its appeal to an illusory unity, caught Lafayette's fancy. Though the shining symbol of republicanism, he was still something of a courtier, still a hapless prisoner of his aristocratic heritage, and had declined to act on Jefferson's advice to burn his instructions as a noble and declare for the Third Estate. Encouraged to develop his suggestion, Jefferson sketched a proposed charter, which he sent to Lafayette and St. Etienne the next day. It embraced, with liberal amplifications, the propositions he had advanced in January. Habeas corpus and free press laws were now definitely included; the Estates General was accorded exclusive power to legislate, with the King's consent; and fiscal privileges and inequities were abolished. The nobles had consented to the last in principle; the King had vaguely promised the rest. If all parties would endorse a reasonable compromise on this plan, then disband for a time, Jefferson said, they would accomplish "more good than was ever effected before without violence, and . . . stop exactly at the point where violence would otherwise begin. Time will be gained, the public mind will continue to ripen and to be informed, a basis of support may be prepared with the people themselves." And he assured his friends that this proposal stemmed from "an unmeasurable devotion for your nation and a painful anxiety lest despotism, after an unaccepted offer to bind its hands, should seize you again with tenfold fury."

Jefferson's "charter of rights" has little importance in the history of the French Revolution, but it has considerable interest for the history of Jefferson's opinions. It marked another advance in his conception of the revolution, an advance still grounded, however, on an accommodation of king, nobles, and commoners. The Bourbon monarch was to come forth at Versailles, like William of Orange in England a century before, with a charter of compromise between tradition and progress, feudal privilege and equal rights, absolutism and republicanism. Jefferson detested monarchy in theory, yet he seemed to think the French people should enter into a contract with the King in return for certain liberties. He was no longer fond of the English "balanced constitution," at least in American affairs, yet this was his model for France. Thirty years later, when he wrote his personal account of the coming of the French Revolution, he felt that events had vindicated his judgment, and proved the "lamentable error" of those, whoever they were, responsible for the rejection of this compromise. "For after thirty years of war, foreign and domestic, the loss of millions of lives, the prostration of private happiness, and the foreign subjugation of their own country for a time, they have obtained no more, nor even that securely." He was right only if one granted that compromise such as he had advocated was politically feasible in June 1789.

The King rallied to the noblesse. "The King is honest and wishes the good of his people, but the expedience of an hereditary aristocarcy is too difficult a question for him." Had Louis been master of his own house, the issue might have been different, Jefferson thought; unfortunately, the Queen and the court held absolute sway over him. "I have ever believed," he wrote in retrospect, again disclosing his blind spot, "that had there been no Queen, there would have been no revolution." When the Third Estate constituted itself as the National Assembly and proceeded to transact the public business, the King declared its actions null and void, and, at last, in a *séance royale*, offered a program intended to unite all parties. While in line with the reforms he and the nobles had pledged—reforms such as Jefferson had advocated—the program ranged the Crown on the side of the noblesse. The King would become a constitutional monarch, but traditional orders and many privileges would be preserved. "The Nobility were in triumph, the people in consternation," Jefferson observed. A solution the Third Estate might have regarded as a victory several months, or even weeks, earlier was now completely unacceptable. "Instead of being dismayed with what has passed they seem to rise in their demands, and some of them to consider the erasing every vestige of a difference of order as indispensable to the establishment and preservation of a good constitution." Jefferson remained apprehensive as the Third Estate stood its ground against the alliance of King and nobles. Suddenly, on June 27, only four days after the *séance royale*, the clergy and nobility took seats with the Third, thus completing the union of the three orders in a single assembly. Only now did Jefferson fully embrace the radical goals of the French Revolution.

He hoped these goals might be realized peacefully through the establishment of a stable constitutional government, relying on the moderate elements in the National Assembly, backed by the King. The opportunity was real. But at the moment of their prostration at the feet of the National Assembly, the King and the "Turkish despots" around him resorted to force, provoked the violence of the populace, and dug their graves in the ruins of the Old Regime. Troops, many of them foreign, were concentrated around Paris and Versailles. Necker's abrupt dismissal on July 11 set off the explosion in Paris. Jefferson was a close observer of the events of the ensuing five days—the encounter between unarmed populace and German cavalry at the Place Louis XV, the possession of arms at the hôtel des Invalides, the storming of the Bastille—ending with the recall of Necker and the King's apparent capitulation. On the 17th the King went in a procession to Paris. "About 60,000 citizens of all forms and colors, armed with the muskets of the Bastille and Invalides as far as they would go, the rest with pistols, swords, pikes, pruning hooks, scythes, etc., lined all the streets thro' which the procession passed, and, with the crowds of people in the streets, doors and windows, saluted them everywhere with the cries of 'vive la nation.' " The King stuck the national cockade in his hat at the hôtel de Ville, "such an *amende honorable* as no sovereign ever made, and no people ever received," and he returned to Versailles amidst the joyous acclaim of "vive le roi et la nation."

Once again, and for the last time, the precious occasion was lost. The King's weakness and duplicity, the flight of refugees, reports of aristocratic conspiracy and foreign intervention—the "Great Fear"—raised the vengeful fury of the populace and it spread without check. "The cutting off heads is become so much à la mode," Jefferson wrote with grim humor to Maria Cosway, "that one is apt to feel of a morning whether their own is on their shoulders." The savage murders of particularly obnoxious aristocrats and the parading of heads stirred no counter-revolutionary feelings in him, as they did in Morris. The tumult would subside once the populace had tasted blood. "I have been through it daily, have observed the mobs with my own eyes in order to be satisfied of their objects, and declare . . . that I saw so plainly the legitimacy of them, that I have slept in my house as quietly thro' the whole as I ever did in the most peaceable moments." Considering the provocation, he thought the populace behaved well, and sought to correct exaggerated reports of violence in the English press.

The aristocracy had conspired in its own destruction, Jefferson wrote at the beginning of August, "and the nation has made a total resumption of rights, which they had certainly never before ventured even to think of. The National Assembly have now as clean a canvas to work on here as we had in America." So he saw now the *democratic* revolution and also compared it with the American case. The Assembly, acting in effect as a constitutional convention, first wiped the canvas clean by abolishing feudal rank, order, and privilege. It then emblazoned the new standard of freedom and equality in the Declaration of the Rights of Man and Citizen. Jefferson had collaborated with Lafayette in drafting a declaration of rights which the Marquis introduced in the Assembly early in July; and the monumental document finally enacted bears traces of the American's influence. The formation of a constitution gave much more difficulty. All parties agreed, even the most fervent republicans, that France should retain its monarch. But how far should his executive powers extend? Should he have an absolute or merely a suspensive veto of legislation? And should the legislature be constituted in one or two houses? If the latter, should the upper house be formed as a kind of aristocratic check on the people? These questions divided the Patriots, whose unity Jefferson considered essential to the Revolution. When Lafayette proposed a dinner meeting of the principal leaders at Jefferson's house, he consented at once. "The discussions began at the hour of four," he recalled, "and were continued till ten o'clock in the evening; during which time, I was a silent witness to a coolness and candor of argument, unusual in the conflicts of political opinion . . . . The result was, that the King should have a suspensive veto on the laws, that the legislature should be composed of a single body only, and that to be chosen by the people. This Concordate decided the fate of the constitution. The Patriots all rallied to the principles thus settled, carried every question agreeably to them, and reduced the Aristocracy to insignificance and impotence."

Jefferson's account, while not inaccurate, slides too easily over one of the most significant issues in the comparative history of the American and the French Revolutions. Turgot, a chief mentor of the Patriots, had sharply criticized the revolutionary constitutions of the American states for dividing the legislative power and creating an independent executive. This imitation of the English constitution, as he saw it, made no sense in a country where the people *en masse*, undifferentiated by rank or order, were sovereign, and it could only weaken the authority of the nation. John Adams undertook his three-volume *Defence of the American Constitutions* to refute Turgot. Adams presented his friend across the Channel with the first volume of this cumbersome work when it appeared in 1787. Jefferson's own *Notes on Virginia*, published in London at the same time, incorporated his 1783 draft constitution for Virginia which provided for a strong governor and an upper house of more distinguished character than the lower house. (The draft constitution did not appear in Morellet's translation of the *Notes*, perhaps because he agreed with Turgot, but Jefferson saw to its French publication in the *Encyclopédie.*) In short, Jefferson's opinion at this time was not far from Adams's. He at once arranged for French translation and publication of Adams's volume. None appeared, however, until 1792, and that abridged. Very likely Jefferson lost interest, and may, in fact, have read the *Defence* attentively for the first time when several of his liberal friends in Paris—Mazzei, Dupont, Condorcet, and others—attacked Adams for Anglicanism, aristocratic prejudice, and distrust of the people. In 1789 Condorcet and Dupont brought out a French translation of the American John Stevens's pamphlet, *Observations on Government,* which blasted the "heterogeneous jumble" of monarchy, aristocracy, and democracy in Adams's system. The French editors supplied notes and commentary that expanded the ephemeral pamphlet into a substantial book. The work was often cited in the constitutional debates of the National Assembly to support a unicameral legislature and a weak executive against English ideas. The Patriots prevailed, as Jefferson said; but did he agree with them? A month or two earlier he would surely have sided with the minority on this issue. But the Revolution had leaped forward since then, and Jefferson, unlike Adams, went with it. The defense of "aristocracy" in America, where there was none, was quite a different matter from the perpetuation of aristocracy in France, where it was the great obstacle to reform. The establishment of an elitist upper house, even if not committed to the nobility, would provide a fortress for conservative groups against the democratic revolution. Jefferson had come to see this by August. He also believed that the French people, once they had won the stake in democracy, would come to see the wisdom of a divided legislature on the American, not the English, model.

Soon after the Patriot conference at the hôtel de Langeac—a diplomatic indiscretion for which the Minister made apology the next morning to Montmorin who, as it turned out, entirely approved of his good offices—Jefferson suffered a siege of illness. From September 1 to 9 he wrote but two letters, one of them addressed to Madison, though not sent to him for several months. This was an epistolary disquisition on the principle "that the earth belongs in usufruct to the living." It had been suggested to his mind, he said, in the course of reflection on the principles of a just society in the preceding months. The idea that one generation of men in civil society cannot bind another had extensive applications and consequences, especially in France. It was a favorite idea of Jefferson's physician, Dr. Richard Gem, an elderly Englishman, friend of the philosophes, ardent champion of the Revolution, and in the patient's recollection thirty years later, the best physician he ever met. He may have prompted Jefferson, during his illness, to consult the mortality tables, calculate the life of a generation (19 years), and develop the practical application of the idea. But it had been germinating in his mind for some time. Perhaps it began with the "little attendrissement" of a poor woman encountered on a walk near Fontainbleau in 1785. Her melancholy tale, and her tears of gratitude for the sous Jefferson gave her, first brought home to him the wretchedness produced by the unequal division of property in Europe. Returning to his fireside, he shared his reflections with a friend at home. "Whenever there is in any country, uncultivated lands and unemployed poor, it is clear that the laws of property have been so far extended as to violate natural right. The earth is given as a common stock for man to labor and live on," he wrote. It was too soon to say that American laws of property, omitting slavery, trespassed on human rights; but legislatures could not invent too many devices for dividing property from generation to generation. This was simply a more radical statement of Jefferson's well-developed principles of land tenure, which, to go farther back, stemmed from the Lockian theory of the natural right to land. The general notion was not original with him. Adam Smith, for instance, arguing from the same premises, had asserted the principle "that every successive generation of men have . . . an equal right to the earth, and to all that it possesses."

But the formulation of the principle that generations, as well as individuals, have natural rights, the application of it to the fundamental conditions of civil society, and the effort to reduce it to mathematical precision: this was at once the most original and most radical idea in the Jeffersonian catalogue. It could not have matured in America. It grew out of the European situation, specifically the situation of France in 1789. It expressed the speculative fervor of the French Revolution, the rage against the past, the assault on inequalities that amounted to a tyranny of the dead over the living; and in this light, the theory helped Jefferson justify the Revolution to his own reason. "It enters into the resolution of the questions, whether the nation may change the descent of lands holden in tail? Whether they may change the appropriation of lands given anciently to the church, to hospitals, colleges, orders of chivalry, and otherwise in perpetuity? Whether they may abolish the charges and privileges attached on lands, including the whole catalogue ecclesaistical and feudal? It goes to hereditary offices, authorities and jurisdictions; to hereditary orders, distinctions and appellations; to perpetual monopolies in commerce, the arts and sciences; with a long train of et ceteras." One generation may not form a constitution for another, or contract debts to be paid by another, or bind its successors by commitments of any kind.

The pertinence of the doctrine to France is self-evident. The issue between prescriptive rights—all the sanctions of tradition—and the "sovereignty of the living generation" would be pointedly drawn in the controversy of 1790–91 between Edmund Burke and Thomas Paine on the French Revolution. At the end of his letter— more essay than letter—Jefferson suggested that the principle would "furnish matter for a fine preamble to our [i.e. the United States] first law for appropriating the public revenue; and it will exclude at the threshold of our government the contagious and ruinous errors of this quarter of the globe, which have despots with means, not sanctioned by nature, for binding in chains their fellow men." So the doctrine gave a bearing to the United States as well, immediately with regard to the public debt, which should not be allowed to descend to the next generation. Yet this American reference had the appearance of an afterthought. In time, Madison wrote a long and cogent refutation of Jefferson's generational theory, proving its impracticability (generations are flowing waves, not fixed mathematical points) and even its elements of injustice. But, of course, the essay addressed the European more than the American condition; and Jefferson never intended rigorous application of the doctrine in public law, meaning it rather as a moral directive to society. In this sense he adhered to the doctrine throughout his life, and it entered into the spirit, if not the law, of American institutions.

The French Revolution had a long way to go when Jefferson left Paris near the end of September. The Assembly groped toward a constitution, disorders continued, bread was still scarce, civil war and foreign war threatened to upset the Revolution. Disquieting though these signs were, Jefferson radiated optimism. The juridical revolution was complete; the mass of the nation was united, with force at its disposal; public enlightenment and republicanism marched hand in hand. He felt he had witnessed, as twenty years before in America, the commencement of a new era in Europe. "I have so much confidence in the good sense of man, and his qualifications for self-government," he declared, "that I am never afraid of the issue where reason is left free to exert her force; and I will agree to be stoned as a false prophet if all does not end well in this country. Nor will it end with this country. Here is but the first chapter in the history of European liberty."

Jefferson's appointment as Minister to France still had two years to run in 1789. He returned to the United States on a six-month leave of absence, fully expecting to resume his duties in Paris after that time. He had gone to Europe on a commission of two years; events had prolonged his absence to five. Personal affairs required his attention in Virginia, and he was anxious to restore his daughters to their home and friends. Patsy was just turning seventeen, educated in the best Continental manner, but deserving now the opportunity for domestic happiness only to be found in her native country. Jefferson felt genuine affection for many French women, but the comparison of Woman in the two worlds was "a comparison of Amazons and Angels." Ironically, in Patsy's case the European temptress was Angel rather than Amazon. According to the family tradition, she had, while under the influence of the Abbaye de Pentemont, written her father for permission to become a nun, a request he had answered by abruptly withdrawing her and Polly from the school and burying the subject in awful silence.

Jefferson left everything in Paris on the assumption of an early return to his post. The business of the legation was put in the capable hands of William Short, though Congress had not seen fit to give him an official title. The lease on the hôtel was renewed; and, of course, Jefferson's books, furniture and household effects were left there. Even so, his baggage totaled 38 boxes, several trunks, and objects too bulky to pack. There were many hampers of wine, a box of food (macaroni, Parmesan cheese, raisins, almonds, dates), plants of every description, boxes of books (for Madison and Franklin and others), copies of Houdon busts, guitar, harpsichord, portraits of American discoverers (copied in the Uffizi Gallery) and of the noble trinity, Bacon, Newton, and Locke (obtained from Trumbull in London), phaeton, saddle and livery, and the handsome "crane neck" carriage made in London. There was no need for ceremonial leave from the court or sad farewells to European friends. Some of them had joined with American residents in Paris to pay tribute to the Minister on the Fourth of July. The complimentary address, after thanks for many kindnesses, lauded him as "the proper minister of that enlightened people whose cause is the cause of humanity."

In carriage and phaeton, Minister, daughters, and servants rode to Le Havre, where they were to catch a boat to Cowes, thence aboard the *Clermont* to Norfolk. At the French port the equinoctical gales descended with a fury that delayed their crossing ten days. Jefferson made his family as comfortable as possible at the British Hotel, where Nathaniel Cutting, an American merchant, offered friendly assistance. At the port Jefferson made inquiries touching the last concession he had gained for American commerce, one that permitted American ships to load salt at Honfleur, opposite Le Havre, at mercantile rates. He roamed the city, continued his correspondence, and amused himself with his children. A shepherd dog "big with pup" was added to the party; bitch, and litter, accompanied the Jeffersons to America. They crossed the Channel on October 7: "26 hours of boisterous navigation and mortal sickness." Another delay, of two weeks, at Cowes: more walks and excursions, more letters, more chats with Cutting, soon to leave "this worthy family" with regret. Jefferson penned an affectionate adieu to Maria Cosway, hoping they might enjoy a reunion in Paris with the first swallow of the spring. Trumbull, in London, had looked after Jefferson's accommodations aboard the *Clermont*, including arrangements for clearing his baggage and the convenience of boarding at Cowes. "There are two large staterooms . . . . There are *quarter galleries*, and a very good quarter deck for walking: she is new and a good sailor." In this fine vessel Jefferson sailed for home on October 23.

386

In the course of reassuring an American father about his touring son in Europe, Jefferson said, "He is likely to return home charged, like a bee with the honey gathered on it." Jefferson, certainly, returned home "charged"—with ideas, experiences, plans, pleasures, friendships. After five years Paris had become a second home to him. The artistic splendor of Paris, the society of his friends, their cultivated tastes and sensibilities, their speculative and humanitarian concerns, had become, not a substitute for the simpler society he had known but, like the delicacies of the French table, such an addition to his happiness that henceforth he would never feel quite complete without them. Yet, in a deeper sense, Europe had made him more profoundly American. For all the amenities of European civilization, it presented to him "no other picture than that of God almightly and his angels trampling under foot the hosts of the damned." The more he saw of it the more lustrous his image of America became.

His frame of reference was America, not Europe. This was truer in an elementary sense when he went to Europe than when he left it. Despite the sweeping clauses of the creed set forth in the Declaration of Independence, despite the rationalism and cosmopolitanism that informed his work, he had no thought, in 1776 or even in 1784, of his young country becoming the torchbearer of liberty to the world. Europe's enlightened philosophers were kindred spirits, of course, but on the entire continent, tyrannized by kings, priests, and noblemen, there was little leverage for change. As the French Revolution came on, he saw that change was possible after all, that France, if unprepared for liberty on the American plan, was nevertheless marching under the colors of 1776, and that his own country had an important stake in this political reformation of Europe. The frame was still America, but by 1789 Europe, above all France, was part of the picture. And so it remained during the next decade until finally, the hope blasted, Europe was erased and he formed a new image of American destiny in a world apart.

His business in Europe was diplomacy, not philosophy or revolution. France was an ally; she had helped the United States win its independence, which merited American gratitude whatever her motives may have been. And since the peace and independence of the new nation was still at hazard, the friendship, the power, and the prestige of France were vital to the United States. Without France the country was a cipher in the scales of European politics, with her a power of considerable weight. So Jefferson approached all questions in France, including those of reform and revolution, not as a republican dogmatist, not as a visionary theorist, not as a missionary diplomatist, but, fundamentally, as the representative of an American national interest that, in his view, was involved with the interest of France. Trade offered the most promising avenue of Franco-American co-operation. As a nation just emerging from colonial status, rich in agricultural surpluses but little else, unless possibly the carrying trade, the United States had a large stake in the liberalization of commerce, together with the whole enlightened movement for humane and pacific intercourse among nations. France sought entrance into the American market; the United States sought markets outside the old imperial system. Jefferson's commercial diplomacy found favor at Versailles. While he scored no spectacular successes, he helped to open new routes of trade and riches for his country. Easily assuming that monopolies and restrictions would fall with the progress of liberty and self-government, Jefferson believed the French Revolution would clear the way to the promised new epoch of commercial freedom. In this, too, he was destined to be disappointed.

Jefferson had impressive talents for diplomacy. He was cool, adroit, supple, resourceful, and patient. He approved Franklin's rule, "never contradict anybody." A disputant, he said, never wins an argument but only widens the gap of disagreement. So it is much better to tolerate differences, insinuate doubts, ask questions, and in this good-humored fashion discover workable grounds of co-operation. He was a very different man from his predecessor, yet he had Franklin's easy confidence and ability to relate gracefully to any situation, above all the wit to slide around rough corners without losing sight of his object. His self-possession was remarkable. William Smith, Adams's secretary, said he knew no man better qualified to pass over difficulties because "he makes his calculations for a certain quantity of imposition, which must be admitted in his intercourse with the world. When it shows itself in high colors, he has only to count ten and he is prepared for the subject. Happy state of mind—." "The quantity of imposition" at Versailles was tolerable. Jefferson genuinely liked his position, preferring it to a domestic one more exposed to the buffetings of politics. "The attaching circumstance of my present office," he remarked, "is that I can do its duties unseen by those for whom they are done." He returned home a thoroughly accomplished diplomatist, trained in Europe's leading school, yet not hardened or narrowed by the constraints of this old profession, and still faithful to the larger "cause of humanity."

He returned home persuaded that neutrality and non-entanglement in Old World politics was the true policy for the United States, yet with such strong attachments to France and Revolution that they gave a turn to his political posture. While France had nurtured his Americanism, it had also extended his vision of America's responsibility to the hopes of mankind. His attachments were founded in commercial policy; in feelings of gratitude, feelings that, in the diplomatic code of Europe, supposedly had no place in the determination of national conduct but that the young republic, acting on the principle of "but one code or morality for man whether acting singly or collectively," should not proscribe; in the reality of Revolutionary France, where he had seen American authority "treated like that of the Bible"; and finally, in the personal delights of his sojourn there, the benevolence of the people, the warmth of their friendships, the vivacity of their minds, the charm of their society. These things hung in his memory thirty years later, long after the other attachments had passed. "So, ask the travelled inhabitant of any nation, in what country on earth would you rather live? Certainly," Jefferson answered, "in my own, where are all my friends, my relations, and the earliest and sweetest recollections of my life. Which would be your second choice? France."

CHAPTER SEVEN

Secretary of State

Amidst the contentions of party, the interests of the public, even the maxims of justice and candour, are sometimes forgotten; and yet those fatal consequences which such a measure of corruption seems to portend, do not unavoidably follow. The public interest is often secure, not because individuals are disposed to regard it as the end of their conduct, but because each, in his place, is determined to preserve his own. Liberty is maintained by the continued differences and oppositions of numbers, not by their concurring zeal in behalf of equitable government. In free states, therefore, the wisest laws are never, perhaps, dictated by the interest and spirit of any order of men: they are moved, they are opposed, or amended, by different hands; and come at last to express that medium and composition which contending parties have forced one another to adopt.

Adam Ferguson, *An Essay on the History of Civil Society, 1767.*

WHEN JEFFERSON disembarked at Norfolk on November 23, 1789, the newspapers at once informed him of his nomination by President Washington to the high post of Secretary of State in the new government. The honor, unexpected and unwanted, placed Jefferson in a delicate position. Several months before, when Madison sounded him out, he had declared his aversion to any post in the domestic administration, and his determination soon to retire altogether from that "mere mouser of time," public service. He soon realized that in the eyes of his Virginia countrymen, if not of his own, the President's call admitted but one answer. Official welcomes tendered the returning envoy, first in Norfolk, then by the General Assembly in Richmond, pointedly congratulated him on "the important station you are now called to by a grateful country." Jefferson responded politely but ignored the calculated persuasions of these addresses. As he journeyed westward, canvassing six years of change in a familiar society, taking stock of his friends' hopes and fears for the new government, the burden of decision weighed heavily on his mind.

The President's letter and commission reached him at Eppington on December 11. His acceptance would be very gratifying, Washington said, though he respected Jefferson's wishes in the matter. For four days he pondered his reply. He could not flatly refuse the appointment; neither was he prepared to accept it. So far as the question depended on himself, Jefferson wrote, he much preferred his post in Paris. It was familiar, its lines well charted. The new office of Secretary of State, on the other hand, embracing a mass of domestic administration together with the foreign, presented a boundless sea of troubles, which he would enter with "gloomy forebodings from the criticisms and censures of a public" easily misinformed and misled, and from which he would wish to withdraw the moment the torrent rose. "But it is not for an individual to choose his post. You are to marshal us as may best be for the public good." Jefferson thus threw the decision back to Washington, uncertain of what the outcome would be, but inasmuch as Washington had consulted his wishes, expecting he would be allowed to remain as he was.

Visiting all the way home, Jefferson and the girls reached Monticello two days before Christmas. What a tumult greeted the returned master! "The Negroes discovered the approach of the carriage as soon as it reached Shadwell . . . ," Martha recalled. "They collected in crowds around it and almost drew it up the mountain by hand. . . . When the door of the carriage was opened, they received him in their arms and bore him to the house, crowding round and kissing his hands and feet—some blubbering and crying—others laughing. It seemed impossible to satisfy their anxiety to touch and kiss the very earth which bore him." Household fires again burned at Monticello. Friends and relations—Carrs, Eppeses, Skipwiths, Jeffersons—came from all around, and in the midst of this happy reunion Jefferson labored to straighten out his private affairs. Martha, meanwhile, lost no time acquiring a suitor for her hand. She gave it to young Thomas Mann Randolph, a second cousin she had romped with as a child, the son of Jefferson's boyhood friend Colonel Randolph of Tuckahoe. Jefferson was delighted with the match. A perfectly polished Virginian, tall, handsome, studious, amply endowed with fortune and family, recently returned from Edinburgh where he had opened a correspondence with Jefferson in regard to his studies at the University, Randolph qualified as the ideal son-in-law. Marriage settlement and wedding were quickly arranged. Within little more than a month Jefferson managed to put his own affairs in order and attend to his daughter's happiness, the two main concerns of his leave.

How the leave was to be concluded, whether in New York or in Paris, remained a dilemma. One of the first callers at Monticello was James Madison, who came not only as a friend and neighbor but as the President's emissary. Anxious for the success of the bantling Constitution, disturbed by the Anti-Federalist complexion of Virginia politics, and encouraged by the public response to Jefferson's nomination, Madison regarded his friend's association with the Washington administration as a matter of "infinite importance" to the country. He was distressed by Jefferson's coolness to the office and supposed it arose mainly from a mistaken view of the quantity of domestic business annexed to the foreign department. He returned to Orange, thence to New York to report to the President, uncertain of the success of his mission. Washington soon wrote to the reluctant nominee. He had been irritated by Jefferson's gloomily compliant response to the letter bearing the commission, and now told him plainly that the decision was his alone. At the same time, cued by Madison, he endeavored to overcome Jefferson's aversion to the new office. Its duties would be less arduous than Jefferson imagined. While it was true that Congress had combined home and foreign affairs in one department, the latter, for which Jefferson was preeminently suited, was more important by far, and a division might be made should experience suggest the need. Jefferson could not mistake Washington's desire, nor be indifferent to it; yet his repugnance to the office increased "so as to oppress me extremely." No matter in what light it was viewed, the domestic post had no charms for him.

Jefferson was also feeling the force of pressures nearer home. A committee of the local citizenry, no doubt with Madison's connivance, prepared a ceremonial address to welcome the return of Albemarle's distinguished son. He received the text in the middle of January. Extolling his long career in the public councils, the citizens sympathized with his desire to remain among them and then pointedly alluded to the present crisis: "But America has still occasion for your services, and we are too warmly attached to the common interest of our Country, and entertain too high a respect for your merit, not to unite with the general voice that you continue in her councils." Jefferson pondered the appeal for three weeks before offering his response in ceremonies at Monticello on February 12.

He seized the occasion, with its complicated political overtones, for an elevated summation of his philosophy. "We have been fellow labourers and fellow sufferers, and heaven has rewarded us with a happy issue from our struggles. It rests now with ourselves alone to enjoy in peace and concord the blessings of self-government, so long denied to mankind: to shew by example the sufficiency of human reason for the care of human affairs and that the will of the majority, the natural law of every society, is the only sure guardian of the rights of man. Perhaps even this may sometimes err. But its errors are honest, solitary and short-lived.—Let us then, my dear friends, for ever bow down to the general reason of society . . . ." In this lofty response Jefferson associated the sentiments of a public he was bound to respect with the new venture in government to which their cause and his—"the holy cause of freedom"—was now committed. As all must lay aside their objections and "bow down to the general reason of the society," so he too must bow down to "the will of my country."

The die was cast. Two days later Jefferson wrote a cheerless letter of acceptance to the President. A swirl of pressures had sucked him into a position of national leadership against his will. He tried to be philosophical about it. In farewell letters to friends abroad, he stated repeatedly that the desires of others had obliged him to go into an office he neither liked nor wanted. "But these things not being created for our convenience," he grandly explained, "we have

393

no right to decline the post in which the public authority marshals us for public service." At another time, after the agonies of the Virginia governorship, he had labeled such a proposition ridiculous. Nor was he fully reconciled to it now. The conviction that he had suffered himself to be "overpowered" accompanied him into the office of secretary of state, and he was determined to leave it as soon as decency and circumstances would permit.

He set out for New York with as little delay as possible. Martha's wedding was advanced several days. Polly was hustled off to motherly Aunt Eppes with instructions to mind her Spanish. Once again Nicholas Lewis was put in charge of affairs at home. Jefferson took to the road on March 1, accompanied by the newlyweds, who planned to settle on one of the Randolph properties, Varina, fronting the James below Richmond. At Richmond, Jefferson executed bonds for the discharge of his debts, both his own and his share of the Wayles's debt, which totaled approximately £6000, and from which, if all went well, he would be free at last in the year 1797. After bumping his way to Alexandria by stage, he laid over a day to attend a testimonial dinner in his honor. The merchants of the Potomac port lauded him for his labors at Versailles: "You have freed commerce from its shackles, and destroyed the first essay made in this country towards establishing a monopoly." Phaeton and horses, brought from Monticello, awaited him in Alexandria; and while there he purchased the noble steed Tarquin, "got by Eclipse out of Peyton Randolph's roan mare who was of the blood of Monkey, Othello and Dabster." But a heavy snow had fallen, causing Jefferson to change his mode of travel. He left the phaeton to be sent by water, and continued his passage by stage, horses following behind. Occasionally he would mount Tarquin to relieve the monotony of the coach. Thus he went, buffeted along at a pace of five or six miles an hour, stopping briefly at Baltimore, then Philadelphia, where he had a last memorable visit at Franklin's bedside, and to his journey's end at New York on March 21.

It was a Sunday. The tired traveler waited on the President after his return from church. The reunion of the two Virginians must have been a happy one. Only the President's esteem for Jefferson can explain his extraordinary patience to obtain him as secretary of state; only Jefferson's loyalty to Washington can finally explain his submission to the halter. He had brought with him two sets of medals struck in France to honor victorious commanders in the Revolutionary War; and he now presented Washington with his gold medal, authorized by Congress in 1776, together with those intended for the other officers. It was a piece of unfinished business from the Revolution, like the new government Jefferson had come to serve. After an hour's conversation, he retired to the City Tavern. Here he lodged until he could find a house. Congress was in session—few houses were to be had. He rented an "indifferent" one in Maiden Lane, going to live there on the first of June. And so, "harnessed in new gear," Jefferson set forth on still another career.

Agenda in New York

The new Secretary at once plunged into the work of his department. John Jay, newly appointed Chief Justice of the United States, had stayed on for several months as caretaker of the foreign department, but much business had been put aside for Jefferson's arrival. His staff was already complete: two chief clerks, two assistants, and a part-time translator—the entire personnel of the Department of State, which had an annual budget of about $7,000, one half of it representing the salary of the Secretary. The mission of the department in foreign affairs was reasonably clear; most of its other duties, as an unglorified "home office," had yet to be disclosed by Congress. Just before Jefferson came, it was charged with taking the census, a little later with the granting of patents and copyrights, still later with the supervision of the mint. These, together with the keeping of the seal, publication of the laws, law enforcement through district attorneys, pardons, federal relations with state and territorial governments, made a strange medley of responsibilities no minister could comprehend or, with a staff numbered on one hand, adequately attend to. The trifling ones took care of themselves, the others suffered from neglect, as the Secretary necessarily devoted nine-tenths of his time to foreign affairs.

There was as yet no "cabinet." The head of each department, State, Treasury, and War, along with the part-time Attorney General, transacted his business independently with the President. The

Constitution vested all executive powers in him. He relied heavily on the initiative and advice of his subordinates, of course, but nothing of consequence was done without his approval. The preparation of papers for the President, consultation with him (often over the breakfast table), followed by the implementation of decisions, formed the basis of Jefferson's daily routine. The President's responsibility was particularly evident in foreign affairs, not only because of their paramount importance but because he alone could speak for the entire nation. Jefferson was more of a stickler on this point than the President himself. It offered no difficulties. The relationship among the departments, on the other hand, was fraught with difficulties from the start. The shadowy lines between them, their overlapping jurisdictions, the inevitable intersections of public business occasioned administrative conflict, which then became enmeshed in personal and political differences. Washington took pains to secure a harmonious administration. The mere fact of his presence at the helm was perhaps the surest guarantee of harmony, for he commanded the loyalty of the whole nation when other forces and symbols of loyalty were still inchoate. Issues of moment touching more than one department called for concerted advice and, if possible, concerted action. As the need increased, a formal consultative body, the cabinet, was evolved. But the more the department heads were thrown together, the more vexatious their differences became; and Washington's scheme for harmonious and, as he believed, non-partisan administration collapsed.

Cordiality was the keynote in the spring of 1790. Alexander Hamilton, Secretary of the Treasury, was already the young lion of the administration. He had nailed his flag to the mast the preceding January in his Report on Public Credit, and Congress, though hesitant and divided, prepared to steer by it. Jefferson knew Hamilton principally as Madison's collaborator in *The Federalist*, the celebrated defense and exposition of the Constitution. The partnership had not withstood the shock of the minister's report, and no doubt Madison had put his friend on guard against Hamilton's aggressive leadership. The military dash and bravado of the little New Yorker, who played at the games of a Caesar, made a startling contrast to the tall, easy-gaited Virginian. There was an air of insouciance about the Secretary of State, as if he were tired or half-hearted, while Hamilton still burned with the relentless ambition that had taken him, a mere lad, from the West Indies to New York in 1773, then into the Continental Army, where his services as Washington's secretary and aide-de-camp opened up a remarkable career that had yet to satisfy his dream of grandeur for his adopted country. Jefferson had traveled the road to fame; it still lay ahead of Hamilton. Jefferson was secure in his Americanism; Hamilton flaunted his, like the nouveau he was. Jefferson's political instincts were to conciliate; Hamilton's were to command. Although Treasury was the giant among the departments, with by far the largest staff and the most influential constituency, it could not contain his energies. Treasury, too, had an access to Congress and a degree of executive independence not possessed by State, set up wholly as an arm of the President. But Jefferson did not see Hamilton as a threat in 1790. Still less did he anticipate troubles from his other colleagues. Henry Knox, the portly and amiable Secretary of War, knew guns and soldiering but little else. Like Washington and Hamilton, a veteran of the Continental Army, Knox could be counted on to take high Federalist ground on every question. He was offset by Edmund Randolph, the gifted Attorney General, who was an old Virginia friend and, in some sense, a protégé.

For several weeks Jefferson spent long hours poring over files of correspondence and bulky documents, and conferred almost daily with the President to set the course of a reinvigorated foreign policy. There was little room for complacency. Seven years after the treaty of peace, the new nation was still besieged by European empires, the Spanish to the southwest, the British to the northwest, who together occupied or controlled one-half the land area of the United States. Except for the Kentucky spearhead, the United States had still to make good its claim to the western country from the Floridas to the Great Lakes. Indian resistance, aided and abetted, as the Americans believed, by the colonial powers, checked the advance of settlement and took a frightful toll of lives. The economic loss to the nation was incalculable. Indian hostilities, together with British occupation of the posts below the Lakes, cut American profits from the fur trade, while Spain's blockage of the Mississippi navigation turned every westerner into a potential conspirator in the separatist schemes of frontier adventurers and Spanish agents. The redemption and pacification of the West constituted the paramount problem of American foreign relations. Scarcely less important in Jefferson's eyes was the release of American commerce from European thralldom, British in particular. There was no immediate prospect for the settlement of these problems. Relations with Britain remained in limbo; since Adams's departure from London two years before, formal contact between the two countries had disappeared. Similarly with Spain—nothing had occurred since the collapse of the Jay-Gardoqui negotiations, and Carmichael, in Madrid, had not even been heard from for a year. Viewing the situation broadly, the Secretary of State sometimes felt like praying for a European war, which, with all its risks, would strengthen America's bargaining power in foreign courts and enable the New World to "fatten on the follies of the Old."

The one bright spot in the picture was revolutionary France. Of the major powers only France had made important concessions to American commerce, and Jefferson expected further gains from the progress of liberal principles in Paris. In order to deal with Britain and Spain, the United States needed a place to stand in European politics. The French Alliance, while not an unmixed blessing, provided it. With France there were no critical problems; on the contrary, every step brought the two countries closer together. The Revolution had suffered some setbacks since Jefferson's departure, but as he philosophized to Lafayette, "we are not . . . to be translated from despotism to liberty, in a featherbed." He did not doubt the ultimate result. In letters of adieux to friends in Paris, written after his arrival in New York, Jefferson declared his love for France, his faith in the Revolution, his assurances of American good will, and explained that although he had reluctantly assumed a domestic station, he was reconciled to it by "the most powerful . . . opportunities it will give me of cementing the friendship between our two nations." He was far too experienced in the uncertain reckonings of the national interest to tie his foreign policy to the French kite; yet it glittered in his eyes and he hoped his country might soar with it. The political imperative of the national interest happily conspired with the obligation of fidelity and principle to France.

The first item on the Secretary's agenda was the diplomatic establishment of the United States. It was discussed in the early conversations with the President. Jefferson saw no need for representatives of a higher grade than chargé d'affaires at any court except Versailles, where only a minister carried dignity. It was agreed, however, that Britain too should receive a minister whenever the prospects for negotiation improved. Gouverneur Morris was then in London, under instructions from the President to sound out the British ministry. Although Jefferson advocated a small and unpretentious diplomatic establishment, confined to four or five countries (the others being Spain, Portugal, and, possibly, Holland) he wanted it to be respectable. The salaries of American envoys should be raised; they should be allowed outfits and private secretaries. Washington agreed. But it would not be easy to reverse the niggardly course set by the old Congress. The President worried about the scope of his authority with respect to diplomatic appointments. Could the Senate, under its power to approve persons nominated for diplomatic posts, reject the destination and the grade of the appointment as well as the person? Jefferson gave his written opinion that the Senate could not. "The transaction of business with foreign nations is Executive altogether." His strong line on this question overcame the President's caution. The Intercourse bill finally passed by Congress adhered generally to Jefferson's recommendations.

On behalf of this bill, the Secretary made his first, and last, appearance before a Senate committee. Senator William Maclay of Pennsylvania, a churlish soul who disapproved foreign embassies altogether and labeled any salary above a pittance "princely," undoubtedly voiced his opposition to Jefferson's opinions in committee; but the encounter was memorable because of the description this austere republican recorded of the Secretary of State. "Jefferson is a slender Man," Maclay wrote. "Has rather the Air of Stiffness in his Manner. His cloaths seem too small for him. He sits in a lounging Manner on one hip, commonly, and with one of his shoulders elevated much above the other. His face had a crany Aspect. His whole figure has a loose shackling Air. He had a rambling Vacant look and nothing of that firm collected deportment which I expected would dignify the presence of a Secretary or Minister. I looked for Gravity, but a laxity of Manner, seemed shed about him. He spoke almost without ceasing. But even his discourse partook of

399

his personal demeanor. It was loose and rambling and yet he scattered information wherever he went, and some even brilliant Sentiments sparkled from him. The information which he gave us respecting foreign Ministers &ca. was all high Spiced. He has been long enough abroad to catch the tone of European folly . . . . He took his leave," Maclay concluded, "and the Committee agreed to strike out the specific sum to be given to any foreign appointment, leaving it to the President to account, and appropriated 30,000 doll. generally for the purpose." The amount was later raised to $40,000.

The appointments would be made in due course. Carmichael remained in Madrid, in baffling silence that tried Jefferson's patience; and, in the interim, William Short was commissioned chargé d'affaires at Versailles. Short was "cruelly disappointed." He had counted on Jefferson's influence to secure him the permanent post at Versailles, as minister he had hoped. To leave Paris now, he said, "would be to me like quitting the most interesting spectacle at the end of the third act." And besides, though there was no need to explain it to Jefferson, he had fallen hopelessly in love with the young wife of the venerable Duc de la Rochefoucauld. Jefferson did not in the least doubt Short's abilities, and he did his best to make them known to the President. Unfortunately, Short had no political qualifications. Jefferson could only repeat the friendly advice he had given him many times before. If he wished any public career at all, he must make a name for himself in his own country. Short was an astute observer, well regarded in French ruling circles; but his woeful refrain grew tedious, and he never fulfilled the high expectations Jefferson had for him.

With Short's help Jefferson wound up his affairs at the French capital. His lease must be terminated, his servants discharged, all except the invaluable Petit who should be prevailed upon to come to the United States as Jefferson's housekeeper. Furniture and other items, some yet to be acquired—an elegant mantle clock set between marble obelisks, an oval looking-glass, dozens of rolls of wallpaper (sky blue, pea green, crimson, brick) "eight best and thickest hair mattresses," many foods, wines, books, plants, a new copying press, pairs of Angora cats, Angora goats, bantam fowl, and as many sky larks and red-legged partridges as Petit could manage—all this, and much more, must be sent. In addition to this private business, Short was instructed to present Jefferson's letter of recall at Versailles. There was a delicacy in this, for the Comte de Montmorin and the principal officers of the *corps diplomatique* must be told, in such a way as to avoid offence, that Jefferson could not receive the customary present of the King to a retiring minister. He detested this diplomatic convention, together with the reciprocal gratuities expected of him. While in residence he had paid the usual "court fees," of course; and he now asked Short to bow to the etiquette of the court by presenting gold snuff boxes to the Secrétaire and the Introductteur des Ambassadeurs. As to the royal gift, however, which Franklin and American ministers at other courts had received before him, Jefferson thought it mercifully prohibited by the new Constitution.

But the problem was soon complicated by the discreet suggestion of the French chargé that the American government should, after many years' neglect, present some mark of its esteem to the first minister, Luzerne, and presumably to Moustier, who had recently gone home. Although deeply averse to introducing the Old World diplomatic custom into the United States, Jefferson was more anxious to avoid embarrassment with France. So he promptly worked out a policy compatible with European practice. The American present to foreign diplomats would consist of a gold medal, which Jefferson designed for execution in France, and a chain of 365 links, its gold value proportioned to the length of a minister's service in this country. Having thus committed the United States to the policy of presents, Jefferson could hardly refuse a gift from Louis XVI. For, in truth, the constitutional bar was not absolute. He might accept the gift as something demanded by custom, and following the example of Arthur Lee, deposit it in the public funds. Or he might accept it after obtaining the consent of Congress; but he had no thought of being "laid on the gridiron of debate in Congress for any such paltry purpose." The dilemma pressed upon him. What he finally did was devious, stealthy, and perhaps irresponsible. He accepted the present under the fiction it was a private matter, then turned it into cash to cover the costs of his own gifts to the King's servants. The business was confided to Short. The present, a diamond studded portrait of Louis XVI, was secretly stripped of its value, the diamonds sold, the unadorned picture sent to Jefferson.

When he balanced the account he discovered that he had, quite unintentionally, realized a neat profit. The transaction was never disclosed. It set no precedent. Neither did the policy of gifts to foreign diplomats retiring from this country. Fittingly, the fourth French Minister, Edmond Charles Genêt, who shattered so many precedents in the diplomatic line, occasioned the demise of this one.

While engaged with these endings and beginnings of diplomacy, Jefferson also gave his attention to several items of domestic policy and administration. All the reports and opinions he wrote during these early weeks in office fell on the side of a strong national government and a strong executive. His first official report dealt with the old problem of coinage. Congress had received proposals from an enterprising American connected with Matthew Boulton, in England, for supplying the American government with copper coins manufactured with Boulton's steam on the plan of Jean Pierre Droz, the inventor Jefferson had met in Paris and hoped to send to the United States, only then to watch the English snatch him from under his nose. Congress referred the proposals to Jefferson. He opposed the project. "Coinage is peculiarly an attribute of sovereignty. To transfer its exercise into another country, is to submit it to another Sovereign:" The government ought to mint its own coins, he said, which was all that was wanting "to banish the discordant pounds, shillings, pence and farthings of the different states, and to establish in their stead the new denominations" on the approved decimal ratio. A year later Congress authorized the mint; and Jefferson, meanwhile, made a second unsuccessful attempt to entice Droz to America. The chaos in the nation's coinage continued for many years.

The uniform chain of connection between coins and weights and measures, all reduced to the decimal rule, had long appealed to Jefferson's reason. He was pleased to discover in the pile of papers that awaited him in New York a two-month-old resolution of Congress requesting the Secretary of State to draw up a comprehensive plan of weights, measures, and currency. The idea of deriving a universal standard from nature, the same the world around and forever, and arranged on the simplest arithmetic, was a commonplace of the Enlightenment. Entertaining this idea, with the rational hope it embodied, Jefferson was not original; but in the precision and the scope he gave to it, he was unexcelled among the philosophical statesmen of his age. "I believe you are the first nation that ever produced statesmen who were natural philosophers," wrote an English savant after reading Jefferson's Report on Weights and Measures. It was this conjunction of philosophy and statesmanship that made the Report an expression of both the national spirit and its promise of universality. Actually, of all the Western nations the United States had the least need to legislate uniform standards. A gallon in the Carolinas was the same measure as a gallon in New England. But this happy uniformity, so far as it extended, ought not be left to accident. Besides the convenience that would attend the introduction of the decimal ratio, a comprehensive system of weights, measures, and money, tied to an unchangeable standard fixed in the order of nature, "accessible to all persons, in all times and places," might become the model for the entire world.

In preparing the Report, Jefferson brought himself abreast of the latest literature, profited from Madison's guidance, and checked his calculations with David Rittenhouse and other "mathematical friends." The first and most difficult problem was to determine the natural standard of measure that would "give law through the whole system." The common idea was to derive this standard from the motion of the earth on its axis. Sir Isaac Newton had determined the precise length of a pendulum in the latitude of London which would make its vibrations in one second of mean time. Finding some imperfections in this second's pendulum as a standard, Jefferson adopted the suggestion of a Philadelphia watchmaker, Robert Leslie, whose manuscript Madison showed to him, to substitute a cylindrical rod of iron, of such a length as would oscillate in a second's time. He originally proposed the 38th degree of latitude—the latitude of Monticello—but at once saw the error of this when he received from Short the plan presented by Talleyrand, the Bishop of Autun, to the National Assembly. It proposed to base the standard on the latitude of $45°$, equidistant between the equator and the poles, thus equally acceptable to all nations. Jefferson revised his plan and his calculations accordingly. Once the standard was settled, the rest was arithmetic. "Let the Second rod then . . . be the Standard of measure; and let it be divided into five equal parts, each of which shall be called a *Foot*." Such a foot would be one-quarter of an inch shorter than the current measure; it would be divided into ten inches, each inch into ten lines, each line into ten points; ten feet would make a decad, ten decads a rood, ten roods a furlong, ten furlongs a mile. The unit of capacity would be one cubic foot, to be called a bushel, though less than the common bushel. The standard of weight would be fixed by the weight of a cubic inch of rain water, the ounce, with greater and lesser weights going by the rule of tens. In order to embrace the money unit, or dollar, within the system, Jefferson proposed a slight increase in the silver content to give it a weight of one ounce exactly.

Jefferson wanted Congress to adopt a complete and integrated plan of this character, and in the original draft of his Report it was the only plan presented. But thinking that Congress would balk at "changing the established habits of a whole nation," he included a modest alternative in the final Report. The alternate plan, for which he showed no enthusiasm, would achieve invariable and uniform standards at the cost of perpetuating the bewildering arithmetic of vulgar weights and measures. Thus the gallon would be 270 cubic inches, eight gallons to a bushel or firkin, of which two would make a strike or kilderkin, of which two equaled a croom or barrel, of which two equaled a quarter or hogshead, one and one-third hogsheads a tierce, and so on. How much more difficult this system than the temporary inconveniences that would accompany the system of reason! Congress adopted neither plan. Only once, in 1792, after repeated promptings by the President, was Jefferson's Report seriously considered. It was printed, of course, and the savants of two continents joined in praise. To the end of his days Jefferson championed the cause of uniformity of weights and measures; but the moments for great innovations in society are few and far between, as he appreciated, and in the case of this one the moment quickly passed after 1790. More urgent business claimed the attention of Congress; commercial intercourse settled habits of reckoning; the spirit of national reformation gave way to intense partisanship; and the dream of universality founded on the plain dictates of reason and nature faded from councils of state. Only revolutionary France registered progress in this area by the adoption of what became the metric system. Jefferson, interestingly enough, viewed the French system as a setback. Its unit of measure was based on a quarter of a meridian of the earth as determined within the limits of France, which, aside from other difficulties, made it unacceptable internationally.

The Report on Weights and Measures was prepared, Jefferson later said, "under a severe attack of periodical headache which came on every day at sunrise, and never left me till sunset. What had been ruminated in the day under a paroxysm of the most excruciating pain was committed to paper by candlelight, and then the calculations were made." The attack came on early in May, resisted the usual dosings of "the bark" (quinine), and though it let up from time to time, kept the Secretary from his desk for most of a month's time. He was not alone in his misery. The spring was "uncommonly wet and cold," Mrs. Adams reported. Influenza swept through the city; the Adams's house on Richmond Hill became a mere hospital. The President was stricken with pneumonia. "Yesterday (which was the 5th day) he was thought by the physicians to be dying," Jefferson wrote to Monticello on May 16. But Washington sweated out the crisis, and the nation breathed easier. Both men, President and Secretary of State, were well on the road to recovery three weeks later when they joined Hamilton and several others in a fishing expedition off the coast of Long Island.

Jefferson's illness furnished the occasion, though not the cause, for his retreat from the polite society of the upstart capital. Many years later he could scarcely find words to express the shock his initiation had given him. He had left France but six months before, the watchwords of revolution fresh on his lips. Cordially received in New York, wined and dined in the best circles, he was at once placed in the city's society. "But I cannot describe the wonder and mortification with which the table conversation filled me," he recalled. "Politics were the chief topic, and a preference of kingly over republican government was evidently the favorite sentiment. An apostate I could not be, nor yet a hypocrite; and I found myself, for the most part, the only advocate of the republican side of the question." New York had been a haven of Loyalists during the war, of course, and continued to show Tory proclivities beyond most cities. Jefferson escaped his embarrassment by losing himself in the work of his department.

Government was inevitably imbued with the tone of society. Jefferson's friend the Vice President, John Adams, had started a rage for honorific titles. While still in Paris he had learned from Madison—"the most superlatively ridiculous thing I ever heard of" —the title the Senate proposed, on Adams's prompting, to give the President: "His Highness, the President of the United States of America, and Protector of their Liberties." (The House, mercifully, held out for the simple title "The President of the United States.") Adams, with many others, thought that some of the pomp and majesty of Old World courts was needed to impress the people with the dignity and authority of the new government. The flavor of a court, albeit a republican one, was everywhere. In the pompous formality and sycophancy of the "court" newspaper, the *Gazette of the United States*, for example. John Fenno, its editor, gushed flattery on the President, extolled every ceremony, chronicled the doings of every "His Excellency" and "Most Honorable" and their "Ladyships." Plain and unassuming Mrs. Washington was "the amiable consort of THE PRESIDENT." (Returning to New York in May, she was "conducted over the bay in the President's barge, rowed by thirteen eminent pilots, in a handsome white dress; on passing the Battery a salute was fired.") It was all very silly, this emulation of royalty in the American republic. The spectacle revolted Jefferson, who prayed for the disappearance of all titles but "Mister."

The President, Jefferson thought, was more the victim than the agent of these follies. Washington was used to adulation, of course, expected it, and naturally took an interest in the forms and ceremonies befitting his high office. He had himself become a ceremony— and perhaps the presidency was little more. The honor he felt in his own person reinforced his sense of the respectability owing to the chief of state. It scarcely occurred to him that an elegant state carriage, drawn by six white horses, smartly attended by liveried servants and outriders, ruffled republican sensibilities. In his character, pride and diffidence, gravity and dignity, combined to smother familiarities. Senator Maclay, after sweating out one of the President's weekly dinner parties, put him down as "a cold, formal man." "No cheering ray of convivial sunshine broke through the cloudy gloom of his settled seriousness." Jefferson revered Washington: "never did nature and fortune combine more perfectly to make a man great." Such was his considered judgment. He knew the President out of harness, shared his enthusiasms as a Virginia planter, glimpsed his convivial side, and sensed the basic simplicity of his character; yet the dominant impression for Jefferson, as for others, was one of high-toned austerity. It made the President an easy mark, Jefferson thought, for the sycophants who would surround him with the tinsel splendors of royalty.

Washington's icy Tuesday afternoon levees drew the most complaint. The three o'clock visitor to the house on Broadway was conducted past liveried servants at the entrance to the formal dining room, and there presented to the President. He stood "clad in black velvet; his hair in full dress, powdered and gathered behind in a large silk bag; yellow gloves on his hands; holding a cocked hat . . . . He wore knee and shoe buckles; and a long sword, with a finely wrought and polished hilt, which appeared at the left hip; the coat worn over the sword . . . . The scabbard was of white polished leather." The President received the visitor with a dignified bow; as others came they formed a circle around the room; at a quarter past three the door was closed and the President toured the circle, exchanging a few words with each caller. "When he had completed his circuit, he resumed his first position, and the visitors approached him in succession, bowed and retired. By four o'clock this ceremony was over." It suited Washington's personality, his convenience, and his conception of the presidential office. But it did not suit plain republicans. They supposed Washington had been duped by the high-flying Federalists of New York. Sometime later, in the fires of partisan controversy, Jefferson expressed similar sentiments; still later, he thought that the pomp and ceremony had a deeper basis in Washington's doubts for the strength and durability of republican government. "He was naturally distrustful of men, and inclined to gloomy apprehensions; and I was ever persuaded that a belief that we must at length end in something like a British constitution, had some weight in his adoption of the ceremonies of levees, birth-days, pompous meetings with Congress, and other forms of the same character, calculated to prepare us gradually for a change which he believed possible, and let it come on with as little shock as might be to the public mind." But in 1790, with a surer faith in Washington's republican character, Jefferson clung to him as the rock of national salvation.

Jefferson was more troubled by opinions than by forms. Part of the difficulty was simply one of reliable political intelligence. In Paris he had discovered that the news of the United States came filtered through the English press; now, at the other end, he found the same "lying" distortion of European events, especially of the French Revolution, and he again applied a corrective. The most authentic channel of European intelligence was the famous *Gazette de Leide*, to which he and Mazzei, in Paris, had sent communications on American affairs. The translation and publication in New York of extracts from its pages would counteract the tyranny of English opinion. For this purpose Jefferson entered into an arrangement with John Fenno, whose *Gazette of the United States*, while distasteful to him, already had the reputation of an administration organ. Toward the end of April, Fenno began to publish translations from the *Gazette de Leide*, along with other items of European news, furnished by the Department of State. The strange alliance lasted only three months. By the time newspapers and letters arrived from the Continent, the events they analyzed were ancient history; and before Jefferson could arrange for their transmission by speedy English packet, Fenno's paper had become unreceptive to the views he espoused. When the seat of government moved to Philadelphia, Jefferson found another vent for European intelligence sympathetic to the republican cause.

The dissolution of the tenuous connection with Fenno points to the beginnings of political discord in Washington's administration. When Jefferson arrived on the scene, the prospects of unity were bright, and further enhanced by his presence. The wrangling in Congress was ominous, however. In the House of Representatives a long and angry debate on the abolition of the slave trade—inferentially of slavery—was just drawing to a close. It raised a fever in the South and recalled to some minds the Cassandra warnings of Patrick Henry and others against overreaching power in the new government. "A spirit of jealousy which may prove dangerous to the Union, towards the Eastern states, seems to be growing fast among us," a Virginian warned the President in March. The "Northern phalanx" seemed to bear down all opposition. Northern congressmen, on the other hand, viewed their colleagues south of the Potomac as willful obstructionists, panderers of popular vices, "violent republicans," which, according to Fisher Ames of Massachusetts, was but another name for "the republicianism of the aristocracy of southern nabobs." The slavery debate was no more than an interlude in the controversy of far greater import on the plan submitted by the Secretary of Treasury in January for the funding of the public debt.

The belief that the new government would pay the debts of the United States was unquestionably one of the foundations of its support. Hamilton divided the whole debt, principal and accumulated interest, into three parts. First, the foreign debt amounting to approximately $11,700,000; second, the domestic debt of the Union amounting to $40,400,000; third, the debts of the several states, estimated at $25,000,000. He proposed that the federal government assume the state debts, and by a system of funding secure the whole at face value in specie. Under the funding system, public creditors would exchange their old securities for new federal "stock" bearing annual interest of something over 4 per cent on the average. Only a small portion of the stock would be eligible for redemption annually. Even under the best of circumstances, it would be many years before the debt was retired; its support, meanwhile, would represent roughly three-fourths of the entire cost of the federal establishment. Beginning in this way, "the way other nations have ended," the French chargé predicted, the Americans "will be decrepit before arriving at manhood." But the burden of so large a debt, for so long a time, held no terrors for Hamilton. Quite aside from the overwhelming importance of national credit to the power and respect commanded by a government—a point on which most statesmen were agreed—Hamilton believed this public bane, the debt, could be turned into a public blessing of incalculable magnitude. By the magic of funding—so the theory went—the debt acquires stable value, augments the productive capital of the country, and answers all the purposes of money. The Midas touch thus given to the enterprise of the moneyed class secures, in return, the consolidation of its interests with the interest of a strong national government. Servicing of the debt necessitates taxes, fiscal administration requires a national bank—the powers of the Constitution are called forth in amplitude. Viewed as a political engine, the funding system combats the centrifugal tendencies of the federal polity by creating a "union and concert of views among the creditors," which acts in some measure as a republican substitute for the Old World establishments of clergy, nobility, royalty, army and navy, and so on. These considerations of national power were of such importance in Hamilton's statecraft that, had the public debt not existed, he would have had to invent an "engine of government" equally efficacious.

The Report on the Public Credit laid the foundation of what history remembers as "the Hamiltonian system." The plan was a bold one, and Congress, anxious for direction, hastened to implement it. No difficulty arose on the provision for the foreign debt, nor indeed on the principle of funding the domestic debt of the Union. But justice was revolted by the proposal to put the original and present holders of this debt on the same footing. In the course of depreciation over the years the debt had become an article of speculation. The needs of the original creditors—soldiers, farmers, traders—for ready cash had gratified the avarice of moneyed men; the securities had been bought and sold at a fraction of nominal value. Speculation rose high after the adoption of the Constitution until, in 1790, the entire $40 million was concentrated in perhaps 15 to 20,0000 holders, of whom probably no more than one-fifth were original creditors of the Union. Hamilton's plan appeared to sacrifice the substance of justice to its shadow. Why should speculative greed be rewarded by the government? Why should the poor and the ignorant be taxed to support the nominal value of securities "filched" from them at several shillings in the pound? Their case was "a hard one," Hamilton conceded, but he flatly rejected "as equally unjust and impolitic . . . as ruinous to the public credit" the idea bruited about of a discrimination between the two classes of creditors. Madison, who had earlier rejected the idea, now took it up in Congress. Original holders should be paid in full, holders by transfer at the market value, with the difference made good to the primitive creditors. The proposal furnished a standard of justice around which opponents of Hamilton's plan rallied. They were few, however, and discrimination met defeat in February by a vote of three to one.

"This game was over, and another was on the carpet at the moment of my arrival," Jefferson recalled years later. The new game was assumption of the state debts. Had he been earlier on the scene, he would probably have concurred with Madison on the question of discrimination, though, as with him, this would have required a change of front, justified on the ground that speculation and fraud, both inside the government and in every state and town country-wide, had accompanied the introduction of Hamilton's program, thus turning the scales of justice all around. At a later day he insisted that Hamilton's debt was "artificially created" and saddled on the country by a "corrupt squadron" in Congress, many of whose members were personally interested in the public funds. In any event, it was assumption, a far more explosive question than discrimination, that agitated the Congress on Jefferson's arrival in New York. Since the Revolutionary debts of the states had been incurred in the common cause, justice and policy, said the advocates of assumption, recommended equality of treatment of state with national creditors. The measure had the further merit of doing away with the dangers of competition between two sets of creditors, one looking to the states, the other to the federal government, for command of the public revenues. But eager national creditors worried lest the addition of the mass of state debts put so great a burden on the infant government as to injure their claims. Some states, moreover, Virginia among them, had made substantial progress toward liquidating their debts, while others, Massachusetts and South Carolina in particular, still groaned under enormous debts and threatened to break the Union unless they were promptly taken up as a common charge. The problem of inequities among the states gave the most trouble. But trouble came too in other forms: jealousy of the central government, suspicion of Hamilton's purpose, fear of moneyed influence. "The Secretary's people scarce disguise their design," Maclay crankily noted in his journal, "which is to create a mass of debts which will justify them in seizing all the sources of government, thus annihilating the state legislatures and creating an empire on the basis of consolidation." The question came to a vote in the House on April 12. Assumption was narrowly defeated.

Several more weeks passed before Jefferson took any part in this "most bitter and angry contest." "I arrived in the midst of it," he wrote a quarter-century later. "But a stranger to the ground, a stranger to the actors on it, so long absent as to have lost all familiarity with the subject, and as yet unsure of its object, I took no concern in it." There is no reason to doubt his statement. He was ill much of the time; for the rest, as he told friends in Virginia, he was too much occupied with the affairs of his department to meddle in questions outside his competence. The political scene *was* strange to him; its games did not amuse him, and it was several months before he could follow them. He had come to New York "neither federalist nor antifederalist," yet persuaded by his observations in Virginia that the principal danger to the Constitution, "the wisest ever yet presented to men," proceeded from demagogic Anti-Federalism. This was the enemy, not Hamilton, whose tangled skein of credit and power he had yet to unravel.

The storm over assumption raged for more than two months, reducing Congress to a shambles, before Jefferson was drawn into it. "No assumption, no funding," its advocates cried. If they could not "milk the cow their own way, they would not suffer her to be milked at all." But the majority held firm, vote after vote, until it prevailed finally the middle of June, and sent the funding bill, *sans* assumption, to the Senate. Deadlock now settled on the upper house. As it happened, however, the Senate was already deadlocked on the residence bill—the old labyrinth of the seat of government—and this would make all the difference. Hamilton saw the opportunity to strike a bargain: the national capital in exchange for funding with assumption. But who could preside over a transaction of this magnitude? Perhaps the Secretary of State: a Unionist, a Virginian deeply interested in the location of the capital on the Potomac, an innocent bystander in the funding controversy.

As Jefferson recalled the momentous encounter, he was going to the President's one day when he was waylaid by Hamilton, "somber, haggard and dejected beyond description," who took him by the arm and walked him backwards and forwards before the President's door for half an hour. They made an odd pair: the lanky Virginian, cool and imperturbable, the brisk little New Yorker, more agitated than Jefferson had ever seen him. "He painted pathetically the temper into which the legislature had been wrought; the disgust of those who were called the creditor states; the danger of the secession of their members and the separation of the states." Nothing was said of the capital, but Hamilton begged for help to avert calamity and suggested that some of Jefferson's friends in Congress might be induced to change their votes so as to permit assumption, with the funding system, to become law. "I told him that I was really a stranger to the subject . . . but that undoubtedly, if its rejection endangered a dissolution of the Union at this incipient stage, I should deem that the most unfortunate of all consequences, to avert which all partial and temporary evils should be yielded." He asked Hamilton to dine with him the next day in the company of a friend or two. It was impossible that "reasonable men, consulting together coolly, could fail, by some mutual sacrifices of opinion to form a compromise which would save the Union." The discussion took place, Hamilton and Madison the principals, Jefferson the mediator. The Union was more important than assumption; some members must change their votes to carry the measure. "But it was observed that this pill would be peculiarly bitter to the Southern states, and that some concomitant measure should be adopted to sweeten it a little to them." The sweetener was the capital. It would go to the Potomac after a temporary residence of ten years in Philadelphia, which should appease the Pennsylvanians. The principals now undertook to obtain the votes to close the deal. Two Marylanders and two Virginians, one "with a revulsion of stomach almost convulsive," swallowed the pill; and both bills, residence and funding with assumption, became law in July.

Jefferson soon came to regret his part in this sectional bargain as the worst error of his political life. He had been "duped" by the Secretary of Treasury and "ignorantly and innocently made to hold the candle" for his fraudulent scheme to throw $20,000,000 or more of state debts to "the stock-jobbing herd." His national feelings had been enlisted to forward a system far more injurious to the Union, he came to believe, than the selfishness of congressmen and speculators whose threats Hamilton had so cleverly used to fan his fears in 1790. Perhaps Jefferson was right in this assessment; but he was neither as ignorant nor as innocent as he portrayed himself. A bystander he was, but he had eyes and ears. Speculation in the state debts was a public scandal. The full import of assumption escaped him; yet he had opinions, and while they were not favorable to the measure standing by itself, they presented no bar to compromise. "I have been and still am of the opinion," he wrote to Monroe at the time of the backstairs maneuvering, "that Congress should always prefer letting the states raise money in their own way where it can be done. But in the present instance I see the necessity of yielding . . . to the cries of creditors in certain parts of the Union, for the sake of union, and to save us from the greatest of all calamities, the total extinction of our credit in Europe." In short, he preferred to leave the debts with the states, who were perfectly capable of discharging them, but not at the price of funding, of credit, of government. The circumstances called for "mutual sacrifice and accommodation." The Potomac site, while perhaps dispensable, was a useful consideration; for aside from the political advantages of a more southerly and westerly location of the national capital, Jefferson estimated it would circulate half a million dollars annually in Virginia. Moreover, the assumption as finally passed fell several million dollars below the figure Hamilton had proposed, and the fund was scrupulously allotted among the states so as to prevent injustice to any one. Virginia, Madison assured his constituents, "will consequently pay no more to the general treasure than she now pays to the state treasury." It was only a question of who was the paymaster. But, of course, that is always the critical question in politics. Assumption opened Pandora's box, rather Hamilton's box; and whatever justifications Jefferson and Madison found for their actions in the summer of 1790, they appeared meager a year or so later.

Jefferson had actually received his first lesson in the evils of the Treasury system before he submitted to its establishment. The occasion was a minor issue, involving the paltry sum of $40,000 voted in the previous session to pay arrearages due veterans of the Virginia and North Carolina lines. Eight months passed and the money still lay in the Treasury. Theodorick Bland, of Virginia, declared on the floor of the House that a list of the soldiers to whom payments were authorized had been improperly obtained from a public office and that a parcel of knowing scoundrels was cheating the soldiers, ignorant of their claims, by purchasing assignments of pay at a fraction of value. The speculative odor was stifling in this instance. A committee reported, and Congress adopted, a series of resolutions directing the Secretary of Treasury to get on with this business, and in every case to make payment to the original claimant, unless an assignee could produce power of attorney duly attested by two justices of the peace. The resolutions were more than critical of the

Secretary: they suggested fraud, and in the context of the debate that produced them, collusion of the Treasury in the fraud. Stung to the quick, Hamilton dashed off a report to Washington. If fraud had been committed on individual claimants, Hamilton said, their redress was to the courts. To annul all contracts, the good assignments with the allegedly bad, would be to usurp the authority of the judiciary and strike at the foundation of private property. The question was a difficult one for the President. Hamilton was persuasive, as always; but, unsure of the ground, Washington turned to Jefferson for his opinion. The resolutions were passed, Jefferson said, to defeat an alleged fraud which arose, in the first instance, from improper access to Treasury information. He did not doubt that such a fraud had occurred, but neither did he furnish proof of it. He confined his argument to Hamilton's objection: that the resolutions would annul valid contracts. Under the common law, at least in Virginia, he said, the conveyance of a debt not actually in possession is void. So, contrary to Hamilton, the legislation was not retrospective. It merely directed the Treasury to refuse disbursements on invalid assignments. Law and justice commended the resolutions, and Jefferson pointedly concluded that their defeat was "solicited only to support a fraud." Washington signed the resolutions. His two secretaries had crossed swords, and the opening encounter was, as Julian P. Boyd has said, "symbolic of all that was to follow." As yet, however, neither man had taken measure of the other, and their relations remained cordial and co-operative for many months.

Further premonitions of difficulty came in Jefferson's own province of foreign affairs. All summer long Britain and Spain rocked on the verge of war. The affair took its name from Nootka Sound on the far Pacific coast, where the Spanish struck at British intruders. The United States could not be indifferent to any conflict between the great empires ringing its borders. Should the incident erupt in war, as Jefferson expected, France would be involved under the terms of the Bourbon family compact. Belligerency might be forced on the United States either from its commitments to France or in defense of its own territory. War between the European powers held both dangers and opportunities for the infant republic. On balance, Jefferson thought the opportunities outweighed the risks. A paramount object of the new government, in his view, was to enable the nation to avail itself "of the wars of others to open the other ports of America to our commerce, as the price of our neutrality." As a neutral trader the New World might indeed "fatten on the follies of the old." "Our object is to feed and theirs to fight. If we are not forced by England, we shall have a gainful time of it." This was a dangerous "if," turning on the chance of British conquest of the Floridas and Louisiana. "What a tremendous position would [British] success in these objects place us in! Embraced from the St. Croix to the St. Marys on one side by their possessions, on the other by their fleet, we need not hesitate to say that they would soon find means to unite to them all the territory covered by the ramifications of the Mississippi." On the other hand, Britain might be induced to forego conquests in the Spanish colonies, yield American claims under the treaty, and possibly offer commercial concessions in exchange for neutrality. But if the awful prospect of encirclement materialized, the United States must join in the war on Albion. This, too, might be turned to America's advantage. If he played his cards right, Jefferson thought he could win high stakes from Spain, perhaps the Floridas, perhaps the Mississippi trade. Surveying all the possibilities, the Secretary of State, like a canny broker of the national interest, prepared to negotiate with both sides and, if the developments dictated, sell to the highest bidder.

Such was the advice he embodied in a memorandum to the President on July 12. It was prompted by indirect British overtures in the person of Major George Beckwith, who had been sent to New York by Lord Dorcester, Governor of Canada. While on a similar side-wind of diplomacy a year before, Beckwith had established close connections with Hamilton. He talked to Hamilton now, holding out the bait of a treaty of commerce in exchange for American support against Spain. Hamilton reported to Washington and Jefferson. An essentially non-committal response, conforming to Jefferson's opinion, was agreed upon. Hamilton wished, with Jefferson, to exploit the crisis for America's advantage, but he was far more convinced than his colleague that the advantage lay on the side of connection with Britain. His system was bottomed on peace and commerce with that power; and the Mississippi was a subordinate object. In reporting the government's answer to Beckwith, Hamilton was reassuring on the point of negotiations, and he stepped over official bounds to warn the British agent of the obstacle Jefferson was likely to present. Should the hoped for negotiations occur, Hamilton wished to be informed of any difficulties so that they might be explained away. This was only the first instance of Hamilton's maneuvering behind the back of the Secretary of State. Not only did he disclose to British diplomacy a division of opinion within the administration, but he also offered himself as the channel for thwarting the Secretary's policy toward Britain.

Jefferson moved quickly to implement the policy of inducing Britain and Spain to bid for American guarantees. In the event of war, Gouverneur Morris was directed to assure the British of American neutrality, "*if they will execute the treaty fairly and attempt no conquests adjoining us.*" Jefferson made no mention of an alliance, though Hamilton had improperly hinted that to Beckwith. Nevertheless, Jefferson threatened Spain with an Anglo-American alliance if she failed to heed American demands. David Humphreys was sent to Madrid with instructions for Carmichael. Spain must immediately recognize the American right to navigate the Mississippi. From this point negotiation should proceed to the question of an entrepôt at the mouth of the river, and finally to the cession of the Floridas. Spanish obstinacy would be met by American force, either alone or in concert with Britain; compliance, on the other hand, would secure American friendship and protection of Spanish sovereignty in Louisiana. "In fine," Jefferson said, "for a narrow slip of barren, detached and expensive country [the Floridas] Spain secures the rest of her territory, and makes an ally where she might have a dangerous enemy." To make himself heard in Madrid, Jefferson counted on the friendly persuasions of the French foreign ministry. Short was told to press the Mississippi question at Versailles when, and if, war broke out.

Soon after the dispatch of these instructions to the three foreign capitals, Washington learned that Lord Dorcester contemplated, at the opening of hostilities, a request to the United States for the unmolested passage of British troops through American territory to the Mississippi. What should he say to such a request? Washington put the query to his advisers, in this instance Hamilton, Jefferson, Knox, Adams, and Jay. Hamilton's opinion was hopelessly snarled in narrow points of international law, but it finally came down to ac-

417

quiescence in the anticipated request. The country could not risk war, least of all against Britain, with whom its interests were closely identified and whose naval power ought to be a protection. Jay's opinion was similar; Adams took a somewhat stronger line; only Knox advised peremptory refusal of the application, though he would not resist if the British marched. Jefferson advised the President to return no answer at all. He was stalling for time to give the mills of diplomacy a chance to grind. Outright rejection of the application would commit the United States prematurely. If time ran out, neutrality could be protected by granting the same privilege of passage to both belligerents. If the troops in Canada marched without our leave, the United States might keep up an altercation with Britain until events should decide whether war or peace was the more advantageous. Fortunately, Washington was not compelled to choose from these divided counsels. The application never came, and the Nootka Sound affair, after a most threatening appearance, was amicably settled in the fall. Thus American foreign policy was pivoted on the chance of an event that failed to happen. Jefferson reconciled himself to the loss of initiative but stuck to the policy.

After the dispatch of diplomatic instructions the second week of August, he accompanied the President on a tour of Rhode Island. The laggard state had rejoined the Union in the spring, and the President wished to welcome it, as he had the other New England states on an extensive tour the previous year. Crowds and ceremonies, dinners and speeches—the tour held little interest for Jefferson. A week passed and he was back in New York, drafting more papers on the foreign crisis and preparing to move his department, with the rest of the government, to Philadelphia. At the end of August he climbed into his phaeton and, with Madison's company, commenced the long journey homeward. They stopped in Philadelphia several days, then proceeded to Georgetown to reconnoiter the site of the future capital. The grandeur of the task, uniting conceptions of architecture and nationality, had an irresistible appeal to Jefferson. He turned his mind to it, and the planning of the capital occupied many of his hours as Secretary of State. From Georgetown to Mt. Vernon, via Fredericksburg to Orange and Albemarle: Jefferson was home on September 19. It was a brief visit, not much longer than the time spent on the road coming and going. Before the oaks curled their leaves in November, he and Madison returned to Philadelphia.

Conflict in Philadelphia

If he must be a prisoner of office, Jefferson was glad he could serve his time in Philadelphia. It was familiar ground. It was civilized beyond any other American city. Where else could he find so many kindred spirits, men who united wit and learning and republican principles? The beloved Franklin was dead now, Hopkinson lingered at the door, but old friends like Rush, Rittenhouse, and Thomson welcomed him into a widening intellectual circle. Philadelphia was a city of doctors—a veritable Edinburgh. William Shippen, whose son Jefferson had shepherded in Europe, taught and maintained an elegant practice; portly James Hutchinson mixed in the rough-and-tumble of politics; Rush and Caspar Wistar were scientists of note; and George Logan, abandoning the profession, had become a pioneer agriculturist on his ancestral estate, Stenton, several miles north of the city, where Jefferson spent many diverting hours. The American Philosophical Society, newly installed in a fine brick building on Independence Square, continued to be the center of many-sided scientific activity. Jefferson was at once reunited in the Society's endeavors, becoming one of its three vice presidents. (In a paper read to the Society in May 1792, Benjamin Smith Barton named the species of a new plant family, *Jeffersonia binata,* now *Jeffersonia diphylla,* not because of his political eminence, Barton said, but because of his pre-eminence in natural history.) Jefferson had complained in New York of the lack of books and libraries. It was much less of a problem in Philadelphia. In the Natural History Museum, the personal creation of the painter Charles Willson Peale, the city boasted a new marvel of science. Here could be seen, and studied, "a vast variety of monsters of the earth and main, and fowls of the air . . . in perfect preservation and in their natural shape and order," "a great collection of bones, jaws, and grinders of the incognitum," ferocious snakes, baboons, and monkeys, Indian scalps, wampum and tomahawks, a six-footed cow and other natural curiosities, together with the portraits of eminent American and French patriots. Peale idolized Jefferson, and added his portrait to the gallery in 1792. The College (soon to become the University of Pennsylvania), William Bartram's botanical garden on the Schuylkill, the Library Company, a wax works, an equestrian circus, even a theater (over Quaker objections) which some thought the equal of Paris houses—Philadelphia was not Paris, but it offered an environment in many ways congenial to Jefferson.

The city had a Quakerish reputation for coldness and reserve, but with the coming of the national government society frolicked in fashion and splendor. Philadelphia, Mrs. Adams said, was "one continued scene of parties upon parties." A young Frenchman who had yet to make his name in the world of letters, François René de Chateaubriand, arrived in 1791 in quest of the Northwest Passage. "A man landing, as I did . . . full of enthusiasm for the ancients, a Cato, who sought everywhere the rigidness of early Roman manners, must have been greatly scandalized on meeting everywhere the elegance of dress, the luxury of equipages, the frivolousness of conversation, the inequality of fortunes, the immorality of banking and gaming-houses, the noise of ball-rooms and theatres. In Philadelphia I might have believed myself in an English town. There was nothing to announce that I had passed from a monarchy to a republic." The President and his lady set the official tone, as high and formal and, in the opinion of some, as regal as before. The Philadelphia Assembly, to which Jefferson subscribed, sponsored a ball every fortnight. More elegant, however, were the soirées of the first ladies of society, Mrs. Morris, wife of the financier, and the beautiful Mrs. Bingham, whose infatuation with French fashion had made Jefferson wince even as he had admired her in Paris. Morrises and Binghams and others of their class were high-toned Federalists, of course, but politics had not yet split society in two. There was still a pleasing levity about it, reminiscent of Parisian drawing rooms before the Revolution. Jefferson might be seen at these splendid gatherings, hair powdered and scented, attired in the finest silks, blue coat, black breeches, ruffled shirt—all in the Paris mode—scattering information, amusing the company with anecdote, and charming the ladies with courtly flatteries.

He had rented a fine, large brick house on Market (High) Street, one of the city's broad thoroughfares soldiered with poplars.

The building occupied by the State Department was only three doors down and across the street; the President's establishment and the Hall of Congress were nearby. Jefferson lived on the third floor of the house for months while it was remodeled to suit his taste and convenience: a stable for five or six horses and adjoining room for three carriages, a long gallery for books, an enlarged dining room and antechamber, a veranda and garden house, and so on. The house was furnished, the gallery filled up, with the things he had acquired in Paris. They arrived, 86 packing cases, in November. Six gold leaf sofas, 44 gold leaf chairs with damask coverings, elegantly decorated tables, mirrors and commodes, blue and crimson draperies, wallpaper, statuary, and other items too numerous to mention, but all suggesting that Jefferson's house exhibited a French style beyond any other in Philadelphia. The cuisine was also French, or as nearly so as he could make it. Good French cooks were scarce, and some of the gourmet tastes he had grown accustomed to were simply unachievable. When Petit finally arrived in July, he searched the city for vanilla without success; Jefferson had to order his stock from abroad. Macaroni, too, came in this way. Guests at Jefferson's table were introduced to favorite French recipes he had copied in his own hand. His tastes were expensive. Wine was always a major item in his budget; similarly, the hired servants, who numbered four or five, and the expenses of the stable. The house rent was £100 a quarter—more than he had paid in New York. His salary never covered his expenses. The books were balanced quarterly by other income, chiefly from the sale of tobacco.

When the Secretary returned to his desk, he realized that he could not, for the present, pitch his hopes in foreign affairs on the doubtful blessings of a European war. The revised calculus of foreign policy which he made in the winter months was especially notable for the reliance placed on American commerce as a weapon of diplomacy. Jefferson had long been impressed with the potential of this weapon, whether directed to a state of war or of peace in Europe. But only with the coming of the national government could its potential be exploited. Jefferson proposed to use it, extending or withholding commercial favors as circumstances offered, with a view to advancing both the wealth and the security of the United States.

The course was set in several reports prepared between the opening of Congress in December and the following February. One of these, the Report on the Mediterranean Trade, had only an indirect bearing on Jefferson's European diplomacy. The Algerine problem remained as Jefferson had left it in Paris. All he could do was to lay before Congress the options available: war, tribute, and ransom. He continued to advocate the first, which, if successful, would permanently open the Mediterranean to American trade and command respect for the new nation in Europe. A year and a half later Congress chose the other course, voting funds to ransom the captives and to secure peace by a modest—an unrealistically modest—tribute. The riches of the Mediterranean trade continued to elude the Americans.

More central was Jefferson's Report on the Tonnage Law, prepared for the President, who later submitted it to Senate. The Tonnage Act of 1789 levied a per ton duty on foreign ships entering the ports of the United States. Although it discriminated in favor of American ships, it placed the vessels of all foreign nations on the same footing. Madison had attempted to introduce a discrimination between the vessels of nations in and out of treaty with the United States. This conformed to the abortive commercial policy of the Confederation, and Madison could rightly argue that the new government was committed to its realization. His object, of course, was to combat British restrictions while at the same time encouraging American shipbuilding and navigation. Failing in 1789, Madison resumed the fight, not once but twice, in the next session. Jefferson followed the debate in Congress with deep interest. American independence from British commercial bondage had been the goal of his strivings in France, and he hoped now to reach it through the power of the national government to legislate a system that had heretofore floundered on the contingencies of foreign treaties. From behind the scenes in the State Department, he worked to promote commercial discrimination. He and Madison defended the policy as, in fact, one of reciprocity, since it only aimed to counter British discriminations, particularly in the West Indies, and would be modified as these discriminations were removed. But to Georgia and South Carolina planters dependent on British ships and credit, to importing merchants and shippers tied into the old channels of trade, to warm friends of Britain, above all to treasury men eying the revenue collected on British tonnage and imports—to these assorted interests, Madison's project of a navigation act looked like a declaration of commercial war on Britain, and it was conveniently sidetracked during the political maneuvers over residence and funding.

Britain's gain was France's loss. The French chargé d'affaires, Louis Guillaume Otto, watched the proceedings in Congress with mounting concern. He shared with Jefferson the expectation that the revolution in American affairs, together with the Revolution in France, would bring to fruition the commercial alliance between the two countries. But the Tonnage Act, renewed in 1790 after patient deliberation, struck at the hopes of liberalization by placing the friendly commerce of France on the same basis as a commerce loaded with pains and penalties, hence, in effect, discriminating against France. In December, Otto lodged a protest with the Secretary of State. The Act, his government charged, violated the treaty of commerce of 1778, specifically by its failure to reciprocate the tonnage exemption allowed to American vessels in French ports. The protest was made under the threat of retaliation.

Jefferson reacted quickly, finishing his report within five days after he received Otto's letter. He disagreed with the Versailles construction of the treaty. The exemption from alien tonnage duties was not a special favor to the Americans but merely an application of the "most favored nation" principle, and no equivalent had been asked of the United States because it levied no such duties when the treaty was made. But diplomacy could not be threaded through the needle's eye of legal technicality. Jefferson faced a dilemma. If in the spirit of the treaty the point was conceded to France, the United States would be compelled to grant the same tonnage exemption to other countries with whom it had "most favored nation" treaties. Yet the consequences of refusal, jeopardizing the favorable standing of American commerce in France, were equally bad. Jefferson sought escape through an act of Congress that would place French vessels on the footing of natives in consideration of favors granted by the decrees of 1787 and 1788. No other nation could claim the same privilege without equal concessions. Once again he was backing into a navigation act.

Hamilton opposed the recommendation. The concession was too

high a price for the favors France had granted, and since it appeared gratuitous and voluntary, it would excite unfriendly feelings in Britain. Moreover, as he reminded Jefferson, the fund from the tonnage duty was mortaged to the payment of the public debt. "I feel a particular reluctance to hazard anything in the present state of our affairs which may lead to commercial warfare with any power . . . ." Hamilton's policy was locked in the vise of the funding system. The revenue of British trade filled the Treasury. Until the United States could manufacture for itself, Britain was its surest supplier, almost its only creditor, and its best market; and for the sake of American peace and commerce and credit, Hamilton was reconciled to the subordination entailed by the British connection. In his advocacy of the Constitution three years before, he had hailed the prospect of vigorous commercial retaliation to force the opening of British ports to American trade. Now he sang a different tune, one not unfamiliar to Jefferson but one he had not expected to hear in the highest quarters of the new government. For the first time, in the winter of 1790–91, Jefferson and Hamilton confronted each other on a major issue. For Jefferson it involved the question whether the United States would persevere in the liberal commercial policy of the American Revolution or, trapped in the web of fiscalism, acquiesce in British maritime dominion. The President approved the Secretary's report and sent it to the Senate. There Treasury influence defeated his recommendations. Jefferson thus had to scramble with the French as best he could. With Otto he took a hard line, justifying the tonnage law under the terms of the treaty, but softened the blow by holding out the prospect of a navigation act. Otto understood Jefferson's predicament. The estimable minister, he had earlier reported to Montmorin, "ought to be particularly dear to us by the affection he never ceases to show for France and by a sort of enthusiasm he communicates to persons in office for everything which concerns us."

All the while Jefferson remained hopeful for the emancipation of the French commercial system. The breakdown of French authority in the West Indies and the real distresses of the planters there gave new grounds, as he instructed Short, to press the American claim to freedom of trade with the islands. The ultimate object was a new treaty that would create a virtual commercial union between the two countries. In March 1791, when Franco-American amity was embarrassed by the tonnage question, Jefferson achieved a diplomatic *tour de force* by his official response to the homage the National Assembly of France had rendered to Benjamin Franklin. Perhaps never before in history had the death of a private citizen of one country been so solemnly mourned in another. It was a dramatic testimony of the bonds between the two nations, Jefferson said, and ought to become the occasion for cementing their friendship. Joining in these sentiments, the National Assembly called for the negotiation of a new treaty of commerce. Moustier's long-awaited successor, Jean Baptiste Ternant, departed for the United States three weeks later. Unfortunately, as Jefferson soon learned, he was not instructed to negotiate the promised treaty. And even before he arrived in the summer, it became apparent that Franco-American commerce, far from approaching a new epoch, was sliding back into an old one. It was more than Short could do to maintain previous concessions, let alone obtain new ones. The French merchants had never accepted the liberal commercial policies of ministers like Vergennes and Montmorin, philosophers like Condorcet, physiocrats like Dupont, and Americanists like Lafayette. They reaped few rewards from the American trade. Indeed, Short wrote Jefferson, they regarded it as a losing proposition, only made worse by the tonnage law, and they pointed to the evidence of seven years to show that every sacrifice made by France had done nothing to shake British supremacy in the American market. The Revolution brought these merchants of the commercial cities to power in the National Assembly. Jefferson had not understood this bourgeois animus of the Revolution. Freedom at home, protection abroad, was the merchants' cry. The evidence first came on the crucial article of tobacco. The Farmers-General was abolished, but the Assembly imposed a discriminatory duty, nearly prohibitive, on tobacco carried in American ships. Jefferson was outraged: Britain had not ventured so far! French nationalism seriously embarrassed his commercial diplomacy. He did not abandon it, but he would never find the opportunity to bring it to fruition.

Of course, Britain was incorrigible. Another key report, in December 1790, dealt with the failure of Gouverneur Morris's informal mission in London. With the passing of the Nootka crisis, this diplomatic kite fell to the ground. It had been useful nevertheless, removing all doubts as to the disposition of the British ministry. Jefferson concluded that the United States should not again renew propositions for a treaty of commerce or an exchange of ministers or for the delivery of the Northwest posts. The President concurred in this analysis, which he transmitted in a special message to the Senate in February.

At about the same time, Jefferson sent Congress his Report on the Cod and Whale Fisheries. Couched in strong language, it appeared to the British consul in Philadelphia, reporting to Whitehall, "to have been designed as the introduction or a series of proceedings calculated to promote measures very hostile to the commercial interests of Great Britain." The plight of the New England fisheries was a familiar subject to Jefferson. British bounties and trade restrictions caused much of the difficulty. "The *ex parte* regulations which they have begun for mounting their navigation on the ruins of ours, can only be opposed by counter regulations on our part." Jefferson viewed the French, on the other hand, as "co-operators against a common rival." "Nor is it in the interest of the fishermen alone, which calls for the cultivation of friendly arrangements with that nation; besides five-eights of our whale oil, and two-thirds of our salted fish, they take from us one-fourth of our tobacco, three-fourths of our live stock . . . a considerable and growing portion of our rice, great supplies, occasionally, of other grain . . . ." The fisheries had an added importance from their connection with sea power and the carrying trade. Jefferson suggested various remedies; in the main, he called for a system of counter regulations, prohibition opposed to prohibition. The British consul was not wrong in his estimate of Jefferson's report: it was part of a concerted campaign against the British commercial system.

The first gun had been sounded in Washington's annual message to Congress. One paragraph, drafted by Jefferson, recommended measures to foster the independence of American commerce and navigation. The reports on the Morris mission, the tonnage act, and the fisheries followed in rapid succession. Their cumulative effect, together with pressures exerted by interested groups in foreign trade, led a committee of the House to report a bill barring the importation of non-British goods in British vessels. Like previous attempts at a navigation act, the bill was sidetracked, principally on the Federalist plea for negotiation; and on February 23 the whole subject of commercial policy was referred to the Secretary of State for study and report. The threat of retaliatory legislation prompted the British government, at long last, to commence normal diplomatic relations with the United States; and that in turn (the news reached Philadelphia when the navigation bill was in second reading) took all the steam from retaliation. The new minister, George Hammond, arrived in August. The leading objects of his mission were, first, to obtain satisfaction of British demands under the treaty of 1783 as the *sine qua non* of withdrawal from the Northwest posts; and second, to combat the movement against British commerce. Hammond was apprised of the "extremely discordant" rift in the administration and he would seek to exploit it.

Jefferson held no illusions of British readiness to enter into reciprocal commercial arrangements with the United States. Before Hammond arrived he came into possession of a highly secret report on London's policy. This report, which was submitted in January 1791 by the Committee of the Privy Council for Trade and Foreign Plantations, gave a flattering picture of the American trade since the Revolution. Britain's share of the shipping had increased; the tonnage and tariff duties of the United States were actually less by about one-half than those levied by the states individually in 1787; British exports to the former colonies had fallen off about one-sixth, but the loss was more than offset by expanded markets in other North American colonies; and since imports from the United States had declined drastically, the balance of trade was even more favorable than before the war. The report might have been titled, "How To Grow Rich by Losing an Empire." It was a thorough vindication of the architects of British policy in 1783-84. "Government has indeed not been altogether deceived—the new system [of the Constitution] is certainly more favorable to British navigation. And there can be no doubt from the proceedings of Congress, and from all that passed in their debate during the last two sessions, particularly in the American Senate, that a party is already formed in favor of a connection with Great Britain, which by moderation on her part, may perhaps be strengthened, as to bring about in a friendly way, the object in view." The object: to detach the United States from France and to strengthen the connection with Britain. Negotiation was advised chiefly as a check on retaliatory measures, for nothing was to be conceded; as for the West Indian trade, it was not even open for discussion. Such were Hammond's instructions, as Jefferson surmised, with respect to commerce.

The Privy Council report confirmed with facts and figures Jefferson's opinion of British obduracy. He had recently learned that the Commissioners of the Treasury refused to admit as American vessels naturalized in the United States though built elsewhere. Of small moment in time of peace, the regulation would injure American neutral trade in time of war. Earlier, during the Nootka crisis, he had had a nasty taste of British impressment of American seamen. What perhaps disturbed him most in this show of British power, however, was the confession in a state paper of the highest importance of collusion with a party in the government of the United States. Many things in the early months of 1791 persuaded him that such a party existed and that Hamilton was its leader—the secret British intelligence added a crowning touch. Without knowing of Hamilton's machinations with Beckwith, Jefferson soon suspected his liaison with Hammond, and became convinced of Hamilton's unlimited hostility to his commercial diplomacy. The financial system was probably at the bottom of it. Indeed, for the first time, Hamilton's measures began to assume the character of a system in Jefferson's mind, a system permeated with fiscalism, and from what he had seen of France and learned of Britain, fiscalism was the parent of monopoly and oppression. The funding of the national debt was a necessary measure, but government should not be lashed to the predatory wheels of credit. The system was very partial in its distribution of benefits, enriching a few eastern merchants and speculators, holding nothing material for southern planters dependent on foreign markets, and, in general, checking the nation's agricultural expansion. In foreign affairs it tied the government into British politics. Despite new British encroachments on American commerce, Jefferson wrote to Monroe in April, Treasury takes the line of "passive obedience and non-resistance, lest any misunderstanding with them [the British] should *affect our credit, or the prices of our public paper.*" He was nevertheless sanguine about the prospects of commercial legislation, and he began to gather data for the report

Congress had charged him to prepare. Surprisingly enough, his principal aide in this enterprise was a Treasury officer, the Pennsylvanian Tench Coxe, an ardent economic nationalist who worked both sides of the street, Jefferson's and Hamilton's, not only because he had an eye for the main chance politically, but also because there were two distinct sides of economic nationalism, one basically fiscal, the other basically commercial, one oriented to credit, the other to markets, one British-centered, the other non-British and mainly French.

Commerce was a subordinate issue in Jefferson's Spanish diplomacy. The danger from Spain came not from strength but from weakness, which had led the colonial governors into alliances with desperate Indians and frontier adventurers and had made Louisiana and the Floridas convenient pawns on the chessboard of European politics. Yet the illusion of North American empire persisted in Madrid. A new policy came to the rescue of the old. By land grants, commercial privileges, and promises of freedom, Spain now sought to attract colonists from the borderlands. The policy struck Jefferson as rather like "settling the Goths at the gates of Rome." He wished a hundred thousand Americans would accept the invitation: "It will be the means of delivering us peaceably, which may otherwise cost a war. In the meantime we may complain of this seduction of our inhabitants just enough to make them believe we think it very wise policy for them, and confirm them in it." While still dangling the prospect of a commercial treaty before the Americans, the Spanish court declined to discuss the southern boundary or the Mississippi question. Jefferson's position was just the reverse. He was willing to discuss trade provided it in no way prejudiced the principal point to be gained, the navigation of the Mississippi. In March he boldly sketched the plan of a four-power commercial entente against Britain. To Short, Carmichael, and Humphreys, in Paris, Madrid, and Lisbon respectively, he proposed a concert along the lines of the navigation act lately debated in Congress. Could the three European countries be induced to adopt similar measures, Jefferson said, "it will form an epoch in the history and freedom of the ocean." "We would not wish to be declared the excitors of such a concert of measures," he continued, but by appealing to motives of self-interest the American ministers should "insinuate it with all the discretion and effect" they could muster. It was a long shot. Nothing came of it. In the succeeding months Jefferson's perturbations of the Mississippi question got through to the Spanish court. Two commissioners were sent to Philadelphia, and at the end of the year Jefferson learned of the court's desire to negotiate all differences in Madrid. He leaped at the opportunity, instructing Short to join Carmichael in a special mission to Spain.

Thus, over a period of twelve months, the renewed initiative in diplomacy opened promising lines of negotiation with the major powers. Whether they would reach their objects remained to be seen. Jefferson was most eager with respect to Spain. Success there would be a boon to his country commensurate with the pain and trouble of serving it. He was less hopeful of overcoming British recalcitrance; but in sending a minister His Majesty's government took the first forward step in Anglo-American relations since 1783. Continued firmness on the American side, backed by a navigation act, would surely bring results. Jefferson was little alarmed by the frictions and frustrations of the French alliance. The decree of the National Assembly calling for a new treaty of commerce, Ternant's arrival, the final establishment of a constitutional government in September—these were good omens. He was, however, disturbed by Washington's peremptory choice of Gouverneur Morris, "a high-flying monarchy man," as United States Minister to France. The Senate reluctantly consented, and Versailles hid its fears. Poor Short, awarded the consolation prize of The Hague, just as he was ordered to Madrid, vented his rage in a stream of letters to Jefferson. Thomas Pinckney, of South Carolina, soon undertook the ministerial duties at the Court of St. James's. The diplomatic establishment was at length completed.

All these developments occurred against a background of mounting tension abroad and chronic disturbance on America's frontiers. The French Revolution convulsed Europe and plunged Santo Domingo, the queen of the Indies, into a devastating slave insurrection against the French masters. If in the shifting sands of international politics the monarchs of Spain and Britain united against France, or if France, with her hands full at home, invoked the American pledge to defend her West Indies possessions, the peace and security of the United States would be jeopardized. Early in December, just as Jefferson was beginning talks with Hammond and preparing for the Spanish negotiations, reports reached Philadelphia of General St. Clair's shattering defeat by the Ohio Indians. The same fate, though less disastrous, had befallen General Harmer the year before. St. Clair's orders were to push the Indian boundary further west, which was sufficiently provocative in itself. But every American, beginning with the President and Secretary of State, believed the British incited this cruel warfare; and as they grew bolder with each success, so too did the Spanish in the Southwest. While still in New York, the government had neogtiated a new boundary with the troublesome Creeks in Georgia. But land speculators and adventurers encroached on the receding lands of the Indians. Jefferson consistently advocated a strong national line, including the use of force against intruders on the Indian lands, even if it collided with state authorities. More was involved than the rights of the Indians and the paramount authority of the national government with respect to them, for Spain exploited every disturbance on the brawling southern frontier. Indeed, no sooner had the news of St. Clair's defeat reached these quarters than the newly appointed Spanish governor, the Baron de Carondelet, dropped the pacific immigration policy of his predecessor and returned to the older policy of Indian alliance to check the Americans. The result proved embarrassing to Jefferson's Spanish negotiations, just as the Indian warfare in the Northwest spread a pall over his discussions with Hammond. Peace on the American frontiers was thus involved in peace with Britain and Spain.

The conduct of foreign affairs was inevitably enmeshed in domestic politics. The question of commerical discrimination, for example, could not be considered apart from its bearing on competing interests at home. Nor were Jefferson and Madison oblivious to these considerations. The policy was calculated to win friends in every section—from shippers chafing under the restraints of British navigation acts, from struggling manufacturers, from planters seeking wider markets—and it appeared to offer an alternative to the narrowly based fiscal program around which Hamilton's political strength was organized. It was too early to speak of parties and party conflict in 1791, but the administrative rivalry between Jefferson and Hamilton grew in intensity. The interconnections of issues of commerce and diplomacy and finance, the lack of firm policy direction from the President, the confused division of authority between the principal departments created a fluid situation which drew men who were temperamentally and politically averse into one collision after another as they competed for initiative and influence in vital areas of national policy.

The course was probably irreversible after the conflict in February 1791 on the question of the United States Bank. In the second of his great reports to Congress, Hamilton had recommended the creation of a national bank modeled on the Bank of England and combining, like that century-old institution, public convenience with private advantage. As the financial arm of the government the bank would assist in the collection of taxes and the management of the public debt. It would serve as a ready lender to the treasury. It would also constitute a fund for mounting a large paper circulation in the form of bank notes, thereby multiplying the active capital of the country and stimulating its trade and industry. This was particularly necessary in the United States, Hamilton argued, because of the deficiency of coin and credit, the retarded state of manufactures, and the settlement of the West, which soaked up capital without producing any early returns. One great bank, incorporated and fortified by the government but propelled by private enterprise and the desire for profit, would lift the economy over its difficulties. The bank was a logical corollary of the funding system, and that system alone made it possible. The government would furnish but one-fifth of the total capital of $10,000,000, the rest being subscribed by private investors, three-quarters of it in the form of public securities. The convertibility of the funded debt into bank stock would both enhance its value and augment "the *active* wealth of the country." In effect, the tiny knot of public creditors would be privileged to incorporate as a bank, empowered to engage in commercial business, and blessed with the largest account in the economy, that of the federal government. Congress enacted the Bank bill virtually as Hamilton had drafted it. Although it was strongly contested in the House of Representatives, where Madison led the fight, only twenty votes could be mustered in opposition, and fifteen of these came from the southern states.

Jefferson watched the progress of the bill with deep concern. Its introduction coincided with the remonstrance of the Virginia assembly against the assumption of state debts. That measure was designed to "perpetuate a large monied interest," the memorialists charged, and it must eventually produce one of two evils, "the prostitution of agriculture at the feet of commerce, or a change in the present form of federal government, fatal to the existence of American liberty." Hamilton greeted these resolutions with gestures of defiance: "This is the first symptom of a spirit which must either be killed or will kill the constitution of the United States." Jefferson, on the other hand, after making allowance for their origin in Henry's "implacable" hostility to the new government, viewed the resolutions as a manifestation of widespread fears aroused by Hamilton's measures. He did not doubt the constitutionality of assumption; but it was precisely on this ground, where Virginia drew the line, that Madison fought the Bank bill in Congress and that Jefferson, upon its passage, sought its defeat at the hands of the President.

The constitutional question being brought to the fore for the first time, Washington was uncertain whether to sign or to veto the bank charter. While it was true that even the old Congress, under the Articles of Confederation, had chartered a bank, it was also true that the convention of 1787 had pointedly declined to include the power of incorporation among those enumerated in the Constitution. The question, therefore, became one of construction. The Attorney General's opinion, the first sought, was adverse. Jefferson's was then requested. With the crisp and categorical logic of one who had entered the realm of constitutional certitude, Jefferson presented a *prima facie* case against the bill. The Constitution was laid in the principle of the Tenth Amendment, then in the course of ratification: "all powers not delegated to the United States by the Constitution, nor prohibited by it to the States, are reserved to the States respectively, or to the people." No power to incorporate a bank was delegated. It could not be found in any of the enumerated powers, as Jefferson proceeded to show, nor could it be legitimately inferred from either of the general clauses appealed to by the bank's advocates. The power of Congress to provide for the "general welfare" was only a power to lay taxes for that purpose; the power to enact laws "necessary and proper" for carrying the enumerated powers into execution must be construed strictly or it would "swal-

433

low up all the delegated powers, and reduce the whole to one power." Jefferson acknowledged the *convenience* of a national bank but not its *necessity* for effecting the clearly defined objects of the Constitution. "To take a single step beyond the boundaries thus specially drawn around the powers of Congress," he warned, "is to take possession of a boundless field of power, no longer susceptible to definition." Not only would the creation of a bank breach the limits of the Constitution; it would also, "for a shade or two of *convenience*, more or less . . . break down the most ancient and fundamental laws of the several states," such as those against monopoly, fraud, mortmain, and alienage. No shadow of doubt crossed Jefferson's mind; yet, in conclusion, he counseled the President to bow to the will of Congress unless in his judgment the bill was clearly unconstitutional.

Washington turned finally to Hamilton, presenting him with Jefferson's and Randolph's objections for rebuttal, and meanwhile asked Madison to draft a veto message should his decision go against the bill. In a long and discursive opinion, which lost none of its force from its endless windings, Hamilton refuted every constitutional objection. Through it all ran one fundamental idea: "That every power vested in a government is in its nature *sovereign*, and includes, by *force* of the *term*, a right to employ all the *means* requisite and fairly applicable to the attainment of the *ends* of such power, and which are not precluded by restrictions and exceptions specificied in the Constitution, or not immoral, or not contrary to the *essential ends* of political society." This doctrine of *implied powers* blurred the sharp line Jefferson had drawn between the ends and means of government; every power he had strictly defined opened itself to almost limitless development. The utility of a national bank in the execution of the powers of Congress to tax, to borrow money, regulate commerce, and so on was easily shown. And it was decisive in Hamilton's judgment. Washington concurred. On February 25, within two days of receiving the opinion, he signed the bill chartering the Bank of the United States.

The issue expressed the fundamental conflict between Jefferson and Hamilton on the Constitution. Both wished a strong Union, but one sought its strength in the trust of the states and the people, the other in the amplitude of the general government's powers. Hamilton thought the Constitution "a shilly shally thing," too frail to survive. It needed every possible reinforcement. Jefferson feared an overreaching centralism. He believed in federalism as the only secure foundation of the Union; his antagonist, though he took the name Federalist, had little faith in the principle and worked incessantly to shrink the powers of the states. One viewed the Constitution as a superintending rule of political action; the other viewed it as a point of departure for vigorous statemanship. One believed that private interest corrupted public good; the other—the ghost of Mandeville looking over his shoulder—exploited selfish interests for national purposes. Jefferson, with a profound conviction in the powers of free men, was radical in the ends he pursued but generally conservative in his choice of means. Hamilton was the reverse. Untouched by Jefferson's vision, the means he employed—of organization and innovation, energy and command—disclosed a radical tendency which in time must produce radical effects.

The debate inevitably took shape on the constitutional question, but it involved much more, of course. Jefferson would almost certainly not have enunciated such a niggardly view of federal powers had he approved of the Bank as a financial institution. Tied into the funding system, the Bank would give permanence to the reign of debt and speculation and fraud. "We are ruined, Sir," he wrote to Monroe, "if we do not overrule the principles that 'the more we owe, the more prosperous we shall be,' 'that a public debt furnishes the means of enterprise,' 'that if ours should be once paid off, we should incur another by any means however extravagant' etc. etc." He took the commonsense view. A public debt was no more of a blessing than a private one, except to creditors and stockholders whose profits were wrung from the people in taxes. The Bank of the United States was only an abomination of the evils Jefferson ascribed to all banks of note issue. He loosely equated bank notes payable on demand with paper money, like the bills of credit of Revolutionary times. Either one drove out gold and silver and introduced fluctuating values into the life of trade. Commerce and industry were insecure when suspended, in Adam Smith's phrase, "upon the Daedalian wings of paper money." Bankers and public creditors had no stake in the prosperity of agriculture, commerce, and manufactures, except as they produced taxes and interest to enrich themselves. Banks ran people into debt, supported luxury and extravagance, created delusory values and delusory expectations. They did not create capital, as Hamilton implied, but diverted it from useful economic pursuits into gambling ventures in paper and stock. Jefferson recoiled from "the spirit of gaming," "the rage of getting rich in a day," which he observed in the speculative scramble for the stock of the Bank of the United States in the summer months. His friend Benjamin Rush described Philadelphia as "a great gaming house." Some men lost their reason, others their appetites, the good doctor noted with clinical interest. "The great speculators become talkative and communicative or dull, sullen, silent, and peevish." The depravity of the scene bore no resemblance to Jefferson's vision of a virtuous republican society.

He was probably most alarmed, however, by the political effects of the Bank charter. Piled on top of funding and assumption, it increased the sectional imbalance. The southern states, whether wisely or foolishly, felt little interest in a national bank. Few southerners acquired stock in it. It was designed for the convenience of merchants, not planters and farmers. The excise tax on whiskey, passed at about the same time in order to service the assumed debt, also spread resentment in southern and western quarters. The Anti-Federalist spirit still hovered over Virginia politics. Jefferson decided a week or so before he advised rejection of the Bank bill that the government should not risk further alienation of southern opinion. "There is a vast mass of discontent gathered in the South," he confided to one correspondent, "and how and when it will break God knows. I look forward to it with some anxiety." And to others he did not disguise his basically political approach to the issue. "Whether these measures be right or wrong abstractedly [sic]," he said of Hamilton's program, "more attention ought to be paid to the general opinion." "Government being founded on opinion, the opinion of the public even when it is wrong, ought to be respected to a certain degree." Treasury was "driving too fast." The precipitancy of the bank measure, when other means of financial management were available, proved it. Jefferson could not approve of the measure in the abstract or in the face of the Constitution; even more, he was convinced it was politically unsound, and he would not, in the interest of administrative harmony, take any responsibility for it.

436

Nor would he place himself at the head of the growing opposition to Hamilton's system. Madison was the recognized leader of this opposition; and in the reciprocity of influence between the two Virginians, it was Madison who held the edge at this time. Jefferson's position in the administration, his undiminished confidence in the President, and his aversion to political combat acted as powerful restraints. He made no effort to dramatize or publicize his quarrel with Hamilton. He was apprehensive, nevertheless, and began in February quietly to insinuate his concern to prominent men in different parts of the Union. To Robert R. Livingston in New York: "Are the people in your quarter as well contented with the proceedings of our government, as their representatives say they are?" To George Mason in Virginia: "What is said in our country of the fiscal arrangements now going on?" And after Congress adjourned early in March, to Harry Innes of Kentucky: "What is said with you of the most prominent proceedings of the last Congress?" Such inquiries were usually followed by appeals to his friends to exert their influence to change the complexion of Congress. Probing opinion, Jefferson also sought to shape it.

In the spring he was unwillingly thrust on the stage as a political gladiator against his old friend John Adams. The controversy between Edmund Burke and Thomas Paine on the French Revolution supplied the background. American opinion of the Revolution, favorable at the outset, had already begun to divide when the English polemics reverberated across the Altantic in the early months of 1791. Burke's *Reflections on the Revolution in France* captured conservative feelings for the cause of order, tradition, church, privilege, and royalty in France. No sooner was Paine's vigorous democratic reply, the first part of the *Rights of Man*, received on this side of the water than arrangements were made to publish it. John Beckley, Clerk of the House of Representatives and political accomplice of his fellow Virginians, had this purpose in hand, but before sending the pamphlet to the printer, he lent it to Madison, who then passed it on to Jefferson with instructions to return it to Beckley. But that gentleman called before Jefferson had finished. He promised to hurry Burke to his grave and then send the murderous tract to Jonathan B. Smith, whose brother was to print it. Smith was a stranger to Jefferson; so, as he later explained, "to take off a little of the dryness of the note" transmitting the pamphlet, he expressed his pleasure "that something was at length to be publicly said against the political heresies which had of late sprung up among us, not doubting but that our citizens would rally again round the standard of Common Sense." It was a casual piece of courtesy. He was dumbfounded the next week when, "without the least information or suspicion it would be published, out it comes . . . at the head of the pamphlet." Jefferson thus appeared before the public as the unqualified champion of the French Revolution. He could not disavow the endorsement, for he had indeed written it, and he rejoiced in Paine's triumph. He decided to remain silent, except as private explanations might ease his embarrassment.

The embarrassment came less from the association with Paine and his radical opinions than from the veiled reference to the "political heresies" of the Vice President. Though the gentleman was unnamed, no one mistook Jefferson's object. He candidly acknowledged it to Washington and Madison. "I tell the writer [Adams] freely that he is a heretic, but certainly never meant to step into a public newspaper with that in my mouth." The alleged heresies had filled the columns of Fenno's *Gazette* for months. The *Discourses on Davila*, as Adams called these rambling reflections on government, attacked democratic ideas of equality, progress, and popular rule. Political man was a creature of passions, Adams said, above all "the passion for distinction." To channel this selfish passion into works for the public good was the principal problem of government. A system of checks and balances founded on the different orders of society was necessary. Because of inequality of birth, of wealth, and talent in every society, a division between the few and the many was inescapable. Liberty could be had only by erecting a political balance between the two orders of *aristocracy* and *democracy*, then adding, as a presiding genius and symbol of eminence, the third order of *monarchy*. Adams's casual use of these galvanizing abstractions made him an easy target. While he did not mean, as some inferred, that nobility and kingship should be instituted in the United States—a majestic president and a high-toned senate satisfied him—his image of American government was plainly derived from the English model that Paine satirized as "this, that, and t'other." The theory had been stated earlier in the ponderous *Defence of the Ameri-*

can Constitutions, excoriated by Jefferson's friends in Paris. Now Adams was riding his hobby horse again, this time with priestly admonishment against the overbearing influence of democracy drawn from the "levelling" and "fanaticism" of the French Revolution.

Adams was hurt by Jefferson's thrust. Major Beckwith expressed astonishment that the American Secretary of State could recommend a political tract branded as seditious in England. Hamilton was "open-mouthed" against his colleague, viewing the prefatory note as an attack on both the British and American governments. As everywhere men declared themselves partisans of Burke or Paine, it became apparent that the ideological division existed in the government of the United States.

While the controversy simmered in the press, Jefferson went off on a month-long "botanizing excursion" he had earlier arranged with Madison. Their itinerary took them from New York up the valley of the Hudson to Lake George and Lake Champlain, across to Vermont and down the Connecticut River Valley, returning by way of Long Island. This was fresh country to the Virginians. The *flora* and *fauna* of the region, its scenic beauty, historic sites of Revolutionary fame—Saratoga, Ticonderoga, Crown Point, Bennington —all this was interesting to Jefferson and Madison. As they bounced along in leisurely fashion, their conversation must have turned occasionally to politics, and they probably did not overlook the opportunity to make political inquiries in the towns where they stopped. In the view of some New York Federalists the secret purpose of the Virginians' tour was to cement an alliance between the Madisonians of the South and the Clintonians of the North. The collapse of the powerful family alliance of the Schuylers and the Livingstons in January had weakened the Federalists. Robert R. Livingston, the Chancellor, seeing that the landed aristocracy he represented was becoming but a poor relation of the moneyed aristocracy headed by Hamilton's father-in-law, Philip Schuyler, joined forces with the popular Clintonians and helped elect the venturesome upstart Araon Burr over Schuyler to the United States Senate. Hamilton was troubled by this development; and the information he received from a friend in New York "that there was every appearance of a passionate courtship between the Chancellor, Burr, Jefferson and Madison, when the two latter were in town," did nothing to ease his anxiety.

Hamilton and friends imagined political intrigue where there was none. Governor Clinton, still the leader of the state despite his Anti-Federalist past, seems not to have noticed the touring Virginians, nor did they call on him. If any alliances or bargains were struck, with Livingston, Burr, Clinton, or anyone, they were very secret indeed, for they left no trace. The excursion bore fruit not in deep-laid schemes but in the innocent delights of science and agriculture, as in a grove of sugar maples Jefferson planted at Monticello.

When he returned to Philadelphia in the middle of June, the political pot had come to a boil. Caught in the polemical battle between "Burkites" and "Paineites," Jefferson found himself shamed on one side, applauded on the other. "Some persons here are insinuating that I am Brutus, that I am Agricola, that I am Philademus, etc., etc. I am none of them . . . ." The letters of "Publicola," emanating from Boston, caused the most interest. They defended the alleged "political heresies" of the Vice President, defended the English constitution from Paine's sarcasm, and lashed out at his extreme views of popular sovereignty and democratic revolution in which the Secretary of State was implicated. By his endorsement of the *Rights of Man*, Jefferson seemed, said Publicola, "like the Arabian prophet, to call upon all true believers in the Islam of democracy to draw their swords, and, in the fervor of their devotion, to compel all their countrymen to cry out, 'There is but one Goddess of Liberty, and Common Sense is her prophet.' " Publicola added to Jefferson's chagrin, for this latest gladiator was thought to be John Adams.

After Adams went home to Braintree in July, Jefferson addressed him a long letter. "I have a dozen times taken up my pen to write you," he began, "and as often laid it down again, suspended between opposing considerations." He then gave his account of the painful episode. Although they differed on the best form of government, he hoped they might differ as friends in the privacy of their own conversation. Nothing had been further from his intention than public controversy, and lest Adams suspect him of masquerading in the press under a Roman name, Jefferson declared he never had and never would. Adams's reply was friendly. He was grateful for Jefferson's letter and gave entire credit to his motives. "It was high time that you and I should come to an explanation with each other," he wrote. "The friendship that has subsisted for fifteen years between us without the smallest interruption, and until this occasion without the slightest suspicion, ever has been and still is very dear to my heart." With respect to political ideas, Adams was not aware that he and Jefferson had quarreled or, for all that, ever had a serious conversation on the subject. If Jefferson assumed that he, John Adams, wished to introduce aristocracy and monarchy into the United States, he was entirely mistaken. Adams denied authorship of *Publicola*, omitting to disclose its true author, his son John Quincy, with whom Jefferson had perambulated in Paris a few years before, now a promising young attorney in Boston. The New Englander wrote as always with an open heart; yet he could not suppress a reproach to Jefferson for giving circulation to a false or misleading interpretation of his writings. Jefferson might better have left the matter there; but, believing he was "as innocent *in effect* as . . . in intention," he sought to absolve himself entirely. Had it not been for *Publicola*, he said, his opinion of Paine's book would have gone unnoticed; furthermore, in alluding to "political heresies," he had not had Adams's writings in view. This little piece of mendacity aimed at closing the wound had the opposite effect. Jefferson protested too much, as Adams suspected. He made no answer, nor did the old friends correspond again for several years.

As the fog of political rhetoric thickened, neither man could see the other except as an enemy of the American republic. Jefferson, for his part, became a victim of volatile abstractions like "aristocracy" and "monarchy." He was correct in perceiving that a change had come over John Adams. If his system was basically unchanged, he had grown distrustful of the people, shifted the accent from democracy to the privileged orders, and, indeed, by his obsession with these European categories disclosed a treacherous intellectual flaw. It was impossible to separate the Adams of *Davila* from the reactionary tendency of Burke's *Reflections*. Yet Adams was not, even now, an uncritical advocate of the old order against the new, however frightening its appearance. His polititical vocabulary blurred the difference for Jefferson and many others. Adams, for his part, grew more distrustful still of the fickle populace and felt that Jefferson, from his delusions about the French Revolution, had become a tool of democratic malcontents and Francophiles bent on running him down as an Anglican, aristocrat, and monarchist.

Jefferson placed Adams's heresies, bad as they were, on a different plane from Hamilton's. Many years later he recalled a dinner-table conversation with these men in the spring of 1792. Of the English constitution, Adams observed, "Purge that constitution of its corruption, and give to its popular branch equality of representation, and it would be the most perfect ever devised by the wit of man." Hamilton interjected, "Purge it of its corruption, and give to its popular branch equality of representation, and it would become an *impracticable* government: as it stands at present, with all its supposed defects, it is the most perfect government which ever existed." The exchange stated their differences exactly, Jefferson thought. "The one was for two hereditary branches and an honest elective one: the other, for an hereditary King, with a House of Lords and Commons corrupted to his will, and standing between him and the people." Believing in the power of ideas, Jefferson believed these theoretical preferences had a profound bearing on the future of republican government in the United States. And beginning to discover, with Madison, "a sympathy between the speeches and the pockets" of congressmen, he formed the conviction that the sophisticated "corruption" of the funding system looked to the subversion of American liberty. Hamilton denied this, of course. But he made no secret of his political convictions. In August he talked freely to Jefferson about the Vice President. He disapproved of *Davila* not because the opinions were wrong but because their publication was imprudent, tending to weaken confidence in the administration. "I own it is my own opinion," he declared to Jefferson "though I do not publish it from Dan to Beersheba, that the present government is not that which will answer the ends of society . . . and that it will probably be found expedient to go into the British form." In testimony concerning his arch rival, Jefferson scarcely qualifies as a disinterested witness; but in this instance, as in others, his own report of Hamilton's views tallies with friendly witness. The enduring effects of the Hamiltonian system lay in the directions of nationalism and capitalism. On this long view the idea of its "monarchical tendency" has often seemed the work of a demented imagination or an unprincipled demagogue. But effects and intentions, retrospective judgments and judgments in historical context, are entirely different things; and Jefferson, acting in the circumstances of his time, making the linkages authorized by the works, utterances, and sympathies of his political foes, fairly detected an animus in the proceedings carrying the government beyond the republican limits of the Constitution.

The Jefferson-Adams *contretemps* injected the ideological issues of the French Revolution into American politics. Henceforth, though the problems of the government were as mundane as before, they were increasingly colored by the hopes and the fears, the twin hysterias of enthusiasm and denunciation, sent up in the progress of an event far from American shores. Jefferson, though he regretted the personal embarrassment, thought the public controversy surrounding Paine's book was salutary. It helped "to separate the wheat from the chaff," he wrote to Paine. It dramatized the connection between the American experiment and the French Revolution. "I consider," he had earlier said, "the establishment and success of their government as necessary to stay up our own, and to prevent it from falling back to that kind of half-way house, the English constitution." He hoped "so beautiful a revolution" would "spread through the whole world." And despite revolutionary excesses that soon repelled other partisans of the cause, despite the career of exile and death that opened before many of his friends in Paris, despite evidences of official distemper toward the United States, Jefferson remained a champion of the French Revolution. The commitment was justified, but the interpolation of Revolutionary ideas and passions into American politics did as much to obscure issues as to clarify them. "The characteristic difference between your revolution and ours," the Comtesse de Houdetot suggested in a melancholy letter, "is that having nothing to destroy, you have nothing to injure, and labouring for a people, few in number, uncorrupted, and extended over a large tract of country, you have avoided all the inconveniences of a situation, contrary in every respect." Jefferson knew this truth, but the winds of European doctrine often clouded his view of it.

While thus thrust into public prominence as the champion of revolutionary democracy, Jefferson continued his intramural quarrel

443

with Hamilton. The New Yorker took the opinion against the national bank as a personal affront. The ambitions of Jefferson and his friends were first disclosed, he thought, on a bill placing the Secretary of State next in line to the Vice President in succession to the presidency. The bill failed in January 1791; revived a year later, Hamilton spurred the Federalists to defeat it as "a measure of self-defence." (Succession was fixed upon the president pro tempore of the Senate.) In his Report on the Establishment of a Mint, Hamilton opposed Jefferson's plan to conform the unit of coin to the unit of weight. Here, too, he was successful, though in other respects his ideas on mint and coinage agreed with Jefferson's, whose influence he acknowledged. He believed Jefferson's personal animosity was aroused by disagreements such as these, the small with the large; and perhaps it was, for Jefferson proceeded in the following months to snipe at Hamilton's department. When the Treasury's second officer, the Comptroller, died in April, Jefferson at once urged Washington to appoint Tench Coxe to the place. Hamilton suspected Coxe's loyalty, the more so from Jefferson's pushing his candidacy. Washington followed Hamilton's advice and nominated the Auditor, Oliver Wolcott, a stern Connecticut Federalist. Several months later the Postmaster General resigned. Jefferson espoused Paine's appointment to this office within Hamilton's department. "It seemed to be a fair opportunity for a declaration of certain sentiments," Randolph observed to Madison. In Jefferson's eyes the Post Office had great importance as the only means of circulating political intelligence. The snail-like movement of the mails retarded public discussion and posed a serious challenge to popular government. Believing he could speed up the mails, anxious, too, to lessen the influence of the Treasury, Jefferson coveted the Post Office for his own department. He was not so naïve as to expect the President to nominate Paine, or Paine, happily tooting his horn in Paris, to accept. The Massachusetts Federalist Timothy Pickering got the job. But Jefferson kept his sights on the Post Office.

It was in connection with his effort to improve the circulation of news that he helped Madison and Henry Lee in 1791 to establish a national newspaper at Philadelphia under the editorship of Philip Freneau. The uncrowned poet laureate of the American Revolution lived on the edge of poverty in New York by writing for the *Daily*

Advertiser. Madison and Lee, former classmates of Freneau at Princeton, interested Jefferson in finding an office for him. The part-time position of translator clerk became vacant when the government moved to Philadelphia. In March Jefferson offered the post to Freneau. The annual salary was only $250, but the duties of the clerkship were so inconsiderable, he said, "as not to interfere with any other calling the person may choose." It was understood that Freneau wished to establish his own newspaper, and had already made tentative arrangements to do so in Monmouth, New Jersey. Retirement to the Jersey moor appealed to him—the din of war and politics and cities had never suited the poet's true nature. He declined Jefferson's offer. But Madison refused to accept this decision as final. He was impressed by Freneau's combination of literary and polemical talents, and to enlist these in the republican cause, rather than simply to help an old friend and deserving poet, now became a major object. Preceding Jefferson to New York in the spring, he talked with Freneau there. "The more I learn of his character, talents and principles," he reported, "the more I regret his burying himself in the obscurity . . . chosen for himself in New Jersey." Madison persisted, and Freneau finally agreed to go to Philadelphia to talk with Jefferson. But stopping in New Jersey along the way, he never reached the capital city. Jefferson got his first glimpse of him, a smallish man of forty years with a touch of sadness in his deep dark eyes, from across a boarding house breakfast table in New York in May. Nothing developed then; but Madison, with Lee's assistance, resumed the negotiations in July. Jefferson added his persuasions. And Freneau, hesitant and torn between competing desires, finally agreed to trade the quiet seat in Monmouth for the prospect of fame and fortune in Philadelphia. In August, Jefferson appointed him to the clerkship, and the *National Gazette* commenced publication on the last day of October.

Because of the political storm that some months later raged around the *National Gazette*, Jefferson's motives in attending its birth assumed unexpected importance. He recognized that the republican cause, as he defined it, was making no headway in Congress and not much in the administration. Hamilton and his followers were in command and, though the President was a steadying influence, there was no limit to which they might go. Jefferson thought it necessary, therefore, to go outside the government, broadcast the issues, and form a responsive public opinion. What was needed, he told his son-in-law in May, was a national journal that "might go through the states, and furnish a Whig vehicle of intelligence." Fenno's obsequious gazette was, in Jefferson's opinion, "a paper of pure Toryism." Benjamin F. Bache's *General Advertiser* provided a mild republican antidote in Philadelphia, but, a daily, it was not suited to national circulation, and Bache declined Jefferson's overture to make it "a purely republican vehicle" for general distribution. He wished by a *national* gazette to penetrate the public mind, articulate the issues of the government in Philadelphia, and interpret European events. The plan of publishing extracts from the *Gazette de Leide*, briefly tried with Fenno, had not been forgotten. Jefferson offered Freneau access to the foreign newspapers of the State Department. But the establishment of such a newspaper was only half the battle. To get it into the hands of the people throughout the Union was the more difficult part; and so Jefferson was attentive to seemingly small matters of post offices, post roads, and postal rates, as well as a willing solicitor of subscriptions to the new *National Gazette*.

The newspaper was not begun as a party organ, for no *party* centered on the "republican interest" had as yet been organized; nor was it begun with Jefferson's auspices, for he had no editorial supervision of the newspaper and the money came from Freneau's former employer in New York. Of course, knowing Freneau's reputation as a "good whig" and a plain-speaking and hard-hitting journalist, Jefferson could rely on the *National Gazette* to combat the "political heresies" afloat in the government. Only in this sense can his intervention be described as partisan. But as the conflict within the government deepened, as the press dramatized it in bolder and bolder terms, the *National Gazette* contributed immensely to the rise of the Republican party and to the public recognition of Jefferson as its leader.

Struggles with Hamilton

It had been a torrid summer in Philadelphia. On September 2, 1791, Jefferson paid ten dollars for an odometer, fixed it to the phaeton, and journeyed home with Madison, making precise notations of the mileage from place to place along the route. He was a grandfather now. Martha and her husband and seven-month-old baby Anne were living at Monticello. The arrangement was temporary, but Jefferson would see to it that they never strayed far from his fireside. While in Philadelphia he usually wrote home every Wednesday, alternately to Randolph, Martha, and Polly; and from them he exacted the same punctuality, so that the post could complete the circuit every three weeks. But neither post nor loved ones lived up to his expectations. His letters dwelt on many things: housekeeping, the nursing of infants, news of friends abroad (to Martha especially), politics, farming, tobacco markets (for Randolph's benefit), the weather and seasonal events of frogs and bluebirds and strawberries (especially for Polly, his "botanical and zoological correspondent"). "Tell me when you shall have peas, etc., up," he had written Polly at the first hint of spring, "when every thing comes to table; when you shall have the first chickens hatched; when every kind of tree blossoms, or puts forth leaves; when each kind of flower blossoms." Not a breeze blew, not a flower bloomed, at Monticello uninteresting to him. He was there only a month and took Polly away with him. Now a lovely girl of thirteen, Polly was ready, like her sister before her, to receive the polished graces and literary refinements of Philadelphia.

The route traveled by the Virginians passed through Georgetown, close by the site of "the Grand Columbian Federal City." As became his habit, Jefferson stopped to witness its progress. This was not a casual interest. From the first Jefferson acted as the President's chief assistant in the planning and supervision of the capital city. Details relating to the purchase and sale of property, the procurement of laborers, machinery for cutting and polishing stone, even the determination of place names, received Jefferson's attention in the close liaison he maintained with the three-man federal commission on the site. Of course, the design of the city and its buildings stirred his imagination. His first suggestions were included in a comprehensive series of notes prepared for the President in August 1790, after the passage of the Residence Act. Construing the statute in all possible latitude, he proposed that sufficient land be acquired for a capital city, not simply a seat of government. The nation that

447

had declared its own principles, formed its own government, cast its own future, ought to erect its own capital—on a scale and in a style consonant with its civic ideals. Many thought the idea ludicrous, especially in a situation as remote and unpromising as the falls of the Potomac. Jefferson helped the President to determine the exact location of the city within the constitutional "ten mile square"—several thousand acres between Rock Creek and the eastern branch of the Potomac—and to enlist the interest of the landowners in its development. The city envisioned in his early notes would be generously laid out in streets at right angles, in a checkerboard pattern, as in Philadelphia. A restriction he thought, should be placed on the height of houses, as in Paris: "it keeps the houses low and convenient, and the streets light and airy, fires are much more manageable . . . ." And he objected to the "disgusting monotony" and inconvenience produced by a uniform setback of houses and buildings. A rough sketch, made in March, was the germinal conception of the mall, the location of the capitol and executive mansion, with surrounding walks and gardens.

Major Pierre Charles L'Enfant, the French engineer who had served under Washington in the war, arrived on the Potomac about this time to lay off the city under the commission's direction. At L'Enfant's request Jefferson forwarded such plans of cities as he possessed—cities he had visited in France. But none was comparable, in his opinion, to "the old Babylon" Penn had re-created in Philadelphia. The Frenchman did not agree. The rectangular plan lacked, he said, "a sense of the real grand and truly beautiful." In June, L'Enfant unveiled his splendid scheme of radiating axes and cardinal points, together with lavish gardens, monuments, fountains, and a cascading waterfall forty feet high under the base of the Capitol. L'Enfant incorporated Jefferson's idea of a central mall, but as with everything else raised it to the nth dimension. Jefferson would have preferred more of the simplicity of Philadelphia and less of the grandiosity of Versailles. But he put aside his reservations and joined with the President in approving the L'Enfant plan. It was incredibly ambitious, indeed quite impossible of execution in the manner the egocentric Frenchman demanded. Not a lot should be sold, he argued, until the public buildings, parks, and avenues were provided; yet without the income from real estate very little could be built, and in the meantime last-ditch opponents of the Potomac capital might prevail. Thus began the conflict between L'Enfant and the commissioners, the dreamer and the realists, which rapidly threw the whole enterprise into confusion and uncertainty.

The first lots were sold at auction when Jefferson stopped at Georgetown in October. A month later the commissioners reported that L'Enfant, without a stitch of authority, had demolished a bothersome house belonging to a prominent citizen. It was apparent, Jefferson advised the President, that L'Enfant must either co-operate with the commission or be dismissed. But the temperamental engineer regarded the commissioners as a set of unprincipled politicians and speculators. Jefferson valued L'Enfant's services, and he was as interested as any man in the creation of a national capital attuned to national ideals; but law and politics, finance and administration, set limits to conceptions of grandeur. The conflict mounted to a climax in February 1792. L'Enfant's arrogance became intolerable, and Jefferson had the painful task of informing him, on the President's orders, his services were at an end. A rocky road still lay ahead.

The next step, the design of the Capitol and the President's House, also absorbed Jefferson. He wished the former to be built on one of the ancient models, like the Virginia Capitol. Architect prizes were offered for both buildings. For the President's House, he submitted, anonymously, his own porticoed and domed design based on the Villa Rotunda of Palladio, but the prize went to the professional architect James Hoban. James Thornton, an amateur like himself but less imitative of classical models, won the competition on the Capitol. Jefferson was captivated by Thornton's plan: "It is simple, noble, beautiful, excellently distributed, and moderate in size." Many thought it immoderate, however. Jefferson called in a group of architects for advice. One of them, Stephen Hallet, made the necessary alterations in scale. This was in July 1793. Jefferson's contribution to the shaping national capital, though but an episode of his tenure as Secretary of State, was perhaps more gratifying than any of his major undertakings.

Traveling from Georgetown though "five days of northeast storm," Jefferson arrived in Philadelphia on October 22, just two days before Congress convened. Polly was soon settled with a housekeeper and tutors. "She has made young friends enough to keep

449

herself in a bustle," Jefferson informed her sister. Among several items of unfinished business claiming the Secretary's attention was a report to Congress arising from the patent application of one Jacob Isaacks for a method of distilling fresh water from the sea. The first superintendent of patents did not fully subscribe to the principle of the system. He questioned that ingenuity is "spurred on by the hope of monopoly," and thought "the benefit even of limited monopolies . . . too doubtful to be opposed to that of their general suppression." Few patents were applied for, fewer still granted—only thirty-seven during Jefferson's tenure—partly because he scrupulously guarded the privilege and investigated every claim to satisfy the statutory test of originality. In the case of Isaacks, Jefferson called in Rittenhouse and the Doctors Hutchinson and Wistar to observe demonstrations of the elaborate apparatus (a still and furnace fed with hickory logs) that had been set up in his office. This galaxy of philosophers concluded after five separate tests that Isaack's discovery marked no advance over methods already known for rendering sea water potable. The patent was denied. Jefferson's lengthy report reviewed the history of this subject, of so much interest to a seafaring nation, and proposed that the approved method of distillation be described and illustrated on the back of clearance papers given to shipmasters, with the request that all trials be reported to the Secretary of State. Although his interest in new inventions was insatiable, the care he bestowed on this and other patent claims was demanded by a jealous statute. Partly through his efforts Congress simplified the system in 1793 so as to permit the issuance of patents without the test of originality or usefulness and on the sole responsibility of the Secretary of State. Registration replaced investigaton, which overcame an intolerable burden at the price, to Jefferson's chagrin, of widening the opportunity for limited monopolies.

The year 1791 closed in a perfect siege of business. Jefferson was readying his report on commerce. There were renewed negotiatons with each of the powers. L'Enfant, public lands, Indian affairs—the latter, especially involved much time and trouble. Jefferson supported the campaign afoot against the Ohio Indians, but after giving them a good drubbing, the government should adopt, he thought, the more humane and economical policy of bribes. The cost of St.

Clair's expedition "would have served for presents on the most liberal scale for one hundred years; nor shall we otherwise ever get rid of an army, or of our debt." St. Clair's terrible defeat in November, necessitating still another expedition, buttressed his opinion on this point, as well as on the superiority of militia to regulars in frontier warfare, an opinion involved in his fears of standing army and debt. Indian affairs, primarily, caused the President to consult collectively with department heads toward the end of the year. The cabinet as a convening body was born. Increasingly thrown together with Hamilton in these meetings, "like two cocks in a pit," as Jefferson later said, the result was to intensify the rivalry between the secretaries.

Among the early subjects discussed in the cabinet none was more important than the line to be pursued in the negotiations with the British minister. George Hammond was a cocksure young man who had served his diplomatic apprenticeship at several of the European courts including Versailles, where Jefferson had had a casual acquaintance with him. He presented his credentials in November. Informal talks began. Hammond would have liked to continue these exchanges across the table; but Jefferson, averse to mixing the politeness of conversation into hard-headed diplomatic maneuver in this instance, quickly switched the negotiations into the more formal medium of written communication. He made short work of wringing from Hammond the admission that his instructions gave him no leeway with respect to commerce. What remained—it was enough —was the settlement of the issues left over from the treaty of peace. Hammond's instructions were clear: he was to obtain the execution of those articles of the treaty dealing with unpaid debts and Loyalist property as the *sine qua non* for the abandonment of the Northwest posts. On December 15 Jefferson handed Hammond the American "assignment of breaches." They were basically two: not only the posts but also the slaves carried off by the British after the cessation of hostilities. Much was made of this second grievance in the South (Jefferson had lately received a resolution of the Virginia assembly on the subject) partly because it took off some of the odium attached to the southerners on the point of the debts. Hammond agreed to furnish a counterstatement of the British position. With the cards on the table, negotiation might proceed.

Weeks, then months, passed, and nothing came from Hammond.

Jefferson suspected Hamilton's interference. At a cabinet meeting near the end of December, Jefferson had stated his intentions of recommending commercial retaliation against Britain in the report slated to go to Congress. "Hamilton opposed it violently," he subsequently wrote, "and among other arguments, observed that it was of more importance to us to have the posts than to commence a commercial war." Struck by the force of this reasoning, not wishing by commercial threats to wreck the negotiations if they held hope for the surrender of the posts, Jefferson agreed to defer the report he had promised, at least until Hammond filed his answer. From the moment this was decided in Hamilton's presence, the British minister studiously put off the counterstatement. If Hamilton had actually tipped the government's hand, it was probably not the first time, Jefferson noted. "It was observable, that whenever, at any of our consultations, anything was proposed as to Great Britain, Hamilton had constantly ready something which Mr. Hammond had communicated to him, which suited the subject and proved the intimacy of their communication; insomuch, that I believe he communicated to Hammond all our views, and knew from him, in return, the views of the British court." Jefferson felt he had again been taken in by Hamilton, whose connivance with the British minister seriously embarrassed American diplomacy. At length the President lost patience with Hammond and told Jefferson to jog him. He did so at the assembly honoring the President's birthday. Hammond delivered the statement on March 5.

The bulky memoir charged that the United States had wantonly violated the treaty from the first with grave injuries to British subjects, which were detailed in five appendices. Ninety-four charges were cited, none of them documented. "I flatter myself, my Lord," Hammond boasted to Grenville, the Foreign Minister, "that this Statement will be found . . . to contain a body of proof so complete and substantial as to preclude the probability of cavil and contradiction on the part of this government." How wrong he was! Jefferson worked nearly eight weeks on his rebuttal of Hammond, amassing quantities of data from public records and public officials, reducing them to order, and finally writing a diplomatic note of 17,000 words, plus elaborate appendices, the whole running to 250 manuscript pages, six times the length of the British memoir. It was a masterful performance, conceded even by his enemies when it was later made public.

Jefferson wrote as the American Secretary of State, not as a disinterested analyst. The memoir, while exceedingly vauable as history, ought to be read, above all, as a brilliant piece of advocacy. He did not scruple to shade the evidence within the perimeters of truth and honor. He did not refrain from fruitless recriminations. An acrimonious tone pervaded the whole. Such had been the style of Anglo-American relations, and Jefferson's production did nothing to change it. But it answered, with document and testimony, nearly all of Hammond's charges, beyond "cavil and contradiction," then went on aggressively to put the British government in the wrong. Jefferson denied the accusation of perfidy against the United States for failure to execute the article of the treaty which pledged Congress to *recommend* to the states the restitution of Loyalist property. Careful examination of the documents showed that both parties understood the nature of this article, as a sop to English opinion, with no expectation Congress would or could enforce obedience on the states. Congress made the recommendation and, as Jefferson noted in detail, the states complied in surprising degree. The provision against future confiscations of British property had not, contrary to Hammond, been violated in a single instance. It was true that several of the states had violated the fourth article by impeding the collection of British debts. However, there were mitigating circumstances. The debts could not have been paid at once; and certain questions, such as the allowance or disallowance of interest during the war, belonged to the discretion of the courts. Moreover, it could no longer be claimed that legal impediments existed. Jefferson quoted state laws, court decisions, and authoritative testimony to refute Hammond's evidence to the contrary. He was right in the main, though the persistent opposition to British creditors, especially in Virginia, received scant notice in his account. He justified any waywardness on the American side by British infractions of the treaty. Not only had the British government refused to abandon the Northwest posts, as it was obliged to do "with all convenient speed," but in violation of the same article British commanders had deliberately carried off 3000 Negro slaves during the eight months following notification of the treaty. Jefferson's conclusive proof of

453

the latter charge fixed the onus of first breaking the treaty on the British. "It may safely be said then that the treaty was violated *in England* before it was known in America; and, *in America*, as soon as it was known." Yet Whitehall appealed to the retaliatory acts of the states as an excuse for further obstinacy, "and inverting the natural order of cause and effect, alleged that these proceedings of ours were the cause of the infractions which they had committed months and years before."

Hammond was stunned by the memoir. Having gained the upper hand, the Secretary invited the Minister to dinner, and after the cloth was removed they discussed their differences in a familiar way. Hammond said his government had heretofore heard only one side of the dispute; Jefferson's statement placed it on new ground, requiring new instructions from London before he could proceed. Jefferson surmised from the conversation "that it had not at all entered into the expectations of his court that they were to deliver up the posts." The point was pivotal for American policy, of course. Although he did not appreciate the extent to which British occupation of the Northwest was dictated by obligations to the Indians, Jefferson was justified in his suspicion of Whitehall's intentions. In March, not long after delivering his note, Hammond received from London the project for the creation of an Indian reserve and neutral barrier state in the lands above the Ohio. This was the ministry's response to St. Clair's disaster. It was hoped that Hammond's diplomacy would back up the force of Indian arms, and thus bring the Americans around to the British plan for settling the problem. But the plan was wholly unacceptable, as Hammond realized. Nothing could be done with it in the face of Jefferson's memoir. The plan never came to the attention of the American government.

Unfortunately, the force of Jefferson's *coup* was subverted by Hamilton. Several days after the "solo dinner" at Jefferson's house, when he had seemed visibly shaken by the Secretary's thrust, Hammond sent a reassuring report to his government. From Hamilton he had learned that Jefferson's paper did not represent the views of the administration, that its "intemperate violence" was regretted, that the President had not read it, nor had the cabinet agreed to it. This was misleading, in part downright false. Randolph and Hamilton read Jefferson's paper in draft. The latter suggested only one significant change, on the subject of state impediments to British creditors. Randolph, too, criticized his friend's complacent view of this subject and detected "a peculiar asperity" in the note generally. Jefferson sent his colleagues' views, together with his own, to the President, who approved the document as it was written and then submitted to Hammond. Although Jefferson's suspicions were aroused, Hamilton's underhanded conduct on this occasion never came to official notice. Had Washington learned of it, the consequences may well be imagined. Month after month passed, and Hammond made no reply to the American note. "He says, he waits for instructions," Jefferson wrote wearily in 1793, after one of his periodic needlings of the Minister, "which he pretends to expect from packet to packet. But sometimes the ministers are all in the country, sometimes they are absorbed in negotiations nearer home, sometimes it is the hurry of impending war, or attention to other objects, the stock of which is inexhaustible, and can therefore never fail those who desire but that things shall rest as they are." The British ministry buried Jefferson's memoir for a number of reasons, some of them extraneous. But the decision was a tribute to his performance as well as to Hamilton's treacherous interference; for if the former was unanswerable, the latter ensured that no answer was necessary. Nor was one ever given. Jefferson would leave office without resolving a single issue in Anglo-American relations.

He encountered inertia of different kinds in his dealings with France and Spain. Between him and the French minister Ternant, a veteran officer of the American Revolution, roughly of Jefferson's age, communication proved difficult. Both were reserved and circumspect men, to which the Frenchman added unreasoned fears of Jefferson's negotiations with Hammond. The principal object on the American side was a new commercial treaty; but, as already noted, Ternant lacked positive instructions. Under the circumstances Jefferson could do little more than lodge protests against new French restrictions, meanwhile awaiting more favorable developments. But Hamilton saw in the business of a French treaty the opportunity for forcing Jefferson into commercial negotiatons with Hammond. Let Jefferson and Ternant agree on the terms of a treaty, he said, then send it to Paris for approval or disapproval. Ternant was willing. So was the President. "I disapproved of it," Jefferson stated, "observing, that such a volunteer project would be binding on us, and not on them; that it would enable them to find out how far we would go, and avail themselves of it. However, the President thought it worth trying, and I acquiesced." He prepared the plan of a treaty exchanging the privileges of natives and fixing maximum duties on principal articles of commerce. Now it was Hamilton's turn to object. He disliked Jefferson's liberal plan and proposed instead a tariff of duties ranging upwards to 50 per cent on French goods. A treaty on this basis was impossible, as Hamilton well knew. He disclosed his little game at a subsequent cabinet meeting. Since the business of a treaty had been taken up with Ternant, he argued, it ought also to be taken up with Hammond, who was similarly uninstructed. "His scheme evidently was," Jefferson noted, "to get us engaged first with Ternant, merely that he might have a pretext to engage us on the same ground with Hammond, taking care at the same time, by an extravagant tariff, to render it impossible we should come to a conclusion with Ternant: probably meaning at the same time, to propose terms so favorable to Great Britain, as would attach us to that country by treaty." Jefferson promptly dropped the matter, though a commercial treaty with France remained a leading object. Morris was urged to press it in Paris. Jefferson later revived it with Ternant. Pending the submission of his report calling for commercial retaliation against Britain, it was highly desirable to place Franco-American trade on a more liberal footing. Otherwise, either Britain would not be singled out for discrimination or France would fail to reap the rewards. All his efforts were unavailing until war forced revolutionary France to recognize the vital importance of American trade.

Jefferson's heaviest stake was in Spanish diplomacy. A settlement with Spain opening up the Southwest would alone make his tenure in office memorable. On the American side the chance rested with the joint commissioners, Short and Carmichael, in Madrid. In March, Jefferson detailed their instructions. The paper showed more ingenuity than force of argument. Legal, historical, and moral reasons were offered in support of the American boundary claim to the 31st parallel, as provided in the treaty of 1783 with Britain; but Spain was a bystander to this treaty, while under her own accord with Britain she recovered West Florida to the 32nd parallel. Equally specious was Jefferson's plea for the American right to navigate the Mississippi. Here, too, the claim rested on a treaty engagement empty without Spanish recognition, and the dons were neither obliged nor inclined to give it. From this impasse Jefferson flew to the elevated heights of "the law of nature and nations." "If we appeal to this" he asked rhetorically, "as we feel it written on the heart of men, what sentiment is written in deeper characters than that the ocean is free to all men, and their rivers to all their inhabitants?" The right of the upper inhabitants of a river to navigate its whole length to the sea was founded in nature and reason. Indeed, said Jefferson, the segment of the Mississippi occupied by Spain ought to be considered not as part of the river but as "a streight of the sea." He went on to argue that the right to ply the river necessarily gave the right to use its shores—for mooring vessels, depositing goods, and so on. Thus was the venerable doctrine of natural rights mustered into the service of American expansion, making manifest the territorial destiny of the nation as it had earlier made manifest its freedom.

There was justice in Jefferson's position, and he buttressed it with citations to the authoritative texts in international law and to the Roman law of riparian rights; but that the "heart of men" should overrule treaty claims, that a river should suddenly become an ocean strait, that Spanish sovereignty in Louisiana should be washed away in the waters of the Mississippi—all of this only evoked smiles and sneers in Madrid. As feeble as she was in North America, Spain still gloried in empire and still weighed in the scales of European power. It was all the dons could do to suffer the upstart Americans. Yet time was on their side. If reason and justice failed to impress the Spanish court, Jefferson told the commissioners, other means of doing so would not be wanting. "The present turbid situation of Europe cannot leave us long without a safe occasion of resuming our territory and navigation, and of carving for ourselves those conveniences on the shore which may facilitate and protect the latter effectively and permanently." Unfortunately, the vessel carrying his instructions sank beneath the Atlantic, and though the diplomatic pouch was saved, it was many months in reaching its destination. Then, no sooner did the commission begin its work early in 1793 than the balance of power shifted ominously.

457

Spain was thrown into the scale with Britain, upsetting all of Jefferson's calculations. The Spanish negotiations, so boldly conceived, spun out in tedious charges and counter-charges on the conduct of the two governments toward the Indians. The Spanish governors in the Southwest linked the four major tribes in a defensive confederacy against the American intruders. Carondelet, in West Florida, actively incited the Indians to border hostilities which, in addition to angering Philadelphia, cost Spain the sympathies of many westerners disgruntled with the American government for its failure to secure the navigation of the Mississippi. In time, talk and protest must give way to war; by the middle of 1793, certainly, Jefferson lost hope of averting it. Not even war came to his rescue, however. In nothing he undertook did he meet with greater frustration and disappointment than in his Spanish diplomacy.

Domestic politics grew warm in 1792, lines of division hardened, and the quarrel between Jefferson and Hamilton broke into public controversy. Differences within the administration on foreign policy hastened the development, but it occurred mainly on the issues of fiscal and economic policy. The Report on Manufactures, submitted to Congress in December 1791, furnished the capstone of Hamilton's system. In this brilliant state paper, the manifesto of American industralism, Hamilton showed the advantages to the nation of industrial employments and technology, of a balanced economy embracing manufactures with agriculture and commerce, and of a home market for the varied productions of American enterprise. The principal objections to manufactures were answered in convincing fashion. If a regime of "perfect liberty of trade" prevailed among nations, the Americans might pursue agriculture to the virtual exclusion of manufactures. But, as Jefferson too had said, national policy must deal with an imperfect economic world. Viewed realistically, the goals of national wealth and power can only be attained through industrial manufactures on a large scale. And since this development works against natural currents which, together with fallacious ideas, give an unfortunate predominance to landed enterprise in the United States, the aid and patronage of the national government is required on a comprehensive plan. Banks and funded debt already made provision for investment capital; further inducements should be given to the investment of foreign capital. Labor shortage should be overcome by immigration, by the employment of women and children in factories, and by the liberal encouragement of labor-saving inventions. Roads and canals should be built to facilitate the exchange of products. Nothing would prove more efficacious, Hamilton thought, than a system of bounties: the modest protective duties collected on given foreign imports should be defrayed as subsidies to their domestic competitors. For the authority of the government to engage in these and other activities—export prohibition, drawbacks, inspection of manufactured goods, and so on—Hamilton appealed to the "general welfare" clause of the Constitution.

Jefferson disapproved of Hamilton's Report on Manufactures less as a political economist than as a republican constitutionalist. It never became a clear-cut issue between them. Hamilton's design of an industrial society was much too radical for Congress. It was, in fact, hopelessly unrealistic in 1792 in both its political and economic aspects; and the course of events in Europe soon opened unprecedented opportunities to the nation's foreign commerce, checking the incipient growth of American manufactures for nearly twenty years. So Jefferson was not required to come to grips with Hamilton's Report, and he did not. Its tendency was nevertheless disturbing. He could not help but see it as a challenge to his own system of political economy based primarily on agricultural expansion and the enforced liberalization of foreign commerce. He was not at all averse to simple manufactures of a private, or household, variety, only to large-scale enterprises publicly encouraged against the natural order of things and necessarily partial in the distribution of benefits. His interest in transportation improvements and in mechanical invention, his concern to check the adverse balance-of-payments resulting from overindulgence in imported manufactures, his passionate commitment to economic independence from Britain—in certain respects, at least, Jefferson had better credentials than his rival to espouse the cause of domestic industry and the home market. In theory, of course, he continued to favor an agricultural economy, which was especially conducive to republican virtue and to the diffusion of power among the people. But in another policy context than Hamilton's, modest proposals for the encouragement of manufactures would probably have won his support. As it was, the proposals, far from modest, had to be seen in their relations to other parts of Hamilton's design. Bounties and other aids to manufactures would perpetuate the debt. Reliance on funded debt and bank stock for the provision of capital would further enrich the privileged financial class at the expense of the mass of people. The attraction of foreign capital, from Britain undoubtedly, would add new links to the chain of bondage. For better or worse, the southern states felt little interest in manufacturing enterprise and would, presumably, reap few of the rewards. These would go to the section of the country already favored by the national government with a lavish hand; and the growth of cities and factories in the Northeast would divert the energies of the country from its westward course of empire. Hamilton planned for America as if it were England. Jefferson had a different vision of American society, more austere, more democratic, more spontaneous, more attuned to the unique task of mastering the continent. It was also more realistic in 1792 and for several decades to come; only in the longer run of history would it seem archaic.

Considerations such as these formed the shadowy background of Jefferson's thinking; the foreground was monopolized by the constitutional question which, as in the case of the Bank, was conclusive in itself. Nothing in the Constitution authorized the government to encourage manufactures except indirectly by the levy of duties on imports. Jefferson thought additional duties should be laid equal to the bounties paid by the exporting country. But the government was not free to adopt the Old World mercantilist practices championed by Hamilton. The decision on the extraordinary proposition to aid manufactures under color of the "general welfare" clause would "let us know," he said, "whether we live under a limited or unlimited government." The Bank question, touching an incident to a delegated power, was small by comparison. For Hamilton now meant to establish the doctrine, Jefferson told the President, "that the power given by the constitution to collect taxes to provide for the *general welfare* . . . permitted Congress to take everything under their management which *they* should deem for the *public welfare*, and which is susceptible to the application of money; consequently, that the subsequent enumeration of their powers was not the description to which resort must be had, and did not at all constitute the limits of their authority." The inference was warranted from Hamilton's proposition, and that had no warrant at all in the intentions of the Constitution's framers. What confidence could be placed in a government that transformed a jealously guarded constitution into a boundless charter to legislate for the "general welfare"? Leading Federalists in Congress complained that the southern contingent had conjured up the bugbear "consolidation" to paralyze the government. "The practice of crying out 'this is unconstitutional,' is a vice that has grown inveterate by indulgence." It was selfish, parochial, against the national interest, said Fisher Ames, whose own politics smelled of fish and dripped molasses. The opposite cry, "this is constitutional," also had its dangers. To force a centralizing administered system of economic development on the young country would greatly impair the national consensus. Madison once remarked that the Constitution had two enemies, "one that would stretch it to death, and one that would squeeze it to death." For him, as for Jefferson, death by stretching was the danger in 1792.

On the very day Hamilton presented his Report to the House of Representatives, the *National Gazette* printed one of Madison's occasional articles, entitled "Consolidation." Here was a more penetrating statement of Republican nationalism than any Jefferson himself wrote at this time. Earlier, before the Constitution, the danger had come from the dissolution of the central government; now, Madison warned, it came from the consolidation of the states into one big government. Congress could not regulate the infinitely varied objects of state and local concern in all the latitudes of the American Union. If it made the attempt government must become "self-directed," for the sense of so many millions of people spread over a vast surface could never be collected apart from the provincial organs of government; and, in addition, such an accumulation of powers must be vested in the executive head as to make him a virtual monarch. Governmental consolidation multiplied the causes of dissension among the people, defeating the very object most wanted: "that a consolidation should prevail in their interests and affections." In this view, strict construction and state rights served the cause of one nation. Thus, Madison concluded, "let it be the patriotic study of all, to maintain the various authorities established by our complicated system, each in its respective sphere; and to erect over the whole, one paramount empire of reason, benevolence, and brotherly affection." The alternatives were to consolidate power and divide the people or to consolidate the people and divide power. The latter offered the only sure foundation of national union.

March brought startling confirmation of still other fears—fears evoked by the mania of speculation and monopoly. A financial panic rocked New York and reverberated through the eastern cities. Its principal author was William A. Duer, a former Assistant Secretary of Treasury, a princely speculator in land and stock, Hamilton's bosom friend and his associate in a mammoth manufacturing enterprise. Playing a bullish game with public and bank stocks—by "cornering" them to create a phenomenal rise in prices—Duer borrowed money and contracted purchases on a lavish scale. When he failed to meet his obligations, the stocks collapsed, breaking Duer, sending him to prison, and ruining his numerous creditors. Losses were estimated at three million dollars. "Men are often seen to weep in the streets. Fighting and boxing are common in the Coffee house." Money was scarce. Trade sickened. Public securities slipped to dangerous lows and were, with difficulty, propped up by Hamilton. Nothing like it had been known before in the United States. Jefferson compared the panic to the South Sea Bubble of English fame and, with Republicans generally, blamed it on the Treasury system, which had given ample field to the tribe of speculators. "This nefarious business is becoming more and more the public detestation," he wrote, "and cannot fail, when the knowledge of it shall be sufficiently extended, to tumble its authors headlong from their heights." Once in an age at least, he philosophized, the people seemed "doomed by nature" to receive such painful lessons from "cunning and unprincipled men," and they would, he trusted, "now come about and get back into the tract of plain, unsophisticated common sense which they ought never to have been decoyed from."

The panic aggravated Jefferson's opposition to the Secretary of Treasury. He objected to the measures taken by the Secretary to cushion the shock. Dipping into the government's sinking fund, Hamilton threw $100,000 into the securities market to purchase federal stock at par in order to uphold the government's credit and ease the panic. Jefferson, who sat as a commissioner of the sinking fund, felt the unprecedented action looked primarily to the relief of the speculators. The stocks, he thought, should have been purchased at the depreciated market price so as to expedite the sinking of the debt. He was aware of Duer's Treasury connections but did not directly implicate Hamilton in the speculator's schemes. He accused Hamilton of wrong policy, not of wrong-doing. Yet the Secretary had contributed more than Jefferson realized to Duer's outrageous adventures. The would-be titan's downfall was precipitated by a suit brought in federal court for recovery of a debt in excess of $200,-ooo, the amount still outstanding in his account with the government as Secretary of the Treasury Board of the old Congress. Oliver Wolcott, the Controller, took this face-saving action when he learned of Duer's precarious situation. Hamilton did not intercede in Duer's behalf; however, for three years he had freely permitted Duer to speculate with money owed to the United States government.

Jefferson could not trace all the ramifications of the panic, but it provided him with as convincing proof as he ever wanted of the nefarious effects of Treasury's alliance with stockjobbers and adventurers. It drew out all his deep-seated fears of a society floated on the treacherous seas of money and privilege. His censure extended to manufacturing enterprise, for it was part of the same movement and must show the same effects. Hamilton and Duer were, in fact, associated with their friends in a great moneyed corporation, the Society for the Encouragement of Useful Manufactures, which was intended to exemplify the wisdom of the Report on Manufactures and attract federal largesse on top of the privileges of its New Jersey charter. SUM and the Report, the Duer panic, the whiskey excise—all brought Hamilton and his policies under mounting criticism in 1792. Despite his financial wizardy, said a New York newspaper, Hamilton had failed to reach "the heads and the hearts of the people." He had inscribed "the hieroglyphs of money" on the escutcheon of liberty and enticed men to abandon "the ordinary walks of life . . . for the golden dreams of speculation." Ironically, the nation was "on the verge . . . of ruin, by reason of prosperity"!

Political alignments in Congress began to assume a definite form in 1792. In March, for the first time, Jefferson spoke of "the heats and tumults of conflicting parties" and introduced the pronouns "we" and "they" into his political correspondence. Madison was still the leader of the "republican interest," but Hamilton and company spread suspicions of the Secretary of State. "Mr. Jefferson," Wolcott reported, "appears to have shown rather too much of a disposition to cultivate vulgar prejudices; accordingly he will become popular in ale houses, and will do much mischief to his country by exciting apprehensions that the government will operate unfavorably." A pamphlet appeared, the first in a long line of diatribes, assailing Jefferson's character and politics. (He consoled himself that he had been spared obloquy for so long, and said that its author did not half so much wish for his retirement as he did.) The press beat the drums of partisanship. The *National Gazette*, after a mild beginning, showed its true colors early in March with a violent attack on the funding system. The rival *Gazette of the United States* screamed "mad dogs," "audacious scribblers," "propagators of calumny," exhausting the vocabulary of political invective.

After Congress adjourned in May, Hamilton unbosomed himself to a friendly Virginian, Edward Carrington. His long letter on the state of the parties, afterwards reiterated in Fenno's *Gazette*, voiced opinions of Jefferson and Madison that would soon become stereotyped in Federalist discourse. As the *locus classicus* of the Federalist image of Jefferson, the epistle to Carrington has immense importance. Hamilton regarded Jefferson as the evil genius of the Virginians' partnership—a partnership in faction "subversive of the principles of government and dangerous to the Union, peace, and happiness of the country." About Madison he was frankly puzzled. Whether his apostacy was the result of Jefferson's influence or the seductions of Virginia politics, Hamilton did not know; but he was sure the older man exerted a strange hypnotic power over the younger, showed a deeper hostility to sound government, and was the more dangerous foe. Jefferson was "an avowed enemy of the funded debt," anxious for any crisis (the recent panic, for instance) that might embarrass the national credit and overturn Hamilton and funding together. Jefferson, with his friend, constantly worked for commercial warfare against Britain; if left to themselves the Virginians would embroil the United States in open war within six months. "They have a womanish attachment to France and a womanish resentment against Great Britain." Indeed, France was at the root of Jefferson's opposition. "In France, he saw government only on the side of its abuses. He drank freely of the French philosophy in religion, in science, in politics. He came from France in the moment of a fermentation, which he had a share in exciting, and in the passions and feelings of which he shared both from temperament and situation." In this intoxicated state, he could not understand the "imbecilities" of government that had occasioned the Constitution, and toward it he entertained "many doubts and reserves." The controversy on the succession bill proved, said the New Yorker, "that Mr. Jefferson aims with ardent desire at the Presidential chair." To realize this ambition the government must be rendered odious, to which nothing could prove more effectual than the subversion of its main source of energy, the Treasury. As yet the enemies of government had enjoyed no success, but failure after failure made them desperate and willing to hazard everything for power. The danger to republican government, Hamilton asserted, came not from men who, like himself, gave it order and dignity, but from political adventurers who thrived on popular fears and faction and anarchy. Jefferson was at the head of the tribe. "I read him upon the whole thus: 'A man of profound ambition and violent passions.' "

The truth or falsity of Hamilton's opinion is of less importance than the fact that he and a growing number of his followers seemed to believe it. Hamilton's doctrine on the Secretary of State not only expressed the basic assumptions of a party but set up an anti-hero for Federalist vilification. William L. Smith, a leading Treasury spokesman in the House of Representatives, provided the first outright example in *The Politicks and Views of a Certain Party Displayed*. The whole complexion of American affairs changed, Smith argued in this anonymous pamphlet, when Jefferson returned from France. Then a system was formed "as wicked, profligate and malevolent as ever disgraced the most corrupt and abandoned government." Its object: to make Thomas Jefferson President of the United States. Adams was easily cornered and demolished as a serious rival, but against Hamilton's splendid qualifications, Smith asked, what had Jefferson to offer? Charm of conversation, military exploits at Monticello, the discovery that the blacks secrete less from the kidneys, the invention of the wirligig chair—these satirical touches left indelible marks on the public image of Jefferson. Lacking legitimate claims on the public, Jefferson resorted to trickery and deception. He raised a "pretended outcry against Monarchy and Aristocracy," took on a "ridiculous affectation of simplicity," and

465

built up a "monstrous system of detraction" in order to persuade the people they were oppressed by the Secretary of Treasury, from whom he would rescue them. As pamphlet and newspaper warfare raged in 1792, Jefferson found himself brought forward—less by his friends than by his enemies—as the "generalissimo" of a political party on which he meant to mount his own ambitions at the hazard of government itself. His fate was sealed in July when Hamilton, alarmed by the whirlwind of criticism, threw himself headfirst into the public prints against his arch rival. Thereafter, willing or no, Jefferson could not escape the leadership role thrust upon him.

It was not a role he coveted in 1792. From the first of the year his thoughts were on retirement, and the heats of politics only increased his longing for the tranquil shades of Monticello. Broaching the subject to Washington at the end of February, he said he was "heartily tired" of the office he had entered reluctantly and with a resolution to quit at the earliest opportunity. When the President, some months before, dropped the hint of his intention to retire at the end of his term, Jefferson decided "to make that the epoch of my own retirement." Washington was distressed to hear this. While reasons obliged him to retire, his example, if followed by the department heads, would send a shock through the public. He alluded painfully to "symptoms of dissatisfaction" that had lately shown themselves. Jefferson seized the opening to press his political views on the President. Treasury was the cause of these discontents, he said. A system had been contrived "for withdrawing our citizens from the pursuits of commerce, manufactures, buildings, and other branches of useful industry, to occupy themselves and their capital in a species of gambling, destructive of morality, and which had introduced its poison into the government itself." It was a fact, he continued, that congressmen "had feathered their nests with papers, had then voted for the laws, and constantly since lent all the energy of their talents, and instrumentality of their offices, to the establishment and enlargement of this system; that they had chained it about our necks for a great length of time, and in order to keep the game in their hands had, from time to time, aided in making such legislative contructions of the constitution, as made it a very different thing from what the people thought they had submitted to . . . ." Washington listened but held his political reserve. He shrank from recognizing the rift between the two secretaries. They were equally necessary to his conception of a government without parties. The resignaton of either one would tend to force a partisan character on the administration and unleash the opposition. With his Olympian conception of leadership, founded in loyalty to himself as the point of harmony and union, Washington seemed not to understand that the differences between the two secretaries went to the root of principle and, accordingly, were irreconcilable.

As the rift deepened, and without relenting in his decision to retire, Jefferson appealed to the President to stand for re-election. The public mind, comparatively calm in February, could not now, in May, endure the shock of Washington's withdrawal. Confidence in the government had slipped dangerously. Jefferson hastily summarized the causes of discontent—debt, excise, banks, panic, corruption of the legislature—hackneyed in the press. It was the belief of the "republican party," he wrote, that Hamilton's measures aimed at "a change from the present republican form of government to that of a monarchy, of which the English constitution is to be the model." The calamitous course might be reversed in the Third Congress, soon to be elected on a more numerous basis of representation by a people at least partially alerted to the issues. Nothing ensured this happy outcome, however; and since the political division in the country tended to run along geographical lines, disunion was a real danger. When we consider, Jefferson said, that most of the original opposition to the Constitution lay in the southern states; that the leading measures have favored northern interests; that the "monarchical federalists" have adopted the very constructions of the Constitution they had renounced in championing it against violent Anti-Federalists; "that the republican federalists who espoused the same government for its intrinsic merits, are disarmed of their weapons; that which they denied as prophesy, having now become true history, who can be sure that these things may not proselyte the small number which was wanting to place the number on the other side?" And this, Jefferson declared to his chief, "is the event at which I tremble, and to prevent which I consider your continuing at the head of affairs as of the last importance." In the final analysis, then, he feared the "monarchical federalists" would produce a reaction to Anti-Federalism, driving the country backwards into an-

467

archy, violence, and disunion. It could not occur so long as Washington was at the helm. "North and South will hang together if they have you to hang on," Jefferson concluded his impassioned appeal.

The question of retirement or re-election, bristling with political thorns, was almost more than Washington could endure. On July 10, just a day before his summer's retreat to Mount Vernon, he took up the subject where Jefferson's letter had left it. After recurring to the reasons he had offered for retirement—ardent desire, physical disability, professions honorably made to his countrymen—he said Jefferson's political fears were greatly exaggerated. He did not believe there were monarchical designs on the government. He was disturbed, on the other hand, by the efforts of opposition newspapers, particularly Freneau's, to stir up discontent. If monarchy came to the United States it would come as a sequel to anarchy and discord, which the newspaper agitation tended to produce. The attacks on his administration were attacks on him, and he resented them. But he doubted that the discontents reached much beyond Philadelphia; so far as he had been able to observe, as on his travels to and from the Potomac, the people were calm and happy. In reply Jefferson went over the ground he had covered before. It was well known, he said, that the funding measures had been carried by representatives and senators personally interested in their passage. With the assistance of Madison and Beckley, perhaps others, he had been compiling the names of this "corrupt squadron," but presumably he did not show the list to Washington, who kept a stony silence on the point. The President defended assumption, however. Jefferson, with most Republicans, argued that the state debts would have been more fairly, cheaply, and easily discharged by the state governments themselves, while the Treasury plan so far inflated the national debt as to make it virtually permanent and to call forth the odious excise. A few stockjobbers grew rich on the taxes extracted from the people. He had prepared a table showing the ratio of public debt to annual revenue for several European countries in given years, from which he concluded, with a good deal of guesswork, "that tho' the youngest nation in the world we are the most indebted nation also." If he showed these figures to the President they made no impression. Finding him decided on the fiscal system, Jefferson refrained from useless argument. Three days later, on July 13, he purchased fiddle strings and muslin, paid his servants, received 1500 half-dimes of the new coinage, and, Maria in tow, followed the President's tracks for Virginia, this time for two leisurely months at Monticello.

But there was no vacation from politics in the summer of 1792. Charge and countercharge, each more reckless than the last, issued from the Philadelphia gazettes, which usually arrived at Jefferson's door in eight days, thanks to the cross-post from Richmond recently opened though his efforts. By dramatizing the divisions within the government, newspapers the country over helped to give partisan tone and character to the electoral campaigns then going on. Jefferson took no part in them. Asked to endorse his old friend Charles Clay, a candidate for Congress, he politely but firmly declined on the personal rule "never to intermeddle with elections of the people." He kept a tight rein on his partisan feelings. Some weeks before he left Philadelphia the heated New York gubernatorial contest between Governor Clinton and John Jay ended in a disputed election. Although "Clintonians" and "Jayites" were practically synonymous with "Republicans" and "Federalists" in New York, Jefferson thought, on the merits of the case, Clinton should decline an ignoble victory. The Governor's reputation as an Anti-Federalist and political manipulator troubled Jefferson. "I really apprehend," he told Madison, "that the cause of republicanism will suffer and its votaries be thrown into schism by embarking it in support of this man, and for what? To draw over the antifederalists who are not numerous enough to be worth drawing over." Though he remained on the sidelines, leaving the leadership to Madison, Jefferson was constantly solicitous for the "cause of republicanism."

Early in August the post brought news of a turn in the political warfare at Philadelphia. Fenno's *Gazette* had taken the offensive and trained its big guns on the Secretary of State. After two opening salvoes announcing that Freneau, the vilifier of the government, was also its hireling, the *Gazette* blasted Jefferson as the author of this wicked experiment, the head of a party, and the secret disturber of the public peace. "Can he reconcile it to his own personal dignity and the principles of probity to hold an office under [the government] and employ the means of official influence in opposition?" The assailant signed himself "An American." Jefferson and his friends surmised from "the style, matter . . . [and] venom of the pieces" he was Hamilton. Searching for a means to strike back at his critics, Hamilton had learned of Jefferson's association with Freneau in the founding of the *National Gazette*. It suited his purpose exactly. With his rare polemical gifts, Hamilton exploited its hints of venality, subversion, and abuse of trust, in the process crediting Jefferson with a larger part in the newspaper's establishment than was his due, with an editorial influence he never had, and a party leadership he neither coveted nor possessed. Freneau was crippled but far from beaten. If government patronage was the issue, he threw back at his accusers, the pittance he received as translator clerk was not to be compared with Fenno's income as printer for the Treasury and the Senate. Before the mayor of Philadelphia, Freneau signed an affidavit swearing that Jefferson had "at no time urged, advised, or influenced" his establishment of the newspaper or "ever, directly or indirectly, written, dictated or composed for it." Hamilton, still under cover of "An American," denounced the statement as equivocal and surreptitiously sent to New York for counter-affidavits.

Meanwhile, at Monticello, Jefferson held council with his Virginia confederates, Madison, Monroe, and Randolph, on this startling turn of affairs. The boldness of Hamilton's attack amazed them. The *National Gazette* was fair game, of course, and Freneau's onslaught had angered Hamilton. But it was another thing for a minister to vent cabinet dissensions out-of-doors and make a public target of the Secretary of State. Hamilton scored heavily under a crowd of disguises. Jefferson kept a dignified silence, while his friends put their pens to work, not only in Philadelphia but in New York, Boston, and other places. Hamilton soon had his hands full, trading blows with more scribbling foes than he could count, yet never meeting the one foe who really mattered. Jefferson's refusal to enter the field of combat infuriated Hamilton. Seated on his lofty perch, wrapped in the mantle of philosophy, primping himself on his official dignity—how could Jefferson be revealed for what he was, "the heart and soul of faction," "the intriguing incendiary," "involved in all the obscurity of political mystery and deception"! Jefferson was sly, devious, inscrutable—a Machiavellian democrat. Hamilton could neither draw him out nor trace his tracks. Conclusive evidence incriminating Jefferson in the affair of the *National Gazette* eluded him; and as he busily passed from one journalistic mask to another (Catullus, Scourge, Caesar) Hamilton brandished new accusations. Jefferson had opposed the adoption of the Constitution—a charge Madison quickly refuted by the publication of edited extracts from the accused's letters to him from Paris. Hamilton, alias "Catullus," stamped "treachery" on Jefferson's proposal of 1786 to transfer the French debt to Holland, labeling it a scheme to swindle Dutch creditors for the enrichment of the French treasury. Since the charge was supported by a passage quoted from Jefferson's letter to the Board of Treasury, it could not be treated as windy invective. But Jefferson at once produced his copy of the letter in question (he suspected Duer, secretary of the old board, of putting Hamilton on to the original) which showed that the accuser had doctored the extract passed off as genuine and cleverly twisted the meaning of Jefferson's proposal. If it was treacherous to seek the removal of a source of friction with France, while at the same time pledging to preserve inviolate the faith of the United States to all creditors, then John Adams, who endorsed Jefferson's plan, shared the infamy.

While the battle of the gazettes raged, Washington fussed at Mount Vernon to bring his quarreling secretaries to heel. Like an overindulgent parent, he found it difficult, indeed impossible, to tighten reins of authority so long slackened. His last standoffish interview with Jefferson suggested the problem was graver than he had imagined. No doubt he reflected about it, and pondered, too, Jefferson's letter of May 23; for at the end of July Washington sent to Hamilton a list of twenty-one charges made against him by "sensible and moderate men," charges, in fact, drawn almost verbatim from Jefferson's letter. Hamilton replied at length on August 18. His answers repeated for the most part what he had previously written in public defense of the funding system. On some particulars, for instance the refutation of the naïve idea that bank bills banished specie, Hamilton was clearly right. But since most of the charges turned on questions of opinion and judgment, it was not a case in which one side could be proven right and the other wrong. Hamilton denied that the debt had been "artificially" created, that the country was over-taxed, the excise odious, the Constitution violated —none of these answers touched the real grounds of Jefferson's complaint. In the New Yorker's opinion, speculation in federal securities was beneficial to the mass of citizens since the stock, operating as capital, "promotes among them industry, by furnishing a larger field of employment." The corruption charge was "malignant and false": Hamilton knew of no stockjobbers and paper-dealers in Congress, though many members owned securities. Clearly the question of what constituted improper influence on legislators, or what today would be called "conflict of interest," took a different shape in Hamilton's mind than in Jefferson's; and while the former counted the selfish interests of men a legitimate, indeed an essential instrument of legislation, his rival squeamishly recoiled from this vicious principle. Panderers to the vices of the people were "the true artificers of monarchy," said Hamilton, reiterating the time-worn conservative opinion of democracy. He flatly denied the holding of "monarchical opinions" or their advocacy in the Constitutional Convention. If the institution of hereditary kingship and nobility was the issue, the denial carried conviction; but, of course, the nub of the charge so roundly stated for political convenience lay against the tendency of Hamilton's system to transform the "pure" republican government of the Constitution into something approaching the cherished English model. And on this ground Jefferson and his friends found Hamilton's opinions, measures, and administrative conduct more English than American. The Secretary concluded his long essay with several observations on the alleged inequities of funding in the sectional balance. Even if the benefits lay predominantly in the northern scale, which he doubted, it was no argument against the policy. National credit had to be established regardless of other considerations; the government could not be blamed if forces of a political and economic character caused the benefits to flow more to one section than to another. The entire defense was calculated to appeal to the President. He shared Hamilton's national outlook and, from long acquaintance, could not doubt his loyalty to the Constitution. Moreover, the administration and the country were too far committed to Hamilton's measures for the President seriously to question their merits.

Washington had probably just received Hamilton's letter when, on August 23, he wrote to Jefferson. After alluding to fresh reports of Spanish and British intrigues on the frontiers, he again appealed for moderation and conciliation in his official family. "How unfortunate, and how much is it to be regretted then, that whilst we are encompassed on all sides with avowed enemies and insidious friends, that internal dissensions should be harrowing and tearing our vitals." Without more charity and forbearance, especially on measures fairly decided, he did not see how the government could go on. "And . . . the fairest prospect of happiness and prosperity that was ever presented to man, will be lost, perhaps forever!" Washington addressed a similar plea to Hamilton. Neither of the wayward ministers, despite nods of assent to the patriarch's wisdom, showed a disposition to reform.

Again, but with the added vexation of the journalistic outrage in Philadelphia, Jefferson went over the now familiar ground with the President. Hamilton's system, he repeated, "flowed from principles adverse to liberty, and was calculated to undermine and demolish the republic, by creating an influence of his department over the members of the legislature." Although the danger justified vigorous opposition from him, he had limited himself to private expressions of dissent, neither meddling in legislation (except when "duped" by Hamilton in 1790) nor intriguing to defeat measures he disapproved. He invited the President to compare this example of forbearance with the aggressions against him—in Congress, in the press, in the affairs of his own department. The last of these, touching the administrative rivalry between the two men, was obscured by the pyrotechnics of the gazettes. The public knew little of the intramural issue, and Washington seemed insensitive to it. But it rankled Jefferson, not because his standard of official propriety was higher than Hamilton's, though it was, not primarily because he resented the greater power and influence of the Treasury Department, though he did, but because Hamilton subverted his policy in foreign affairs, "my system," which was founded on the differential treatment of Britain and France. Supposing the President had always concurred in this system, Jefferson thought he ought to know that Hamilton's cabalistic influence forced the country into one exactly the reverse, resulting in the French stab at our navigation and continued British intransigence. On whichever ground Hamilton was judged, his own policies or his opposition to Jefferson's, he was the aggressor. The *National Gazette* episode offered further proof, Jefferson said. He explained his relations with the newspaper, hiding nothing material, praised Freneau as a "man of genius" who merited the modest patronage he had received, acclaimed the freedom of the press, and said the virtues or the faults of Freneau's gazette did not concern him. "He and Fenno are rivals for the public favor. The one courts them by flattery, the other by censure . . . . But is not the dignity, and even the decency of government committed," he asked, "when one of its principal ministers enlists himself as an anonymous writer or paragraphist for either of them?" As to the future, he again stated his determination to retire in March of the next year. "I look to that period with the longing of a wave worn mariner, who has at length the land in view, and shall count the days and hours which still lies between me and it." Meanwhile, he would mind his business, only reserving the right to appeal to his countrymen when he dropped anchor. "I will not suffer my retirement to be clouded by the slanders of a man whose history, from the moment history can stoop to notice him, is a tissue of machinations against the liberty of the country which has not only received and given him bread, but heaped honors on his head." There spoke the conceit of the Virginia aristocrat against the arrogant upstart!

Jefferson lingered at Monticello through most of September. There were the usual cares of family and estate. With habitual optimism he had overestimated the ability of his plantations to meet the scheduled installments on his debt. He sold lands occasionally, and was finally pushed to the awful extremity of selling several families of slaves. (Not wishing to have his name linked publicly with a transaction of this kind, he arranged to have the slaves sold at some distance from their Bedford plantation.) At the same time, looking forward to his retirement, he inaugurated elaborate improvements at Monticello. He had an infant grandson now, Thomas Jefferson Randolph; and little Anne, "with whom even Socrates might ride on a stick without being ridiculous," was the joy of his heart. Her illness, and the new arrival, detained him at Monticello longer than he had expected. On the road at last with Polly, he stopped at Gunston Hall to talk with George Mason, who told him anecdotes of the Constitutional Convention well suited to Jefferson's politics. Hamilton, declared Mason, had "done us more injury than Great Britain and all her fleets and armies." The old Roman died not long after—

Jefferson would miss him. Mount Vernon was virtually next door. Before breakfast the next morning, scarcely time to readjust his political senses, Jefferson sat down with Washington for a long talk.

The two Virginians were more deeply divided than they realized, but neither had difficulty appreciating the yearning of the other for retirement. Washington nevertheless confessed his willingness to make a further sacrifice to the public if necessary. Jefferson assured him "there was but one voice" on this point. As for himself, he would not recede from the decision he had made. After expressing surprise at the extent of the division within the administration, Washington said he wished to put an end to it. As Jefferson reported the conversation, "he thought it important to preserve the check of my opinions . . . in order to keep things in their proper channel, and to prevent them from going too far." Clearly, he did not think things had already gone too far. Clearly, his faith in Hamilton had not been shaken. Jefferson again tried to open his eyes to ministerial domination, corruption of the legislature, and the pantings after monarchy. All to no avail. "He finished by another exhortion to me not to decide too positively on retirement, and here we were called to breakfast."

The discussion was never resumed. The problems it addressed were abandoned to the winds of politics. Back in Philadelphia, Jefferson found the political scene more oppressive than ever. "Party animosities have raised a wall of separation between those who differ in political sentiments," he noted. Old friends, finding themselves partisan foes, crossed the street to avoid unpleasant encounters. Congress reconvened early in November. The less done in this "lame-duck" session the better in Jefferson's opinion, for the Republicans had scored impressively in the recent elections. "I think we may consider the tide of this government as now at the fullest," he wrote to Pinckney in London, "and that it will, from the commencement of the next session of Congress, retire and subside into the true principles of the Constitution." Jefferson saw encouraging signs in, among other things, the House defeat of a Federalist motion to admit department heads into its proceedings, thus crippling Hamilton's ambition to become a kind of prime minister. But the Virginia Republicans spurned Fabian tactics looking to reinforcements in the Third Congress, and impatiently launched a campaign to drive

Hamilton from the government. "Virginia moves in a solid column, and the discipline of the party is as severe as the Prussian," Ames remarked. Doubting the time was right, Jefferson nevertheless cheered the campaign from the rear. He scribbled the objectives on a scrap of paper: divide Treasury (between customs and internal revenue), abolish the Bank, repeal the excise, lower the impost, repeal the irredeemable clause in government securities, place government transactions on a hard cash basis, exclude paper-holders from Congress, and condemn a recent Treasury report. As the campaign went shakily forward in Congress, Jefferson resumed his fencing with Hamilton in the cabinet, and also in the commission on the sinking fund, which he wished to convert from a fund employed to keep securities aloft to one that actually sank the debt.

All the while he was preparing to leave office in March. He gave up the lease on his house and began to pack his furniture. Then, near the end of January, he decided to stay on. "It happened unfortunately," he explained to his son-in-law, "that the attack made on me in the newspapers came out soon after I began to speak freely and publicly of my purpose to retire this spring, and from the modes of publication, the public were possessed of the former sooner than of the latter: and I find that as well those who are my friends, as those who are not, putting the two things together as cause and effect, conceived I was driven from my office either from want of firmness or perhaps fear of investigation." How long he would continue he did not know; it would depend on those who had troubled the political waters. "When they suffer them to get calm, I will go into port." In short, wishing to avoid any repetition of the mistake he had made in 1781, he would not retire under circumstances likely to injure his reputation or the Republican cause. But why at the eleventh hour did this cloud suddenly appear so much larger than before? In fact, it was not. Hamilton, far more than Jefferson, was under attack in January. He faced investigation by Congress; Republican leaders had uncovered (and suppressed for the present) a juicy scandal in his private life; and on the very day Jefferson wrote to Randolph of the change of plans, the Senate, with an assist from the President, gave Hamilton a stinging defeat on the bill to extend funding to the small unassumed portion of the state debts. Could it be that Jefferson was moved by these brightening prospects? Or by the flattering appeals of Republican scribes, who called him "the colossus of liberty"? Philadelphia had become a ghastly inferno, he insisted; yet he found it much too interesting to leave. The demon of politics possessed him even as he yearned for retirement.

That demon drove him hard in the waning days of the Second Congress. Ignoring his earlier counsels of caution and delay, as well as his boasted standards of official propriety, Jefferson secretly joined the Virginia column in its final maneuver to discredit Hamilton. The move took the form of a series of resolutions introduced in the House by William B. Giles, a truculent young Virginian, whose "frothy manners," fondness for drink, and tendency to discourse on "canvas-back ducks, ham and chickens, old Madeira, and the glories of the Ancient Dominion" seemed not to inhibit his talents as a legislative pugilist, which had caused Madison to bring him forward as the Republican champion in the assault on the Secretary of Treasury. Giles's motives were partisan, of course, but they were not unworthy. Hamilton managed the Treasury as a private domain. A million dollars was shuffled between two continents; funds were manipulated at convenience; accounts with the Bank were veiled in obscurity. The President did not pretend to understand these intricate operations; but congressmen opposed to Hamilton's fiscal system, suspicious of his motives, baffled by his methods, demanded a close accounting from the high-handed minister. In a feat of labor his friends described as herculean, Hamilton filed a series of reports vindicating his fiscal management. The Virginians were still not satisifed. Many questions remained unanswered, and besides it would not do to leave Hamilton in command of the field.

Entering the Virginia councils at this point, Jefferson drafted a set of resolutions that indicted Hamilton's conduct and declared him unworthy of his office. It was this indictment that formed the basis of Giles's resolutions—the second set—of February 27. Even Giles could not go all the way with Jefferson. Stripped of the latter's accusations of speculative malice and fraud, the final resolutions arraigned Hamilton for technical violations of the appropriation laws, unwarranted assumption of power in fiscal management, and contempt of Congress. There were grounds for these charges, but the Republicans were drubbed on every count. Jefferson attributed the defeat to the Hamiltonian phalanx of stockjobbers, Bank directors, and devoted partisans, aided and abetted by faint-hearted Republicans. Since the result was predictable on his own reckoning, he had, in fact, committed a grave political blunder. He never acknowledged any connection with the ill-fated resolutions. The Federalists were sure he was the culprit, of course, and from the basest motives. To himself and his political intimates he justified the resolutions, not because he expected them to succeed, but because their rejection would educate the public in "the desperate and abandoned dispositions with which their affairs were conducted." If this was political wisdom, it was a curiously perverse kind. Vindicated at the hands of Congress, Hamilton appeared to occupy an impregnable position at the end of Washington's first term.

The quarrel between Jefferson and Hamilton, after threatening to wreck the administration, ended in perpetuating it for an uncertain term. Washington never offered himself for re-election, but in view of partisan dissensions his withdrawal was unthinkable, and he silently bowed to the inevitable. Jefferson and Hamilton stayed in uneasy harness. The President was much relieved and spoke optimistically of the "coalition" between the two ministers. Jefferson sought to disabuse him of this notion. Neither he nor Hamilton would yield his system and principles to the other. Pulling in different directions, each assured of the other's enmity, each accusing the other of designs to subvert the government—Jefferson to anarchy, Hamilton to monarchy—it was little short of miraculous they were kept in harness at all.

The controversy between them had yet to run its course. Beginning as an internal administrative conflict, associated with competing congressional interests and national ideologies, it assumed a much larger importance when it penetrated the public mind and became the catalyst of party conflict. Where the advantage lay in 1793, it was not easy to say. Hamilton had given direction to the government, aligned it with powerful interests, and the President, as much as he respected the Secretary of State, was committed to Treasury policies. Jefferson began to wonder if perhaps he, the President, had not become Hamilton's captive. On the other hand, for all his influence in Congress and with the executive, Hamilton had revealed himself to be a bungling political artist. The laurels of journalistic combat were frail indeed; they did not win elections, and far from making Jefferson an enemy in the eyes of the American public, Hamilton, like a wayward press agent, built up his rival as the friend and champion of the people. Against the tide of democratic opinion, rising like a force fated in nature, Hamilton was helpless. Power was in the people, in the wholesome energies of free individuals, not in the machinery of government. Forty years later Alexis de Tocqueville wrote of the American democracy: "the grandeur is not in what the public administration does, but in what is done outside it or without it." Jefferson understood this genius of democracy, Hamilton never.

The Ordeal of Neutrality

The year 1793 made its entrance to roars of acclaim for the victorious armies of revolutionary France. After a most disturbing appearance, the "conspiracy of kings" marshaled in the invading forces of the Duke of Brunswick had been turned back, and the newly proclaimed republic took the offensive, vowing never to rest until the fires of "liberty, equality and fraternity" set the whole of Europe ablaze. Jubilation swept the country. John Adams counted twenty-two "grand civic festivals," fifty-one of a lesser order, and 193 public dinners, all in celebration of the French victories. "I believe from my soul there have been more cannon fired here . . . than the French fired in achieving them." Men cropped their hair, stuck the tricolor cockade in their hats, and in deference to all that was French, made their bows to "Citizen" and "Citess." *Yankee Doodle* and the *Ça Ira* blended in song. As if to exemplify the sublimity of republican brotherhood spanning the Atlantic, the celebrated French astronaut Jean Pierre Blanchard ascended to the heavens, gallantly waving the Tricolor and the Stars and Stripes, while thousands cheered in Philadelphia.

Jefferson invested five dollars in Blanchard's feat. No doubt he witnessed it with the rest of the populace, and shared too in the rejoicing for the happy turn of affairs in Europe. The turn in his own affairs—the decision to continue in office—may have been influenced by European events. Persuaded that the republican cause in America

479

was bound up with the fortunes of the French Revolution, that success or failure abroad would tip the political scales at home, Jefferson could not view those events with cool detachment. Reports came to him in the winter months of Gouverneur Morris's open hostility to the new republican government, whose ministers he cursed as "a set of damned rascals," and, more surprising, of Short's rancor against the extremists in France. Detecting the same sentiments in Short's letters, Jefferson pointedly censured his friend and defended the course of radicalism on what amounted to a plea of revolutionary necessity. The crimes against implacable royalty, while deplorable, were as nothing compared with the preservation of the Revolution. "The liberty of the whole earth was depending on the issue of the contest, and was ever such a prize won with so little innocent blood? My own affections have been deeply wounded by some of the martyrs to this cause," Jefferson said, alluding to the many friends he and Short numbered among its victims, "but rather than it should have failed, I would have seen half the earth desolated. Were there but an Adam and an Eve left in every country, and left free, it would be better than as it now is." Such were the sentiments, Jefferson informed the envoy, of 99 of every 100 Americans. This was hyperbole, of course, and Jefferson's brutally frank declaration conveys the misleading image of an *enragé;* but republican fevers soared in 1793, and so did Jefferson's.

February brought news of the King's execution. "Louis Capet has lost his caput" was the hardy jest of the Republican press. Jefferson shed no tears for Louis. Many Americans did, however. The ladies of Philadelphia—the ladies especially—"are open-mouthed against the murderers of a sovereign," Jefferson reported. Leading Federalists no longer concealed their enmity to the French Revolution. Despite polemical skirmishes, like the one between Jefferson and Adams two years before, the Revolution had not been a leading issue in American politics. Public opinion generally supported it, while opponents generally kept their opinions to themselves. With the execution of the King, reaction set in, and it rapidly acquired political character when France declared war on Great Britain. Contrary dispositions toward these powers were woven into the texture of American politics. Latent hostility to revolutionary democracy burst forth in the Federalist ranks as ties of affection and interest with the old country were threatened. But the mass of Americans hated and feared Britain, remembered France as a gallant ally, applauded her revolution as an extension of their own, and coupled every patriotic feeling to her beleagured cause. Jefferson recognized the political implications of this fact. It was a godsend to the Republicans. He was soon writing to Monroe: "The war has kindled and brought forward the two parties with an ardour which our own interests merely, could never excite." War and revolutionary frenzy gave the Republicans the popular initiative they had failed to gain in their opposition to Hamiltonian measures. The cause of France became "the touchstone," Republicans said, for trying the principles of men. But it was a risky game, playing politics with these combustible materials. Jefferson, as Secretary of State, endeavored to curb his partisan feelings and to meet his responsibility to the national interest. Between his roles as revolutionary ideologue and minister of state, he was caught in a cruel dilemma. While he could not resolve the dilemma, he managed it magnificently, and in the face of formidable trials emerged from the ordeal in statesman-like triumph.

Near the end of March a vessel from Lisbon brought first reports of the Anglo-French war. War had been freely predicted for two months past, even before Louis's death on the guillotine, as the certain outcome of Britain's blockade of the French coast. Jefferson kept the President informed at Mount Vernon, and when the reports were later confirmed, urged "that we take every justifiable measure for preserving our neutrality, and at the same time to provide [to the belligerents] those necessaries for war which must be brought across the Atlantic." The desire for peace and profit was as universal as it was ardent; but to realize it, to turn the European crisis to American account in all possible ways, was a task beset with difficulties. If neutrality was the policy, the French alliance might prove embarrassing. France had appointed a new minister to the United States, a young Girondin zealot, Edmond Charles Genêt, whose arrival was expected momentarily. "He has . . . more of genius than of ability," Morris had written of Genêt, "and you will see in him at first blush the manner and look of an upstart." Upstart indeed! But Jefferson cheered Genêt's coming. Diplomatic contact with France had virtually ceased. Ternant, on hearing of the King's death, had gone into "deep mourning" and discontinued his visits to the Secretary of State. Morris was, unofficially, *persona non grata* to the French republic. Washington felt enough concern for this situation to ask Jefferson to go to Paris. He would not hear of it and pointed out to the President that Genêt's coming would shift the scene of diplomacy to Philadelphia. By this time, in February, he had learned that Genêt's instructions were very cordial to the United States.

Washington hurried back to the capital. On April 19 the cabinet met at his house. Two basic questions were before the executive. In what manner, if at all, should Genêt be received? And how should the President act to maintain American neutrality? Always the aggressor, Hamilton had prepared the agenda, though it was copied in Washington's hand. Jefferson surmised the fact and called the paper merely a skeleton on which to hang the argument "that our treaty with France is void." Hamilton revived the issue of the legitimacy of the French government and, inferentially, of American commitments under the alliance of 1778, an issue Jefferson had supposed settled and laid to rest several months earlier. When the National Convention assembled after the fall of the monarchy, Jefferson took the position that this body expressed the will of the nation, and therefore ought to be recognized as the legitimate government of France. "We certainly cannot deny to other nations that principle whereon our government is founded," asserted the author of the Declaration of Independence, "that every nation has a right to change these forms of its own will; and externally to transact business with other nations through whatever organ it chooses, whether that be a King, Convention, Assembly, Committee, President, or whatever it be. The only thing essential is the will of the nation." The principle was novel, like the republic from which it sprang. Hamilton opposed it but Washington assented. Appropriate instructions went out to American embassies; payments on the French debt (briefly suspended) were resumed; and Morris was ordered to present his credentials to the French republic. In sum, this *recognition* principle, "the will of the nation substantially declared"—an enduring legacy to American government—was already operative when Hamilton used the impending arrival of the French minister as the excuse for reviving the question.

Hamilton saw a dangerous chain of troubles in the simple act of receiving Genêt. Unless pointedly qualified, the act was tantamount to recognition of the French republic; recognition admitted the continuing force of the treaties of 1778; these treaties contained articles incompatible with American neutrality, thus courting British displeasure. Under the Treaty of Alliance the United States was pledged to defend the French West Indies, while under the companion Treaty of Commerce French armed vessels were permitted to come and go freely in American ports—privileges denied to France's enemies. Anxious to avoid war with Britain at all costs, doubting the legitimacy or the virtue or the permanence of the French republic, regarding the treaties as contracts with a deposed sovereign, Hamilton thought they should be declared void, though he was willing to settle for their suspension.

Jefferson stood by the treaties, of course, including the unfettered recognition of Genêt and his government. Opinion was divided in the cabinet; the question was adjourned, and the officers, excepting Knox, turned in written opinions. Jefferson's closely reasoned argument displayed his mastery of the law of nations, his keen sense of the demands and the limits of responsibility in foreign relations, and his deep conviction that American conduct toward other nations should be founded on its own first principles. A treaty is made between nations, not between their governments, which nations may change as they please without impairment of obligations. The duties between nations are the same as between individuals. They may be excused from solemn compacts only when their performance becomes impossible or self-destructive, Jefferson said. Thus far the dangers from the alliance were imaginary. *If* affairs in France issued in "rawhead and bloody bones," *if* the West Indies guarantee threatened to engage us in war, then the United States might place its own survival above treaty obligations. Britain could not fairly complain of Article XVII's granting privileges to the belligerent vessels of France; for under the terms of the Anglo-French commercial accord of 1786 Britain granted the same privileges to the French in the case of war with the United States. Under Article XXII of the Franco-American treaty, the enemies of the former could not fit out privateers or sell prizes in the ports of the latter; but no danger was apprehended from this provision, since it did not prevent the United States from making a similar denial to France, as ought to be done. Jefferson then appealed to the leading authorities on international law (Grotius, Puffendorf, Wolf, and Vattel), ranging the pertinent passages from their works in four parallel columns. At least three of these authorities agreed on the sanctity of treaties regardless of changes in the form of government; Vattel allowed for renunciation when such a change rendered an alliance "useless, dangerous, or disagreeable," supposing, however, that the change in question was to a form of government which the other party disapproved, a supposition Hamilton had conveniently overlooked in citing this "ill understood scrap" of Vattel. It could hardly be argued, Jefferson thought, that an alliance contracted with a despotic France became "useless, dangerous, or disagreeable" when France passed into a republic. In the circumstances American neutrality would be breached, not by adherence to the treaty, but by renunciation or suspension. "An injured friend is the bitterest of foes," Jefferson warned. It was the height of folly to give France cause for war upon the American republic. Let the alliance stand, he pleaded. Washington's vote gave Jefferson the majority. Genêt would be received, the alliance maintained, trusting to events to keep them compatible with American neutrality.

But what should be done to secure that neutrality? Hamilton called for an immediate proclamation by the President. Jefferson objected so far as it would involve executive determination of a question belonging to the legislature. Viewing a declaration of neutrality as the negative side of a declaration of war, he thought the decision belonged to Congress. He had earlier supposed Congress should be summoned into special session, but on April 19, and for some time to come, he agreed with his colleagues in opposing this measure. He yielded on the question of an executive proclamation, with the understanding, however, that it simply declared the President's intention to keep the United States at peace pending action by Congress. The constitutional basis of Jefferson's position was clear. Yet he was not usually so scrupulous in his view of presidential powers. The real basis of his opposition to Hamilton's proposal lay elsewhere. He wished to keep the options open, the belligerents in suspense, and thereby force them, especially Britain, to "bid for our neutrality." Jefferson thought Britain would pay a price for neutrality both because of the contingencies of the French alliance and because of her wartime dependence on American commerce to supply her colonies, feed her soldiers, and carry her goods. France was similarly dependent, though to a lesser degree, being more of a land animal. So Jefferson favored a waiting game, withholding American neutrality as a weapon of bargain. He had a particular end in view: British recognition of "the broadest neutral privileges," such as those embodied in American treaties of commerce. Some of them—"free ships make free goods," for example—had found their way into the Anglo-French accord. The fact that these *modern* principles had not gone unrecognized even by Britain, historically their major opponent, together with the pressing exigencies of war, buoyed Jefferson's hopes of a diplomatic *coup* from American neutrality.

History remembers the presidential proclamation of April 22 as the Proclamation of Neutrality. It was at once so regarded. Yet in deference to Jefferson's wishes, the word "neutrality" did not appear in the text, and he afterwards denied that it was meant to commit the government to neutrality in the strict sense. The proclamation pledged "a conduct friendly and impartial" toward the belligerents, warned citizens against hostile acts, and denied the protection of the United States for offences against "the *modern* usage of nations." The adjective was Jefferson's. He at once advised Pinckney to inform the authorities in London of the American desire for neutrality "on condition that the rights of neutral nations are respected in us, as they have been settled in *modern* times." Jefferson meant to practice this idea. By *modern* he meant—what everyone meant—a narrow definition of contraband, the security of non-contraband cargo on neutral vessels, and a realistic rule of blockade. As the leading naval power, Britain had generally refused to recognize these principles. If Britain persisted, adhering to the older rules of the *consolato del mare*, Jefferson did not mean to go to war but rather, as he explained to Madison, to adopt stiff economic sanctions against the aggressor and thereby "introduce between nations another umpire than arms."

At the same time he voiced his approval of the proclamation in letters to Virginia. "I fear that a fair neutrality will prove a disagreeable pill to our friends," he wrote soothingly to Madison, "tho' necessary to keep out of the calamities of a war." And to Monroe: "I wish we may be able to repress the spirit of the people within the limits of a fair neutrality." A "fair neutrality" was one compatible with the French alliance, on the one hand, and with the neutral rights claimed by the Americans on the other. To Hamilton, of course, Jefferson's "fair" or "manly neutrality" squinted toward France. As it worked out, however, Jefferson felt that Britain got most of the benefits while yielding nothing in return. He bitterly resented this "sneaking" Anglophile neutrality managed by his rival. And so, finally surrendering to his friends' violent opinions against the proclamation, Jefferson also called it dishonorable, unconstitutional, and impolitic, and deplored its shameful appeasement of Britain. He was embarrassed to explain his part in the birth of this prodigy. To Madison he said its intent was good, aiming only at the preservation of peace with the belligerents; unfortunately, it had been badly drawn by the Attorney General. When shown the draft, Jefferson said, he had hastily run his eye over it to see that it omitted "neutrality," not stopping to realize that even without that fateful word it might be construed as a definitive proclamation of neutrality. And so it was. Again he had been outmaneuvered by Hamilton. He was saddled with the administration of a policy he could not wholly approve and a policy condemned by the Republican friends of France.

Anxieties about the proclamation were offset in the spring by the booming public reception of Citizen Genêt, the glittering symbol of republican France, as he passed from ovation to ovation on his leisurely journey northward to Philadelphia. Landing in Charleston the second week of April, Genêt lost no time implementing his instructions to commission privateers against British commerce and to foment hostilities against the Spanish colonies. At Richmond he learned of the proclamation. It daunted him not at all in the heady acclaim he was enjoying. Reports of his precipitate actions, the popular demonstrations, the rousing appeals to French sympathies, reached Philadelphia ahead of Genêt. Already, protests from the British minister against unneutral acts of the French flag piled up on Jefferson's desk. He was mildly concerned. A good cause could be injured by too much zeal. But he was happy in Genêt's triumph. "All the old spirit of 1776 is rekindling," he exulted. Though it must be kept within the limits of neutrality, he was glad for this testimony of the people against "the cold caution of their government." In the rage for Genêt the people found their voice. "For our constituents seeing that the government does not express their mind, perhaps rather leans the other way, are coming forward to express it themselves." Not only France but the Republican party had an interest in this development.

Philadelphia gave Genêt a delirious welcome on May 16. Cannon boomed. Bells clanged. From Gray's Ferry to the City Tavern, he rode through a cheering throng. The next evening several hundred citizens met in the State House yard, acclaimed an address, then paraded noisily through the streets, swelling their ranks as they went, to make the presentation at Genêt's lodgings. "You ask who were its promoters," Hamilton wrote testily to a friend. "I answer that with very few exceptions they were the same men who have been uniformly the enemies and the disturbers of the government of the United States." The reception continued for days. "I live in the midst of perpetual festivals," Genêt remarked. The lavish banquet at Oeller's Hotel was unsurpassed in the memory of Philadelphians. A battery of artillery saluted each spirited toast; the diners, numbering perhaps 200, donned red liberty caps, hymned the *Marseillaise*, and roared approval when Genêt himself burst into patriotic song:

> Liberty! Liberty! be thy name adored forever
> Tyrants, beware, your tottering thrones must fall;
> One interest links the free forever,
> And Freedom's sons are Frenchmen all.

From other quarters, all the old Tories, as Jefferson described them —fashionable aristocrats, paper-men, merchants trading on British capital—came pledges of support for the President and neutrality. Jefferson remained aloof from the spectacle, but he was far from being a disinterested spectator.

In the midst of the furor, the youthful minister presented his credentials to the Secretary of State. For all the Girondin dash and bravado of the little Frenchman, there was about him, as Jefferson must have seen at once, the delicate aura of one who had grown up in the courtly world of Versailles. Jefferson, after a cordial exchange of greetings, took him to the President's house. The scene changed dramatically. Portraits of his late sovereign and queen hung on the wall. The President showed a cold and haughty manner. The contrast between the huzzas of the masses and Washington's chilly reception spoke volumes to Genêt. Fortunately, the Secretary of State understood him, loved France, loved the Revolution, and would espouse his cause in the government. In Charleston, Ralph Izard, an old friend of his father, had sought to disabuse Genêt of this preconceived idea of Jefferson. Izard, a leading Federalist, described the Secretary as "an ambitious and intriguing demagogue" who, together with Madison, would use Genêt so long as he was serviceable to their crooked schemes, and then drop him. "Place no confidence in them," Izard warned. Genêt would later feel Izard had prophesied his destiny, but the warning made no impression in the spring of 1793. "Tomorrow," he wrote just after his official reception, "I will have my first conference with . . . Mr. Jefferson . . . . His principles, his experience, his talents, his devotion to the cause which we defend, inspire in me the greatest confidence, and make me hope that we will reach the glorious goal which the cause of humanity in general must make us desirous of achieving."

Minister and Secretary met on a friendly footing, as men engaged in a common cause. Genêt was conciliatory in regard to his hasty actions at Charleston before the proclamation of neutrality. He was instructed, of course, to obtain every possible favor for French shipping and commerce, but he promised to respect American neutrality. Indeed, France preferred her ally as a neutral rather than as a belligerent. She had no intention of invoking the guarantee clause of the Treaty of Alliance. The West Indies ports, he announced, were thrown open to American trade. His assurances respecting the treaty vindicated Jefferson's judgment in the cabinet, while the liberation of the island commerce fulfilled a decade-long objective of American diplomacy. Genêt was also instructed to negotiate a new treaty of commerce on Jefferson's favorite plan of mutual naturalization. Alas, such a treaty would now be incompatible with American neutrality. Jefferson quietly tabled the proposition. Yet, at this juncture, Genêt appeared to embody the old dream of Franco-American commercial empire. It was the Girondin dream too, but crazily mixed up with frenzies of war and conquest troubling American peace. The danger from the French side was apparent. Could neutrality co-exist with the French alliance? Jefferson felt reassured after his first talk with Genêt. "It is impossible for anything to be more affectionate, more magnanimous than the purport of his mission," he wrote to Madison. "In short he offers everything and asks nothing." But would his colleagues in the cabinet meet Genêt fairly? He feared not. "Under pretense of avoiding war on the one side [they] have no great antipathy to run foul of it on the other, and to make a part in the confederacy of princes against human liberty."

The cabinet was becoming an established institution. "This sets almost every day on questions of neutrality," Jefferson said in May. These questions were vexing to the last degree. The statute book offered no help, though some might be found in the customary law of nations. Every question as it arose became the subject of discussion in executive conclave, testing the wits, tiring the patience, gnawing the feelings of its members. Agreement on the applicable principle —and this was often the case—was frequently accompanied by an exasperating inability to agree on details of implementation. It was unanimously agreed, for instance, that France should not be permitted to fit out privateers or sell prizes in American ports. (Article XXII of the treaty of commerce decided the question as to France's enemies.) But should the ruling be retrospective, forcing the suppression of privateers Genêt had commissioned at Charleston and the surrender of their prizes? Did the prohibition extend to the mounting of arms furnished by the belligerent as well as those acquired in the United States? Must belligerent vessels abstain from recruiting their own nationals in American ports? Were citizens of the United States barred from selling vessels armed for war to the belligerents? The negative vote Jefferson gave on each of these questions leaned to the French side. He was not for that reason any less neutral than the two, sometimes three, officers who voted affirmative. True neutrality was unattainable. Every decision, however fair its grounds, had an unequal effect on the belligerents. Jefferson bent American policy one way, Hamilton the other; and in this they represented the clash of opinion in the country at large. As the dominant naval power, without the benefit of treaty, Britain favored strict and cautious American neutrality, while France pressed the advantages not only of the Treaty of Alliance but of national sympathy for the republican cause. Neutrality was a fiction, exploited by both sides, but more effectively by the British and their friends, primarily Federalists, as the means of negating the French alliance. This was the real issue, as Jefferson had insisted from the start, though it was rapidly obscured by the unreal issue of neutrality.

Nothing so well demonstrated Jefferson's inability to direct foreign affairs the way Hamilton personally directed fiscal affairs than the fact that, largely because the maintenance of peace transcended administrative jurisdictions, the rules and regulations governing neutrality were hammered out in executive council by majority vote. The cabinet met, either at the President's house or one of the executive offices, Hamilton, lean and quick, Knox, fat and slow, on one side, Jefferson on the other, and poor Randolph more often than not in between. This is to speak figuratively. When not at Mount Vernon Washington usually attended, listened to the different opinions, and invariably bowed to the majority or cast his own vote to make a majority. Until the frenzy whipped up around Genêt, Jefferson believed the President's "penchant" was toward a "fair neutrality," and he relied on him to check the Anglicism of the Federalists. Washington tried to strike a just balance. He never seriously entertained Hamilton's project to scrap the French alliance. Although Hamilton had set his foot in Jefferson's domain, he had not supplanted the Virginian's authority in the President's eyes. But what Hamilton had failed to accomplish would be at least partially accomplished by Genêt's audacity and the invective of the Republican press. Several days after the ministerial reception, Washington called Jefferson to task for using the term "republic" to describe the governments of both France and the United States in an official letter acknowledging Ternant's recall. The irritant was the *National Gazette*, which flaunted that otherwise innocent word in attacks on the administration now aimed directly at the President's person. Freneau was a Francophile, bitterly opposed to the neutrality proclamation, and linked politically with the Secretary of State. Jefferson took the President's outburst as a hint to curb the Republican editor. "But I will not do it," he scrawled in his private record. "His paper has saved our Constitution . . . ." The President's *sang froid* was shaken. The more he was attacked from Republican quarters, and the more insolent Genêt became, the more closely he drew to his Federalist advisers.

Not the President but the Attorney General was Jefferson's

chief affliction. Edmund Randolph belonged to the inner circle of Virginia Republicanism. Jefferson had contributed to his success at the bar and in politics, and Randolph, like a grateful friend and protégé, had enrolled himself in Jefferson's cause. But he seemed less than ardent in the neutrality councils in 1793. Jefferson could endure the obstinacy of Hamilton and Knox—it was known and expected. Randolph quibbled and vacillated. Jefferson described the alignment in the cabinet as two and one-half to one and one-half, the split vote being Randolph's, which, making the majority, carried the day. "Everything . . . now hangs on the opinion of a single person," he confided to Madison in May, "and that the most indecisive one I ever had to do business with. He always contrives to agree in principle with one [Jefferson] but in conclusion with the other [Hamilton]." The affront which brought on Jefferson's disgust occurred on the question of the enforcement of neutrality. He objected to Hamilton's plan to use his customs' officers, as it would convert that service into "an established corps of spies or informers against their fellow citizens" and also add "a new and large field to a department already amply provided with business, patronage, and influence." The responsibility properly belonged in his own department, Jefferson said, utilizing the regular machinery of district attornies, grand juries, and federal judges. On this issue Randolph conceded Jefferson's point, yet sided with Hamilton. "E.R. found out a hair to split, which, as always happens, became the decision." His old friend now appeared as a political chameleon. He was angered in July when Randolph, returning from a mission to sound out Virginia opinion of administration policy, gave the President a favorable report. Outwardly, Jefferson kept up friendly relations with the Attorney General; but within the close knit Virginia circle, he threaded his distrust, causing Randolph to lose political caste there two years before the Federalists completed the wreckage of his career. Randolph was some of the things Jefferson said he was. He shilly-shallied, he split hairs, he trimmed. His irresolution favored Hamilton's ascendancy in the cabinet. Yet his offences were not of the proportion Jefferson imagined, and they arose from a conscientious effort to follow Washington's lead in striking a just balance of American neutrality. Jefferson expected dutiful obedience from his junior friend and colleague. When he did not give it and acted with seeming indifference to political considerations, Jefferson felt betrayed and responded in sullen anger.

While the administration gradually hammered out a system of neutrality, the public debate raged on, drawing fresh fuel from Genêt's antics, from the assaults of both belligerents on American commerce, from street brawls between French and English sailors, the violence of the press, and the determined effort of political foes, Federalist and Republican, to transmute all this emotion into party capital. When summer came Pennsylvania's Republican chieftains organized a Democratic Society modeled loosely on the political clubs of Paris. Soon these clubs, which championed the French Revolution, agitated public issues, and served as a kind of auxiliary of the Republican party, appeared in every part of the country. Jefferson kept to his official station, but encouraged anything tending to advance the Republican and the French cause. Society in Philadelphia was spoiled by the heats and tumults of politics. The amusement he had found in the homes of fortune and fashion turned to ashes. Old friendships were strained or broken. He had often seen John Trumbull, his artist-friend and companion in Europe, since he returned to the United States, still "collecting heads" for his historical canvases. Sometime in the early months of 1793 Jefferson invited Trumbull to dinner. Giles was in the company, and he at once, according to Trumbull, "began to rally me upon the puritanical ancestry and character of New England." At Jefferson's table the voluble Virginian launched into a tirade against Christianity and other miserable delusions in the broadest French style, "Jefferson in the meantime, smiling and nodding approbation on Mr. Giles." Trumbull roundly declared Giles a scoundrel, rose and left the house, and thereafter had only a "cold and distant" acquaintance with Jefferson. Political passions in 1793 bared all the edges of mental discord.

After giving up his house on Market Street, Jefferson found a quiet country refuge on the banks of the Schuylkill. Most of his books, furniture, and other household possessions—a total of fifty crates—were packed and shipped to the James in April, when he moved to the country. He had fewer visitors and never entertained in style. The silks and ruffles were put away in favor of more republican garb—Jefferson began to appear the Jacobin his enemies imagined him to be. Polly came to his retreat on weekends. "She passes two or three days . . . with me, under the trees," he wrote to Martha, "for I never go into the house but at the hour of bed. I never before knew the full value of trees, good grass below, and under them I breakfast, dine, write, read, and receive my company. What would I not give that the trees planted nearest round the house at Monticello were full grown." Official duties drove him hard, "like a horse under whip and spur from the start to the poll," but his thoughts turned more and more to Monticello. He needed a farm manager, tenants, workmen in different lines, and he gave what time he could to the search for them. Intending to become a plain, practical farmer at last, he talked over his plans with Dr. Logan, "the best farmer in Pennsylvania," and in correspondence with his son-in-law. Styling himself "but a tyro in agriculture," he was eager to experiment with new methods and new machinery, such as a model threshing machine he had ordered from Scotland.

Madison contemplated Jefferson's retirement with dismay. It surely ought to be deferred, he advised, until it could be "marked with justifying circumstances which all good citizens will respect, and to which your friends can appeal." Jefferson brushed aside this political appeal, retorting in language of unprecedented severity in his correspondence with Madison. "What must be the principle of that calculation which should balance against these [pleasures of private and domestic life] the circumstances of my present existence! Worn down with labors from morning to night, and day to day; knowing them as fruitless to others as they are vexatious to myself, committed singly and in desperate and eternal contest against a host who are systematically undermining the public liberty and prosperity, even the rare hours of relaxation sacrificed to the society of persons in the same intentions, of whose hatred I am conscious even in those moments of conviviality when the heart wishes most to open itself to the effusions of friendship and confidence, cut off from my family and friends, my affairs abandoned to chaos and derangement, in short giving everything I love, in exchange for everything I hate, and all this without a single gratification in possession or in prospect, in present enjoyment or future wish.—Indeed my dear friend," he closed, "duty being out of the question, inclination cuts off all argument, and so never let there be more between you and me, on this subject." At the end of July he notified Washington he would retire on September 30.

Meanwhile there was no escape. In June, Hamilton, as "Pacificus," commenced a series of articles in the *Gazette of the United States* in defense of the proclamation of neutrality. He upheld its constitutionality, declared the Treaty of Alliance in abeyance, pooh-poohed sentiments of gratitude for France, and denounced her revolution. Jefferson was shocked by the gloss Hamilton put on the proclamation. "For God's sake, my dear sir," he implored Madison, "take up your pen, select the most striking heresies and cut him to pieces in the face of the public. There is nobody else who can and will enter the lists with him." Madison had not needed Pacificus to show him the terrible mischief of the proclamation. "It wounds the national honor, by seeming to disregard the stipulated duties to France. It wounds the popular feelings by a seeming indifference to the cause of liberty. And it seems to violate the form and spirit of the Constitution . . . ," he had written to Jefferson. But simmering under the July sun of the Virginia piedmont, Madison took up the task of reply with faint heart. "I can truly say I find it the most grating one I ever experienced." In five articles over the signature "Helvidius," he never got beyond the constitutional issue. Jefferson saw to their publication in Philadelphia. The argument of Helvidius was a detailed elaboration of Jefferson's original position: that because the power to decide between war and peace belongs to Congress, the President cannot initiate a policy which, in effect, confronts Congress with a *fait accompli*. As against Hamilton's sweeping claim of executive prerogative in foreign affairs, no other position could stand the scrutiny of the Constitution; but the Constitution did not cover all exigencies, as even the Virginia Republicans were to discover in time.

The achievement of what Jefferson styled a "fair neutrality" demanded the prudent co-operation of the French minister. In this regard, first impressions had been deceiving. Within a week of his reception Genêt boldy challenged administration rulings. When Jefferson informed him that American ports could not be used for the arming of French vessels, Genêt affirmed the right from its negative as to the enemies of France in Article XXII of the treaty, an inference Jefferson had earlier rejected in his defense of the alliance. On June 5, Jefferson presented Genêt with a careful restatement of the government's position. The United States must prohibit acts within its borders injurious to Britain, a nation with which it was at peace. The privateers commissioned at Charleston would have to depart (a ruling Jefferson had not approved), and the granting of military commissions to American citizens would have to stop (a ruling he had emphatically approved). A week later the cabinet met to consider the cases of the brigs *Polly* and *Catherine*, the former a French privateer seized by Governor Clinton for arming in New York, the latter a French prize taken in American waters. Both, it was decided, would be held by the United States and committed to the federal district attorney for settlement at law. Genêt protested. Again Jefferson patiently stated the American position, showing it to be in accord with treaty obligations and the law of nations. The Frenchman met Jefferson's reasoning with defiance and contempt. What had he to do with "diplomatic subtleties" and "aphorisms of Vattel"! The American people would not tolerate this treatment of the French nation. "Our treaties have been unfavorably interpreted. Arbitrary orders have directed against us the action of the tribunals; indeed, my diplomatic reception excepted, I have met with nothing but disgust and obstacles in the negotiations I have been charged with."

Questions of consular jurisdiction and the French debt also gave difficulty. The consuls presumed to hold courts of admiralty on prizes. When Jefferson, in May, pointed out that the consular convention of 1788 gave no such jurisdiction, Genêt acknowledged the error and promised to correct it. Instead, he again embarked on it. After repeated warnings, the administration was finally obliged to order the withdrawal of privileges from refractory consuls. For some time before Genêt's arrival the government had been advancing payments of its debt to France in order to furnish relief for the slave-ravaged island of Santo Domingo. Genêt was instructed to improve this friendly gesture by obtaining payment of the entire balance, about $2,500,000, to be laid out in provisions. Jefferson would have liked to comply with this request, but finally agreed with Hamilton that the financial risk was too high. The decision helped to cripple the French Minister. He protested it without avail. Although the Treasury continued to make advances on annual installments, he never received sufficient funds for his larger undertakings. Moreover, hard pressed as he was, he broke faith with American creditors who had furnished supplies to Santo Domingo by diverting funds set aside on their account to new purchases for France. For this he drew another reprimand from the Secretary of State.

By the end of June, Jefferson was agonizing over Genêt's performance and wondering what to do with him. Dazzled by the brilliance of his public triumph, the little hot-head presumed to set the government itself at defiance. "I am doing everything in my power to moderate the impetuosity of his movements," Jefferson wrote to Monroe, "and to destroy the dangerous opinion which has been excited in him, that the people of the U.S. will disown the acts of their government, and that he has an appeal from the Executive to Congress, and from both to the people." Wishing at all costs to avoid a break, he gently reasoned with Genêt, coaxed and placated him, in an endeavor to set him on the right path. The envoy took Jefferson's confidence and manifest good will at face value and continued to view him as a friendy coadjutor, differentiating him in this role from his official role as Secretary of State in which he must be the agent of the President. The quaint courtesies and supple manners of the Virginian, who expressed pleasure or displeasure only in varying degrees of assent, confused the Frenchman. Yet in his most ambitious scheme Genêt might rightly claim to have had the compliance, if not the encouragement, of the Secretary of State.

As early as February Jefferson had learned vaguely of the ruling Gironde's clandestine support of Francisco de Miranda, the Venezuelan adventurer, in his efforts to foment revolution in Spanish America, as well as of Genêt's secret instructions to enlist the Kentuckians in a combined land and sea expedition against Louisiana; but nothing directly touching these matters reached the Secretary. Genêt then, late in June, asked him to furnish André Michaux, the French botanist, with a letter of introduction to the governor of Kentucky. Jefferson happily complied. He knew and admired Michaux, who had been in the United States for several years collecting botanical specimens for introduction into France—a scientific enterprise dear to Jefferson's heart—and he had only recently penned Michaux's instructions for a Trans-Mississippi expedition under the

496

auspices of the American Philosophical Society. Unknown to Jefferson, however, the enterprise had taken on a political character since Genêt's arrival in Philadelphia. Grasses, mammoth, and the Missouri route to the Pacific were still the stated objects of Michaux's expedition, but as Genêt's appointed agent he would also go in quest of support for the western venture against the Spanish colonies. For this reason Genêt was dissatisfied with Jefferson's first letter, which simply introduced Michaux as a botanist. Jefferson obligingly tore it up and wrote another recommending the botanist as a man in the confidence of the French Minister. About a week later Genêt called on Jefferson. Making a show of speaking to him "not as Secretary of State, but as Mr. Jefferson," he read the instructions prepared for Michaux, as well as an address to the inhabitants of Louisiana, another to those of Canada, and disclosed the plans afoot to free the Mississippi, take Louisiana, and establish it as an independent state "connected in commerce with France and the United States." Jefferson responded coldly: "I told him that his enticing officers and soldiers from Kentucky to go against Spain, was really putting a halter about their necks; for that they would assuredly be hung if they commenced hostilities against a nation at peace with the United States. That leaving out that article I did not care what insurrections should be excited in Louisiana."

Perhaps Jefferson would not have made this last disclaimer, which Genêt took as a backhanded endorsement of the western project, had he known of the alliance formed between Britain and Spain several weeks earlier. Even so, the sharp distinction he made between French machinations in Kentucky and insurrections in Spanish Louisiana, while perfectly valid in law, had little support in western realities, for the Mississippi linked Kentuckians in treachery and conspiracy through all its muddy waters to New Orleans. As interested as he was in commercial union with France, he had no desire to see that ambitious nation seated at the mouth of the Mississippi. He hoped to secure the Floridas and New Orleans for the United States, on his own terms, with as little risk to peace and honor as circumstances would admit. The matter was still in the course of negotiation with Spain in the summer of 1793. But the prospect of success dimmed with each dispatch from Madrid, and the twin marplots in Philadelphia, the Spanish commissioners Viar and

Jaudenes, made such a trumpery of the United States' incitement of the Indians that a rupture seemed imminent. Already, perhaps on the possiblity of Girondin revolution in the Spanish provinces, Jefferson had told the ministers at Madrid to withhold the defensive guarantee of Louisiana earlier tendered in exchange for the navigation of the Mississippi and the Floridas. In this situation, his patience worn thin after several years of negotiation with Spain, Jefferson was little inclined to suppress French irritants. He did not lay Genêt's scheme before the President, nor did he ever make his knowledge of it a part of the official record. Near the end of August, however, the Spanish commissioners, having learned of the enterprise and the involvement of prominent Americans, such as Jefferson's old friend George Rogers Clark, brought it to official notice. Speaking for the President, Jefferson at once assured the commissioners that the United States would act to prevent American aggressions. On the same day he directed the governor of Kentucky to take appropriate measures, and when this met with an indifferent response, he wrote again in stronger terms. By then the Girondins had fallen in France and Genêt in America, and the once-postponed expedition against the Spanish colonies could not be revived. Toward it Jefferson had taken an ambivalent, perhaps even ambiguous line, which would enable him to maneuver as changing circumstances might require. It was all inconsequential, so it is difficult to say whether or not his line was the right one.

Jefferson's trust in the French Minister, ebbing fast for several weeks, finally ran out in the case of the *Little Sarah*. At a meeting of the department heads on July 5, several hours before Genêt made his startling disclosures of New World liberation in Jefferson's office, it was agreed to ask the governor of Pennsylvania, Thomas Mifflin, to determine whether or not this French prize lying in the Delaware between the city and Mud Island was arming as a privateer. Mifflin reported the next day that the merchant brig had been brought in with four guns and now mounted 14, with several swivels, and a crew of 120, some of them American. Alexander J. Dallas, secretary of the commonwealth and a leader of the Democratic Society, understood that the brig, rechristened *La Petite Démocrate*, was about to put to sea. Later that night he called on Genêt to persuade him to detain the vessel. He angrily refused, complained of

498

ill-treatment, promised to meet force with force if it came to that, and, according to later reports of the conversation, threatened to appeal over the President's head directly to the people. The alarm reached Jefferson at his country place the next morning, which was Sunday. He hurried to the city, conferred first with Dallas and Mifflin, then went to see Genêt. He renewed Dallas's appeal: detain the vessel until the President, then at Mount Vernon but expected in the capital on Wednesday, could decide the case. Genêt flew into a rage, traversing an "immense field" of complaint, the sum of which was that the treaties had been violated, the administration had acted unconstitutionally, and he had been checked in every endeavor. The turbulence smothered Jefferson's efforts to reason with the Minister. He refused to give any assurances but said the vessel would not be ready to sail before Wednesday anyway. Taking this as a face-saving declaration, Jefferson went away confident the matter would await the President's decision.

The case of the *Petite Démocrate* was already becoming celebrated. On Monday morning the public woke to the possibility of a serious breach of neutrality. Merchants of the city held a meeting at the coffeehouse and urged strong measures. The spotlight of publicity, the scene of the challenge under the very noses of the government, made the case peculiarly delicate. Mifflin, who was charged like all governors to use force if necessary to prevent the arming of privateers, wished to know what steps he should take at this juncture. The three secretaries (Randolph was also in Virginia) met in Mifflin's office at the State House. In the opinion of Hamilton and Knox, a battery should be set up at Mud Island under a party of militia with orders to fire on the privateer if she spread sail before the President's pleasure could be known.

Jefferson dissented. Summarizing his argument in a memorandum written for the President the next day, he began with the more specific reasons and proceeded, with rising eloquence, to the more general. He felt confident the brig would not sail. The erection of a battery might "produce the fact it is meant to prevent"; if so, and if the guns fired, he warned, "it is morally certain that bloody consequences would follow," slamming the door on peace. This was too great a responsibility to be assumed by subordinate officers when the chief magistrate, to whom the people had committed their safety, was within forty-eight hours of the opportunity of judging the question for himself. Hamilton had emphasized the consequences of adverse British reaction to a breach of neutrality so flagrant as to make a mockery of the government. To this Jefferson said that Britain would have no right to complain. If the breach occurred it would be contrary to the assurances of the French Minister, and the United States would then demand satisfaction from France. In view of the evidences of good faith already given to the British, in view of American sufferance of their damnable practice of impressing our seamen to bear arms against our friends, Whitehall was not likely to make a capital case of the *Petite Démocrate*. Having borne for ten years "the grossest insults and injuries" from their late enemy, the American people ought not "to rise at a feather against their friends and benefactors," Jefferson continued with mounting indignation. "I would not gratify the combination of kings with the spectacle of the only two republics on earth destroying each other for two cannon; nor would I, for infinitely greater cause, add this country to that combination, turn the scale of contest, and let it be from our hands that the hopes of men received their last stab." In his judgment, clearly, the explosive potential of the case placed it on an altogether different footing from the generality of cases, thus making the arbitrary application of the general rule unwarranted and unwise. Hamilton also realized the stubborness of this particular transaction; indeed, for that reason, Jefferson suspected, he had seized upon it to provoke an incident fatal to the French alliance. At bottom, Jefferson's position, no less than Hamilton's on the opposite side, was dictated by commitments outside the straight-and-narrow path of neutrality. In the present instance, peace and neutrality were better served by the course Jefferson advocated.

By the time Washington returned to the capital the succeeding Thursday, the *Petite Démocrate* had hoisted anchor and fallen down the river several miles to Chester. She had not departed, but the maneuver pretty well eliminated the possibility of coercive action. The President found the relevant papers on his desk. Rage was an emotion he reserved for extraordinary provocations. He felt it now. "What is to be done in the case of the *Little Sarah*, now at Chester," he demanded of the Secretary of State, who had taken to the country with a fever. "Is the Minister of the French Republic to set the acts of this Government at defiance *with impunity?* And then threaten the Executive with an appeal to the People? What must the world think of such conduct, and of the Government of the United States in submitting to it?" He summoned the cabinet to meet the next day. Jefferson found him considerably calmed, though apparently sorry the brig had not been fired on—an action Jefferson doubted he would have ordered had he been on the spot. The President and his officers decided to refer the difficult legal questions of American neutrality to the justices of the Supreme Court, expecting in the meantime that the *Petite Démocrate* and a half-dozen vessels in indeterminate status would remain in port. But the Court declined to intervene. Left to work out its problems alone, the executive promulgated nine rules governing belligerents early in August. Long before then the *Petite Démocrate* had gone to sea. Hammond offered no protest. Jefferson might console himself in this, and in the thought that the defeat was insignificant when compared with the risks of a confrontation in arms. But he could no longer take any consolation whatsoever in the French Minister.

"Never in my opinion, was so calamitous an appointment made, as that of the present Minister of France here," Jefferson confided to Madison on July 7, the day of his disheartening interview with Genêt. "Hot headed, all imagination, no judgment, passionate, disrespectful and even indecent towards the President . . . urging the most unreasonable and groundless propositions, and in the most dictatorial style etc. etc. etc." Toward him personally Genêt was respectful and willing to listen to advice; but then at the first opportunity he would rear and buck like a wild colt. "He renders my position immensely difficult." In discrediting himself, Genêt discredited Jefferson's foreign policy pegged to friendship with France and struck at the hopes of Republicans to bury the Federalists under an avalanche of popular enthusiasm for the French Revolution. By mid-July Hamilton was moving for Genêt's recall. It was the Federalists' turn now to appeal to the people, unaccustomed though they were to that tribunal. "They know too well that the whole game is played into their hands . . . ," Jefferson remarked. Finding Genêt "absolutely incorrigible," as he reported to Madison, he saw "the necessity of quitting a wreck which could not but sink all who should cling to it." Genêt must be abandoned. The Secretary's job was to salvage what he could of the cargo.

On August 1 the four gentlemen of the cabinet took "family dinner" with the President, then got down to the business of what should be done with the Frenchman. A full and documented statement of his conduct to be prepared in the form of a letter to the American Minister in Paris for communication to the Executive Council of the French republic: agreed to unanimously. An immediate recall to be required: agreed to unanimously, Jefferson for tactful, the others for peremptory, expression. A letter to Genêt informing him of the recall action and the grounds: Jefferson against, as further incitement of the envoy, but overruled by the others. A publication of the whole record "by way of appeal to the people": Hamilton passionately advocating it, Randolph opposed, and the question adjourned to the next day. Hamilton again took up the subject, answered now by his inveterate rival. The appeal was a brazen party maneuver. Its real object was to rally the populace against France, throw the country into the arms of Britain, and destroy the incipient democratic societies. Jefferson was unusually outspoken. The measure, he asserted, "was calculated to make the President assume the station of the head of a party, instead of the head of the nation." Washington, nevertheless, favored the appeal. Knox barged in, exhibiting a pasquinade lately printed which jested with Washington's death on the guillotine. "The President was much inflamed; got into one of those passions when he cannot command himself; ran on much on the personal abuse which had been bestowed on him . . . [declared] that *by God* he had rather be in his grave than in his present situation . . . [condemned] that *rascal* Freneau," and so on. When he finished there was some difficulty resuming the question. After awhile the President said it could be deferred, and the stormy meeting ended.

Several days later Washington called at Jefferson's place in the country. The Secretary's pending resignation stared him in the face. Once again they went over the familiar ground. Washington was full of apprehension. The retirement of the minister who had become the national symbol of Republicanism would open the government to unmitigated partisanship. Jefferson alluded to the uneasiness of his situation, obliged by the laws of society "to move exactly in the circle which I know to bear me peculiar hatred." He sought to overcome the President's fears. The Republican party was sound, aiming to save, not to destroy, the Constitution; the new Congress would attempt nothing material but to establish its independence of Treasury influence; as for Genêt, though the affair caused some embarrassment, "he would be abandoned by the Republicans the moment they knew the nature of his conduct." Washington conceded the purity of the mass of Republicans, but spoke uneasily of their obsessive fears of monarchy, and he wondered if they could stop the political machine they had put in motion. He then went into the question of Jefferson's successor. Several possibilities were discussed but none suited. Like a man going to the gallows, as Washington described his predicament, he wanted to put it off as long as possible. He implored Jefferson to stay on until the end of the year. By then affairs might show a brighter prospect. Could not Jefferson readjust his own plans by a flying trip to Monticello in the fall? The Secretary demurred but agreed to think about it. Between the President's convenience and his own there was perhaps not much to choose. He consented; and without further ado proceeded to dismantle his modest household as a precaution against yielding another time.

His desk piled high with letters, newspapers, and other damning evidence bearing on Genêt's recall, Jefferson sweated over the exacting letter to Morris through torrid August days. The rough draft was taken to the cabinet on the 15th, the finished draft on the 20th. After a thorough analysis of the issues that had led to the diplomatic impasse, Jefferson indicted the French envoy for his presumption "to put himself within the country on a line with its government, to act as co-sovereign of the territory." Genêt was granted the dubious privilege of convicting himself out of his own mouth. The cabinet officers could find no fault with this masterly statement of the case. But the studied propriety of Jefferson's language, the exclusion of Genêt's provocative words and actions outside the diplomatic line, the pointed distinction between the Minister and his government—in this character the letter rankled Hamilton. Writing as "No Jacobin," he had recently presented the public his own account of Genêt's activities, premised on the assumption that the envoy was the loyal servant of his Jacobin masters in Paris whose secret purpose was to drag the United States into the war. Hamilton wished to take the same high ground toward the government as toward the minister. The issue in the cabinet discussion finally came down to a single electric phrase from Jefferson's pen. Genêt's conduct threatened to embroil the two republics and draw upon them the terrible reproach of history, Jefferson wrote, "that of liberty warring on herself." The phrase was meant, in a letter otherwise cold and forbidding, he said, "to satisfy France not only of our friendship for her, but our attachment to the general cause of liberty, and to hers in particular." But was the cause of France the cause of liberty? Hamilton denied it; even if the proposition were true, there was no need to offend France's enemies, or gratify her American friends, by asserting it. Knox agreed. So did Randolph. The President, surprisingly, favored the expression, declaring his attachment to France above any other nation and his confidence in the ultimate triumph of liberty there; then adding, as Jefferson himself would have added at this juncture, that that embattled nation sometimes failed to understand the best means of reaching the end of its strivings. Yielding to the majority, Jefferson struck the expression. For the rest, the letter was dispatched as Jefferson had written it, together with 35 documents and 32 copies of newspapers.

None of this was communicated to Genêt for several weeks. The Republican sun still shone for him as he waited impatiently for the assemblage of Congress. "We will soon be avenged," he assured the Foreign Ministry in Paris. The little firebrand had gone to New York where the French fleet, driven from Santo Domingo, mutinous, embroiled in factional quarrels among refugees, lay at anchor. While harassed with these problems, which were more than sufficient to defeat his plans for using the fleet in New World ventures, Genêt suddenly found himself arraigned in the press for threatening to appeal from the President to the people. That he had made the rumored threat was certified by Chief Justice Jay and Rufus King, the New York senator, who had got the story from Hamilton, who had got it from Mifflin and Jefferson, who had got it from Dallas, the witness to Genêt's midnight harangue on July 6. Genêt at once wrote to the President, asking that august personage to repudiate the charge. The letter was routed to Jefferson's desk. With cold formality he told the Minister he was to address his communications to the

Secretary of State; as for the present case, it was beneath the dignity of the President to interfere. Nothing abashed, Genêt promptly gave the correspondence to the newspapers. He has "thrown down the gauntlet," Jefferson told Madison, "thus forcing that appeal to the public, and risking that disgust" he had hoped to avoid.

Some weeks earlier Jefferson would have deplored the political artifice used by the Federalist chieftains to expose Genêt. Now, near the end of August, he had abandoned the wreck and wished the mass of Republicans to do likewise. So he viewed the partisan attack on Genêt with a measure of equanimity. Public addresses in support of the President against the envoy poured into Philadelphia from all parts of the country, even from Richmond, where Jefferson's sturdy republican mentor George Wythe had chaired the meeting. In the Secretary's calculation Genêt was a necessary sacrifice to preserve American neutrality, the French connection, and the Republican interest; on the other hand, the systematic campaign launched by Hamilton and his friends threatened to sink the Republicans under the weight of popular opprobrium directed against Genêt. If unopposed they might carry everything before them. Jefferson's anxieties still focused on the first danger, Genêt, when Madison, hundreds of miles from the scene and baffled by the hero's fall from grace, called the Virginia cadre into action. "The Anglican party is busy . . . in making the worst of everything, and in turning the public feelings against France, and thence in favor of England." Madison hoped through Republican assemblages in several counties to call out the true feelings of the people. This was fine, but Madison and Republicans generally did not seem to realize the necessity of abandoning Genêt. Jefferson finally got the message across and Madison toned down his resolutions. Several meetings were held and resolutions adopted, all enforcing a line of separation between the French nation and the tarnished envoy. But it was a disappointing rearguard action. The Federalists had scored heavily.

A disease more mortal than politics, the yellow fever, struck Philadelphia, mercilessly infesting the city near the end of the torrid summer until all life seemed about to stop. No movement at the wharves, streets deserted, the theater darkened, newspapers suspended, and the burial ground beginning to look like a freshly plowed field. "The fever spreads faster," Jefferson wrote on September 12. "Deaths are now about 30 a day. It is in every square of the city. All flying who can. Most of the offices are shut or shutting. The banks shut up this day. All my clerks have left me but one: so that I cannot go on with business." Washington went home on the 10th. Knox was going away, and Hamilton lay ill with the fever. Jefferson accomplished nothing by staying in the plague-ridden city. He withdrew with Polly to his house on the Schuylkill, attended to several items of business, and left for Monticello on the 17th, two weeks ahead of schedule.

Just before leaving he notified the French Minister of the request for his recall and enclosed copies of the papers sent to Morris. Genêt, stunned, replied at once with a long, ranting letter that furnished further evidence, if further evidence was needed, of his utter recalcitrance. He had only done his duty. Every obstacle had been thrown in his way. The treaties had been falsely construed. The President could not demand his recall against the will of the people. The idea of Jefferson's perfidy now entered his tortured mind. His letter suggested at least the suspicion of betrayal by the official who had pretended to be his friend. With furious energy, Genêt composed another vindication of his conduct for home consumption and sent it by special courier to Paris. (Anticipating this move Jefferson had purposely delayed notification of the Minister, thus ensuring priority for the government's case in Paris.) But the envoy was already out of favor at home. The Jacobins had come to power. Robespierre's foreign minister had already dispatched a sharp reprimand to Genêt for permitting "the brilliance of a false popularity" to place him at odds with the American government. The Jacobins wished for quiet in America; they disowned the dazzling ocean-girdling ambitions of the Girondins, sent to the guillotine in October, and pressed all-out war—at home and abroad, commercial and military—against Great Albion. The Jacobins would be happy to recall Genêt. No argument from Morris was needed. They would like the envoy's head too. Morris did not object, but this would be denied. Thanks to the generosity of the government he had abused, Citizen Genêt would be permitted to live out the remainder of a long life in the United States, a respected New York farmer and son-in-law of Governor George Clinton.

In the months and years ahead, as he reflected on his fate and learned the extent of Jefferson's complicity in his downfall, Genêt became convinced that this Janus in the cabinet had sacrificed him on the altar of political ambition. Such was the judgment he made in a vindictive autobiographical letter addressed to Jefferson in 1797, and such was his plea at the bar of history. It could not be denied that Jefferson had confided in Genêt, sympathized with his cause, egged him on, then tried to restrain him, and finally collaborated in his destruction. But neither could the over-all consistency of Jefferson's conduct be denied. He sought always to balance American peace and neutrality with the French alliance and republican ascendancy. Genêt could not be expected to appreciate the artful management this twofold commitment required of the Secretary of State. Nor could he, a man without subtlety or modulation in his own person and incapable of perceiving it in others, be expected to understand Jefferson. About America the Frenchman was incredibly obtuse, making everything of popular effusions, next to nothing of constituted authority, and supposing that true republicans, like Jefferson, were revolutionary ideologues first and patriotic Americans second. The wisdom of a later French minister was never vouchsafed to Genêt. "Jefferson, I say," wrote Pierre Adet in 1796, "is an American and, by that title cannot be sincerely our friend. An American is the born enemy of all European peoples."

Jefferson's last two months in office was like an epilogue to a turbulent drama, adding little but giving finality to the whole. The government took up temporary quarters in Germantown, out of the way of the fever. President and Secretary of State, who had met on the road, arrived there on November 1, just as rain and cold struck down the epidemic. Refugees from the city crowded Germantown. "As a great favor," Jefferson said, "I have got a bed in the corner of the public room of a tavern." Where congressmen, soon to arrive, would lay their heads he could not imagine. The cabinet met regularly. Questions of neutrality that could not be resolved under the standing rules occupied the executive officers. The question of Genêt's discharge or suspension, pending his recall, caused further discord along the usual lines, as did the discussion of the President's message to Congress. Jefferson was back in Philadelphia by the first of December. The fugitives returned. Government and life in the city resumed their accustomed rounds. But the fever had taken a huge toll. Among the victims was Jefferson's good friend and leader of the Philadelphia Republicans, Dr. James Hutchinson. He wondered "whether the Republican interest has suffered more by his death or Genêt's extravagance." Another casualty was the *National Gazette*. The paper had never paid for itself, and Freneau, who stood by Genêt to the bitter end, now gave it up, resigned his clerkship, and withdrew to rural quietude in New Jersey at last. Actually, despite casualties of this kind, the epidemic helped the beleagured Republicans. The public outrage over Genêt sickened and died, like nearly everything else in the capital, and the general disruption upset Federalist plans to exploit the affair nation-wide.

In these final months the Secretary of State endeavored to bring the British problem back into the foreground of public attention. The subordination of that problem was part of the catastrophe wrought by Genêt. Since few British privateers frequented American waters, since Hammond was on his best behavior, British infractions of American neutrality were neither dramatic nor pressing. Against all of Jefferson's calculations, the natural balance of American diplomacy was reversed in 1793. He had expected neutrality would be delicate and difficult, not with respect to France, "temperate, forbearing, and without designs on us," but with respect to the old enemy, whose "extraordinary pride, constant course of injustice and propensity to eternal war" promised trouble. "No moderation, no justice, on our part can secure us against the violence of her character, and that we love liberty is enough for her to hate us. . . ." The course of events ran to the contrary while Genêt was on the scene.

Yet the differences between Britain and the United States on neutral rights were more basic, more threatening to peace, than the issues posed by the wayward French envoy. Determined to starve the enemy into submission by blockade, the government of William Pitt formed a convention with the governments of Russia, Prussia, and Spain to cut off the supply of provisions to France, and on June 8 issued an order in council for the seizure of neutral vessels ladened with grain and flour for France and the indemnification of their cargoes in British ports. News of this "provision order" reached the

United States before the government dispersed in September. The cabinet unanimously favored protest by the Secretary of State. He wrote to Pinckney and took up the matter with Hammond. The order forced the United States into an unneutral position toward France. Britain justified it on the ground provisions were contraband and the withholding of these supplies was one of the means employed to defeat the enemy. But this was an absurd pretension, Jefferson said. "She may, indeed, feel the desire of starving an enemy nation; but she can have no right of doing it at our loss, nor of making us the instrument of it."

Before the imposing reality of the Royal Navy, Jefferson had placed in suspension the historic American principle of "free ships make free goods." He had done so reluctantly, not only because he cherished the principle together with the profits it brought to the American carrying trade, but also because this tactical retreat implicated the United States in British seizures of French goods on American vessels, with most lamentable results in the case of the Santo Domingo refugees. Genêt had wrangled at length on this point. If the United States did not take steps to protect French persons and property in American bottoms, by arms if necessary, he would advise his government to repudiate the principle written into the treaty of 1778. (In the sequel France did, in fact, revoke the principle.) Jefferson informed Genêt of his efforts to force British concurrence in the *modern* rule. He hoped the minister would desist, for as long as Britain adhered to the ancient rule, *consolato del mare,* making enemy goods liable to seizure regardless of flag, the United States was helpless to oppose her at sea. But Genêt was adamant. The British seizures assailed American neutrality—let the government bring Albion to justice on the seas. It became necessary to oppose Genêt rather than Britain. "He thus obliged us," Jefferson sadly observed, "to abandon in the first moment the ground we were endeavoring to gain, that is to say, his ground against England and Spain, and to take the very ground of England and Spain against him." The British seizure of American grain as contraband was another matter, however. Even Hamilton, who had advocated American abandonment of "ill-founded" pretensions of neutral rights, opposed this arbitrary extension of British policy.

Jefferson scarcely expected the Pitt ministry to revoke the provision order on American demand. It did not; instead, in November, it adopted a stiffer order against neutral carriers, which was applied with devastating effect in the West Indies just after Jefferson left office. Even so, diplomatically, the demand helped to balance accounts with France. Politically, it deflected some of the rising acrimony from France to Britain. Jefferson thought the matter ought to be laid before Congress, as it would be in the legislators' power to soothe France by adopting some form of commercial retaliation against Britain.

Early in December, when he was retouching the long deferred report to Congress on commercial policy, Jefferson received from the Mediterranean new evidence of British perfidy. Death had taken successive envoys, John Paul Jones and Thomas Barclay, sent to ransom the prisoners and purchase peace with Algiers. The mission, with its niggardly purse, might have failed in any event; yet while Portugal policed the Gibraltar gate the Barbary nation was perhaps sufficiently desperate to listen to American overtures. Humphreys was ordered to take up the ill-starred mission. Before he could reach Algiers, he learned of the treaty that nation had signed with Portugal. He hired a Swedish vessel to speed the alarming news to New York. The treaty was credited to British intervention. Jefferson believed that Britain aimed in this way to cripple American trade. Once again the corsairs sailed through the Strait of Gibraltar to prey on American vessels, and only the American, as other nations navigating the Atlantic were at peace with Algiers. Jefferson reported on this state of affairs to the President, who laid it before the House in a confidential message. By voting money for a naval force, Congress at last moved toward the implementation of a policy Jefferson had advocated for nearly a decade.

The retiring Secretary was largely successful, over Hamilton's opposition, in determining the substance and tone of the President's communications to Congress on the country's relations with the major powers. The unpromising state of the negotiations with Spain gave no room for disagreement. The special mission to Madrid had become a casualty of the shifting balance of European politics, and the Spanish officials' incitements of Indian aggression under a covering barrage of accusations against the government in Philadelphia had caused Jefferson to send a sharp note to the Spanish court, from which he hoped to force clarification of the issue for the decision of Congress. Waiting almost to the last day for the courier to return from Spain, Jefferson had finally to leave the matter in the same ambiguous state he had found it. With respect to France, he was reconciled to the submission and the publication of his correspondence with Genêt. To counter the partiality of this measure, however, he insisted that his correspondence with Hammond, together with the papers on the provision order, also be made public. The negotiation with Hammond was clearly at an end. The people had a right to be informed and Congress to act. Hamilton objected strenuously. It was Jefferson's last desperate effort to embroil the United States with Britain, Hamilton felt. He viewed the disputed points—the treaty, commerce, and neutral rights—as still pending, and implied that they might be amicably settled once Jefferson's influence was removed. But Washington unreservedly sided with the Secretary of State. On the question of airing the provision order, Randolph joined Hamilton and Knox in opposition only to be overruled by the President. This was the first instance Jefferson recalled of Washington's deciding on the opinion of one against three.

The publication of these documents added luster to Jefferson's name and enabled him to retire with wide acclaim. At a later day even his enemies paid him a backhanded compliment in saying he was only fit to be Secretary of State. Against Genêt he appeared as the staunch defender of American peace and neutrality, the more remarkable because of his known sympathies for France. Against Hammond he appeared as the champion of all Americans—frontiersmen, planters, merchants, shippers, and manufacturers—still under the British yoke. Documents relating to the Spanish negotiations were confided to Congress; they too offered proof of Jefferson's quickness to defend American honor and his untiring pursuit of national objectives.

Yet, while an impressive record, it included no diplomatic triumph or break-through. After the labors of nearly four years, the advance in foreign relations could be measured in inches. The movement might be considered preliminary to great strides in the future, but it did not mark the kind of achievement Jefferson had set for himself. With Spain nothing had been settled, though the mere process of inertia—the flow of rivers and people and grain—overcame the failings of diplomacy in the moribund remnant of the Spanish empire. The same process could not be relied upon with respect to Britain. Jefferson had badgered and bargained, threatened and blackmailed, but Britain was unmoved. He expected no favors from Britain and gave none. With France he had hoped to build an alliance into a transatlantic fortress of freedom. When he retired the alliance was in a shambles and only the insolence of Britain could restore it. The deterioration in Franco-American relations was an unmitigated disaster from Jefferson's standpoint. He was not responsible for it and, indeed, managed to prevent it from becoming total; but the effects on his political system were irreparable.

He was not prepared to accept this conclusion. In his last major act as Secretary of State, he placed the capstone on that system seemingly outmoded by events and shaken to its foundations. His Report on Commerce culminated a decade's work to develop a national system independent of Britain, allied with France, and directed ultimately to a reign of free exchange and pacific intercourse among nations. The Report had a curious history. It was made in compliance with a resolution passed by the House of Representatives after setting aside a navigation act in February 1791. Jefferson worked up the Report in the ensuing recess of Congress and planned to present it in the fall session; but, "taken in" by Hamilton, he deferred the recommendation of measures unfriendly to Britain until Hammond could return an answer to the demand for evacuation of the Northwest. The Report lapsed into the catalepsy of the British negotiations. Jefferson was again prepared to submit it, newly revised, expanded, and updated, at the close of the Second Congress in February 1793. But the timing troubled him. His recommendations would almost certainly get a better hearing from the Third Congress, and in the interim Genêt would have the opportunity to present the liberal propositions he was thought to be bringing from Paris, thus strengthening the case for differential treatment of the commerce of Britain and France. Cued by Jefferson, the Republican leadership in the House decided not to call for the Report. Genêt did, of course, propose a new and liberal treaty, but the circumstances of war and his own monumental ineptitude blocked the way. Urgent problems of neutrality usurped the place previously occupied by the long-range problems of peacetime commerce. A discriminatory commercial policy was one thing in 1792, when the leading maritime powers were at peace; it was another thing altogether in 1793, when they were at war. For it must then, whether founded in treaty or in statute, have the color of an unneutral act. Moreover, the injuries to the United States as a neutral were different from the injuries suffered by American trade in peacetime. In the waning hours of his ministry, Jefferson must have pondered what to do with his twice-deferred Report. He finally decided to submit it without further revision, based on the conditions of American commerce in 1792. It was a gesture of summation. But for renewed British violence on the seas, it might have passed unnoticed— a faded piece of unfinished business. Not only was the Report saved from this fate, but falling in with the turn of events, it gave form and direction to the amorphous Republican party by setting forth a counter-system to Hamilton's, "my system," as Jefferson said, which justified in hard fact and high principle aggressive opposition to the reign of Treasury policy.

"The report," it has been well said, "is an extraordinary example of the reduction to simplicity of a complicated subject." The subject is the relationship of the American economy to Europe. As an agricultural-commercial nation, its internal trade undeveloped, its industrial base exceedingly narrow, the United States must cherish its navigation, penetrate foreign markets, and seek its economic well-being in the transatlantic trading orbit. Economic policy is inseparable from foreign policy. Trade is a weapon of diplomacy—the only potent weapon in the American armory—to be employed in pursuit of the national interest, including in that term not only the security and independence of the United States but also the widening acceptance of liberal commercial principles in the international community. "Instead of embarrassing commerce under piles of regulating laws, duties, and prohibitions," Jefferson wrote in paraphrase of Adam Smith, "could it be relieved from all its shackles in all parts of the world, could every country be employed in producing that which nature has best fitted it to produce, and each be free to exchange with others mutual surplusses for mutual wants, the greatest mass possible would then be produced of those things which contribute to human life and human happiness; the numbers of mankind would be increased, and their condition bettered." Ideally, trade should be free; in fact, it is burdened with restrictions harmful to the United States and to mankind. Jefferson described these burdens, nation by nation, and drew up the balance sheet of American commerce.

The account was fairly drawn, partial to no nation other than his own; yet it required no clairvoyance to see that, in Jefferson's judgment, the principal culprit was Britain. On liberal principles it was simply absurd that an island should rule the commerce of the world. Three-quarters of American imports came from Britain; she took one-half our exports, re-exported the greater part, prohibited what she pleased, practically monopolized the navigation, and left everything at the hazard of executive decree. France too was restrictive, embarrassingly so for Jefferson's purpose; yet France neither profited from American trade nor held the nation on its tether. "But if particular nations," Jefferson wrote, "grasp at undue shares, and, more especially, if they seize on the means of the United States, to convert them into aliment for their own strength, and withdraw them entirely from the support of those to whom they belong, defensive and protective measures become necessary on the part of the nation whose marine resources are thus invaded; or it will be disarmed of its defence; its productions will lie at the mercy of the nation which has possessed itself exclusively of the means of carrying them, and its politics may be influenced by those who command its commerce." To correct this unnatural condition Jefferson proposed counter-prohibitions, regulations, and duties, working reciprocally on all nations, but in the necessity of the case working hardest on Britain. She refused to accept vessels not built in the United States as American: we should do the same as to vessels naturalized in Britain. She refused to permit American merchants to reside in her colonies: we should refuse residence to English merchants. She admitted nothing but the domestic productions of the United States in our carriers: we should admit only British productions in theirs. She excluded, with some exceptions, both the productions and the vessels of the United States from her colonies: we should prohibit American exports in British vessels. She imposed high duties on American products: we should do the same on British manufactures. And here Jefferson, although making no concession to Hamilton in principle, gave his blessing to the encouragement of manufactures in consequence of a national strategy aimed at commercial freedom and independence. "The oppressions on our agriculture, in foreign ports, would thus be made the occasion of relieving it from a dependence on the councils and conduct of others, and of promoting arts, manufactures and population at home." Ironically, the factories and workshops he had preferred to keep in Europe would the more likely result from his commercial system than from Hamilton's fiscal system. The latter reinforced Anglican connections and its political thrust was counter-revolutionary in the great conflict raging in the Western world.

No nation could object to his system, Jefferson thought, since it was founded on perfect reciprocity. Its inconveniences were nothing when compared with the loss of wealth and of power attending the current indiscriminate policy. "Free commerce and navigation are not to be given in exchange for restrictions and vexations; nor are they likely to produce a relaxation of them." But by granting favors where favors were due, by meeting prohibitions with prohibitions, the United States might, in the course of serving its own interest, bring other nations to the liberal standard.

The Report on Commerce was read in the House on December 19 and ordered to the committee of the whole. Jefferson, said the Secretary of Treasury, "threw this FIREBRAND of discord into the midst of the representatives . . . and instantly decamped to Monticello." Early in January, Madison introduced a series of resolutions based on the Report. France was stamped on its face, the Federalists charged. The movement for discrimination stemmed from the old unreasoning hostility to Britain, revived now solely for political effect. Whatever the disadvantages of the British trade, Federalists said, they were more than offset by the rewards in capital and credit, federal revenue, and dependable markets and supplies. Representatives of the eastern carrying states opposed discrimination, though they presumably had most to gain from the policy, while southerners, who had trembled at the grant of congressional power to legislate in this sphere, furnished the main support. As the anger against Britain mounted, so too did the prospect for the resolutions. But it mounted too far, bringing the two countries to the verge of war, causing the resolutions to be sidetracked in favor of a temporary embargo, and leading finally to the mission of John Jay, whose famous treaty consummated the British-centered policy of the Federalists—an astounding defeat for the Jeffersonian system.

Jefferson would observe these developments from his summit at Monticello. His retirement ended Washington's plan of a "coalition" government. For all its difficulties it had served the new nation well, checking extremism, balancing interests, commanding that element of unity so necessary if the government was to survive. But with the rise of political parties, the plan outlived its usefulness. Washington was reluctant to abandon it, and he knew this must be the consequence of Jefferson's withdrawal. One last appeal failed. He accepted Jefferson's resignation with assurances "that the opinion which I had formed of your integrity and talents, and which dictated your original nomination has been confirmed by the fullest experience, and that both have been eminently displayed in the discharge of your duty." In the critical year just passed the President had grown in Jefferson's estimation. He had failed to shake Washington's confidence in Hamilton and Treasury policy, a defeat so shattering that it robbed his partial victories in foreign affairs of character; but only later, from his Olympian perch, did he yield to his fears and view the President as a helpless captive of party. It never seemed to trouble him that he had helped to make this development inevitable.

Jefferson insisted his withdrawal from the public stage was final. He had been in the spotlight long enough, and as he wrote to an old friend, in the course of eighteen years he had had but two years at home. "It will be the second time my bark will have put into port with a design not to venture out again; and I trust it will be the last. My farm, my family and my books call me to them irresistibly." To these resolutions his Republican friends politely demurred, while the Federalists simply refused to believe them. The vauntings of pastoral quietude covered a poisonous ambition Jefferson dared not acknowledge even to himself. The retirement was only an interlude, John Adams mused. "Jefferson thinks by this step to get a reputation as an humble, modest, meek man, wholly without ambition or vanity. He may even have deceived himself into this belief. But if the prospect opens, the world will see and he will feel that he is as ambitious as Oliver Cromwell." If vanity is a qualification for seeing it in others, then Adams was a good judge. History would bear him out. While there is not the slightest reason to doubt the sincerity of Jefferson's motives in seeking retirement, had he planned it as an elaborate political stratagem he could not have planned more wisely.

Jefferson lingered over goodbyes in Philadelphia, discharged his servants, gathered the few things he had not sent by boat, took in the Friday meeting of the American Philosophical Society, and on the following Sunday, January 5, set forth, bumping his way by stage, private conveyance, and on horseback to his journey's end at Monticello on the 16th. He had, he thought, closed the last political chapter of his life.

CHAPTER EIGHT

Withdrawal and Return:

Vice President

But there have been many and still are many who, while pursuing the calm of soul of which I speak, have withdrawn from civic duty and taken refuge in retirement. Among such have been the most famous and by far the foremost philosophers and certain other earnest, thoughtful men who could not endure the conduct of either the people or their leaders; some of them, too, lived in the country and found their pleasure in the management of their private estates. Such men have had the same aim as kings—to suffer no want, to be subject to no authority, to enjoy their liberty, that is, in its essence, to live just as they pleased.

Cicero, De Officiis.

IN HIS MIND'S EYE Monticello had long been the scene of a pastoral idyl that only now, in the ripeness of his years, took full possession of Thomas Jefferson. Successive calls of public duty had carried him far from his element and robbed him of selfhood. Too long had he lived in what he hated; too long had he neglected the things he loved—his farm and family and books. Return to the orange-red highlands of his native Albemarle—"the Eden of the United States"—was a return to the paradise of his soul.

In letters to his friends he depicted himself as a plain farmer, an "antediluvian patriarch" among his children, and a political innocent who, with Montaigne, had found "ignorance the softest pillow on which a man can rest his head." He was still capable of outraged ejaculations on the conspiracy of kings, nobles, and priests against European liberty. "I am still warm whenever I think of these scoundrels," he said, "though I do it as seldom as I can, preferring infinitely to contemplate the tranquil growth of my lucerne and potatoes. I have so completely withdrawn myself from these spectacles of usurpation and misrule, that I do not take a single newspaper, nor read one a month; and I feel infinitely the happier for it." For years he had been accustomed to writing a dozen letters a day; now weeks passed without setting pen to paper as, farmer-like, he put off letters 'til a rainy day. "My next reformation," he said, "will be to allow neither pen, ink, nor paper to be kept on the farm. When I have accomplished this I shall be in a fair way to indemnifying myself for the drudgery in which I have passed my life."

Jefferson was now fifty years of age. His hair was turning gray, but his body was as strong and trim, his countenance as mild, his mind as nimble as in his youth. After a bout with rheumatism in the fall of 1794, he imagined for a time that age had caught up with him. But the torment passed. His habits bordered on the ascetic. He rose early: the sun never caught him in bed was his boast. He neither smoked nor drank, except light wines at dinner and a single glass of water a day. He ate moderately, giving vegetables the first place in his diet. Always busy, "a miser of his time," he expected the same diligence of others, and partly for this reason would not permit games of cards under his roof. He took his own amusement on horseback, riding solitary an hour or two every day regardless of the weather. "He was an uncommonly fine rider—sat easily upon his horse, and always had him in the most perfect control." From the first breath of spring to the last gasp of autumn he spent most of his waking hours in the open air, inspecting his grounds and shops and riding over his farms. "I live on my horse from an early breakfast to a late dinner, and very often after that till dark," he said. His ruddy skin flaked and freckled under the Virginia sun. He dressed plainly, put on no airs, and in every outer aspect was the image of the Virginia farmer he professed to be.

An eminent Frenchman came to visit this American Cato in June

1796. "I found him in the midst of the harvest," the Duc de La Rochefoucald-Liancourt wrote, "from which the scorching heat of the sun does not prevent his attendance." The Duke was one of those enlightened noblemen who in the declining years of the Old Regime had woven fact and fancy into the gossamer dream of America. In 1789 the dream seemed about to materialize in France. Liancourt was a leader of the Revolution. He it was who upon informing the King of the true state of affairs just before the fall of the Bastille heard the amazed cry, "But it is a revolt!" and retorted, "No, Sire, it is a revolution!" When Jefferson last saw the Duke he was president of the National Assembly and the principal author of the so-called abolition of the feudal system. Three years later the dream turned to ashes; he lost his estate, the head of the family, La Rochefoucald, was murdered; and Liancourt went into exile, first in England and then, in 1794, in the United States. From his base at Philadelphia he made five "voyages" which took him to Canada and to Georgia and most parts in between, studying the land and the people not as in a dream but as they appeared to a keen and friendly sojourner. He included Monticello in his itinerary as a matter of course. The house on the mountain's summit gradually acquired the fame of its master. Already travelers in number beat a track to Jefferson's door. A hard-headed Irishman, Isaac Weld, had stopped in March, and the Comte de Volney, perhaps the most celebrated traveler of the time, had just ended a leisurely visit when his compatriot in exile came upon Jefferson in the harvest field.

Although there was a political bond between the Frenchman and the American, they were men disenchanted with politics who at once found more interesting things to talk about. "In private life," Liancourt recorded, "Mr. Jefferson displays a mild, easy and obliging temper, though he is somewhat cold and reserved. His conversation is of the most agreeable kind, and he possesses a stock of information not inferior to that of any other man. In Europe he would hold a distinguished rank among men of letters, and as such he has already appeared there; at present he is employed with activity and perseverance in the management of his farms and buildings; and he orders, directs and pursues in the minutest detail every branch of business relative to them." These employments were dear to Liancourt's heart. An agricultural reformer before he was a revolutionist, an innovator of crops and tillage and stock on his own estate, a founder of the French Royal Agricultural Society, he at once recognized in Jefferson the republican counterpart of Europe's "improving landlord." Compared with his guest, the Virginian was a poor amateur. Eight bushels of wheat to the acre was hardly impressive; the ancient Romans had done better. Nevertheless, in his farming as in his politics, Jefferson had escaped from the tyranny of habit into the freedom of knowledge, and this was impressive in a country where bad practice had hardened into a system. "Above all," Liancourt wrote, "much good may be expected, if a contemplative mind like that of Mr. Jefferson, which takes the theory for its guide, watches its application with discernment, and rectifies it according to the peculiar circumstances and nature of the country, climate, and soil, and conformably to the experience which he daily acquires."

Jefferson's zeal for innovation and improvement extended to his house as well as to his fields. Monticello was in noble disarray. Jefferson was tearing down his house in order to make a better one, and the visitor had to keep a lookout for flying bricks. "Monticello, according to its first plan, was infinitely superior to all other houses in America, in point of taste and convenience; but at that time Mr. Jefferson had studied taste and the fine arts only in books," Liancourt observed. "His travels in Europe have supplied him with models; he has appropriated them to his design; and his new plan . . . will be accomplished before the end of the next year, and then his house will certainly deserve to be ranked with the most pleasant mansions of France and England." In fact, whatever its merits, the work of "re-edification" upset Jefferson and his family for quite a number of years.

The patriarch directed his domestic establishment with the same exactness and system he had shown in public affairs. "As he cannot expect any assistance from the two small neighboring towns, every article is made on his farm; his Negroes are cabinet-makers, carpenters, masons, bricklayers, smiths, etc." In the cares of the household he was assisted by two amiable daughters. The Frenchman thought the younger, Miss Maria, now seventeen, "remarkably handsome"— something of an understatement if the testimonies to her exquisite beauty are to be credited—and he hoped that Jefferson might find the philosophy to accept her loss in marriage and the good fortune to add a second worthy son-in-law to his family circle. Martha and her husband—more son than son-in-law, Liancourt thought—were at Monticello with their children every summer and much of the time in between. Never reconciled to their living at Varina, the distant James River plantation, Jefferson had induced Randolph *père* to part with Edgehill, a 1500-acre seat near Monticello; and despite a bitter feud between father and son the deed was done in 1792. Young Randolph soon began farming at Edgehill, though it was several years before the family actually settled there. Jefferson remained an over-anxious third party to this marriage. Martha had grown into a copy of her father, tall, bright-featured, gentle, and, from all accounts, the soul of matronly virtue. She still adored her father, once in a letter to him scolding "those who dare to think that any *new* ties can weaken the first and best of nature." On most points the new tie, Randolph, was her exact opposite. A restless, impulsive, and tormented man, whose unpredictable flights of temper were to make him a legend among his neighbors, Randolph sometimes felt like a "silly bird" among the swans at Monticello. Perhaps the "silly bird" should have taken his little swan and flown away, but his own affections were too deep to permit that, and it would have killed Jefferson. For Randolph, at least, the triangle was unhealthy. It shattered his self-esteem and threw him into fits of depression. In the summer of 1796, during Liancourt's visit, he was still suffering from a strange undiagnosed malady of body and mind that descended not long after Jefferson's retirement. The heart of the patriarch overflowed with love, but it was not selfless; and his need to remain the center of all domestic affection and management introduced a hidden flaw into the seemingly idyllic family circle at Monticello.

Jefferson's summit afforded no certain refuge from the political commotions of the world. He said his scheme was to pay no attention to them, but the world would not leave him alone and he had been too long in it to resign himself to the stoical politics he liked to imagine were his. He had been in retirement only eight months when President Washington asked him to go as a special envoy to Spain. He responded, from his bed of rheumatism, in terms that could not be misunderstood. There were earlier reports that he had actually arrived in Europe to negotiate with one or another of the great powers. The critical state of American foreign relations, together with the Whiskey Rebellion and other signposts of discontent on the home front, proved a severe test of Jefferson's political abnegation. The strife of nations and parties broke over the walls he had raised, and before a year passed he was making an experiment to determine the fastest postal route between Philadelphia and Albemarle.

Yet it was a retirement. His principal business of life now was not politics but the management of his estate. "The land left to the care of stewards has suffered as well as the buildings from the long absence of the master," Liancourt observed; "according to the custom of the country, it has been exhausted by successive culture." Jefferson hoped under his own management to make his lands bounteous again; and the outcome of this trial, so long deferred, must decide whether he and his children were to trudge through life mortgaged to British merchants or to enjoy the freedom of a great estate. His debts in 1794 were in excess of £7500, and another £1000 would be added the following year by a new judgment against the Wayles' heirs. (Randolph inherited a similar debt from his father.) The goal of debt freedom by the end of 1796 was apparently out of reach. He did not give up on it but was still struggling to reach it years later when he entered the presidency. Under so crushing a burden a man might lose the courage to pursue his vision. Jefferson, however, went ahead with his elaborate plans for Monticello at the same time that he labored to exact a profit from his lands. "I expected when I came home to be quite at my leisure," he wrote in 1796. "On the contrary, I never was so hard run with business." For all the rewards of retirement, it had its disappointments too; and he never found at Monticello the tranquility he sought.

Farming

Jefferson's land roll of 1794 shows that he was the lord of 10,647 acres. The property was divided more or less equally between Albemarle and the counties of Bedford and Campbell eighty or ninety miles to the southwest. The latter plantations, which he called collectively Poplar Forest, were under the supervision of a trusted manager, and Jefferson seldom went there. About 800 acres were under cultivation, chiefly in the prime money crop, tobacco. The lands in Albemarle were divided into several plantations, lying on either side of the Rivanna River, nearly all contiguous, and all directed from Monticello. Jefferson wanted to place Shadwell and the adjoining farms across the river under tenants, leasing his laborers with the land; but he could not perfect this system. He tilled more than 1200 acres in Albemarle. His total force of slaves numbered 152 on the roll he took in November, a decrease of about one-quarter from the roll of eleven years before. He held on to his land more tenaciously than to his slaves. In 1793 he sold Elk Hill, the James River plantation, as a contribution to his debts, though neither deed nor money passed hands for four years. After this he made only minor adjustments in his landholdings, except for handsome conveyances to his children.

Viewing his native country as a virtual Eden, Jefferson had an exalted opinion of its capabilities for agriculture. No landscape was lovelier than that upon which he gazed from Monticello—an endless panorama of fields and forests and hills—no climate was as mild and healthful, nor had nature been niggardly in her supreme gift of the soil. Perhaps he communicated his enthusiasm to his visitors; at any rate, they too formed a good opinion of the land. William Strickland, an English agriculturist who called in 1795, later wrote, "a richer district by nature there cannot be, than all those counties which lie at the eastern front of the Blue Ridge." In truth, the natural assets were matched by appalling liabilities. The surface soil, while fertile, was shallow and underlaid with hard clay almost impenetrable by the plows of that day, thus hindering the replenishment of plant food and constantly exposing the loose upper layer to leaching and erosion. The hilliness of the terrain accentuated the latter evil. The normal rainfall was quite sufficient for piedmont crops, but too often it came in huge downpours that drowned the fields and washed the precious topsoil into muddy streams and rivers. Jefferson spoke of "such rains as never came since Noah's flood," and moderately estimated the loss of soil during one summer at a year's rent. At other times the earth was so hard and dry it could not be plowed; and his well atop Monticello failed with distressing frequency. The winters, mild as a rule, sometimes froze his wheat in the ground. The land and the climate, for all their charms, were less suited to cultivation than Jefferson supposed.

He was right, nevertheless, in seeing the problem as one of art rather than of nature. Certainly he was under no illusion about the condition of Virginia agriculture, nor indeed of American husbandry generally. It was a scandal to enlightened farmers everywhere. The Virginia lands had been worked for quick profits, exhausted, then abandoned or left to beggar the wretched men who persisted in cultivating them. Bad as the situation was in New York or Pennsylvania, where the older lands yielded little more than those in Virginia, it was there at its worst, "the lowest state of degradation," in Strickland's opinion. The degradation had spread from the tidewater westward to Jefferson's Eden. A new settler described Albemarle in the 1790's, barely half a century after it had been redeemed from the wilderness, as "a scene of desolation that baffles description— farm after farm worn out, washed and gullied, so that scarcely an acre could be found in a place fit for cultivation." The causes of this rapid deterioration naturally invited speculation. Slavery was prominently mentioned. Jefferson's opposition to the institution had not abated, and he sometimes wondered if he was master enough to succeed at farming with slave labor; yet, recognizing the futility of making slavery the scapegoat, he wasted little time on the subject. Besides, he had demonstrated to his own satisfaction (though to no one else's) that Virginia slave labor was considerably less costly than English (and surely American) free labor, so the real cause of the agricultural malady lay elsewhere. The management of large estates required the employment of overseers, a class of men all too conveniently blamed by Virginia planters for the ravaging of their lands. Jefferson had the usual trouble with overseers. Seven had come and gone at Monticello during the decade of his absence. In 1793 he took pains to recruit one in Maryland, supposedly uncorrupted by the habits of the Virginia class, only to have to discharge him after a year's sorry experience; and he went through four more before 1801. But he drew up no indictment of overseers. Virginia estates lacked sufficient capital for large-scale improvements. This was part of the explanation. Another part was political: laws and policies which enriched merchants, stock-jobbers, bankers, and speculators at the expense of the landholding class. But Jefferson the farmer never gave as much weight to these political evils as some of his friends; nor did he, with some others, trace the degeneration of Virginia agriculture to democratizing laws, such as those for the divisibility of estates, which he had inspired.

Jefferson ascribed the malady primarily to a system of culture that could not fail to desolate any country where it was pursued, as in his own, over two or three generations. "The highlands where I live," he explained, "have been cultivated about sixty years. The culture was tobacco and Indian corn, as long as they would pay the labor; then they were turned out. After four or five year's rest, they would bring good corn again, and in double that time, perhaps, good tobacco. Then they would be exhausted by a second series of tobacco and corn." This remorseless "cropping" impoverished the earth. Tobacco was the first evil, "a culture productive of infinite wretchedness," but corn, especially under shallow plowing straight up and down the hillsides, was a close second. The former, it was said, enriched the planter and ruined the soil, the latter ruined both. Tobacco had been abandoned for wheat in Jefferson's part of the country. He had shifted to wheat in Albemarle in 1790 on the expectation of the rising market in Europe. He was not disappointed; but he could never get away from tobacco in Bedford, and corn was such a staple of the plantation economy he had to conquer his aversion to it. The common rotation began with wheat, followed by corn, then a year's fallow, the cycle repeated until the fields died. While exhaustion might be slower under this "three shift system," it was no less certain than under the barbarous system it replaced.

The restoration of the soil was the starting point of all improvement. Jefferson believed with the scientific agriculturists of the time that the soil held a given quantity of plant food, that it was gradually depleted under cultivation—more rapidly by some growths than by others—but that it could be constantly replenished by restorative crops in proper rotation. He had not himself been a scientific student of agriculture. He was, of course, acquainted with the agricultural revolution inaugurated in England sixty years before by Jethro Tull's famous work, *Horse-Hoeing Husbandry*. He knew some of the prolific writings of Arthur Young and opened correspondence with this great reformer's associates on the government chartered Board of Agriculture, one of whom, William Strickland, stopped at Monticello in 1795. "Should you pass by," Jefferson wrote to a neighboring farmer soon after his retirement, "you will find me more eager to talk of Home [Lord Kames] and Young than Grotius and Vattel." Like the gentlemen farmers in England, he was enchanted by the Romans, whose theory and practice had yet to be surpassed. Adam Dickson's *Husbandry of the Ancients,* a two-volume compilation of the Latin writers, was a favorite among his many books on agricultural subjects.

But he was a practical farmer, not a bookish one, and he probably learned more from George Washington and George Logan, progressive farmers like himself, than from all his books. For several years they had been applying the "English system" to their own lands. Jefferson had observed the results. Dr. Logan's careful experiments at Stenton had proven the superiority, at least in that locality, of a system that employed red clover as the principal soil improver in a nine-year rotation. Listening to the good doctor, seeing the richness of his place, Jefferson became an enthusiast for cover crops, especially red clover. The substitution of clover for unproductive fallow protected the tired lands from the baking sun and drenching rains; it enriched the soil; it furnished fodder to support livestock which, in turn, supplied the farmer with manure for his fields. Since the progressive husbandry did away with pasturage altogether, working the fields more or less continuously, the production of manure was an essential element in the plan of rotation. It also went to the principles of deep plowing first championed by Tull, for the application of manure dissolved the soil particles, thus permitting the pulverization believed necessary to good husbandry. In his own practice Jefferson was attentive to these matters of plowing and manuring, but his experimentation centered on the determination of the right crops in the right rotation. This, he thought, "the most important of all questions a farmer has to decide."

Before he left Philadelphia he had decided with Logan's advice on an eight-cycle rotation, the last three in clover. On second thought he dropped one year of clover, made other adjustments, and ended with a seven-year rotation. The plan called for the division of his farms into seven fields all equal. "In all successions of crops," he instructed Madison, "the fields must be supposed equal, each field to go through the same succession, and each year's crop to be the same. On these data the laws of combination pronounce that the number of fields and number of years constituting a complete rotation, must always be equal." Since he had 280 acres in tillage at Monticello, each field would be 40 acres; each would have its own granary, and be allotted four men and four women laborers, four horses and four oxen, a complement of plows, other implements, and so on. Such a farm on his crop rotation would support about 90 head of cattle; they, in turn, would make manure enough for spreading every field once in seven years. By commencing the rotation in each field at successive points in the seven-year cycle, the aggregate produce would be the same from year to year. The rotation ensured a balance between exhausting grain crops (wheat, rye, corn) and soil amelioratives (peas, clover, succory, vetch). It would also provide an annual crop of turnips and potatoes, primarily as animal food, though Jefferson promoted the latter, a genuine American article, as a substitute for corn in the human diet.

Such was the general system of farming Liancourt observed in Albemarle in 1796. Of course, Jefferson's plans were never fully realized. Nor is it easy to imagine under what circumstances they might have been. They expressed a rage for order and system sure to be embarrassed in the untidy and unpredictable business of farming. If agriculture were a species of architecture—if the structuring of fields and rotations were more important than the day-to-day cultivation of crops—then Jefferson would have been a superior farmer. A farmer who thinks like a mathematician is an easy object of ridicule—too easy, for ridicule diverts understanding. In farming, as in politics, Jefferson made allowance for the gap between theory and practice and seldom found it necessary to betray his responsibility to either one. The plans, the diagrams, the mathematical calculations he made for his farms served him as blueprints, rather like the architect's; and in the execution he simply did the best he could, relying on experience to correct his errors. This was the way of the thinking reformer. And in a science so little known as agriculture, reform, though it must proceed on a constructive plan, must also give a large berth to laborious methods of trial and error. Jefferson did. Still he was disappointed that his plans fell so far short of execution. His fields, sloping and irregular, were "too rough even to please the eye," he complained in 1796, "and as yet unreclaimed from the barbarous state in which the slovenly business of tobacco making left them." He never had enough cattle, usually let them forage for themselves, but not on tilled ground, thus losing the dung altogether. This was a common defect of American husbandry and certainly of Jefferson's. The slackness of slave labor, the caprices of the weather, the fluctuations of the market—all helped to upset his well-laid plans. Hopes continued to run high, but the profit account was discouraging. Two years after his return to public office he resumed the detestable culture of tobacco in Albemarle: a poignant confession of failure.

"His system is entirely confined to himself," the Duc de Liancourt noted; "it is censured by some of his neighbors, who are also employed in improving their culture with ability and skill, but he adheres to it, and thinks it is founded on just observations." Plainly, the Frenchman was not sure that it was. He admired Jefferson's "science" but thought less of his "skill." It was scarcely creditable that a man of Jefferson's knowledge should decline to enclose his fields, preferring instead to divide them by rows of peach trees—an aesthetic extravagance he could ill afford—or should allow his cattle to graze in the woods, or make no effort to control the drainage on his hillsides.

One prominent Virginian who dissented from leading points of Jefferson's system was John Taylor of Caroline. Searching for a good drilling machine in 1794, Jefferson opened an agricultural correspondence with this former political cohort. "There is a spice of fanaticism in my nature upon two subjects—," Taylor confessed, "agriculture and republicanism, which all who set in motion are sure to suffer by." Taylor did run on, dropping useful hints on many things, and Jefferson, lacking that "spice of fanaticism," had difficulty upholding his end of the account. At Hazelwood, on the Rappahannock River, Taylor had been working for years to restore his worn-out lands. His experiments led him to reject the "English system" of cover crops and manure and long rotation. He did not doubt the importance of manure; on the contrary, the best system of agriculture was that which produced the most manure. But English ideas on this subject were inapplicable to America, where it was cheaper to buy an acre of new land than to manure an old one.

Taylor had no confidence in green crops, held a high opinion of corn, and practiced a simple four-shift rotation, half in wheat and corn, half in fallow. Unmoved by these strictures, avoiding argument, Jefferson viewed his differences with the Caroline planter as more verbal than substantial. "You keep half your lands in culture, the other half in nurse; so I propose to do. . . . My years of rest, however, are employed, two of them in producing clover, yours in volunteer herbage. . . . I think that the important improvement for which the world is indebted to Young is the substitution of clover crops for unproductive fallow." In the passage of time the two Virginians, Taylor the hard-headed practitioner and Jefferson the constructive theorist, approached a middle ground.

Jefferson exchanged ideas with many persons, American and European, and not only ideas but plants, seeds, devices, and implements of husbandry. This continued an old enterprise, more directly related now to his own immediate purposes. Whenever he learned of a promising innovation in farming, he was eager to try it at Monticello and, if the experiment succeeded, to share the benefits with his fellow cultivators. He got from Washington in 1794 the seed of the succory, a "green dressing" which flourished at Mount Vernon. Planted in Albemarle it was an indifferent grower the first year but luxuriated the second. Jefferson become an ardent champion of this humble plant and awarded it a place in his rotation. On the other hand, he was disappointed in lucerne (alfalfa), giving it up after a brief trial. He never knew—no one knew—why one plant flourished and another failed; the best the agriculturist could do at this stage of the science was to follow the tedious methods of trial and error experimentation. His greatest success was with Logan's clover, but almost any ameliorative aroused his interest. For example, the "true winter vetch," a European plant he had observed in his travels abroad and wished to try at Monticello. Unable to obtain it from Philadelphia, where it was unknown, he asked Thomas Pinckney to send the seed from London. Nothing came of this, but Strickland, on his return to England sent him the vetch. Apparently, after these efforts, the plant failed, for it never entered into his rotation. During his visit the English agriculturist had given him the seed of the Swedish rutabaga, earlier imported into England, and now through Jefferson disseminated in the United States. Sheep turned turnips into manure and supplied the plantation with mutton and wool. So it went—each innovation was a link in the chain of improved husbandry. Taking a hint from Arthur Young, Jefferson began raising sheep at Monticello in 1794; but some years passed before he, with a few other Americans, turned his attention to improving the breed.

If he could be accused of negligence toward animal husbandry, the same could not be said with respect to farm machinery. Here, too, progress was painfully slow and the rewards were poor compensation for the time and money spent in securing them. He was alert to any improvement in the plow and perfected his own moldboard of least resistance; he kept a lookout for better seed drills (Young said there wasn't a good one in England); and he put the Scotch threshing machine to work in Virginia. A scale model of this horse-powered machine, sneaked out of England under Pinckney's auspices, finally arrived at Norfolk near the end of 1793. Jefferson could hardly wait to see it in action. But to construct the machine with his own labor was a much bigger job than he had counted on. It took three years. The clumsy contraption of gears and revolving beaters was mounted on a wagon and carried from one field and farm to another. While its performance was below expectations, and Jefferson hoped to find a better one, it was still a great advance over the almost universal practice of "treading" the grain from the chaff. His wheat was cleaner than his neighbors'. On the basis of his own time studies, the machine doubled his output. Earlier and speedier threshing eliminated infestation of the grain by the weevil; it also released one-half his laborers, previously employed on the treading floors, to begin the season's plowing. Jefferson never really understood machinery, only what it could do, but he liked to tinker. One of the products of his tinkering was a seed-box for sowing clover, constructed on the basis of a hint in an agricultural journal. The seed-box, he informed Taylor, "reduces the expense of seeding from six shilling to two shilling and three pence the acre, and does the business better than is possible to be done by the human hand."

Jefferson was a meticulous observer of farm operations. As Albert Jay Nock has said, his mind had something of the quality of the modern efficiency engineer.

Julius Shard fills the two-wheeled barrow in 3 minutes, and carried it 30 yards in 1½ minutes more. Now this is four loads of the common barrow with one wheel. So that suppose the 4 loads put in at the same time viz. 3 minutes, 4 trips will take 4 × 1½ minutes = 6, which added to 3 minutes filling = 9 minutes to fill and carry the same earth which was filled and carried in the two-wheeled barrow in 4½ minutes. From a trial I made with the same two-wheeled barrow, I found that a man could dig and carry to a distance of 50 yds, 5 cubical yds of earth in a day of 12 hours length. Ford's Phil did it; not overlooked and having to mount his loaded barrow up a bank 2 f. high and tolerably steep.

This little study reflects Jefferson's approach to plantation management. He recorded his observations in his Farm Book, a volume of blank pages with chapter headings on every phase of farming. Here, too, was the calendar of his works and days: the fall's plowing and sowing and gathering of potatoes, corn, fodder; in the winter, clearing land, cutting firewood, repairing fences and roads, hauling wheat and floating it to market; in the spring, oxen and men set to plowing as soon as the sun warmed the earth, then planting corn, clover, peas, and so on; summer, harvest. Practically the whole force of slaves was employed in the harvest. In 1795, 17 were cradlers, 5 reapers, 7 stackers, 36 gatherers, plus cooks and loaders and carters. Working from dawn to dusk through 320 acres of wheat and rye, on both sides of the river, the harvest was finished in 10 to 11 days. The performance did not measure up to Jefferson's standards. There had been waste motion, idle time, and bottlenecks. On the basis of his inspection he drew up a new plan under which "the whole machine would move in exact equilibrio" so that the same acreage would be harvested with fewer hands in six days. But, alas, men were not machines and harvests could not be reduced to mathematical rule. The harvest the next year, though better, took the same muscle and the same time as before.

Despite the irrelevance of some of Jefferson's plans and calculations, the disjointed empiricism of others, all were informed by a unifying purpose: the improvement of agriculture for human welfare. Agriculture was his livelihood, but his zeal for improvement was actuated by interests larger than his own. By taking upon himself "the risk of a first experiment," he hoped to be more useful to his neighbors, who could not afford the risks but whose lands also cried for reform. His correspondence reached far beyond the neighborhood, of course, and so, too, might the ambit of his usefulness. The progress of agriculture and the increase of human happiness were all one. "Science never appears so beautiful," he wrote to an English coadjutor, "as when applied to the uses of human life, nor any use of it so engaging as those of agriculture and domestic economy." His idealized husbandman held the sum of human happiness. He sought it for himself, but not, after all, in the antique guise of a pastoral poem. He sought it in the modern guise of agricultural science. He really believed with Jonathan Swift "that whoever could make two ears of corn or two blades of grass to grow upon a spot of ground where only one grew before, would deserve better of mankind and do more essential service to his country than the whole race of politicians put together."

Whatever the public benefit of Jefferson's services, they probably made little if any difference in his account of profit and loss. He kept a day-to-day record of his financial transactions down to the last penny. He was forever calculating costs. (The habit stayed with him to the very end: on his deathbed he noted, "a gallon of lamp oil, costing $1.25 has lighted my chamber highly 25 nights, for 6 hours a night which is 5 cents a night & 150 hours.") Still he was not a good accountant—and anything but frugal. Prudent in small expenditures, he was lavish in large ones. His concern with costs, as with efficiency generally, seldom rose above the level of petty detail. The practice of plantation accounting, later developed to a fine point, was still in a primitive state. Jefferson itemized everything but seemed to know nothing of debit and credit accounting; hidden costs, such as depreciation, rarely entered into his reckoning; and he never actually balanced, or closed, his books. Annual income from wheat and tobacco fluctuated wildly. For the seven years 1794–1800, it probably averaged between $4000 and $5000. Since most of the Bedford tobacco was mortgaged, he looked to the produce of his Albemarle lands, to wheat primarily, for personal income. Prices were high. The crop improved in 1795, and the bumper harvest of 1796 helped to indemnify earlier losses. Then the elements turned against him. A severe winter succeeded a dry fall. (On December 24 the thermometer plunged to five degrees below zero at Monticello, breaking the low point he had stated in the *Notes on Virginia*.) In desperation he planted tobacco again, at first on a small scale but in 1798 almost exclusively. In that year the price at Richmond soared to $13 a hundred pounds. Jefferson paid $2000 on his old debts with comparative ease. The temptation to go entirely into tobacco was irresistible. But the market was a fickle temptress. The price collapsed the following year, and Jefferson, after withholding his tobacco for several months in anticipation of a rising market that never came, finally had to sell for seven dollars. He got only six dollars in 1800. If his total crop approximated 50,-000 pounds, as seems likely, the gross was only $3000. His annual account with Richmond merchants for supplies and services exceeded that amount. Clearly, after making allowance for other income, he was hard-pressed. On the whole, any net profits realized in these years took the form of capital improvements at Monticello.

His plantations were a good deal less self-sufficient in these years than later. Only the most basic supplies could be obtained locally, in Charlottesville or in Milton, the latter a now forgotten village located on the Rivanna at the head of navigation; other things came from Richmond and Philadelphia. Cash was a rarity in this rural community, and Jefferson, like other farmers, necessarily engaged in barter. He traded the work of his blacksmith for beef and butter, some of his wheat for store supplies, and a few bushels annually for whiskey. He seems never to have had a sufficiency even of corn. Clothing was a major item, for his spinners and weavers met only a fraction of the annual requisitions. Nor was he self-sufficient in labor. His records list eleven hired slaves in 1795, which represented a cost in excess of $400 a year. Many of his own slaves were mortgaged to his creditors, and, as before, he occasionally sold slaves in the effort to meet his debts. Such were his financial straits in 1796, when the new judgment on the Wayles estate went against him, that he had to mortgage away what little equity he had accumulated in his slaves in order to protect his creditors. As the old slave Isaac said of his former master, "he want rich himself—only his larnin."

In the management of his slaves Jefferson encouraged diligence but was instinctively too lenient to demand it. By all accounts he was a kind and generous master. His conviction of the injustice of the institution strengthened his sense of obligation toward its victims. It was chiefly with a view to placing his slaves "on the comfortable footing of the laborers of other countries" that he had gone outside Virginia for an overseer in 1793. It was a costly experiment, apparently without mitigating effect. There were limits to his own superintendence, but within them he would not allow his slaves to be over-driven, or whipped unless at the last resort, preferring rather to penalize the lazy and reward the industrious. He kept detailed records on his slaves, not only because it was part of good management, but because he cared about their health and welfare. The practice was to put the children to work at ten years of age, the boys at the nail forge, the girls at the spinning wheel. When they turned sixteen—and about one-half of his slaves were under sixteen—they went into the fields or learned a trade. The field hands lived in log huts clustered at convenient places over his farms, while the artisan families were similarly housed on the slopes of the mountain near their work. The house servants were privileged, of course. A number of them belonged to the Hemings family, part of the Wayles legacy, for whom Jefferson showed particular affection. He let Bob Hemings buy his freedom in 1794, the employer to whom he had been hired for a number of years having advanced the purchase price of £60. And James Hemings, who had been with him in Paris and Philadelphia and learned to cook in the French manner, won his freedom upon fulfilling the pledge to teach his art to a worthy successor. In 1796 Jefferson gave him his freedom papers and $30 to get to Philadelphia. He might have done the same for others as faithful, skilled, and enterprising as James, but the state of his affairs would not permit this indulgence, and to turn loose the mass of slaves would have been, in his eyes, an act of heartless cruelty. Until the institution itself could be extinguished, slavery was an evil he had to live with, and he managed it with what little dosings of humanity a diabolical system permitted. His anxiety for a solution to this problem increased after the horrendous slave revolts in Santo Domingo. The storm there was a portent of things to come in the southern states, he thought. He was pleased that younger Virginians, like St. George Tucker, whose *Dissertation on Slavery* he read in 1797, were reviving the plan of gradual emancipation long associated with his name. "But if something is not done, and soon done," he warned, "we shall be the murderers of our own children."

Jefferson called himself a nail-maker as well as a farmer. Realizing it would be some time before his farms were restored to profitable operation, he had, while still in Philadelphia, cast about for a modest business to help him through this trying period. He at first thought of manufacturing potash at Monticello, but finally decided in favor of nails. The manufacture was simple and required little capital; Negro boys, otherwise a nuisance, might be employed in it; and it would be useful to his neighbors. "My new trade of nail-making," he remarked, "is to me in this country what an additional title of nobility or the ensigns of a new order are in Europe." The naillery, together with the blacksmith's shop, formerly at Shadwell, was established on Mulberry Row, which ran along the southerly slope of the mountain below the mansion. Here was no pastoral Eden but belching smoke and clanging hammers. He began with one fire, turning out nails by hand. With the acquisition of a cutting machine in 1796, he added two more fires and raised the output to 10,000 nails a day. Usually a dozen boys were employed, "overlooked" by the smith, Great George, though the master himself supervised the entire operation and was frequently at the forge. According to Isaac, a blacksmith, Jefferson enjoyed making things—keys, locks, chains, and so on—in iron and brass.

The naillery was a modestly successful business, at least in the early years. It kept his family supplied with "groceries," that is store-bought goods—coffee, tea, sugar, rice, brandy—some obtained locally, some from Philadelphia, amounting altogether to $400 or $500 a year. He sold or bartered his nails at Richmond wholesale prices, counting the saving of the freight to give his product a preference with the retailers in the upper country. The system worked for a time, but then, just as he expanded his output, the merchants who dealt in English hardware caught on to his scheme and persuaded the local retailers to refuse the Monticello nails. "The two importing houses at Milton have . . . brought a deluge of British nails with a view, as is said, of putting down my work." To defeat this typically British artifice, Jefferson devised a new system. His nails were sold on consignment to single dealers in Charlottesville, Milton, and Staunton, across the mountains in the Shenandoah Valley. The dealers, each with a monopoly in his town, retailed the nails at the Richmond wholesale price plus a 5 per cent commission. The plan was not the unqualified success he had hoped for. He continued to be plagued by British competition; the consignees took the nails on credit and were slow to pay, while he had his own bills for nail rod to meet in Philadelphia; the price of the rod went up and he had trouble keeping it in stock. When the nail money stopped he was "painfully embarrassed" to pay his grocery bills. But he survived these hardships, and the nail factory operated for many years.

Jefferson had plans upon his retirement of undertaking improvements in local navigation and commerce. "I wish to heaven the spirit of mill-building and manufacturing . . . could spread itself to Albemarle," he wrote to a fellow Virginian in 1793. "We are miserably circumstanced . . . as to the disposal of our wheat. We can neither manufacture nor sell it there, and tho' we have five mill seats at the head of the navigation of the Rivanna, we cannot get mills built." The grain of the country would be worth a good deal more if it could be carried to Richmond in the form of flour; thus the importance of mills. But capital was scarce, enterprise sluggish, and engineering skills non-existent. Years before Jefferson had embarked on a project to restore the gristmill at Shadwell destroyed in the flood of 1771. This involved construction of a canal three-quarters of a mile long and eventually, as it turned out, a new dam as well. Costly and difficult, the work was repeatedly suspended. He was determined to resume it in 1793, having in the meantime incorporated a manufacturing mill in his plan. Three years passed before the work actually resumed. The first stage, the canal, was finally completed in 1803 at the astronomical cost of $20,000.

"I have sometimes asked myself," Jefferson wrote in a memorandum to himself, probably about 1800, "whether my country is the better for my having lived at all?" And he answered, "I do not know that it is," but then went on to list a number of services. The Declaration of Independence, the Statute for Religious Freedom and other acts of the Virginia Assembly—these were mentioned, of course. First in time, however, and therefore at the head of the list, was his work in opening the Rivanna to navigation. The amazing fortitude he showed in this enterprise over the years, and the manufacturing connected with it, stemmed from the conviction that it was useful to his country. He also named the introduction of olive plants from France and of upland rice from Africa. "The greatest service which can be rendered any country is, to add a useful plant to its culture; especially, a bread grain; next in value to bread is oil." Jefferson made no great discoveries in agricultural science, and indeed on his record as a practical farmer "science" established no certain superiority to common sense; yet time would vindicate the faith he exemplified in the improving sciences' works for human welfare.

Monticello Renewed

Monticello was the name of a mountain, the name of a farm, above all the name of a house. The house was an ideal: the congealed expression in brick and mortar and wood of a man's capacity to humanize his environment. As an ideal it would never be finished. Jefferson had worked a dozen years to create his first conception of Monticello—the "elegant" house described by the Marquis de Chastellux, the house where his wife died, and which he left in 1783. It no longer pleased him when he prepared to return to the mountain a decade later. He was born with an irrepressible urge to build, felt it in every house he lived in, and indulged it on every possible occasion, public or private. His passion for architecture was exuberant. Monticello did not contain it, though there it flowed long and lavishly. "They was forty years at work upon that house before Mr. Jefferson stopped building," old Isaac recalled. Monticello was the work of a lifetime, not simply a building but a continuing act of creation and recreation; "and so I hope it will remain during my life," Jefferson himself said, "as architecture is my delight, and putting up, and pulling down, one of my favorite amusements."

Perhaps there is no need to probe further into Jefferson's reasons for remodeling in the 1790's. "Architecture is my delight." Added to this personal pleasure was the satisfaction found in the instruction of his countrymen. To produce a reformation in this most useful of the fine arts, to elevate the public taste, to raise on the American landscape a shining model of republican dignity was a work of "permanent improvement" scarcely less important than improvements in agriculture. His example, to some extent his teachings, inspired the first generation of professional architects in the new nation. Men like Benjamin Latrobe and Robert Mills were his disciples even if he was not, in any formal sense, their teacher. He had learned the art almost exclusively from books, above all from the great folio volumes of Palladio, whose influence fixed Jefferson's style before he set foot outside his own country. In Europe the noble designs he had admired from afar came alive. He never saw an authentic Palladian villa—the master's creations lay beyond Jefferson's hurried steps in Italy—but Roman classicism was the fashion in Paris and several of the elegant new town houses incorporated Palladian features. He was "violently smitten" with one of these, the hôtel de Salm, which he visited almost daily, perching himself on a parapet of the Tuileries nearby and twisting his neck around to view the object of his delight. When he drew his plan for the President's House in Washington, he at first thought to take this pavilion splendidly columned in front and rear for his model, then laid it aside in favor of the purest Palladio, the Villa Rotunda near Vicenza, which he had never seen and which had, in fact, more than a decade before been his model for the Governor's House in Richmond. The neo-classical buildings he saw in Paris, in Amsterdam, and in London too, though he thought English architecture "wretched," offered a profusion of suggestion without in any way unsettling the style he had derived from books. If anything, he turned more unreservedly than before to the chaste forms of Palladio and, as in his adaptation of the Maison Carrée, beyond them to the ancient fountainhead itself. At any rate, it was while in Europe that he began to revise his conception of Monticello. Planning commenced in 1792, and all was in readiness months before he retired from office.

The house as it stood was a two-story center block with shallow wings terminating in octagonal bays. Porticoes adorned both fronts. The entrance hall, stairs on either side, led into a grand salon, or parlor, as Jefferson called it, which projected half its length toward the western portico in the form of an octagon. The dining room was in the wing to the right, the drawing room and master's quarters in the wing to the left. His library was nicely accommodated in the spacious quarters above the parlor. The "attic" space under the low horizontal roof line and above the wings on either side of the central mass contained several small bedrooms. According to the master plan of 1772, the basement was to connect at either end with long L-shaped wings sunk into the northern and southern slopes and covered with terraces on a level with the main floor of the house.

But these "dependencies" had not yet been built. Nor had the second of the two small "outchambers." "Honeymoon Lodge" stood alone at the southwest corner of the garden front.

Handsome as it was, this house no longer met Jefferson's needs on the points of size, convenience, and taste. He wanted more room to acommodate Martha and her family, Maria's when she married, at such times as they could be at Monticello; also his sisters, who often visited the highlands in the summer, and the many friends and strangers to whom he extended his hospitality. Personal convenience was probably a consideration in the expansion of his quarters on the first floor. Other considerations were aesthetic, even at the expense of convenience. In Paris he had admired the low, unpretentious elegance of houses that seemed to have but one story. He had seen second floors constructed as mezzanines with great advantage to the first. He had fallen under the spell of domes and seen how they could be managed with becoming modesty in a private residence. None of these features was novel; they were Palladian, but he had not fully understood them before. His upright center block lost its appeal, and he determined to incorporate the features he now admired in an enlarged Monticello. There was some awkwardness in this, for although these features were Palladian, like the original, he could not start over from the ground up. He had to build on to what he had.

The new design did away with the second story of the original and doubled the width of the house. This meant tearing down and rebuilding the entire east front, remounting its portico, and erecting a mezzanine floor across the length of the new portion. The one-story effect was achieved by ingeniously blending the windows of the main floor with those of the mezzanine floor. Octagonal bays at both ends of the new front duplicated an existing feature, though Jefferson sacrificed the effect of the octagons by uniting the pair at either end with arcaded loggias. The doors from the east portico led into a spacious and lofty hall. Corridors to the right and left gave access to the new rooms—three bedrooms and a library. In the former Jefferson provided for alcove beds, another Parisian touch. The space between the alcoves was barely enough to accommodate two narrow stairways to the mezzanine. Jefferson did not care for elegant staircases. By eliminating this feature he saved space and money

—one of his few gestures toward economy—and also ensured the privacy of the bedrooms above. There were five of these, accessible from corridors that joined in the open gallery above the entrance hall. There were still other bedrooms on a skylighted upper floor well obscured from outside by an ornamental balustrade that encircled the roof of the house. Only one change was proposed in the west front, the addition of a dome, but it was the crowning touch. The dome rose upon the walls that had been Jefferson's library in the old house. He apparently intended to put the dome, or "sky room," to some use, but what it was, or what use it ever actually had, is still a matter of conjecture.

Such was the new Monticello. The plan was not matured all at once, but it was fully embodied in a drawing Jefferson made in 1796. As the work progressed he figured the specifications down to the last detail. In a notebook kept for this purpose are sketches, computations, and builder's directions for cornices, columns, dome, friezes, dados, fireplaces, mantles, chimneys, windows, curtains, and so on. The house would thus become an unrivaled, and quite inexhaustible, statement of his own personality. It had no prototype. Combining elements derived from ancient models, from the Palladian revival, and French neo-classicism, all beautifully articulated with the natural setting and practical requirements of the master, it had an architectural integrity wholly its own, and so can only be described as Jeffersonian.

The new façade was an extraordinary achievement. The house clung graciously to the mountain eminence in self-assured serenity; white columns, dome, and woodwork brilliantly accented the quiet charm of native red brick; and, though the dimunitive appearance was deceptive, the treatment of the windows and the perfect symmetry of line and proportion throughout achieved coherent form scaled to the human life contained within. By the same token, however, the interior arrangements were not altogether satisfactory. Here, too, especially in the public rooms, the taste was classical. Jefferson gave the same attention to the order of his columns on the inside as on the outside; and it might be noticed that they progressed from the sturdy Doric of the portico, through the more graceful Ionic of the hall, terminating in the elegant profusion of the Corinthian in the parlor. In the disposition of his rooms he was remarkedly free from Palladian rigidities and sought, rather, his own convenience. Part of the problem was that he was remodeling, which set limitations to his freedom; besides, as a working architect Jefferson tended, even in Monticello, to sacrifice livability within to stylistic effect out of doors. The dome cost him the spacious room that had been his library, for which the elongated octagonal quarters on the first floor was a poor exchange. Being adjacent to his bedroom, the new library was a gain in convenience, of course, as were all the added rooms downstairs. But those upstairs, reached by cramped lateral stairs, poorly ventilated, and lighted from windows near the floor or from skylights, had less to recommend them.

It was many years before the house took something like a finished form. As in most of his undertakings, public and private, Jefferson refused to be intimidated by temporary obstacles and inconveniences, and he expected greater efficiency in the execution than circumstances would permit. The demolition of the east front, first scheduled for the spring of 1793, did not actually occur until three years later. Meanwhile, thousands of bricks were baked on the premises, stone and lumber brought up the mountain, and orders placed in Philadelphia and London for window frames, glass, and other articles. The old walls had been built solid; pulling them down was as big a job as putting up new ones. Jefferson had counted on completing both jobs before the return of winter, but the house was only partially covered-in when the first blast came in November and suspended building for the season. The roof was still on, so the place was habitable, if anything but comfortable. Rains poured in, brickbats flew, and once Maria tumbled through the floor into the cellar, "miraculously" without injury. When Martha came in August she took up quarters in the "outchamber" and soon gave birth to another daughter, Ellen Wayles. The walls were in place the next summer. Now the old roof had to come off and the new one laid before another winter. Jefferson's duties as Vice President interrupted his personal supervision, however, and things lagged more than usual at Monticello. Whether or not Maria was wed to John Wayles Eppes in October 1797 under her father's roof or under the blue sky above Monticello can only be guessed; but the house was both roofless and tenantless the ensuing winter and the next. There were recurrent problems of workmen and materials. "Scarcely a stroke has been done towards covering the house since I went away . . . ," he wrote to Maria on his return in March 1799. "It seems as if I should never get it inhabitable." The roof was soon finished, new floors began to be laid, and the entire family was together again at Monticello that summer. Still the house was far from finished, interior and exterior, when Jefferson became President. And although he had made several improvements in the grounds, planting trees and encircling the hilltop with several roundabouts, work had not yet begun on the gardens or on the winged dependencies of the house.

It never occurred to Jefferson to include Monticello in his record of services to his countrymen. Home, like religion, was a personal matter. Yet it had public significance of the highest import. It made certain innovations in American domestic architecture, of course, and contributed to a style still recognizable today in country mansions, especially in Virginia. More important was Jefferson's vision of human habitation formed to the life of free men. The architectural style was in itself of small consequence, though it was probably the only form the ideal could have taken at that time. Nothing luxurious, sensual, or ostentatious would do. Simplicity of line, reasoned order and proportion, a chaste dignity, at once ancient and new, beautiful and virtuous, served the civic culture of the young republic. Jefferson's classic columns rising before the wilderness framed an ideal of workmanship, beauty, and civility in the rough and tumble American world. Whether or not the Americans could appropriate it was another question. The conquest of the continent gave but narrow scope to the humanizing arts. The distance between Jefferson's cultural ideal, as stated at Monticello, and the insistent realities of American life increased with the passage of years. The Americans mastered their environment but little heeded Jefferson's example of raising it high on the scale of human values.